WINNING
INDEPENDENCE

Apostles of Revolution: Jefferson, Paine, Monroe, and the Struggle Against the Old Order in America and Europe

Whirlwind: The American Revolution and the War That Won It

Jefferson and Hamilton: The Rivalry That Forged a Nation

Independence: The Struggle to Set America Free

The Ascent of George Washington: The Hidden Political Genius of an American Icon

Almost a Miracle: The American Victory in the War of Independence

Adams vs. Jefferson: The Tumultuous Election of 1800

A Leap in the Dark: The Struggle to Create the American Republic

Setting the World Ablaze: Washington, Adams, Jefferson, and the American Revolution

John Adams: A Life

The First of Men: A Life of George Washington

Struggle for a Continent: The Wars of Early America

A Wilderness of Miseries: War and Warriors in Early America

The Loyalist Mind: Joseph Galloway and the American Revolution

WINNING INDEPENDENCE

The Decisive Years of the Revolutionary War, 1778–1781

John Ferling

BLOOMSBURY PUBLISHING

NEW YORK · LONDON · OXFORD · NEW DELHI · SYDNEY

BLOOMSBURY PUBLISHING
Bloomsbury Publishing Inc.
1385 Broadway, New York, NY 10018, USA

BLOOMSBURY, BLOOMSBURY PUBLISHING, and the Diana logo are trademarks
of Bloomsbury Publishing Plc

First published in the United States 2021

Copyright © John Ferling, 2021

Maps created by Ortelius Design

ISBN: HB: 978-1-63557-276-6; eBook: 978-1-63557-277-3

LIBRARY OF CONGRESS CATALOGING-IN-PUBLICATION DATA IS AVAILABLE

2 4 6 8 10 9 7 5 3 1

Typeset by Westchester Publishing Services
Printed and bound in the U.S.A. by Berryville Graphics Inc., Berryville, Virginia

To find out more about our authors and books visit www.bloomsbury.com and sign up
for our newsletters.

Bloomsbury books may be purchased for business or promotional use. For information
on bulk purchases please contact Macmillan Corporate and Premium Sales Department at
specialmarkets@macmillan.com.

For Peter Ginna,
who took a chance on me,
stuck with me,
and was always a kind and gentle teacher and editor

CONTENTS

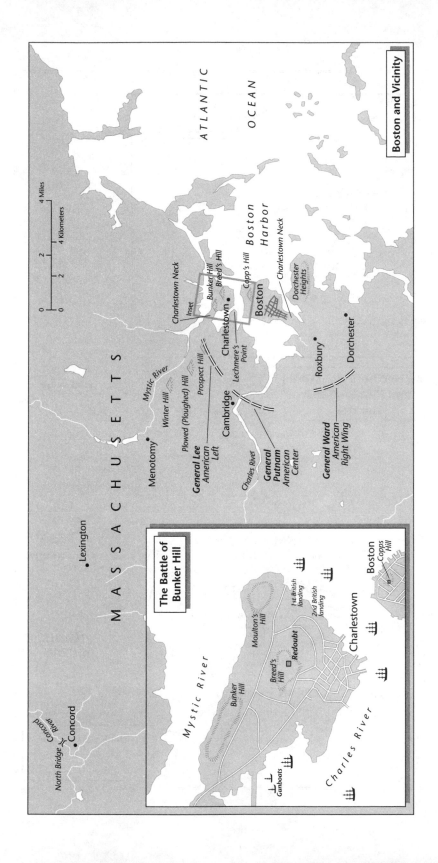

Boston and Vicinity

ATLANTIC

OCEAN

Boston Harbor

Charlestown Neck

Inset

Bunker Hill
Breed's Hill

Copp's Hill

Boston

Dorchester
Heights

Charlestown Neck

Charlestown

Lechmere's
Point

Mystic River

Winter Hill

Prospect Hill

Plowed (Ploughed) Hill

General Lee
American
Left

Cambridge

Charles River

General Putnam
American
Center

Roxbury

Dorchester

General Ward
American
Right Wing

M A S S A C H U S E T T S

Menotomy

Lexington

4 Miles

4 Kilometers

0   2   4

The Battle of Bunker Hill

Concord

North Bridge

Concord River

Mystic River

Bunker Hill

Moulton's Hill

1st British
landing

2nd British
landing

Breed's
Hill

Redoubt

Charlestown

Boston

Copps
Hill

Gunboats

Charles River

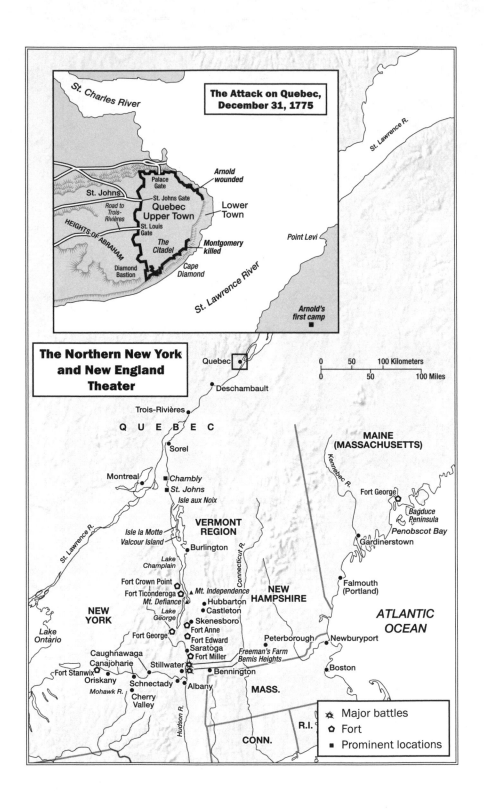

The Attack on Quebec, December 31, 1775

St. Charles River

St. Lawrence R.

Palace Gate

Arnold wounded

St. Johns

St. Johns Gate

Road to Trois-Rivières

Quebec Upper Town

Lower Town

HEIGHTS OF ABRAHAM

St. Louis Gate

The Citadel

Montgomery killed

Point Levi

Diamond Bastion

Cape Diamond

St. Lawrence River

Arnold's first camp

The Northern New York and New England Theater

Quebec

Deschambault

0   50   100 Kilometers
0   50   100 Miles

Trois-Rivières

Q U E B E C

Sorel

MAINE (MASSACHUSETTS)

Montreal

■ Chambly
■ St. Johns

Isle aux Noix

Kennebec R.

Fort George

Bagduce Peninsula

Penobscot Bay

Isle la Motte
Valcour Island

VERMONT REGION

Burlington

Lake Champlain

Gardinerstown

Connecticut R.

Fort Crown Point
Fort Ticonderoga
Mt. Defiance

▲ Mt. Independence

NEW HAMPSHIRE

Falmouth (Portland)

NEW YORK

Lake George

● Hubbarton
● Castleton

Skenesboro
Fort Anne

ATLANTIC OCEAN

Lake Ontario

Fort George

Fort Edward
Saratoga
Fort Miller

Peterborough

Newburyport

Caughnawaga
Canajoharie

Freeman's Farm
Bemis Heights

Boston

Fort Stanwix
Oriskany

Stillwater

Bennington

Mohawk R.

Schnectady

Albany

MASS.

Cherry Valley

Hudson R.

R.I.

CONN.

✴ Major battles
⬠ Fort
■ Prominent locations

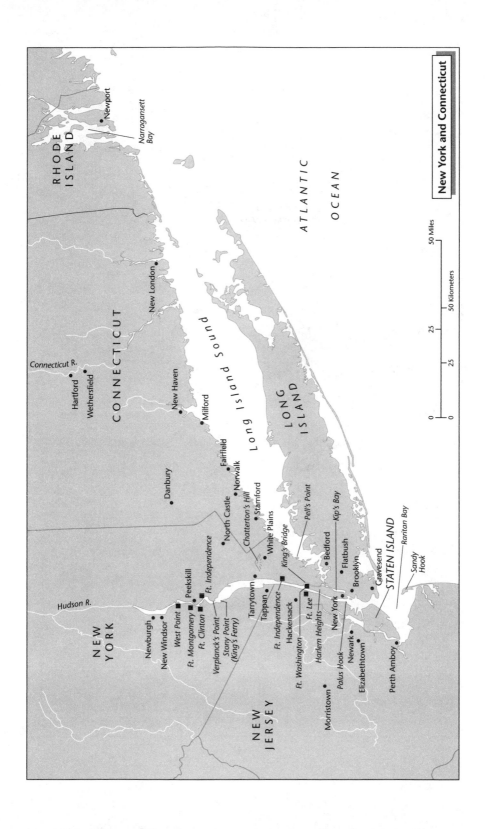

New York and Connecticut

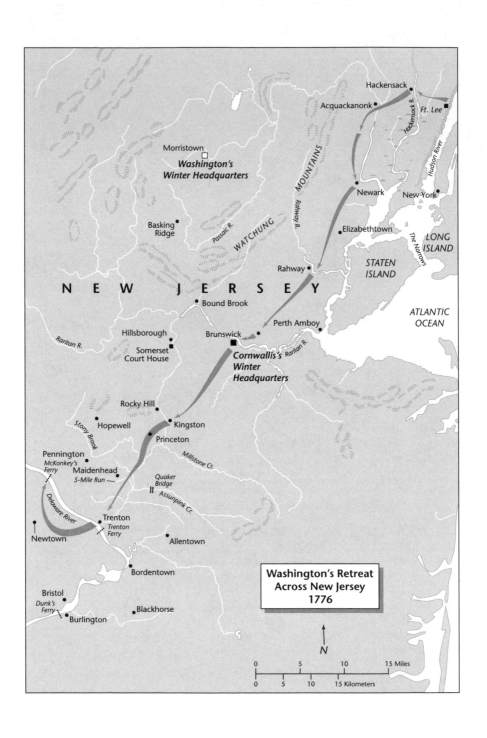

Hackensack

Acquackanonk

Hackensack R.

Ft. Lee

Hudson River

Morristown

*Washington's
Winter Headquarters*

Newark

New York

Basking
Ridge

WATCHUNG   MOUNTAINS

Rahway R.

Elizabethtown

Passaic R.

LONG
ISLAND

N E W   J E R S E Y

Rahway

STATEN
ISLAND

The Narrows

Bound Brook

Perth Amboy

ATLANTIC
OCEAN

Hillsborough

Brunswick

Raritan R.

Raritan R.

Somerset
Court House

*Cornwallis's
Winter
Headquarters*

Rocky Hill

Hopewell

Kingston

Stony Brook

Princeton

Pennington

Millstone Cr.

*McKonkey's
Ferry*

Maidenhead

*Quaker
Bridge*

5-Mile Run

Delaware River

Assunpink Cr.

Trenton

*Trenton
Ferry*

Newtown

Allentown

Bordentown

Bristol

*Dunk's
Ferry*

Blackhorse

Burlington

**Washington's Retreat
Across New Jersey
1776**

N

| 0 | | 5 | | 10 | | 15 Miles |
| 0 | 5 | | 10 | | 15 Kilometers | |

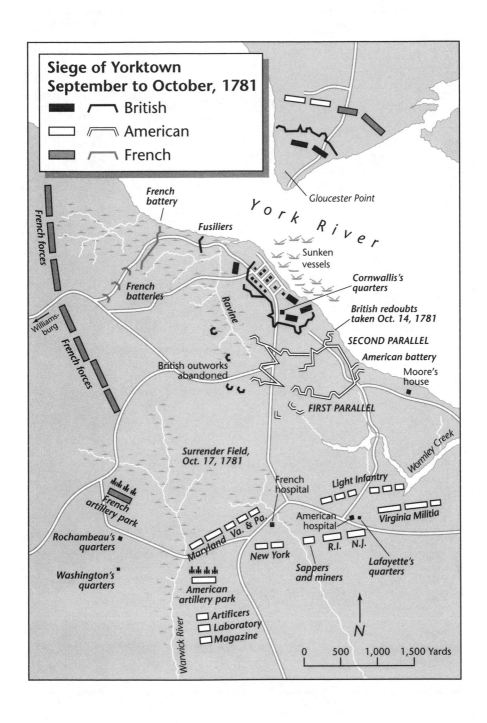

**Siege of Yorktown
September to October, 1781**

British
American
French

French battery

Fusiliers

French batteries

Ravine

French forces

Williamsburg

French forces

British outworks abandoned

York River

Gloucester Point

Sunken vessels

Cornwallis's quarters

British redoubts taken Oct. 14, 1781

SECOND PARALLEL

American battery

Moore's house

FIRST PARALLEL

Wormley Creek

Surrender Field, Oct. 17, 1781

French hospital

Light Infantry

French artillery park

Rochambeau's quarters

American hospital

Virginia Militia

Maryland, Va. & Pa.

New York

R.I.

N.J.

Lafayette's quarters

Washington's quarters

Sappers and miners

American artillery park

Artificers
Laboratory
Magazine

Warwick River

N

0   500   1,000   1,500 Yards

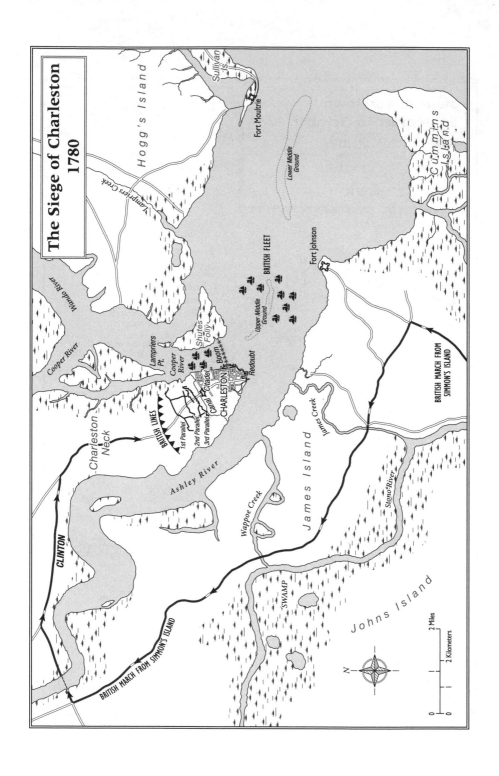

The Siege of Charleston
1780

Hogg's Island

Vanderisters Creek

Wando River

Cooper River

Lampriers Pt.

Shutes Folly

Cooper River

CHARLESTON

Citadel

Canal

1st Parallel

2nd Parallel

3rd Parallel

BRITISH LINES

Charleston Neck

CLINTON

BRITISH MARCH FROM SIMMON'S ISLAND

Ashley River

Wappoe Creek

SWAMP

Johns Island

Stono River

James Island

James Creek

BRITISH MARCH FROM SIMMON'S ISLAND

Fort Johnson

Upper Middle Ground

BRITISH FLEET

Boom

Redoubt

Sullivan Is.

Fort Moultrie

Lower Middle Ground

Cummins Island

N

2 Miles

2 Kilometers

0

0

1

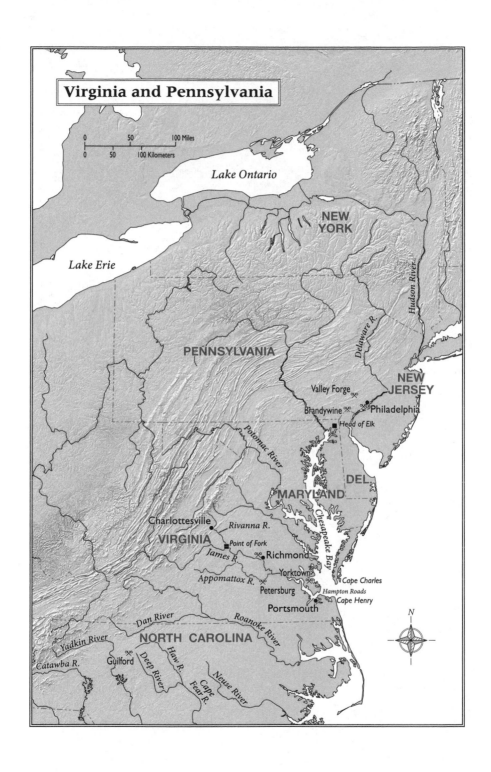

Virginia and Pennsylvania

0   50   100 Miles

0   50   100 Kilometers

Lake Ontario

NEW YORK

Lake Erie

Hudson River

PENNSYLVANIA

Delaware R.

NEW JERSEY

Valley Forge

Brandywine   Philadelphia

Head of Elk

Potomac River

DEL.

MARYLAND

Chesapeake Bay

Charlottesville   Rivanna R.

VIRGINIA   Point of Fork

James R.   Richmond

Appomattox R.   Yorktown   Cape Charles

Petersburg   Hampton Roads

Portsmouth   Cape Henry

N

Dan River   Roanoke River

Yadkin River   **NORTH CAROLINA**

Catawba R.   Guilford   Haw R.

Deep River   Neuse River

Cape Fear R.

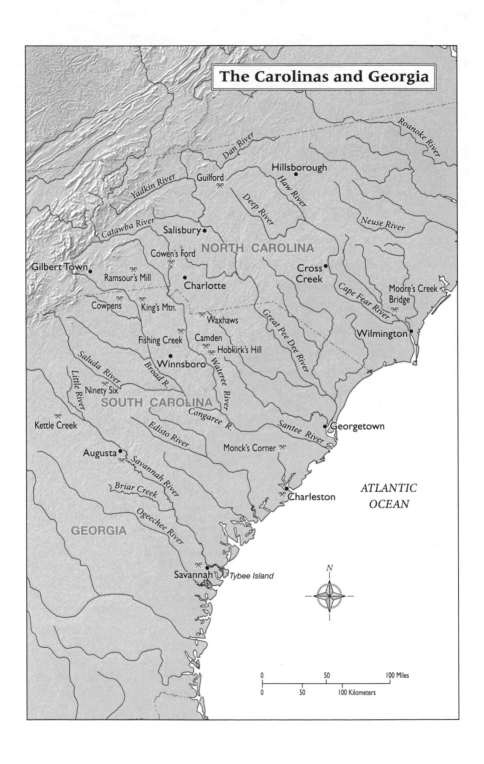

The Carolinas and Georgia

Roanoke River

Dan River

Hillsborough

Yadkin River

Guilford

Haw River

Deep River

Neuse River

Catawba River

Salisbury

NORTH CAROLINA

Cowen's Ford

Gilbert Town

Cross
Creek

Moore's Creek
Bridge

Ramsour's Mill

Cape Fear River

Charlotte

Cowpens

King's Mtn.

Waxhaws

Great Pee Dee River

Wilmington

Fishing Creek

Camden

Saluda River

Hobkirk's Hill

Winnsboro

Broad R.

Little River

Ninety Six

SOUTH CAROLINA

Wateree River

Kettle Creek

Congaree R.

Santee River

Georgetown

Edisto River

Monck's Corner

Augusta

Savannah River

Briar Creek

ATLANTIC
OCEAN

Charleston

Ogeechee River

GEORGIA

Savannah

Tybee Island

N

0   50   100 Miles

0   50   100 Kilometers

PREFACE

IN THE LAST days before the outbreak of the Revolutionary War, a majority of Americans—or at least most of their representatives in Congress—hoped against hope that war with Great Britain could be avoided. John Adams, a delegate from Massachusetts to the First Continental Congress in the fall of 1774, concluded that most of his colleagues were "fixed against Hostilities," fearing that the "Flames of War" would engulf "the whole Continent" and "might rage for twenty year, and End, in the Subduction of America, as likely as in her Liberation."[1]

The fears of Adams's fellow congressmen were not misplaced, though the War of Independence did not last twenty years. It went on for eight years and was America's longest war before Vietnam. Fighting occurred in each of the thirteen colonies, and Americans also fought and died west of the Appalachians, in Canada and East Florida, and at sea. Nor had the members of Congress been mistaken in worrying whether the colonists could defeat Great Britain. In January 1781, six years into the conflict, leaders on both sides regarded the war's outcome as very much in doubt. Indeed, only a short time earlier George Washington confessed that he had nearly lost hope in America's chances of winning the war.

Many on both sides had thought the war was nearly over when the large British army under General John Burgoyne surrendered at Saratoga in October 1777. They reasoned that the British government would now see the American war as a hopeless cause. But Britain persisted, changing its strategy from attempting to quash the rebellion in the northern colonies to one of seeking to regain control of two or three, or more, southern provinces. Within twelve months of Saratoga, the war was stalemated.

During the years that followed Saratoga, most of the fighting was in the South, and that was where the war's outcome was finally determined. Yet Bunker Hill and Trenton and other engagements fought in the North between 1775 and 1777 are ensconced in America's historical lore and are better remembered today than crucial battles in the southern theater such as Cowpens and Guilford Courthouse. This may be because northern authors and poets in the early nineteenth century were more zealous than their southern counterparts in celebrating events of the Revolutionary War. Furthermore, while southern writers, with a few exceptions, were preoccupied with the Civil War deep into the twentieth century, northern writers and scholars continued to write extensively about Revolutionary War episodes from New England to near Philadelphia. History isn't always neat, and the way subsequent generations remember the past isn't always accurate or balanced. Some of the imbalance in the recollection of the War of Independence has been redressed within the past generation or two, though far and away the most popular books treating the war during the past quarter century—worthy offerings by David McCullough, David Hackett Fischer, and Rick Atkinson—have focused nearly exclusively on hostilities in the North.[2] Yet fighting in the South was a pivotal part of the Revolutionary War. Hostilities in the Carolinas and Virginia laid the cornerstone for the decisive clash at Yorktown in the autumn of 1781, the war's pivotal engagement that at last secured American independence.

The period of campaigning and fighting after Saratoga was nearly twice as long as the war that preceded Burgoyne's surrender. Twice as many Americans died in combat in the four years between Saratoga and Yorktown as had perished on battlefields in the initial two and half years of hostilities, and when the death toll includes all causes—such as disease—two thirds died after Saratoga. Nearly all who died after 1777 perished somewhere in the South. If the death toll of Americans who fought for the British after

1777 is included, nearly 75 percent of Americans who died in the War of Independence lost their lives in the wake of Saratoga.

In 1776, Thomas Paine, in his sensational pamphlet *Common Sense*, wrote that America had the numbers, strength, and unity "to repel the force of all the world."[3] Contemporary readers of his tract might have almost felt sorry for Great Britain at having taken on so powerful an adversary. It soon was evident that the rosy picture painted by Paine was illusory. The primitive American economy collapsed two years into the hostilities, the new United States never had the manufacturing capabilities to sustain a long war, and morale waned as the war dragged on with no end in sight. Less than a year after predicting America's inevitable triumph, Paine took up his pen again. This time, in the last desperate days of 1776, he sought to bolster America's will to continue the struggle: "These are the times that try men's souls," he wrote in *The American Crisis*. He added: "Tyranny, like hell, is not easily conquered; yet we have this consolation with us, that the harder the conflict the more glorious the triumph."[4] This time Paine was correct. An American victory would not be easy. In fact, as Paine well knew, winning would become more difficult the longer the war continued.

John Adams, who supported going to war in 1775, also learned how problematic and grueling it was to gain the eventual victory, and he wondered if his descendants would fully understand the formidable demands that had been encountered in the fight to win American independence. "Posterity! You will never know, how much it cost the [Revolutionary] Generation to preserve your Freedom," he later wrote.[5]

This book is the story of the seemingly interminable struggle waged by both sides during the four years after Burgoyne's army surrendered at Saratoga. For both Great Britain and America it was a war with more twists and turns, ups and downs, than a roller-coaster rider might experience. Luck, good and bad, played a role. There were missed opportunities on both sides that might have turned around the course of the war. Soldiers on both sides in the southern theater endured incredible hardships. Continentals, militiamen, and British regulars in the field suffered unimaginable privation. Nor were those who bore arms the only ones distressed by hostilities. Vast numbers of American civilians suffered and sacrificed to a degree seldom experienced by those on the home front in any other conflict in American history. By 1780, the war in the South was being waged with a savage intensity, as both rebel and Loyalist partisans resorted to what today would be called terrorism. By then, this war had become America's first civil war, as Americans who fought for their king battled Americans committed to independence. General Nathanael Greene, who fought in both the North and the South, advised fellow officers in the northern theater that until they experienced hostilities in the South, they could not know the full ghastly meaning of warfare.

In an age when nations typically fought their wars with professional armies, both sides in the Revolutionary War actively solicited the service of civilians. The British put their American recruits into newly formed provincial regiments and royal militia companies. Time and again the American states summoned militiamen to active duty and recruited, or conscripted, men to serve in the Continental army. Eventually the percentage of free adult males who bore arms exceeded that in the United States in either World War I or World War II. As in all wars, soldiers coped with the loneliness of separation from everything that was familiar and faced demands to do things that were unthinkable in peaceful civil pursuits. The war was far removed from the lives of most of England's citizenry, but it touched nearly all Americans. Families were separated and all too often lost loved ones. Some watched forlornly as husbands, sons, fathers, and brothers came home no longer the whole men they had been when they had gone to war. Wives and children at home were pressed into unfamiliar roles to keep families afloat. Many families—especially farm families—not infrequently watched helplessly as the army of one side or the other seized their crops, livestock, wagons, and tools. People in both urban and rural areas suffered scarcities and paid staggering taxes unlike anything they had faced in peacetime. Civilians were caught up in the fighting to a degree seldom seen during hostilities in Europe or the American colonies in the century before the War of Independence. In the years after Saratoga, two major southern cities were attacked and occupied by the army of Great Britain and a third suffered extensive damage. Raids on coastal hamlets and backcountry settlements produced horror, panic, losses, death, and destruction. Warriors on both sides pillaged the homesteads of those they deemed their enemies, sometimes committing unspeakable atrocities. Like many wars, this one uprooted countless civilians, sending them fleeing for safety and inspiring thousands of enslaved people to risk flight in hopes of deliverance from bondage.

The expectation that Saratoga was the breakthrough that would soon lead to an American victory was, like's Paine's fanciful prognosis of a certain victory, incorrect. By late 1778, when it was clear that the war was stalemated, American, British, and French leaders were faced with difficult choices. How military leaders made these opaque choices is the linchpin of this book. It scrutinizes the ongoing travail of the rival commanders— George Washington, commander of the Continental army, and Sir Henry Clinton, commander in chief of Britain's armies in North America—as they coped with the impasse. Both sought the means of ending, or surviving, the stalemate. Both sought to understand if time was an ally or an enemy. Both wondered whether it was preferable to forego risks or to roll the dice on a hazardous undertaking.

Washington and Clinton were not the only leaders faced with difficult choices. The book also treats Comte de Rochambeau, commander of the French army that arrived in America in the summer of 1780; Lord Charles Cornwallis, who commanded the British army in the South after June 1780; Benjamin Lincoln, the leader of America's army in the South in 1779 and 1780; and Nathanael Greene, who was in charge of American forces in the southern theater in the year leading to Yorktown. Nor was it solely high-ranking military officers who faced trying decisions. Ordinary men chose whether to bear arms and on which side to serve. The Continental Congress, the ministry and Parliament in London, and the French government in Versailles were confronted with options that could have momentous results.

Many have pronounced Saratoga the turning point of the war. Its impact was crucial, but in long wars there is seldom a single turning point. More often there are numerous little turning points. Unlike, say, World War II, the War of Independence was peculiar in that at the beginning of 1781, the seventh year of hostilities, neither side appeared to be any closer to winning the war than it had been three years earlier. Britain had achieved more than its adversary since Saratoga. It had retaken Savannah and Charleston; a large swath of South Carolina was occupied by British troops; and the pro-independence legislature and governor in Georgia had been ousted and the province was once again a royal colony. General Clinton was more optimistic about the war's outcome than General Washington was in January 1781. Had Las Vegas bookies existed at that time, they might have established incredible odds against an Allied victory. The oddsmakers might even have posted good odds on the war remaining stalemated, leading in 1782 to a negotiated peace in which two or more southern provinces remained in Great Britain's possession. In that event, the United States—if it existed at all—would have been a nation of fewer than thirteen states. This book argues that Great Britain could have—and should have—crushed the colonial rebellion in 1775 or 1776, or possibly even 1777. Thereafter, Britain's difficulties increased, but losing the war, as finally occurred at Yorktown in October 1781, was never inevitable.

Not a few historians have scoffed at the southern strategy pursued by Great Britain after 1778, depicting it as a fool's errand. In the end, it didn't succeed, but that is not to say that it couldn't have succeeded. This book argues that Sir Henry Clinton, Britain's commander in chief in North America after May 1778, developed a thoughtful and realistic strategic plan for winning the war in the South. Had Clinton's plan been fully implemented, and had it carried the day, Britain would have repossessed South Carolina and Georgia, in addition to East Florida (today a substantial portion of Florida, Alabama, and Mississippi), which it had controlled since the end of the Seven Years' War in 1763. Britain might even have reclaimed North Carolina. While reestablishing control of the provinces above the Potomac River was beyond Britain's grasp, which the imperial government realized in the wake of the debacle at Saratoga, the successful implementation of Clinton's strategy would have led to a United States that consisted of as few as ten states. Furthermore, the United States might possibly have been surrounded by British-held Canada, several southern colonies that had been restored to royal rule, and Britain's trans-Appalachia. The small and girdled United States would have faced a most uncertain future.

With its explanation of why Clinton's carefully constructed strategic conception failed and its reassessment of his generalship, this book is the first comprehensive reexamination of Clinton as commander of Britain's army in North America to be undertaken in the past seventy-five years. Many in England scapegoated Clinton following the Allies' decisive victory at Yorktown. For several generations he has been virtually without a defender among historians, to some degree because of the persistent influence of a devastating psychological profile of Clinton put forward in the 1960s by his principal biographer. That study argued that Clinton's subliminal demons destined his failure. Other scholars, reading history backward, have played on decisions made, or not made, and actions taken or not taken, by Clinton that might have headed off the disaster that befell Britain's armed forces at Yorktown. The time is long overdue to take another look at Clinton, one not tainted by a dubious psychological evaluation of a subject who cannot be interviewed and who left for posterity the scantest of personal letters that might have opened a window onto his inner self. It is time, too, to consider Clinton's decisions in light of what he knew and did not know at the time he made his choices. This book argues that Clinton was a better general than most historians have believed. But Britain did lose the war at Yorktown on Clinton's watch, and the book confronts his responsibility for the disaster that has blackened his reputation.

In addition, the book probes why the war was stalemated and why it remained a standoff for so long thereafter. Of course, it explains why the deadlock was broken in 1781. It contemplates the options available to the assorted leaders in the years after 1778, their strategies, and possible actions that were not attempted. It explores who deserves credit for ending the stalemate and where blame should be laid for the British catastrophe at Yorktown. It questions whether the Allied victory was inevitable.

Hindsight, as the saying goes, is twenty-twenty. The principal leaders—Washington, Clinton, Rochambeau, Cornwallis, and Greene—were not clairvoyant. Throughout this book I have sought to evaluate these leaders on the basis of what each knew when making crucial decisions. What information, good and bad, did they possess? What pressures, real and imagined, did they face from their civilian masters? How much latitude did each have in making decisions? What hazards did they believe could flow from acting or not acting? What were the perils they foresaw in the course they contemplated? How did the realities of eighteenth-century warfare dictate the limits of what could be attempted?

While Washington and Clinton were polar opposites in many respects, their generalship after 1778 was not always dissimilar. Both largely avoided risks, waiting month after month, year after year, for the arrival of just the right turn of events. For Washington, it would come when the French at last were prepared to act in concert with him. Clinton, the more active of the two, was pressed into trial-and-error expediencies in the South while simultaneously preparing for what he believed would be an inevitable Allied campaign to retake New York.

The book is not solely about the leaders. It is also about their soldiers. The severe winter ordeals experienced by Washington's soldiers in northern states—at Trenton in 1776 and Valley Forge two years later—are imbedded in the American story. The torments borne by those on both sides who fought in the South in 1780 and 1781 are less well remembered. They served in a region of miasmic heat and humidity. Disease stalked the land to a degree largely unknown in the North. If southern winters were not a match for those to the north, there were wintry episodes in the Carolinas, and both British and rebel soldiers sometimes campaigned in bitter conditions that included seemingly endless rain, freezing nights, and the perilous necessity of crossing cold, swollen rivers. Both the king's soldiers and those fighting for American independence endured punishing marches and, not infrequently, destitution. Soldiers on both sides at times coped with inadequate shelter, scarce provisions, and insufficient clothing and shoes. And, of course, danger was never far away, whether from fearful diseases, the terrors of the battlefield, or ghastly atrocities that were part and parcel of the civil war in the South.

The book offers a look at the nature of waging war in the eighteenth century. Armies traveled on foot (though field-grade officers sat astride horses), and the men often marched for days on end and in all kinds of weather. Some soldiers trekked more than a thousand miles in the course of a campaign lasting a few months. Armies on the move stretched for miles, accompanied by horse-drawn wagons laden with food, ammunition, and equipment. Even when hurried, the armies moved slowly by today's standards. Nearly six weeks were required for the Allied armies in 1781 to make the trip from just north of New York City to Virginia. Not infrequently, armies on the move had to forage for food, descending like a horde of locusts on the nearby farms of unlucky yeomen. In the northern theater, the campaign season more or less resembled today's baseball season, commencing in the spring and ending in October or November, when the onset of wintry weather rendered primitive roads impassable. Thereafter, the armies went into winter quarters. In the South, where winters were less severe, fighting continued year-round. The slowness of communication was a fact of life that every leader had to deal with. Letters exchanged by Washington in New York or New Jersey and the French commanders in Rhode Island were in transit for about five days. Fifteen days or more might be required for a letter sent from British headquarters in New York to reach Charleston, after which several more days might elapse before the message was delivered to an officer in the field. General Washington, not having the luxury of sending communications by sea, knew that a month or more could be expected to pass before a missive that he sent to South Carolina would reach its recipient. British packet ships regularly sailed between New York and the Caribbean, but nearly a month's lag in communications was customary. Leaders were often several days, even weeks, out of touch with a region for which they were planning strategy. Government officials in London sent directives to General Clinton based on information about the course of the war that was three or four months old, and often erroneous.

This is a book about choices made and not made, roads and risks taken or not, plans good and bad that were made and sometimes attempted, sometimes never ventured. It is about grievous mistakes, incredible heroism, and spectacular gambles. It is about the gruesome horrors of war. It is about shrinking from a daring choice and acting with incredible audacity. It is about victory and defeat—and the thin line that often separated one from the other. It is about making decisions, and why those decisions were made.

It is a book that I first considered writing years ago, and that I eventually undertook when the six volumes of Earl Cornwallis's papers for 1780–1781 were recently published. Modern scholarly editions of George Washington's papers and those of General Nathanael Greene are in print as well, and so, too, were a vast number of accounts by soldiers on both sides, many of which were reissued—or published for the first time—during America's celebration of the bicentennial of the American Revolution. Recent years have witnessed the publication of both a multitude of documents culled from Colonial Office records in London—including correspondence between Britain's civilian and military leaders on both sides of the Atlantic—and the diaries and letters of members of the American Congress during the war. The eighteenth-century memoirs of many participants in the war, some including important documents, are now available electronically. In the aftermath of the war, Sir Henry Clinton wrote extensively about the conflict and his role in it, and some of his books and pamphlets contain important documents. Finally, a huge collection of Clinton's papers are at hand at the William L. Clements Library at the University of Michigan.

When the seemingly endless slog from Saratoga to Yorktown ended in a decisive Allied victory, Thomas Paine—after heaving a sigh of relief—looked back and compared the war to a "long and raging hurricane." But the American victory, he claimed, had always seemed to him to be "probable." Paine has been echoed by many historians who have argued that Britain was destined to fail because of the size of America or the monumental logistical hurdles or the number of enemies that it faced. Neither General Clinton nor General Washington would have agreed, and this book takes issue with the conclusion that British failure was inescapable. Clinton thought a succession of preventable mistakes on the part of Cornwallis and the Royal Navy—and the misinformed meddling of the king and government officials in London—in the months preceding Yorktown had sealed Britain's fate in this war. At war's end, Washington remarked that the American victory was astounding, even miraculous.[6] Paine, Washington, and Clinton were not historians, and each had an ax to grind. I hope that the perspective of time and the massive documentation now available have enabled me to offer a fresh judgment on the reasons for the war's outcome.

THE BOOK OPENS with a sweeping analysis of the war from its inception in April 1775 through Saratoga in October 1777, with particular emphasis on the point that Britain could have, and should have, won the war during this period. The second chapter covers the response of Britain's leadership to the news of Saratoga, its decision to continue the war, and the evolution of the government's commitment to a southern strategy. The great bulk of the book, chapters three through fifteen, focuses on the war during 1778–1781, and especially on the period beginning with the British siege of Charleston in the spring of 1780. Nearly half the book centers on 1781, the pivotal year in this war and one of the most consequential years in all of United States history. The concluding chapter offers an assessment of the leaders and the reasons for the war's outcome.

A couple of words of explanation. I frequently use the term "rebels" in describing those who fought for American independence. That label might rile some readers, possibly even leading some to suspect me of a bias toward Great Britain. I tried not to use an "Americans versus British" terminology because during the last few years of hostilities a considerable number of Americans were fighting for Great Britain and against other Americans. During some of that period, in fact, more Americans were serving in the British army than in the Continental army. Second, when quoting from those involved in the war, I left their spelling intact, unless it clouded the meaning of what they wrote.

CHAPTER I

BRITAIN'S WAR TO WIN,

1775–1777

"BLOWS MUST DECIDE whether they are to be subject to this country or independent," said King George III late in 1774 as Britain's ministers discussed the use of force to suppress the American insurgency.[1] The monarch was correct. By then neither the colonists nor the imperial government would peacefully submit to the other. In the absence of a capitulation by one or the other, leaders on both sides saw war as the only solution to the decade-long Anglo-American crisis.

Serious imperial troubles had begun after 1763 when Parliament sought to tighten its control of the American colonies, steps that included inhibiting the flow of population across the Appalachians, securing revenue through parliamentary taxation, and more stringently regulating colonial trade. Britain's new colonial policy aroused violent and destructive protests, and several provincial assemblies adopted statements denying Parliament's jurisdiction over the colonies. London answered that Parliament possessed the right to legislate for America "in all cases whatsoever."

Parliamentary taxation and regulation aroused concerns of economic adversity among colonists of all stripes, from wealthy and politically powerful merchants to land-speculating planters, from land-hungry farmers to artisans, sailors, and dockhands. The more ambitious colonists already chafed at their cramped opportunities within the British Empire. Because they were colonists, the doors to Britain's highest political and military offices were shut to them. Some had also discovered that when the interests of colonists clashed with those of influential figures in England—over issues of trade, say, or rival claims of land companies—the imperial government invariably sided with those at home, an awareness that fueled a longing for greater autonomy among colonists. The panoply of British policies in the decade leading up to 1774 convinced many in America that the mother country had fallen prey to corrupt and tyrannical leaders bent on exploiting the colonists. Concluding that monarchy and titled nobility were at the root of Britain's despotism, not a few came to think that republicanism was a superior—even liberating—form of governance.

For years, the imperial government sought to placate the colonists by repealing some of its objectionable legislation, but it never backed off its position as the unquestioned sovereign authority. In 1768, two thousand British soldiers were sent to Boston to ensure that imperial laws were enforced in Massachusetts. Thereafter, the threat that the government in London would seek to have its way by resorting to force hung like a saber over the colonists. Nevertheless, before 1774 British officials never came close to turning loose their country's army against the colonists, and things were so quiet in America in the early 1770s that the royal governor of Massachusetts rejoiced that the "incendiaries are much fallen." He even dared to believe that the imperial crisis was over.[2]

But London's American troubles had not ended. Descent toward war was sparked by the ministry's decision in 1773 to enforce the sole parliamentary tax yet on the books, a duty on tea. Resistance to the Tea Act was immediate and widespread in the colonies, and in Massachusetts, in December, it resulted in the Boston Tea Party. A cold fury swept over England at the news of renewed colonial recalcitrance and the destruction of the East India Company's tea. Essayists denounced the forbearance of earlier British governments and some proclaimed that the time for military action had come. With winter hanging over London in the first weeks of 1774, the ministry of Frederick Lord North debated its options. The use of force was on the table, and the ministers, in secret, discussed for perhaps the first time what might happen if war came. Some, fully aware that Britain's army, which had consisted of two hundred thousand men in 1760, had shrunk to a mere thirty-six thousand, were skeptical of the army's ability to quash the insurgency. Instead, they advocated for a naval blockade, a form of economic warfare that would be free of danger, as the colonists lacked a fleet with which to respond to the challenge. However, most did not see much that could go wrong if the army was called on to suppress the disaffected Americans. The colonists had militias, but neither a national army nor a navy; the colonies had seldom cooperated with one another during earlier eighteenth-century wars against the French, Spanish, and Indians; and the colonists' performance as soldiers in the most recent war—the Seven Years' War in the 1750s—had hardly been exemplary. Indeed, the watchword in London was that Americans were a "poor species of fighting men." Even if that jaundiced view was incorrect, few imagined that callow militiamen would stand and fight against Britain's highly trained regulars. And in the event that colonial soldiers were hardy enough to give battle to regulars, what would they fight with? Given the dearth of arms and munitions manufacturers in the colonies, the colonial soldiery would face an appalling shortage of muskets, powder, and cannon. It was widely presumed among officials in London that a war would be over within weeks and would consist of only one or two engagements. Some thought a handful of frigates or even as few as one thousand British army regulars could defeat the Americans. A marine colonel, posted in Boston, informed the folks at home, "One active campaign, a smart action, and burning two or three of their towns, will set everything to rights." General Thomas Gage, the commander of the British army in America, advised officials that the Americans would "be lyons whilst we are lambs but if we take the resolute part they will be very meek." To this, he added that the first engagement would be of crucial importance. If the Americans were humiliated at the outset, he advised, the colonial rebellion would likely wither on the vine. However, Gage also cautioned that the colonial rebellion was widespread and that a large army would be necessary to suppress the insurgency, a force well in excess of the five thousand men who were posted in Boston in 1774. North's ministers brushed aside the more unpleasant aspects of Gage's advice.[3]

The ministers did not opt for war in 1774. Lord North and a majority in his cabinet yet hoped to avoid hostilities. North—cheerful, amusing, modest, and, above all, well liked—had inherited the American crisis on coming to power in 1770. From the outset, he had doubted that the colonial troubles could be peacefully resolved. His policy—to the extent that he had a policy—had been to avoid any step that might roil the Americans. To his surprise, the Tea Act resurrected the American problem, leading the prime minister to conclude in 1774 that the tipping point in imperial relations had been reached. North did not imagine that Britain could lose a war against the colonists, but he felt that gaining victory would be a more difficult slog than many in his cabinet realized. At the same moment, he believed that conciliation had failed and that something new must be tried. George III backed North, telling him: "we must not retreat." Hitherto, the monarch had hardly intruded in the crafting of colonial policies by his assorted ministries, but in this instance he took a more active part, somewhat from rage over the destruction of the tea in Boston and partially from concern over the colonists' growing embrace of anti-monarchical republicanism. The king leaned on North to be resolute, and when the prime minister conceived the Coercive Acts—a series of nonmilitary measures designed to harshly punish Massachusetts for the Tea Party—the monarch applauded the step. In the cabinet debates that followed early in 1774, some ministers continued to argue for using force, but after a month of discussions the ministry agreed on peaceful coercion, not war. Most were convinced not only that the epicenter of the colonial rebellion was centered in Massachusetts, but that the American rebellion would collapse in the face of the imperial government's adamant stand.[4]

Some colonists, notably George Washington and Samuel Adams, had earlier spoken in private about going to war to defend their rights, but armed resistance had not been publicly discussed.[5] Since 1765 the weapons wielded by the colonies had been petitions and economic boycotts. Once the details of the Coercive Acts were learned in May 1774, momentum gathered behind the notion of holding a national conclave to determine a unified response. Although Massachusetts alone was to be punished, the feeling was widespread that Britain was pursuing a divide-and-conquer strategy. Massachusetts was to be chastised by the Coercive Acts, but tomorrow it could be the turn of another province. Many were also confident that Britain would back down if it understood that it faced the unified resistance of all thirteen colonies. There were those, too, who feared that further defiance would provoke Britain into using force. Should that be the case, it was imperative to determine the degree of unity that actually existed among the thirteen colonies. Unity was essential if the colonists were to meet force with force.

The First Continental Congress, as it came to be known, met during September and October 1774 in Philadelphia. Virtually every delegate was committed to a national boycott of British trade until both the Tea Act and Coercive Acts were repealed. The congressmen were not of one mind regarding whether Parliament possessed any legal authority over the colonies, though in the end Congress adopted a Declaration of Colonial Rights and Grievances that conceded Parliament's right to regulate imperial commerce but otherwise denied its authority over America. In its final days, Congress debated war preparations. After several bruising sessions, it asked each colony to ready its militia, but Congress stopped short of voting to provision the militiamen. Congress's actions made clear that the colonies were ready to once again defy the mother country, though private discussions among the delegates revealed to more than one delegate that American independence was an idea "which Startles People here." A majority of congressmen hoped to remain within the British Empire, but with greater autonomy and immunity from parliamentary taxation. It was additionally apparent that most delegates desperately hoped that war could be averted. Richard Henry Lee of Virginia concluded that most of his colleagues in Congress "had not the spirit" for war. John Adams of Massachusetts saw things more clearly. The delegates, he said, were "fixed against Hostilities and Ruptures, except that they should become absolutely necessary."[6] Britain's response to the actions taken by Congress would determine if hostilities erupted.

Unofficial word of Congress's defiant stand trickled into London in November, thanks to a loose-lipped congressman or two who violated the body's rule of secrecy. The "dye is now cast," George III predicted on learning that an illegal American congress was to meet. It was when he became aware of the defiant stand taken by Congress that the king told North that "blows must decide" the issue.[7] North's ministry did not take up the use-of-force matter until January 1775, when every member had returned from the holidays and official word of what Congress had done finally reached London. In the interim, North, who yet clung to the hope of sidestepping war, had sought without success to persuade the king to send a peace commission across the sea to seek a negotiated settlement. Several factors disposed North to seek peace, among them the realization that Britain was hardly prepared for a tough war, if hostilities in America came to that. But the king was ready for war, and he was not alone. Most ministers had opted for coercion a year earlier in the hope that it would provoke an American capitulation short of war. That had not been the case. The mood of most ministers now mirrored that of the king.

The cabinet came to its fateful decision in the course of three meetings in eight days. Deliberations included a reprise of the previous year's discussion regarding whether Britain could easily win a war against the colonists. The answer was the same, though a few troubling points arose. One or two ministers were skeptical about the ability of Britain's army to suppress the rebellion, with one cynic allowing that it was "as wild an idea as ever controverted common sense." Concern was aired over the possibility of French intervention on the side of the Americans, though most thought the war would be over before France would finally decide to enter the conflict. Another awkward matter was the vast size of America, but the prevailing wisdom was that once the rebellion was suppressed in Massachusetts—often characterized as the "head of the snake"—the insurgency would collapse in the other provinces. Some were uneasy about how to supply a British army campaigning deep in America's interior. That worry, too, was given short shrift. The majority believed that control of Boston (and, if need be, other port towns) would sow sufficient economic hardships throughout the hinterland to bring on the collapse of the rebellion. The conviction that hostilities would be brief also overrode doubts that the Royal Navy possessed sufficient ships to effectively blockade the seemingly endless American coast. In the end, the ministers opted to wage a war primarily of land operations, feeling that it was the quickest and cheapest means of crushing the rebellion, and the least likely to nettle the French. But the ministers were heedless of General Gage's strident warnings that all thirteen colonies were in rebellion and that a huge British army was needed for winning the war. Some, including the king, concluded that Gage was a defeatist who should be removed and replaced.[8]

As the discussions within the ministry moved inexorably toward using force, others outside the cabinet advocated a peaceful approach. Members of Parliament from manufacturing districts feared the loss of trade that would inevitably accompany hostilities. The most admired political figure in England, William Pitt, Earl of Chatham, introduced a plan in the House of Lords for "settling the Troubles in America." He called for the removal of the British army and recognition of the legitimacy of the Continental Congress—which North's government had branded as criminal—but he thought Parliament must continue to regulate imperial commerce. As for the reach of Parliament, Pitt ambiguously proposed that it no longer exercise its powers in matters where the colonists were able to govern themselves, presumably including raising revenue.[9] Soon thereafter, Edmund Burke, a member of the House of Commons, proposed that London make concessions. Given what he called the "fierce spirit of liberty" that burned in America, Burke predicted that the colonists would yield nothing. What Burke recommended hardly differed from Chatham's propositions, but he argued that if war came, Britain would in time lose its American colonies and much, if not all, of its lucrative North American trade. Should that come to pass, said Burke, the disaster could be laid at the feet of "those vulgar and mechanical

politicians, who have no place among us and [are] far from being quali-
fied to be directors of the great movement of empire."[10]

Aside from a couple of ministers who counseled against war—and, like
Gage, were branded milksops and ejected from their posts—North's
government voted overwhelmingly to use force to end the American rebellion. The order to apply "a vigorous Exertion of . . . Force" was adopted on
January 27, 1775. Gage was advised that reinforcements were coming, but
it would take a year to bring his army up to the twenty thousand men he
had once said that he needed to wage this war. The ministry's directive
added that Gage's present army should be sufficient for coping with the
rebels in Massachusetts, given that the American troublemakers were "a
rude Rabble without plan, without concert, & without conduct." Victory
might be garnered after "a single Action," and it might not require even
that. The show of force alone might bring about the colonists' capitulation
"without bloodshed."[11]

The ministers' errant presumptions about the coming war are easily
discernible today. However, these officials were not taking their country into
an inevitably doomed enterprise. Some of their assumptions about the colonists' war-making liabilities were correct, especially the Americans' lack of
weaponry. Benjamin Franklin subsequently noted that when the war began,
there was "not five rounds of powder a man" in America, and he was not
exaggerating. Only one in four New Hampshire militiamen had a musket,
and each man with a gun had only enough powder for fifteen rounds.[12] The
colonists were woefully prepared even for a very short war.

None in America had known for sure how North's government would
respond to the Continental Congress, but throughout the cold winter of
1775, militia units marched and drilled on muddy fields from very nearly
one end of colonial America to the other. The answer that all had waited for
came on April 19 when Gage, in Boston, carried out his orders by dispatching
several companies to destroy a colonial arsenal in Concord, about twenty
miles west of the city. Before the day ended, it was evident that the expectations of the North ministry regarding the colonists' conduct had been
ill-founded.

Although Gage had earlier spoken of the crucial importance of the first engagement, he lacked the manpower with which to score a crushing win against the Yankees during the mission to Concord.[13] Instead he sought to surprise the militia in Concord, but his best laid-plans went awry when rebel spies in Boston learned of the undertaking before the first British troops marched out of the city. Gage's problems were compounded by his commitment of too few men. He deployed 900 men, about 20 percent of his total army, and he failed to include his 225 dragoons, mounted infantry armed with muskets, swords, and pistols.[14] If Gage was without the numbers necessary for thoroughly humiliating his New England foes, he possessed—but did not initially utilize—sufficient manpower to prevent his army from suffering a chastening defeat on the first day of hostilities.

Gage's force of regulars first encountered militiamen in Lexington, a few miles east of Concord. The militiamen did not resist, but the redcoats killed eight and wounded nine of them in an event that historian Rick Atkinson aptly characterized as "not a battle, or even a skirmish, but an execution." The first blood of the Revolutionary War had been spilled. From there, the redcoats marched to Concord and, unmolested, destroyed the arsenal. But as the regulars were completing their task, a force of Massachusetts militia-men offered resistance. A brief firefight ensued in which three of the king's soldiers were killed and several were wounded on or near the North Bridge that spanned the Concord River. In the wake of that fateful incident, the regulars set out for Boston on what would be a march into hell. Militiamen from throughout Massachusetts, alerted by dispatch riders such as Paul Revere, descended on the redcoats. Dozens of ambushes and skirmishes occurred throughout the long, bloody afternoon as militiamen, hidden behind walls and trees, poured a deadly fire into the regulars. Had not the British commander in the field early on sensed the danger that was brewing and called for reinforcements—which finally arrived late in the day—it is conceivable that the entire British force would have been wiped out. As it was, by the time the regulars reached Boston in the gathering darkness, around 70 had been killed and some 270 wounded, including numerous officers.[15]

Gage's woes had only begun. By dawn the next morning thousands of militiamen from throughout Massachusetts and the neighboring colonies of Connecticut, New Hampshire, and Rhode Island had descended on Boston. Some twelve thousand colonial soldiers had taken up positions on the flanks of the city. In mid-June, the rebels occupied Bunker Hill in Charlestown, high ground on a peninsula connected to the mainland by a narrow isthmus. From that elevated site, the few artillery pieces in American hands could be trained on Boston's harbor, the lifeline for the regulars in the city. Gage had to do something. The promised reinforcements would not arrive for months, but in late May three major generals dispatched by London had sailed into Boston Harbor aboard the *Cerberus*. William Howe was the oldest and senior in rank. John Burgoyne and Henry Clinton were the other two veteran officers. As soon as he learned that Bunker Hill was in rebel hands, Gage summoned a council of war.

The generals agreed that the hill must be taken. The question was how to gain the victory. Clinton proposed that while Britain's main force landed on the beach below the hill, he would lead another five hundred men ashore west of Charlestown, sealing off the rebels' exit through the isthmus. Clinton envisaged that with every American on Charlestown Heights trapped, Gage would score a largely bloodless victory. Lives would be saved, and the operation would confirm the deadly expertise of the king's military, prompting the colonists to think again about casting their lot with amateur martial leaders.[16] But Gage ignored Clinton's plan. The Concord debacle notwithstanding, Gage still doubted the courage of colonial militiamen. Nor was he in a mood to spare an enemy that had shown no mercy toward his redcoats on their march back to Boston from Concord. Gage wished to demonstrate in the harshest manner possible the misplaced folly of waging war against a formidable world power. He opted to assault the rebel entrenchments at the top of the hill. Gage gave responsibility for the attack to Howe, one of the loudest voices urging a frontal assault, and an officer known for his dependability.

Tall, burly, and athletic, the dark-complexioned, forty-six-year-old Howe carried himself like a soldier, and indeed during more than twenty years of service he had acquired a deserved reputation for valor, daring, common sense, tactical dexterity, and quick thinking under pressure. Time and again, it was Howe that superior officers turned to when faced with a difficult assignment. Though Gage did not imagine that taking Bunker Hill would be especially demanding, he knew that Howe was the man for the job.[17]

The regulars marched up the gently sloping hill and into a cataclysm. Three assaults were needed to take the hill from the Americans, who chose to fight, not flee. There were times during the unfolding calamity when Howe feared that Britain's entire light infantry in America would be destroyed. Viewing the carnage from Boston, where he had been posted, Clinton risked censure by violating his orders and crossing to the scene of the fighting. He valiantly rallied stragglers and, as a diversion, led them up the periphery of the battlefield. In the end, the British succeeded principally because their foe ran out of ammunition. By day's end, 226 regulars were dead and 928 had been wounded, the greatest loss of men that Britain would suffer in a single engagement in this war. Fifty percent of the redcoats who fought that day were killed or wounded. Fully 40 percent of the officers in Gage's army were casualties. In the space of two months Gage had lost nearly 1,500 men, more than one-fourth of the number he had commanded when the decision to use force was made in London.

Gage was shaken, and more than one British official, including General Clinton, noted that a "few more such victories" as Bunker Hill would "put an end to British dominion in America." The bloodbath unsettled Howe. He subsequently acknowledged that securing the hill was "too dearly bought" and spoke of the "horror" of the battle. In the aftermath of the fighting, Howe walked the blood-soaked hillside, stepping over bodies and listening to the groans and anguished cries of the wounded. Seemingly shattered by his responsibility for the butchery, he thereafter alluded to Bunker Hill as that "unhappy day," and ever afterward was hesitant to order his men to make a frontal assault against an entrenched adversary. In Bunker Hill's aftermath every British leader, whether soldier or civilian, should have concluded that this war wouldn't be a cakewalk. Major General Hugh, Earl Percy, spoke for many when he remarked soon after the debacle that "our army is so small we cannot even afford a victory, if it is attended with any loss of men." The fighting that spring also brought home to the colonists the costliness of hostilities, as roughly 450 Americans had died or been wounded in the two engagements.[18] Nevertheless, Yankee militiamen had seemingly proved themselves capable of fighting regulars and exacting an appalling rate of attrition. Of no less importance, the British had failed in the crucial early stage of hostilities to score a devastating victory that might have shaken the rebels to their core.

Even though the Crown and ministry went forward with the plan to recall General Gage, the opening engagements had demonstrated the wisdom of his admonition that a huge military force would be needed to crush the colonial rebellion. When news of the twin military calamities eddied across the Atlantic, a greater sense of reality was awakened within ruling circles in London. By summer's end, North's government had begun to take steps to bring to more than thirty thousand the number of redcoats in North America, though a year or more would be required to get all these men across the Atlantic. In the meantime, Gage was scapegoated for all that had gone wrong and replaced by Howe, who had the support of nearly all military men and most civilian leaders, for he continued to be looked on as the general with the most successful record of service. The Earl of Dartmouth, one of the few cabinet ministers who had questioned many of the assumptions leading to the use of force, was also sacked.[19] His successor as American secretary—essentially the minister of war for land operations—was Lord George Germain, who had never countenanced concessions toward the colonial insurgents and since the Boston Tea Party had been an unflinching advocate of quashing the insurgency through the use of military force.

Now sixty, large and strapping, Germain remained strikingly handsome and continued to look like the soldier he once had been. Following studies at Trinity College Dublin, Germain had entered the army. He fought in two wars and additionally served in the suppression of the Jacobite rebellion in Scotland. On two occasions he had been seriously wounded in battle. However, his conduct at Minden in the Seven Years' War resulted in his court-martial and dismissal from the army, presumably ending for all time his public service. But Germain fought his way back, winning a seat in Parliament and gradually rising to prominence. His success was not due to a winning personality, as many found him to be remote and haughty. The intolerant scorned him for his homosexuality, which was an open secret. On the other hand, he was an imposing figure, considerably taller than the average English male of that day, and he was an excellent speaker and effective debater. His long-standing hawkishness toward the colonial rebels convinced many that he was the man to preside over the conduct of the war, and others presumed that given his army background, he possessed administrative skills that would be a prized asset when managing a war being fought there thousand miles away.[20]

BRITAIN'S GOVERNMENT HAD at last awakened to an understanding that a considerable army would be required for crushing the colonial rebellion, and in the fall of 1775 it took the preparatory steps for war that it should have taken eighteen months earlier when it enacted the Coercive Acts. Nearly a year would elapse after Bunker Hill before Britain's readiness was more or less complete and the king's armed forces could at last take the field. As a result of London's mismanagement, the colonists were afforded a grace period of several months, during which they raised a large army, both soldiers and officers received some training, and local committees of safety identified and often disarmed those who opposed the rebellion. The avoidance of providing breathing room to an adversary is an elementary axiom of waging war, one that Abraham Lincoln sought to convey to his generals a few decades later: "By delay the enemy will relatively gain upon you—that is, he will gain faster by *fortifications* and *re-inforcements*, than you can by re-inforcements alone."[21]

While Britain belatedly geared up for war, the Continental Congress moved rapidly after the first day of fighting in April 1775 to create a national army. The Grand American Army, as newspapers dubbed the New England militia units that had besieged Boston since the day after Lexington and

Concord, was unsustainable. The four Yankee colonies lacked the means of maintaining a large army for a prolonged period, an undertaking made all the more difficult by a blockade of their region by the Royal Navy. Nor could New England see any reason why it should bear the burden for a war that involved all of America. Furthermore, many inside and outside New England concluded that far too many officers in the Grand American Army owed their appointment to politics, not merit. Believing that a national army would solve all those problems, Congress in mid-June created the Continental army. A day later, it appointed George Washington as its commander.

Washington was not the only colonist with command experience, but his credentials were compelling. Beginning at age twenty-two, he had commanded Virginia's army for nearly five years in the Seven Years' War in the 1750s. He appeared to be prudent and thoughtful, and unlikely to make hasty or baseless choices. As he had served for years in Virginia's assembly and was currently a delegate to Congress, it was presumed that Washington could work well with Congress and provincial governors. He was forty-three and in good health, and appeared certain to possess the stamina required of his demanding post. Atop these virtues, at nearly six feet, four inches tall (at a time when the average full-grown American male stood five feet, seven inches), Washington was an imposing and awe-inspiring figure. He evinced both a polished side and a tough, forceful demeanor, and the latter indicated that he would have the mettle to "new model," or reform, the army he was inheriting, readying it for war. Furthermore, as he was not a New Englander, Washington's selection was thought to be helpful in the recruitment of a truly national army.[22]

Washington's selection was easy. The choice of a bevy of general officers was vexing, and when the job was done the Continental army, like its predecessor, was laden with political appointees. Nevertheless, some worthy veteran soldiers were chosen. Washington personally asked Congress to appoint Charles Lee and Horatio Gates, former officers in the British army who had resigned their commissions and moved to Virginia in recent years. Connecticut's Israel Putnam and New York's Philip Schuyler had soldiered in the Seven Years' War for about the same number of years as Washington, though in less consequential capacities. Nathanael Greene of Rhode Island turned out to be the biggest surprise among the dozen selected, as he was devoid of military experience and rightly thought to be "the rawest, the most untutored" among the initial general officers. Yet almost from the beginning, Washington, a shrewd judge of men, divined something in Greene that few others saw.[23]

Congress was additionally busy acquiring weaponry. New England merchants had begun trading hard currency and foodstuffs for arms and powder a year or more before the war commenced, a brisk commerce conducted for the most part through Amsterdam and obliging Caribbean ports, including French Martinique and Saint-Domingue, Dutch St. Eustatius, and Spanish Santo Domingo.[24] After hostilities broke out, Congress took up the quest for guns and munitions, and before long it was in secret contact with the French.

Eager to avenge its defeat by Britain in the Seven Years' War, France had carefully followed the American insurgency and proceeded to rebuild the navy it had lost in that earlier conflict. However, the French foreign minister, Charles Gravier, Comte de Vergennes, was wary of open commitment. The last thing he wanted was for France to find itself alone in another war with Britain, but Vergennes was emboldened by the valiant performances of the militiamen in Massachusetts. Furthermore, when George III, in August 1775, declared the colonies to be in a state of rebellion that must be suppressed and the "traitors" brought to justice, Vergennes concluded that the Anglo-American war was likely to be protracted. Wishing more information, he dispatched Achard de Bonvouloir, an army officer, to Philadelphia. Disguised as a businessman, Bonvouloir arrived near the end of the year. No time passed before he met with a handful of congressmen in talks so secret that not all members of Congress were aware of their existence. When he returned to Paris in the spring of 1776, Bonvouloir reported that the Americans were fervent for war but needed arms, munitions, and military engineers. Soon thereafter the French monarch, Louis XVI, authorized the dispatch of four army officers from the engineering school in Metz.

At almost the same moment, Congress sent one of its members, Connecticut's Silas Deane, to France to formally request assistance. Eighteen months into the war, France's first shipment of arms to the American rebels crossed the Atlantic under a cloak of secrecy. It was the end result of a complex chain that primarily involved congressional credit and the exchange of American tobacco for French weaponry and equipment. Between April and December 1777, French ships arrived in America with over two hundred pieces of artillery of assorted sizes, tons of powder, and thousands of cannonballs, bayonets, mortars, grenades, muskets, flints, tents, blankets, suits of clothing, and yards of wool and coarse linen for shirts and stockings. Not long after the first arms shipments arrived, four French generals—one of whom was the nineteen-year-old Marquis de Lafayette—disembarked in Philadelphia. Although Vergennes had acted boldly, he hesitated to enter the war, preferring to wait and see how the Americans performed in the campaign of 1776.[25]

Following his appointment, General Washington had hurried northward to take command of the army besieging Boston. He arrived in July, a couple of weeks after Bunker Hill. Fortune smiled on Washington throughout his nine months near Boston. Reinforcements sent by London trickled into the city, but not in sufficient numbers for Howe to act. Washington was free to devote his energies to fashioning the Continental army into a force capable of standing up to Britain's professional soldiers. He broke some officers and elevated others, and introduced a severe disciplinary code.[26] The siege of Boston ended bloodlessly in March 1776 when Howe quit the city, convinced—as Gage before him had concluded—that campaigning in the interior of New England was filled with insurmountable difficulties. Howe's army sailed for Nova Scotia to await further reinforcements that would enable him to take the war to New York.

While the thirteen colonies were largely freed from attack for a year after Bunker Hill, Canada was the scene of campaigning. Reports that reached Congress in the weeks following the first day of the war indicated that Canada—which Britain had gained from France only a dozen years earlier—was lightly defended and its almost entirely French residents would welcome the colonial rebels with open arms. For some congressmen, hope abounded that the loss of Canada would induce London to negotiate a favorable settlement ending the war. By late summer two divisions of the rebel invasion force were on the move. General Richard Montgomery, once a British officer who, like Gates and Lee, had moved to the colonies, commanded an army that advanced on Quebec through New York's Champlain Valley. Colonel Benedict Arnold, noted for his tenacity, combativeness, and facility for leading men, simultaneously led the second force toward Quebec through Maine. Congress was optimistic, though it understood that success probably depended on the two armies rendezvousing at the gates of Quebec long before the fierce Canadian winter set it. But snow was in the air when both reached their destination, and neither force was in good shape following their long and difficult treks northward. In the course of his advance, Montgomery had come to think of his motley, untrained band as more reminiscent of a mob than an army. Men quaked at the prospect of encountering Indians, panicked at unfamiliar sounds, feigned illness, plundered frightened civilians, and deserted in droves. Montgomery described his soldiery as "a set of pusillanimous wretches." Few armies in history encountered greater travail than that faced by Arnold's men. Mostly greenhorns unaccustomed to the wilderness, these men faced a journey of several hundred miles by foot and bateaux through formidably tangled forests and up dangerously swirling rivers. In no time, much of the food was lost in boating accidents. Snow fell on the nineteenth day of the expedition, and a short time later a hurricane blew through. A month into the enterprise an entire battalion—roughly 50 percent of the force—defected and marched home.

What was left of the two American divisions merged in December outside snowy Quebec. Only about a third of the men who had set off for Quebec were still with the army, and they were poorly supplied. Montgomery ordered a siege of the small British garrison inside the walls of the citadel high above the St. Lawrence River. But with most enlistments due to expire on January 1, it was one of the briefest siege operations ever undertaken. Choosing to attack rather than to return home without having given battle,

Montgomery ordered a strike on December 31. It was the first great battle since Bunker Hill, where the Americans had made a determined stand. But at Quebec they were the attackers, and the result was a disaster—nearly a Bunker Hill in reverse. Charging forward during a blinding snowstorm, the men advanced only a few yards before they were cut to pieces. Montgomery was killed and Arnold seriously wounded. Sixty Americans died and over four hundred were captured. When the last shot was fired, only some four hundred American soldiers remained in Canada.[27]

News of the disaster in Canada shocked a Congress that had begun to inch toward declaring independence. Although hostilities were eight months old, to this point a majority of congressmen had continued to oppose a break with the mother country. They had gone to war to force Britain to reconcile on America's terms. Opposition to independence was built largely on fear. It would be "a leap in the dark" some said, a jump into unchartered territory.[28] Others warned that a social revolution would inevitably accompany a lengthy war, and still others predicted that a weak, independent American nation would be vulnerable to conquest by predatory European powers. The strongest advocates of reconciliation also maintained that once America scored a few victories, Lord North's ministry would be replaced by a government willing to make the concessions demanded by the First Continental Congress. But if independence was declared, Britain would pour all its might into the war. The conflict would be long and desperate, and the outcome far from certain.

The reconciliationists prevailed in Congress deep into the spring of 1776, but the tide was running against them. The war radicalized many colonists, turning anger toward Great Britain into hatred of the mother country. Growing casualty lists and a host of sacrifices brought on by the war turned some who initially favored reconciliation into proponents of an indelible break with Britain. So, too, had a late 1775 proclamation issued by the last royal governor of Virginia, John Murray, the Earl of Dunmore, that offered freedom to rebel-owned enslaved people willing to fight for Britain. Dunmore's step aroused boiling fury among many white southerners who feared both the loss of chattel and slave insurrections. Dunmore had done more "to work an eternal separation between Great Britain and the Colonies, than any other expedient," declared a congressman from South Carolina.[29] For many, American independence looked attractive for an entirely different reason. The war had elevated many colonists to positions of authority that would have been unthinkable prior to hostilities, whether it was a seat in Congress, a colonial assembly, a post on a local board of safety, or a lofty rank in the Continental army. Virtually all of those positions would be forfeited the moment the colonies reconciled with the mother country.

In January 1776 Thomas Paine's *Common Sense* hit the streets. Paine, a native of England who had been influenced by the flourishing radical reform movement in his native land, immigrated to Philadelphia in 1774. In *Common Sense*, he denounced monarchy and aristocracy and urged independence. Perhaps even more important, Paine gave new meaning to the American rebellion. It was not simply a struggle against taxes, he said. It was an epochal historical event that would usher in "the birthday of a new world," a republican era devoid of kings and titled nobilities and characterized by peace and prosperity.[30] Paine's influence was critical, but it was the war—and in particular the continuing horrors in Canada—that after fifteen months of hostilities led Congress to declare independence in July 1776.

Following the colossal American defeat at the gates of Quebec on the last day of 1775, Congress quickly rushed reinforcements to its tiny, ragged army camped outside the city. Throughout the winter and spring it continued to send additional units northward. Congress's initial objective was to maintain the siege of Quebec, hopeful that the starving British garrison would be compelled to surrender before additional troops arrived from England. Congress also sent a team of observers that included Benjamin Franklin for a closer look. Their reports, which reached Philadelphia in May, painted a picture of an army that was rotten to the core and a supply system that might have been even worse. Left unsaid was the conclusion that America could not win this war by itself. But as Paine had emphasized in *Common Sense*, no European foe of Britain would provide truly meaningful assistance so long as America's war aim was reconciliation with Britain. However, if America broke away, the British Empire would be weakened, a welcome turn of events in the eyes of Britain's enemies.

Congress hardly had time to digest the dire assessments of Franklin and his colleagues before more bad news from Canada arrived. A British flotilla carrying supplies and five thousand redcoats under General John Burgoyne arrived at Quebec in early May 1776. Whatever discipline existed in the American army vanished at the sight of the royal squadron. Panicked soldiers, including officers, broke and ran. Before order was restored, the army was halfway back to the Champlain Valley. Reinforcements had brought the rebel army up to about five thousand men, though disease and deprivation had rendered many unfit for duty. Those who could fight faced a considerable army of regulars supplemented by Canadian militia and Indian allies and assisted by a powerful naval arm. For the first time since Bunker Hill, British armed forces were presented with the means of wreaking a monumental drubbing on their enemy, a defeat of sufficient magnitude that it might possibly be the turning point in Britain's campaign to destroy the American rebellion.

If the British military response in Canada had been left to Burgoyne, whose long military career evinced splashes of courage, valor, daring, and innovation, the bedraggled American force might have been eradicated. But Sir Guy Carleton, the governor and captain general in Canada, and Burgoyne's superior, responded with excessive caution. He was content to merely reclaim what had been lost in the American invasion the previous autumn. The American force slipped back toward New York, some 250 miles away, a retreat that temporarily ended at mosquito-infested Isle aux Noix, where disease and desertion largely accomplished what the British force might have done. While its soldiers died in droves—bringing to more than one thousand the number who had perished in the nine-month Canadian campaign—Congress hurriedly declared independence. John Adams summed up the thinking of most of his fellow congressmen: "The importance of an immediate Application to the French Court is clear." William Ellery, a delegate from Rhode Island, also reflected the thinking of his colleagues. It "is one Thing for Colonies to declare themselves independent," he said, "and another to establish themselves in Independency." That is, the United States would have to win the war to become an independent nation.[31]

ON THE DAY before it declared independence, Congress learned that a British armada of more than 130 ships had been sighted off Long Island. It was bearing Howe's reinforced army. The news was not surprising. Long before the British abandoned Boston in March, it was widely presumed that they would shift their focus to New York. John Adams had advised General Washington that Manhattan, together with the Hudson River, was the "Nexus . . . of the Colonies, as a Kind of Key to the whole Continent." Washington hardly required Adams's advice. He had already anticipated the enemy's invasion of New York, aware that if the British succeeded, the war was lost, for the four New England colonies and the state of New York would be irrevocably detached from the eight remaining American provinces. Britain's first step would be to take New York City, together with Long Island and all of Manhattan. Howe, not without reason, was confident that he would succeed. Howe knew that by late summer he would command the most powerful army that Britain had ever sent to America, a force of 31,600. Britain had succeeded in recruiting only some 7,000 men in the past year, but it had concluded several treaties with German principalities through which 18,000 mercenaries were hired. (Few things angered the colonists more than Britain's decision to hire the "Hessians," as the Americans persisted in calling the mercenaries. The Declaration of Independence denounced the king for having taken that step, outrage captured by a New England officer who observed, "O Britons, how art you fallen that you hire foreigners to cut your children's throats.") About two-thirds of the hirelings had reached New York and were part of Howe's army in August. Washington's army totaled 28,500, about equally divided between Continentals and militiamen.[32]

Washington doubted the worthiness of militia, but he was persuaded that a year's training had made the Continentals into decent soldiers. Events would soon demonstrate that Washington was wrong. From top to bottom, the American force that defended New York was not up to the task. Few officers, and even fewer of their men, had ever experienced combat. No one was less prepared for the challenge than Washington, who throughout the New York campaign blundered time and again. Prior to the fighting, Washington overestimated the capabilities of his raw soldiery and no less injuriously misjudged the crucial importance of his five-hundred-man troop of cavalry, first deploying them far from the likely site of battle and ultimately sending them home.[33] Once the fighting commenced, Washington magnified his mistakes through indecisiveness. But the greatest error of all was to defend New York. To attempt to defend two islands—Manhattan and Long Island—against a foe that possessed total naval superiority was to invite catastrophe. Even in the unlikely event that America's raw and untested army performed well, the enemy, with its "canvass wings" (as an American officer characterized the great vessels in the Royal Navy), could move rapidly.[34] But Congress wanted New York defended, and Washington thought his army was up to the task. General Howe, on the heels of the Canadian fiasco, was presented with a golden opportunity to deliver a cataclysmic, war-ending blow.

Howe came to New York prepared to act with vigor, or so he said. His goal was not to conquer territory, but to destroy Washington's army, for that was "the most effectual means to terminate this expensive war." To accomplish this end, Howe said, he was prepared to run every hazard.[35] But Howe blanched when he glimpsed the rebel defenses. During the preceding eight months the Americans had labored over an elaborate system of batteries and entrenchments in the city, across Manhattan, in Brooklyn, and along the Hudson River. Howe glimpsed multiple redoubts and breastworks "very advantageously placed" and "more than 100 pieces of Cannon" that awaited his army in New York City alone.[36] Seeing what the rebels had fashioned during the months of British inactivity, Howe realized that frontal attacks might replicate the results on Bunker Hill many times over. That indeed was exactly what Washington originally planned. Convinced that his army was far superior to the scruffy force that had mowed down the redcoat attackers at Bunker Hill a year earlier, Washington had set out to make his adversary pay a forbiddingly high price to take New York. But things did not go quite as Washington had imagined. Howe had no stomach for even one more Bunker Hill, let alone many repeat performances. In addition, as Washington had no way of knowing where Howe would strike first, he divided his army, posting half on Manhattan and half on Long Island. Washington's decision assured that the British would enjoy considerable numerical superiority wherever they landed.

Howe chose to launch his campaign on Long Island. Although Washington had posted seven thousand defenders near Brooklyn, he had not only failed to properly reconnoiter the area but also scattered his troops along a six-mile-long ridgeline, a distance far too great for that number of men to defend. Seeing this, many of Howe's officers proposed a straightforward frontal attack. However, General Clinton, who had gone to the trouble of exploring the region, had found a "gorge about six miles" to the east of the obvious landing site through which the army could pass undetected, after which it might loop around behind the entrenched enemy. Howe had spurned Clinton's plan for avoiding a pitched battle on Bunker Hill, but he warmly embraced this new plan, sensing that his subordinate had once again conceived the means of avoiding heavy casualties while presenting the rebels with the option to "quit directly or be ruined." Howe's ploy was for a small portion of his army to make a diversionary attack on the American defenders while the principal British force circled the enemy's left flank. The strategic plan that Howe put in place was incredibly simple, so elementary in fact that, in the words of historian Edward Lengel, "European generals would have seen through it easily."[37] But America's amateurs took the bait. The engagement was over within two hours. Some American units had fought valorously; some had not. Even had all performed courageously, the outcome would have been an American disaster. The British scored an easy victory. Over three hundred Americans were dead, hundreds wounded, and more than one thousand captured, including three generals. Those who survived took flight, running as hard as they could until they reached the entrenchments on Brooklyn Heights. Britain's only failure that day, said

Howe's secretary, was that the redcoats "could not run so fast as their Foes," whom he characterized as "Poltroons" who "ran in the most broken and precipitate manner at the very first Fire."[38] Howe's losses were in the neighborhood of four hundred, which he thought acceptable.[39]

The rebels may have thought they were safe inside Brooklyn's redoubts, though that was hardly the case. The 9,500 Americans in Brooklyn—Washington implausibly sent reinforcements to replace those who had been lost—were trapped. Their back was against the East River, which the Royal Navy controlled, while a British army of more than 20,000 men was poised to launch a frontal assault. Within hours of its first test, Washington's army appeared to be on the cusp of suffering the loss of more than 40 percent of its soldiery.

Some British officers urged Howe to attack immediately. The thinking of many of these men had been shaped by the harsh suppression of the Scottish Jacobite uprising a generation earlier. They scorned "false humanity towards these wretches" and advocated the restoration of British "dominion of the country by laying it waste, and almost extirpating the present rebellious race."[40] But Howe was not cut from that cloth. He had come to New York convinced that the American army was not "to be despised," for it contained "many European Soldiers, & all or most of the young men of Spirit in the Country, who are exceedingly diligent & attentive to their military profession." Howe later said that he believed he would suffer upwards of 1,500 casualties through a frontal attack on Brooklyn Heights, losses that would be "criminal" given that he could gain the same end through a nearly bloodless siege operation.[41] His estimate of casualties was probably accurate. That Howe shrank from the prospect was a legacy of Bunker Hill. Howe desperately hoped to avoid ever again having to experience what he had witnessed on Charlestown Heights. The qualities that once had made him a profoundly effective soldier and leader were gone. The British army on Long Island had the means of scoring a hugely decisive victory that could extinguish the American rebellion. But it was led by a commander no longer capable of ordering the cold-blooded steps necessary for doing his job. To attack the heavily fortified rebel lines in Brooklyn Heights would have been bloody, but given Howe's superior numbers and the additional firepower provided by the Royal Navy, the assault almost certainly would have culminated in a catastrophe for the Americans, possibly even a rebellion-ending calamity. Howe shrank from ordering the assault, later candidly telling London that an attack would have succeeded but that he "would not risk the loss that might have been sustained." He opted instead for a siege operation, telling himself that if the rebels were defeated, but not humiliated, colonial moderates would regain power and end the war.[42]

While Howe prepared to besiege the snared Americans, Washington acted quickly to extricate them. When a nor'easter struck and idled the British fleet, Washington gathered every available craft and sent them from Manhattan to Brooklyn to rescue his penned soldiery. His desperate gamble worked. Acting at night during thunderous downpours and later under cover of an eerie yellowish fog, Washington extricated his apparently doomed men and their weaponry. Howe subsequently said the rebels had "quitted" their refuge in Brooklyn in the "utmost silence." Rescuing nearly ten thousand men was a near impossibility, but it was accomplished and the fatal trap overcome. For the third time since that first day of hostilities along the road from Concord to Boston, a British army had lost its chance to inflict a crushing blow on its enemy.[43]

Washington's army had survived one snare only to immediately find itself in another. Convinced that Congress still wanted New York City defended at all costs, Washington kept 3,500 men in the city at the bottom of Manhattan while most of his remaining army was posted several miles to the north in Harlem Heights. It was an invitation to the enemy to strike midway between the American divisions, and that was precisely what the British did on September 15. Early that Sunday morning a landing force of four thousand redcoats came ashore virtually unopposed at Kip's Bay on the eastern side of Manhattan. The capture of every man garrisoned in the city was within Howe's grasp, for Manhattan in this sector is barely two miles wide and no American force stood between the British landing site and the Hudson River on the west side of the island. What is more, six hours passed between the redcoats' landing and the American army's retreat northward from the city to a point perpendicular to Kip's Bay. The British had ample time to seal every avenue of escape. Clinton might have accomplished the feat with the four battalions of grenadiers available to him. But his orders were to secure the high ground not far inland, and he complied. Indeed, the British stuck to the by-the-book formula for an advancing army. Audacity and innovation were not to be seen. Every rebel soldier in the city escaped, led by young Colonel Aaron Burr, a Manhattan native who guided his comrades up a country lane to an eventual rendezvous with their companions in Harlem Heights.[44]

Some 15 percent of Washington's army had been saved, but his entire American army remained on Manhattan Island and in grave danger. Shaken by events, exhausted, burdened by unimaginable stress, and no longer certain whose counsel he could trust, Washington was confused and woefully irresolute. He told Congress that he would henceforth pursue a Fabian strategy, avoiding pitched battles or putting at risk his entire army in an engagement. At the same moment, however, he set his army in Harlem Heights to digging entrenchments, in effect daring Howe to risk another Bunker Hill in a grand showdown. Washington appeared to relish a climactic face-off, even though he privately acknowledged that it could only end in a bad outcome: Either he would be starved into submission and forced to surrender following an attack (as had been the fate of the rebels atop Bunker Hill), or his trapped army would be compelled to attempt to fight its "way out under every disadvantage."[45] Howe, a professional soldier, must have foreseen the same results, yet with the most tantalizing prize of all within his sights—the destruction of Washington's army—day after day passed and the British army did not move. Nor did Washington's army budge. It stayed put in his death trap. Howe continued to shrink from ordering a frontal assault on an "enemy . . . too strongly posted to be attacked in front." Nor did he act when Clinton urged an amphibious night-time landing in the rear of the rebel army. There were "innumerable difficulties . . . in our way of turning him on either side," Howe protested. Ultimately, Howe's inaction saved Washington yet again. When General Charles Lee, sent to Manhattan by Congress, arrived early in October, he instantly sized up the situation and urged Washington to get his army off Manhattan. Lee had been a professional soldier with years of experience, and Washington took his advice. Four weeks after Kip's Bay, the Continentals made a run for it just as Howe at long last moved to put units ashore behind the American forces, the course that Clinton had earlier recommended. Washington's army barely escaped before the British sealed the exit routes. Britain had lost another chance to administer a likely war-ending defeat to its enemy.[46]

The Continentals may have made their getaway, but they were not out of the woods. They were in exceedingly poor shape, having abandoned much of their food and nearly all their tents when they set off on their hasty flight from Manhattan. The army's supply system was primitive at best, and while the soldiery was on the run it was even less reliable. Moreover, if the British relentlessly pressed them, Washington's men would in no time face a severe shortage of munitions. This was an army vulnerable to attack, but during the rebels' twenty-mile sprint to White Plains, and defensible high ground, the enemy's pursuit was nearly as sluggish as it had been following the Kip's Bay landing. In this instance, however, the Americans had a hand in slowing the regulars, for Washington repeatedly deployed units to delay his adversary. The Continentals reached White Plains in five days. The British got there in ten, and discovered that in the interim the rebels had constructed strong entrenchments anchored by a lake on one side and a hill on the other. Probably thinking that this was his last opportunity to have at his enemy before winter set in, Howe chose to do what he had not done previously. He attacked. There were times during the daylong brawl that the British appeared close to victory, and as night fell Howe spoke of launching a frontal attack in the morning. But rainstorms drenched the area for twenty-four hours, and for a time thereafter the waterlogged terrain precluded the movement of heavy artillery and wagons. Washington took advantage of the enemy's paralysis to escape. He retreated farther north, going ever deeper into the hinterland. More than two months had elapsed since the engagement on Long Island. Howe had taken Manhattan, but he had failed to destroy his foe, the stated aim of his New York campaign. Howe doubted that he could overtake and have at his retreating adversary, a course of action that a London newspaper compared to "a cow catching a hare." Above all, Howe thought the dangers were too great to chase Washington through a backcountry filled with Yankee militiamen. The British commander opted to march his army back to Manhattan.[47]

Howe was not finished for the year. He contemplated a campaign to capture control of Rhode Island, though first he turned to a prize ripe for the picking on Manhattan. After his hairbreadth escape early in October, Washington unwisely opted to leave a bit more than three thousand Continentals garrisoned in Fort Washington, a post that overlooked the Hudson River in the rural northwestern reaches of Manhattan. It was an absurd decision. Having already demonstrated that it was incapable of thwarting enemy traffic on the river, Fort Washington served no useful purpose. Furthermore, as the installation had no well, it was doomed in the event of an enemy siege. Washington should have known that the men inside Fort Washington were destined for a horrid outcome. If he assumed that Howe's demonstrated hesitancy to launch a frontal assault guaranteed the safety of the fortification, he was wrong on that score as well. Perhaps because he had accomplished so little in terms of inflicting profound damage on his adversary, Howe chose to act, even though getting at the fort required ascending a rugged and precipitous hill. It was "exceeding difficult of access," was the way Howe put it. That he threw hazard to the wind was due to the pressure that he felt to achieve something before 1776 ended. He struck Fort Washington on November 16. The battle was savage, but the outcome was never in doubt. Within a few hours, the British had taken the installation. The Americans suffered 149 killed and wounded, and 2,900 were captured. As studies have shown that in this war between 50 and 70 percent of Americans prisoners of war perished, it is likely that upwards of 1,800 taken at Fort Washington died during internment in sordid British prisons in and around New York City. The defense of Fort Washington was unjustifiable, and in its aftermath General Washington took pains to convince Congress that Nathanael Greene was responsible for the catastrophe. It was a habit that Washington had fallen into when things went wrong back in the Seven Years' War and a behavioral pattern on his part that persisted through the Revolutionary War. It was difficult to imagine something worse than the Fort Washington disaster, but seventy-two hours later the British captured nearby Fort Lee, a huge American supply depot directly across the Hudson. Washington had taken no steps in the interim to remove its treasures. Already dogged by shortages of every imaginable sort, the Continental army lost 30 cannon and 2,800 muskets as well as a veritable gold mine of ammunition, tools, and flour.[48]

For a time, Howe was energized by these two conquests. He saw an opportunity to restore royal rule in the eastern portion of New Jersey, a province that together with New York, Delaware, and Pennsylvania had been the most reluctant to declare independence six months earlier; in addition, he wanted another shot at Washington, who was nearby with a tiny army. In the wake of its narrow escape from Manhattan and the one-day engagement at White Plains, the Continental army had been broken into four parts. Washington and his generals had agreed to station four thousand men in the Hudson Highlands above Manhattan. Another division of seven thousand men had been deployed not far from White Plains and was to assist the army in the Highlands or help with the defense of New England should the British invade that region. The third segment was the three thousand men improvidently left at Fort Washington. Washington had taken the remaining two thousand Continentals—who he hoped would be augmented by state militia—and during the second week in November he had crossed the Hudson into New Jersey. When Washington entered the state he had no way of knowing whether the British would come after him, but following the fall of Fort Washington and Fort Lee he suspected that, given the Continental army's precarious situation in New Jersey, Howe would strike. He was correct. Howe gave Charles Lord Cornwallis ten thousand men and tasked him with catching and destroying Washington's army. In contrast to the enticing prizes at Howe's fingertips in August and September, the decimation of Washington's tiny force would be less consequential. But it would not be unimportant, for yet another debacle would make it decidedly more difficult for America to recruit a new army and continue the war in 1777.

In selecting Cornwallis for the assignment, Howe had turned to an unquestioned fighter. Thirty-seven years old and a twenty-year army veteran, Cornwallis had won acclaim for valor—almost reckless courage in fact—under fire during the Seven Years' War. He had quickly risen in the ranks. He was a colonel in command of his own regiment by age twenty-six, and when he arrived in America early in 1776, Cornwallis was a major general. Staid, thoroughly professional, innovative, daring, determined, compassionate, and considerate of his men—and respected by them to an extraordinary degree—Cornwallis was a soldier's soldier, a man who could be relied on for a worthy performance and, like many another, an officer who chased the dream of winning military glory.[49]

Cornwallis had shown what he was made of on Long Island, leading his men in a perilous assault that he thought featured fighting every bit as bitter as any he had experienced in Europe. He shined again in taking Fort Lee, as his men scaled steep, craggy, and rain-slick cliffs on the west side of the Hudson to get to the installation. Whereas the British had all too often dawdled in the New York campaign, Cornwallis immediately demonstrated that a new day had arrived. Aware that he possessed a three-to-one numerical superiority over Washington, Cornwallis sent out dragoons in search of the Continentals before sunset on the very day that Fort Lee fell. They reported that Washington's army was crossing into Hackensack, some seven miles away. Cornwallis put his army in motion the next morning, leaving behind tents and heavy baggage that would slow his progress.[50] The Americans had a considerable head start, but Cornwallis drove his men and steadily closed the gap, even though his adversary felled trees and destroyed bridges to slow his advance, and at times rebel artillerists laid down a deadly fire to shield their retreating comrades.

Seven days in, Cornwallis thought he could bag his foe, and he was confident that he could destroy Washington's force if he could catch it. In all likelihood, his conviction was spot-on, for even the adjutant-general of the

Continental army acknowledged that Washington commanded "the wretched remains of a broken army." On December 1, Cornwallis pushed his army to cover twenty miles, expecting to overtake the rebels in Brunswick on the Raritan River. But the Continentals were gone when Cornwallis reached that hamlet. Cornwallis had cut the distance between the two armies to a mile or so, but Washington continued to elude him and had put another river between his army and that of his pursuer. Cornwallis reluctantly paused at Brunswick. His men and horses were exhausted. He planned only a temporary respite, but word arrived from Howe to go no farther until he could join the force and have a firsthand look. Precious days passed before the chase resumed, and when it began again, with Howe at the helm, the army moved at a painstakingly measured pace. Always before, there had been a plausible, though not necessarily wise, basis for the choices that Howe had made. In this instance, however, the unhurried advance that Howe ordered was an act of folly. Not only was Washington's army badly outnumbered and in deplorable shape, but Howe was aware that the rebels were crossing the Delaware River into Pennsylvania, a dangerously slow undertaking that soldiers looked on as a time of maximum peril.

No one was more aware of the danger he faced than Washington, and he later remarked that with "a little enterprise and industry" Howe could have destroyed "the remaining force which still kept alive our expiring opposition." Whether Howe could have quashed the American rebellion by destroying Washington's tiny army is conjectural, but a British victory in the immediate aftermath of the capture of three thousand men at Fort Washington would have inflicted a crumpling blow. The damage to American morale from the loss of roughly one-third of the Continental army in a span of three weeks might have been irreparable. But for all practical purposes Howe terminated the chase, later pleading that he feared his force was being led into a trap. It was not a convincing argument. Howe possessed a vast superiority in numbers, his adversary was eviscerated and ill-equipped, Pennsylvania's militia was in Pennsylvania, and New Jersey's militia had remained largely invisible all month.[51]

Aside from his anxiety at being overtaken or assailed while crossing the Delaware River, Washington's paramount nightmare during his flight was that the British would land a second force at Perth Amboy. Should that occur, Washington's forlorn army would be menaced by Cornwallis from the north and the additional British pursuers from the east. As Manhattan was not threatened, it was a logical step, but it ran afoul of Howe's hopes of taking Rhode Island. General Clinton, who continued to see the situation with greater clarity than his commander, urged Howe to scrap the Rhode Island campaign and focus instead on Washington's army. After all, he said, the rebellion was "on the brink of being wholly crushed by the annihilation of [Washington's] corps." Clinton proposed two options: a landing on the New Jersey coast—the very threat that kept Washington awake at night—or having the navy transport a considerable force up the Delaware River. The latter might be a diversion to tie down the Pennsylvania militia, or with luck and sufficient manpower, it might take Philadelphia. Had Howe heeded Clinton's advice, Washington almost certainly would have been compelled to march his army into winter quarters at Morristown, if his force could get there. But Howe rejected Clinton's recommendations, instead dispatching him to take Newport, Rhode Island, an end that was achieved before the year closed.[52]

When Howe and Cornwallis at last reached the gray-green Delaware River in Trenton around 4:00 P.M. on December 8, they learned that the last American soldier had made it across about eight hours earlier.[53] Now that the enemy had arrived, Washington was presented with another worry. While he doubted that the British would immediately attempt to cross the Delaware, he brooded over the prospect that during the coming winter Howe would send an army over the frozen river and strike at Philadelphia, where Congress was sitting. Howe never considered such a bold and risky enterprise. Instead, with bad weather on the horizon, he put his army into winter quarters, content to finish off the enemy in the spring. That the war could not be won in 1776 was a conclusion Howe had reached long before. In September, while Washington still occupied his self-made trap on Manhattan, Howe had informed Germain that he had "not the smallest prospect of finishing the contest this campaign."[54] It was a remarkable admission with weeks of the campaign season still remaining, but given his excessive caution it had been borne out by December. Capping months of imperfect leadership, Howe carved up Cornwallis's army into seventeen separate units that were garrisoned in cantonments scattered far and wide throughout southeastern New Jersey. One cantonment containing 1,500 Hessians was located in Trenton, just across the river from Washington's army. This was dangerous business. But as Howe believed that Washington would likewise conclude that a winter campaign presented too many difficulties to be seriously considered, he felt that the small, isolated garrisons were safe. Years later Howe claimed in doubtful, exculpatory remarks that he had thought the presence of numerous cantonments strewn throughout New Jersey would encourage the "many loyal inhabitants" in the province to rally to the service of their king, producing such a sufficient force "that we might possibly have taken possession" of Philadelphia "in the course of the winter." What is known for certain is that Howe rode to Manhattan, hoping to spend a comfortable winter basking in the glow of having been made a Knight of the Bath by the king, an honor bestowed on him for what in due course would be seen as his inconsequential victory on Long Island in August.[55]

Howe had conducted a desultory campaign in 1776, the result mostly of his excessively cautious mindset. But he also had to cope with serious hindrances. He often campaigned in rugged, heavily wooded areas that bore little resemblance to Europe, where he and his officers had learned the art of war. His officers frequently complained that America's primitive conditions were unfavorable for operations, and Howe himself later attributed many of his troubles to a landscape that abounded in mountains, rivers, swamps, and thick forests. In addition, he was dogged by a lack of good maps and a hastily improvised and inadequate intelligence network. As his supply base was three thousand miles away, Howe often faced serious shortages of needed materials. Several supply ships that set off for North America in 1776 never reached Howe before his army took the field in August, and some that made the Atlantic crossing arrived with a ruined cargo. For instance, of the nearly one thousand horses sent from England in the summer of 1776, fewer than half were capable of taking part in the opening of the campaign for New York.[56] Howe's impairments were real, but they paled in contrast to the monumental encumbrances facing his adversary. Howe's worst enemy was Howe himself. When he reverted to his resolute earlier manner of leadership, as he did in ordering the attack on Fort Washington, he scored a great victory. But that conquest stands out amid a colossally long list of missed opportunities that sprang from a lack of audacity, even hard-hearted pitilessness. The British army's light infantry units were superb, and the soldiery as a whole was capable of enduring incredible privation and casualties without the loss of morale. Wars can be lost through imprudence. They can also be lost through tentative leadership.

When Howe put the army in New Jersey into winter quarters in December 1776, he thought there would be no further action until the spring. However, since crossing into Pennsylvania, Washington had wrestled with the idea of launching a surprise attack against the Hessian cantonment just across the river in Trenton, though it would be feasible only if his meager force was joined by sufficient reinforcements. Throughout December, Washington's manpower totals slowly increased. First, the Pennsylvania militia turned out. Soon thereafter the remnants of the army that had invaded Canada joined him, a step that could be taken because in the six months since its retreat from Quebec, General Carleton had failed to advance to New York's northern border. A substantial number of the Continentals posted near White Plains also appeared. Near Christmas, Washington's force had inched above eleven thousand, though not all were able and fit to serve. Nevertheless, should he choose to act, Washington could deploy a force that was three times or more greater than the number of Hessians garrisoned in Trenton.[57]

Washington chose to act. He felt that he had to do something, and so did most of his advisors. One of his officers advised the commander in chief that "even a Failure cannot be more fatal than to remain in our present

Situation. . . . [S]ome Enterprize must be undertaken . . . or we must give up the Cause."[58] Washington planned a strike against the Hessians in Trenton on Christmas night. It would be an act of incredible boldness, a roll of the dice to resurrect America's sinking morale and, perhaps, to save himself. Doubts and concerns about Washington's capabilities had grown since September, and he was all too aware of the simmering mistrust. Driven by a sense of apocalypse for America's cause and his own undoing—disquiets that had never harried Howe—Washington took his army into the lion's den, crossing the Delaware and hoping against hope that the Hessians would be taken by surprise. The odds against success increased when the weather fell apart during his army's long, circuitous trek toward the cantonment. It rained, then sleeted, and finally snowed, and throughout a keening wind cut through the men, nearly all of whom were inadequately clothed. An unspecified number even lacked shoes, and some of those unfortunate men purportedly left bloody footprints in the snow.

Getting an army across the river was no easy task, and the abominable weather only added to the difficulty. Yet the army's leaders pulled it off. Crossing on ferries, heavy freight boats, and an assortment of smaller vessels, about 2,400 men in twenty-eight infantry regiments and seven artillery companies—together with eighteen cannon, upwards of one hundred horses, and several ammunition carts—were on New Jersey soil by 2:00 A.M., about twelve hours after the van of Washington's little force had set off.[59] The men had already marched some ten miles and faced an additional trek of roughly similar distance to reach their target. They arrived on the periphery of Trenton behind schedule but before the first feeble light of day appeared in the eastern sky. There was adequate time for the various units to be organized for the assault. At 8:00 A.M., with snow still falling, Washington gave the order to attack. No American army would again fight a major engagement in such brutal wintry conditions until the Battle of the Bulge in World War II. Though the men were miserable, the deplorable weather may have been helpful. Thinking a rebel strike was unlikely given the dastardly elements, the Hessians let down their guard.

They were taken by surprise. After an hour of bloody fighting in which over 150 of the enemy were casualties and 900 captured (against barely a dozen American losses), Washington had gained what he justly proclaimed "a glorious day for our country." It was a day that would never have occurred had Washington been compelled to retreat into winter quarters earlier in the month.[60]

Washington was not finished. Within the week, he took his army back across the Delaware. Faced with the imminent expiration of enlistments of many of his men, Washington knew that if he wished to act again, he must do so immediately. His focus was the British cantonment at Bordentown, twenty miles downriver from Trenton, where another 1,500 Hessians were garrisoned. They were a tempting target, for Washington was convinced that one more victory on the magnitude of that at Trenton would eradicate whatever loyalty to the king lingered within New Jersey. However, the rebel army was hardly back in New Jersey before Washington learned of an unexpected development. Cornwallis, only ten miles away in Princeton, was made aware of Washington's second crossing. Quickly gathering some 8,000 men, Cornwallis set off for Trenton, hoping for another shot at Washington. When joined by Pennsylvania militiamen, Washington had a force of about 6,800. Spurning a Fabian strategy, he opted to make a stand. He had a sizable force and an awesome number of artillery pieces, the most thus far employed by the Continentals in a battle. He posted his men on a hill behind the Assunpink Creek just outside Trenton. The Delaware River was at his back. If the artillery and infantry could not hold off the enemy, the Americans would be trapped. Washington's decision to fight was somewhere between boldness and recklessness, and some of his soldiers thought their situation was "most awful."[61]

With darkness an hour away on January 2, Cornwallis assembled about 1,500 of his men in a sector where he believed the creek could be crossed and ordered an attack. It was a foolhardy act. Like Gage at Bunker Hill, Cornwallis had only to seal off every possible lane of escape and his adversary would be doomed. But Cornwallis was keen to have at the foe he had been unable to catch. Nor could he shake the implacable notion that a rude rebel army was no match for regulars. He was wrong. What followed was a reprise of Bunker Hill. Wave after wave of redcoats were gunned down. When darkness descended on the blood-soaked creek, Cornwallis had lost 365 men. Previously, he had lost roughly 150 men to the pickets that Washington had posted along the road from Princeton to Trenton. The Second Battle of Trenton had claimed 5 percent of Cornwallis's army.

Cornwallis was confident that he would finish the job the next day. "We've got the Old Fox safe now. We'll go over and bag him in the morning," he allegedly declared. But during the cold, dark night, Washington again wiggled out of the noose. While the British slept, Washington's army marched northward to Princeton, led by one of its officers, Joseph Reed, who had attended college in the little New Jersey hamlet and was aware of backcountry routes. With Cornwallis miles away on the Assunpink, Washington assumed that Princeton would be lightly defended. The rebel army neared the village at 8:00 A.M., not too long after Cornwallis discovered that his prey was gone. Two miles outside town, Washington and his men encountered a party of 700 British soldiers, reinforcements summoned overnight by Cornwallis. The odds were heavily in Washington's favor, and he made the most of it. Before the day's fighting in Princeton was concluded Washington had scored another victory. The British lost 450 men against only 37 suffered by the Americans. When the fighting ended, Washington at last started his men for Morristown and winter quarters.

In the nine days beginning at Christmas, British losses exceeded 2,000. The Americans had lost a tenth of that number. Since the initial engagement on Long Island in August, British losses totaled nearly 4,400 difficult-to-replace soldiers. In the nearly two years since Gage had been ordered to start a war that some in London thought might consist of no more than one battle, the British army had suffered more than 6,000 casualties. The Americans had also paid a price. Total American battlefield losses during that period were almost identical to those of the British, but in addition a considerable number of Continentals and militiamen had perished from camp diseases, and 4,430 more languished in captivity as prisoners of war.

Not for the last time, a war that many on both sides had thought would be short, and not especially bloody, had become quite gruesome.[62]

THE BRITISH HIGH command did not see Trenton-Princeton as a sign that the war was lost. They viewed the recent engagements as rather minor affairs in the grand sweep of things. That is not to say that the American victories were without an impact. In July, Ambrose Serle, Howe's secretary, had characterized Washington as "a little paltry Colonel of Militia at the Head of a Banditti of Rebels." On Christmas Eve, hours before Trenton, Serle was convinced that the campaigning in 1776 had produced the "dying Groans of Rebellion" in America. In the aftermath of the engagements at Trenton and Princeton, Serle declared that Washington's recent electrifying actions had "revive[d] the drooping Spirits of the Rebels and increase[d] their Force." At last, General Howe came to understand that the war could be won only through the application of unrelenting force that would cripple and dispirit his foe. London, too, realized that changes were necessary. The ministry augmented its North American fleet, sent over an additional 6,000 troops—its army was to be six times larger than on the day the war began—and stripped languid Carleton of his military authority in Canada.[63]

Howe would have greater resources, but he would also have to overcome a stronger adversary than he had faced in 1776. Washington, whose self-confidence had suffered in the face of repeated setbacks in New York, had performed brilliantly and seemingly put to rest questions regarding his ability. Furthermore, his officers were now more experienced, and Washington had a better sense of which ones he could rely on. The army was also altered. Whereas men had enlisted for only one year's service in 1775 and 1776—and most had departed for home the minute their obligation was fulfilled—Congress at Washington's behest had ordered a standing army. Henceforth, recruits were given an option. They could take an enlistment bonus of $100 and serve for three years or opt for a postwar land grant and serve for the duration of the war. If those enticements did not work, men could be conscripted. In time, some states, and even towns, sweetened the tender by offering greater cash bonuses in order to procure volunteers, and in desperation many provinces permitted men to enlist in state lines for a six-month tour of duty. Lengthened terms of service altered the composition of the army, once composed mostly of property-owing farmers and artisans who, to some degree, had been stirred by patriotic fervor to bear arms. From 1777 onward the Continental army soldiery was for the most part a motley band of German and Scotch-Irish immigrants, indentured servants, the landless poor, a handful of Native American New Englanders, and, after another year, growing numbers of African Americans. Faced with a standing army, Congress revised the Articles of War to allow harsher punishments, including an increase in capital crimes. The goal was not only a well-disciplined army composed of battle-tested veterans but a considerably larger force. The number of Continentals in 1775 and 1776 may never have topped 23,000, but Congress envisaged an army of 75,000 men in 1777. (That proved to be wishful thinking. The army peaked in October at 39,443.) Thanks to the secret French aid that would arrive during 1777, America's army would also be better equipped. By autumn, 90 percent of the arms and ammunition in the hands of the Continentals had been manufactured in France.[64]

The British would face a more daunting task in 1777, though their chances of scoring a decisive victory and winning the war remained good if a realistic strategy could be put together and implemented in a timely and vigorous manner. Howe drafted a plan in November, changed it a month later, altered it again after three additional weeks, and in April cobbled together a fourth plan. Meanwhile, Lord Germain, in London, put together a plan of his own, and a sensible one at that. Germain envisioned an army under General Burgoyne invading New York from Canada. It was to advance southward toward Albany while Howe was to take his army northward from Manhattan to Albany. Germain was certain that Washington would have to gather virtually the entire Continental army near Albany to prevent a linkage of the two British armies. The American secretary believed his plan offered the best chance of destroying the American army and taking control of the Hudson River, and he was correct.

Other plans were floated, including one by General Clinton, whose clarity of vision had been demonstrated during the past two years. Clinton's thinking was akin to that of Germain, though he leaned toward diversions by Howe rather than an attempt to rendezvous with Burgoyne. Clinton would have had four thousand men conduct coastal raids in New England, another ten thousand launch an offensive in the Connecticut River Valley, and ten thousand additional troops strike at rebel fortifications on the Hudson north of Manhattan. Clinton's objective was to draw away both Continentals and New York and Yankee militia so that Burgoyne would have a good chance of reaching Albany. It is not clear whether Clinton ever presented his plan to Howe, but the commander was aware of Germain's plan and ignored it. Howe decided to have his army seek to take Philadelphia. Burgoyne was to be left to cope on his own. Germain was dismayed, but due to the time lag between the colonies and the imperial seat, officials in London had always given their commanders in America considerable leeway in making strategy. Germain deferred to Howe. Nevertheless, he informed Howe that the king expected him to launch his Pennsylvania endeavor early on so that there would be "time for you to cooperate with the army ordered to proceed from Canada."

It was delusional to think that Howe could take Philadelphia and thereafter transport his army to Albany. The advance on Philadelphia would be a time-consuming undertaking, followed by a campaign certain to face worthy resistance by rebel defenders. Once Howe's mission in Pennsylvania was accomplished—and no one could know how long it might take—his soldiery and tons of weaponry and supplies would have to be conveyed to Albany some 250 miles to the north. Moreover, to reach Albany, several rebel installations on the Hudson would first have to be taken. Even if Howe acted with greater gusto than he had displayed the previous year, it was highly unlikely that his army would ever get close to Albany during the campaign season in 1777. Furthermore, British officials were consenting to a stratagem that guaranteed Burgoyne's army would remain alone and unaided deep in an American backcountry that had not been hospitable to the British in this war. Seldom in warfare had a more flawed strategic plan been devised.[65]

It was late May, five long months after Trenton-Princeton, before any British soldier took a step toward rebel-held territory. Burgoyne's men were the first to take the field, though he was disappointed in the size of his force. He had 7,250 regulars, a thousand fewer than he had wanted, fewer even than Howe had posted in New Jersey as an occupation force. Further, Burgoyne had expected to have about 2,000 Canadian militiamen and Loyalist volunteers, but had gotten only 300. He had about one-third the horses and wagons he had anticipated and only half the Native Americans he had thought would rally to his side. There was also a serious shortage of laborers needed for clearing roads and innumerable other chores. Nevertheless, Burgoyne remained optimistic. He, too, believed the amateurish rebels would be no match for his regulars. He also looked forward to being joined by hordes of New York Tories eager for the reinstatement of royal rule. He possessed 138 artillery pieces, an amount, he was convinced, that his adversary could not match. He had detached Colonel Barry St. Leger with some 3,000 redcoats, militiamen, and Indian allies on a diversion through the Mohawk Valley, a ploy designed to draw New York militiamen away from the main British army. In addition, Burgoyne had been assured by London that he could expect Howe's "cooperating army at Albany," a pledge that led him to believe that at the very least the approach of the army from Manhattan would draw away large numbers of enemy militiamen.[66]

Burgoyne had been on the move for only two weeks when he learned from Howe that he would be receiving "no direct assistance" from the main British army.[67] Burgoyne was stunned, but the jolting news did not stop him from pursuing his initial objective, Fort Ticonderoga, situated near the juncture of Lake George and Lake Champlain. Burgoyne's army arrived toward the end of June and found easy pickings. Though the installation was garrisoned by more than three thousand Americans, its commander, Arthur St. Clair, abandoned the fort and its supplies without a fight. (It was a decision that led John Adams to muse that American success might not come "until we shoot a general." None was ever shot, and St. Clair was eventually exonerated by a court-martial.) Within a week of taking Ticonderoga, Burgoyne and a small portion of his army had moved well south of it. Albany was barely seventy miles away. Such chaos accompanied the rebels' retreat from Ticonderoga that in mid-July General Philip Schuyler, commander of the Continental army's Northern Department, had no idea where his army was or even if it still existed. Nor did Burgoyne know his enemy's whereabouts. At the very moment Burgoyne was trying to make up his mind about what to do next, Schuyler confessed to Washington that the "prospect of preventing" Burgoyne from reaching Albany "is not much."[68]

Burgoyne faced difficult choices. His safest option would be to post his army at Ticonderoga and await the campaign of 1778, when Howe surely would come north. Another option was to send forward the light infantry units, trained to move rapidly and live off the land. It would be risky, as Burgoyne did not know the location or strength of his enemy, but the odds were that his adversary was in disarray. If this was his choice and his gamble succeeded, his army could quickly follow, perhaps breaking through to Albany within a matter of days. Such a choice appeared in step with his temperament. At age fifty-four, he had a long and distinguished record in Britain's army, so meritorious that he had shot upward in no time to the rank of brigadier general. Atop all his virtues as a soldier and leader, one quality in his makeup was particularly alluring to those in London who felt that an aggressive recklessness on Howe's part would have paid dividends. All knew that Burgoyne was addicted to the gaming table. He was a risk-taker. During his recent winter visit to London, Burgoyne had not been shy about letting those in high places know that he possessed the enterprise and audacity to make good things happen. He had noised about that he was "an officer with a sanguine temper" for "timely" action, the polar opposite, he seemed to say, of Carleton and Howe. But when the moment to act arrived, Burgoyne proved to be little different from Howe. He displayed gumption in rejecting the alternative of posting his army at Ticonderoga and calling off the year's campaign. But he shrank from the perilous course of hazarding his light infantry. Burgoyne opted for what under the best of circumstances promised to be a ploddingly slow advance that could devolve into a fatally ponderous operation. He ordered down supplies and his heavy artillery and called in the portions of his army that had scattered in search of the fleeing rebels. Three long weeks elapsed before Burgoyne's army was ready to move. These may have been the three most important weeks of the war.[69]

The Americans that fled Ticonderoga gradually came together during the reprieve provided by Burgoyne's immobility. Atrocities committed by Britain's Native American allies, as well as the threat posed by the invaders, also sparked New York militiamen to rally to arms in an unprecedented fashion. Moreover, General Schuyler, whose management of the Northern Department had all too often been sluggish, sprang into action. He put his men to work felling trees across roads, destroying bridges, constructing barriers, burning crops, driving away livestock, and damming streams to make them too shallow for bateaux. The steps taken by Schuyler would add crucial days to Burgoyne's advance. In the interim, rebel reinforcements were arriving. But the men who were gathering to one day fight Burgoyne would not be commanded by Schuyler. Many in Congress had never cottoned to Schuyler, and others thought the loss of Ticonderoga—the latest disaster on his watch—was the final straw. Early in August, Congress replaced Schuyler with General Horatio Gates.[70]

By then, Burgoyne had gotten a taste of campaigning in the back-country. His men were tired, having spent an exhausting two months in the field even before they set off from Ticonderoga. Thereafter, they daily muscled their way through steamy forests and labored to clear Schuyler's obstacles. Hunger was soon added to their miseries, compelling Burgoyne to detach a large force to seize a rebel supply depot at Bennington. The twenty-mile trek was about the same length as had faced the men sent by Gage to Concord two years earlier, but the outcome for the British was even worse. Both Burgoyne's raiders and a relief party were routed by Yankee militia, mostly citizen soldiers from New Hampshire who, at the war's beginning, had been nearly without weapons and who now were heavily armed. Burgoyne lost 900 men. Those losses were added to the 200 casualties the British had suffered in an earlier engagement at Hubbardton against a rebel force that had retreated from Ticonderoga. As Burgoyne had left behind one-fifth of his army to protect Ticonderoga and other American installations that he had taken, and to guard his supply line, he had to summon additional reinforcements to bring his army back up to about 7,500 men. The rate of attrition was disquieting, though Burgoyne did not panic. After all, he expected to soon be joined by St. Leger's victorious force.

Four days after Bennington, Burgoyne made a fateful decision, one that would rank with the most ruinous choices made by Britain's commanders in this war. Burgoyne chose to cross the Hudson, a step that would cut his link to his supply line. As his army prepared for the crossing, Burgoyne wrote two remarkable letters to Germain on the same day. Although he insisted, "I yet do not despond," each missive exuded an air that mixed doom with hope. Burgoyne confessed that if the worst came to pass, "fighting [his] way back to Ticonderoga" would be problematical. He advised Germain that he was basing his hazardous choice on the notion that when joined by St. Leger, his army would be capable of meeting any threat posed by the enemy. Furthermore, as he neared Albany, Burgoyne expected to find a "country in a state to subsist my army." His plan, he said, was to fortify his position near Albany "and await Sir William Howe's operation."[71] With that, Burgoyne continued his descent. Eight days after penning the letters, Burgoyne learned that St. Leger, faced with wholesale desertions by his Indian allies, had retreated to Canada.

Without a meaningful intelligence arm, Burgoyne had no idea of his enemy's strength. He was in fact leading his army down the road to misfortune, and he at last appears to have sensed as much, if he did not know it for certain. In the nearly eleven weeks since Ticonderoga's fall, the American army that Gates now commanded had grown by leaps and bounds. Gates had cavalry, engineers, scores of artillery pieces—nearly every one of which had been given to the United States that year by France—and ten thousand men. Throughout the month, militia continued to join the American ranks.

General Israel Putnam once advised Washington, "Give an American army a wall to fight behind and they will fight forever."[72] Gates and his men were entrenched and waiting.

Before Bennington, Burgoyne had predicted that he would reach Albany during the third week in August, and in his correspondence with General Clinton, who had been left in command in Manhattan while Howe was en route to Pennsylvania, Burgoyne did not ask for help. But in the wake of the disaster in Vermont, Burgoyne's sense of the trouble he faced gradually became indisputable, and he wrote Clinton again, this time asking that he send help. "Do it, my dear friend, directly," Burgoyne implored. Eight days passed before Clinton received the communiqué, but on the same day that he heard from Burgoyne, 1,700 reinforcements from England reached New York. Clinton acted. Early in October, with 3,500 men, he undertook an arduous and risky campaign in New York's Highlands. He was extraordinarily successful. Clinton's force captured three rebel forts well up the Hudson, two of which—Forts Clinton and Montgomery—were taken after an overland march through the mountains. According to one account, Clinton spurred on his men during the attack on Fort Clinton by "scal[ing] the top of the mountain, himself carrying the British colors, which he kept holding aloft, while his troops descended the steep rock, crossed the 'creek,' and carried the post." Clinton thereafter destroyed the American batteries on Constitution Island, opposite West Point, and razed Kingston, New York, roughly halfway between Manhattan and Albany. His incredible achievement removed "all the obstructions on the river between us and Albany," Clinton announced. But he lacked the manpower and the naval arm—not to mention the orders from Howe—needed to proceed to Albany.[73]

Clinton's masterful campaign did not help Burgoyne, who, it turned out, was already trapped. Burgoyne's army could neither retreat nor sustain itself for a prolonged period, and it could not fight its way through Gates's army. Burgoyne tried to break through twice, once in September in the Battle of Freeman's Farm and once in October in the Battle of Bemis Heights. He was beaten both times, and in the aftermath of the second defeat his forlorn army was surrounded at Saratoga. On October 17, Burgoyne's army of 5,895 surrendered, though Britain's total losses during the invasion of New York—including St. Leger's and the attrition suffered by Burgoyne since May—was close to 8,000. The American victory, proclaimed a rebel soldier at Saratoga, was "the greatest Conquest Ever known." His British foes similarly understood the magnitude of what had occurred. A sorrowing British lieutenant wept at the surrender ceremony, though he thought it "unmanly" to do so, and in his anguish he cursed "the stupid inaction" of Howe that had permitted "the crime" of catastrophic defeat to occur.[74]

LATE IN JULY, nearly three months after Burgoyne's army had begun its descent from Canada, General Howe loaded his army onto a flotilla of 267 ships and sailed for Philadelphia. Eight months had passed since he halted Cornwallis's pursuit of Washington, effectively ending the British campaign of 1776, and three months were gone of what should have been the campaign of 1777. Howe knew that any possibility of cooperating with Burgoyne was out of the question.

Washington had expected Howe to "form a Junction" with Burgoyne near Albany.[75] Like Germain and General Clinton, Washington thought no other strategy made sense. Howe, of course, saw things differently. His reasoning was not entirely without foundation. He believed that if he could make Washington fight, he could destroy a huge portion of the Continental army. Howe further believed that Washington would not dare permit Philadelphia—home to Congress—to be taken without a fight. Howe had earlier stated that he was "still of opinion that peace will not be restored in America until the rebel army is defeated," and he was angling for one additional chance to take on the Continental army.[76] He was further persuaded that if Britain held both New York and Philadelphia, the mid-Atlantic backcountry would suffer such economic adversity that support for the rebellion would dwindle in several states. As the four mid-Atlantic states had been the soft underbelly of support for independence a year earlier, Howe was led to think that those provinces might give up the fight altogether should Britain occupy those two key urban centers. The great flaw in Howe's thinking was that he convinced himself that an unaided Burgoyne could succeed in taking Albany. With hindsight, all things are crystal clear. Nevertheless, it is nearly impossible to understand how Howe could not have foreseen the profound dangers that Burgoyne would face on his descent from Canada. After all, Howe would sidestep having his army march the seventy-five miles from Perth Amboy to Philadelphia, fearing repeated ambushes and the difficulties he would face in securing his supply line across a long stretch in the New Jersey and Pennsylvania hinterland.

The naval transport of Howe's army was a thirty-two-day nightmare in which twenty-seven men and around 325 horses perished. Many of the equines were to have been mounts for the cavalry that Howe had hoped to utilize. When the expedition dropped anchor at Head of Elk, Maryland (fifteen miles farther from Philadelphia than he and Cornwallis had been when they reached the Delaware River the previous December), the survivors were in such poor shape that Howe had to wait three weeks for them to recover before he could put his army into action. As he lingered at the top of Chesapeake Bay, Howe wrote Germain that he would be unable to cooperate with Burgoyne. Typically, Howe assumed no responsibility for this turn of events. There would not be time for him to get his army to Albany, he disingenuously claimed, because he would be "impeded" by the nearly universal "enmity against us" on the part of the inhabitants of Pennsylvania.[77] On September 11—eighteen days after his army disembarked in Maryland and eight days before Burgoyne's first attempt to fight through Gates's lines—Howe's army squared off against Washington's at Chadds Ford on Brandywine Creek, about thirty miles west of Philadelphia. The engagement that followed was characterized by what one American officer thought was "the most severe action that has been fought this war."[78] Things were playing out as Howe had imagined, for Washington had jettisoned his Fabian tactics and was prepared to make a stand with some fourteen thousand men against Howe's sixteen thousand.

Howe's battle plan was a carbon copy of the one that had succeeded on Long Island. While roughly one-third of his men under General Wilhelm von Knyphausen struck at the center of Washington's lines at Chadds Ford,

Howe, astride a pitiful horse that was reduced to skin and bones, personally led his main army to the left on a flanking maneuver. The Americans had risen to the bait a year earlier, and Washington once again fell for the ruse at Brandywine, in some measure because he had neither adequately reconnoitered the area nor secured information from area residents about the lay of the land. He remained convinced that the most viable site for crossing Brandywine Creek was at Chadds Ford, where the water was waist-deep and the creek narrowed to roughly fifty yards.[79] Washington posted the bulk of his army at that location. Prior to the fighting, Howe had spent far less time than Washington near what was to be the site of the engagement, but he found local Loyalists that tipped him to a ford upstream. Throughout the morning and deep into the afternoon of the fray, Washington ignored intelligence reports warning of an impending enemy assault on his right flank. Heedless, Washington continued to plug additional units into his center. Around four o'clock in the afternoon, following a march of several hours on this hot, late-summer day, Howe struck. For the Continentals, this was a moment of supreme peril. In some respects, Washington's army was up against the greatest danger it would face during the war. If Howe—who had twice as many men as his surprised adversary on the flank—blasted through the American right, he might envelop and destroy Washington's entire army. Or if Knyphausen, suddenly strengthened as Washington rushed reinforcements from his center to shore up his right flank, was able to break through the rebel lines at Chadds Ford, he and Howe might jointly engulf the American army. Given Washington's irresolution, the British came within a whisker of scoring a decisive victory.

But Howe was now up against a better, more battle-hardened army than he had faced the previous year. The fighting was savage. The American right buckled, but it held off Howe's assaults until Washington tardily rushed in reinforcements. The fighting continued until the last glint of sunlight. Some on both sides speculated that with one more hour of daylight Howe would have won a pivotal victory that might have changed everything in this war, including Washington's continuance as commander and even America's commitment to carrying on hostilities. It appears that Washington reached the same conclusion, for during that stygian night his army retreated to safety.[80]

The members of Congress soon fled imperiled Philadelphia, though some made it clear that they expected Washington to continue to fight to prevent the fall of the city. In 1776, Washington had obsequiously followed Congress's wishes that New York be defended, and in risking his entire army at Brandywine, he must again have followed what he presumed the congressmen wished. But following his close brush with disaster at Chadds Ford, Washington turned a deaf ear to the entreaties of the legislators. Although he told Congress that he would either make a stand outside Philadelphia or fall on the enemy's rear as it crossed the Schuylkill River, Washington wisely permitted Howe to capture the city without another fight. When the redcoats crossed the Schuylkill unmolested, Washington fibbed to Congress that the enemy had gotten across because of the poor intelligence he had received. Four days later, on September 26, the British army—with Lord Cornwallis at its head—marched into Philadelphia, stepping briskly to the cadence of a military band playing "God Save Great George Our King." Large, jubilant crowds cheered the triumphant British in some neighborhoods, while in others "Everything appeared still & quiet."[81]

The British army's celebratory victory parade came midway between Burgoyne's two desperate attempts to fight through to safety, not that Howe was aware of his comrade's plight. Even had Howe known of his fellow general's predicament, there was nothing he could have done to help. He still faced what was certain to be a long, difficult campaign to clear the Delaware River of rebel forts, an unavoidable task if his army was to be supplied. Howe divided his army. Half the soldiers were put into the field for the dangerous work of taking the Delaware forts. The other half were posted in Germantown, north of the city between the Delaware and Schuylkill Rivers. A month before Philadelphia's fall, John Adams, who had never soldiered, saw what Howe could not see. Said Adams, "all that [Howe] could gain by a Victory would be the Possession of this Town which would be the worst Situation he could be in, because it would employ his whole

Force by Sea and Land to keep it." Once the British army took the city, Adams—again on target—commented that "Howe is compleately in our Power."[82]

Aside from clearing the Delaware River below Philadelphia, Howe had no further plans for 1777. As in 1776, however, Washington was not through. He contemplated a surprise attack on the British garrison at Germantown, hoping for another magnificent year-ending victory. Washington drafted a complicated plan and struck on October 4. The enemy at Trenton had been surprised, and that had been a crucial factor in the American victory. But the British in Germantown were not taken by surprise. Numerous other impediments to success arose, too, including Washington's egregious blunder in misusing an entire brigade for an hour in a needless firefight far from the real fulcrum of the engagement. Some of Washington's field-grade officers were infuriated by their commander's conduct. One went so far as to say that the battle had been "shamefully lost" due to Washington's mistaken action. Some British officers concurred. A dismayed wag in a London newspaper opined that at Germantown "Any other General in the World than General Howe would have beaten General Washington, and any other General in the world than General Washington would have beaten General Howe." In fact, victory for either was a long shot, though the jester's quip had come closer to the truth with regard to Washington, who squandered whatever opportunity for success was available.[83]

Thereafter, Howe withdrew his entire army into Philadelphia. Washington was under pressure from some in Congress to assault the enemy's defensive lines in the city or to mount a "vigorous Effort" to save the American forts. For a time, it appeared that he might again bend to pressure. Instead, Washington listened to the counsel of General Nathanael Greene, who prudently maintained that both endeavors would be unwise.[84] The campaign of 1777 was over, and in December, Washington's army marched into winter quarters at Valley Forge, twenty miles outside Philadelphia.

British losses for the year came to nearly nine thousand. Since that first memorable day of hostilities thirty months earlier, the British army had lost approximately fifteen thousand who were killed, wounded, or captured, three times the size of Gage's army in Boston in April 1775, a force the ministry had thought adequate for crushing the American rebellion. To this juncture, Britain's price tag for having gone to war was twenty million pounds, an expenditure many times greater than the revenue Parliament ever anticipated raising from the tax levies it sought to impose on the colonies.[85] Three years into the war, Britain held New York City, Philadelphia, and Newport, but virtually every other square inch of what had been the thirteen colonies east of the Appalachians remained in American hands.

A war that Britain might have won many times had come to this. Fateful choices led to three disasters—along the road from Concord to Boston, on the slope of Bunker Hill, and at Saratoga—and missed opportunities to inflict crushing defeats that could have been fatal to the American insurgency. When word reached England late in 1776 that Howe had failed to score a decisive victory in New York, the news prompted a despondent London pamphleteer to lament that it could mean only "a French war [is] brought upon us."[86] That had not been the case, but when the imperial capital learned of Burgoyne's surrender late in 1777, the king "fell into agonies," certain that a wider, more desperate war was at hand. Not a few of his subjects concluded that the two flawed campaigns under Howe's direction *"have cost Great Britain America."* It was the "unanimous sentiment" of New York's Loyalists, said one Manhattan Tory, that Howe's "gross and mortifying blunders" had denied Britain the victory it could have had. Even some of Howe's senior officers attributed the failure to crush the rebellion to his "monotonous mediocrity." Whatever, or whoever, was responsible for the alarming military situation that was Great Britain's lot at the end of 1777, many would have agreed with Horace Walpole, once a member of Parliament, who predicted that the "end of the American war" was approaching and that his country would not be victorious. In America, such a sentiment was more a hope than a conviction. While still in Saratoga,

General Gates privately remarked, "If Old England is not by this lesson taught humility, then she is an obstinate old slut, bent upon her ruin."[87]

No one in America knew what England would do, though the prevailing wisdom was that the former mother country's choice would be dictated by what France did. There were those like John Harvie, a Virginia congressman, who was confident that when word of Burgoyne's surrender reached Paris it would "Operate powerfully in our favour." The president of Congress, Henry Laurens of South Carolina, was less sanguine, and his assessment appeared to be the most prevalent. France, he told Washington, would enter the war only if Great Britain declared war on her, and that was unlikely. William Ellery, the congressman from Rhode Island who had cautioned that once independence was declared, it must be won on the battlefield, also doubted that France would enter the war. Ellery surmised, "We must fight our way to Independency alone," though he added: "We should be abundantly competent for it."[88]

CHAPTER 2

A NEW WAR COMING

AFTER SARATOGA, THE next step was up to the British government. It could continue to fight, with either General Howe or someone else in command of its army in North America. It could pursue victory through some new strategy. It could open serious peace negotiations with America. It could opt for peace, recognizing American independence.

Suggestions were not long in coming. Lord Germain's initial reaction, offered only one day after word arrived of Burgoyne's staggering defeat, was that Britain should abandon its attempts to destroy the Continental army and shift to tightening its naval blockade and launching destructive raids against American ports that were, among other things, havens to privateers. Parliament, meanwhile, rocked with recriminations against both the ministry's long-standing American policies and General Howe, who, according to one member of the House of Lords, "deserve[d] to be brought home in chains." Others, unaware of how the flawed strategy for 1777 had come about, savaged Germain. A member of the Commons asserted that "no man with common sense would have placed two armies in such a position as from their distance made it absolutely impossible that the one should receive any assistance from the other." The American secretary was denounced as "so soiled a character," one who was "unworthy" of his office, and an official who "through willful blindness [had] lost" America. Many argued against continuing the war, some asserting that the "reduction of America by force of arms is impossible." Burgoyne's fate, it was said, "evinced the folly of attempting a conquest" of America. Another predicted that the continuation of "the accursed American war" would result in the "havoc and ruin" of Britain's economy, and perhaps much more. Some were for immediately granting the colonies their independence. Britain's minister to Prussia offered a unique option. He favored not only independence for the colonies but also simultaneous attacks on French and Spanish Caribbean colonies, a step that would "force a free trade in the Gulf of Mexico." George III staunchly opposed independence and initially insisted that the war must be waged as previously. Soon, however, he called for a review of British strategy, though he radiated confidence that the war could yet be won. He told Lord North that the "present misfortune" was "not without remedy," ruminated about sending an additional five thousand men to America, and reminded others that Britain had triumphed in the Seven Years' War after a bad start. The monarch said little about what was on everyone else's mind: the gloomy apprehension that France and Spain would enter the conflict.[1]

Time would tell what England's two traditional European rivals would do. Meanwhile, Lord North, who for some time had quietly harbored reservations about Britain's ability to win the war, wrestled with offering generous peace terms to the Americans. Peace would terminate a costly and uncertain war in North America and, at the same moment, prevent a destructive war with France. North held on to the hope that the colonies might accept a peace settlement short of independence. After all, New York, Newport, and Philadelphia were in British hands, thousands of prisoners of war languished in British jails, and the colonists had suffered in the neighborhood of twelve thousand battlefield casualties atop untold numbers that had perished of diseases. Although the Americans were celebrating the victory at Saratoga, North suspected that many were weary of war. Some militiamen had been summoned to duty time and again, forcing long and painful absences from their farms and workbenches. The same maladies that had killed soldiers had here and there coursed into the civilian sector, taking a heavy toll.

Americans were groaning under burdensome wartime taxes, and thanks to the Royal Navy's blockade, many precious commodities were no longer available. If all this was not sufficient to bring the colonists to the bargaining table, North believed that the Americans understood that if the war continued, it might go on for a great many more years. He knew, too, that in 1776 the colonists had been deeply divided over declaring independence, and he felt that a serious peace offer might reopen those fissures, provoking sufficient disunity to make it difficult to continue the war. (Not for nothing did General Washington curse North's "art & villainy" when he learned of the prime minister's plans to offer peace terms.)[2]

While still mulling over what to include in his peace plan, North quietly dispatched emissaries to confer with Benjamin Franklin, one of three United States envoys sent by Congress to Paris. North appears to have believed not only that Franklin favored an accommodation, but that he had spoken favorably of a French alliance merely as leverage for extracting a more generous offer from England. Early in January, Franklin had indeed remarked that "America is ready to make peace. If Great Britain desires to make peace, let her propose the terms." In reality, Franklin most certainly favored both an alliance with France and American independence. Fully aware that nothing was secret in Paris, Franklin's real objective in openly appearing to be receptive to a peace overture by London was to have the French government believe that America would come to terms with England if a Franco-American alliance was not forthcoming. North's envoys sought to persuade Franklin of the dangers that America would face in putting its trust in France. The French, said one to Franklin, have "no affection for America nor have they shown any when the alarms of America were at the greatest."[3] Franklin was not swayed. He was also noncommittal. After hearing from the diplomats who had made contact with the American emissary, North knew only one thing for certain: Britain's peace offering would have to be exceedingly generous in order to compete with a tender of a French alliance, should that in fact materialize.

North waited patiently before showing his hand. He wished to gauge sentiment in Parliament and to learn France's intentions. At last, in mid-February, the prime minister was ready to act. By then, he knew not only that the Commons had rejected a motion that would have prevented the dispatch of additional troops to America, but also that intelligence from Paris indicated France would offer the American envoys a treaty of alliance. North, an adroit politician, also knew that the prospect of French belligerency would boost support for his stab at reconciliation, as many in Parliament desperately wished to avoid war with both France and America. Some seventy-five days after word of Burgoyne's surrender reached London, North—in a two-hour speech that one observer labeled a "confession and humiliation"—unveiled his plan to bring the colonies back into the British Empire.[4]

The prime minister opened with a mea culpa. Not only had the "war in America . . . turned out very differently" than he had imagined, but the Coercive Acts had "produced effects which he never intended." Thereafter, he introduced his plan for Britain's reconciliation with its colonies. In essence, he offered the Americans what the First Continental Congress had demanded six months prior to hostilities:

> Parliament would never attempt "to tax them again";
> the colonists might make "some reasonable and moderate
>   contribution to the common defence";
> all American legislation enacted by Parliament since 1763 would be
>   repealed;
> the American Congress was permissible so long as it did not breach
>   Parliamentary sovereignty;
> Britain would not station a standing army in the colonies in
>   peacetime;
> the Crown would never again change a colonial charter without the
>   colonists' consent;
> Americans would be given preference when colonial offices were
>   filled;
> the customs service would be staffed solely with Americans; and
> aid would be extended to help the colonists reduce their war debts.

North insisted that Parliament must regulate all imperial commerce—which the First Continental Congress had been willing to accept in 1774—and "the claim of independency set up by America" was off-limits. The prime minister also spoke of sending commissioners to America to conduct negotiations. Peace was his goal, but he assured Parliament that if the colonists spurned his offer, hostilities would continue. He added that Britain yet possessed the means of winning the war: "We might raise many more men": the "navy was never in greater strength"; and Britain's "revenue [was] very little sunk." Before the month was out, Parliament approved the prime minister's peace plan and his appointment of the multi-member Carlisle Commission, the team of envoys to be sent to America to seek reconciliation based on North's initiative and, if necessary, to agree to an armistice while negotiations were conducted.[5]

A FEW DAYS before his conciliatory speech, Lord North learned that France and the American envoys in Paris had signed treaties of alliance and commerce, though those pacts would not go into effect until approved by the Continental Congress in Philadelphia. The accords came two years after France opted to provide secret aid to the Americans, assistance that was vital to Gates's victory at Saratoga. In 1776, Louis XVI had approved steps to ready France for war. During the following year French officials had made the decision to enter the war within about twelve months, unless America suffered fatal disasters in the interim. For years, France had been rebuilding its navy, which had been decimated by Britain in the Seven Years' War, and all along the target date for completing the rearmament program had been 1778. Throughout 1777, as France inched toward hostilities, it sought to persuade Spain to also enter the war, a step that would give the Allies naval superiority.[6]

Serendipitously for Comte Vergennes, France's foreign minister, word of Saratoga reached France in December 1777. So, too, did news of Germantown. It had not been an American victory, but when John Adams arrived in France as an American diplomat soon thereafter, he discovered that the combination of Washington's boldness and daring in undertaking yet another surprise attack and Gates's magnificent victory had convinced the French that they would not be betting on a loser in allying with the United States.[7] Vergennes was no less struck by the reality that in three years of war Britain had been unable to suppress the American insurgency. The Americans had endured, and their army was led by what the French saw as an audacious commander. To Vergennes, entering the war would be a winning bet: France could gain revenge for its humiliating defeat in the Seven Years' War, win valuable prizes in the Caribbean, weaken Great Britain's hand in European affairs, and capture a share of American trade. Moreover, it appeared that France would have no need to commit troops to North America. The blend of French naval prowess and Washington's boldness would be sufficient for coping with Britain's armed forces.

Franklin and his colleagues—Silas Deane and Virginia's Arthur Lee—met with Vergennes immediately after word of Burgoyne's surrender reached France. Serious negotiations were underway by mid-January, two weeks before North's envoys met with Franklin. From the outset, the American diplomats pledged that if a formal alliance with France could be reached, and if France soon thereafter entered the war, Congress would reject any British offer of reconciliation. Early in February, Vergennes learned that Spain would not enter the American war. Even so, France was prepared to go it alone, and in February the Franco-American treaties were signed in Paris. More than a month later, the French ambassador in London officially notified North's government of the alliance. Great Britain soon declared war on France.[8]

Once London learned that France had offered to ally with the American rebels, virtually no British official—with the possible exception of Lord North—expected the Americans to accept Britain's peace terms. (Horace Walpole, a perceptive observer, prophesized that the members of the Carlisle Commission were on a journey "to make a treaty that will not be made." To that, he added, "Acts of Parliament have made a war, but cannot repeal one.")[9] With the continuation of hostilities a virtual certainty, North spent much of the spring fighting off attempts by the opposition in

Parliament to end the war by recognizing American independence, a step that many found more appealing than ever now that French belligerence was assured. Some maintained that peace was essential for the "dearest interests of this undone, disgraced country." Edmund Burke called for peace with America on the grounds that the colonies were in reality already independent. Others asked how Great Britain, which had failed in the course of three campaign seasons to conquer the colonists, could possibly win a war against both France and the United States. One member of the House of Commons, who had taken his seat after serving as an army officer in America since the war's beginning, asserted that Britain could not put down the rebellion if it sent fifty thousand soldiers across the sea. North America was just too large, he said. Others in the Commons had heard from despondent officers in America who counseled that the war could not be won given that the colonists were "almost unanimous" in their antipathy to Great Britain. Nevertheless, the ministry's nearly two-to-one majority held. If peace did not result from the negotiations pursued by the Carlisle Commission, the war in North America would go on. It would continue, said one in the Commons who reflected the sentiment of many, "so long as there was a prospect of success or any real advantage from conquest."

But Britain's conduct of the war would no longer be based on the illusions of 1775. "The Americans had . . . been always represented as cowards; this was far from being true," confessed one member of the House of Commons in 1778. Another, who reminded his colleagues that the colonists had once been seen as "lawless, desperate adventurers," declared them to be "men of the most exalted sentiments." In addition, not only had General Washington won the respect of Britain's leaders, but the notion that militia-men would shrink from fighting regulars had been laid to rest.[10]

Nor could Britain's old military strategy be maintained. Both Saratoga and the looming war with France necessitated a strategic reappraisal. Opinion in Parliament was divided over the proper course. One faction, in which Germain was a major player, emphasized that wars were unpredictable and that the loss of the thirteen mainland colonies might yet be prevented. The First Lord of the Admiralty, John Montagu, the Earl of Sandwich, was the paramount figure in the second faction.

After Eton and Cambridge—and an unhappy marriage at age nineteen, followed in midlife by years of living openly with a mistress who was twenty-seven years his junior—Sandwich had served as a diplomat and in assorted ministerial posts. In 1771, at age fifty-three, he embarked on his third stint as First Lord of the Admiralty, a position he would occupy throughout the Revolutionary War. Sandwich proved to be a commendable administrator. Prior to 1778, he had offset inadequate funding for increasing the size of the fleet by initiating reforms that added years to the life span of the ships of the line. French belligerency spurred spending for the navy, and Sandwich gradually increased the number of ships of the line from thirty-six to ninety. Even so, the navy was saddled with waging war in several theaters. From day one, it was apparent that the navy was overextended, as it faced the necessity of defending Britain's interests at home as well as in the Mediterranean, South Seas, North America, and the West Indies. In North America alone, the navy had to cope with some two thousand rebel privateers, blockade the lengthy Atlantic coast, assist the army, protect convoys, and defend against the French adversary.[11]

In the late winter and spring of 1778, as the cabinet debated how to wage the war, Sandwich correctly suspected that France would focus its primary energies in the West Indies. Great fortunes had been built in England from these tropical islands. Rum and sugar from what many termed the "sugar islands" were more valuable commodities than any products exported to Britain from the mainland provinces, and in addition coffee, chocolate, ginger, cotton, indigo, and textile dyes also flowed from the tropics throughout the British Empire and into Europe. A vast slave trade, now a century and a half old, was central to the wealth of the islands and the riches of entrenched interests in England. Not surprisingly, powerful political forces in England urged that greater stress be placed on the defense of Britain's West Indian possessions than in recovering the North American colonies. Sandwich and his confederates accurately observed that England's grip on its Caribbean islands was tenuous. Not only was France thought to already have five times as many troops in place in the region as did Britain, but the Royal Navy would be stretched to the limit if it had to simultaneously seek to restore British control in the mainland colonies while defending Britain's colonies in the West Indies.

Given the daunting multiple tasks that faced the navy, Sandwich had to make choices. He wished to concentrate naval prowess on the western periphery of Europe—which had been the Admiralty's successful strategy in two previous wars—and in the Caribbean, and he advocated Britain's withdrawal from North America. But some important figures were unwilling to turn their back on the thirteen colonies. The king, Lord North, Germain, and William Eden, the undersecretary of the Northern Department and a close friend of the prime minister, all believed that if mainland North America became only a secondary object in the war, Britain would in time lose not only its thirteen colonies but Canada, Nova Scotia, and the Floridas as well. In the wake of the lack of success since 1775, and the pending opening of new theaters of action that would inevitably strip away resources from waging war in North America, those who thought it still possible to salvage something in mainland America had no choice but to conceive a new strategy.[12]

Ministerial officials slowly moved toward a policy of bolstering Britain's armed forces in the West Indies while remaining active against the American rebels, albeit with fewer troops. Early on, it was understood that many units would have to be sent to the Caribbean, including some currently posted in the thirteen colonies, and in March, Germain ordered that five thousand troops in occupied Philadelphia be detached for a pending invasion of France's West Indian island of St. Lucia. Another three thousand were to be sent to Canada, Nova Scotia, Newfoundland, and East and West Florida. As those deployments would reduce the prowess of Britain's army in the mainland colonies, the American secretary also ordered that Philadelphia be abandoned. The units that were not slated for redeployment elsewhere were to be posted in Manhattan, but if New York could not be secured, it, too, was to be relinquished, and the army was to retreat to Halifax and await further orders.[13] With the British army in the thirteen colonies slated to be much smaller than when the campaign for New York had commenced eighteen months earlier, Britain's government had in effect scrapped all plans for the reconquest of the northern provinces.

Once the overall game plan for coping with two enemies in separate theaters was resolved, it fell to Germain to make strategic recommendations for Britain's army in North America. Germain clung to the notion of the army continuing its attempts "to bring Mr. Washington to a general and decisive action." He additionally urged repeated coastal raids from New York through New England, ruinous sorties that would bring the war home to civilians and erode morale.[14] But all the while, the American secretary's thinking was turning in another direction. His focus shifted to the southern provinces, where he glimpsed the possibility of Britain coming away from this war with something of considerable consequence. Turning southward, however, would depend on French strategy. Sandwich had been arguing that France would neither attempt to regain Canada nor provide much help to the Continental army. Instead, it would focus on India, West Africa, and the Caribbean. If Sandwich were proved correct, Germain thought it conceivable that Britain could undertake an offensive strategy in the South. This was not the first time the South had beguiled military planners in London. Late in 1775 the British had readied a naval task force to assist what North Carolina's royal governor had described as a teeming throng of Loyalists chafing to fight for their king. Not much came of the endeavor, as the Loyalists had been defeated by rebel forces during the flotilla's Atlantic crossing. Thereafter, the South had remained on the back burner, though it was never entirely forgotten.

Germain was intrigued by the possibilities in the South. For one thing, the South supposedly overflowed with inhabitants who had never been swept with enthusiasm for American independence. Some were thought to have remained loyal to the Crown as a result of their Anglicanism, some from fear of losing their slaves in the course of a republican revolution, and some from their bountiful prewar trade within the British Empire. Nor was it a secret that deep divisions separated the backcountry residents in the Carolinas from the coastal elite who had long dominated the two provinces and exploited the small farmers in the hinterland. For instance, in the late colonial period, three-fourths of South Carolinians resided in the back-country, but the region had been allotted a tiny fraction of the seats in the provincial assembly. Backcountry residents had complained that they were overtaxed, bridges that they needed had not been constructed, and they had been provided insufficient protection against the Indians. Germain and others felt that Britain might take advantage of the sectional discord.[15]

By the spring of 1778, Germain had begun making plans for imple-menting what would come to be called the "southern strategy." His was "a view to the conquest and possession of Georgia and South Carolina," where many inhabitants were eager "to return to their allegiance" to the Crown. He contemplated raising units of Loyalists, a step the British had largely overlooked in the initial three years of fighting. These provincial regiments, as they came to be called, would become part of the British army that recon-quered lost territory. The army was to be augmented by Loyalist militia, some of which was to serve as an occupation force in liberated areas. During the spring, Germain additionally broached the idea of committing a "corps of 2000 men" to retake Savannah, after which Indian allies and troops from Florida might pacify the Georgia backcountry. Crushing the rebellion in Georgia, he added, would lead "great numbers of the back[country] inhab-itants" in South and North Carolina to enlist in newly forming Loyalist units. Thereafter, while a large British army campaigned "to reduce Charleston," these expanding Loyalist detachments would subdue "that tract of pineland which separates" South Carolina's low country and the piedmont, cutting off "all succour and retreat" for Charleston's defenders. In the meantime, diversions should be made into Virginia and Maryland to prevent those colonies from aiding their fellow rebels in South Carolina. Success was something "we may reasonably hope for," Germain predicted. Reclaiming Georgia and South Carolina—and possibly North Carolina as well—might turn the war around. At the very least, the British armed forces in the Caribbean could draw essential supplies from those reconquered southern provinces. What is more, retaking these southern colonies would impede the long-standing rebel practice of trading low-country rice and

Chesapeake tobacco for war materials from Europe, a step that would adversely impact America's prosecution of the war.[16]

Germain had conceived a strategy that, if successful, could at minimum leave Great Britain at war's end in possession of a vast American empire that swept from Newfoundland's valuable fisheries to Canada's rich interior farmland; from the splendid agrarian heartland in trans-Appalachia to the inordinately beneficial tobacco and rice colonies in the South; from Florida, with its long growing season and access to the Atlantic and the Gulf of Mexico, to the fortune-making sugar islands in the Caribbean. Furthermore, with Britain in possession of all this, the United States would at best be a diminutive union of perhaps ten states hemmed in by British dominions to the west, north, and south. The postwar United States would be so weak and uninviting that in time the citizenry's "distress [would] bring them back to their duty"—that is, rekindle the desire to reconcile with the Crown. Germain knew the southern strategy could not be put into play immediately, but he was confident that before long it could be set in motion. He was no less convinced that his design would succeed if only the commander of Britain's army adhered to his plans.[17]

But who would command Britain's army in North America? A successor to General Howe had to be found, as during the winter he had sent home his letter of resignation. The government first offered the position to Lord Jeffrey Amherst, who had commanded Britain's army in America during the Seven Years' War. He thought a military conquest of America was impossible unless the British army was increased to forty-four thousand, almost a third again larger than the number of men Britain had deployed in the thirteen colonies in 1776 and 1777. When Amherst learned that such numbers would not be available, he declined the tender and counseled that under the circumstances naval operations offered the only hope of success. But neither the king nor the ministry were willing to jettison the land war, and Germain eventually settled on General Henry Clinton, who had earlier been his choice to lead the campaign to take Albany. Some were uneasy because of Clinton's lack of command experience, but in military circles he was renowned as a strategist and his record in taking Newport and attempting to rescue Burgoyne had been exemplary. Germain spoke of Clinton's "gallant behaviour" and the "royal confidence" in him. One of Clinton's friends, dissembling somewhat, reported that he had been "the favorite of everybody" to take command of Britain's army in America. Clinton accepted the post.[18]

AMERICANS HAD FOLLOWED the campaign of 1777 with great apprehension, and never more so than in the early going when it appeared that Howe would attempt to link up with Burgoyne, a prospect that led one congressman to wring his hands over the "calamities [that] betide us." Even after it was apparent that Burgoyne was on his own, no one breathed easily. Members of Congress pinned their hopes on General Horatio Gates and a sizable turnout of Yankee militiamen. John Adams, a Yankee himself, had exhorted his fellow New Englanders to rally to arms. "Now is the Time to Strike. New Englandmen! strike home," he urged. Another delegate to Congress predicted that if Gates "gives a check to Burgoyne his name & memory will ever be dear."[19]

Burgoyne's setback at Bennington aroused hopes among many. Richard Henry Lee of Virginia immediately predicted that if Burgoyne did not "retire very quickly" to Ticonderoga, "his destruction" was certain. But as Gates's clashes with Burgoyne neared, others, including Adams, worried that the British general would "deceive" him: "Oh, Heaven! grant Us one great Soul! One leading Mind [to] extricate the best Cause, from that Ruin which seems to await." Within days, word arrived that Burgoyne had failed in his first attempt to break through. Maybe there would be "a Happy issue of the Campaign" after all, allowed a New York congressman. Two weeks later news reached Pennsylvania that Burgoyne had been "beaten in two pitched battles" and that his army was "shattered." Hard on the heels of that disclosure came word "of the Captivity of General Burgoyne with his whole Army," a revelation—exalted one congressman—that God had "remarkably favoured our Cause." It was "a glorious close to this campaign," he added.[20]

Congress was so delighted that it awarded the messenger who had brought the news of Burgoyne's surrender a shiny set of spurs. Understanding that Gates had taken command of a dispirited army, restored morale, and drawn huge numbers of New England militiamen to his side, delegates lavished praise on the victorious general for his "critical and decisive" win, told him that his "Name . . . will be written in the breasts of the grateful Americans of the present Age & sent down to Posterity in Characters which will remain indelible," and wished him "many happy Years enjoyment of the Fruits of your great Labours in peace hereafter."[21] Congress quickly dispatched a fast ship to France with word of America's victory. One American soldier, posted downriver from Albany, later recalled that when news of Gates's victory arrived, "the ground trembled" with cheers from the soldiery. In their ecstasy, he said, the soldiers picked up stones and hurled them at a British vessel nearby in the river, an act that led the ship's captain to retaliate with a broadside that forced the Continentals to dive for cover. There were celebrations in New England's coastal cities and towns, with "a general discharge" of the shore batteries and the guns on all the ships in the ports. Some states declared a day of thanksgiving. Saratoga also inspired a host of patriotic songs and poems, some lampooning Burgoyne as "Jack Brag" for the menacing proclamations he had issued during his army's advance southward from Ticonderoga. One ditty proclaimed:

> HERE'S a health to the States,
> And the brave General Gates,
> Whose conduct in history will shine;
> In the year seventy-seven,
> With the assistance of heaven,
> He defeated th' important Burgoyne.[22]

As the drama in upstate New York unfolded, every congressman had prayed that Washington could likewise "destroy" Howe's army and "put an End to a most unnatural & inhuman War." Although he failed to accomplish that feat, Washington was not criticized for his lack of success at Brandywine and Germantown. Most recognized that he had faced a larger, better army than Gates had beaten. However, some in Congress were not happy that Howe had been able to take Philadelphia "without a Battle" after Brandywine, a turn of events that compelled Congress to flee to backcountry York, Pennsylvania, a "most disagreeable Town" in the estimation of many delegates. More than Washington's failure to defend Philadelphia provoked rancor. Some, inside and outside Congress, had not forgotten his many mistakes in the New York campaign, and others were roiled by Washington's unwillingness to do more to oppose Howe's offensive against the Delaware River forts following the occupation of Philadelphia. Some, swept off their feet by Gates's heroics and his ability to inspire militiamen, were certain this more experienced former British field officer was better equipped than Washington to command the Continental army. In 1776, Washington had learned of criticism of his generalship, but the number of critics had been minimal in contrast to the swelling chorus of detractors and the sulfurous quality of the caviling in the winter of 1777–1778.

"We want a General," groused one congressman, expressing a viewpoint with which many others concurred. Much had been "sacrificed to the Insufficiency of our Commander in Chief," another charged. In time, as more was learned about the engagements at Brandywine and Germantown, some charged that Washington had committed "Blunders as might have disgraced a Soldier of three Months Standing." The commander's indecisiveness was fodder for complaints. Others thought he shrank from taking risks or carped about the soldiery's lack of discipline. Critics blasted Washington's failure to rectify the army's administrative deficiencies, which included a disgraceful supply system, deplorable intelligence-gathering network, and woefully managed medical department. (One exasperated faultfinder remarked that the surest way to defeat the British army was to entice the redcoats "through any of the villages . . . where we have a [Continental army] hospital, and . . . in 6 weeks there shall not be a man of them alive or fit for duty.") Still others were nettled by Washington's devotion to a standing army, inveterate distrust of militiamen, and what they believed was his proclivity for surrounding himself with sycophants. The secretary of

Congress privately remarked that Washington was "deficient" in those "marks of true greatness" exhibited by history's most successful generals. So many delegates had grown jaded that Washington's opinions were said to be "treated with . . . much indecent freedom & Levity" within the halls of Congress.

Inevitably, word of the disaffection got back to Washington, who concluded that a vast conspiracy by a "malignant faction" both inside and outside Congress wished to see him replaced by Gates. His aide-de-camp Alexander Hamilton, probably reflecting Washington's outlook, referred to the cabal as a "monster" of the "most extensive" size. Washington was convinced that Gates was part of the plot and that Thomas Mifflin, once his aide-de-camp and later the quartermaster general, and Thomas Conway, a colonel in the French army who had arrived in America early in 1777 as a volunteer, were deeply involved in the intrigue to "ruin [his] reputation and influence," and ultimately to remove him. Shaken and angry, and convinced that Gates, Mifflin, and Conway were only the chiefs among the schemers, Washington was driven to spending portions of his busy days poring over anonymous letters that rebuked him in hopes of learning the identity of his other critics.

Washington overestimated the threat of his removal, as nearly every congressman understood that he was "too well established" to be removed without incurring fatal domestic divisions. Furthermore, some worried that his removal, or any attempt to oust him, might lead France to shy away from allying with a country that appeared to be torn by internal discord. Summing things up, a Pennsylvania delegate remarked that should Washington be "sported with . . . his Country & his Country's Cause will inevitably suffer." Another despaired that Congress was stuck with Washington, leading him to conclude that in the end the cause might "sink with him."[23]

Those who truly wished to oust Washington never constituted a majority in Congress. Most in Congress continued to see him as the best man for the job. He had made mistakes, but he had not abused his power, no hint of scandal hung over him, and he had worked well with Congress and state officials. He had also faced a Herculean task, preparing an army of callow soldiers and officers to take on a large, well-equipped professional British adversary.

But Washington did face opposition. As historian Mark Edward Lender has demonstrated in an important recent work, Congress never sought to overthrow Washington, but it did wish to establish greater control over the army. It hoped to institute administrative reforms leading to greater civilian influence over strategic goals and the army's organization, including decisions over personnel and the assignment of theater commanders. Above all, it aimed to overhaul the army's supply system. The motive for these moves was the belief that in at least some areas Washington was incapable of adequately reforming the army and that without proper reforms the army would be incapable of winning the war. While Washington exaggerated the danger he faced in being removed, he eventually came to understand that the real threat was the loss of some of the power he wielded as commander in chief of the Continental army. He fought back. His talents as a political infighter have often been underestimated. He marshaled those talents, and many of the officers who surrounded him—and had hitched their wagons to his star—joined with him in the fight, heaping invectives on the putative schemers. (Hamilton wrote letters characterizing the plotters as "villainous" and "vermin.") Some men of influence, including Robert Morris and Gouverneur Morris, powerful merchants and congressmen, believed in Washington, or feared that the proposed reforms would be ruinous to the war effort, and did what they could to thwart those who had moved to limit the commander's jurisdiction. Those on both sides were driven by patriotic motives. Washington believed that unity of command in the army was essential to victory. Those on the other side were convinced that only drastic change in the structure of the army could bring victory. In the end, the move by Congress to exert greater control over the army largely collapsed, dying in the face of opposition from within the army, a body that was not to be trifled with in the midst of a desperate war, and from fear that the Pandora's box that was to be opened was likely filled with fatal uncertainties. By

March, General Greene noted that "the late faction . . . vanishes like a mist before the warming beams of the sun in a summer's morning."[24]

THROUGHOUT THE WINTER of 1778, as rumors swirled about French intentions in the wake of Saratoga, many a congressman scratched his head over the "Misterious Conduct of the French Court." While nearly everyone in Congress thought France would continue to provide sufficient aid to keep America from losing the war, many doubted that the French would agree to an alliance, principally from fear that Britain was "still so formidable." Some devotees of realpolitik believed the French would be happiest if both England and the United States were "well beaten" so they could collect the spoils. Just before Christmas 1777, a leader in Congress said privately that he felt the French—whom he labeled "our artful, specious half-friends"—were "playing off these Infant States as puppets" for their own benefit. He expressed a widely held view in forecasting that France would become a belligerent only if Britain declared war on them. Nearly five months after Saratoga, a Rhode Island congressman fumed that France "still pursues her old equivocal line of conduct," telling America's envoys in Paris that they must be content with "an assistance as underhanded as it is efficacious."[25]

But just as spring was bursting out in rustic York, Pennsylvania, the surprising news arrived that treaties of alliance and commerce had been signed with France. From America's point of view, the terms were more than generous. Each country had agreed not to make a separate truce or peace with Great Britain, and France pledged not to lay down its arms until American independence was recognized; France additionally renounced all claims to Canada. These bountiful terms sparked an instantaneous reversal of opinion toward France. An effervescent mood seized the country. Many now lauded the "magnanimity and goodness" of Louis XVI or praised the "Wisdom and Magnanimity" of the French. A Yankee congressman called the French king "the great protector of the Rights of Mankind." Another said he was "the most wise, most just and most magnanimous prince, not only in the world [but] in history." Some gushed that France did "not . . . take advantage of our situation so as to obtain unequal advantage" of American commerce. "[W]e chuse [who] to trade with," one congressman exalted. It was, said a Pennsylvanian who spoke for most congressmen, an accord that "far exceeds my most sanguine expectations."[26]

A great many Americans cherished the hope that not only would the alliance guarantee American independence but that the war would end in the near future. An ecstatic Pennsylvanian captured the prevailing sentiment when he wrote his congressman that the "arduous contest for American Independence is near at an end . . . & that [the] Brilliant Revolution is accomplished." As the treaty demonstrated that America had "taken her rank among the Nations," not a few believed that Spain and Holland would also soon enter the war as American allies. Thomas Paine, like many others, thought England would immediately recognize American independence and make peace in order to avoid a wider war. New York's Gouverneur Morris foresaw peace within three months. Patrick Henry expected the war to continue, though he thought that because of the alliance America had escaped "a dreadful precipice." The new nation's ultimate triumph, he said, hinged on "our holding fast [to] our attachment" to France. A Continental staff officer thought that General Washington, who was unsurpassed in hiding his emotions, was near tears of joy when a messenger brought the news of the French alliance. Although Washington did not predict the war's immediate end, he acknowledged that the alliance would "give a most happy tone to all our affairs." The commander added that affairs were "verging fast to one of the most important periods that ever America saw," for the war now was "verging fast to a favourable issue." Washington jubilantly added, "This is great, 'tis glorious News and must put the Independency of America out of all manner of dispute." In place of the "dark and tempestuous Clouds which at times appeared ready to overwhelm us," he continued, "serenity" was in America's future. As peace was seemingly imminent, some thought the United States should act hurriedly to seize Canada and Nova Scotia, and possibly East Florida as well. If it dragged its feet, they said, the peace treaty might block the capture of those territories. Ecstatic at the prospect of peace, spontaneous celebrations occurred throughout the country. An observer of the revelry in New Bern, North Carolina, noted that a "great plenty of liquor" flowed and "Universal joy appeared in every countenance" among the celebrants.[27]

Henry Laurens, the president of Congress, saw things somewhat differently. Anticipating a protracted war, Laurens feared that America would find itself in a "more serious contest than any we have experienced" thus far. Henceforth, the "whole [British] Nation will be engaged" against America" and "the whole Nation is Mighty," he advised. That was one of two dangers that Laurens foresaw. The other was that "we shall lull our selves into a fatal security in the mistaken" belief that Britain was now fatally weak and France was all powerful. Going forward, he cautioned, the American people should perhaps be "afraid of ourselves." Washington concurred, warning that now the greatest dangers were "supineness on the one hand, or impetuosity on the other." America must not be duped into indolence by a belief that the war was as good as won. It must also guard against being led into ill-advised behavior by its new ally. A "reverse" from doing too little or from foolhardiness, Washington warned, could have a fatal impact on the public's will to continue.[28]

Recklessness had never characterized Washington's conduct, though he had taken risks, most notably in both battles at Trenton and his surprise attack at Germantown. As John Adams had observed, it was Washington's audacity that the French most admired about him, so much so that it was a crucial factor in France's decision to ally with the Americans. But with France's entry into the war, Washington manifested an unabashed wariness that had not previously been so conspicuous. It may have been that French belligerence made him more circumspect. Maybe he was thinking that he now had to worry about not only America's staying power but France's as well. Perhaps he felt that time was on America's side, that the costs Britain faced in continuing to wage war—both in terms of manpower and financial losses—would eventually drive it to make peace. In that case, victory was assured, unless the United States, through imprudence, stumbled into defeat. Or perhaps the war had taken its toll on him. Washington's numerous failures in the New York campaign, and again at Brandywine and Germantown, and his awareness that many disparaged his abilities, may have eroded his self-assurance. He may have deeply, implacably, feared that he would fail again, perhaps disastrously, a turn of events that could wreck his country's quest for independence and embolden those who harbored "a disposition . . . to see me superceeded in my Command by Genl G[ate]s," as he put it.[29] Washington's cryptic vow not to act rashly may have meant that for the remainder of the war he would be reluctant to take a bold step of surpassing importance unless he acted in concert with the French and with their explicit blessing.

IN JUNE, MORE than a month after Congress had ratified the treaties with France, the members of the Carlisle Commission completed their crossing of the Atlantic. They immediately discovered there was no hope that Congress would accept Lord North's peace plan. Congress, in a resolution, made clear that it would not meet with the commissioners until Britain recognized American independence and withdrew its armed forces from the United States. That Congress would spurn the prime minister's peace offering had been foretold in an address that it sent to the American people shortly before the commissioners arrived: "That God of battles, in whom was our trust, hath conducted us through the paths of danger and distress to the thresholds of security. . . . [I]f we have courage to persevere, we shall establish our liberties and independence."[30] With Congress a dead end, the peace commissioners sought to appeal to the public, hoping that war-weariness, Lord North's generous terms, and lingering anti-Catholic and anti-French sentiment would bring success. But euphoria triggered by the belief that the French alliance ensured victory was sweeping the American provinces. In the end, the peace commission was a casualty of Saratoga and the French alliance, but the open secret that Britain's army in America was to be severely reduced in size and Philadelphia abandoned also sealed its fate. The disappointed and angered members of the peace commission were convinced they had been sent on an impossible mission by a government that had hidden from them its decision to curtail its army in North America. Said one commissioner: Britain's new military strategy consigned their mission to "a mixture of ridicule, nullity and embarrassments."[31] Nevertheless, the commissioners remained in America for five months. In the event that the United States suffered a sharp military setback during 1778, Congress might be more willing to talk.

Opinion in Britain was divided over the wisdom of persevering, but those Americans who had always supported the insurgency were nearly unanimous in their positive outlook about the war and the belief that hostilities would not last much longer. After all, Britain had been unable to crush the rebellion when the United States stood alone. That it could possibly make gains against the combined might of France and the United States was surely out of the question. Victory and peace, it was thought, lay on a near horizon.

CHAPTER 3

FROM HOPE TO CONSTERNATION

GENERAL WASHINGTON IN the late spring of 1778 may have been happier than he'd been at any other time during his three years as commander of the Continental army, and not solely because of the high expectations aroused by the French alliance. He was elated that what he believed to have been either a conspiracy to remove him from command or an attempt by Congress to curtail his authority had failed. According to one observer, as the episode had backfired, Washington now felt safe in his position so long as he avoided inexcusable mistakes. Indeed, from this point forward none dared to publicly criticize him. But the new spirit in Congress went beyond that. Benjamin Rush of Philadelphia, who had signed the Declaration of Independence, said that Congress now saw it as a "state necessity" for America to have an unassailable great man who his countrymen could look to. John Adams concurred. All along, Adams argued, Congress had concealed Washington's flaws and blunders, even representing his "every defeat as a victory and every retreat as an advance." Now, said Adams, Congress "agreed to blow the trumpet of panegyric . . . to cover and dissemble all faults" of the commander. Washington was made to be "the central stone in the geometrical arch" that in the public mind was the United States. Others also took steps to transform Washington from a respected figure to one who was revered. He was to be the glue that would hold together this new nation that nearly alone in the western world did not have a monarch around whom the populace could unite.

Washington's birthday was now noted in almanacs and publicly celebrated, and for the first time he was exalted as the "Father of his Country." As never before, he was toasted at banquets and styled "the best man living" and "our Glory and Pride." Several contemporary books were dedicated to him, one referring to him as the "Saviour of his Country, the Supporter of Freedom, And the Benefactor of Mankind." Some Continental army officers, avid to display their devotion, had fought duels against those who had dared cavil about the commander's shortcomings. By springtime, Washington was widely seen as an iconic figure, the first inductee into the American pantheon of heroes. Some were unhappy with the veneration of Washington, including some who had never supported his removal as commander in chief. Samuel Adams did not like it, and neither did his fellow Massachusetts congressman James Lovell, who grumbled that Congress had fashioned a "Demi G[od] . . . whom no citizen shall dare even to talk about" in a critical manner. An anonymously authored pamphlet, *The Thoughts of a Freeman*, assailed Congress for its "Idolatry by making a man their god."[1]

Washington was happy, too, because his army—or most of it—had survived its winter in Valley Forge. Washington had never wanted to post his army there. He had preferred to scatter his soldiers among several cantonments from Reading to Lancaster, safer sites given their distances from Philadelphia, and each more easily supplied than one central encampment. However, congressmen from Pennsylvania, New Jersey, and Delaware demanded that the army remain close to British-occupied Philadelphia in order to defend the region from the enemy's foraging expeditions and other detrimental actions. Washington complied, but he was angry and for one of the few times in the war made no attempt to hide his fury toward Congress. Saying that it was "time to speak plain," he lectured Congress that it "is a much easier and less distressing thing, to draw Remonstrances in a comfortable room by a good fire side" than, like a soldier, "to occupy a cold bleak hill, and sleep under frost & snow without Cloaths or Blankets."[2]

The army's ordeal at Valley Forge gave Washington something of the appearance of a seer. In fact, he was well situated to see what was coming. Two months before entering Valley Forge, Washington had advised Congress that the army needed 3,084 coats, 4,051 waistcoats, 6,148 trousers, 8,033 stockings, 6,472 pairs of shoes, 6,330 shirts, 137 hunting shirts, 4,552 blankets, 2,399 hats, 356 overalls, and 1,140 knapsacks. He had not been at Valley Forge a week before he reported to Congress that the army "must inevitably be reduced to one or other of these three things, Starve—dissolve—or disperse, in order to find subsistence in the best manner they can." Many of the woes suffered by the Continentals in Valley Forge resulted from the long-standing scarcities that Washington had earlier reported. Finding ample supplies of food might have been a problem no matter where the army spent the winter, but going into a cantonment so close to Philadelphia was, as Washington had warned, particularly unwise. The area had been picked over in the late summer and autumn campaign, and it continued to be stripped clean from December onward as both the British and American armies scoured the region for provisions. In addition, during the Valley Forge winter, the army's shoddy supply system was plagued by corruption, bad weather, and shortages of wagons, horses, and teamsters. Severe food scarcities dogged the encampment on three occasions in a span of two months, and throughout the winter the men suffered from inadequate supplies of clothing, blankets, and shoes while living in substandard, hastily erected log cabins. The soldiery, said Washington late that winter, had "encountered every species of hardship that cold, wet, & hunger, and want of Cloaths were capable of producg." The appalling conditions turned Valley Forge into a death trap. Some 20 percent of the Continentals who marched into the camp in December were dead by spring, a mortality rate far in excess of that experienced by American armies in some of the costliest engagements in World War II.[3]

With good reason, Washington worried that word of the travail of his army would reach General Howe—who remained in command of Britain's army until deep into the spring—and prompt a British attack. In fact, Howe was made aware of the plight of his adversary at Valley Forge. Much of Howe's intelligence was provided by the Loyalist Joseph Galloway, who doubled as police commissioner in occupied Philadelphia and an army spymaster, and his reports were uncannily accurate. Early on, Galloway advised that more than 1,000 Continentals had deserted and 2,500 had died, together with most of the American army's horses. In March, he reported that Washington would be hard-pressed to field 4,000 able-bodied soldiers. If anything, Washington's army was in even worse shape than Galloway's intelligence reports suggested. Scores of officers quit during January and February, a time when Washington advised Congress that he might be incapable "of holding the Army together much longer." Galloway and other Tories pressed Howe to attack.[4] No one can know how a British strike at Valley Forge would have played out. Undertaking a winter assault would have been difficult, and a twenty-mile march to Valley Forge (the same distance that General Gage's men had marched from Boston to Concord) could have ended in yet another British disaster. But sometimes risk-taking pays off handsomely, and it is not inconceivable that Howe might have dealt the Americans a crippling blow. However, Howe was no longer given to chancy undertakings, if he ever had been. He had submitted his resignation and, as he awaited his successor's arrival, America receded further and further from his mind. According to a captured American officer who observed him, Howe, by now thoroughly "confounded and stupefied," "shut his eyes . . . drank his bottle [and] had his little whore."[5]

The reprieve from armed conflict afforded Washington the opportunity to reform his army. It was something that he naturally wished to do, but it was also something that Congress had leaned on him to undertake. A few weeks before the army entered Valley Forge, a congressional committee visited headquarters and made clear that it believed a thorough overhaul of the army was long overdue. Later, other committees came to camp and pressed for streamlining the army in numerous ways. Washington was a good manager of the army but an inexperienced administrator. One historian who meticulously studied the structure of the army during Washington's first thirty months at the helm found that it was "plagued by incompetent staff, poorly defined departmental responsibilities, and intersecting chains of command." Washington may or may not have been familiar with all the army's deficiencies, but he was aware of many, and during the Valley Forge winter he turned to both professional French officers who had crossed to America in 1777 and talented Continental officers for guidance in reshaping the Continental army.[6]

Regiments and battalions were consolidated in the belief that they would be more easily controlled in the field. In addition, with the arrival of Friedrich Steuben, who passed himself off as a former Prussian general, both the men and their officers were exactingly trained in what many referred to as "the Prussian drill." The soldiers were schooled in camp hygiene and the care of weapons, and officers learned how to organize baggage trains and move the army. Steps were taken to improve medical services, and though horses and equipment remained in short supply, a cavalry arm took shape. The quartermaster corps was the focus of much of the remediation efforts. General Nathanael Greene, a prewar businessman who understood the army's needs, reluctantly agreed to become the quarter-master general and, in the words of historian Stephen Taaffe, he "got things done." Greene established a train of magazines and supply depots from Virginia and Maryland to the Hudson River, found wagons for the army, and improved the quality of work by his deputy quartermasters by paying them by commission rather than a fixed salary.

Recruiting also went forward through the early months of 1778. At its low ebb, Washington's army dipped to around seven thousand effectives, but by May it had swelled to about fifteen thousand men, with another two thousand or so expected by early summer. The army grew in part because some states had resorted to conscription to meet their assigned quotas, but also as some northern provinces welcomed Black enlistees. Blacks were serving in the army in 1775 when Washington assumed command, but he had objected to their presence and wished to dismiss them. Congress had resolved that those in the service could remain in place but that no addi-tional Blacks were to be permitted. The manpower shortage in early 1778 led some states to ignore the congressional edict, and Washington quietly acquiesced. Connecticut moved tentatively, enabling slave owners to enlist their chattel as substitutes, but Rhode Island permitted Blacks to join the army on the condition that they served until the war's conclusion. So many African Americans enlisted in Rhode Island's First Battalion—soon known as the "Black Regiment"—that 25 percent of the state's adult male slaves ultimately soldiered in the Continental army. By the end of the Valley Forge winter the army was well clothed, with the men sporting an array of colorful uniforms, some manufactured in France and some in Spain, which had secretly opened commercial connections with the United States, though it had not entered the war. The army's pantry was better provisioned, too, and the men enjoyed a rare abundance of munitions and weapons, as French Charleville muskets were delivered to the camp. Given the capture of General Burgoyne's cannon at Saratoga, the artillery corps commanded by General Henry Knox now had a plentiful supply of large guns.[7]

Washington lost officers at an alarming rate during the Valley Forge winter. Some three hundred resigned their commissions and departed for home. Some had wearied of the harshness and dangers of army life, but many departed because of economic necessity, fearing the eventual loss of their property at home if the war dragged on indefinitely. To staunch the loss of experienced officers, Washington threw his weight behind a half-pay pension for life for officers following the completion of their service at war's end, benefits that would be extended to each officer's family following his demise. Congress approved the plan. Washington neither requested better pay nor a pension for common soldiers, and when some argued for public assistance for the families of enlisted men—who had not been paid for ages—Washington denounced the notion as "robbing the public and encouraging idleness."[8]

As spring blossomed and the wretched Valley Forge winter receded into a never-to-be-forgotten memory, Washington knew that his army was vastly improved. Although the Continentals had not been victorious at Brandywine and Germantown, they performed better than they had in New York in 1776, and Washington was convinced that his officers and men would be even better soldiers in 1778. But Washington had no idea what tests his army might face. In 1776 and 1777 he had fairly easily predicted the enemy's strategy. But now, with France a belligerent and rumors swirling that Howe had resigned, what the British might do in 1778 was a riddle.[9]

When appointed, Washington had been instructed by Congress to make his most substantive decisions after listening to the advice of councils of war, bodies consisting of the general officers at hand. He was not required to follow their recommendations, but he was to solicit their advice. While still in Valley Forge, Washington in mid-April sought his generals' thinking regarding the proper strategy to pursue. At that juncture, half favored an attempt to recover New York City, one-third called for an attack on the British in Philadelphia, and another third—all of whom were Europeans—leaned toward remaining in camp at Valley Forge until the "future motions of the enemy" became clear. The commander sided with the Europeans. Three weeks later, at Congress's direction, Washington convened a second council of war. After a lengthy discussion, the generals overwhelmingly embraced the wait-and-see option, advising Washington to "put nothing to the hazard" before learning what steps France might take.[10]

Weeks would pass before word of French plans reached Washington, but five days after meeting with his generals Washington for the first time received intelligence reports that the British planned to abandon Philadelphia. That news arrived just as the Continental army was celebrating a day of "General Joy," a festival Washington had proclaimed for rejoicing both the alliance with "a powerful Friend" and, now that an enchanting spring sun brightened the Pennsylvania countryside, the army's survival following 125 grim days in the winter encampment. The men paraded, field artillery (all of which was of French or English manufacture) boomed, and after each cannonade the soldiery cheered, "Long Live the King of France," "God Save the Friendly Powers of Europe," and "To the American States."[11]

IF WASHINGTON LEARNED through spies that the British might evacuate Philadelphia, he read in the newspaper that General Howe had resigned and sailed for England in late May. Before his departure, British officers feted him with a bizarre farewell fling they dubbed a "Mischianza," a term derived from the Italian words meaning "to mix" and "to mingle." Howe alighted from a vibrantly decorated riverboat and walked under a misnamed "triumphal arch." There was music and dancing, medieval jousting, fireworks, fine food, and an abundance of wine and liquor. Toasts were raised to nearly every imaginable thing, save for a truly crowning British victory, a feat—the arch notwithstanding—that had eluded Howe during his two years as commander in chief.[12]

Howe's successor, General Henry Clinton, was already in town. Lord Germain had settled on Clinton early in the year, though it was not until May that the American secretary's letter notifying the new commander of his appointment arrived in New York. It was then that Clinton learned that he was to abandon Philadelphia and redeploy roughly 30 percent of his army to assorted other sites in the Caribbean and throughout North America. Five thousand were to be immediately redeployed to St. Lucia and the remainder scattered to other sites in North America, but chiefly to Florida. Though vested with a suddenly shrunken army, Clinton's orders were to "prosecute [the war] with the utmost vigour," seek to retain Britain's hold on New York and Rhode Island, endeavor to bring Washington to battle, and initiate "an attack . . . upon the southern colonies" with the goal of repossessing Georgia and South Carolina. The American secretary broke the news of the reduction of the army and the disconcerting laundry list of objectives to be pursued in a letter to "our trusty and well beloved Sir Henry Clinton." Germain closed his weasel-wordy missive by remarking that the diminution of Britain's armed forces "may be productive of some ill consequences."[13]

The newly designated British commander in America was doom-ridden from the start, convinced that the American secretary's orders "ruined all my hopes" of totally crushing the colonial insurgency. Not only was he in effect being asked to fight with one arm tied behind his back, but Clinton faced a more sweeping mission than his predecessor had been ordered to undertake, and with fewer troops. Where Howe had been expected to stamp out the rebellion in the northern colonies, Clinton was to defend what

Britain still possessed in the North while seeking to regain lost provinces in the South. What is more, unlike Howe, Clinton would have to contend with both colonial rebels and the French. "My fate is hard," Clinton exclaimed with good reason. He felt that he had been given a command "so hopeless" that "neither honor nor credit" could be reaped from his assignment. Given the hand he was dealt, Clinton took on the assignment haunted by the premonition that one day he would be saddled with "a considerable portion of the blame" for Britain's "inevitable" lack of future success. Clinton's gloomy outlook was shared by many of his officers. One thought that "inactivity, disgrace, or a retreat seem[ed] inevitable," while another privately remarked that henceforth he would refer to the "rebellious colonies" as "what I may now venture to call *the United States of America.*"[14]

The forty-eight-year-old Clinton had spent about half his youth in Manhattan, the son of an aristocrat, admiral, and New York's royal governor. Clinton entered the army at fifteen and was a grizzled veteran by the time of the Revolutionary War, having already served in two wars. During the War of the Austrian Succession, in the 1740s while Clinton was still an adolescent, he served at Louisbourg, at the mouth of the St. Lawrence, and survived both an ambush by a party of French and Indian soldiers and the region's bone-chilling spring weather. In his early thirties, Clinton soldiered in the European theater during the Seven Years' War, serving as a volunteer in an Allied corps. Its commander, Charles, hereditary prince of Brunswick, the nephew of Frederick the Great, saw something he liked in Clinton and selected him to be his aide-de-camp. In his second year at the front, Clinton was seriously wounded in the Battle of Frieberg in 1762. Clinton thought that having been "hacked by an ignorant German surgeon" in the field hospital had caused more damage than the gunshot wound itself, and in the years ahead he was at times hobbled to the point that he could barely "stir from my bed to my chair."

Three years before the Revolutionary War, Clinton suffered the loss of his twenty-five-year-old wife, Harriet, who perished in her fifth pregnancy during their five-year marriage. Though the couple had often been separated given his postings abroad, Clinton had been devoted to her, and her demise plunged him into a deep, guilt-ridden depression from which he did not emerge for two years. Time, and a 1774 trip to the Balkans to learn more of warfare by observing hostilities between Russia and the Turks, gradually enabled him to overcome his melancholia. His old ambitious self once again, Clinton, now a major general, welcomed his appointment as the third in command in America in 1775. Leaving behind his four surviving children, whom he loved deeply—but would see only for a brief time in 1777 and not again for another five years—Clinton sailed to Boston with Howe and Burgoyne, arriving about thirty days after the war began.[15]

A man of average height, Clinton in his middle years was paunchy and balding, and much of his hair that remained had gone to gray. Intellectually curious, Clinton was a voracious reader on myriad topics, though military history, the art of war, and studying flora and fauna were his passions. Throughout his career he avidly discussed military history and tactics with any officer willing to chat. He daily set aside time for his beloved violin, and by the time he arrived in America, Clinton was regarded as a laudable amateur musician. As an officer, he was diligent, contemplative, and cautious. Many observers thought Clinton unsurpassed in his ability to see the big picture, and not a few regarded him as the best strategic planner among Britain's generals. He had few peers when it came to courage under fire. In battle, he habitually exhibited a personal recklessness, causing some to worry that he was "sporting away [his] life." His admirable qualities were counterbalanced by less attractive attributes. He was unassuming and hardly extroverted—he once oddly described himself as a "shy bitch"—and could be both quarrelsome and hypersensitive to criticism. Throughout his lengthy career Clinton formed long-standing friendships with some fellow officers, but making friends did not come easily for him. Clinton seemed happiest when he secluded himself and found the time to read, think, study nature, or play his violin.[16]

By 1778 Clinton had achieved a worthy record in this war. At several crucial junctures he had unsuccessfully offered commendable advice to Gage and Howe that might have refashioned the course of the war. On three occasions Clinton had borne the responsibility of command in important undertakings. The first had occurred in 1776 a few weeks prior to the fighting in New York. Prompted by reports that eastern North Carolina teemed with Loyalists eager to "take up arms in the King's cause," the British government late in 1775 readied an expedition under Commodore Peter Parker that was to assist the Tories in reclaiming the colony. The task force included more than three thousand soldiers, ten thousand small arms, and six cannon for the Loyalists, and it was to sail from London around December 1, 1775. Clinton, whom General Howe named to command the army, departed Boston early in 1776, hoping to rendezvous with his army and the naval arm at Cape Fear in mid-February. London's thinking was that the operation in North Carolina would be completed before the South's unhealthy summer arrived and in plenty of time for Clinton to rejoin Howe for the New York campaign. However, Britain's well-laid plan, including its time line, went askew.

Clinton discovered on his arrival at Cape Fear in March that a sizable Loyalist contingent had indeed assembled, but shortly before Christmas it had been decimated at Moore's Creek Bridge in a brief encounter with a smaller force of rebel militiamen. Nor was Parker's fleet anywhere to be seen. Weeks passed, leaving Clinton to spend his time studying the coastal plant life and rethinking the planned operation in light of the defeat of North Carolina's Loyalists. Clinton thought it best to scrub the enterprise for reclaiming North Carolina. Instead, he wished to establish two British bases in the Chesapeake, one at Albemarle Sound and the other on or near the Elizabeth River. Guarded by a couple of frigates, each site would be "a secure asylum" for Loyalists. Armed with the cache of weaponry in the cargo holds of Sir Peter Parker's vessels, the Loyalists could make destructive and morale-abrading sallies against the rebels in Virginia and North Carolina. Furthermore, once New York had been retaken and Washington's Continentals annihilated, Howe could bring his army southward, retrieve the Loyalists from their sanctuaries, and reclaim the Carolinas and more.

Commodore Parker's entire armada at last arrived deep in May, having sailed seventy-four days later than scheduled and made a slow and difficult Atlantic crossing. Parker was not smitten with Clinton's Chesapeake plan. He preferred to go after Charleston, which intelligence reports—some provided by Loyalists—characterized as weakly defended. Clinton hardly fought for his alternative, in some measure because Howe, in a letter that arrived in late May, also contended that Charleston was an alluring target.

Clinton was obsessive when it came to carefully planning every operation, whether large or small, of which he was part. But in this instance he went into the Charleston foray "blindfolded," as he later put it. He and Parker knew next to nothing about Charleston and its defenses, which historian Rick Atkinson characterized as "the most heavily fortified city in America." Nor did Clinton and Parker have a definitive objective in mind. Depending on what they found, they might wind up blockading the city, destroying it, or capturing it, though both knew that the British and their Loyalist allies—if there were any Loyalist allies—could not long maintain control of Charleston. The best they could hope for was to capture Sullivan's Island at Charleston Bar, a few miles out from the city. It might serve as a refuge for Loyalists and a site from which the thousands of weapons that Parker had brought along could be put in the hands of the king's American friends. In the end, in what largely became a naval operation, nothing was accomplished. South Carolina troops, garbed in dapper blue coats faced with red, "acted like Romans in the third century" in defending the city, in the estimation of General Charles Lee, the ranking Continental officer in the southern theater. In no time, Parker's ships fired seven thousand rounds, used up more than twelve tons of powder, and suffered some eighty casualties; in addition, several Royal Navy vessels sustained extensive damage. "We never had such a drubbing in our lives," said one of the surviving British sailors. In July, Clinton sailed for New York. Never again would he enter into a campaign with such haphazard planning.[17]

Later that same year, just days after the conquests of Forts Washington and Lee, General Howe ordered Clinton "to make a descent" on Rhode Island to secure "full possession" of Newport, regarded by many Royal Navy officers as the "best and noblest harbor in America." While Clinton agreed with that assessment of Newport's value, he thought he and his men could be put to better use in November 1776 by joining Cornwallis in pursuit of Washington's bedraggled force across New Jersey. The approach of winter notwithstanding, Clinton also thought that campaign should be continued until Philadelphia was taken. But orders were orders, and Clinton—once again in concert with Commodore Parker—sailed for Rhode Island on December 1 with four battalions, half British and half Hessian. There were a few rebel defenders present, and they "retired with precipitancy," as Clinton put it, when they spotted the approaching enemy squadron. Everything had gone wrong in the Carolinas, but the Newport initiative could not have been carried off more smoothly, and in its aftermath George III lavished praise on Clinton for his part in the conquest.[18]

Clinton's third opportunity to command had occurred in October 1777 when he daringly, and brilliantly, had responded to General Burgoyne's pleas for help, though in the end he had been unable to rescue his beleaguered fellow officer. He might have come closer to achieving that end, but Howe—who was having his own problems in Pennsylvania—summoned "without delay" three regiments and two battalions who were with Clinton in New York. Clinton's achievements that autumn were the only real successes that the British could relish, and as a result his popularity soared in England. Clinton always looked back with pride on the part he had played in attempting to forestall the disaster at Saratoga, perhaps most of all relishing the "universal admiration and applause" his actions had won.[19]

CLINTON ARRIVED IN Philadelphia on the frigate *Greyhound* two days after Washington's day of joy at Valley Forge. He was immediately confronted with critical decisions. One involved Germain's order to waste no time in redeploying men for the planned attack on French St. Lucia. Clinton's first decision as commander was prudent and gutsy. He ignored Germain's order. He would comply with the order to abandon Philadelphia but thought it best to keep his army intact in order to get it safely to New York.

Next, Clinton had to decide how to get his army to New York. Several factors led him to eschew making the return trip by sea. Crucial to his decision was an awareness that a French fleet had sailed for North America. Given the "dispersed situation of the [British] fleet," his entire force would be a sitting duck if it had the misfortune to run upon the French squadron. In addition, he feared that if "detained by contrary winds," Washington might respond by "making a decisive push" against lightly defended New York. Still another factor to consider was that there would not be sufficient room in the available vessels for both the army and Philadelphia's many Loyalists who wished to escape. As the Tories were "objects of vengeance to the enemy," Clinton shrank from leaving them to an unsavory fate. One other consideration was paramount in his final decision to march his army to Manhattan. Germain had urged an attempt to bring Washington to battle, and Clinton was ardent for taking on his adversary. Clinton knew that if Washington summoned all his resources—units scattered through New Jersey as well as militia—the redcoats would face a formidable foe, though the British commander was confident that his men's "spirit and discipline" would be equal to the challenge. With France now in the war, Clinton guessed that Washington would shrink from risking a set-piece battle, but it was likely the rebel commander would seek a "little triumph" through a "partial blow," most likely a strike at the British army's baggage train. Clinton felt that he could safely get his army to New York through an overland march, and if fortune smiled, he might get a crack at Washington on a battlefield.[20]

More than three weeks elapsed after Clinton's arrival before Britain's soldiers took their first step toward New York. Ships had to be loaded not only with baggage but with soldiers too ill to march and perhaps as many as five thousand Loyalists—including some seventy-five Black men and women who had served the British during the occupation—and their possessions. It was during this phase of the evacuation that the members of the Carlisle Commission docked in Philadelphia and unhappily discovered that the British government had long ago made the decision to abandon the city. Their anger and indignation was shared by some in the British army.

The quartermaster general declared his shame at relinquishing the city that so many British soldiers had died in taking barely eight months earlier. But London's orders were to abandon Philadelphia. The army and a great many displaced Pennsylvanians pushed off on foot for Manhattan on June 18. Some 20,800 people—of which about 85 percent were soldiers—were to make the hundred-mile tramp, accompanied by 5,000 horses, countless wagons, and a vast train of artillery. They were organized in two parallel divisions of roughly equal size that stretched for miles. Lord Cornwallis, who seemed to be everywhere, commanded one of the two divisions.[21]

Clinton expected Washington's army to stay on his heels, throw "every obstruction . . . in [his] way," and at some moment during the trek assail the "vulnerable" rear of his army.[22] Washington may have thought along the same lines, but he was slow to respond to the intelligence reports about the British evacuation of Philadelphia. As a result, the British had already begun to cross into New Jersey before Washington, on June 17, summoned his third council of war within sixty days. Washington wished to know his officers' thoughts on the wisdom of pursuing and attacking his adversary. If the generals favored an attack, Washington asked whether they wished a general engagement or only a strike against Clinton's rear guard. The commander wanted their answers in writing. The responses were all across the board, save for the matter of a general engagement. Only two of fifteen advocated risking all in a full-blown battle. Not all the others even wanted to shadow the British retreat across New Jersey. The one thing on which the great majority agreed was that with the French entering the war, this was not the moment to unduly imperil the army.[23] As the British were already on the move, the next morning—before he received the first written response from any of his generals—Washington ordered his army to march. Presumably, he would digest their recommendations in the course of the pursuit.

Washington kept his army north of the Delaware River in the early going while Clinton's marched on the other side. But within four days both armies were on the same side of the river, though the late-starting Americans were nearly twenty-five miles behind the redcoats. Nevertheless, the Americans could move more rapidly, for the British were encumbered by a huge baggage train and slowed by the rebels' obstructionist tactics. Meanwhile, Washington stripped down his force for speed, jettisoning his baggage and tents. Each day the rebel soldiery cut the distance that separated the two armies, and it was not long before small firefights were occurring. The two armies slogged ahead in the midst of an uncommonly torrid early-summer heat wave. The temperature daily climbed to near one hundred degrees and the humidity soared as well, leading to torrential late-afternoon thunderstorms that turned the roads into a sticky ooze. Both armies were awakened each day around 4:00 A.M. and set off in the feeble light of sunrise, and both paused now and again for a gulp of tepid water and respite from the searing sun in the warm shade of leafy trees. Even so, the merciless heat was inescapable, and men on both sides died daily from heatstrokes. (An officer in an elite Hessian unit said that 20 of his 210 men "dropped dead from the great heat and fatigue.")[24]

A week after he began stalking his adversary, Washington, on June 24, held yet another council of war. Five generals stuck to the balky conviction that it would be unwise to engage the British in any fashion. Their argument was that it would be imprudent to run unnecessary risks before the French arrived. Some among them additionally questioned the wisdom of squandering the lives of soldiers in a battle that would likely be inconsequential. Although none advocated a full-blown engagement in which the entire army was put on the line, a majority favored assailing the rear of the enemy force. It was an alluring target. As the British force included over 1,000 wagons and nearly 2,000 noncombatants—primarily Tories, but also the wives, girlfriends, and servants of some officers—Clinton's army was strung out over eight miles, seemingly assuring that Washington's army would have a considerable numerical advantage when making the assault.[25] An assault not only might inflict heavy losses, but it could result in the destruction or capture of valuable stores in the enemy's baggage train near the rear in the line of march. Some of their arguments reverberated with an unmistakable political ring. The Marquis de Lafayette said that "the honor of the american army" required that it strike what he called a "happy blow"; he added that it would be "disgraceful and humiliating to allow the enemy to cross the Jerseys in tranquility." General Greene, who was thought to be the commander's closest confidant, advised that to end the chase "without attempting to do the enemy the least injury" would cause many to believe that "our courage faild us. . . . People expects something from us & our strength demands it."[26] Greene had a deft understanding of political realities and an even better feel for what Washington was probably thinking. Washington sided with those who favored a strike at the enemy's rear. It appeared to be a relatively safe undertaking. Counting available militia, Washington had some 13,500 men with him. Intelligence reported Clinton's strength at no more than 10,000—it was actually 17,600—and the British van was far away and on the move, and unlikely to see action unless the fighting lasted for more than a day.

During the two days that followed the latest council of war, the American army continued to close in on the redcoats. The rebel force was only ten miles away when the British, late on Friday, June 26, reached Monmouth Courthouse. Clinton's army had doggedly marched sixty miles in the blistering daily heat since leaving Philadelphia. It faced a march of another thirty miles before it reached the coast, and safety. On Saturday, Clinton did not move. He gave his weary men a day of rest. He also hoped for a battle and thought his pause would provoke Washington to attack. Clinton's plan worked. Washington felt this was his best opportunity. He ordered a strike against the tag end of the British army once it began to move again on Sunday morning.

Washington offered General Lee, the second-in-command, the opportunity to lead the forward elements into battle. Lee declined, remarking that such a small-scale endeavor was better suited for a junior officer. Washington next turned to Lafayette, who had not yet turned twenty-one and was woefully inexperienced. He was spectacularly brave and nearly unrivaled in the art of ingratiation, and those two qualities likely swayed Washington, even though back in the spring Lafayette had botched an important assignment and succeeded—as Washington put it—in getting "caught in a snare" of his own making.[27] Lafayette also mismanaged this assignment. His force somehow got hopelessly lost and was fortunate not to blunder into the enemy, a turn of events that might have resulted in a severe drubbing. Given Lafayette's close brush with disaster, General Lee—who may have been prodded by some of his shaken fellow generals—suddenly offered to take command. Washington, perhaps with a hidden sigh of relief, consented.

Considerable confusion characterized the American high command in the final hours prior to the Battle of Monmouth. Given the change in command, Lee had little time to prepare. Washington, who could be indecisive or methodical, also lacked the time to map out a well-conceived plan of attack. Aside from selecting the units that would available to Lee— what the commander would label "a select and strong detachment"—it appears that from necessity Washington gave Lee, an experienced professional soldier, a free hand to improvise. Lee was on the move not long after sunrise, though little time passed before he encountered snags. For one thing, Lee was leading his force into an area that had not been reconnoitered. He immediately discovered several deep ravines that coursed through the terrain. Should a retreat be necessary—a contingency that would cross the mind of any veteran officer—Lee's army could be decimated while attempting to cross one of those gaping, gnarled gorges. In addition, Lee knew neither the exact location of some of his brigades nor whether all his units would even arrive in time to participate in the looming battle. (As it turned out, the vaunted riflemen under General Daniel Morgan, who had played a crucial role in Burgoyne's defeat, did not reach the battlefield in time to join in the fighting.) No less disturbing, while Lee was aware of the location of the enemy's rear, he was uncertain of the exact position of the bulk of Clinton's army. He knew only that most of the redcoats had departed Monmouth, and he also believed that the 4,500 men he commanded would be twice the size of the likely number of redcoats in the enemy's rear. Lee knew that in battle things almost never play out as planned, but his objective was to swiftly envelop the British rear guard and wrap up the fighting before Clinton could bring reinforcements into play. If he succeeded, he would inflict heavy losses on the

British army, including the capture of at least a portion of its valuable baggage train.

Lee had earlier counseled against risking an attack, but he struck the enemy's rear guard as ordered. Lee radiated confidence early in the fighting, cheerfully telling Lafayette, "I think these people are ours." Speed was crucial to success in this operation. Washington had said that success hinged on assailing the enemy "before they get into strong grounds."[28] But Lee had unavoidably required nearly an hour to organize his force, precious time during which Clinton divined what was unfolding. The British commander rushed in reinforcements that were not as far away as Lee had been led to believe. Within an hour of Lee's having gotten his force into position to act, the numbers swung in Clinton's favor, and with each minute Britain's numerical superiority seemed to grow. Some American detachments began falling back, in some instances because they faced a real threat, though some units retreated despite having occupied highly defensible positions. At first the retreat was on only one flank. However, when Lafayette ordered a retreat, a dumbfounded Lee realized that both his right and left were giving way. Lee had no choice but to withdraw and organize a defensive stand, a move that probably saved his advanced units from annihilation. He sent a French brigadier general of engineers to select the perfect site for withstanding the coming enemy blow. As the Americans fell back, Clinton glimpsed the opportunity to strike and turn the flank of his adversary. Lee was compelled to order another withdrawal. His new plan was to place his force behind one of the ravines. Retreats during a battle can sow panic, and disaster, but both of Lee's fallbacks were orderly.

At this juncture, some three hours after the fight commenced, Washington—who earlier had been nearly four miles away enjoying a leisurely breakfast at the home of a local physician—arrived on the scene. Lee had failed to keep the commander adequately informed of the swiftly changing developments in the engagement. Washington had assumed that no news was good news. But on reaching the periphery of the battlefield and realizing that the army was retreating, Washington was not a little perplexed that what had seemed like a simple operation was ending in a withdrawal. He appears to have jumped to the conclusion that Lee, who had opposed giving battle in several councils of war, was deliberately sabotaging the operation. It was a nerve-racking moment, and Washington had a terrible temper. Thomas Jefferson, who witnessed Washington's volcanic fury on more than one occasion, once spoke of Washington having "got[ten] into one of those passions when he cannot command himself."[29] On this day, on this battlefield, Washington's temper snapped and his suffocating rage, like a spreading fever, took control of him. Witnesses said that Washington cursed Lee. The most voluble of men, Lee was so astonished that he fell nearly mute. The acrimonious encounter was brief, and it culminated with Washington removing Lee from command and taking charge himself.

With Clinton's men advancing rapidly—they were but half a mile away and bearing down on the Americans "with great Spirit"—Washington did exactly what Lee had set out to do: he fell back behind a ravine and organized a defensive position. Acting decisively, Washington hastily summoned substantial reinforcements. What was supposed to have been a small-scale engagement had turned into a major confrontation that would continue for several more hours. Washington laid out his force so that it was secure against a frontal assault, leaving Clinton to seek to turn the enemy's flanks; he first struck Washington's left wing, then his right. The fighting was desperate. Casualties were heavy from spirited infantry attacks, including bayonet charges, and thunderous cannonades, all played out in the merciless heat. Monmouth may have been the longest day of fighting during the entire war, a contest that began just after sunrise and continued until after the lengthy shadows of late day crept over the battlefield. Expecting a second day of battle, Washington and his men slept that night on what one called "a field of Carnage and Blood." But this fight was over. Under cover of darkness, Clinton's army slipped away—as Washington had so often done—and resumed its march to New York, its long column of horses, wagons, and humanity churning a thick, choking dust.

Monmouth, a brawl that occurred near the third anniversary of Bunker Hill, was to be the last major battle fought above the Potomac in the war. It took a grim toll on both sides. The Americans had some 450 men killed and wounded, the British about 600. (From the moment his army departed Philadelphia until it reached New York, Clinton's losses—from combat, desertion, and days of searing heat—soared to nearly 2,000.) Neither side won the bitter encounter at Monmouth, but both sides claimed victory. "We forced the Enemy from the Field," said Washington. Clinton told Germain that not only had his exposed baggage train survived an attack by a "strong corps" that he wildly overestimated to have totaled 20,000 men, but that his outnumbered army had driven the rebel "corps . . . from two strong positions" and regained every inch of territory lost in the earliest moments of the clash.[30] Despite the exaggerations of the two commanders, the engagement was a standoff that had no immediate impact on the course of the war.

Nevertheless, the engagement was not without importance. The American army, a more veteran army than ever before, had performed well in the wake of the retreats, vindicating the exacting training the soldiers and officers had received at Valley Forge. Even a high-ranking British officer praised the Continentals' "boldness and resolution" at Monmouth. The battle also enhanced Washington's standing, as the public accepted his claim of a "Victory obtained over the Arms of his Britanick Majesty." Some who had backed the commander during the previous winter's supposed conspiracy now spread the story that Washington's heroics had prevented disaster. Hamilton circulated the message that Washington's "coolness and firmness" had saved the day. Countering those critics who had earlier assailed the commander's indecisiveness, Hamilton stressed that the general "instantly took measures for checking the enemy's advance." Hamilton added: "I never saw the general to so much advantage. . . . America owes a great deal to General Washington for this day's work." In "any other hands," said Hamilton in a barb unmistakably aimed at Lee, the outcome would have been "dismay and disgrace." Washington, he added, had "directed the whole with the skill of a Master workman." Others also portrayed the commander as having "turned the fate of the day," saving the army from "disorder arising" from Lee's retreat.[31]

While Washington's stock rose following Monmouth, Lee, who was extremely popular in many quarters—not a few in Congress thought him the best general in the Continental army—self-destructed. Lee had long quietly (and sometimes not so quietly) thought Washington beyond his ken in the post of commander. He once acidly remarked that "Washington was not fit to command a Sergeant's Guard." To have been stripped of his command on the battlefield by Washington, and to have been chastened and discredited in the process, ate at Lee until, a couple of days following the battle, he demanded a court-martial to clear his name. It was an unwise move. He could not win a fight with Washington, especially in the midst of a war and in the new environment that came into being following the Valley Forge winter. Predictably, Lee was convicted and suspended from command for one year, and thereafter some officers who sought to safeguard Washington's reputation—and curry favor with the commander in the process—publicly disparaged Lee.[32]

Monmouth may have been important in one additional way. A month before the battle, Washington had spoken of the imprudence of running risks now that the alliance with France seemingly assured victory. At Monmouth, he had gambled despite the warnings of several generals. Things had gone quite differently from what Washington had imagined, something that seemed to happen in nearly every engagement. In the wake of the battle, he spoke of his unexpected "hour of distress" before "affairs took a favourable turn." He knew that the battle could have ended disastrously, in some measure due to his mistake of having committed his army in stages to an ill-defined mission.[33] Following Monmouth, Washington's aversion to risk-taking would be greater than ever.

WHEN WASHINGTON ORDERED the attack at Monmouth, he did not know—and would not know until thirteen days after the battle—that America's new ally, France, had dispatched an armada to North America. (The French foreign ministry had not shared that information with Benjamin Franklin and America's other envoys in Paris.) A squadron of twelve ships of the line, three frigates, and some four thousand marines under Vice Admiral Comte d'Estaing had sailed from Toulon nearly two months before the day of joy at Valley Forge. The French fleet contained three more ships of the line, the great battleships of the day, than the Royal Navy possessed in New York. With luck, d'Estaing might score a colossal victory, even a war-ending triumph. Alas, d'Estaing had no luck whatsoever. He sailed for Philadelphia, where Clinton's army and a large number of British ships were known to be. But unfavorable winds and Versailles's vacillation over sending the naval force caused it to arrive six days after all the Royal Navy's vessels had sailed from Philadelphia to New York. Otherwise, declared Charles James Fox, a long-standing foe of Lord North's American policy, d'Estaing would have "destroyed our naval force in America" and France would have established "a decided superiority in the . . . seas."[34] D'Estaing next proceeded northward to the New Jersey coast, only to discover that Clinton's army had come and gone seven days earlier, completing its long march to New York City. The French navy, by a whisker, had missed pinioning much of what remained of the British army in America between itself and Washington's army, virtually assuring its destruction and almost certainly ending the war.

Washington was in touch with d'Estaing immediately, and through Hamilton and Lieutenant Colonel John Laurens, two young French-speaking aides he sent to meet with the Allied admiral, the two commanders discussed a campaign to recapture New York. The potential prize would be colossal: the crippling of Britain's fleet and possession of New York. Washington rejoiced that the "ruin of Great Britain" would soon be "reduced to a moral certainty." But once again luck—with an assist from Sir Henry Clinton—abandoned the Allies. The inferior British fleet refused to budge from New York Harbor, and soon enough d'Estaing's pilots concluded that the channel was too shallow for France's heavy warships to enter the harbor. (The "elements so remarkably befriended us" was how Fox put it in Parliament.) In breaking the bad news to Washington, d'Estaing added a heaping ladle of treacle: "[Y]ou are too good a patriot and too great a soldier" not to understand the situation, he said, and not to realize the necessity of "going to seek elsewhere an opportunity of injuring our common enemy." D'Estaing did not mention that had he moved more quickly, Britain's control of New York still might have been seriously imperiled. It was Clinton who moved rapidly, dispatching 1,800 men and howitzers to occupy a region that commanded the approach to New York Harbor and prevented d'Estaing from bringing in batteries that might have so jeopardized the Royal Navy that it would have been compelled to yield its anchorage. The second in command of the Royal Navy in New York later lauded Clinton's swift action, arguing that it had doomed the French to "lose their ships if they should attempt the harbor." Rather than making an attempt, d'Estaing spoke of looking elsewhere for a better target.[35]

Washington was bitterly disappointed, but two options existed. Since before the Continental army marched into Valley Forge, both Congress and the Board of War—a congressionally created panel charged with oversight of the army—had urged yet another invasion of Canada. At one point Congress unanimously approved what some called an "irruption" into Canada, but Washington balked. He pronounced the idea a "child of folly" that was too hazardous for serious consideration. It would have been a risky undertaking, though unbeknownst to Washington, Canada's governor at this very moment was telling his superiors that a United States army would have "many advantages over us." The invaders, said the governor, would have superior numbers, and the British defenses on the approach to Canada were "miserable . . . and in bad condition." He added that neither the Canadians nor the "savages" could be "depended upon," and the "fortifications of Quebec are entirely rotten" and "in a very defenceless state." It is conceivable that had the United States made preparations for a Canadian invasion—which could not have been hidden—Clinton might have been forced to decide which was the most crucial: New York or Canada. Holding both might not have been possible. But another Canadian venture was not going to be pursued, especially after Washington advised Congress that his real reason for opposing such an enterprise was his fear that the conquest of Canada would result in France's retaking the region, despite its pledge of disinterest in the Treaty of Alliance. Washington's powerful argument, and the congressmen's newfound unwillingness to challenge the commander, silenced sentiment within Congress in favor of an invasion of Canada.[36]

The second option, which Washington immediately embraced, was a Franco-American campaign to retake Newport on Aquidneck Island, now occupied by some 4,700 enemy troops under Sir Robert Pigot. Washington thought such an operation had "a less hazardous complexion" than attempting to regain Quebec; it "seems to promise more success," he allowed, particularly if it could be put in motion before British naval reinforcements arrived. D'Estaing readily concurred. He, too, understood the importance of rapidly completing the operation, but his departure from New York was sluggish, and his voyage to Newport, slowed by headwinds and a fruitless attempt to fool Britain's admirals through time-consuming feints, consumed six long days. On July 29, nine days after he and Washington made the decision to go after Newport, d'Estaing's fleet at last arrived off Aquidneck Island. It was not the first fleet to arrive. Clinton once again had acted with extraordinary speed. On July 9, eleven days before the Allied leaders concurred on a Rhode Island campaign, Clinton deployed more than 1,800 troops under General Richard Prescott to Newport, together with artillery and sufficient provisions to sustain the British garrison in the event of a lengthy siege. Clinton's reinforcements, which swelled Pigot's army to 6,500 men, were in place two weeks before d'Estaing arrived. Clinton was being confronted with his second great crisis within thirty days of his arrival in New York, a test of mettle that no other British commander in chief faced so soon after taking command, and he had deftly met the challenges.[37]

The commander of the 360 Continentals in Rhode Island, nearly half of whom were part of the Black Regiment, was General John Sullivan. Among the first batch of general officers chosen by Congress three years earlier, Sullivan—a New Hampshire lawyer without prior military experience in 1775—had been a purely political choice. His wartime performance had done little to remove doubts about his capabilities. Sullivan had blundered into what was nearly a disastrous encounter with John Burgoyne during the retreat from Canada in May 1776. Moreover, some in Congress believed that Sullivan's errors in the Battle of Brandywine had nearly led to a British victory; in the wake of that engagement, one North Carolina congressman even declared that his state would never again permit its soldiers to serve under Sullivan. Washington had privately acknowledged that Sullivan was prone to make bad choices, but he stuck with him, and now that Rhode Island was to be the scene of a crucial campaign, he continued to stick with him. There were those who thought that he should have replaced Sullivan with Horatio Gates, the hero of Saratoga and a general with a proven record of rallying militiamen to take up arms. At first blush, Washington's decision was perplexing, but those around him understood why he acted as he did. Washington hated and feared Gates, and as General Greene remarked that summer, the commander in chief was not about to give "a doubtful friend" the opportunity to win further laurels. Washington knew that he was running a considerable risk, and he took pains to encourage Sullivan to "pursue every measure in your power." The success of "the enterprize . . . will depend . . . on the promptness & energy of its execution," Washington advised.[38]

Washington deployed Lafayette with two thousand Continentals to reinforce Sullivan and temporarily pulled Greene away from his quartermaster duties and sent him to his native Rhode Island, where he might "render very essential services" with local officials. Washington further advised Sullivan to call on the three other New England states to raise thousands of militiamen, moves that altogether would bring the Allied force up to roughly ten thousand men. Raising militia could not be achieved overnight. Two days passed before Washington's communiqué reached Sullivan, who in turn dispatched couriers with appeals to the governors of the three states. The chief executives followed with orders to their militia commanders, though they did not always respond quickly; Connecticut's governor, burdened with inconsolable grief at the recent death of his son, did not act for five days. The state militia commanders next sent directives down the chain of command. Ultimately, word reached the villages that had been targeted to supply troops, but that was not the end of the process. Citizen soldiers, for the most part scattered on distant farms, had to be notified to muster. Thereafter, the local units advanced to a rendezvous site or sites, after which the soldiery marched to Rhode Island. Even if everyone moved with alacrity—and when does that occur?—it was a time-consuming process.

The provinces eventually raised one thousand more militiamen than Sullivan had requested, and ever so gradually the men were on the march to the front. Two long, anxious weeks passed following d'Estaing's arrival while Sullivan awaited the appearance of the full force of militia. He was idled, too, by a search for transport vessels that would get his force onto Aquidneck Island. In all, nineteen crucial days passed between the moment when Washington sent the first orders to Sullivan and the day that the Allies were prepared to act.

Each day that passed was a day when Pigot strengthened his defenses and Sullivan grew more worried about the "Motley and disarranged Chaos of Militia" that he commanded, convincing him that they needed additional training before being put to the test. D'Estaing was impatient to act. His men needed fresh water and he wanted to put them ashore, as most had not walked on land in four months. The two Allied commanders agreed to strike on August 7. On the eve of D-Day, Sullivan asked for a two-day postponement. The plan was for the American force to land on the east side of Aquidneck Island, their ally on the west side; the two leaders envisioned a pincer movement designed to cut off British troops in remote posts outside Newport. Thereafter, they were to assail Pigot in his entrenchments in Newport. By August 9 all was ready, and Sullivan's men began going ashore on the island. The Allies had nearly a two-to-one numerical advantage. Affairs looked so promising that General Greene gushed to Sullivan: "You are the most happy man in the World. What a child of fortune. The expedition going on against Newport . . . cannot fail of success."[39]

But on August 9, the day of the landing, a powerful British fleet was spotted on the horizon, a task force that had sailed from New York during the lengthy period of Allied inactivity. It contained four more fighting vessels than d'Estaing possessed and far more guns. D'Estaing immediately forgot about Newport and focused on a pending naval battle with the Royal Navy. As the sky lowered and the wind stiffened, the two squadrons maneuvered. But before either fired a shot, what might have been a hurricane churned out of the Atlantic and overpowered the vessels. Both fleets were "much disabled" by the storm's howling winds. When the tempest abated, Sullivan desperately beseeched his ally to return to the business of capturing Newport and the British garrison within the city, but d'Estaing hurriedly departed for Boston to repair his tattered squadron. He also told Sullivan that his orders were to seek the safety of Boston should he be outnumbered. Sullivan, brimming with anger and disappointment, was not assuaged, and he sent off an intemperate message to d'Estaing that in essence said that the still-salvageable operation had been doomed by the admiral's "refus[al] to assist." Nor were those the last of Sullivan's injudicious comments. Feathers were so ruffled within the ranks of the French naval officers that Washington, who understood the indispensability of his ally's commitment to America, wrote d'Estaing explaining that the "thinking part of Mankind" understood his withdrawal from Rhode Island. Washington additionally sought to mollify Lafayette, believing that many of the French officers "look up to him as their Head." He exhorted Lafayette to "take no exceptions at unmeaning expressions, uttered perhaps without Consideration, & in the first transport of disappointed hope." To that he added: "America esteems your Virtues & yr Services—and admired the principles upon which you act. . . . I, your friend, have no doubt that you will use your utmost endeavors to restore harmony that the honour, glory, and mutual Interest of the two Nation's may be promoted and cemented in the firmest manner."[40]

D'Estaing was gone, but as both the American force and Pigot's entrenched army remained on the island, Clinton immediately spotted an opportunity to score a major victory. He remarked that he was hopeful of "reducing General Sullivan to something like the Saratoga business"—that is, offsetting the losses that Burgoyne had suffered ten months earlier—after which his British army would "destroy all that was at Providence."[41] Clinton acted swiftly. He gathered seventy-seven vessels and a force of 4,300 men, which he would personally lead toward Newport. Clinton's plan was to occupy Bristol Neck—across from the top of Aquidneck Island—and block Sullivan's escape. It would be Sullivan who was caught in a pincer between Pigot advancing from Newport in the south and Clinton funneling in troops to his north. Clinton sent word ahead to Pigot that his force would sail the next day, August 27. He hoped for a swift passage that would deliver him to his destination before Sullivan, left in the lurch by the French, realized his predicament and retreated off the island.[42]

If Clinton expected Sullivan to withdraw within days of the departure of the French squadron, Sullivan had other ideas. Clinging to the misbegotten belief that the refurbished French fleet would soon return, Sullivan ordered the establishment of batteries within a few hundred yards of the outer British lines. His objective was to drive all the enemy defenders into the entrenchments within Newport, where Pigot's force would be vulnerable once d'Estaing's fleet reappeared. It was a risky plan and all the more dicey as Sullivan's militiamen had begun to desert in droves in the aftermath of d'Estaing's departure. By August 26, the day before Clinton's potent detachment sailed from Long Island, Sullivan knew that his army had shrunk by three thousand men in two days—the Yankee militiamen "desert by shoals," said one of the American officers—leaving him with only a slight numerical majority against Pigot's entrenched army of regulars. Sullivan persisted, however, alternating between plans for a siege and a surprise assault that he hoped might pierce the enemy's defenses. But by August 28, with his army having shrunk by another one thousand men and incidents of disease increasing among the troops, who were living in the open without tents and often consuming tainted water, Sullivan ordered a pullback to his own entrenchments farther north on the island.[43]

When Sullivan ordered a retreat, Pigot—who, given the ever-present lag in communications, had not yet learned that Clinton's considerable force was en route—came after the rebel army. On August 29 the two armies clashed in a daylong, seesaw engagement. Clinton had hoped to arrive that very day, but as luck would have it, his voyage was "retarded by calms and contrary winds." Meanwhile, the rival armies were locked in a furious fight, and for a time, it appeared that the Americans would suffer a ghastly defeat. But Sullivan's army succeeded in reaching the redoubts on Quaker Hill and twice stopped British advances. At day's end, Sullivan's army had retreated to the northern tip of the island and was largely intact. During the battle, Sullivan learned that Clinton's relief force was on the way. It had been spotted as it passed Block Island, ten miles off the Rhode Island coast; by utilizing a system of signals, the information was rapidly transmitted to Aquidneck Island. Moreover, on August 30, Sullivan received unequivocal information that d'Estaing would not be returning. The Americans began an immediate withdrawal from Aquidneck, and by the next morning, August 31, the last of Sullivan's troops were off the island.[44]

Less than twenty-four hours later, Clinton's reinforcements arrived and the British commander in chief was rowed ashore. He was "much chagrined," according to a witness. In fact, Clinton was livid and in "a very ill humour" and "not a little disappointed . . . to find that the Rebel army had entirely quitted the Island." His anger was directed at Pigot for having gone to battle with the rebels, a decision, he mistakenly believed, that had finally pried Sullivan off Aquidneck and "saved him . . . from being very critically circumstanced." By the slimmest of margins, Britain's commander in chief had missed inflicting a crushing blow to his adversary, and the Americans had avoided a colossal defeat.[45]

The great Atlantic storm got both Sullivan and Washington off the hook, for many believed that the regrettable timing of the gale had prevented a sure American victory. That was the tack taken by Washington, who for public consumption claimed that Sullivan was on the brink of taking Newport when the "unfortunate storm . . . blasted" the "certainty of success." Some knew the full story but said nothing publicly. For instance, General Greene, who had earlier thought it impossible for Sullivan to fail, later seemed surprised only that Sullivan somehow escaped condemnation. "He is ever unsuccessful . . . and yet comes off free from disgrace," the perplexed Greene blustered. Most thought it best to say as little as possible about the disappointment and America's close brush with disaster. The preferable line, one taken by a Rhode Island congressman, was that "the Arms of America far from being sullied, have reaped Glory & Honor in the attempt" to retake Newport.[46]

AS THE SUMMER of 1778 faded away, both Clinton and Washington understood that the opportunity for decisive action that year was slipping through their hands, and both contemplated major undertakings while it was still in their power to act. Clinton for certain, and probably Washington as well, foresaw that without a pivotal victory in the coming weeks this war was destined to go on for a very long time, and time might not be a friend. Even into early autumn, Clinton still possessed the army that he had inherited back in the spring, much of which he had been ordered long before to redeploy to other sectors. It was not as if he had deliberately snubbed Germain. Once d'Estaing's powerful fleet arrived in American waters, Clinton needed every man for the defense of New York. Even after that threat faded, he hesitated to act as long as d'Estaing remained in the vicinity. During the summer, with his army intact, Clinton had pulled out all the stops to gain a major victory in Rhode Island, and he came closer to success than the American public realized. That was not the end of his audacious thinking. Hoping to utilize his army before much of it was redeployed, Clinton proposed a land and sea operation that would have included an amphibious landing in Boston and a naval assault on the badly damaged French fleet that was refitting the city's harbor. Clinton knew that the eradication of d'Estaing's force could be pivotal in countless ways, not least in that it might cause Congress to rethink opening talks with the Carlisle Commission. In the end, Clinton—who often planned more boldly that he executed—wisely shelved his Boston scheme as too dangerous. Shortly thereafter d'Estaing took advantage of yet another Atlantic storm that immobilized the Royal Navy for a spell and slipped out of Boston Harbor. His destination was Martinique. With d'Estaing gone, Clinton took what he called the "heart breaking" step he had so long dreaded. Off went division after division of his army, some men sailing for Florida, others for the West Indies, and still more to assorted stations in Canada. Within days, his army "dissolved," as he put it. He was left with between thirteen thousand and fourteen thousand in New York, a site that in his estimation required at least fifteen thousand for a proper defense.[47]

Before the emasculation of his army, Clinton had been dauntless. Thereafter, he knew that any hazardous move was not in the cards for the foreseeable future. That was not the case with Washington, who presented two daring options to his generals. Following the abortive end to the Newport affair, Washington asked his generals to consider marching the army—augmented by militia—to southern New England in the hope of drawing the British into a clash. His other notion was to strike the northern defenses of Manhattan, an operation perhaps not unlike what he had attempted at Germantown. The Americans would have numbers on their side, and though it was unlikely to produce a decisive action, a victory might galvanize those in England who were disenchanted with the war. Washington's generals, as was usually the case, offered mixed advice, but those that the commander most trusted counseled against any rash action for a variety of reasons, not least because they suspected that French belligerence would force the redeployment of a sizable portion of Clinton's army. Given the expected dwindling of the adversary's army, several generals advised that better opportunities might lie down the road, though they might have to wait until the arrival of better weather in the spring.[48]

Washington probably anticipated the provident approach of his generals, men with whom he was thoroughly familiar, and their advice tallied with the risk-averse strategic thinking he had broached back in the spring. If anything, the events of 1778 had hardened Washington's unwillingness to engage in precarious moves, unless accompanied by a powerful French naval force. He was now thoroughly versed in the unpredictability of battles. Furthermore, the advantages afforded the enemy by its naval capabilities had once again been on display in Rhode Island, as Clinton in the blink of an eye had transformed a numerically inferior body of British defenders into an able fighting force. By the end of 1778 Washington must also have known that Clinton was a more dangerous adversary than Howe had been. Clinton had acted aggressively in an effort to save Burgoyne a year earlier, his speedy action had perhaps prevented a disaster in New York Harbor, and at Monmouth and in Rhode Island he had been eager for a fight. It took no arm-twisting for Washington to see eye to eye with the generals who had counseled against risky actions for the time being.

As 1778 inched toward its conclusion, the ebullient optimism that Washington had exuded earlier in the year was nowhere to be seen. D'Estaing's behavior opened his eyes to the realization that France would act in its own interest. The alliance was helpful, to be sure, but the United States had to be self-reliant, and it was possible that it might have to stand alone in 1779. That prospect was all the more troubling as he was convinced that in the coming year Britain's operations would have to be "vigorous & decisive" to "hold their present posts in the United states." Atop this was something far more concerning. By early autumn, Washington was profoundly aware of what would become a nightmare for the United States—a collapsing economy. Unless "some remedy can be soon, and effectually, applied" to the "depreciation of our money . . . the total stagnation of all purchases" would be the result, he warned. Well before the year ended, Washington raised with an acquaintance a gloomy question that he had not addressed since the darkest days of late 1776: "Can we carry on the War much longer?"[49]

Clinton, meanwhile, was equally dismayed. Having been stripped of what he called "the very nerves of his army," he knew that he had too few men fit for duty to adequately defend either New York or Newport, or both simultaneously. Two years earlier, General Howe's army in New York alone had contained more than thirty thousand men. Clinton now had about two-thirds that number, most in New York, some in Newport. He feared that he was too weak to maintain what Britain still possessed, and that due to his weakness his army was likely to have to "remain on a most strict defensive next year." What made this all the more agonizing, in Clinton's estimation, was that the enemy might be vulnerable as never before. The Americans, he believed, were not only "tired of the war" but disillusioned with their leaders for having provided inadequate assistance to their new French ally, especially in Rhode Island. "One more vigourous campaign" would win the war, he predicted as 1778 drew to a close. But he knew that was not to be. Given that the "future vigour" of his army was sadly compromised, a despondent Clinton requested that he be relieved of his "mortifying command" and allowed to return home.[50]

CHAPTER 4

LAUNCHING THE SOUTHERN STRATEGY

THE DOCKS IN Watering Place on Staten Island had bustled with activity for days in early November 1778. Stevedores had been loading a six-vessel flotilla that soon would sail. Provisions of every sort had been hoisted aboard, teams of horses had been led onto the vessels, and company after company of soldiers had ascended the gangplanks in preparation for the voyage. But a "melancholy" accident due to "Inattention"—in the words of a high-ranking British officer—delayed the loading of the artillery for two weeks.[1] All the while, rumors buzzed through the city about the destination of the expedition, but orders from on high mandated that the "strictest Secrecy" was to shroud every aspect of the undertaking.

On the evening before sailing, the commander of the expedition, Lieutenant Colonel Archibald Campbell, was invited to dine with Sir Henry Clinton and Rear Admiral James Gambier. Ushered into the dining room, Campbell found about twenty guests in attendance. Some were military men he knew. The others, all strangers, were likely New York City Loyalists. Before the meal was served, all drank to the king's health. Gambier then offered a toast: "Success to Colonel Campbell against the Town of

Savannah!"² The British campaign to retake Georgia and South Carolina, the notion that Lord Germain had first broached some nine months earlier, was about to become a reality.

Germain's plan for a southern strategy had lain idle seemingly for ages, but once d'Estaing's French fleet sailed for the Caribbean early in November, Clinton felt free at last to launch at least a limited campaign in the South, beginning with a move to reclaim Georgia, the youngest and smallest of Britain's thirteen mainland colonies. Clinton had initially been unenthusiastic about the departure in how Britain was to wage the war, though once it was clear that luring General Washington onto a battlefield was unlikely, the British commander had warmed to the idea of the reconquest of southern provinces. He thought Washington might respond by deploying a "considerable reinforcement to the southward," a step that would make it more difficult for Britain to "be able to keep" whatever territory it conquered. On the whole, however, Clinton was confident that so long as Britain retained its naval superiority, it could destroy any armies that the rebels detached to the South. Clinton radiated optimism about seizing Savannah, though he had added a thousand troops to the number that Germain advised would be sufficient for the undertaking. All in all, Clinton believed that if the "temper of the people" meshed with what the American secretary foresaw—that vast numbers of southerners were Loyalists who would soldier for their king—then he, too, felt that the British had a good chance of succeeding in Georgia and the Carolinas.³

Colonel Campbell, forty years old and a soldier since he was nineteen, was thought by some to be gracious and refined, while in the stinging judgment of others he was looked on as haughty and imperious. Throughout his long career as a soldier he had served almost entirely in the Corps of Engineers in stations in the West Indies, East Indies, and India, but in 1775 this native of Scotland had been made a battalion commander in the Seventy-First Highlanders regiment. In the spring of the following year, unaware that General William Howe had abandoned Boston, Campbell and his men put to sea for the city. They sailed into a snare. Campbell and a considerable portion of his men were captured as they neared Boston

Harbor. He spent more than two years in captivity, and it was no bed of roses. According to Campbell, his Yankee captors treated him with a "shameful and unprecedented Barbarity" that "disgraced human Nature." Finally liberated in a prisoner swap, Campbell rejoined the British army in New York late in the spring of 1778. In no time, he was named commander of the Highlanders and led it in several foraging operations along the Hudson River in New York and New Jersey, some of which included skirmishes with rebel forces. Clinton liked what he saw in Campbell and, for that matter, so did the king, who had told Germain that here was an "able and prudent" officer. The members of the Carlisle Commission, still biding their time in New York, were also impressed with Campbell. They authorized him to proclaim that Georgia was again part of the British Empire as soon as Savannah fell and, giddy with optimism, named him the royal governor of South Carolina should he succeed in pacifying that colony as well.[4]

On November 26, a raw autumn day, Campbell's fleet weighed anchor and set off for Georgia with a fresh wind in its sails. Colonel Campbell, on board the *Phoenix*, sailed with mixed emotions. He was overjoyed that his compensation was to be that of a brigadier general, but fearful and angry in the wake of Admiral Gambier's ill-advised toast revealing the destination of the expedition to a room that included strangers. (Privately, Campbell raged that the admiral's blunder was consistent with the "Folly and Weakness" of those whom London repeatedly sent to conduct this war.) Some three thousand men were crammed into the holds of the ships in the little squadron. Fewer than half were British regulars. The bulk of the force consisted of two Hessian regiments (which Clinton, in private, trivialized as steadfast but neither as zealous nor as hardy as British regulars) and four Loyalist battalions raised in recent months in New York and New Jersey. The British had mostly utilized provincial troops in the Seven Years' War for garrison duty and securing supply lines, but the downsizing of Britain's army following France's entry into the war meant that Loyalist units were now to be depended on in major operations. Clinton would have welcomed more Loyalists, but their recruitment in the North in 1778 had lagged, a fact of life that he shrugged off with the comment that they were not inclined "to add to their other sufferings those of a military life."[5]

Colonel Campbell commanded the force that was sailing south, but he was outranked by Brigadier General Augustine Prevost, who commanded the British army in East Florida and was to play a role in the conquest of the South. A native of Switzerland, the fifty-five-year-old Prevost was nine years older than Washington, though he had begun his career as a soldier at the same time as the Virginian, having been commissioned in an English infantry regiment that was earmarked for the American theater in the Seven Years' War. Prevost was sent back to America in 1776 to command a regiment posted in St. Augustine, very much in the backwater of the Revolutionary War. But as 1778 wore to a close, that was about to change. Clinton had notified Prevost of the pending operation to reclaim Savannah, and—at the instigation of Germain—also urged him to do his best to stir up the Indians, a move aimed at tying down Georgia's militiamen. In addition, Prevost at the earliest moment was to bring as many men as "could be spared with safety at St. Augustine" and link up with Campbell's force.[6] Prevost had not stirred much of late. He thought he had grown prematurely old and blamed Florida's heat and humidity for his every malady, but he had also suffered a dangerous wound in the Seven Years' War that still troubled him. It had additionally left him with a disfigured face that prompted some of his men to secretly call him "Old Bullet Head." His afflictions notwithstanding, Prevost was a soldier who followed orders, and he made preparations to assist Campbell.[7]

While awaiting word on the outcome of the campaign for Georgia, Clinton learned that the king would not hear of his recall. He was to remain in America and in command of Britain's army. Germain broke the news in one of his patented sugarcoated missives. Given Clinton's "great military talents" and the king's "entire reliance upon your zeal and ability," not to mention the majestic job he had done in seeing to the "valour and discipline" of his troops, George III refused to sanction the general's resignation. Indeed, given that reinforcements were to be sent, the monarch looked forward to active campaigning in the coming year. As Britain's victories piled up, Germain continued, Clinton would bask in the "particular honour" that would be his due.[8]

Whether or not he believed Germain's twaddle is unknown, but when the American secretary's letter arrived, Clinton was wrestling with a matter of considerable urgency. His army faced a severe supply crisis. In mid-December, Britain's army in New York had only a two-week supply of flour, and its cache of meat and vegetables would be gone in about seven weeks. As his "military chest . . . is empty," as Clinton said, he lacked the means to purchase provisions or pay the farmers who tended the army's gardens on Manhattan, Long Island, and Staten Island. Nor was it solely the British soldiers who had to be fed. The army was dependent on thousands of horses, and each day the equines with Clinton's army collectively consumed six tons of hay. Clinton was additionally responsible for seeing that food was available for a multitude of prisoners of war incarcerated in or near the city, and he was at least morally accountable for the welfare of the civilian population in New York, which had swelled dramatically as countless Tory refugees from the backcountry flooded in. The army itself consumed staggering quantities of food. Each man's weekly allowance was seven pounds of bread, seven pounds of beef or four pounds of pork, three pints of peas or half that amount of oatmeal, six ounces of butter, half a pint of rice, and some eight gills of rum spread out over the week. (The liquor allotment amounted to roughly a gallon per man per month, or in today's terms, a bit more than a fifth of rum each week.) Provisioning the British army in America was not a new problem, and Clinton had done everything he could since July to find additional supplies. Thousands of men had been in the field in New Jersey and the periphery of Manhattan scouring the countryside for provisions and fighting the rebels who sought to deny their success, and as 1778 closed, Clinton gloomily suspected that his supply difficulties were likely to be habitual. However, good news accompanied his despair. Clinton learned from his intelligence officials that divisions were rife in the

American congress and "great discontent . . . prevail[ed] in the [rebel] army owing" to the collapse of the enemy's economy.[9]

GENERAL WASHINGTON, LIKE his opposite number, was worn down with the burdens of command. Unlike Clinton, he never considered resigning, though during the darkest days of 1776 he all but said that he would never have accepted the post had he known what he was getting into. Washington longed to escape headquarters and return for a spell to Mount Vernon, his home in Virginia, which he had not seen in more than three years, but he dared not risk a vacation. The army, he said, required "constant attention & . . . care . . . to keep it from crumbling."[10] Clinton's intelligence gatherers had discovered disaffection within the Continental army, and to be sure Washington knew that trouble existed and could mushroom quickly. Washington also feared that discontentment among civilians would swell the longer the conflict continued. After all, he, too, was disappointed, even disillusioned, as the fourth year of the war approached. He had thought the alliance with France and the arrival of d'Estaing's fleet signaled an early peace, but the optimism he once had manifested had long since disappeared. When he learned in October that d'Estaing was sailing to the Caribbean, Washington managed to hide his displeasure, though with crystal clarity he let the admiral know that he wished him to return for the summer campaign in 1779.[11]

At the dawn of that year Washington faced several problems, and some were unlike any that he had dealt with earlier in the war. Previously, Washington had always had a reasonably good feel for what his adversary would attempt in the coming campaign, but late in 1778 he had sighed that the "designs of the Enemy . . . are mysterious." In the short, dark days of late autumn, informants in Manhattan notified Washington of the dockside bustle on Staten Island. He knew the enemy was planning something. For a brief moment he clutched at the hope that they were abandoning "future operations in this country," though from the outset he thought that was unlikely. He expected his adversary to stay the course, hoping to prevent

American independence either through a military victory or an unexpected "chapter of *accidents*" along the lines of army mutinies or the total breakdown of civilian morale. But why were the British loading transports? Washington was "in suspence & baffle[d]," he acknowledged. Were they planning a campaign to take the Hudson Highlands? Were they sending still more of their army to the West Indies? As early as September 23, intelligence notified Washington of British plans to invade Georgia and South Carolina, but he thought such a step unlikely. His devious enemy must have leaked word that their sights were set on the South merely to "perplex & confound" him, he said.[12]

Among the "chapter of accidents" that Washington feared the enemy might exploit was America's gravely troubled economy. In fact, it was front and center among Washington's anxieties. Currency depreciation had first been evident late in 1776, but inflation grew at an alarming rate the following year as both Congress and the states issued paper money without adequate provision for its redemption. As the value of Continental money fell to a rate of 5 to 1 of specie, Congress in the summer of 1777 took remedial steps. It asked the states not to issue additional money, and it requisitioned revenue from the states. The measures largely succeeded in staunching the slide for a few months, but when Congress learned that d'Estaing's task force was sailing to America in the spring of 1778, it needed money, and quickly, in order to cooperate with the new ally. Congress made a fateful choice. Gambling that French belligerence meant that the war would not last much longer, it turned loose the printing presses. Inflation returned with a vengeance, triggering the most rapid rate of depreciation in American history. The value of Continental money suddenly slipped to about 10 to 1 of specie, and that was only the beginning. Horses that could be had for under £10 a head at the outset of hostilities cost £200 or more at the outset of 1779. A gloomily apprehensive Washington noted not only that the value of money was "melt[ing] like Snow before a hot Sun," but that a "wagon load of money will scarcely purchase a waggon load of provision." (More pithily, a Connecticut Yankee opined that a Continental dollar was "fit for nothing but Bum Fodder"—toilet paper.) Washington warned that the United States could not continue to wage the war much longer "unless some measures can be devised, and speedily executed, to restore the credit of our Currency."[13]

Washington had little experience with currency depreciation or how to cope with it, and at least initially he reached the conclusion that this potentially lethal turn of events had been brought on solely by the "variant tribes of money makers" in quest of windfall profits. In several private letters brimming with his tightly wound outrage, he called those seeking to profit from the war "speculators," "stock jobbers," "monopolizers," "forestallers," and "engrossers." He charged that this devious crew, driven by their "thirst for gain," had deliberately run up prices on "those articles which the army cannot do without" and the public did not wish to give up. To be sure, war profiteering was not unheard of among American merchants, and it contributed to soaring prices. In 1778, the price of domestic foodstuffs and imported goods such as tea, rum, and molasses had risen by more than 1,000 percent. As the cost of vital commodities soared to levels beyond the reach of ordinary citizens, the very real danger grew that morale on the home front would collapse. Worker-dominated price-control committees sprang into being in Philadelphia, but powerful business interests resisted government regulation and in time succeeded in rolling back public policing. Washington never endorsed price controls and was careful not to wax on about the profiteers in his communications with Congress, in some measure because of his steadfast wish to maintain the separation between the civil and military spheres. He also likely said nothing publicly because one or two powerful members of Congress were among the engrossers that he privately berated. But he made no attempt to hide his sulfuric feelings when writing to family members or trusted acquaintances who did not sit in Congress. He raged that avaricious businessmen were the "murderers of our cause," the "pests of Society," and the "greatest enemies we have," and charged that they possessed "little virtue & patriotism." He said that he wished each state would hang one of these unsavory characters as an example to other miscreants. That never happened, but had the hangman been put to his grisly work, it would not have solved America's economic problems.[14]

The unsound economy was not Washington's problem to solve, but he had to cope with its menacing impact on the army. Currency depreciation not only had sent the cost of supplies needed by the army spiraling into the stratosphere; it led many ordinary citizens to refuse to sell their goods to the American military. Instead, many otherwise patriotic farmers who lived near British-occupied territory trafficked with the enemy, which paid in sound currency. Nor were those the only complications brought on by the growing economic crisis. The enlistments of roughly 8 percent of the soldiery were due to expire at year's end. Those men had to be persuaded to reenlist or, if that failed, to be replaced. For certain, replacements would be needed for those who had died or were too incapacitated to any longer bear arms. Men had rushed to serve in 1775 and 1776. But as the reality of war set in, it had become increasingly difficult to find new recruits. As early as 1777 both the states and Congress were offering cash bounties to lure men into the ranks and to keep "our Army upon a respectable footing," as Washington put it. But the depreciated currency that was offered in the winter of 1778–1779 was hardly alluring. A concerned Washington wondered how long the army could stay in the field in the face of "ruined finances." Before the end of 1778 he advised Congress that it must either solve the economic quandary or raise and maintain the army through conscription.

Yet another danger brought on by the economic crisis was that many officers, suddenly faced with penury as a result of hyperinflation, were quitting the army and returning home to save their property. (Washington complained to the Board of War that officers could hardly afford "to pay . . . for a servant," an untoward remark at a moment when many enlisted men lacked blankets, coats, shoes, and a nutritious diet.) Hundreds had resigned their commissions during the Valley Forge winter, leaving the army with a dearth of experienced officers. Washington was convinced that had the French alliance not encouraged the belief that the war would soon end, so many officers would have resigned their commissions that the nation would have been left with a mere "shadow of an Army." Of course, the war had not ended and the mounting economic malaise throughout 1778 had further "Soured the temper" of many officers. Nor was the army alone in suffering from the woes of the economy. Washington was keenly aware that civilians also faced increasing austerity, and at the very moment that many were being asked to join the army or face danger as militiamen. With yet another year looming of what had become a seemingly interminable war, Washington advised Congress that "the people and the Army appear to grow dayly more tired of the War."[15]

Better than most, Washington understood that a robust army "must depend" on the "state of our finances." If the financial crisis could not be brought under control, he feared that the army could do little more than "lie quiet" in some unassailable place and hope to confine "the enemy to their present posts." The year 1778 had begun on a high note, but as it wound down, Washington expressed concern that "the wretched state of our currency" would furnish the enemy with "exultation and renewed hope." (At nearly that very moment Clinton predicted that "the Rebellion is near its end," a conclusion he reached based on America's economic miseries and Lafayette's departure for home; Clinton thought the marquis was abandoning a hopeless cause, when in fact he had returned to France in the hope of contributing to his country's success in the European phase of this war.) The revival of British optimism, Washington went on, would spur Clinton to action to cultivate ever more dangerous "internal dissentions" within America. Among other things, Washington now expected his adversary to make "predatory war" on the nation's coastal towns and along the frontier. In the meantime, Washington despaired that there was little his army could do that would have a substantive impact on the course of hostilities. He could only hope that d'Estaing returned in the near future or that Spain would enter the war, a step that might compel Britain to "renounce her American projects" in order to defend the homeland.[16]

While Washington never let up on the ruinous practices of profiteering, toward the end of the year he had reached a strikingly new conclusion with regard to what posed the fundamental threat to the war effort: It was

America's "political system." The states were too powerful and the central government too weak. Like a clock, he said, "it answers no good purpose to keep the smaller Wheels in order if the greater one which is the support & prime mover of the whole is neglected." An "entire reformation" of the powers of Congress and those of the states must be tended to, he said. Driven at this point by the rather sudden and deadly slipping of the value of Continental money, and faced with a most uncertain future, Washington asked to meet with Congress. But the economy was not all that was on Washington's mind. He wished to share his thoughts concerning campaign strategies for 1779 and to broach the need for additional administrative reforms within the army. Congressmen who had ideas of their own concerning "the affairs & operations of the army this ensuing year" were eager to meet with the commander. Washington departed headquarters in Middlebrook, New Jersey, on Christmas Eve morning and was received by Congress later that same day in the Pennsylvania State House (Independence Hall) in Philadelphia.[17]

Washington had spoken with a sprinkling of congressmen when he passed through Philadelphia en route to his encounter with the enemy at Brandywine, but he had not met with the full Congress in nearly three years. Nor had he been away from his army during the past thirty months. He remained in Philadelphia for five weeks and much that he encountered was an eye-opening experience.

Although a few who had been delegates since the time that Washington had served in Congress in 1774 and for a few weeks in 1775 were still in their seats—including Samuel Adams, Richard Henry Lee, and Roger Sherman—Washington mostly met men he did not know. Some he had served with, such as John Adams and Benjamin Franklin, were away on diplomatic assignments, but most had returned home and were serving, if they were serving at all, in state offices. Washington unfairly concluded that the majority of congressmen at the outset of 1779 were second-raters, even though men on the order of Elbridge Gerry, James Duane, John Jay, Gouverneur Morris, and Henry Laurens were delegates. Perhaps more accurately, he also felt that Congress spent too much of its time on "trifling" provincial issues rather than on national "matters of great moment at this critical period." Whereas his army duties forced him into an unrelenting schedule day after day, the impatient Washington surmised that a good bit of the congressmen's time was squandered in "idleness and dissipation."[18]

Washington had not been in town long before he discovered that some congressmen wanted help from his army. The Georgia and South Carolina congressional delegations, suspecting that their provinces were the likely targets of the British expedition under Colonel Campbell, hoped to persuade Washington to aid in defending against the coming invasion. Congressmen from New York and Pennsylvania were no less eager for a helping hand from Washington's army. Their beleaguered frontiers were under attack from Iroquois who believed—as the Mohawk war chief Joseph Brant put it—that the colonial insurgents had "in great measure begun this Rebellion to be sole Masters of the Continent." The Iroquois joined with Loyalists to form vigilante bands that plundered tiny hamlets and solitary farms in the Mohawk Valley and elsewhere. They hoped to drive away those who were foes of Great Britain. Raiding increased during 1778, sparking brutal reprisals by pro-Revolutionary settlers and militia that, in turn, precipitated equally cruel raids by the Loyalists and Indians. Early that summer—about the time of the battle at Monmouth—a sortie against the settlement of Wyoming, Pennsylvania, by several hundred Seneca and Cayuga Indians and Tories resulted in the deaths of more than 225 settlers and militiamen, and some Continental soldiers who had been posted there to protect it. "I had worked so hard with my tomahawk and scalping knife that my arms were bloody above the elbows," said one Indian warrior. By late in the year seven frontier villages in and around the Mohawk Valley in New York had been laid waste, and hundreds of settlers had been killed or taken captive.[19]

The entreaties of the congressmen may have caused Washington to recalibrate the plans for 1779, as three weeks passed before he finally shared his thinking with Congress. What he submitted was disingenuous. He presented his proposals in such a manner that Congress was virtually guaranteed to reject two of the three choices. He claimed that his preferred course of action was to launch simultaneous attacks against the enemy in Rhode

Island and New York. This would be a major undertaking that would require an army of twenty-six thousand men, more than he had possessed at the outset of the New York campaign thirty months earlier. If that were not sufficient for dooming that alternative, Washington ticked off two additional drawbacks to his own plan. Britain's naval arm gave it the ability to so speedily redeploy troops that any attack was likely to be met with the "united opposition" of Britain's armed forces in New York and Rhode Island. Furthermore, the "insular situation of the Enemy's posts" presented "obstacles not easily overcome." He might have mentioned, but did not, that his generals had previously argued against such an endeavor.

A second possibility, said Washington, would be a campaign to take Niagara. Success would secure the northern frontier and "open a door into Canada." Yet Washington had been a steadfast foe of another Canadian venture and only weeks earlier, in secret, had advised the president of Congress of the many perils that he believed would accrue from yet another incursion into Canada. On this occasion, Washington cautioned that Niagara was one of Britain's "strongest fortresses in America" and it could be taken only if the United States "gain[ed] a superiority" on Lake Ontario, which he knew was out of the question.

The third possible course—the one he truly favored—was for the bulk of the army to remain "intirely on the defensive," save for the dispatch of a small expeditionary force to pacify the northern frontier.[20] Washington leaned in this direction for several reasons. He had long since concluded that if at all possible he wished to undertake no risky operation without the cooperation of the French fleet, and this choice would assure the availability of the lion's share of the Continental army in the event that d'Estaing suddenly reappeared. Additional factors added to the beauty of this option. Pennsylvania and New York, the two states ravaged by the fighting on their frontiers, had furnished vast numbers of men and precious comestibles to the Continental army. Washington's army would be seriously weakened should the two provinces turn inward to cope with their domestic problem. Washington's willingness to act against the Indians and Tory vigilantes also stemmed from his belief that the timing was favorable. Not only was

Clinton's army in winter quarters and unlikely to take the field anytime soon, but it was doubtful that d'Estaing would return before summer—if he returned at all—when the hurricane season commenced in the West Indies. What is more, Washington understood that sowing terror among the northern Indians might keep the indigenous peoples on other frontiers quiet for the duration of the war.[21]

Five days after Washington's presentation, the Committee of Conference, the panel that Congress had created to meet with the commander, agreed "to lay . . . entirely aside" both the Rhode Island–New York and Niagara choices in favor of "operations on a smaller scale against the savages" and Tories who have "infested our frontier."[22] Washington had secured congressional backing for his preference. Back in the spring, while still in gloomy Valley Forge, he had warned of the hazards of risk-taking, and now, at the very outset of 1779, he was assured that the army would not be squandered on a perilous venture. It would be intact and capable of joining with the French fleet if d'Estaing brought it northward.

Even before departing Philadelphia, Washington set about planning a campaign on the northern frontier, hopeful that it might be put in motion while snow still covered the landscape. Acting quickly proved to be unrealistic, forcing Washington to shift toward a spring launch. Early in March, he asked General John Sullivan to command "an Expedition of an extensive nature agt the hostile tribes." But Washington never took his eye off New York City, and from the outset he made it clear to the congressmen that the frontier campaign "will be carried into execution . . . if no unexpected event takes place."[23]

Washington was convinced that retaking New York offered the best hope for the decisive victory, but he was also aware that the loss of the Hudson River would have ruinous consequences. With that in mind, he wished to assure that the cause was not jeopardized by the relentless siphoning of parts of his army to other theaters, including to wherever Campbell's fleet was bound. If Washington could consolidate authority in his hands, he could largely assure that the army would not be fatally weakened by having detachments sent hither and yon. Thus, while in

Philadelphia he told Congress that he needed to have the "controuling power" necessary to guarantee the army's focused response to any opportunity of consequence. Congress quickly assented, a step that in the words of one historian truly made Washington the "commander in chief of all the Continental army," as he now possessed greater control over "army affairs" in every theater.[24]

Washington had also wished to meet with Congress in order to show the delegates how the army was menaced by the disintegrating economy, and he spelled out the dangers in more than one report. He warned that the "state of our finances"—which he categorized as the "depreciated state of the paper currency and the consequent high prices of every necessary"—inevitably "regulated" the army's "Every undertaking."[25] But while he had come to town to open the eyes of the congressmen, Washington's awareness of the acute dangers haunting the army were also enhanced during his stay in Philadelphia. Night after night the general and Martha, who had joined her husband, were dinner guests in the homes of the city's wealthiest inhabitants, citizens who lived as if there were no war raging. While the Continental soldiery went hungry, the cream of Philadelphia's society enjoyed multicourse meals and every conceivable delicacy. In private, Washington variously said that the lifestyle of Philadelphia's elite was indicative of an "extinction of public spirit," "declining zeal" for the cause, and a bewildering "rapacity." This "tribe of gentry," he added, mostly viewed the war as an opportunity to acquire "a little pelf." According to Philadelphia's Joseph Reed, who at the start of the war had been an aide to Washington and who, many times over, had seen what the commander now saw, it was customary for the city's wealthiest inhabitants to host parties at which "public Frugality, Spirits, and Patriotism [were] laugh'd at." A disgusted Samuel Adams had witnessed it, too, and he lamented that "Foppery" had become the "ruling Taste of the Great." To Adams's mind, and Washington's as well, the "Spirit of '76"—the ethos of sacrifice for the national well-being—was dead among many affluent Philadelphians. A spirit of hedonism now prevailed. Washington, who had often watched as his soldiers suffered ghastly privations, was indignant and fearful that high society's indifference toward those who bore arms would ultimately prevent the United States from winning its independence.[26]

A year earlier, Washington had been happier than at any time during the war. But by early 1779 a shaken commander in chief had come to believe "that our Affairs are in a more distressed, ruinous—& deplorable condition than they have been in Since the commencement of the War." He added that "the common interests of America are mouldering & sinking into irretrievable (if a remedy is not soon applied) ruin."[27] So great was the crisis that only "Men of abilities" could staunch the "decay of public virtue" that was at "the root of all our misfortunes" and lead the country through the difficult months—and possibly years—ahead. But where were those men of abilities? In letters to important individuals back home, Washington asked why some Virginians who had been active early in the American Revolution had "not come forth to save their country?" Where, he asked in a condemnatory manner, are "Jefferson & others?" (Besides Jefferson, the "others," he told a confidant, included George Mason, George Wythe, Edmund Pendleton, Thomas Nelson, and, a bit surprisingly, Robert Carter Nicholas, the long-time treasurer of the colony, who supported the war but opposed American independence.) Are they willing to stay home and permit the "noble struggle [to] end in ignominy?" Congress, he declared, must be composed of our "ablest men" who could lead with "cool & dispassionate reasoning." He added that the "crisis . . . requires no small degree of political skill," as well as "steady perseverance in our national duty."[28]

Soon after he left Philadelphia and returned to headquarters, Washington drafted one of his most passionate and moving letters, an urgent sigh of despair: Does not America "possess virtue enough" to sacrifice for

the essential rights & liberties of the present generation, & of millions yet unborn? shall a few designing men for their own aggrandizement, and to gratify their own avarice, offset the goodly fabric we have been rearing at the expense of so much time, blood, & treasure? and shall we become the victims of our own abominable lust of gain? Forbid it heaven! Forbid it all, & [in] every state in the union. . . . Our cause is noble. It is the cause of mankind! and the danger to it springs from ourselves.[29]

Later in the war, Washington on occasion sent out circular letters to state officials, knowing that his thoughts would be published. He did not take such a step in this instance, as he hoped to keep the enemy in the dark as much as possible about the disturbing trends on the home front.

IN THE SPRING of 1778 most members of Congress had shared Washington's optimism about the course of affairs, especially after the army survived its horrid experience at Valley Forge and word arrived of the French alliance. Virginia's John Banister, a close friend of Jefferson's, thought the Valley Forge crisis had been a rejuvenating spark that "gave Life & animation to every thing. The Army recruited, Supplies became certain instead of being precarious. Discipline began to prevail. . . . Providence save[d] us here again. I think we should be grateful." Still bubbling with optimism that summer Banister proclaimed: "the Remainder of the Conflict will be easy to us."[30]

But by autumn, in the wake of the failure in Rhode Island and d'Estaing's departure, the members of Congress understood that if the nation faced a protracted war with an ailing economy, the United States was looking at a grave crisis. Congressmen spoke of their "great anxiety" at the "truly alarming" financial calamity, and by the time Washington arrived in Philadelphia the delegates were preoccupied with the financial malaise. Before the commander departed, Congress had acted. Congressional leaders understood, as a New Yorker put it, that "Too much paper money is our great Evil." Somehow, much of it had to be taken out of circulation. Congress took two steps. Thinking that "nothing will answer the purpose but large Taxes," Congress in January set quotas and asked each state to impose new levies on its citizenry. It envisioned removing fifteen million dollars, one-sixth of the money in circulation. In addition, Congress issued public securities called bills of credit. Those who invested in the new securities would earn 6 percent interest. Congress hoped the step would take an additional thirty million dollars out of circulation. Sounding very much like Treasury secretary Alexander Hamilton a bit more than a decade later, New York's James Duane characterized the new debt as "properly funded." There was yet another reason for the new initiative. The money raised was to be set aside for paying the soldiery and sustaining the army. But as no one thought a sufficient amount could be raised to satisfy the needs of the army, Congress also agreed to seek a loan from France. The congressmen were optimistic. France had a stake in America's continued belligerence, as otherwise it alone would have to deal with its powerful archenemy. A French loan was to be used for "cloathing, Arms, Artillery and Ammunition." A loan by Versailles would additionally help assure France's staying power, as America would have to gain its independence in order to meet its debt obligation.[31]

"Time will prove [the] efficacy" of the steps Congress had taken, said one delegate, to which another answered that the plan would work if the states complied. On the whole, the congressmen were optimistic at the beginning of 1779. "Economy, Taxation & Open Ports"—that is, trade with Europe's neutrals—will be "infallible" is how one put it.[32]

The tone of Washington's letters early in 1779 suggests that he was far from sanguine that the states would do their part to rectify the economic crisis, but he was too savvy to put his ideas in writing. He simply said that the states would do their part if they "are not lost to every thing that is good & virtuous." But before the first warm days of spring arrived, Washington in private carped that the states were neither activating their militias nor meeting the quotas stipulated for the number of troops to be furnished to the Continental army. He was also aware that the steps taken by Congress in January had been ineffective in preventing "the further depreciation of *our Money.*" Indeed, the exchange rate for Continental money had slipped further, its worthlessness doubling in the first one hundred days after Washington departed Philadelphia.[33]

The mounting evidence that the war was nowhere close to ending, as well as the swelling financial troubles, moved Thomas Paine to take up his pen. *Common Sense* and the first installment of *The American Crisis* in 1776 had established Paine as America's premier writer. He had produced five additional installments of his *American Crisis* series in 1777 and 1778, each for the most part designed to sustain support for the war and praise General Washington. But by late 1778 Paine, no less than Washington, was aware that the war had taken an ominous turn. Like the commander in chief, he, too, understood that economic disorders and the self-serving ethos that was overtaking the fabled sacrificial Spirit of '76 would eat away at America's ability to wage war. Washington was shocked at what he encountered in Philadelphia. Paine, who resided in the city, had long been convinced that many powerful businessmen cared more about increasing their fortunes than an American victory. Like Washington, Paine believed that these merchants were war profiteers who inflated prices to maximize their profits, and during the summer of 1778 he not only had sat on price-control committees but had published several newspaper essays assailing the pervasive corruption that threatened the war effort. "We have been sinking from one stage of public virtue to another, till the whole body seems to want a re-animation, a calling back to life," he wrote. Sounding strikingly similar to what Washington in his private musings was saying, Paine publicly proclaimed: "We are not the same People nor the same Congress that we were two years and a half ago. The former wants reinvigorating, the latter purging."[34]

Although Paine did not meet with Washington during the commander's stay in Philadelphia, their outlooks were comparable with regard to what they saw as the breakdown of virtuous behavior.[35] That was hardly surprising, for both had made exceptional sacrifices for America's cause. Washington served without pay and daily bore the incessant weight of command; Paine, in 1776, had risked his life as a soldier and donated nearly all his substantial earnings from *Common Sense* for the purchase of clothing for the soldiery. The two thought alike on another matter. Paine, like Washington, now understood that America faced a prolonged war. As was the case with Washington, Paine knew that a country saddled with a disintegrating economy and sagging morale would be severely challenged in a drawn-out war. Paine wished to address the matter but not to tip the enemy to America's snowballing adversities. He had two ends in mind. He sought to convince his countrymen that they could outlast their enemy. In addition, he hoped to break down the English peoples' confidence in victory. He knew that he had an audience in England. He knew, too, that war-weariness was growing in England, as were doubts that victory could ever be won in the American war. Paine, for the first time, sought to influence thinking in the enemy's lair.

He began *The American Crisis VII* with a question for the English people: "why is it that you have not conquered us?" He answered that "either you are not able or heaven is not willing." Thereafter, Paine played on England's lack of military success and the damage caused by remaining at war. He observed that in 1776 and 1777—when England was "at rest with the whole world" and the new American nation, standing alone, had to form governments and raise and train the Continental soldiery—the Crown had sent over huge armies and a colossal fleet. Those armed forces had failed to score a decisive victory. Now, four years later, America had an experienced army and was allied with France, the British army in America was smaller, and England was groaning under mounting indebtedness brought on by this conflict and the multitude of wars that preceded it. In contrast, he fibbed, there "is not a country in the world so capable of bearing the expense of a war as America." You "spend your substance in vain," he advised the English, for "America is above your reach." Moreover, many in England, and especially "the mercantile and manufacturing part," stood to gain nothing from a continuation of this war. This was a war waged by and for the monarchy and aristocracy. They have "an interest to pursue, distinct from, and opposed to" that of the ordinary Englishman and England's businessmen. "Your present king and ministry will be the ruin of you." You "had better risk a revolution . . . than be thus led on from madness to despair, and from despair to ruin." But if England made peace and recognized American independence, many throughout England would be "enriched" from a flourishing United States that would be eager for trade.[36]

ON THE DAY before Washington arrived in Philadelphia to confer with Congress, the lookout on board the *Phoenix*, the ship of the line in Colonel

Campbell's flotilla, spotted the deer-colored dunes and wind-scoured beach along Georgia's coast. The fleet had been dispersed by rough weather during its twenty-eight-day voyage, though most of the vessels had come together again two days previously off Cape Fear. Even as he awaited a rendezvous with the other ships in his task force, Campbell remained busy. He sent *Alert*, an armed schooner, ahead to scout the lower Savannah River, and he issued a bevy of orders. Campbell told his men that they were on a mission to liberate Georgia from the "savage Oppression" of the American revolutionaries, and he pledged an "equitable division" among both soldiers and crewmen of all proceeds realized from the seizure of any vessels taken in Savannah. As he had been led to expect that "a considerable Body of Loyalists are happily disposed to join the Royal Standard" throughout the South, he took special pains to warn against pillaging or harming civilians. Campbell cautioned that not only would pilfering be severely punished but that soldiers "who straggle in Quest of Plunder" might encounter "some lurking villain" bent on killing or capturing them.

By evening the next day, Christmas Eve, all the ships in the flotilla—save for "two horse sloops" that were still missing—were at anchor in the Savannah River at the foot of the Tybee Island lighthouse. The next morning, with the salty tang of the sea heavy in the air, a white flag with a red cross fluttered from the masthead of the *Phoenix*, the signal for disembarkation. Infantrymen on wobbly sea legs were the first to go ashore, tasked with searching for American soldiers or Georgians who could provide information on Savannah's defenders. Artillerymen, horses, and women (the wives and girlfriends of some of the soldiers) remained on board their ships. They would not land until the time came for fighting, or even later. The men who noisily clambered onto Georgia's sun-bleached shore spotted no sign of the enemy or of any residents. Again the next day no American soldiers were sighted, but as the troopers fanned out through the shaggy, waterlogged coastal fields, they apprehended a white overseer and Peter, an African American enslaved male. Peter talked, offering a wealth of information, much of which turned out to be quite reliable. He informed Campbell that there were 1,200 Continentals and 600 militia under arms in Savannah, and that the enemy possessed ten artillery pieces. Even if Peter had considerably overestimated the rebel's strength, Campbell knew that he possessed a huge superiority in both manpower and weaponry. He decided not to wait for General Prevost's arrival, a fortunate decision as Prevost had not yet left St. Augustine. Campbell knew that acting immediately would not violate Clinton's orders, for he had been directed to waste no time in taking possession of Savannah. On December 28, after further reconnaissance, Campbell ordered his men back on board the vessels. His plan was to sail upriver and put the men ashore at Girardeau's Landing about two miles below Savannah, the first viable site near the city for landing his army.[37]

The American force that was about to be tested was led by Brigadier General Robert Howe. The same age as Washington, Howe was a rice planter of considerable wealth who owned a handsome plantation house in southeastern North Carolina. He had possibly studied in England, and if so, that may explain why some thought he exuded suavity and "good breeding." (A worldly-wise French general officer was impressed by his "cultivated mind.") But some were put off by what they saw as his unsavory traits, including financial irresponsibility, insufferable egotism, stubbornness, heartlessness, and incessant womanizing. (A female visitor from abroad characterized Howe as a "woman eater," but she also acknowledged that she had met few colonials who were his equal as a gentleman.) Some males appear to have envied Howe for his ability to sweep any woman off her feet, though Janet Shaw, the Scottish sister of a royal official, concluded that Carolina's bumpkins "overrate his merits." Years before, Howe had soldiered in the Seven Years' War, after which he served in his colony's assembly and militia. When Congress created a Southern Department in the Continental army, Howe—who had won accolades in the first months of hostilities for his leadership during the defense of Norfolk against a small royal force—was named a general officer. Whatever his foibles, Howe was widely praised for gallantry and soldier-like qualities. The president of Virginia's assembly described him as "brave, prudent & spirited," and North Carolina's legislature called him "manly" and "warlike." Howe had served under Charles Lee when Sir Henry Clinton threatened Charleston in 1776, but during the next thirty months the war had seldom intruded on the southern theater. Howe did see action, however, resisting Tory raiders from Florida and in 1778 leading what was to be an invasion of East Florida, an operation that was abandoned after two months of floundering in Georgia. Early that autumn, as evidence mounted that Clinton was preparing to send a force to the South—possibly to take Charleston, but more likely to go after Savannah— Congress appointed General Benjamin Lincoln to command the Continentals in the Southern Department. As Lincoln had not yet reached Charleston in mid-November, Howe marched to Savannah with two regiments.[38]

Howe did not have much to work with. Contrary to what Campbell had been told, Howe had only some six hundred Continentals and one hundred militia under his command. Early on, too, Howe had discovered that most of the cannon in Savannah were not operational and that the city's defenses, erected years before to protect against Spanish attacks, had fallen into a state of hopeless disrepair. Long before Campbell's arrival, Howe, in his best fey manner, told the authorities in Georgia that Savannah was "not defensible for half an hour." Two weeks before the full British flotilla reached Tybee Island, he learned from a British deserter who had fled the *Neptune*—a transport from Campbell's storm-tossed armada that had reached Georgia well before the other ships—that a formidable enemy squadron was coming. Howe summoned a council of war to determine a course of action. Though the odds against success were long, the council did not see resistance as doomed to fail. It recommended defending the city, advice that stemmed from the belief that if the enemy could be held off for a few days, General Lincoln might arrive from Charleston with reinforcements. Howe consented and posted a small galley near Tybee to watch for the invasion force. Probably on Christmas Day—when the Highlanders in their green plaid kilts and red tunics and the Hessians in their blue uniforms first came ashore to gather intelligence and walk out the kinks after several weeks at sea—Howe called in his scattered men in preparation for the coming engagement.

Howe guessed that the enemy, not wishing to run the gauntlet of the few serviceable artillery pieces that guarded Savannah Harbor, would land downriver and approach the city by an overland route. Like Campbell, Howe thought Girardeau's Landing was the best site for putting men ashore. Not only did a narrow causeway sluice through rice fields and connect Fair Lawn plantation to the river three-fourths of a mile away, but a road ran from the estate to the city.

Fair Lawn plantation stood on Brewton Hill, a forty-foot bluff that looked down on the probable disembarkation site, an expanse of watery rice fields and swamps that was anchored on the east by the river. Some of Howe's officers urged him to assemble his force atop the steep little hill and flood the landing zone, rendering the road impassable and compelling the enemy to assault Brewton Hill. Spurning the recommendation, Howe stationed only about fifty South Carolina Continentals on the knoll. He positioned the bulk of his force in a long V-shaped line that ran from the river to the road leading to Savannah and beyond into impassable wooded swamplands. As neither Howe nor Jean Baptiste Ternant, a French army engineer serving with the Continentals, found any trails that the enemy might use to flank the American line, Howe was confident that Campbell would have no choice but to assail the center of the American line. Though outnumbered, Howe had constructed a daunting defensive position. Two South Carolina Continental regiments, as well as ranger and rifle units, composed the force on Howe's right; Georgia riflemen and militia, accompanied by artillery, made up the left wing. Forbidding swamps anchored each end of Howe's line. The British strike would have to be made at the strongest point of the rebel's line of defense and in the face of an enfiladed fire. All the ingredients were in place for the coming encounter to replicate that bloody day when Cornwallis's army had been mowed down when attempting to break through Washington's defenses on the Assunpink Creek.

The British force swung into action during the inky-black night of December 29, but the plan went awry. Expecting his adversary to post most of its firepower on Brewton Hill, and fearful that a rerun of the Bunker Hill catastrophe might be in the offing, Campbell opted to put his men ashore at night and in the "utmost silence." He handpicked experienced units with his best marksmen to serve as shock troops. Once ashore, they were to await the first pink streaks of daylight before assaulting the rebel-held bluff. When it was taken and the American artillery immobilized, the remainder of the army could disembark.

That was Campbell's plan. But the tide did not cooperate, and several vessels ran aground. Campbell had to improvise. The night landing was shifted to an early-morning operation. Soon after sunrise the assault troops—including Campbell himself—jostled ashore. To Campbell's surprise, and joy, he discovered that the hill was only lightly defended, allowing his men to come ashore without incident. Campbell soon found, too, that the rebels posted on Brewton Hill were not combat-hardened veterans. Combat, among other things, is a test of the limits of a soldier's courage. On this warm winter morning, self-preservation trumped valor among the rebel defenders. They fired one volley. Thereafter, at the sight of fierce-looking enemy soldiers mounting a bayonet charge, the Americans' boldness faltered and they fled. The hill was taken with minimal losses. Campbell could not understand Howe's thinking in not having heavily fortified the hill. With "four Pieces of Cannon" and five hundred men, Campbell said later, the Americans could have "destroyed the greatest part of [the] Division" assigned to take the bluff. Campbell had been lucky. His good fortune continued. Morning had burned into midday before the entire British force completed its disembarkation under a blue sky scudded with fleecy white clouds. Campbell expected that the real test was about to come. His men would have to fight their way through the Americans' defensive line. Instead, thanks to an obliging enslaved person, Campbell learned of a hidden path through the swamp on Howe's right wing.

The British commander seized the opportunity. In an action that nearly duplicated the surprises that Washington had experienced on Long Island and at Brandywine, a contingent of regular light infantry and New York Volunteers—a Loyalist regiment—took the secret path and circled behind the unsuspecting rebels, who were busily engaged in laying down a blistering fire against the advancing British. The moment the British in the rebels' rear peppered their enemy with an opening salvo, Howe realized that his force soon would be totally enveloped. He ordered a retreat, which before long dissolved into a helter-skelter flight toward Savannah. ("Their Retreat was rapid beyond Conception," said Campbell, a master of understatement.) Terrified men raced through thick woods lanced by sunlight. Toward the end of this long, ill-fated day, frightened American troops sprinted through the streets and squares of the city with the ecstatic enemy hard on their heels. In the last golden light of sunset, Campbell's troops occupied Savannah, which it had lost some thirty months earlier. There was no pillaging, and the Americans were prevented from burning the town, if in fact they contemplated doing so. Eighty-three Americans were dead, most having perished in the battle outside town, though perhaps as many as thirty drowned in a misbegotten attempt to avoid capture by swimming across Yamacraw Creek. Eleven rebels were wounded and 453 taken captive. Among the prisoners was George Walton, a signer of the Declaration of Independence and now a militia commander who had suffered a serious leg wound in the day's fighting; Walton wisely never volunteered the information that his name was on what the British regarded as a treasonous document, and his captors never learned his secret. Campbell had additionally seized forty-eight American cannon—only four of which had been utilized by Howe in the brief battle—mortars, powder, stores, and every vessel docked in the port of Savannah. All had been gained with the loss of only twenty-four of the king's men. It was a victory, the ecstatic Campbell remarked, that "ripped one star and one stripe from the rebel flag of America."[39]

SINCE TAKING COMMAND, Sir Henry Clinton had believed that if Britain was to win this war, victory would come in the North against Washington's army, and he despaired that he lacked the troops to take the field and force his adversary's hand. However, Campbell's decisive success exhilarated Clinton. "The province of Georgia is ours," Clinton exalted when word of the outcome at Savannah reached New York. It was of the "utmost importance to us," he thought, as Britain's possession of Georgia secured East

Florida, paved the way for taking South Carolina—which now seemed to be a realistic possibility—afforded hope of raising swarms of Loyalist volunteers, and "dispel[led] the cloud" that had settled over the British following France's entrance into the war. If taking Savannah also compelled Washington to transfer some of his soldiery to the South, New York City would be less vulnerable and Washington's army weaker. Clinton did not abandon his dream of a showdown with Washington, but he glimpsed a radiant hope for Britain in the South.[40]

Throughout the autumn, Washington had been dismissive of Britain's plans for the South, thinking his adversary might raid a coastal city or hamlet in hopes of reducing the population's will to fight on, but nothing more pivotal. When he provided Congress with an overview of the likely actions to be taken by Britain's armed forces in 1779, Washington never mentioned the southern theater, though he offered his thoughts seven weeks after Campbell's task force sailed southward. Not long after Campbell's men had chased the panicked American soldiers through downtown Savannah, Washington remarked that the British army's conquest of Savannah "will contribute very little to the brilliancy of their arms."[41]

Although Washington did not immediately see it, an ominous new phase of the Revolutionary War had begun.

CHAPTER 5

THE YEAR OF MARKING TIME

IN MARCH 1779, EVEN after learning of Britain's success in Savannah, General Washington thought the war had arrived at a point somewhere between "an immediate and glorious peace" and "one more campaign." He knew that France's entrance into the war had provoked sufficient anxiety in England that some wanted Lord North's government to focus entirely on protecting the homeland and Great Britain's interests in Europe. They were "now on tiptoe," Washington remarked, meaning that many in Parliament were torn between launching one more overseas campaign and immediately terminating the American war. Washington obviously hoped for the latter, but feared that America's economic troubles and its sagging morale—neither of which could be fully hidden—might tip London toward staying the course for an additional shot that summer at salvaging something from this war. Washington no longer believed that Britain could win the war through military means and, for that matter, did not think that the British any longer contemplated victory in the sense of thoroughly quashing the American rebellion. But a spate of recent bellicose speeches by British cabinet officials led Washington to conclude that the British would wage another campaign in 1779 in hopes of compelling the Americans to accept a negotiated peace settlement, probably on terms along the lines that Lord

North had proffered a year earlier. Washington remained confident that the United States could withstand the enemy in 1779 and gain its independence, and he went so far as to advise some of his field officers to hang on for one more year so they could share the honors that would be showered on the army when the sublime peace was won.[1]

Washington made an uncannily good conjecture regarding Britain's plans for the coming campaign. He anticipated what he called "predatory" raids along the northern coast, and probably in the South as well, while General Clinton would seek to draw him into battle. Clinton would be disappointed on the latter score, Washington as much as said, unless the Continental army had to risk all in the defense of West Point. While Washington appeared to think that the enemy would have to be satisfied with a holding pattern in the northern theater, over the course of the winter he came to see that Britain's retaking of Savannah was not a "transient incursion, but a serious conquest." He had been slow reaching that conclusion, slower than Congress, which in February sped quantities of arms and ammunition to Georgia and South Carolina and appealed to the governors of Virginia and North Carolina to furnish assistance to their beleaguered southern neighbors. Nevertheless, while Washington at last understood that Britain's actions in the South were not an unimportant sideshow, he did not yet fully comprehend the enemy's designs. He still thought Britain's gambit had been undertaken chiefly to obtain supplies for the defense of its West Indian possessions and to hurry the South toward a willingness to accept a negotiated end to hostilities.[2]

Washington's overall plan was to wait and watch, and hope Comte d'Estaing reappeared with the French fleet. Otherwise, Washington intended to react in some fashion to the enemy's moves, but he was adamant about avoiding risky ventures and, if at all possible, sidestepping another full-blown confrontation such as that at Brandywine. He shared the sentiments of General Nathanael Greene, who counseled that the paramount goal of the enemy was the annihilation of the Continental army, for if the army was destroyed, "the Country is conquer'd. . . . [T]his Army may be considered the Stamina of American liberty; and our position and measures should be taken upon this principle."[3]

Washington was aware that doing nothing could be as fraught with danger as a hazardous campaign in the field. Acknowledging that war-weariness was stalking the land, he spoke of a "general languor [that] has seized the people." If the war went on and on, the "disaffection" of growing numbers of citizens and the "discontents . . . of the officers of the army" would only increase, and so too would the "want of harmony in our councils."[4] To do nothing might be to court disaster by dangerously lengthening the war. It was a gamble to defer action until d'Estaing arrived, but Washington had reasons for thinking it was a risk worth running.

On May 1, Washington held the first of several conferences with the newly arrived French minister to the United States, Conrad-Alexandre Gérard. D'Estaing's plans figured prominently in those discussions. Gérard had called on Washington at the commander's headquarters in Middlebrook, on the Raritan River not far west of Staten Island, and the American commander rolled out the red carpet for his guest. The Continentals assembled with what one soldier called "martial pomp and style," after which the men performed "field maneuvers and evolutions, with firing of cannon and musketry." The day concluded with a parade past the reviewing stand. In the estimation of one soldier, the pass-by "was conducted with such marked regularity and precision" that Gérard could not but have experienced "the highest degree of satisfaction."[5] Once the festivities concluded, the diplomat and the general conferred. Washington knew that d'Estaing would remain in the Caribbean until the hurricane season commenced in late summer, but when the French fleet came north, the commander pressed to have it sail to New York. If d'Estaing did so, said Washington, he would "make every effort" to cooperate with the French navy in a joint campaign to retake New York. If successful, Washington told Gérard, the Franco-American endeavor would be the "decisive blow" in this war. Next to retaking New York, the best alternative for the Allies would be for the French fleet to recapture Savannah and destroy all British vessels in its harbor. Washington thought that would be a speedy undertaking, so swiftly accomplished, in fact, that d'Estaing might have time to speed to New York before winter set in. Gérard responded that he was unaware of d'Estaing's plans. Washington came away without any assurances, though he felt confident that within one hundred or so days the French fleet would return to North American waters and that at the very least the Allies would score a significant victory at Savannah.[6]

Throughout that spring and into the summer, Washington weighed contradictory intelligence that Clinton was preparing an onslaught against New Jersey or a push against the army's posts in the Highlands above New York City, including a campaign to take the crucial post at West Point. Washington, "extremely solicitous" for its safety, ordered work on West Point's defenses to be "pushed forward with all possible dispatch." Otherwise, he marked time, awaiting Sullivan's readiness to launch his onslaught against the Indians, seeking to divine what General Clinton had in mind, and making plans for the hoped-for joint operation against British-held New York.[7]

CLINTON WAS MARKING time as well. Given the paucity of troops left to him after thousands of his men had been stripped away for redeployment elsewhere, Clinton knew that without reinforcements a major action in the North was out of the question. Back in October, Clinton had dispatched Major Duncan Drummond, his aide and confidant, to London to press for the reinforcements that would enable the British army in New York to take the field in 1779. Clinton also knew that two members of the Carlisle Commission had returned home and would join with Drummond in beseeching the ministry to bolster Britain's army in North America, including even returning to New York the troops that had sailed for the Caribbean in November. The commissioners also planned to appeal for an adequate naval force commanded by a capable admiral or commodore, and Clinton had helpfully mentioned five men that he believed could do the job.[8]

Drummond and the commissioners appeared to have been successful. Whereas in the autumn Lord Germain had merely promised Clinton that "every means" was being taken to find reinforcements "so as to enable you to act offensively" in the spring of 1779, the American secretary now advised his North American commander that 6,600 additional men would be coming later in the year. Given that these reinforcements would be joining the fresh troops raised through the ongoing recruitment of provincial units, an exultant Clinton looked forward to having an army that was very close in size to that which he had been requesting since taking command. As for what Clinton was to do with that army, Germain never backed away from his emphasis on the reconquest of Georgia and South Carolina, though he added that the king and his ministers wanted Clinton to try to bring Washington to battle, and if that failed, he was to keep Washington immobilized in the Highlands north of Manhattan.[9]

Clinton was unnerved by the seemingly bewildering array of objectives that Germain had touched on. Whereas Burgoyne had been assigned a specific goal and Howe had been accorded the freedom to choose what he thought would be a feasible course of action, Clinton had been given numerous missions and a promise—nothing more than a promise—that his army would be adequately increased. Aware that he could not accomplish everything that Germain had mentioned, Clinton was apprehensive that what he did not achieve would be seen as a failing on his part. Usually the model of civility and ready acquiescence, Clinton in exasperation and an uncharacteristic cold fury dashed off an inflammatory response to Germain. He demanded that he be given "every latitude" to decide on feasible courses of action, and he as much as said that too much was expected of him and his "debilitated army." He accused the authorities at home of having been swayed by the "ill digested . . . suggestions" of Tory polemicists, none of whom were military men or "competent judges" of what was possible. He was being painted into a corner, he went on. He was compelled to follow orders with which he might not "agree yet [was] loath to disregard." Should he see an opportunity beyond the bounds of Germain's directives and seize that moment, he risked being scapegoated should his initiative fail. His was a no-win situation. If he followed Germain's orders and succeeded, he would reap no credit, save for having executed someone else's design. Others would bask in the glory that should be his. Clinton insisted he be permitted to design every last detail of his strategy. "I am upon the spot" and can adapt to the "hourly change of circumstances" that occur. "[L]eave me to myself."[10]

It was the angriest letter he ever wrote to his superior and perhaps the most irate missive that Germain received during the war. In all likelihood, much that flowed from Clinton' s pen was revelatory of the mindset of nearly every commander in this war, men who served their country and at the same moment sacrificed and risked life and limb—and their reputations—in quest of glory. The pressures of command weighed heavily on Clinton, leading him to repeatedly apprise Germain of "this difficult command" and how during the past year he had been confronted with "difficulty upon difficulty." He had recently spoken of being "worn down," and some thought him gloomy and despondent. He felt the war had taken a toll on his health, aging him prematurely, and he was haunted with guilt at not having seen his "motherless babes"—his two sons and two daughters—during the past two years.[11] Washington also faced the stresses of leadership, and like Clinton he, too, had once lashed out at his boss, the Continental Congress, when compelled to find winter quarters near Philadelphia in December 1777. Washington's pent-up anger had been unleashed at a moment when he feared not only that Congress was losing confidence in him but also that the congressmen's meddling might destroy the army and himself. Clinton, in 1779, was convinced that the government in London had never had much confidence in his abilities and that to follow the dictates of a faraway ministry would inevitably ruin him and sabotage Britain's slim chances of crushing the colonists' bid for independence.

While Clinton awaited the promised reinforcements, he pondered his strategic options. At "this Stage of the War," he told a friend, "every business" had to be considered, though in the end he adhered to Germain's directives. For months, the American secretary had emphasized that taking Savannah was only a prologue to going after Charleston, a much bigger prize, and that Charleston's acquisition was but the prelude to a campaign to retake all South Carolina. Clinton was more zealous about making war in the South in the wake of Savannah's rapid fall, but he knew that he could not simultaneously strive to lure Washington onto a battlefield and seek the conquest of Charleston. While he was confident that the combined forces of General Prevost and Colonel Campbell could capture Charleston, Clinton did not believe that their small army could hold the city for long. He knew, too, that it would be disastrous for Charleston to be taken, then relinquished, for the Tories who had "declare[d] for us" would see their abandonment as a betrayal. Such a breach of faith would for all time eviscerate any hope of recruiting Loyalists to serve the king. That spring, while Washington planned for d'Estaing's arrival and the campaign to retake New York, Clinton understood that he would have to send a large army to retake Charleston. But taking Charleston would have to await "a proper season," an expression he used figuratively and literally. He would not launch the enterprise until the promised reinforcements had arrived, recruiting of the provincial corps filled his ranks, and Charleston's unhealthy summer was over. During the spring, Clinton anticipated a mid-September start for his campaign to take Charleston.[12]

Even before Clinton was appointed to command the army, Germain had called for strikes on America's coastal towns. The American secretary was certain that the devastation would undermine America's will to persist and that the raids would eradicate America's privateers that preyed on British shipping. Privateering was venture capitalism gone to war. Speculators invested in privately owned crafts that aimed to raid British supply vessels; if successful, the captured cargo was sold, and the profits were divided among the investors and crew of the fortunate privateering ship. Clinton privately deplored coastal raids, largely because most of the pain was inflicted on civilians. However, he acknowledged their usefulness in tying down rebel militia units at home and eroding morale, and in the long run he would order more raids than any other British commander in this war.[13]

Clinton did not think solely of strategic matters that winter. Just as Washington in January had persuaded Congress to consolidate power in his hands, Clinton proposed a somewhat similar administrative reform. Both Howe and Burgoyne had recommended the appointment of a viceroy or lord lieutenant to coordinate military strategy within the North American theaters. Clinton went further and urged not only that the American and West Indian theaters be combined under one commander, but that a supreme commander for North America be vested with authority over both the army and the Royal Navy. This would partially correct the serious administrative flaw that left Britain's army within the jurisdiction of the American secretary while the Royal Navy was under the authority of the Admiralty, with only the civilian prime minister to sort out the problems that arose from the lack of synchronization. There can be little doubt that Clinton was angling to be appointed the commander in chief, but nothing came of his plan, and in time the weakness in Britain's command structure would have an adverse impact on its conduct of the war.[14]

Washington worried about the hazards of a protracted war, and similarly, the core of Clinton's thinking early in 1779 was that time was Britain's enemy. He had long been a proponent of "crush[ing] the rebellion in one campaign" and avoiding a prolonged "land war," which most likely would be "ruinous and unavailing." As opposition to the war had grown in England since Burgoyne's disaster at Saratoga, Clinton appeared to think that Britain must bring the American rebels to their knees in the very near future or lose the war. Success, however, depended on the reinforcements for his army and a larger naval force in American waters. With the two, said Clinton, he would possess the means of sending "separate corps" up the Hudson and Connecticut Rivers, while simultaneously conducting destructive diversionary raids along the northern Atlantic coast and in the Chesapeake. As these actions would threaten American morale, rob the Continental army of much-needed militiamen, and impair rebel recruiting, Clinton felt that "Mr. Washington" would be compelled to quit his unassailable stronghold in New Jersey and take the field. The pot of gold at the end of the rainbow that Clinton envisaged was "a general and decisive action." If he failed to get the showdown with the Continental army that he coveted, Clinton would cap the year with "the conquest of the two Carolinas," for he believed that if he took South Carolina, North Carolina would fall soon thereafter. These assorted actions, he believed, would bring the rebellion to its knees, possibly even by year's end, and oblige the colonists to accept peace terms short of American independence.[15]

WHILE CLINTON AWAITED reinforcements and dreamed of taking the field, Washington feared that his dreams of victory would end in frustration. Just as Clinton carped about his government, Washington in private grumbled about Congress. As Clinton was anxious that his masters in London, swayed by ill-informed Tories, would push him into a disaster, Washington likewise groused about the pressure he felt from congressmen with "a superficial view of the situation & circumstances." By far, however, Washington's greatest worry was the intractable economic crisis. With signs of spring all about and another campaign season approaching, Washington sighed yet again that the economy was taking a toll on recruiting and forcing experienced officers out of the army. Worse, said Washington without elaborating, some former officers returned home and spread "discontent & possibly the seeds of Sedition." Whatever he meant by that cryptic comment, it is a good bet that at bottom Washington's concern was about civilian morale. "I never was, much . . . affraid of the enemys arms," he declared in May, but the staying power of the American people was another matter. Never had morale been "at such a low ebb." Indeed, he spoke of the "disaffection of a great part of the people" and the "lethargy that overspreads the rest" of the citizenry. With Congress and the states unable any longer to "call out the strength & resources of the country" to the degree they had during the initial couple of years of hostilities, Washington felt that America's cause would be severely tested should Clinton be reinforced and take the offensive. In fact, said an uneasy Washington, the nation's ability "to continue the contest" would be sorely tested.[16]

At times, Washington was given to hyperbole, finding it useful in getting Congress to do as he wished. In this instance, however, he was spot-on with regard to sagging morale. Years of sacrifice and deprivation had taken a toll. Unaccustomed scarcities first appeared during the prewar boycotts instituted to protest imperial policies, but the dearth of goods grew dramatically with the advent of hostilities, and all the more so after late 1777 when the collapsing economy put many items and services beyond the reach of much of the population. In September 1777, as the Saratoga campaign was coming to a close, Abigail Adams, the wife of John Adams, lamented, "Our money will soon be as useless as blank paper." A year later, her prediction had come true: A few weeks after the Battle of Monmouth, she declared, "Our Money is very little better than blank paper." Every available article that she had consumed before the war "costs more than double in hard money what it once sold for." Bread, butter, corn, wool, linen, cotton, flour, sugar, molasses, coffee, tea, rum, and cider had become luxury items, she said, and the cost of paying the butcher had become exorbitant. So, too, was the price of securing farm laborers, whose wages, she said, she could not have afforded to pay had she been able to find a man to hire. Lucy Flucker Knox, the wife of Washington's artillery chieftain, Henry Knox, also complained that "there is not a man to be hired" in Boston. "Boys are not to be had," she added, as they can earn much more by working the forts, and standing occasional centrys." "What can be done," Abigail Adams asked, and she additionally wondered, "What is to become" of the workers who struggled to live on their salaries? She had the means of purchasing a few things, but she knew that unbridled inflation had led to prices that many, perhaps most, artisans and laborers could no longer afford.[17]

Sally Cobb Paine, whose husband Robert Treat Paine had sat in the Continental Congress for nearly three years, faced similar problems. Frustrated in her efforts to purchase goods that she wished to lay in for the winter, Paine expressed her exasperation in very nearly the same language that Washington had used when faced with the trials of acquiring goods for the army: "Every thing is So dear here one had need to have a wagon Load of money" for what once had been routine purchases. Abigail Adams meant the same thing when she complained that the worthless "money will avail me not a groat." Both women were driven to "economize with the utmost Frugality," as Adams put it, and both shuddered at the prospect of falling into debt, a possibility they dreaded even more than doing without articles they once had enjoyed. Neither fell into debt, and in fact, as both were relatively affluent, their families largely escaped what Samuel Adams at the time referred to as the "meanness [of] the stings of adversity" that were the lot of the poor and many workers. Nevertheless, affluence had problems of its own. For instance, John Adams was a creditor, having in prewar days so prospered from his legal practice that he made loans to numerous residents of eastern Massachusetts. Many who owed him money never made good on their obligations. However, by 1778, when the provincial currency had lost two-thirds of its value, some debtors whose "pockets [were] full of money"—as Abigail Adams bitterly remarked—seized the opportunity to retire their debts, stiffing the Adamses with cash worth a fraction of its value at the time John had made the loans. Nor were such practices confined to Massachusetts. Historian Woody Holton observed that in "several states a person who owed £1,000 could get out of debt with money that was actually worth only £1."[18]

Whether affluent or not, all Americans had to pay taxes, and the war brought about a staggering increase in taxation. Residents of Massachusetts, which was not vastly different from many other provinces, paid national, state, and town taxes that to many seemed to increase exponentially each year. Indeed, around the time that Washington expressed concern about how long America could continue the war, Massachusetts imposed yet another tax, one that levied a duty on residents in towns that had not met their troop quotas. Not too far down the road, that tax was followed by assessments on grain and hay to pay for the militia and "to furnish a suffering Army with provisions." Abigail Adams was hardly alone in exclaiming that the "burden is greater I fear than the people will bear."[19]

Taxes were onerous, but that burden paled next to the loss of life. Substantial numbers of Continental soldiers and militiamen—citizen soldiers who left home for a few weeks or months of duty during emergencies—had already made the supreme sacrifice, and so, too, had many civilians. Camp diseases, including smallpox and assorted fevers, haunted every army in the eighteenth century, and the maladies had a way of spreading from the soldiers to civilians. During the war's first winter, the time of the siege of Boston, diseases crept from the siege lines to hamlets near the city.

Abigail Adams wrote her husband of the appalling death rate in their hometown of Braintree, a Boston suburb, where "Some poor parents are mourning the loss of 3, 4, & 5 children, and some families are wholly stripped of every Member." Proportionately, more civilians than soldiers in Massachusetts may have died that winter of war-related diseases, and the New Englanders' experience was repeated elsewhere throughout the conflict. No one was immune. Adams lost her mother and a longtime family servant, and one of her children nearly died; one of John's brothers died that first winter of the war while serving in the militia during the siege of Boston. Before the war was a year old, Abigail Adams, as staunch a patriot as could be found, cried out, "Woe follows woe, and one affliction treads upon the heal of another." Grief "presseth me soar," she said, adding, "O my bursting Heart." Her commitment to the cause was tested, to the point that in 1776 she questioned whether having "mount[ed] the Whirlwind" was worth the cost.[20]

Disease aside, Adams was never in personal danger during the war, and her property escaped unscathed. Not everyone was so lucky. Many suffered misfortunes that challenged their commitment to the war effort. Not a few farm families felt as if they had been plundered by their own armed forces when squads of foraging Continentals arrived and demanded precious crops, livestock, firewood, or hay for the army. A Pennsylvania yeoman spoke for many when he raged at the pitiless "ravages and wanton destruction of the soldiery." The farmers were usually compensated for their losses, but by late 1777 the Continentals were paying with IOUs that were universally regarded as worthless. If a farm was in an active war zone, enemy combatants sometimes pillaged at will, destroying crops, taking cattle and household possessions, liberating enslaved people, and sometimes murdering and raping. These personal assaults happened infrequently, but lurid stories circulated about such incidents, heightening apprehensions. Nor were soldiers the only ones who victimized civilians. Women camp followers—sometimes the wives or girlfriends of soldiers, sometimes prostitutes—were known to steal from civilians who had the misfortune to live near an army camp. Outlaws not infrequently skulked in vulnerable areas or hung near an army; there were instances when they robbed and killed to get what they were after, and other times when they passed themselves off as friendly partisans to procure what they wanted.[21]

Every American was touched by the war, but it was when one suffered personal hardship that morale was most likely to be severely tested. Episodic calls to militia duty sparked discontent, particularly when the summons took a farmer away during the planting season or at harvest time, or if a tradesman could not work for weeks. America's citizenry had responded with patriotic fervor at the opening of hostilities, but it did not take long for the reality of war to set in. Some who marched off to war never came home. Some returned disabled. Some were so badly maimed that they could never work again, or they had been so changed by their experiences that they seemed to have become different people. While the men were away on duty, their wives at home took on the tasks that their absent husbands had once performed, including "to plough and hoe . . . and raise bread," and then to get the grains to mills and market. One woman whose husband was posted at Fort Ticonderoga said without rancor that she had "no time for aught but my work." Another, whose husband reenlisted, refused to take it in stride. "Let some body else take your place," she bristled in a missive to her husband, and she reminded him of his wedding vow: "What God has joined Let no Man put asunder."[22] With no end in sight to this war, Lucy Knox complained of her daily "solitary dinner," during which she "reflect[ed] upon [her] past happiness" when her husband had been at home. "Oh horrid war, how hast thou blasted the fairest prospect of happiness. . . . [T]hou art depriving me of the Society of my husband."[23] From the outset, women were anxious when their sons or husbands marched off to danger. When it happened more than once, as it did for many militiamen, despondency frequently accompanied anxiety. As the war grew to seem interminable, and possibly unwinnable, the danger increased that more and more citizens would question the wisdom of continuing.

Washington, in the spring of 1779, was aware that some previously stalwart supporters of the cause were growing less resolute, and Clinton knew it as well. His spies in the field, including some who had pierced both Congress and Washington's headquarters, reported that the surging tide of adversity on the home front was inclining more and more of the citizenry to "very generally declare in [Britain's] favour." The intelligence prompted Clinton to action. In May, he sent off to Virginia a flotilla of twenty-eight sail under Commodore Sir George Collier. To this point, the state had largely been in the backwater of the war, having experienced only localized fighting between bantam-sized units during the initial months of the conflict. Now, however, Clinton was taking the war to Virginia, and when his soldiers landed at Norfolk, the Virginians were taken by surprise. Before authorities could rush in militia, 1,800 British troops had come ashore and sowed destruction. This was just the beginning. Troops disembarked again and again at different sites during the next two weeks. The militia could not keep up with the landings, so that over a wide area tobacco warehouses, rebel magazines, naval craft, and shipyards were destroyed, and acres of crops were torched. Clinton's objective had been to tie down Virginia's soldiery that might otherwise march northward to join Washington or be sent southward to assist in the defense of South Carolina, but he also sought the further erosion of American morale. After two weeks several forts had been razed, the town of Suffolk was in ashes, many dry docks had ceased to exist, 518 slaves had fled to the British, and 137 merchant ships, privateers, and vessels under construction had been destroyed. So much booty had been confiscated that seventeen vessels were needed to haul it all back to New York. Clinton labeled the mission a "great" success that "answered every purpose" of his plan.[24]

Clinton and Collier had jointly planned the expedition and also the one that followed hard on its heels. The spoils that Collier brought back to Manhattan were no more than unloaded before the Commodore's fleet sailed again, this time up the Hudson. Before May ended, the British seized—with the "exchange of a few shot"—King's Ferry and both an unfinished American fort at Stony Point and Fort Lafayette at Verplanck's Point, all on the Hudson and within twenty miles of West Point. Clinton had several things in mind when he ordered the strikes. By gaining control of King's Ferry the British closed a crucial artery to the rebels, somewhat impeding southerly movements and "making the communication betwn the

East & West side [of the river] more circuitous & difficult." (Washington called it "one of the wisest measures" that Clinton had "yet pursued.") Clinton was nearly certain Washington would have to risk "an action [for the] recovery" of what he had lost, and if he did so, Clinton was also convinced that the British would have the stronger hand. Furthermore, if Washington sought to reopen the route to the south, he would—in Clinton's words—have to meet the British "in an angle between the mountains and the river," a site "replete with risk on his part and little or none on mine." In the end, Washington chose not to fight, explaining that it was too dangerous to take the field and adding that all "we can do is lament what we cannot remedy."

Clinton was disappointed, but he had two other things in mind. He was following Germain's long-ago suggestion that he pin Washington in the Highlands, a step that would give the British a free hand to maraud along the coast, as well as in New Jersey and the Connecticut Valley, further sapping American willpower with each destructive step they took. But Clinton's long-term plan was to use the reinforcements promised by Germain for a campaign to take West Point, a stroke that if successful would turn around the course of the war. The action that Clinton took in May laid the groundwork for the offensive that he envisioned following the arrival of the anticipated reinforcements during the summer.[25]

In the wake of Clinton's foray, Washington quickly marched his army from New Jersey to the Clove, a craggy gorge on the west side of the Hudson. He immediately acknowledged that "the posts in the Highland's are of infinite consequence" and that the American cause would be "most essentially injured" should Clinton retain control of what he had gained. But, like his adversary, Washington understood the dangers he would face in campaigning around King's Ferry, a "perplexity," he said, that left him with little means of "counteracting" what Clinton had achieved. While Washington wrestled with his choices, joy was the order of the day at Clinton's headquarters. The British commander was "amazingly elated" by his stroke, and William Smith, the last royal chief justice of New York, a loyalist who appeared to have access to the British commander whenever he wished, was so ebullient that he believed the "wretched State" of both the American economy and the Continental army might induce Congress to seek to "procure Authority from the People to negotiate" an end to the war, their only means of escaping "the Wrath of the Crown."[26]

Judge Smith's reverie on that score was unwarranted, but he may have been on sturdier ground in his belief that the door was now open for Clinton to immediately strike against West Point. Clinton, in early June 1779, had come to one of those consequential moments that in later years would be reckoned to have been more profound than it appeared to be at the time. To have sought to capture West Point, and to have succeeded, would in all likelihood have won the war for Great Britain. To have rolled the dice and failed could have had the most detrimental impact on Britain's war effort. Clinton, as was usually the case, chose caution. He opted not to hazard the war's outcome on a most unpredictable campaign to take West Point.

Clinton's information on the state of West Point's defenses was inadequate at best and at worst so meager as to be close to worthless. Another year would pass before Clinton took the steps that elevated the army's intelligence network from rudimentary to superlative. In the early summer of 1779 he simply had little idea what he would encounter at West Point, aside from the knowledge that Washington would leave no stone unturned in raising the largest possible force to defend the invaluable site. In early June, Clinton believed that Washington could pull together at least sixteen thousand men already under arms at various sites not far from West Point. (In fact, rebel forces in that quarter actually totaled just above eight thousand men; Washington, at that same moment, believed that Clinton commanded thirteen thousand in New York, which was precisely what he possessed.) Clinton knew that once Yankee militiamen were also summoned to Washington's side, the disparity in the rival forces would grow more lopsided in favor of the rebels. But Clinton could never be absolutely certain of the number of men with Washington, and in the end he concluded that putting all on the line—including the lives of his men—in going after such an opaque target would be highly imprudent. These considerations were not all that restrained him. He feared that in amassing a large attack force he would render New York City vulnerable, particularly should d'Estaing's fleet suddenly reappear while much of Clinton's army and a considerable chunk of the Royal Navy were well up the Hudson River.[27]

No one can know what the outcome would have been had Clinton sought to take West Point. Horatio Gates, the hero of Saratoga, believed that Clinton could have captured that key post early in the summer had he acted quickly after taking King's Ferry. Within three weeks Gates felt that Clinton had already waited too long and would be defeated if he struck, a view shared all along by Henry Knox. The post is "too strong . . . to admit even of an Attempt[ted siege] much less a storm," Knox remarked. A Continental officer who saw West Point twelve months earlier was awed not only by the fortress's imposing defenses but by the "dreary forests" and rugged terrain all about—which he described as "wild mountains, craggy precipices, and noble lofty cliffs"—that would pose a daunting barrier to any adversary. A French officer who inspected West Point a year later was amazed by the "wild and warlike" environment and the "formidable batteries" on the approach to the fort, and even more by the "six different forts, all in the form of an amphitheater, and protecting each other," that rose to "lofty heights" at the crest of the hill above the Hudson. How many of these impediments were in place in the summer of 1779 cannot be known, but work to improve the installation's defenses had begun a year earlier under the guidance of Thaddeus Kosciuszko, a French-trained military engineer who had emigrated from Poland to serve the American cause in 1776.[28]

Judge Smith, the Tory, began to turn against Clinton at this juncture, to some degree seeing him and Washington—whom he characterized as "a heavy man of timid Circumstances"—as bookends. When Clinton took no further action that summer, Smith, who had opened channels of communication with numerous high-ranking British officers, concluded that Clinton had become "an Object of Derision." Whether Smith befriended only likeminded officers or if dissatisfaction was widespread isn't clear, but one of his acquaintances called Clinton "a Poltroon and a Rogue," and another wondered "why he has not attempted what he had Force enough to execute." A disgruntled British army surgeon complained, "Nothing surely can be more shameful than our perfect Inactivity," adding that "it is unfortunately our fate to be commanded by a Person that has no Abilities to plan nor Firmness to execute the most trivial military Operations." Some who may have agreed that it was prudent not to go after West Point that summer nevertheless thought Clinton erred in failing to order one sortie after another against small hamlets, remorseless attacks designed "to harass and beat down the Militia," decimate rebel farms, and sap the enemy's will to continue.[29]

Grumbling often finds legs, and Clinton knew of, or uneasily sensed, the displeasure in the ranks and among New York's Tories. Tension was palpable at headquarters. He knew the moment was favorable for action. The enemy's "magazines of flour, corn, and dry forage" collected months earlier were "nearly exhausted," and that year's harvest was weeks away. But he waited impatiently for the reinforcements that Germain had promised. Weeks passed and no action was taken. The soldiers on both sides tended to their duties and, in their idle time, considered the sorts of things that those who bear arms have always contemplated while awaiting an anticipated major showdown. Private Joseph Plumb Martin, now in his fourth year as a Continental, pulled guard duty and otherwise tended to the army's horses but, "being a considerable distance from camp, "diverted" himself by shooting squirrels and birds.[30] Redcoats posted as lookouts watched the sea in vain for sight of the coming naval and army supplements.

June crept past. Clinton brought the posts at Stony Point and Verplanck's Point up to British standards and posted a "respectable force" in each. As the month drew toward a close and with British reinforcements nowhere to be seen—"where, alas" are they? Clinton fumed—the British commander turned to other things.[31] It was summer. The weather was good. There were only a handful of rebel troops south of the Highlands. American farmers, preoccupied by the annual harvest, would not want to be called away for militia duty. The time was right, Clinton reasoned, to carry out raids in eastern Connecticut, forays aimed not just at abrading Yankee morale but at luring Washington's army into the field to defend against the assaults. It would even be a plus, Clinton reasoned, should Washington not respond, for in that case the American commander would be "much blamed" by the Yankees "for neglecting them."[32]

Clinton was not keen on ordering the raids. Among other things, he feared they would anger those in Parliament who shared his contempt for assailing civilian targets. He worried, too, that some in the homeland would suspect the raids only stoked American hatred of Britain, solidifying the colonists' intractability on the issue of a negotiated settlement. But something had to be done. The fifth summer of the war was slipping away, and with it, whatever chance Britain had of salvaging something during the year. Clinton gave responsibility for the raids to General William Tryon, a fifty-year-old infantry officer who had been wounded fighting in France in the Seven Years' War, after which he served as the royal governor of North Carolina and New York. Tryon had earned a reputation as an aggressive leader, and some thought him particularly coldhearted toward the insurgents. Though he knew that Tryon was bent on "inspiring Terror," Clinton did not restrain him. Indeed, when the two discussed the pending raid, Tryon asked Clinton about putting towns to the torch, and the commander responded, "I know you will if I don't forbid it." Clinton did not prohibit it. Aside from ordering Tryon not to keep his troops on the ground for more than forty-eight hours in any location, Clinton gave his subordinate a free hand. Clinton was not unscrupulous.[33] He was a soldier, and like many another warrior in many another war, he sometimes had to make unsavory choices.

Tryon's force set off from Manhattan on July 2 and over a span of nine days descended on New Haven, Norwalk, and Fairfield. Tryon was ruthless, just as Clinton knew he would be. (A New York Loyalist who spoke with Tryon just prior to his departure thought him "fond" of sowing carnage and anguish among civilians.) The soldiers in the raiding parties committed

what one congressman labeled "actions of cruelty hitherto unthought of."
Mills and assorted buildings, including churches, were destroyed, fruit trees
cut down, barns laden with grain burned, and houses and farms ransacked,
with nearly all of Fairfield reduced to ashes. Their "stay was . . . short, but
their rage great," said Connecticut's governor, and a town official in Norwalk
called the redcoats "inhuman & wanton." Elderly men were humiliated.
Women were robbed and "abused . . . with the foulest and most profane
language." Some residents died in the raids. Congress published numerous
depositions given by local residents that recounted the atrocities—including
attempted rapes—underscoring for public consumption Washington's
contention that "plundering and perhaps burning . . . appear to form a
considerable part of [Britain's] present system of War." Tryon subsequently
said that the "usurpers"—his term for the American rebels—had reaped
what they had sown, though he apologized for the destruction of the
churches, which he said were accidental victims of wind-swept fires.[34]

Washington had not marched to the defense of the Connecticut towns—
prompting Clinton to despair that there was "no chance of forcing Washington
to [a general] action"—but the American commander was not inactive.[35]
When intelligence reported that the defenses at British-held Stony Point were
"formidable" yet possibly vulnerable, Washington began to explore the possibility of an attack while Clinton was sidetracked by his "excursions to distress"
civilian sectors in Connecticut. It would be "very disagreeable" for the "reputation of the army" to remain inactive while the enemy rampaged, Washington
said, and he appointed General Anthony Wayne to plan an operation against
Stony Point. Wayne concluded that the installation could not be stormed but
might be taken by a surprise attack. Days of strategizing produced an
immensely risky scheme. Washington thought it might work, and given that
he was "exceedingly mortified" at having been inactive for the past eleven
months, he was willing to gamble. Wayne, with a brigade of about 1,350
men—including 200 carefully chosen volunteers who were to make up a
possibly suicidal advance party ominously dubbed the "forlorn hope"
contingent—were to make a daring midnight assault. Most of the attackers
were to carry unloaded muskets that could be used as clubs. Otherwise, they

were armed with bayonets, swords, axes, and lengthy pikes known as spon-
toons. These men went into battle anticipating hand-to-hand combat. All
knew that success hinged on taking the British by surprise.

The attack took place on the pitch-black night of July 15, and the British
were caught unawares. Within a few minutes the startled and frightened
redcoats cried out for their assailants to call off the butchery. "Mercy! mercy!
Dear Americans, mercy! Quarter! Brave American, quarter! Quarter!" one
rebel attacker recalled the British defenders screaming. The Americans paid
a price for their victory, as nearly one hundred were casualties; above
50 percent of those in the suicidal parties were killed or wounded, and
Wayne suffered an injury to his head. The British fared much worse, with
676 killed, wounded, and captured. But if Wayne is to be believed, his men
heeded the enemy's call for quarter and "scorned to take the lives of a
vanquished foe." At 2:00 A.M. Wayne notified Washington, "The fort &
Garrison . . . are our's. Our Officers & Men behaved like men who are determined to be free." Clinton was nearly as lavish in his praise of the attack.
Wayne, he said, was a "spirited officer" who deserved "applause" for a "bold"
victory that was "a very great affront to us."[36]

It was a pulsating triumph, though neither pivotal on the order of
Saratoga nor transformative as was Bunker Hill. The stalemated war had
reached a point where each side was attempting through the shock of
destructive raids or bold surprises to wear down its adversary. During that
torrid summer, both commanders considered truly major actions, though
Clinton would not move against West Point, or anywhere else, until reinforced, and Washington would not take the field unless accompanied by his
French ally. Following Wayne's success, Washington took fifteen cannon and
an abundance of precious stores from the captured British installation.
Thereafter, he razed the fort, aware that it could not be held should the
enemy counterattack. He made no attempt to reoccupy Fort Lafayette.
Clinton also had no interest in occupying what had been Fort Lafayette, but
he rebuilt Stony Point and once again garrisoned it.

Meanwhile, Washington was eager to score another disheartening blow.
About a month after Wayne's attack, he authorized an assault on

British-held Paulus Hook, a site that was all the more enticing in that it was literally under Clinton's nose. The fort stood directly across the Hudson from New York City. Colonel Henry Lee, a Virginian whose lust for glory was accompanied by a savage streak when his blood was up, was given responsibility for commanding the endeavor. His plan was remarkably similar to Wayne's, save that he lacked the overwhelming superiority in numbers that the Americans had enjoyed at Stony Point. With some 250 Virginia and Maryland troops, Lee, in the inky-dark wee hours of August 19, bore down on the British post, which was occupied by roughly the same number of redcoats. He, too, sought total surprise, but the unavoidable noise made by scores of men splashing through canals and marshes alerted the defenders at the last moment. Nevertheless, without having fired a single shot, the rebel attackers killed, wounded, or captured all but about fifty of the enemy garrison, though they failed to take and destroy the installation. Aside from the attrition suffered by the enemy, the real prize had always been to hack away at the enemy's spirit, and in that respect Lee's attack was successful. Clinton acknowledged his mortification at the "affront," which he labeled "disgraceful."[37]

WORD OF THE assault on Paulus Hook had been unexpected and unwelcome, but it was only the latest in a string of unwanted tidings that cascaded on Clinton during the final weeks of summer, such a sickening avalanche of disquieting news that at one point he despaired for "our . . . drooping cause."[38] On September 1, Clinton learned that Spain had entered the war as an ally of France. In April, the two nations had concluded an alliance in the Treaty of Aranjuez, although Spanish belligerence did not become a reality until June. Given the stalemated American war, due in part to d'Estaing's stunning failure to accomplish the least thing in North America in 1778, Comte de Vergennes, France's foreign minister, had come to realize his country faced a longer war than he had ever imagined when he opted to become America's ally. He knew, too, that the United States was a more troubled ally than it had been eighteen months earlier, and that Washington was no longer the daring commander he had been in 1776 and 1777. Doubtful that France could win a long war against Great Britain, Vergennes was desperate to have Spain on his side. In 1779 the British could man ninety ships of the line, nearly forty more than France. But if Spain, with its approximately fifty-eight ships of the line, entered the war, the Allies would enjoy a coveted naval superiority. Madrid understood Versailles's plight and the demands it made of France were extortionate. Spain hoped to regain Jamaica and East and West Florida, and its foreign minister told Vergennes—perhaps not quite truthfully—that he could obtain these coveted gems from Britain simply by agreeing to remain neutral. Spain also sought the recovery of Minorca and Gibraltar, lost to Britain seventy-five years earlier, and it demanded that France agree to continue to fight until the latter had been retrieved. In addition, Madrid demanded an invasion of England, a necessary step for ending the war before the British could attack Spain's New World possessions.

Vergennes was horrified by Spain's demands, but he was cornered and consented to Madrid's wishes. Meanwhile, he was inching nearer to another crucial decision. At very nearly the moment that Clinton learned of Spain's entrance into the war, Anne-César de La Luzerne, France's new minister plenipotentiary to the United States, called on General Washington. The general met him well above Manhattan at Fishkill and the two sailed upriver together to West Point, with Washington piloting the craft. A squall blew up during their voyage, and the French envoy was left shaken to the core when he discovered that Washington lacked the "required skill and practice" to navigate a vessel under such conditions. But they arrived safely, and during dinner the two talked while an army band, just outside the general's tent, "played military and French airs." In the course of their discussion, La Luzerne, as instructed by Versailles, asked if the United States would welcome a French "squadron and a few regiments attached to it to act in conjunction" with the American army. Washington, perhaps trying to hide his eagerness, replied that additional French help would be "very advantageous." Months would pass before the French foreign minister would make a final decision on committing an army to North America, but if the Allies did not score a military breakthrough in 1779, Vergennes probably already knew what his choice would be.[39]

Both Washington and Clinton understood that Spanish belligerence could be momentous. The happy American commander exulted that the news had given "universal joy" to all who supported the American Revolution while "the poor Tory droops like a withering flower under a declining Sun." But whereas Washington had initially been certain that the Franco-American alliance virtually guaranteed America's victory, he now more guardedly merely expressed his hope that Spain's entrance into the war would secure American independence "in a short time." Clinton, on the other hand, was anything but ecstatic. Not only might his plans for future operations with the Royal Navy be imperiled, but the news that Britain had yet another enemy would likely hamper recruitment among the Tories. What is more, for the first time since the war erupted, British naval supremacy in North American waters might be jeopardized for a fatally prolonged period.[40]

Clinton seemed to get only bad news. Late in the summer he learned that France had taken three of Britain's possessions in the Lesser Antilles, including Grenada, the crown jewel in that string of islands. If that weren't bad enough, d'Estaing's next target was thought to be Jamaica, Britain's most important possession in the West Indian theater. Until then, Clinton had hoped against hope that as many as five of the ten regiments he had reluctantly sent to the West Indies back in November would be redeployed to New York, together with the long-awaited reinforcements from England. He now knew that he would receive no reinforcements from the Caribbean.[41]

The tsunami of unwelcome communications only continued for Clinton. In September he was informed that the homeland of the Iroquois—Britain's ally, who had launched highly destructive frontier raids—had suffered appalling devastation at the hands of American troops. The damage was so great that some royal officials believed that the "Indian alliance . . . must consequentially fall."[42] The American campaign against Iroquois tribes had been in the works since Washington's meetings with Congress at the outset of the year, and before departing Philadelphia he had put General Sullivan in command of the operation. Initially, Washington had thought a winter campaign was possible, but when that proved to be unrealistic he anticipated a spring venture. To his chagrin, that deadline had also passed. Washington was edgy. He wanted the undertaking completed soon so that Sullivan's men would be available to rejoin the main army in late summer in the event that d'Estaing's fleet appeared near New York.

At last, in early summer portions of Sullivan's force began to come together. Much of its initial undertakings were designed to convince the enemy that the rebel army planned to invade Canada. But that was an elaborate ruse. A Canadian invasion was never contemplated. However, the gambit worked, in part because in the spring Germain had warned his North American commanders that intelligence reported that France intended "to throw some troops into Canada." The British commander in chief in Canada was sufficiently worried to request that Clinton detach fifteen hundred men to help guard against yet another American incursion. Clinton complied, though when sending his men he wrote, "weak and miserable as I am, I am obliged to comply with your requisition." Early in August, Sullivan, with some five thousand men, finally began his advance across the frontier. He was virtually unopposed. Britain's regulars were far away in Canada, and the few hundred Iroquois warriors, recognizing the futility of resisting such a powerful force, retreated into Canada. Washington's design was ruthless terrorism that would take these Indians out of the war forever. He ordered Sullivan to "lay waste" to every settlement so "that the country may not be merely overrun but destroyed." Washington defended the gruesome devastation that he had was ordered as a war measure, but, as historian Colin Calloway has argued, the unarticulated purpose of the endeavor included winning control of the Iroquois's lands for postwar speculators and land-hungry farmers. (In 1783, Washington himself purchased a lush tract in this region.)

Sullivan meticulously complied with the directives he had been given, much as Tryon had done a month earlier in his raids in coastal Connecticut. As the Iroquois braves withdrew, they could by day see clouds of gray smoke placidly rising into the blue sky above their villages, and after sunset they beheld a night sky that glowed a fearsome orange. They knew that the American soldiers had torched their homes, corn cribs, and fields. Sullivan's men utterly destroyed 41 Indian towns, upwards of 700 dwellings, 160,000 bushels of corn, and every horse, cow, or pig they could lay their hands on, and even girdled the fruit trees they ran across. Some four thousand hungry, homeless, and nearly naked Indians were compelled to trek into Canada in hopes of finding safety and shelter before the arrival of the region's forbidding winter. The raid succeeded in immobilizing the Iroquois for the remainder of 1779, but within months thereafter they returned to the warpath, driven by a deep-seated desire to avenge their losses. In the first nine months of 1780, Tory and Indian raiders on New York's and Pennsylvania's frontiers killed or captured more than three hundred Americans, destroyed over a thousand houses, burned hundreds of thousands of acres of grain, and drove away more than a thousand head of horses and livestock. The Sullivan Expedition, as it came to be known, did not have a decisive impact on the war.[43]

Around the time that Clinton learned the sullen details of the devastation wrought by Sullivan, he at last received some welcome news. First came word from Germain that the projected Franco-Spanish invasion of England would not result in the "reduction of the forces under your command," though disturbingly the American secretary said nothing about the reinforcements he had long promised.[44] In the autumn, Clinton was informed that the Allies' attempted invasion of England had failed. Spurning the thought of attacking London, the French and Spanish military planners had instead chosen to make a joint landing at Portsmouth, where they expected to encounter fewer defenders and weaker defensive bulwarks. They set a target date of May 15 for uniting their fleets. The two navies finally rendezvoused to form a single armada ten weeks behind schedule. On paper, the invasion fleet was formidable. The armada's 150 vessels outnumbered those in the famed Spanish Armada that had sought to invade England in 1588, but the sailors and soldiers in both navies in 1779 had been decimated by disease during their interminable wait at sea. They were chiefly victims of a virulent dysentery epidemic that swept Europe that summer. Without attempting a landing, the would-be invaders canceled the planned invasion early in September. France's prolonged attempts to bring Spain into the war, crowned by these breathtaking capitulations to Madrid's demands, had yielded nothing to this point. In fact, the misspent time had cost France what might have been a productive year of campaigning. Given the problems that England faced in 1779, France might have achieved more toward knocking its adversary out of the war by sending additional vessels to North American waters and utilizing still others in a spirited campaign to capture enemy convoys. Instead, if Lord Germain was correct, the invasion threat had largely halted the collapse of morale in England, replacing it with "so great a military spirit . . . throughout the people."[45]

Since the reconstruction of Stony Point and the raids on the towns in Connecticut in July, Clinton had remained inactive. He had been preoccupied by what was unfolding in the West Indies, convinced that what happened there would determine what he might do. While he waited, General Cornwallis arrived back in New York in July and took up his old post as second in command. Cornwallis was returning from his second trip to England within ten months. He had crossed to London to tend to personal business a few weeks after the clashes at Brandywine and Germantown, though he had been so eager to get back to soldiering that he had not lingered at home. On that occasion, Cornwallis had landed in Philadelphia just days after Clinton had taken command in the spring of 1778, and he had played a crucial role in the engagement at Monmouth. However, word that his wife was gravely ill led Cornwallis to sail home again that autumn, making the journey in the company of some members of the Carlisle Commission. Cornwallis had crossed the Atlantic thinking he would never return to America, as he had missed his wife deeply and could not bear another lengthy separation. In an age when financial arrangements were crucial in marriages among aristocrats, Cornwallis was an exception. Love, not money, had brought him and Jemima Tullekin Jones together, and their devotion to each other deepened over the years. But other factors also played a role in Cornwallis's unwillingness to return to America. He had soured on the war, chiefly because he despaired that the "Government cannot send out a force" adequate for suppressing the American rebellion. It was bad enough to fight a war in which victory was a long shot, but having to do so without an independent command was not something that Cornwallis wished to undertake yet again. However, Jemima's death in April changed his thinking. Grief-stricken and depressed, Cornwallis wanted out of England and hoped to escape his sorrow by returning to action. He begged Clinton to "send for me," and upon his arrival in New York he promised to serve loyally under the commander in chief. "I come to share fortunes with you," he told Clinton.[46]

Cornwallis and Clinton had long been friends of sorts. They met while soldiering in Germany during the Seven Years' War, and despite the difference in their ages—Clinton was eight years older—a friendship had blossomed and continued, mostly at long distance, over the years. They were reunited in the abortive Carolinas campaign of 1776. A mutual friend, Major General William Phillips, who was aware of Clinton's difficulties in establishing close personal relationships, had at the time exhorted him, "Throw off all reserve, melt [Cornwallis] at once in confidence and friendship." Clinton had done his best to comply, with the result that for a spell their ties remained amiable. However, an unfortunate incident in 1776 strained their relationship forever. Clinton had disparaged General William Howe in the course of a private conversation, and soon thereafter Cornwallis betrayed his trust by divulging to the commander in chief his friend's venom-laced remarks. Clinton was furious. Cornwallis worked hard to win back his onetime friend's affinity, and there were periods in the years that followed when they got along well. When Cornwallis returned to Philadelphia from his initial visit home, he wrote Clinton that he would "do all in my power to contribute to your ease." When he came back to America in August 1779, Cornwallis gushed about his "pleasure" at being

Clinton's subordinate. Clinton seemed to be just as pleased to have Cornwallis at his side, as he believed the veteran officer's "great and liberal assistance" would be of inestimable value. Clinton, in fact, wrote immediately to Germain expressing "how happy" he had been made by Cornwallis's arrival, adding that he treasured his "indefatigable zeal, his knowledge of the country, his professional ability, and the high estimation in which he is held by this army." On departing England, Cornwallis told his brother that his "good intentions and plain dealing" would result in harmony with Clinton, and for several months their association remained close and congenial.[47]

During the same week that Cornwallis came ashore, Clinton at last glimpsed the sails of the British fleet that he had impatiently awaited for months. He could not hide his joy at greeting Vice Admiral Marriot Arbuthnot, but as seemed to be his habitual fate, Clinton was immediately disappointed. He had expected to see 6,600 reinforcements march down the gangplank. Instead, Arbuthnot had delivered only about 3,000, and nearly all of them were in sick bay, victims of a fever that had spread like wildfire during the crossing. Four days before the fleet arrived, Clinton had written London of his plans to open a campaign in South Carolina in October, but in the policy discussions that immediately ensued with the admiral, both Arbuthnot and Cornwallis insisted that Jamaica was the more pressing matter. Although Germain had touted the admiral's strong qualities, one of Clinton's confidants in London had depicted Arbuthnot as honest but said that his advanced age—he was seventy—had rendered him slow and often hesitant to act. Moreover, although Arbuthnot had some command experience at sea in wartime, the navy apparently looked on him more as an administrator than a sailor, as he had spent most of this war in charge of the Halifax Dockyard. At first blush, Clinton found him to be more able and energetic than he had been led to believe, for Arbuthnot jumped at the chance to deliver Cornwallis with four thousand men to the relief of Jamaica. In fact, it was Clinton who at first protested, arguing that d'Estaing would never plan a campaign to take Jamaica during the hurricane season. But in the end Clinton consented. Jamaica was crucial, and in a worst-case scenario

Clinton would pay a heavy price if he had done nothing to save it. A flotilla was prepared and sailed for the tropics on September 16, but within seventy-two hours it reappeared in New York Harbor. The task force had hardly stood out to sea when it encountered a British vessel that passed along word that d'Estaing had not sailed for Jamaica. He was en route to "the North American coast."[48]

Clinton was swept with "alarming apprehensions." For the second consecutive year he feared that he would be faced with an enemy fleet that was superior to anything the British could muster. Clinton did not know the enemy's target. It might be New York or Rhode Island, Halifax or Quebec. Public comments made by d'Estaing when his fleet was in Boston for repairs the preceding autumn seemed to point to France's desire to retake Canada, a supposed craving that the British governor in Quebec took seriously and with considerable dread, as he believed that most of his subjects would greet the French "with pleasure." Clinton sprang to action. He dispatched three battalions to Halifax, but his principal move was to consolidate his army in New York, d'Estaing's target in 1778 and a good bet to be his objective this year. Clinton recalled the troops posted at Stony Point and in a decision that would have crucial long-term implications, he ordered the evacuation of Rhode Island, bringing all the British occupation troops to New York. It was a decision approved by Cornwallis as well as Arbuthnot, who would need every warship he could lay his hands on for the defense of New York. With twenty-twenty hindsight one historian characterized the abandonment of Rhode Island as "one of the colossal blunders of the war," but based on what Clinton knew at the time, his decision was justified. While his men hurriedly dug additional fortifications around New York, Clinton hoped against hope that Washington would forego his "usual caution" and—in expectation that the French fleet would appear—bring his army down to the cusp of Manhattan, giving "me an opening" to "strike at him."[49]

Washington learned on very nearly the same day as Clinton that d'Estaing's fleet had put to sea and was "approaching our coast," though, like his counterpart, the American commander did not know d'Estaing's destination. In the event that the fleet was sailing for New York, Washington immediately wrote the admiral to convey what he knew regarding the strength of the Royal Navy in New York and the size and location of the sundry elements of Clinton's army in and around Manhattan. He also formulated plans for a joint operation to retake New York. Washington did not convene a council of war. There was no need to do so. He had consulted his generals both before and after d'Estaing's prior visit fifteen months earlier and discussed matters with Minister Gérard in the spring. Furthermore, in May, Congress had granted Washington absolute authority over the Continental army's military operations. Above all, Washington did not wish to be hamstrung "by a Majority of votes" or risk having the plans fall into the enemy's hands. "[F]orming conclusions which may be kept secret" was the best option, he declared.[50]

Near the end of September, Washington received word from Congress that d'Estaing had arrived off the coast of Georgia. Given the time lag in communicating from Georgia to Philadelphia, and from Philadelphia to Washington's headquarters, this likely meant that the French fleet had reached Savannah around the beginning of the month. If Georgia's capital was rapidly retaken, which Washington anticipated, d'Estaing might soon arrive off the coast of New York. As signs of autumn's approach were readily apparent, Washington understood that "every instant of time is infinitely precious," for he estimated the operation to retake New York would require four weeks. Washington immediately wrote d'Estaing once again. He pledged his cooperation, promised to act with "dispatch and vigor," and predicted that a campaign to retake New York would require about thirty thousand men, which was pretty much what the combined Franco-American forces could field, as Washington had already called on the five neighboring states to furnish twelve thousand militiamen. Washington emphasized that taking New York must be the "first and Capital object" of the campaign, as the "loss of the [British] Army and Fleet there, would be one of the severest blows the English Nation could experience." On the other hand, to fail to act, or to act and fail, would "damp"

American "spirits" and "diminish its [future] exertions." To avoid the latter, he indicated that plans for a New York campaign had been exhaustively prepared and would be presented to d'Estaing for his consideration upon his arrival.[51]

Washington planned for two contingencies. Should a surprised Clinton be unable to call in his troops from the British garrisons scattered adjacent to Manhattan, posts that housed roughly seven thousand redcoats—almost 50 percent of the British force—Washington planned to open the campaign with assaults on these outlying posts. Some attacks were to be carried out by his troops, some by the marines believed to be with d'Estaing, and some (Staten Island, for instance) as joint Allied endeavors. While those operations were underway, Washington additionally plotted strikes against the remaining British outposts on the Hudson and hoped that d'Estaing could utilize a portion of his fleet to block up all enemy vessels still in Newport. Following the successful completion of this phase, Washington envisaged a siege operation against the remainder of Clinton's army posted on Manhattan. However, if Clinton consolidated his forces on Manhattan before the Allies swung into action, a siege operation would be implemented from the outset. In that event, Washington's army was to make landings at two sites on Manhattan well north of the city, but below Clinton's northernmost forts on the island. Thereafter, those forces would advance southward, eventually forming the center of a siege line near Murray Hill, just west of where the British had landed at Kip's Bay three years earlier. As they did so, d'Estaing was to gain control of New York Harbor and, acting in concert with American units, secure Staten Island. Once it was in safe hands, a joint Allied force would land on Long Island at more or less the same spot that Howe had disembarked his soldiery in August 1776. Seemingly, either an Allied assault or siege operation would be implemented on Long Island. Washington exuded confidence that Clinton would have to capitulate within a few weeks. As speed was of the essence in mounting the campaign, the American commander took steps to secure ample numbers of small craft for the Allied armies, arranged to have pilots standing by to guide d'Estaing on his arrival, and selected trusted officers who were to immediately meet with the admiral and share Washington's plans.[52]

WASHINGTON COULD ONLY wait and hope that d'Estaing completed his work in Savannah quickly and then sailed to New York. Washington would have preferred that the French fleet set sail for New York upon departing the Caribbean, but he had long ago advised Gérard of the significance of retaking Savannah. Nor was Washington alone in stressing the importance of Savannah. D'Estaing had received urgent pleas from the governor of South Carolina, John Rutledge, and the French consul in Charleston to target the city. Both emphasized that Colonel Campbell's capture of Savannah was a precursor to an attempt by the enemy to take Charleston and all of South Carolina. In fact, the British had already made a thrust at capturing Charleston.

General Augustine Prevost had arrived in Savannah several days after the fall of the city late in 1778 and assumed command of all British forces in Georgia. On very nearly the same day, General Benjamin Lincoln, Robert Howe's successor as commander of the Continental army in the Southern Department, reached Charleston. Lincoln's background could hardly have been more different from that of Prevost. Ten years his junior—he was one year younger than Washington—Lincoln had grown up in a small Massachusetts village. After lengthy militia service in the Seven Years' War, he farmed and was active in the prewar protest against the mother country. Lincoln was named a lieutenant colonel in the siege army outside Boston in 1775, but it was not long before Washington came to think highly of him as a worthy leader and administrator. In 1776, he was commissioned by Congress as a major general in the Continental army. Lincoln fought in the New York and Saratoga campaigns, and in the latter his right ankle was shattered by a British ball. Following a long convalescence, Congress put him in charge of the Continental army in the South, leapfrogging him over Benedict Arnold, who had served longer and won greater laurels. Arnold had enemies in Congress. Lincoln did not. Besides, the legislators thought Lincoln's well-known attributes of tact and diplomacy would be useful in the strife-ridden Southern Department. Lincoln's only troubling feature was his narcolepsy, which caused him to suddenly fall asleep, though officers who had served under him insisted that the affliction had never impaired his leadership.[53]

As he had only a small army, no naval arm, and a dearth of siege guns, Lincoln knew that retaking Savannah was beyond his reach. Instead, early in 1779, shortly after Savannah had fallen, Lincoln posted a force of 1,700 at Purrysburg, on the east side of the Savannah River, and waited for Prevost to try to cross into South Carolina. His action replicated that of Washington in 1776, when he had positioned his army on the Pennsylvania side of the Delaware River and waited for Cornwallis to try to cross. There was one major difference. Washington had anticipated—and received— large numbers of reinforcements. Lincoln did not, and he was aware that he would face a vastly superior force that included British and Hessian regulars, Tories who had been recruited for provincial units in northern states, and a handful of southern Loyalists. Despite his manpower advantage, Prevost chose not to immediately move against Charleston. He turned first to the pacification of Georgia, perhaps because the Loyalists in the province had "promised" to "heartedly" join with him when they were assured "that [we] are to be supported." While waiting for the Loyalists to rally to him, Prevost sought to rouse Creeks and Cherokees to also take up arms against Britain's enemy, and less than thirty days after the fall of Savannah, he ordered Colonel Archibald Campbell to take Augusta 120 miles upriver. The Indian tribes turned a deaf ear to Prevost. (Only about seventy turned out, and Prevost characterized those warriors as "so very cautious that no real service can be had of them.") Campbell, meanwhile, took Augusta without much trouble, but he could not hold it. Georgia's Loyalists, outnumbered and fearful of rebel militia, simply refused to turn out. Campbell did raise some eight hundred Loyalists from South Carolina's hinterland, but the Tory force was ambushed and decimated at Kettle Creek while marching to Augusta. It was a crushing blow for the British. Not only was Augusta abandoned, but the disaster at Kettle Creek weakened the zeal for soldiering among many Tories. By the time Georgia's long, hot, humid summer set in—around the time that Commodore Collier struck at Stony Point and Fort Lafayette—Prevost became the latest in a long line of British officers to inform London that its long-anticipated expectation of appreciable assistance from the South's Tory inhabitants was a chimera. "Our successes must depend on the exertions of the King's troops," he advised Germain.[54]

Prevost's discovery led him to abandon his hope of rapidly taking iron-clad control of Georgia's backcountry. Instead, he thought that if he could take Charleston, much of South Carolina's interior could be easily pacified, and that, in turn, would induce Georgia's rebels to fall into line. In February, about the time that Washington completed his meetings with Congress in Philadelphia, Prevost sought to invade South Carolina by making an amphibious landing at coastal Beaufort, about halfway between Charleston and Savannah. The British troops that went ashore were cut to pieces by a South Carolina militia force led by General William Moultrie. However, two months later Prevost spotted an opportunity to get his troops across the Savannah River. Lincoln had withdrawn five hundred men from Purrysburg and merged them with a large American force at Augusta. It was not Lincoln's wisest decision, as Prevost now enjoyed a two-to-one numerical advantage, enabling him to get two thousand men across the river and set off toward Charleston. Thereafter, the Americans under Moultrie fought delaying actions. Like General Schuyler in the aftermath of the loss of Ticonderoga, the South Carolinians felled trees and destroyed bridges to slow the British advance, hoping against hope that Lincoln would have time to deploy sufficient forces in Charleston. But Lincoln did not budge. He discounted the threat posed by Prevost, convinced that the British commander was only making a feint to draw him away from Augusta. Prevost, on the other hand, moved rapidly from the start, and even more quickly as large numbers of Moultrie's dispirited militiamen abandoned the fight and returned home. During the second week in May, eleven days after taking the first step across the Savannah River, Prevost was on Charleston's doorstep.

Prevost knew that taking the city by force was out of the question. He had detached half his men to tend his supply line or to guard against the arrival of Lincoln, who he feared might come at any moment. With only some one thousand men still with him, Prevost knew that his force was too small to fight its way through the stout defenses that guarded the narrow neck leading into the city. Moreover, as Prevost's campaign had been predicated on speed, he had brought too few artillery pieces to conduct a siege. He could only bluff. Prevost demanded that the city be surrendered within four hours or he would destroy it.

South Carolina's civil authorities huddled with the military leaders. Moultrie and his fellow soldiers wished to make stand. Moultrie wildly overestimated the size of the enemy force—he guessed that Prevost commanded an army of four thousand—yet the South Carolinian knew that he had three thousand well-entrenched men. He and his fellow officers foresaw a replay of Bunker Hill in the event that Prevost attacked. However, the civilian leadership, including Governor Rutledge, was anything but resolute. Underestimating the numbers of their own men and vastly exaggerating the size of the enemy army, the timorous governor and a majority of his Privy Council appeared to be mostly committed to saving their property and lives. Led by Rutledge, they offered Prevost a deal: South Carolina would drop out of the war in return for a British pledge to spare the city and take no prisoners. Prevost should have accepted the offer. Had he done so, it was conceivable that the United States would have lost both Georgia and South Carolina, dramatically altering the course of the war. But Prevost spurned Rutledge's tender, continuing to demand the surrender of the city and all the soldiery within it. Moultrie refused to consent to an offer that would have sent his men into a captivity that for many would have been fatal. It appeared to the rebels as if a fight for control of Charleston was inevitable. But the next morning, May 13, as the Americans waited for Prevost's blow to fall, the British force packed up and began its march back to Savannah, plundering what it could along the way. (Prevost did not divulge to Germain the proffer he had rebuffed, simply telling him that Charleston "would have surrendered to us" had his "naval assistance . . . not been so extremely deficient.") Charleston was still in American hands and so, too, was much of Georgia beyond Savannah.[55]

South Carolina and its fainthearted political leaders had escaped, and they wasted little time before pleading with d'Estaing to bring his fleet from the Caribbean and join with Lincoln's Continental army in flushing Britain's armed forces from the South. Earlier, as Prevost was marching toward the gates of Charleston, those same leaders had appealed to Congress for reinforcements. Congress responded with alacrity, inveighing North Carolina to commit one thousand militiamen to its neighbor. At the same moment, Congress entreated Washington to consent to permitting two thousand newly recruited Virginia troops to be sent to Lincoln in beleaguered South Carolina. Washington received Congress's request around the time of his initial meeting with Gérard. He agreed.[56]

A few weeks after learning of South Carolina's travail, d'Estaing received word of Spain's entrance into the war. The latter news led him to abandon his plans for attacking Jamaica, a venture that he felt would best be undertaken someday in a joint Franco-Spanish campaign. In mid-August, with 4,450 troops—including 750 free men of color who had been raised in St. Domingo, the first free Black soldiers to serve in the French military—d'Estaing set sail for Georgia. Two weeks later, on September 1, parts of his armada of twenty-two ships of the line and nine frigates totaling more than two thousand guns, and a few score of transports arrived off Tybee Island, the very spot where the British invasion fleet had dropped anchor eight months earlier. D'Estaing anticipated having a huge numerical superiority over the tiny British occupation force in Savannah, but he soon discovered that General Lincoln had barely 1,000 regulars and some 1,600 militiamen. (The North Carolina militiamen's tour of duty had expired and they had marched home, while barely a quarter of the 2,000 Virginians who were to have been raised had actually been secured.) D'Estaing was so bitterly disappointed that he briefly considered sailing away without a fight.[57] He doubted that his force would have the numbers needed to mount an attack against Savannah's strong defenses. Moreover, as the prevailing notion of the day was that at least a two-to-one superiority in numbers was required to conduct a successful siege operation, d'Estaing suspected that he had come to Savannah on a fool's errand. Yet he stayed, perhaps fearing disgrace at home if he did nothing, especially in light of his having abandoned the enterprise in Rhode Island a year earlier. In addition, he had to have been apprehensive that his departure might deal a fatal blow to the Franco-American alliance or to the staying power of Georgia and South Carolina.

D'Estaing summoned Lincoln, and during the two weeks that passed while he awaited the arrival of all the anticipated American troops, the French commander opted for a siege operation. In the interval, d'Estaing's soldiers and sailors moved the heavy artillery into position near Savannah, grunting and sweating as they labored to wheel ponderous and unwieldy cannon through the intractable sandy soil. D'Estaing figured to have some 7,700 men under his command. The army under Prevost was far fewer than half that number, though, as d'Estaing soon learned, the enemy was entrenched in a complex serpentine arrangement of epaulements and traverses designed by a professional British army engineer who, in Clinton's words, "*understood his business.*" Furthermore, as d'Estaing spent one anxious day after another waiting for additional militiamen to show up, Prevost called in reinforcements from Beaufort. He, too, had to wait, but in the interim Prevost offered to negotiate. D'Estaing took the bait. Days dragged by in fruitless negotiations as Prevost cleverly spun out the talks. All the while, the British improved their defenses. While the talks ground on, Prevost's supplemental troops—eight hundred men in all—arrived following a long, brutal trek from Beaufort. They had marched in scorching heat and fetid air, at times struggling through dark marshes and swamps filled with "Sandfliegen . . . Schlangen und Crocodillen" (sand flies, snakes, and alligators), as an unnerved Hessian noted. Another British soldier— aghast at the "multitudes of alligators lying in the mud like old logs"— opined that the only mammals to have previously successfully struggled through these forbidding morasses had been wolves and bears. But these hearty regulars made it, and their arrival brought the number of Savannah's defenders to 3,200 men fit for action.[58]

On October 4, eighteen long days after putting his army ashore and fourteen days after first calling on Prevost to capitulate, d'Estaing opened the siege with a ferocious bombardment. He hoped it would sufficient to persuade the enemy to run up the white flag of surrender. War is stunningly unfair, and so it was for Savannah's civilians, who disproportionately bore the brunt of the fusillade. Huddled in nauseating fear in cellars or seeking shelter beneath the long, sloping banks of the Savannah River, at least forty residents, including women and children, perished. Meanwhile, Prevost's men, burrowed in earthen shelters, suffered few casualties. When a week of nearly round-the-clock shelling did not lead to the enemy's capitulation, d'Estaing saw his only option as an assault. His highest-ranking officers objected, and so, too, did the Americans, who protested that a frontal attack could not succeed. Besides, they added, Prevost was short of provisions and could not hold out much longer. They urged that the siege continue. But d'Estaing was adamant, and Lincoln—whom the French thought "prickly" but compliant—agreed. French artillerists had estimated that ten additional days of siege operations were probably needed to bring Prevost to heel. D'Estaing did not feel that he could remain in Savannah that long. Nearly six weeks had already passed since his fleet had reached the Georgia coast, and d'Estaing had received warnings that both a British squadron in the Caribbean and a Royal Navy task force from New York were coming after him. After his Rhode Island experience, d'Estaing also worried about a hurricane, a common occurrence along North America's Atlantic coast in October. He believed that he had to attack—and now. D'Estaing ordered the assault for the morning of October 9.

D'Estaing's plan included feints, but the main blow would fall on the British right, the area that d'Estaing correctly judged the weakest part of Prevost's daunting defensive structure. The plan did not unfold as drawn up on paper, but that could be said of the plans for nearly every battle in virtually every war. In this instance, a thick fog had scudded in overnight, which contributed to the perplexities that confronted the attacking soldiery. In the pulse-pounding frenzy of battle, chaotic confusion is often the rule of thumb, and at Savannah the dense, opaque fog only added to the Allies' disorientation. However, the murky, fogbound landscape was but one element in the operation's failure. In fact, most likely the attack was destined to fail because the Allies did not have the numbers to overcome Britain's forbidding defenses. D'Estaing later contended that the reinforcements from Beaufort had tipped the balance to the enemy, and he blamed laxity on the part of the Americans for the success of those additional troops in slipping into Savannah. The splendid performance by Prevost, who had earlier been condemned by Colonel Campbell for being "too old & inactive for this service," should not be overlooked. He had presided over Savannah's defense with energy, shrewdness, and sagacity. Campbell's assessment to the contrary, Prevost's maturity and experience had been crucial. One thing is certain. The Allied attack did not founder because of a lack of courage. Even after being repulsed, the French, the Americans, and even the rebel militiamen regrouped and advanced again and again, pressing on in the face of a deadly artillery barrage and murderous musketry cross fire. No one displayed greater valor than d'Estaing, who personally led the attack and was in the thick of the fighting until he took shrapnel in one arm and a bullet in his leg. Lincoln, too, was valorous, as he joined d'Estaing in the vanguard of the attack. The Allies' last leader was General Casmir Pulaski, a Pole who had been fighting for the Americans since 1777 and commanded Pulaski's Legion, a cavalry troop. When d'Estaing went down, Pulaski, an imperious sort, instantly assumed command and led another charge, only to suffer a mortal wound in a blast of grapeshot.

In the end, as the Americans had feared, Savannah turned into the rebels' Bunker Hill. Lincoln, in the very model of a soldier's careful understatement, reported to Congress that "we were repulsed with some loss." D'Estaing was more candid, describing it as "a frightful carnage." Clinton hit the nail on the head in labeling it a "great slaughter." Roughly 825 Allied soldiers died or were wounded while storming Savannah's entrenched defenders, some 20 percent of those engaged in the assault. This was the greatest percentage of casualties—excluding prisoners—suffered by an Allied force in any major engagement during the war. Another 125 died or were lost to the service in the course of the six-week campaign. The British suffered the loss of 63 men in the attack, atop the 296 lost since the arrival of the two Allied armies.[59]

A bit more than a week after the battle, the American soldiers were back in Charleston and the French fleet had sailed for France, leaving the British in control of war-scarred Savannah. Lincoln had beseeched d'Estaing to stay and continue the siege, to which the admiral replied that his original inclination, based on his interpretation of his orders from at home, had been to "remain on shore 8 days only" and that he had already "spent four times that number."[60] Governor Rutledge, his recent craven behavior notwithstanding, recklessly wrote d'Estaing that he had "not words to express" his "Astonishment & Concern" at the French commander having "blast[ed] all our Hopes" by departing America.[61] But d'Estaing was gone, and for good. Washington was too superb a diplomat to say anything derogatory about the French commander. Besides, either for reasons of diplomacy or because he was persuaded of its truthfulness, Washington must have agreed with Lincoln's assessment that d'Estaing had "the interest of America much at heart" and "in our service he has freely bled."[62]

Washington was bitterly disappointed by what he called the "Disaster at Savannah," and not solely because it "puts matters . . . on a delicate footing in the South." His dream of the "reduction of the enemy's Fleet & army" on Manhattan and Rhode Island was gone once d'Estaing sailed for France. For a time, Washington's letters had brimmed with an uncommonly exuberant tone, but as occurred so many times in this war, his dreams had been dashed. There would be no New York campaign, and the war would continue in 1780. Washington quickly wrote the authorities in several states instructing them to send home the militiamen who had been called to duty, and he sighed, "I do not know what we can do." As the year spiraled toward its end, Washington knew that his army was "dissolving" as enlistments ended, and he feared that the sorry state of American finances had given the enemy "great hopes of terminating the War in their favor" during the coming year. He worried that the enemy might be correct on that score, for he now said that America's teetering morale was "a hundd times more dangerous to our liberties & the great cause we are engaged in" than Britain's military threat.[63]

Washington also knew that a second year since Saratoga and France's entrance into the war—not to mention since the economy had begun to collapse—had passed without a significant Allied victory. The heady optimism he had displayed in the spring of 1778 was long gone. Informing Congress that the term of enlistments of many of his soldiers would expire prior to the opening of the campaign season in 1780, Washington urged national conscription and more substantial bounties to lure volunteers. Only those steps might remedy the "very critical situation of the Army," and they might not meet the challenge of putting effective armies in both the North and the South. He added that he did not feel he could "succour" Lincoln's army in South Carolina, and he as much as acknowledged that he would do nothing without French assistance. To act alone and suffer a disaster, he said, was a turn of events "we must dread."[64]

ON RECEIVING WORD of Prevost's victory and d'Estaing's departure for France, Clinton decided the time had come to invade South Carolina. Clinton knew that he could neither get at Washington nor do anything that would coax him into a general action. He also felt that New York would be safe while he was away, in part because he could leave behind ten thousand troops to defend the city, but also as he was now convinced that Washington was unlikely to undertake a major operation without French assistance. Over time, Clinton had warmed to a Carolina venture. His enthusiasm had increased in the aftermath of Campbell's success in Savannah in 1778, and he was also all too aware that Germain had repeatedly hammered away at the likely success of a campaign to retake South Carolina. Germain had first advocated an invasion of South Carolina nearly two years earlier, and Prevost's march to Charleston in the spring had only whetted the American secretary's interest. Once Prevost reported "indubitable proof" that few of

South Carolina's inhabitants supported the rebel government, Germain was more than ever convinced not only that Charleston could be taken but also that once it fell, both North and South Carolina could be recovered. Those successes would leave Britain in control of everything from Florida to Virginia's southern border. Clinton was now on the same wavelength, and by September he was telling Germain that he would sail for Charleston "as soon as the season would permit." That is, once the hurricane season and South Carolina's blistering summer ended.[65]

New York's Loyalists, who knew little or nothing of Clinton's plans or the scope of the problems with which he wrestled, had waited impatiently throughout 1779 for him to become more active. Judge Smith carped that Clinton was without "any Spirit," raged privately that the commander was "yet about Nothing," and complained to friends of "the General's Indolence." In private, he asked why Clinton had not acted during the entire year. "Certainly he had Nothing to fear all summer from Washington," Smith contended, adding, "People in general shake their Heads at [Clinton's] Conduct." Some of the head-shakers were British officers who carped in secret about their boss, an age-old pastime among those of inferior rank. Some of their fault-finding was merited; much of it was not. One argued that Clinton's military plans were too often weak and imperfect, while another alleged that the commander was always swayed by the last officer to advise him. Yet another insisted that Clinton was too "Fond of praise" and "dreads the Loss of it," a combination that dampened his willingness to take risks. Some grumbled at Clinton's failure to send reinforcements to Prevost, insisting that with "a little Aid" the hard-nosed southern commander could "have put the Carolinas, Georgia and Florida in Peace." "Would to Heaven," said another, that Clinton was more "manly," by which he meant more aggressive and more the risk-taker. A want of spirit within the army was said to be due to the belief that "there is no honor to be obtain'd" in a war that appeared to be going nowhere. If skepticism and ill will were present toward Clinton, his second in command, Lord Cornwallis, was something of a mystery, even though he had fought, and with great ardor, in New York and New Jersey in 1776. Tattle of Cornwallis's supposed willingness to have

Britain give up the fight was ubiquitous among the Loyalists, leading to the widespread view among New York's Tories that he was a "dull, unenterprizing Character."

November brought the long-awaited word of the outcome of the action in Savannah. "The Town is elated," Judge Smith trumpeted when he learned of d'Estaing's defeat. Rumors buzzed that soon "Clinton and Cornwallis leave us" for Charleston, prompting one of the more caustic Tories to acknowledge that if successful in the South, Clinton would "escape Blame" for his supposed shortcomings in the North during the past eighteen months.[66]

While New York's Tories were ecstatic on learning of d'Estaing's crushing defeat in Savannah, Clinton was deliriously happy. He called it "the greatest event that has happened the whole war," and for the British it might well have been. Prevost's victory secured one conquered American province and appeared to open the way for the subjugation of the Carolinas. Clinton had high hopes that within the next few months the number of rebellious American colonies—he still thought of them as colonies, not states—would shrink to ten, as Georgia and the two Carolinas were safely back in the fold. After a largely unavoidable and painfully long period of inactivity, Clinton was charged with fervor and eager to take the field. Seemingly always in the know about decisions made in secret in the Continental Congress, Clinton was aware that the rebels were rushing reinforcements to Charleston. At last, he thought, the great showdown was coming: "This is the most important hour Britain ever knew. If we lose it, we shall never see such another."[67]

Clinton and Arbuthnot put together a huge task force. Clinton's initial plan for the campaign had involved not only the strike against Charleston but the simultaneous dispatch of two thousand men to establish a base in Virginia, a foray that would prevent the Old Dominion from deploying troops to South Carolina and would assist in the reduction of North Carolina following the fall of its sister province to the south. But word that France might send another naval squadron to North America led Clinton to cancel his plans for Virginia. In December, 8,700 men and hundreds of horses clambered aboard 88 transports at anchor off Sandy Hook. All would sail for Charleston in a squadron that included thirty men-of-war. Clinton and Lord Cornwallis, who had enthusiastically endorsed the idea of attempting to take Charleston, were the last two to board the flagship. The next morning, the day after Christmas 1779, the anchors were raised and the great fleet moved majestically into the Atlantic, getting away just in the nick of time. The next morning, New York's waters were choked with ice and, as an observer noted, were "now not navigable."[68] Luck was with the British in sailing when they did. That seemed a good omen for the coming crucial phase of the southern strategy.

A year had slipped away, the second since Saratoga. With the exceptions of the Rhode Island operation in 1778 and d'Estaing's campaign to take Savannah, neither side had launched a major initiative since Burgoyne's surrender. It was clear that Washington had no plans to do so unless he acted in concert with the French, and at this juncture he had no idea when, or if, he would ever again see his ally. Clinton, however, was on the cusp of what might be a pivotal undertaking that could turn around the war.

CHAPTER 6

AMERICA'S SARATOGA

TWO WEEKS BEFORE Clinton's task force sailed, General Washington had been informed by agents in the Culper espionage ring that the enemy was planning an expedition, though its destination was unknown. For days, Washington's best guess was that General Clinton was feinting a move to the tropics or South Carolina and that his intended target was West Point. However, within twenty-four hours of the flotilla's departure, Washington knew that Clinton was en route to Charleston. With striking accuracy, the spies even informed Washington that Clinton planned to return to New York if he succeeded in taking Charleston, leaving Lord Cornwallis to pacify the remainder of South Carolina. The informants erred only with regard to the number of British soldiers in the task force, underestimating by nearly four thousand. They went on to report with greater accuracy that New York's Tories were confident that North and South Carolina, as well as Georgia, would be reclaimed before summer, and one spy advised that Clinton, who lusted to "distinguish himself," would make "a vigorous push" to succeed.[1]

Washington immediately passed along to Congress what he had learned, though the shock of the Allied defeat in Savannah had already spurred the congressmen to act. They had ordered reinforcements for General Lincoln in Charleston, pulled three frigates from the nation's tiny Continental navy and directed that they sail for South Carolina, and once again asked North Carolina's Continentals to march to Lincoln's side. At the same moment, Congress additionally directed the deputy quartermaster general to transport a vast array of military equipment to Lincoln. As it appeared unlikely that Washington would be involved in any major campaign during the coming months, Congress approached him with considerable deference about "reinforce[ing] General Lincoln without delay," though it was left to the commander to "best Judge what troops can *Conveniently* be spared." Washington responded by ordering two regiments of North Carolina Continentals to march to South Carolina, but when Congress also asked him to dispatch a much larger number from the Virginia Line, the commander demurred, pleading his need for troops on the periphery of New York. However, after meeting with Lieutenant Colonel John Laurens, his trusted aide who had recently returned from his native South Carolina, Washington relented and not only ordered the Virginians to hurry southward but dispatched a cavalry regiment as well. Later he sent a professional French engineer to Charleston to assist in preparing the city's defenses.

Altogether, Lincoln could look forward to being augmented by 3,000 infantry regulars and 125 horse soldiers, men that Washington on two occasions told his general—and Congress as well—could be "illy . . . spared" from his army outside New York. Washington wrote Lincoln that the idea of relinquishing those men had been his idea, when in fact he had responded to pressure from Congress and influential South Carolinians. Some in Congress had been as reluctant as Washington to assist South Carolina, though for different reasons. Not a few congressmen were bitter toward the state, as it had provided little help during the dark days of 1777, when fighting raged in the North. Some congressmen also thought it inexcusable that South Carolina had supplied negligible assistance to the rebel force that had defended Savannah against Colonel Campbell's incursion a year earlier. One member of Congress asked "how can South Carolina expect we will send our men to their support, when they will do nothing for themselves. Our men go there, sacrifice their health, their lives, & the So. Carolina

Militia are snug at their own homes. It is too much for them to expect us to fight their battles for them." Boston congressman James Lovell railed that South Carolina never met its assigned quota of Continental army troops and, unlike some northern states, had steadfastly refused to raise Black regiments.[2]

The number of African American soldiers had grown since 1778, particularly within New England units, which enlisted both free and enslaved Blacks, the latter serving with a promise of freedom at war's end. After Britain turned to its southern strategy in earnest, Colonel Laurens, Washington's young aide who had studied abroad and returned home a staunch foe of slavery, pushed a plan to have his home state of South Carolina raise a light infantry force composed of five thousand African American slaves. Laurens departed for South Carolina in 1779, planning to soldier and also to lobby for the enactment of legislation authorizing the enlistment of enslaved people who would be freed following the war. It was an uphill battle, and from the start, Laurens believed that its success hinged on Washington's backing. But Washington refused to endorse the scheme and only a dozen assemblymen voted for the measure. Washington feared that if South Carolina recruited Blacks, Britain would respond in kind, and he knew that the British would have the upper hand in that contest. The British could promise Black recruits freedom regardless of the war's outcome; the rebels' promise of freedom hinged on America winning the war. Washington was additionally aware of both war-weariness in South Carolina and widespread opposition to putting arms in the hands of bondsmen, and he was apprehensive that Laurens's idealistic plan would break the back of support for the war in the Palmetto State. Without Washington's endorsement, the scheme died.[3]

It was in the wake of Laurens's failed attempt to raise an army of Blacks, and after "much altercation" among the delegates, that Congress reinforced Lincoln. To have failed to act would have posed an ominous threat to the quest for independence. Some in Congress who appeared to be intransigently opposed to sending help to the South Carolinians may have been swayed by General Lincoln, who explained the danger posed by losing the state. Should the enemy gain Charleston's harbor and much of backcountry South Carolina, it could funnel invaluable provisions to its armies in the West Indies. Without spelling it out, Lincoln was suggesting that if France suffered irreversible losses in the tropics, it might lose interest in remaining America's ally. Lincoln further warned that should South Carolina fall, Britain's recruitment of Tories would flourish and southern Indians might go to war alongside the British. He hardly needed to say that America's burden was such that it could ill afford to lose a single state in this war, much less the three states that Britain hoped to gain through its southern strategy.[4]

WHILE PREPARATIONS TO defend Charleston proceeded, Washington with some ten thousand men in eleven brigades had taken up winter quarters in Jockey Hollow, a part of the Morristown encampment a few miles west of Manhattan. Today, Valley Forge is remembered for the suffering endured by the troops, but the winter of 1779–1780 at Morristown was worse than its predecessor. Veterans later recalled it as "the hard winter," and at the time, Washington noted that the "oldest people now living in this Country do not remember so hard a Winter." Temperatures plunged and snow began falling while Clinton's task force was slipping out of New York Harbor. It continued to snow for days, and at one point a blizzard hammered the region. Throughout January and February it snowed again and again. With temperatures stuck below freezing, the snow could not melt, and in February drifts reached twelve feet. Day after day, Washington scribbled in his diary: "Very cold," "cold with high winds," "cold & windy," very cold & freezing," "Air keen." Even in March he noted on several days, "Ground hard frozen." Some men endured it while living in tents. Others, in barely heated huts, slept huddled together. The persistent bad weather made it impossible at times to transport stores of food to the encampment. Even after the cold weather finally broke in the spring, the supply system continued to be hindered as the once frozen roads turned into impassable quagmires. For long stretches there was no meat. Washington said the men were eating "horse food," though in fact rice, cornbread, rye bread, or brown bread was the standard fare. However, there were times when the men had no food. One soldier later recollected going four days without a bite to eat. Men, he said, boiled and ate their shoes and gnawed on tree bark. Luckless dogs that drifted into camp hoping for companionship and a handout wound up being someone's dinner. Upwards of 7 percent of the soldiers deserted that winter.[5]

While winter raged, Washington, anxious to do something, hit on the notion that the bad weather provided an opportunity for a surprise attack. Clinton had left behind thousands of men to hold New York, but they were scattered over a huge area. Washington, whose first triumph had come on a freezing Christmas night in 1776 at Trenton, tried to replicate that victory with a night strike against a 3,000-man enemy force posted on Staten Island. As the Arthur Kill and the Kill Van Kull, the waterways that separated the island from New Jersey, were frozen, Washington envisioned a force of 2,500 men storming across the ice to Staten Island and overpowering the surprised defenders. He put the operation in motion in mid-January, but the element of surprise was lost and the attack fizzled. The Americans, not wishing to assail British troops that had retreated behind barricades, withdrew to safety. In exchange for having taken a few prisoners, Washington lost six men who were killed and a dozen or more who were captured, as well as several others who fell victim to frostbite. General Nathanael Greene summed it up best: "It was a noble attempt; but a fruitless expedition. The Enemy have more than doubly punnished us for our presumption."[6]

The British army's payback came a month later, almost to the day. An enemy force variously estimated at two thousand to three thousand infantry and upwards of five hundred cavalry crossed into New Jersey and raided three villages in the vicinity of Morristown. But going after hamlets such as Woodbridge, Rahway, and Elizabethtown was one objective. Another purpose of the operation was to "carry off"—that is, kidnap—General Washington. The British hoped that sufficient numbers of Continentals would be drawn away from Jockey Hollow, enabling some three hundred dragoons to ride into Morristown, where Washington had established his headquarters in the Ford Mansion.

British success was unlikely, as Washington was protected by his Life Guard. He had formed a company of bodyguards during his first year in command of the Continental army. These spit-and-polish soldiers wore dark blue coats with red vests, buckskin trousers, and white bayonet and body belts. They managed Washington's household, moved and guarded his baggage, and of course provided security. Two members of the Life Guard were posted around the clock in front and two in the rear of Washington's headquarters, and in an emergency every soldier in the unit was to immediately spring into action. For the most part, the Life Guard had totaled around 150 members, though in 1779 its numbers had been reduced by nearly two-thirds. (After the 1780 British threat to seize Washington became known, the Life Guard swelled to 180 members.) To have succeeded, the enemy dragoons would have had to have gotten through the rebels' outer defenses and penetrated Washington's headquarters, and the odds against either were considerable. British soldiers did plunder the nearby villages, though the myriad stories of supposed depredations that appeared in rebel newspapers—women and children having been stripped and beaten, and a blind "aged widow" disrobed and subjected to "insults and awful threats"—were likely exaggerated. Meanwhile, the redcoats' attempt to reach Morristown flopped. Not a single enemy soldier got close to Washington, and by 8:00 A.M., three hours after the enterprise commenced, the British commander terminated the action, seeing that the cavalry's horses were unable to gain traction on the ice. Washington gave no sign of having been shaken by the threat. He simply remarked that he felt safe, as precautions had been taken as soon as he learned that the enemy was marauding not far from Morristown.[7]

Aside from the wintertime miseries, Washington's greatest worry during the first several months of 1780 was about maintaining an army that could fight if and when the opportunity presented itself. Faced with a two-front war and an economy that was close to having flatlined, Congress was considering reducing the size of Washington's little-used army. Aghast, Washington immediately informed the congressmen that his army was already shrinking as enlistments expired and the ferocious winter led to a spike in desertions. What is more, as during the Valley Forge winter, many officers were resigning their commissions. (In the vicinity of 136 officers quit the army and returned home during the first six months of 1780.)[8] Nor was that all. Recruiting was lagging in several states. Congress responded by sending a committee to Morristown to meet with Washington, and as was nearly always the case, he played the committeemen like a virtuoso. Congress must act, and quickly, he told his visitors, or the army would be in a "most confused and disordered" state at the outset of the campaign season. He once again urged Congress to increase the bounties offered to recruits and to institute conscription. If those steps were not taken, America's incapacitated army might be unable to act in a hardy manner alongside its French ally. Such an eventuality would be "very unfavourable to us," he warned, as it might not only diminish France's staying power but also encourage Britain "to persevere in the War."

Acting with vigor was only a part of Washington's message. He painted a picture of an army that festered with discontent brought on by episodic supply problems and habitual payroll lapses. He additionally asserted that it was being ripped apart by jealousy. Soldiers from states that were laggard in providing for their troops resented their comrades from states that "pretty amply" furnished their men with clothing and the "many little comforts and conveniences" of life. "An army must be raised, paid, subsisted and regulated [in] an equal and uniform" manner, or troubles would be "endless," Washington lectured. Congress did not tackle the constitutional issue of national versus state sovereignty that he had broached, but it did adopt grand plans for increasing the army. Washington's 10,000-man army was to be increased to 35,211 "exclusive of . . . Officers." Troop quotas were assigned to every state but Georgia, whose government was in enemy hands. Moreover, the committee that Congress had dispatched to Morristown issued a muscular circular letter to the states appealing for action to squelch the smoldering crisis.[9]

> When America stood alone against one of the most powerful
> nations of the earth, the spirit of liberty seemed to animate her sons

to the noblest exertions, and each man chearfully contributed his
aid in support of her dearest rights. When the hand of tyranny
seemed to bear its greatest weight on this devoted country, their
virtue and perseverance appeared most conspicuous, and rose
superior to every difficulty. If then, such patriotism manifested
itself throughout all ranks, and orders of men among us, shall it be
said at this day . . . that America has grown tired of being free? . . .
These reflections arise . . . from the extraordinary backwardness of
some States, and great deficiencies of others, in sending men into
the field. . . . America [must not forget that] she is contending for
liberty, and independence.[10]

With the army in dire straits and Clinton's fleet bearing down on South
Carolina, some searched for ways to counter the sense among growing
numbers that the war was a lost cause. In March, Thomas Paine rushed out
an *American Crisis* essay, his first in eighteen months. For a second time the
people in England were his target audience, although by focusing on the
enemy's problems Paine additionally sought to buck up American spirits by
demonstrating that the war was having a deleterious impact in the enemy's
homeland. Paine argued that England was "rent into parties." The resulting
discord, he contended, threatened fatal divisions. Thereafter, Paine played
on two themes. The first was that English residents of coastal villages would
henceforth be the victim of enemy raiders. John Paul Jones and others had
already conducted raids during the past eighteen months. More were to
come. England had spread "Fire, sword and want . . . with wanton cruelty
along the coast of America." Now retribution was on the way. Soon English
"women and children," like their American counterparts, will wander in the
"severity of winter" and stare at the gutted remains of their once "well
furnished house[s]." Americans at least had an "extended wilderness" into
which they could escape from enemy raiding parties. The English will have
nowhere to "fly to" when their foes arrived to subject them to "unpitied
miseries." Second, Paine sought to convince the English citizenry that they
were being kept in a war that Britain could not win. Forget who was

responsible for having started the war, Paine advised. What mattered now was the reality that "America is beyond the reach of conquest." England was waging a hopeless war that could end in "national suicide" and enormous distress for the people. England's citizenry had already endured war's hardships because a rapacious ruling class profited from remaining at war, Paine declared. He added that there "are men in all countries to whom a state of war is a mine of wealth," loathsome characters who never risk their skin, but fatten on the treasures generated by warfare. He asked the people of England: Are you willing to permit men of this ilk to expose you to great hardships when your only hope of realizing security is through making peace?[11]

Colonel Alexander Hamilton, Washington's aid, also took up his pen, though he pursued a different course. Posing as the fictitious "James Montague, Esqr.," he wrote a long private letter to several influential merchants, including Robert Morris, probably the wealthiest Philadelphian, and to at least one congressman. Hamilton's aim was twofold: remedying the economic crisis and overcoming the paralysis brought on by state sovereignty. Something had to be done to repair the "badness of the (money)" in circulation, he began. As taxation could no longer provide for the "current exigencies of government," there "is but one remedy, a foreign loan. . . . Nothing else will retrieve our affairs." In calling on Congress to seek yet another loan from France, Hamilton was angling for funds for a purpose unlike anything previously attempted. The money would go toward the creation of the Bank of the United States, an entity to be capitalized for two hundred million dollars, half of which would come from the loan, half from investments in the bank's stock. The bank, he went on, could loan money to the United States government and its notes would replace the worthless state and Continental currencies in circulation. Something else was also on his mind. He knew that only the wealthiest Americans could afford to buy shares in the bank. These "men of weight and understanding"—whom he elsewhere called the "moneyed men"—would henceforth be firmly attached to the very survival of the United States, for if the war was lost, they would lose every cent they had invested in the bank's stock. It was a plan that had little chance of success.[12]

The previous March, Congress responded with a dramatic step. It turned responsibility for paying for the army—including arrears of payment—over to the states. It also revalued Continental money at 40 to 1 of specie and asked the states to call in via taxes its proportion of the Continental money, thus driving the existing money out of existence; each forty dollars that the states brought in would be replaced with two dollars in a new bill, 60 percent of which would be kept by the states while the remainder went to the national government. Each member of Congress knew that this was the final stab at making paper currency work. If this step failed, said one member, "we shall be at our wits' end." The states made a worthy effort, but the cost of the war continued to plague the economy, though whereas the currency had depreciated by 50 percent during the initial three months of 1779, it lost less than 20 percent of its value during the last nine months of the year. Nevertheless, money's value did decline, provoking some states to turn to an expedient from which they had previously shrunk—the confiscation and resale of Loyalist properties. Since early in the war states had seized the land and homes of Tories who fled into exile, though in general the expropriated property had been rented, not sold. However, in their desperation for revenue, some states by 1780 had begun to seize property still occupied by Tories and sell that which was impounded. The idea looked good on paper, but it foundered as a revenue raiser. The governments realized only £50,000 in hard money, an inconsequential amount given the staggering cost of fighting this war.[13]

There was one bit of good news amid the gloom of early 1780. Even as Hamilton was writing his proposal about a foreign loan, France's monarch, Louis XVI—who was readying the dispatch of troops to America—agreed to provide three million livres annually for the duration of the war for the purchase of "necessaries" for the Continental army. Chevalier de La Luzerne, the French minister who was based in Philadelphia, passed along word of the benevolence, but he accompanied it by urging Congress in the strongest terms to meet Washington's manpower needs and adequately provision his soldiery. It soon was apparent that French altruism had its limits. France rebuffed Congress's request that it help with the maintenance of American diplomatic missions abroad. (France's rejection led John Morin Scott, a New York congressman, to angrily confront La Luzerne, even intemperately threatening that the United States might "renouncer a l'Independence." Scott was rapidly hushed by his colleagues.)[14]

The cheery side of the news from Versailles did little to alleviate Washington's gloom. By early May, he was convinced that the news from Charleston would not be favorable and, with his army continuing to dwindle, he remained fearful that he might not be able to join the French if they returned in 1780. Washington unburdened himself in a long letter to Fielding Lewis, his brother-in-law in Fredericksburg, Virginia. The obstacles standing in the way of victory might be insurmountable, he acknowledged. After all these years and all his sacrifices, the thought that the war might end short of American independence had given birth to "bitterness [in his] Soul." What he called the "fatal" impediments to victory were not new. They had dogged the Continental army since its inception but had never been properly addressed, and now they had brought the army to a "low ebb." In the sixth year of the war his soldiers yet faced malnutrition and "scarcely as much cloathing as would cover their nakedness." A quarter of the men had "not even the shadow of a blanket." (In an earlier letter he had complained that despite "large importations of cloathing," the soldiers "never see" much of it, for the garments apparently lay "wasting and rotting" in some unheard-of storage facility.)

Washington identified three things that had produced the "disastrous consequences" that plagued the army. One was "a fatal Jealousy . . . of a standing Army." That fear had prevented the formation of a sizable and experienced fighting force that might, by late 1777, have driven the enemy to recognize American independence. In addition, state sovereignty had emasculated the central government. The thirteen sovereign states—what he called a "many headed monster"—hampered the central government's ability to properly meet the "great purposes of War." Finally, at the end of every year since 1777 both the states and Congress had assumed that "Peace must take place in the Winter." This misguided assumption had annually led to "an apathy which lulls" the governments into a sense of "ease and security," resulting in "the most distressing consequences at the opening" of the next campaign season. Only one way existed "to obtain Peace, or insure it," and that is to "be prepared for War." Now, with victory and the realization of independence imperiled as had not been the case since the dark days of 1776, Washington was saying that the "folly of our . . . blunders" had brought America to a point where "the enemy are convinced that we are [not] in a condition to carry on the War." So long as London thinks that is the case, said Washington in closing his disheartening letter, "we shall never have Peace."[15] Washington's worry that independence might be beyond America's reach was hardly the result of a fevered imagination. In midyear, Arthur Lee, one of the three original diplomats sent to France by Congress in 1776, returned home for the first time since before the onset of hostilities. In Boston, of all places, Lee found widespread apprehension that the reconciliationists—the faction that had blocked a declaration of independence during the first fifteen months of the war—might soon regain a majority in Congress and accept an accommodation with Great Britain on terms short of independence.[16]

WHILE WASHINGTON'S MEN suffered through the brutal winter, the men and horses on Clinton's expedition to Charleston endured miseries of their own from the same fierce storms. General Howe's voyage to Head of Elk, Maryland, in 1777 had been a summertime nightmare. The winter journey of Clinton's army was just as bad. He called it a "most harassing and tempestuous" venture. "Storm, rain, hail, snow, and the waves breaking over the cabin," one soldier scribbled in his diary; a few days later that trooper wrote, "Terrible weather! Snow, rain, hail, storm, foaming waves, and bitter cold!" Another soldier, a recent recruit on his initial campaign, recalled that "by the heaving and rolling of the ship, all the beds in which we lay broke loose from the sides of the vessel," and the "ship was so agitated by the wind and waves . . . that our gunnels ran under water, and the guns on the same side broke loose on the quarterdeck." The one thing that was constant throughout, said Clinton, was the "malevolence of the winds."

Misfortune set in at the very outset. While Clinton and Cornwallis got out of New York Harbor just ahead of the plummeting temperature, some ships did not, and seven transports were badly damaged by ice before they reached the sea. The *Lyon*, a vessel loaded with Hessians, got away safely only to have its mizzen masts ripped down by squalls. It wound up being blown all the way to England. Three other ships were lost altogether. On several occasions men had to be transferred from a badly damaged vessel to one that remained intact. Clinton fretted daily over whether the crafts that were swept eastward by the tempests would be prevented by the Gulf Stream from rejoining the armada. He could ill afford to lose men or ships. Clinton had come south with half the number of troops that Howe had commanded when he'd launched the campaign to take Philadelphia, and the navy was one-third the size of the task force that had brought troops to Pennsylvania in 1777. Given that the storms added to the length of the voyage, Clinton also worried that the Americans would have time to rush considerable reinforcements to Charleston, including possibly most of Washington's army.[17]

At the end of January, five weeks after weighing anchor, the first vessels reached the rendezvous spot off Tybee Island. When the lookout in the mast cried "Land," "Every face brightened," one officer noted in his diary. Other ships arrived during the next few days, but some that were expected never came. After a few days, Clinton made an accounting of the "heavy disasters" that his expedition had experienced: an ordnance ship was gone, as were crafts laden with the army's siege guns, horses for the cavalry, and that ill-fated contingent of Hessians. Much of the army's baggage was lost and so, too, were the work horses that were vital to an eighteenth-century army; they had perished or were so badly injured from having been tossed about that they had been thrown overboard. One soldier said that the army had arrived "pretty much in a state of nature." Clinton dispatched ships to St. Augustine, the Bahamas, and St. Kitts in search of replacements for his losses. (General Augustine Prevost in East Florida responded that he would face the "greatest danger" should he relinquish his artillery, to which Clinton tersely replied, "I am sorry," telling him to send what he had and promising that Prevost would receive replacements "as soon as they can be procured.") Clinton was aware that the vessels he sent off in search of necessities, including heavy guns, had to reach their destinations, take on their cargoes, and return to coastal South Carolina, all of which was certain to be a time-consuming undertaking that might fatally delay the commencement of operations. Charleston's defenders might use the additional time to substantially strengthen the city's fortifications—which, Clinton would soon discover, were being constructed by "a vast multitude of Negroes under skillful engineers"—rendering them impregnable. Given his unexpected and unwanted troubles, Clinton ordered reinforcements from New York.[18]

Clinton's concerns about the enemy were well placed. Some of the regulars sent by Congress to South Carolina had reached Charleston. So, too, had the treasure trove of military supplies ordered by Congress, though due to British naval superiority those provisions had made the transit in a torturously slow overland journey. Both General Lincoln and Washington had long since appealed to Thomas Jefferson—who had been elected governor of Virginia in the spring of 1779—and his counterpart in North Carolina, Abner Nash, to furnish Charleston's defenders with whatever supplies they could spare. "Blankets, shoes, and shirts, are now exceedingly wanted here," Lincoln had told Jefferson, who in turn agreed to "send forward all the little aid in our power."[19]

While Clinton waited with growing impatience, Lincoln wrestled with monumental decisions not unlike those that confronted Washington in his 1776 defense of New York City. Lincoln, too, had to choose between defending a soon-to-be-beleaguered city or abandoning it as indefensible. He had been cautioned by Washington as early as September that a British invasion of South Carolina was virtually inevitable. Washington had not recommended a course of action, but in spelling out Britain's "powerful motives" for seeking to take Charleston, he might have led Lincoln to believe that it was imperative that Charleston be defended. Washington had indicated that Britain's conquest of Charleston would imperil all of South Carolina, and that the enemy's acquisition of the province would offset whatever losses it suffered in the tropics, thus sustaining British morale. He also told Lincoln—and Lincoln had repeated it to Congress back in the fall when appealing for men and supplies—that should South Carolina fall into British hands, the province would not only be a source of vital military supplies for the enemy; it would enable the British government to "gain friends [in Europe] for a further prosecution of the war."[20]

The alternative to defending Charleston was for Lincoln to abandon it, retreat into the interior, and hope to draw the enemy after him into the inhospitable backcountry. If he chose that option, Lincoln could also hope that his enemy would experience the same deadly rate of attrition that General Gage had encountered on Concord Road and Bunker Hill, and that Burgoyne had experienced deep in New York's interior. But the losses sustained by Gage and Burgoyne had been due in large measure to the turn-outs of substantial numbers of militiamen, and little in Lincoln's six months in the South led him to believe that ample numbers of Georgia and South Carolina militia were likely to muster throughout the backcountry. That, perhaps, was a factor in his decision to make his stand within the city, a choice that he appears to have made weeks before Clinton sailed.

Several calculations contributed to Lincoln's final decision. As Washington in 1776 had been convinced that he was expected to defend New York, Lincoln felt that was what Congress now wished regarding Charleston, though it never issued such an order. However, Congress ordered troops and vessels to Charleston, and it also sent Chevalier de Cambray-Digny, a French military engineer, to design and oversee work on the city's defenses. If those actions persuaded Lincoln to defend the city, he convinced himself that the city could be successfully defended. The approaches to Charleston Harbor brimmed with long-established defensive installations and six frigates, the three Continental navy vessels sent by Congress and three others that d'Estaing had left behind for his ally. Lincoln knew, too, that an attacking army could seemingly only get at the city via the narrow approach between the Cooper and Ashley Rivers, a geographical blessing in that it enabled the city's defenders to concentrate their forces and defensive bulwarks. Lincoln additionally believed that he would have an army equal in size to that of the enemy. Lincoln anticipated more help from

Washington's army than he would get, more militiamen from North Carolina and Virginia than he would ultimately receive, and, when the pinch came, a more enthusiastic militia response in South Carolina than would be the case. Until the last, he also appears to have believed that Governor Rutledge and his council would meet the crisis by sanctioning the use of Black troops.[21]

For his part, Clinton hoped that Lincoln would defend the city. Though acknowledging that Charleston's defenses would be "by no means contemptible," Clinton was confident that he could take the city through a siege operation. Capturing the city, moreover, would result in the destruction of the army of rebel defenders, something that was far less likely to occur in a backcountry campaign. But with the approach of spring and Britain's army, Lincoln came to understand that he had been let down by those he had depended on to furnish adequate numbers of troops. No amount of cajolery could persuade South Carolina's civil authorities to raise an army of Blacks. At times, Governor Rutledge did not even bother to answer Lincoln's queries on the matter. It was a Pandora's box that he would not consider opening. A greater surprise came when so few South Carolina militiamen turned out to defend the state's most important city. Militia units within the city mobilized, but no more than three hundred militiamen from the backcountry appeared. Rutledge worked tirelessly to spur them to action, even threatening to confiscate the property of those who did not take up arms. Men by the thousands had rallied to Boston's defense in 1775, and subsequently copious numbers of militiamen mobilized to defend New York, Philadelphia, and Albany. But backcountry Carolinians had no love for Charleston, a city dominated by wealthy merchants and planters who had long controlled the province and habitually victimized the residents of the interior with regard to taxes and services.[22]

While Clinton dreamed of "*the capture of all the rebel corps in Charleston,*" Lincoln grew increasingly worried as the showdown approached. He had come to understand that defending the city might be a disastrous choice. He mulled withdrawing to the greater safety of the interior. In January, at nearly the same moment the first vessels in the British fleet anchored at

Tybee, Lincoln wrote Washington an amazingly candid letter in which he confessed that he did not know what to do. "I feel my own insufficiency and want of experience—I can promise you nothing but a disposition to serve my country." Lincoln's letter reads like that of a man desperate for Washington's sanction to abandon Charleston. Although Washington told those around him that Lincoln was "putting too much to the hazard" in attempting to defend Charleston and that he could not "forbear dreading" such a choice, the commander offered no advice to his anxious subordinate. In fact, Washington waited nearly two months to respond to Lincoln, and when he did he mentioned only that the reinforcements Clinton had summoned from New York were on their way, adding that the British army would probably not act until those supplemental troops arrived. If so, the "hot season" might have begun before Clinton acted, and that would be to Lincoln's advantage, said Washington. If anything, Lincoln likely read the letter as an exhortation to stand firm in his plan to defend the city. Washington was a long way away and had never visited Charleston, and both were doubtless factors in his unwillingness to offer advice. More than anything, however, he may have feared that the failure to defend the city would lead South Carolina to quit the war. Washington may have seen it as a Hobson's choice: the certain loss of a state or the possible loss of an army. When Washington had faced a somewhat analogous situation on Manhattan in 1776, he had chosen to save his army, at least after Charles Lee had recommended such a course.[23]

Meanwhile, Clinton had begun his approach to Charleston. Nearly three weeks after reaching Tybee, Britain's troops, having convalesced from their harrowing sea journey, landed on a warm, rainy night on sandy Simmons (now Seabrook) Island, about twenty miles below Charleston. Still awaiting men and supplies, Clinton let two weeks pass before he advanced to James Island, six miles closer to the city. It was a backbreaking undertaking, for given the want of horses the men lugged their heavy supplies and muscled ponderous artillery through unwelcoming swamps and across the uncongenial coastal soil. Neither landing had been opposed, but from this moment forward, rebel cavalry harassed the advancing redcoats. America's horse soldiers were of less concern to most of the British than the "crocodiles sixteen feet long . . . wolves and several species of venomous snakes" that inhabited the wetlands through which they were slogging. While his soldiers kept wary eyes out for the dangerous inhabitants of this low-lying, boggy region, Clinton was reading incredibly accurate intelligence reports filed mostly by Tory operatives. Long before he laid eyes on Charleston, Clinton was aware of the size of Lincoln's army and possessed a sketch of the defensive installations that the rebels were still constructing. In mid-March, nearly a month to the day after the first soldiers had come ashore in South Carolina, an advance force reached the Ashley River and spotted tall church steeples in Charleston. It looked just like New York City, one thought.[24]

During the next two weeks Clinton's army continued its painstaking advance toward Charleston. Clinton himself, a hands-on general, was among the first to arrive at the front lines, and before the end of March he got his initial look at the city's defenses. They were formidable. A two-foot-thick stone wall surrounded by a deep ditch guarded the entrance to the city. Farther out, redans (V-shaped fortifications) and redoubts (earthworks) snaked between the Ashley and Cooper Rivers, and were buttressed by a six-feet-deep and twelve-feet-wide ditch, which in turn was secured by abatis (sharpened tree branches that could impale a charging soldier) and numerous "wolf traps" (deep, concealed holes). A ten-feet-wide and eight-feet-deep man-made canal meandered before the first line of defenses. Clinton had never seriously considered attempting to take the city through an assault, and what he saw confirmed his belief that he must first seek to take Charleston through a siege operation. On April 1, while some British specialists dug wells—the water they produced was "mixed with sand and as white as milk," said one soldier—Clinton's sappers, under fire from the rebels, began digging the first parallel for the siege guns. As the replacements for the artillery lost at sea had not arrived from St. Kitts, Clinton was forced to borrow the guns on Arbuthnot's ships of the line, mostly 32- and 24-pounders that were immense compared with the artillery normally available to an army. Five days later, the bombardment of Charleston began, and almost immediately the "fire of the enemy's advanced works . . . abate[d] considerably," as one British soldier put it.[25]

There were still escape hatches and, as the crisis deepened, Lincoln discussed with the civil authorities the possibility of extricating his army. They demanded that he stay the course. Without a doubt, those discussions led Lincoln to conclude that if he did not defend Charleston, Rutledge and his privy council would abandon the United States, as they had threatened a year earlier. Lincoln also knew that if South Carolina dropped out of the war, Georgia, which in any case was hanging by the slenderest thread, would definitely be lost. North Carolina, which was presumed to have a larger population of Loyalists than its neighbor, might be doomed as well. Lincoln was not alone in that assumption. David Ramsay, a Charleston physician and early historian of the Revolution, wrote that Charleston was the "*vinculum* that binds the three States [Georgia, South Carolina, and North Carolina] to the authority of Congress." Lincoln knew that to fight and lose Charleston would be bad enough. But to abandon the city without a fight would at the very least destroy whatever slim hopes lingered that the Continental army could obtain men and materials from South Carolina. In a worst-case scenario, if Charleston was not defended, it could set in motion a cascading chain of events with catastrophic consequences for America's quest for independence. Lincoln would have been less than human had he not contemplated the price he would pay for exiting the city.

Crazy though it was, only Washington could sidestep a fight and win praise for having done so. Charles Lee's retreat at Monmouth and Arthur St. Clair's relinquishment of Fort Ticonderoga—sound though both steps may have been—had irretrievably blackened their reputations. Lincoln must have presumed that if he made a run for safety, his standing would be ruined. Should two or three southern states be lost to the cause, in the process destroying the nascent United States' bid for independence, much of the burden for having lost the war would come to rest on Lincoln. It would be an insufferably oppressive load to bear. Military leaders, convinced that they are expected to fight, sometimes do so though they are aware that the odds against victory are overwhelming and many of their soldiers will be sacrificed in vain. Against all odds, General Montgomery had chosen to fight at Quebec in 1775, Burgoyne had done so in the Saratoga campaign, and d'Estaing had taken up that option in Savannah. Lincoln, in desperation, had reached out to Washington and hoped the commander would provide a lifeline. Washington had not been so inclined.[26]

Flight from the city remained an option until mid-April, about the time when Governor Rutledge—having done what he could to bring the defenders of Charleston to the brink of doom—took flight. The exit doors had begun slamming shut with surprising suddenness almost immediately following the arrival of Clinton's army. Lincoln was one of the first to see this coming. By the end of February, while Clinton's soldiers were dodging alligators and water moccasins well south of the city, Lincoln was made aware that a major component in his plan for successfully defending Charleston had come unraveled. All along, he had gambled that the quirks of Charleston Harbor would keep the Royal Navy at bay. The Charleston Bar, a long sandbar at the harbor's entrance, posed what was thought to be a nearly unyielding barrier to large warships. An experienced pilot could get a ship through a handful of narrow channels in the bar, but it was a slow, tricky process, and any vessel that made the attempt was thought to be vulnerable to the fire laid down by the six American frigates. In addition to the bar's natural impediments, the British fleet would have to run past Fort Moultrie on Sullivan's Island, an installation brimming with forty guns. Even if enemy craft somehow survived the fusillade laid down by Fort Moultrie and succeeded in crossing the bar, Lincoln assumed that the tiny American navy could keep them at bay until the rebel army slipped out of the city.

Lincoln had gotten his first inkling of real trouble even before Clinton's fleet reached Tybee Island. Commodore Abraham Whipple, commander of the just-arrived Continental frigates, acknowledged that he could not guarantee that the enemy's ships of war could be prevented from entering Charleston Harbor, especially as he balked at making a stand at the bar. However, he agreed to erect a chain of obstructions near Fort Moultrie and predicted they would prove to be the death knell for any foolhardy sea captain. Lincoln thought it a workable plan. However, just as the advance parties of redcoats reached the Ashley, Whipple reported that the obstructions could not be completed in time.[27] Lincoln knew the city would be doomed if Arbuthnot's fleet got into the harbor, for not only would Charleston's defenders be shelled by both Clinton's army and the Royal Navy, but ships from the British flotilla could assist in sealing every exit. The second half of March, a time when Charleston was awash in vibrant spring colors, was the optimum time for the rebel defenders to escape, for neither Clinton's siege guns nor the Virginia troops that Washington had promised in November had yet arrived. Lincoln met with South Carolina's civil authorities in several heated sessions. On April 8, in the midst of those angry meetings, the royal fleet sailed into Charleston Harbor. It had lost only one vessel to Fort Moultrie's booming guns.

That was good news for Clinton, but the day before had not been so good. The Virginia regulars—1,400 men in all—at last arrived in the city, bringing the total in Lincoln's army to 5,660. As they had gotten in, Lincoln's army could still get out. Clinton hurriedly acted to close all exits, including the dispatch of 1,500 men under Colonel James Webster. Their target was a 500-man rebel militia and cavalry force under Colonel Isaac Huger, a South Carolinian who had fought in nearly every major battle in the southern theater since 1776. Huger had been given responsibility for securing the forks of the Cooper River near Monck's Corner, a locale where the river was narrow and shallow and could be easily crossed by Lincoln's army or by British forces bent on closing all roads east of the Cooper that led to North Carolina. As his force neared Monck's Corner, Webster under the cover of darkness sent off his cavalry led by Colonel Banastre Tarleton, a twenty-six-year-old former student at Oxford who had served in the British army since 1775. As the cavalry's customary mounts were at the bottom of the Atlantic, Tarleton's men were aboard ponies and a few "weak, undersized, ill-appointed, and untrained horses" that had been found on Port Royal Island. Aware that his force would be no match for Huger's more mobile dragoons, Tarleton knew from the outset that his best chance of success was to surprise his adversary, and that was exactly what he succeeded in doing. He learned of Huger's location from an enslaved person and approached the rebels in the dark early-morning hours of April 14. Fortunately for Tarleton, Huger had neither posted sentries nor sent out patrols. "[B]loody work we had," said a British soldier, for the Americans, caught unawares, were cut to pieces. Many of the officers bolted to freedom on their horses, but thirty men—mostly enlistees—were killed or wounded, and sixty-five were taken captive, along with fifty wagons loaded with weaponry and munitions, and hundreds of fast cavalry horses that in Clinton's estimation were superior to the equines his cavalry had possessed back in New York. In a matter of minutes, Lincoln had lost his entire cavalry arm east of the Cooper, reducing his chances of both escaping and foraging for supplies. What is more, the river was now shut to inland navigation.[28]

Only one road to safety remained for Lincoln—Lampriers Point, a largely desolate and marshy site just below the junction of the Cooper and Wando Rivers to the east of Charleston Neck. Lincoln rushed men from the now useless Fort Moultrie, together with six cannon, to secure that exit. Clinton countered by sending a force of 2,300 men under General Cornwallis. Thirteen days after the rout of Huger's cavalry—and twenty-two days after the shelling of Charleston had commenced—Cornwallis closed the door at Lampriers Point, killing around forty rebels and capturing another seventy or so, while several others who fled into the aptly named Hell Hole Swamp likely drowned or fell prey to the creatures that called the site home. "Our communication is entirely cut off from the country," a rebel soldier imme-diately notified his wife in a letter that now had little chance of being deliv-ered. Lincoln's long, agonizing quandary over whether to flee or fight was over. His army was going nowhere.[29]

Despite his repeated successes, Clinton's relationship with both Arbuthnot and Cornwallis deteriorated throughout the campaign, for which there would be serious, long-term consequences. Clinton's relations with Arbuthnot had been strained before the task force sailed for South Carolina. The commodore could be tactless, and the sensitive Clinton was the sort to fret over every presumed slight. The intense pressure that both men experienced in the course of the campaign only heightened tensions. Clinton unfairly blamed Arbuthnot for many of the army's woes that arose during the tempestuous voyage from New York. In addition, once the siege commenced, Clinton thought the navy was slow in getting into Charleston Harbor, though he did not make much of an issue of it. However, while the army was sealing off the last exits east of Charleston Neck, Arbuthnot balked at Clinton's entreaties to have the navy sail up the Cooper River. Whipple had sunk ships in the Cooper to block passage, leading Arbuthnot to assert that his vessels would be hopelessly vulnerable should they seek to ever so slowly navigate the river. Clinton regarded that as part of the hazards of battle. Arbuthnot, thinking it an unnecessary peril, wanted the army to close the escape portals. Before the siege ended, Clinton and Arbuthnot were hardly speaking to each other.[30]

Clinton's relationship with Cornwallis suffered as well, though less from the strain of making life-and-death decisions in the course of the campaign. A year earlier, outraged at Germain's intrusiveness, Clinton for a second time had asked to be permitted to resign and return home. Most in the army appear to have believed that the request would be approved and Cornwallis would be named his successor. Cornwallis thought so as well. Uncertain how things would play out, Clinton thought it sensible to consult Cornwallis on every major step in the planning and fulfillment of the Charleston campaign. Clinton had acted judiciously, though he was riled by the belief that many officers were acting as if Cornwallis were already the commander in chief. Not long passed before Clinton suspected that Cornwallis was covertly encouraging the readily apparent behavior of the officers. Things came to a head after March 19. On that day, as the army was still slowly advancing on Charleston, Clinton learned from Germain that his request to resign had been turned down by the king. Clinton would remain the commander. Cornwallis was bitterly disappointed at not obtaining an independent command, and he made little attempt to hide his consternation or even his efforts to turn some within the corps of officers against Clinton. He disrespectfully asked that Clinton no longer ask his opinion on operations. Clinton was outraged. "I do not think his conduct has been military," he remarked in an understatement. With good reason, Clinton thereafter presumed that Cornwallis schemed to persuade officials in London that their commander in chief in North America was unfit to remain in his post.[31]

In April, however, Clinton focused on the business at hand, not his feelings toward Arbuthnot and Cornwallis. Five days after the siege guns opened up on the city. Clinton offered Lincoln surrender terms. Declaring that he regretted the "Effusion of Blood" already spilled, Clinton without specificity promised "mild & compassionate" treatment to those who surrendered. But if the rebels refused to surrender, he added, such magnanimous terms would never again be extended. Ultimately, he warned, Charleston's defenders would have to face "the resentment of an exasperated Soldiery." Lincoln spurned the offer. In subsequent days, British parallels were dug closer and closer to the city, until Clinton's big British guns—and his army's snipers—were barely one hundred yards from the American lines. Life inside the city became a living hell. Civilians and soldiers alike died every day. Mangled and fallen trees dotted the landscape, and the bloated corpses of horses littered the streets. The putrid stench of death hung over the city. Stores and homes were damaged or destroyed. Looting was widespread. Miscreants among the soldiery and residents flourished in this lawless state. Men were assaulted, women raped. With the siege guns booming day and night, sleep was nearly impossible. Food was in short supply, and some had only brackish water to drink. (Nor did the British find their stay pleasurable. They complained of "the intense heat and the innumerable sand flies, whose bites are quite painful," not to mention seemingly daily encounters with "a rattlesnake or some other venomous creature.") Clinton might have made faster work of it had he resorted to incendiary bombs, but he shrank from the imprudence of such a step. It was folly, he said, "to burn a town you mean to occupy." Late in April, Clinton for a second time demanded the surrender of the city. Lincoln agreed, but on the condition that all his soldiers and Whipple's ships be permitted to depart. Clinton's response to the ludicrous request was that only an unconditional surrender was acceptable. The guns roared once again.[32]

By early May, Clinton was coming to the conclusion that the rebels—whom he had taken to calling "Blockheads," both for having defended an indefensible city and for prolonging their inevitable capitulation—would never surrender. If so, Clinton knew the town would have to be taken by an assault. Unlike d'Estaing in facing those dismal odds at Savannah, Clinton was confident an attack would succeed. Not only had the rebel defenses been damaged or demolished by the monthlong bombardment, but Clinton had five times more troops than Lincoln possessed. Clinton had brought 8,700 men south, but early on he had gotten somewhere in the vicinity of 1,500 additional troops from the garrison in Savannah as well as 2,500 men he had summoned from New York. Though Clinton always sought to minimize his losses, he scheduled the seemingly inevitable assault for May 13, less than a week away. In the interim, he intensified the shelling, hoping against hope to break the enemy's will to hold out. On May 10, with preparations for the assault underway, Clinton learned from London that a French fleet "of a very considerable armament" had slipped out of Brest and was en route to America. Its destination was unknown, but Clinton guessed it was New York. He knew that he must return soon. Throughout his more than four-month absence from Manhattan, Clinton had brooded over the possibility of a rebel assault, especially given that Britain's few defenders were so widely dispersed that "on all sides" they were potentially "open to Mr. Washington's attacks." Clinton seemed mystified that Washington had not launched a series of attacks, intimating that had he been in the place of his opposite number, he would have taken the field.

More eager than ever to terminate the campaign for Charleston, Clinton ordered the most intense bombardment of the siege. He referred to it as "very forcible," and for the first time he turned to "hot shot"—incendiary shells—the step he had earlier refused to take. Several houses and other structures immediately went up in flames. Clinton prayed that the shelling would bring Lincoln to his senses and eliminate the need for an assault. His prayers were answered. With over seven hundred rebel militiamen beseeching their commander to end the carnage, Lincoln opened serious negotiations. On May 11, he accepted the British surrender terms that

Clinton accurately characterized as "framed in the mildest spirit of moderation." After all, on two occasions, April 10 and May 8, Lincoln had spurned Clinton's capitulation terms, grounds in the warfare of that day for Clinton to have imposed the most "severe justice" on the conquered army.

Instead, hopeful that "Clemency might yet reconcile to us" the rebels who were laying down their arms, Clinton chose relatively lenient terms. The captured Continentals, both soldiers and sailors, were to "remain prisoners of war until exchanged" and were to "be supplied with good and wholesome provisions" in the same quantity as provided to the British soldiery. But Clinton, who was bent on winning the hearts of the Carolinians, was lenient toward the captured militiamen; to the consternation of more than a few British officers, he agreed that they could "return to their respective homes as prisoners on parole," a stipulation that meant they were free but were never again to bear arms as rebels. The officers could not keep their horses but were permitted to retain their "swords, pistols and baggage." Civil officials "who have borne arms . . . must be prisoners upon parole." Lincoln had requested that his soldiery be permitted to "march out with shouldered arms, drums beating and colors flying," but that was denied. They were to "march out" and "deposit their arms. The drums are not to beat" or "colors . . . be uncased."

The butcher's bill for the ill-advised attempt to defend Charleston was steep. Charleston was America's Saratoga. More than 5,000 men under Lincoln surrendered, almost exactly half of whom became prisoners of war, a captivity that is believed to have been fatal to roughly three-quarters of these unlucky soldiers. In addition, some 225 rebels had been killed or wounded in the siege. (A Continental officer confided to an enemy counterpart that most of the "dead had been killed by rifle bullets," not artillery shells.) The captured rebel soldiers marched out of the city shouting, "Long live Congress," but the only music was provided by British and German bands, as a regiment from Clinton's army marched into the city "flying colors." Governor Rutledge may have slipped away, but some civilian authorities were not so fortunate, including two signers of the Declaration of Independence—Thomas Heyward and Arthur Middleton—who were sent to prison in Florida. The British also took 391 irreplaceable artillery pieces, 6,000 muskets, 3 frigates, 33,000 rounds of ammunition, vast quantities of rum and rice, and the enslaved people owned by rebel soldiers.[33]

Flush with victory, Clinton was exultant. Earlier, he had said that the rebels were risking their army and "the fate of the two Carolinas" by defending Charleston, and when Lincoln capitulated, Clinton almost giddily exclaimed to a friend in England: "we have conquered the two Carolinas in Charleston."[34] He had undertaken a difficult and hazardous operation and triumphed. Two years after taking command, Clinton had carried through two strands in Germain's original orders, the capture of Savannah and Charleston, not to mention that the American secretary's order to maintain control of New York if possible had been realized as well. Furthermore, in taking Charleston and capturing a rebel army nearly as large as Burgoyne had lost at Saratoga, Clinton had won a greater victory than any other British general in this six-year-old war. England was swept with "exuberant and wild" celebrations when word of the commander's crowning success arrived, and according to one onlooker, Clinton was "the most *popular* man in England." Indeed, some believed that Clinton's victory had saved Lord North's ministry, enabling Britain to remain at war.[35]

But there was business to tend to, and in no time Clinton's thoughts turned to the period of peace ahead, leading him to issue a series of proclamations. One made it a crime to "hinder or intimidate" Loyalists and additionally promised the restoration of their property. Another pardoned the militiamen captured in Charleston. Clinton should have stopped there. Instead, he not only demanded that the citizenry swear an oath of loyalty to Great Britain, but stipulated that those who refused to take the oath would be considered rebels. Clinton had blundered egregiously. His decree left no opportunity for citizens to proclaim their neutrality. In essence, they were made to swear that they were Loyalists or proclaim their support for American independence. In a short time the army's officers who were posted in the backcountry readily understood their commander's gaffe. Within a month one addressed the "unfavorable consequences" of the proclamation, contending that many frontier inhabitants who were "ill disposed to us" would never have soldiered against the king's forces, but as a result of the proclamation "nine out of ten of them are now embodied on the part of the rebels."[36]

When Clinton sailed south in December, his focus had been largely on taking Charleston and then pacifying the remainder of South Carolina, but in the course of his nearly four-month stay in the South he had glimpsed the opportunity of accomplishing far more. Clinton came to think that in the aftermath of taking Charleston he would establish coastal bases running southward from Hampton Roads in Virginia to Wilmington, North Carolina. It was not a new idea for him. During his abortive 1776 campaign in the South, Clinton had first contemplated such a scheme, seeing the posts as asylums for southern Loyalists, sources of vital materials for those fighting under the king's banner, launching pads for raids that would keep the southern rebels under "constant alarm," and a means of impeding trade between the rebellious southern provinces and the outside world. But once he received word that spring that a French fleet was crossing the Atlantic, Clinton was forced for the time being to scuttle his plans to establish Chesapeake bases. Instead, in the wake of the capture of Charleston, he centered on rapidly taking control of the backcountry on the periphery of Charleston. The British under General Gage had not been able to do that in Massachusetts in 1775, with the result that the king's army had been pinioned inside Boston. Resolving that his army must not be rooted to the spot in Charleston, Clinton put Cornwallis in charge of pacifying interior South Carolina. As there was no longer an American army in the state to offer resistance, before May ended the British flag was flying again over Georgetown, about sixty miles up the coast from Charleston, in Augusta, and in Ninety Six, some 175 miles to the northwest. Once forts were established at suitable intervals between these sites, the British army would hold a huge arc of territory in the backcountry, something it had not previously accomplished in any state in the past five years.[37]

Clinton simultaneously set his sights on those rebel soldiers who were still in South Carolina. They included a few horse soldiers who had escaped Tarleton's raid near Monck's Corner and some 380 Virginia Continentals and 800 North Carolina militiamen who had arrived after all entrances to the city were sealed shut.[38] Clinton also wished to find Governor Rutledge, who was running for his life and was thought to be "at a bluff" about seventy miles north of Charleston.[39] It took Cornwallis little time to learn that most of the retreating militiamen had crossed into North Carolina, although the Virginia regulars, under Colonel Abraham Buford, were in the Waxhaws, close to the border but still in South Carolina. Only cavalry troopers, riding those speedy horses that had once belonged to Lincoln's army, might overtake them. Cornwallis detached Tarleton with 270 men from his green-clad British Legion, a unit of dragoons composed largely of Pennsylvania, New York, and New Jersey Loyalists that had been cobbled together around the time that Clinton had taken command in 1778. Tarleton and his troopers rode like the wind, covering more than one hundred miles in two days despite the grueling southern heat and humidity. It was a hell-for-leather ride that proved fatal to many of the newly acquired horses, if not to the men. On May 29, less than three weeks after Lincoln surrendered, Tarleton caught up with the Virginians.

Buford had the numbers of his side, some 125 more than rode with the British Legion. But Buford's men were almost entirely infantrymen, and they were without artillery, which had been sent ahead to speed their flight. As Tarleton's dragoons were a mobile force, all Buford could do was form a defensive line. Tarleton was not deterred for a moment. He ordered a cavalry charge at the center of Buford's line. His horses, running full tilt, could reach the enemy in five or six seconds, or less; given that it took around fifteen seconds to reload a musket, the Virginians could get off no more than one shot. The Virginians held their fire until the horsemen were a scant ten yards away. Their salvo did some damage, mostly to the horses. Tarleton himself had his horse shot from under him, but once he was rescued from his mount, which had fallen on him, he, like others under his command, rushed forward swinging his saber. Some Virginians resisted with bayonets or wielded their muskets as clubs, but against men on horses they were for all practical purposes unarmed. It was no contest. Men were trampled, shot, slashed, and stabbed.

Every battlefield displayed dismaying carnage in the aftermath of fighting, but few killing grounds in the Revolutionary War featured so much horror. Whereas somewhere around 6 or 7 percent of combatants were killed or wounded in most battles, nearly 50 percent of Buford's force suffered ghastly wounds ranging from decapitation to crushed skulls, severed limbs to lacerated bellies. Even Tarleton subsequently referred to what had transpired as a "slaughter." In the first moments of the catastrophe, rebel soldiers had cried out, "Quarter! Quarter!" Tarleton neither ordered the bloodbath nor commanded his men to ignore the enemy's pleas for mercy, and in fact nearly 40 percent of the Virginians survived the battle, some unscathed. But some of Tarleton's men were crazed by hatred, much of it doubtless fostered by unsavory memories of the harsh treatment endured by Tories since before hostilities. Cruelty is not a stranger to warfare. Nor is a lust for revenge. Apparently while attempting to surrender, 113 Americans were killed and 150 wounded. This day in the Waxhaws would be indelibly burned into the memory of the southern rebels, again and again recalled as a butchery that need not have occurred. It would lead to reprisals, including other bloodbaths. Southern rebels would henceforth speak of "Buford's Massacre" and "Bloody Tarleton," and not a few from this day forward would go into battle expecting to mete out what they called "Tarleton's quarter" to the unfortunate enemy soldiers who fell into their hands.[40]

During his last two or three days in South Carolina, Clinton learned that Tarleton had "cut . . . to pieces" 263 rebels while Britain's dragoons suffered but 19 casualties. Clinton knew few, if any, details of the carnage in the Waxhaws, save that the "greatest part" of the enemy force had been annihilated. He reacted with joy, and he praised Cornwallis for having "put an end to all resistance in . . . South Carolina."[41]

Clinton's job was done, but before departing he redeployed 1,706 men to Georgia and left Cornwallis with 6,753 men in South Carolina. He was leaving behind 60 percent of the soldiers that had secured the surrender of Charleston.[42] Some subsequently questioned whether Clinton left him with an army of adequate size. At the time, Clinton thought Cornwallis would have a "sufficient force to keep" Georgia and South Carolina "against the world," unless a "superior fleet shows itself." His surmise was based in part on the expectation that Britain's army in the South would swell as southern Tories rallied to arms, some joining provincial corps within the regular army and others serving in militia units. Clinton later contended that Cornwallis agreed, saying that he "wished for no more" and was "perfectly satisfied" with the size of his army.

Since 1778 the members of Lord North's ministry had been convinced that most southerners were what they called the "king's friends" and that they were eager to fight for their monarch. It was a supposition based in part on what the Tories and prewar royal officials in the South had told them, but also on the citizenry's presumed fear of republicanism and that the South's deep and longstanding bountiful commercial ties to the mother country would be sundered by independence. Down to 1780, the extent of southern Toryism had yet to be demonstrated. Even Germain, for all his optimism, had acknowledged that "our utmost efforts" to pacify South Carolina's backcountry "will fail" if the Tories shrank from supporting "a cause which is equally their own and ours." Before the Charleston campaign, Clinton had been more skeptical of Tory support than his masters in London, and while still in the marshes below the city in March he had cautioned the American secretary that it remains "to be proved" that Britain had an ample "number of friends in the interior."

Clinton, however, had seen a ray of hope after the fall of Savannah. Within a month of taking that city, Colonel Campbell reported that roughly 1,100 Georgians in a colony with fewer than 10,000 adult male inhabitants had taken up arms as militiamen for the king. Clinton was even more heartened by the outpouring of royalist sentiment in the wake of the rebels' catastrophic defeat in Charleston. Within weeks, upwards of 3,600 backcountry and low-country Loyalists "offered their services to His Britannic Majesty," as did another 1,861 residents of Charleston. Some who enrolled in British military units had been officers in South Carolina's rebel militia since 1776. More than 200 former insurgents in Charleston also signed a congratulatory letter to Clinton. They acknowledged their earlier opposition to imperial taxation policies, but denied having ever supported independence, insisting that all along they had been repulsed by the American Revolution's democratic proclivities. Several influential South Carolinians—their numbers included a former governor (Rawlin Lowndes), president of the Continental Congress (Henry Middleton), and member of the revolutionary Council of Safety (Charles Pinckney Sr.)—privately petitioned for pardons and the reinstatement of their British citizenship. Clinton was also buoyed by the results of an investigation that he commissioned by James Simpson, formerly the royal attorney general of South Carolina and soon to be Charleston's police commissioner. In mid-May, Simpson reported that the loyal inhabitants fell into four categories, three of which offered great promise for Great Britain. One group—which he acknowledged were "not so numerous as I expected"—had remained steadfastly loyal to the Crown. A second consisted of fence-sitters who had grown disillusioned with the American Revolution and once again adhered to the Crown. The third had supported the insurgency prior to the fall of Charleston, whereupon they concluded that a rebel victory in this war was out of the question. Those in the fourth camp were incorrigible rebels who would have to be dealt with by the occupying army. Simpson did not estimate the percentage of the population that remained unreservedly committed to American independence, but he predicted that it would be "very practicable to reestablish the King's government in South Carolina," though it would "require . . . time" and military service by a great many Loyalists. Furthermore, the Tories who stepped forward in support of their king would have to be protected by the British army.

When Clinton dispatched Cornwallis into the interior, he noted that the operation would "give the fairest opening" for the Tories to exhibit their supposed "loyal dispositions." He expected success, saying that he now had "the strongest reason" to believe that most South Carolinians were Loyalists and that considerable numbers would "take up arms" in support of the king. Whatever Cornwallis thought of that, he knew that his success hinged on either subduing the "violent rebels" or persuading them "to become our friends . . . by convincing them it is in their interest to be so." Mindful that draconian measures could be counterproductive, Cornwallis in his earliest directive strictly forbade acts "of cruelty" to the "wives and children" of rebels, and he admonished his subordinates to "have sense enough to know right from wrong, and honesty enough to prefer the former to the latter"; to underscore what he was saying, Cornwallis stressed to those under him to always act in such a manner that "shall appear to you to be best for the King's Service." What Cornwallis found during his initial weeks in the field confirmed Clinton's thinking. In one of his final missives from Charleston, Clinton informed London that "loyalists in the back parts . . . are arming." That was only a partial reason for his newfound optimism. The mere presence of British troops throughout the province, he predicted, "will call back" most South Carolinians "from their state of error and disobedience."[43]

Clinton also left Cornwallis with detailed orders. He was to see to the defense of Charleston and "its dependencies," though Clinton stressed that he did not mean to "prevent your acting offensively." Indeed, he expected Cornwallis to take steps to "recover North Carolina," so long as doing so was "consistent with the security" of Charleston and South Carolina. Should Cornwallis "succeed in both provinces" and be confident that they are safe from "any attack," he could "assist in operations which will certainly be carried on in [the] Chesapeak."[44]

With that, Clinton, Arbuthnot, and roughly 4,500 British troops boarded ships and on June 8 sailed for New York.

ON MAY 10, THE day Clinton learned that a French fleet had sailed for North America, General Washington received the same news from the Marquis de Lafayette. It was the first time the two had seen each other in more than sixteen months. Lafayette had returned to France early in 1779 in hopes of procuring an army to invade Canada, a plan that Congress had approved but—at Washington's behest—subsequently rejected. On his arrival at Versailles, Lafayette discovered that something much bigger than Canada was in the works—a planned invasion of England. When finally approved, the operation included numerous diversionary raids along the

English coast, the ones that Thomas Paine later wrote about in his *American Crisis* piece. The American sailor John Paul Jones would raid in one region, Lafayette in another, and additional commanders in still other areas. Most of those schemes came to naught, after which Lafayette summoned his considerable energies and diplomatic skills to beseech French officials to send a fleet and an army to America.

Lafayette was hardly the only one urging that France do more to save the Americans, pleas that were given greater weight when word of d'Estaing's failure at Savannah reached Versailles. Benjamin Franklin, America's minister to France, asked the French to commit an army to America, and both Washington and Alexander Hamilton made similar requests to Lafayette, knowing he would make known their wishes. French authorities additionally learned through the accounts brought home by assorted volunteers who had served in the American war that its ally was war-weary. One compared the plight of America's rebels to that of a desperately ill patient struggling to stay alive; another claimed there now was more enthusiasm for the American Revolution in Parisian coffeehouses than in the United States. Lafayette, and probably most supplicants, maintained that unless France acted, Britain would not only win control of all the West Indies, but thwart America's quest for independence. Lafayette urged the ministry to send six ships of the line and 4,000 troops to North America, make another loan to the Americans, and move expeditiously so that France's troops could act in concert with the Continental army in 1780. Lafayette also proposed that he be given command of any army that was sent to North America.[45]

In late January 1780, close to the time that the first vessels in the task force bound for Charleston dropped anchor off Tybee Island, the French government made its decision. France would send six ships of the line and battalions totaling 7,500 men to the United States, as well as 15,000 muskets and clothing for America's ragged soldiery. This was pretty much what Lafayette had requested, save that 3,500 more troops than he (or Franklin) had requested would be crossing the ocean, and the king, Louis XVI, had declined to approve yet another loan to the Americans. Nor had the twenty-two-year-old Lafayette been given command of the French army. That honor went to Lieutenant General Jean-Baptiste-Donatien de Vimeur, Comte de Rochambeau, a fifty-five-year-old veteran of thirty-five years in the French army, and the man who several months earlier had been picked to lead the invasion of England. Charles-Henri-Louis d'Arsac, Chevalier de Ternay, was given command of the naval squadron. Lafayette was ordered to leave soon for America so that he could lay the groundwork for the arrival of what the French government called its "*Expédition Particulière*." Before departing, Lafayette met with Rochambeau and apprised him of conditions in Washington's army. Its needs were gargantuan, and included flour, clothing, and ample amounts of powder and flints. Lafayette added that it would be wise to cram the fleet's cargo holds with bricks for building field ovens for baking bread, leather for making shoes, fabric for fashioning clothing, and even needles and thread.

During the week before sailing, Lafayette—now once again wearing the uniform of a major general in the Continental army—rode to Versailles to bid farewell to the king and his queen, Marie Antoinette, and then to Passy, a Paris suburb, to say goodbye to Franklin. Next it was home for a couple of days with his wife and children, including a son born on the Christmas Eve just past, whom the couple had named after George Washington. During the third week in March, Lafayette began a voyage to America that terminated late in April in his landing in Marblehead, Massachusetts. Two weeks later, just about the time that Lincoln surrendered, Lafayette arrived at the door to Washington's headquarters in Morristown, where he must have received the warmest welcome ever extended to anyone visiting the commander. Not long before, Washington had told the French minister that he loved Lafayette "as my own son." Disentangling Washington the diplomat from Washington the man is impossible, though Washington's admiration of Lafayette was indisputable, not least because the commander saw in the young Frenchman many of the very qualities that he had strived to embody, including honor and courage.[46]

When Washington and Lafayette got down to business, the American commander learned that the French fleet and army were doubtless already at sea and might, with luck, arrive in Rhode Island sometime in June. Lafayette advised Washington that six ships of the line were en route, which was correct, but he also said that upwards of ten thousand troops were coming, which left the American commander to think that three times as many men were on their way as had actually sailed. As instructed, Lafayette also informed Washington that Rochambeau was to "take orders from the American commanding general. . . . It is for General Washington and [his] council of war to decide which operations will be most useful. All the king wishes is that the troops he sends . . . [must] cooperate effectually to deliver them [the Americans] from the yoke and tyranny of the English." Lafayette's orders were to also discuss matters with Congress, but he had been directed to jointly decide with Washington "to what extent he is to reveal to Congress the secret of [French] arrangements." The two opted not to divulge all that they knew about Versailles's wishes concerning operations between the French and American armies. As Washington put it, "Congress is too numerous to act with discretion."[47]

Just as Lafayette and Washington opted to hide from Congress some things they knew, the marquis chose not to familiarize the American commander with the concerns of France's foreign minister, Comte de Vergennes, about how the Continental army had been utilized during the past three years. The "American army . . . before the alliance had distinguished themselves by their spirit and enterprise," Vergennes had told Lafayette, but he was alarmed by its "inactivity" following the Treaty of Alliance. While Vergennes had dismissed as propaganda English claims that the "love of independence is much weakened in America," he confided that "if the Americans do not put more vigor into their conduct one will have reason to believe that they have but a feeble attachment to that independence for which they showed so much enthusiasm at the beginning of the revolution." When the alliance was consummated, France had sent over a fleet under d'Estaing, expecting that it, acting in concert with American forces, would be sufficient to bring the war to a swift conclusion. That had not occurred and now, amid worries that it was being pulled into a dangerously unfathomable vortex, France had felt the necessity to commit troops to the war in America.[48]

CLINTON HAD BEEN aware since April that a fleet and almost certainly a French army had sailed from Brest. Before departing Charleston, he made plans to strike at Washington's army in Morristown, hoping to set the rebels back on their heels before whatever the French were sending reached America. Arbuthnot, displaying more energy than Clinton ever gave him credit for, pressed for a simultaneous naval raid in Virginia and an incursion by Cornwallis's force into North Carolina, though the latter was to be conditional on North Carolina's Loyalists first taking the field. It soon was a moot point, as Clinton quickly brushed aside any idea of immediate action in the Chesapeake or North Carolina. In the dark as to the size and destination of the French task force, Clinton thought it too risky for a British fleet to be out and about. But energized by his victory at Charleston, Clinton was prepared to launch a surprise assault in New Jersey the moment his fleet reached Sandy Hook. He dispatched an aide to New York to alert General Wilhelm von Knyphausen, whom he had left in command in New York, to ready his forces to join in the coming foray. Thinking that Washington's strength was diminished through the deployment of some units to the South, and that New Jersey's militiamen were sure to be "quiet at their respective homes," Clinton felt that a damaging incursion into New Jersey in the immediate aftermath of the rebel catastrophe at Charleston would "depress the friends of independence and make them heartily tired of the war." Perhaps even more could be realized by a foray into New Jersey. If the rebels were taken by surprise, Clinton visualized the destruction of the vital rebel supply depot at Morristown and the possibility that the Continentals might suffer substantial casualties. Hope also sprang eternal that Washington would be lured into battle. Clinton was convinced that huge benefits might be had from what promised to be a not terribly perilous enterprise.[49]

Clinton felt that much depended on the speed with which he made the journey from Charleston to New York, and luck was on his side. He landed after ten days at sea, one-third the time it had taken the fleet to make the winter voyage southward. But that was the end of his good fortune. Clinton discovered that the courier he had sent to New York to notify Knyphausen of the planned attack had never reached Manhattan. Knyphausen, enticed by rosy reports provided by confident Loyalists, had already landed troops in New Jersey, and his endeavor had not gone well. The British advance bogged down from the beginning, and the army suffered heavy losses, with one officer even claiming the action had cost the British more casualties than Clinton had suffered in Charleston. Clinton landed to find what he called "a very unpleasant and mortifying situation." He rushed his force into action to stave off the Continentals and New Jersey militiamen, who had in fact responded rapidly to the threat. Once Knyphausen's men in New Jersey were safe, Clinton withdrew them to Manhattan. With evident displeasure, Clinton scrapped the plans he had formulated for "a sudden unexpected move," since the rebel militia was already in the field and Washington was no longer in "a state of unsuspecting security." Clinton was bitterly disappointed. Given that the combined army would have been much larger than Knyphausen's force, and it would have been assisted by the navy, he believed he might have accomplished something of significance. He was not annoyed with Knyphausen, who never knew of Clinton's plans. But he seethed with anger at the Loyalists. Not for the first time, said Clinton, they had proffered "over-sanguine" information that induced Knyphausen to launch his sally. His wrath fell primarily on the last royal governor of New Jersey, William Franklin, Benjamin Franklin's son, whose "zeal" once again had "out-run" his "prudence."[50]

Clinton received some good news on his arrival in New York. He had worried that the French fleet might reach New York before he did, but it was still at sea. It was supposed to have reached America toward the end of May, but the dockyard at Brest had been deluged with work, principally the rehabilitation of d'Estaing's fleet before it could be sent off for another round of action in the West Indies. Moreover, readying Ternay's fleet was no small undertaking. Stores, equipment, and thousands of soldiers and sailors had to be loaded onto forty-six vessels. Ternay, with Rochambeau's army aboard, did not sail until May 17, nearly one hundred days after the decision had been made to dispatch the task force to America, and it stood out to sea unopposed by the Royal Navy. However, the English knew immediately of its departure, and within two weeks the British Admiralty responded by sending off a force under Rear Admiral Thomas Graves that included six ships of the line. (In the debates over the best size of Graves's squadron, the king had backed those who insisted on half a dozen ships of the line, remarking, "The country that will hazard most will get the advantage in this war.") Despite Ternay's head start, Graves's fleet was the first to arrive, as he sailed in faster copper-bottomed ships. Clinton dared to hope that Arbuthnot, with his augmented fleet, could find and destroy Ternay at sea. But in the event that did not occur, Clinton busily readied a deployment of six thousand men to deal with what Germain had referred to as an "armament"—a French army of indeterminate size—aboard Ternay's vessels. Clinton's plan was for a joint land and sea response to the arrival of the enemy fleet and army. The Royal Navy, if superior, was to contest its adversary; the army was to pounce on the French land forces before they could establish a defensive perimeter. After the licking administered to the rebels in Charleston, Clinton thought it unfathomable that the Allies could remain at war should France's army and navy suffer catastrophic losses immediately upon landing in North America.[51]

On July 5, the *Iris* and *Guadeloupe*, two British cruisers, spotted the French task force off the Delaware Capes. Within two days Clinton had been notified, and given the convoy's course, he guessed that it was bound for Boston or Rhode Island. The next word that a dismayed Clinton received was that the navy had lost sight of the convoy. All he could do was wait. Finally, on July 18, Clinton was told that ten days earlier—it had actually been only seven days—the French had landed in Rhode Island and were "fortifying themselves." This was not the best news he could have received, and he had to have wondered why Arbuthnot had not posted cruisers near Rhode Island to learn immediately of the enemy's arrival. Even so, Clinton had conceived a plan of action. His notion was for Arbuthnot's navy to sail to Rhode Island and seek to learn whose fleet was superior, garner information about the location and strength of the enemy's army, and determine whether substantive fortifications had been completed. If the French were vulnerable, the navy was to "mask the entrance to Newport harbor," neutralizing the French fleet, and the army was to launch a surprise attack. If it was learned that the naval advantage lay with the British but that the French had "throw[n] up works for their defense," Arbuthnot and Clinton were to conduct a synchronized attack on the enemy's ships and troops.

Arbuthnot readily consented, his nerves bolstered by Graves's recent arrival in New York. Virtually certain that he had the stronger fleet—indeed, Arbuthnot could dispatch eleven ships of the line toward Rhode Island, where Ternay possessed just seven—Arbuthnot sailed for Newport on July 19. Clinton simultaneously brought his six thousand men to Huntington Bay, on the north shore of Long Island, to await transport by Britain's navy. From the beginning, Clinton felt that time was of the essence. The French must not be given too much time to prepare their defenses. Intelligence reports led Clinton to overestimate the size of his adversary. He believed Rochambeau possessed six thousand men, one-third more than had actually landed. (He also believed that another three thousand French soldiers were on their way; although those reinforcements were in fact to come, months would pass before they sailed for America.) Clinton was convinced that by throwing a considerable number of Arbuthnot's marines into the mix, the British could muster a decided numerical superiority if they could act swiftly. Arbuthnot quickly discovered that his was the strongest fleet, but he was unable to move rapidly. Contrary winds, and his need to take on fresh water for his sailors, immobilized the Royal Navy, preventing it from rendezvousing with the army until July 28, seventeen days after the French had begun work on their entrenchments. Ample time had passed for a veteran army to buttress itself, especially as the French might be able to utilize some of the bulwarks that the British had created during their presence in Rhode Island. In lieu of an assault, the British were faced with instituting a siege, and Clinton knew that he possessed neither the manpower nor the artillery for such an undertaking.

Clinton subsequently insisted that Arbuthnot, whom he characterized as weak-kneed, was responsible for calling off the attack and causing Britain's armed forces to miss "an Opportunity of attempting an important Stroke." That was not entirely true. Arbuthnot was both cautious and prudent. He feared that Ternay's fleet would soon be reinforced from the tropics, and indeed General Rochambeau expected both a naval augmentation and the arrival of his "second division," which would increase his army by 30 percent. But it had not yet arrived as July turned to August, and at that moment the Royal Navy was vastly superior to its adversary. Arbuthnot, who did not have much wartime command experience, may have been overly tentative, but he was not alone in shunning risk. Clinton wrung his hands over having "no certain intelligence" on the disposition and exact size of the French army, and he was no less anxious about the safety of his own army he had left behind to defend New York, especially if his force in Rhode Island became bogged down and could not speedily return to Manhattan.

Clinton was wary by nature, and in one sense his majestic triumph in Charleston may have made him even more circumspect. Hazarding an attack on the French at this juncture was to risk a defeat that could negate the fruits of his victory in South Carolina. That must have weighed heavily on Clinton, especially as British intelligence was reporting that Rochambeau's army was now "covered by works and a powerful artillery." (Rochambeau would later say that within twelve days "the position was rendered respectable by the labour of all the hands." Thus, five days before the British could have attacked, Rochambeau was confident that his army could defend itself.) Filled with doubts, Clinton summoned a council of war near the end of July. The British generals voted unanimously against either an attack or a siege, and in an instant Clinton put his detachment on the road back to Manhattan. On Christmas night 1776, a critical moment for the American insurgency, Washington had been willing to attempt a chancy undertaking at Trenton. Clinton and Arbuthnot shrank from a hazardous operation in mid-1780, and in the process they may have cost Britain's armed forces an opportunity to score a truly decisive victory.[52]

As Clinton was traveling by ship back to New York, one of the more curious events of the Revolutionary War occurred. He and two staff members became so violently ill following a shipboard meal that Clinton came to believe they had been poisoned, an assumption bolstered by the physician general of the army, who examined their wineglasses and concluded that they were "strongly impregnated with arsenic." Clinton thought the would-be assassin had acted in the hope of bringing forward a new British commander in chief, but he also suspected that William Livingston, the revolutionary governor of New Jersey, may have bribed stewards to lace the wine with poison. Two years earlier, Livingston had vowed revenge against Clinton following an alleged attempt by a British officer to murder him. If, in fact, this strange incident was the result of a murder plot, potential suspects were plentiful, from disgruntled British officers to dismayed Tories to opportunistic rebels. The truth can never be known. It may have been an assassination attempt. It just as easily could have been a simple case of food poisoning.[53]

Although the plan to assail the French in July had not been undertaken, two additional opportunities soon loomed. Early in August, a worried Arbuthnot, sensing that he would be blamed for aborting the Rhode Island operation, suddenly proposed meeting Clinton at Gardiners Bay, at the far eastern end of Long Island, where the admiral was refitting his fleet. Arbuthnot was purportedly amenable to preparing fresh plans for a concerted attack against the French. Clinton was so astounded that at first he doubted the legitimacy of the communiqué, but even "the least hint of a probability of the navy's cooperating" led him to set off on a 120-mile overland journey during a late-summer heat wave. The trip was so arduous that Clinton's driver perished from heatstroke in the course of the trek. But when Clinton reached Gardiners Bay, he discovered that Arbuthnot had sailed away without leaving a single vessel that Clinton might have used to catch up with him. Arbuthnot had left behind only a note saying that Ternay's fleet had sailed and he had set off to intercept it, a chase that would prove to be fruitless.[54]

A month later, on September 14, Admiral Sir George Rodney, commander of the Leeward Islands Squadron, unexpectedly arrived from the West Indies with ten ships. With more than twice the number of ships of the line under Ternay, the British now enjoyed an overwhelming naval superiority, and Rodney and Graves were ready to do their part in assailing the enemy in Rhode Island. In fact, Rodney advised Clinton that he had sailed north for one reason: "to second your efforts towards the Reduction of His Majesty's Rebellious Subjects." Clinton was overjoyed. In their early discussions, Clinton told Rodney that his arrival was certain to have "the greatest effect" on "the affairs of Great Britain in this country," and he added that, based on intelligence reports, the moment was favorable for striking the enemy in Newport. For one thing, yellow fever had supposedly broken out among the French troops. In addition, spies in the field told Clinton that disaffection was rampant among the Massachusetts Continentals in Rhode Island, in part because they had not been paid in six months, but also due to vexation at having to take orders from the French. Finally, Clinton had been informed that Washington's army was in woeful shape—partly from lagging recruiting, partly from a heavy rate of desertion—and was unlikely to provide its ally with much help. Although it would be a risky operation, Clinton—armed with such favorable intelligence—declared his willingness to take a chance should the naval officers approve, and he promised to throw three thousand men into the attack. His men, and the marines with the Royal Navy, would give the British a commanding advantage over the French defenders. However, as planning proceeded, Clinton raised several red flags. He warned that Washington could be expected to muster every available regular and militia-man to guard against a French defeat, and cautioned that the French had been given an undue amount of time to prepare their defenses. If it came down to a siege operation, it would be "impracticable" to expect that a numerically inferior British force could succeed.[55] Although the naval commanders were ready to proceed, Clinton at the last moment pulled back. He abruptly announced his opposition to the undertaking, bringing an end to the preparations.

The outcome of an assault on the French in Newport could not be assured. What was clear, however, was that during the high summer of 1780 the British had been presented with their best opportunity in the North since Brandywine three years earlier to seek to mortally wound their enemy. For their part, the French had feared a shattering blow. A Bavarian-born officer in the French army said that the British threat was "tremendously disturbing to our generals," and a Newport Loyalist subsequently claimed that on learning of Rodney's arrival, the French "gave themselves up for lost."[56]

Why was Clinton suddenly reluctant to go after the French in Rhode Island? A strike against the French had not been the only operation on Clinton's mind during recent weeks. Suddenly changed circumstances during the summer had raised the prospect of an alternative to the Rhode Island venture, an option that Clinton believed held the promise of "great consequences." Fifteen months earlier, he had been made aware through an intermediary that a high-ranking American official "was desirous of quitting the rebel service and joining the cause of Great Britain." For many months Clinton had not known the identity of the would-be turncoat, but he eventually learned that it was General Benedict Arnold. After months of futile discussions, Arnold, in July, "obtained command of all the rebel forts in the Highlands," including West Point. Intelligence informed Clinton that those installations were garrisoned by "near 4000 men." Clinton immediately concluded that "getting possession of these posts with their garrisons, cannon, stores, vessels, gun-boats . . . men etc." was "an object of the highest importance which must be attended with the best consequences to His Majesty's service." The prize before him was nothing less than the long-sought control of the Hudson River from New York City to Albany.

Success against the French in Rhode Island could not be minimized, but once Arnold promised to "surrender himself, the forts and garrison at this instant of time," Clinton was captivated. Not only was it almost certain to be the least costly of the two options, but if the undertaking resulted in Britain's control of the Hudson River, the Allies, simply and starkly, would lose the war. Even if Arnold's treachery failed, the damage to American morale that would result from the defection of a high-ranking general officer in the wake of Britain's capture of Charleston and Lincoln's army—and other rebel setbacks in the South Carolina backcountry—would be colossal. Here, thought Clinton, was an opportunity of "such infinite effect . . . that it was to be pursued at every risk and at any expense."[57]

In addition to the enticement presented by Arnold's offer of treachery, Clinton feared that the proposed attack on Newport had only "the smallest probability of success," a not-unreasonable appraisal. There was no question that the British lacked the manpower to conduct a siege operation, and an assault against an adversary that had been preparing its defenses for two months, and was "covered with a vast Artillery," would have been bloody and perilous. Clinton remembered all too clearly the results of the attack at Bunker Hill against an inexperienced soldiery behind defensive installations that had been prepared less than twenty-four hours earlier. At Newport, his army would face professional French soldiers heavily reinforced by Yankee militiamen. Furthermore, Clinton did not have to be reminded about what those New England citizen soldiers had accomplished along Battle Road from Concord to Boston, and at Bunker Hill, Bennington, and Saratoga. Should Washington, as expected, "assemble the whole force in America" to protect his French ally, Clinton reasoned that he would need upwards of twenty thousand men to carry out a successful attack. To raise a force of that size, Clinton would have to throw every man in New York who was fit for duty into the operation, and that was something he would never have considered doing.

During the past eighteen months the British had been more successful than the Allies. In a stretch during which the British had taken Savannah and Charleston, repulsed d'Estaing's attempt to retake Savannah, and looked with promise on the pacification of South Carolina's backcountry, the Allies had achieved nothing of substance. With Allied morale seemingly on the wane, Clinton's objective was to avoid defeat in the North while continuing to stamp out the insurgency in the South. He turned his back on Rhode Island, judging it too risky, preferring to gamble instead on exploiting Benedict Arnold's proffered treachery.[58]

*　　*　　*

AS THE SUMMER of 1780 unfolded, Clinton felt that a "new epocha in the war" had begun. On the one hand, the British seemed on the verge of bringing two, possibly three, insurgent states under royal control. Yet at the same moment, a French army was now in America, and someday it was expected to have an unfathomable degree of support from France's navy. Without quite saying so, Clinton gave the impression that it was his belief that the remaining four months of the year would tell the tale in this war, and he was reasonably confident. His gambit with Benedict Arnold might pay off. Furthermore, as long as the British fleet remained superior, Clinton felt that New York could be held. Perhaps the best chance of immediate success lay in the Carolinas, though he emphasized to Germain that he was daily "more sensible of the utter impossibility of prosecuting the [two-front] war . . . without reinforcements." He asked for an additional six thousand men and told the American secretary that with those supplemental numbers he thought it possible that eastern Virginia and Maryland—from roughly Annapolis to the bottom of the Great Dismal Swamp at North Carolina's northern border—could "be reduced to obedience" while Cornwallis rolled up similar gains in the Carolinas.[59]

Clinton was not alone in realizing that a new, decisive stage in the war had been reached. Thomas Paine understood that "a crisis, big . . . with expectation and events" had arrived. He had learned that Charleston was "totally gone" and understood the magnitude of the setback, but something else was even more alarming. For six months, Paine had been the clerk of the Pennsylvania assembly, a post that caused him to have to read to the legislators whatever the state's governor thought they should hear. Soon after learning of Lincoln's surrender, Washington had written one of his gloomiest letters to Joseph Reed, Pennsylvania's chief executive. The worst that you can imagine about America's plight "will fall short of the reality," the commander began, and he went on to say that unless the states did more, "our affairs must soon become desperate beyond the possibility of recovery." Washington had said as much previously, but this time he confessed: "I have almost ceased to hope." Paine was stunned. In March, he had written in *The American Crisis VIII* that America was "beyond the reach of conquest." That might be true, but though unconquered it might still lose the war.

Paine sprang to action. He beseeched wealthier Philadelphians to create and voluntarily contribute to a fund to support the army. He additionally urged authorities to levy taxes on Tories and Quaker neutralists who refused to sign an oath of loyalty to the cause. Though almost destitute, Paine pledged five hundred dollars to the fund to help the army. Altogether, more than ninety prosperous Philadelphians responded to Paine's initiative, ultimately raising £300,000 that became the seed money for the first bank in America, the Bank of Philadelphia, which was to help the war effort. (With additional money raised by the merchants, "a quantity of provisions and Rum" was purchased and sent off to the army; Washington was happy to get the supplies, but asked that in the future they send tents.) Paine did not stop there. He crafted *The American Crisis IX*, the first time he had written two *Crisis* essays in such a brief span since the last menacing days of the 1776 campaign. This essay was pure flimflam. "We want rousing," Paine said in private, and his purpose with this essay was to galvanize the country, stirring some men to enlist and others to emulate the Philadelphians who had put up money that might establish the army on a better footing. Paine wrote that the fall of Charleston was a blessing, as it would rekindle the "blaze of 1776," and he encouraged the belief that with proper backing, and French support, the Continental army could inflict "ravages" on the enemy that would banish "the withered head of tyranny" from America.[60]

At about the same moment that Paine's essay appeared, Esther Reed, Joseph Reed's wife, published a broadside in Philadelphia that urged women to be "really useful." Reed went on to organize the Association, a body of female volunteers who made clothing and candles for the soldiers, arranged drives to secure essential items, and appealed for funds to purchase clothing for the men in the army. Within a few weeks $300,000 had been raised from some 1,600 donors, leading to the procurement of more than 2,000 shirts. Ultimately, the Association established chapters in other states. Caught up in the spirit of sacrifice, some churches conducted campaigns to secure items needed by the soldiers. Washington personally thanked Reed for her "nurture" of the soldiers and, before the summer ended, encouraged the Association to deposit whatever money it raised in the Bank of Pennsylvania so that at least some of it might become back pay for Continental soldiers who had not been paid in ages.[61]

It was not merely the disaster at Charleston that gave rise to Paine's activities in June. His hope of arousing his countrymen was sparked in part by an awareness that several Loyalists were working diligently to keep alive England's spirit of perseverance. No Loyalist was more important in this regard than Joseph Galloway, the prewar speaker of the house in Pennsylvania and onetime political partner of Benjamin Franklin. Galloway had attended the First Continental Congress, where in a desperate effort to prevent war he offered a compromise solution to imperial problems. Under what he had called his "Plan of Union," an American congress would become a third house of Parliament, making the colonies more—but not totally—autonomous. Congress spurned his plan and, when war erupted, Galloway declared his neutrality. But late in 1776, when many thought the American insurgency was doomed, Galloway opportunistically offered his help to General William Howe. During the next year and a half, Galloway served the British army as an intelligence official and police superintendent of occupied Philadelphia. When the British quit the city in June 1778, Galloway accompanied Clinton's army to New York. A few weeks later, he and his adolescent daughter sailed for London.

Galloway helped other Loyalists whose world had been turned upside down by the American Revolution, and he simultaneously sought to counter disillusionment with the war in England. He met with British officials, helped drafted petitions to the government, and authored thirteen pamphlets. His essays hammered away at the economic and military importance of keeping the American colonies within the empire, and stressed that the war was winnable. In addition, Galloway put forth his Plan of Union as a viable means toward a negotiated settlement to end the war and preserve America's colonial status. In tract after tract, Galloway argued that Britain possessed the means of preventing American independence. He assailed the generalships of Howe and Clinton—the former for indolence, the latter for not having repeatedly attacked rebel targets in an effort to bring the Continental army into the field. He also censured the Royal Navy for its porous blockade. Despite the gloomy picture that he painted, Galloway insisted that America could still be compelled to accept a settlement short of independence. His prescription for victory included the occupation of all major coastal cities, search-and-destroy missions in the interior, utilization of Loyalist units to occupy conquered areas, and robust campaigns that would compel Washington to fight.[62]

Parliament's support for the war grew stronger during 1780, though Galloway and the Tories had little to do with it. In April, an ambiguous motion that assailed the monarch and Lord North without mentioning the war had carried the House of Commons with the full-fledged support of those who favored American independence. But the ministry weathered the storm and, following word of the rebels' heavy losses at Charleston, Lord North felt strong enough to have the king dissolve Parliament and call for an election. It produced a government victory with an increased majority, a political triumph that was helped immensely by the capture of Charleston.[63]

Meanwhile, there were scant signs of optimism in Congress. News of Clinton's victory at Charleston provoked outrage among many northern congressmen. None denounced Lincoln, but several were unsparing when it came to South Carolina. The "Aristocratic Temper of Mind" among that state's leaders blinded them to the "*general* Interest," exclaimed a representative from Massachusetts. They had pressured Lincoln to defend Charleston, said a New Yorker, implying that it had been indefensible and that the general had made "a brave Defence," but in the end the result was that "to save a town we have lost an Army and a State." Others bristled at the failure of South Carolina's militiamen to turn out in the crisis. All thought the capture of Lincoln's army a catastrophe—"no greater Stroke has befallen us since the commencement of the War," said a New Jersey congressman—and some believed the loss of Charleston guaranteed that Britain would re-exert its control over both Carolinas as well as Georgia. But no one said the war was lost. Some, like Paine, thought the disaster would awaken southerners to the danger they faced. In particular, the "Great Land-Jobbers & Speculators of Virginia" would be galvanized into action, lest they lose their investments, he said. Not a few northerners thought the southern states could be saved only by the North. The "war will . . . be very serious with us" was how a New Englander put it. Another, in June 1780, exclaimed that states from New England southward through Pennsylvania must make "extraordinary Exertions" or "this Year will be filled with our Disgraces."[64]

WASHINGTON, LIKE CLINTON and the congressmen, thought the coming months would probably determine the war's outcome. The "present crisis is by far the most important and delicate that this Country has ever experienced," he said in June in an appeal for help that he circulated to every state. "I am fully persuaded" that "the fate of our cause depends on [our] exertions" during the remainder of the year, he said in another missive that same month. But as he waited impatiently through the last weeks of spring and first days of summer for the arrival of the French army, Washington faced an array of problems. The states were not filling their manpower quotas, and with July in the offing, not a single draftee had come into camp. He hoped to have a plan of action prepared to present to Rochambeau when he landed in America, but so long as the size of the French army remained a mystery, no preparations could be made. That was the least of it. Washington feared that Clinton might take the offensive following his return from Charleston, and—sounding very much like his opposite number—the American commander expressed his apprehension that his army of "a mere handful of men" would be "at the mercy of a formidable enemy." Americans are "dreaming of Independence," Washington scolded, but it cannot be achieved by a "distressed" army that at best could wage an "inglorious campaign." Even if Clinton did not act, Washington feared trouble. His soldiers were so destitute of food and clothing that the army must soon disband or "subsist on the plunder of the people," he cautioned. But that dilemma was a problem for the future. For now, veteran officers, some ill, some bitter from the woes they and their men faced, were quitting the army, leaving it with a less experienced cadre of leaders.[65]

June had been unremittingly gloomy, but July saw hopeful occurrences. Buoyed by word of the efforts of Paine and Esther Reed, and a few from among Philadelphia's elite, Washington spoke glowingly of the "spirit of animation" that "has diffused itself" in several quarters. Furthermore, nearly a thousand new recruits trickled into camp during the first days of July. That was a fraction of what he was longing for, but he hoped it presaged the arrival of an abundance of troops. Maybe his army would yet be "in a Condition" to join with the French in a campaign of "vigor and efficacy." Still, Washington worried. He knew that the moment the French arrived, they would be greeted with the news that Charleston was lost and with it a huge American army. He agonized, too, over the possibility that his ally would be forced to remain inactive for weeks or months because the American army was too weak to take the field. With the clock ticking and perhaps only one hundred days or so days of the campaign season remaining in the northern states, he feared the year would slip away with no action having been taken by the Allies. If that were the case, Washington anguished that the French would lose faith in their ally. Something else troubled Washington. If a showdown with Clinton's army in New York was indeed looming, he wanted America's soldiery to play a vital role. It was essential "to our national character," he said, that American independence not be won by the French. "[O]ur honor demand[s]" that Americans be responsible for winning American independence. It would be a matter of pride for the citizenry in the new American nation to understand that Americans had played the decisive role in winning this war.[66]

In mid-July, Washington told Congress, "So much is at stake, so much to be hoped, so much to be lost" if the Continental army was not ready when the French arrived. The very next day a messenger brought word that the French had landed in Rhode Island five days earlier. Washington responded by telling the governor of New Hampshire, "This is the time for America by one great exertion to put an end to the war."[67]

CHAPTER 7

VICTORIES, SETBACKS, AND MISSED OPPORTUNITIES

GENERAL ROCHAMBEAU, SURROUNDED by grenadiers lest Tories try to kidnap him, had been rowed ashore in Newport on July 11, the French landing that caused Sir Henry Clinton such consternation. Rochambeau found the city's shops closed, the streets deserted, and the wary residents inside their homes, not sure what to make of French soldiers who before the American Revolution had long been New England's hated and feared enemy. A disgruntled French officer said that America's new ally had not received the "reception on landing, which we expected and which we ought to have had." Within a few hours, however, Rochambeau and other officers met with several citizens and put to rest their uneasiness. One thing that smoothed relations almost instantly was that the French army needed horses, wagons, livestock, and colossal amounts of provisions of all kinds, and Rochambeau had brought specie with which to pay for what he got. Newport was soon illuminated to honor the newcomers, and in a matter of days, a merchant who was making money from the city's guests described the French officers as "the most civilized men I ever met." Nor was American help confined to money-making matters. Nearly 2,000 Continentals from the Rhode Island and Massachusetts state lines soon joined the French, as did approximately 1,500 Yankee militiamen. In addition, American physicians, including Dr. James Craik, Washington's private doctor in Virginia who had joined the army, set up medical facilities to care for the hundreds of soldiers who had been felled by scurvy and dysentery during the Atlantic crossing. In no time the officers were intermingling with Newport's residents at dances and other social gatherings, the French were publishing a newspaper on a printing press they had lugged across the sea, and the initial distrust was a distant memory.[1]

As had been prearranged in France months before, Rochambeau used Lafayette as his go-between with Washington, an arrangement with which America's commander was comfortable. ("I confide [in Lafayette] as a friend from whom I conceal nothing," Washington not entirely truthfully informed the French.) Rochambeau had not been in Newport more than a few hours when he wrote Washington to notify him of the landing. An ebullient Washington wasted no time in expressing his gratitude at this "mark of friendship" displayed by Louis XVI and, with the campaign season nearing its halfway mark, suggesting that the two commanders needed to "immediately . . . fix our plan of operations." Washington, in fact, was ready with a plan. Despite his many despondent letters to Congress about his army possibly being too weak to cooperate with the French, Washington and his generals had begun working on a plan of action shortly after it was learned that a French army and fleet were coming. Washington had advised his officers that the French army would fight anywhere in America that the "interest or safety of the states may require," and—unaware at the time of the fate of General Lincoln's army in Charleston—he calculated that there would be several thousand more Allied than enemy soldiers in North America. Within twenty-four hours of learning that the French had landed, Washington put his plan in Lafayette's hands for presentation to Rochambeau.[2]

Since trailing Clinton's army across New Jersey in 1778, Washington's thinking had been riveted on New York, and he proposed a joint operation to retake the city once the Allies possessed naval superiority. This plan bore resemblances to the formula he had conceived when awaiting d'Estaing more than a year earlier, but there were important differences. Once the French navy controlled New York Harbor and the Hudson and East Rivers, Washington suggested that American forces cross to the north side of Manhattan—including some of what today is known as the Bronx—while the French took up positions on the north side in Westchester and to the south in Brooklyn. As he nowhere mentioned a siege operation, Washington appears to have envisioned concerted assaults on assorted British-held sectors.[3]

Before the end of July, about six weeks before Admiral Rodney's fleet arrived in New York, Lafayette laid Washington's plan before Rochambeau and Ternay. It died a quick death. For one thing, Rochambeau's most immediate concerns were to defend his army from a possible attack by Clinton and Arbuthnot and to nurse his ill soldiers back to health. Furthermore, due to what Lafayette called a "great mismanagement in the affair of transports" at Brest, there had been sufficient craft for Rochambeau to bring over only 4,000 men. The general would not consider any step until the remaining men—possibly 2,500, but hopefully 3,500—and additional ships of the line arrived. That might occur within the next four weeks, but the amount of time required to ready an expedition and get it across the Atlantic was always unpredictable. Even if the additional troops, equipment, and supplies arrived within the next few days, Rochambeau in effect replied, his army could not take the field before mid-August, and then it would not assail Clinton's defenses. It would conduct a siege. What is more, it was doubtful that the Allies in 1780 would possess adequate numbers for a siege. Moreover, before any action was taken, Rochambeau said that he expected the Americans to address their "wants of arms and ammunition" and gather an ample supply of boats.[4]

Washington was bitterly disappointed. Soon he was even more distraught. The American frigate *Alliance* had crossed from France and landed in Boston in mid-August, and its arrival was accompanied by good and bad news. Its cargo hold contained two thousand muskets and powder for Washington's soldiers, but no clothing. Worse by far was word that the dozen vessels and additional battalions that Ternay and Rochambeau had anticipated were blockaded in Brest by the Royal Navy. It was anyone's guess when, or if, the remaining French forces would reach America. Washington thought he would be extremely fortunate if the French reinforcements arrived during October, which was perilously close to the time when armies traditionally entered winter quarters.[5]

More than four months had passed since Washington first learned that France was sending an army. He had dreamed of joint operations in the summer, but now the 1780 campaign season was ebbing away. It was likely that a third straight summer and fall would elapse without his army undertaking a major initiative. Frustrated as he was, Washington nevertheless understood. Should Rochambeau's army be hurled into battle against forbidding odds, it—like d'Estaing's forces in Savannah—might suffer a mortifying defeat, and another crippling French setback could be catastrophic for the Allied war effort.[6] Patience was one of Washington's virtues. Lafayette, on the other hand, was young, impulsive, militarily unseasoned, and devoured by hopes of winning glory. He dashed off a twelve-page letter to Rochambeau and Ternay appealing to them to consider a near-term campaign for New York.

Lafayette insisted that time was running out and that something must be done very soon, considering the likely length of the campaign to retake New York. By year's end, he said, Washington would "no longer have militia" and 50 percent of his army "would be disbanded." At present, he went on, the combined Allied armies were greater in number than the fourteen thousand men that Clinton was thought to command in New York. (Clinton at nearly the same moment reported having 11,500 men fit for duty out of a total of nearly 14,000.) It "is very important to take advantage of the times when you find an opportunity for cooperation here," Lafayette lectured the veteran French commanders.[7]

Rochambeau was not amused. All along he had been puzzled by Washington's infatuation with Lafayette, and this only added to his bafflement. Rochambeau remarked to Chevalier de La Luzerne, the French minister in Philadelphia, that he considered Lafayette a "hotheaded" advocate of "extravagant things" that would result in the destruction of the French army by the English navy. Rochambeau was firm but gentle in responding to Lafayette, and the admonition he gave the fame-seeking young officer may in the long run have done him worlds of good. Rochambeau began by saying that he was writing as "an old father . . . to a cherished son whom he loves and esteems immensely." From there, Rochambeau explained that he need not be "roused to action." He would act when the time was right: "[You think] the French are invincible, but I am going to confide in you a great secret based on forty years' experience. There are no troops easier to defeat" than those who have "lost confidence in their commander, and they lose that confidence when they have been put in danger because of private or personal ambition" on the part of their commander. Men had died under his command, Rochambeau acknowledged, but "I need not reproach myself that a single one was killed for my own advantage." He closed with sound advice for the youngster: "the warmth of your feelings and your heart had overheated the calmness and prudence of your judgment. Preserve this last quality in the council, and keep all of the first for the moment of action."[8]

Lafayette was not the only one pushing Rochambeau to act. La Luzerne told the general that restive members of Congress were asking "indiscrete questions"—queries that frankly embarrassed him, he added—about when France's armed forces would do something. If New York was off the table for the time being, the diplomat went on, perhaps Rochambeau and Ternay should consider a winter campaign in the South.[9] La Luzerne's note may have nudged Rochambeau to meet with Washington sooner rather than later, though all along the French commander had mulled over numerous matters that he wished to bring up with his ally. Rochambeau had not been impressed by what he had seen of America's ragged and ill-equipped troops. He was skeptical, too, that Washington would ever have thirty-five thousand men under him, a figure the Americans had of late bandied about. Rochambeau and Ternay had additionally been shocked by America's cascading morale. Lafayette had warned Rochambeau that the Americans were so exhausted they might not be able to campaign in 1781. Rochambeau did not know whether that was true or whether Lafayette had fabricated his report to provoke him to act immediately. As sometime in 1781 was in all likelihood the earliest the French army could take the field, Rochambeau was eager to learn what Washington had to say on that score. Atop everything else, Rochambeau was anxious to size up Washington and to speak with him directly rather than through Lafayette. Washington was no less avid about meeting the French commanders. The two agreed to meet in Hartford on September 20.[10]

As the date of the meeting neared, the plight of Washington's army worsened. He was compelled to bring it near Fort Lee, across the Hudson from Manhattan, in search of food, and it was from there that he set off on horseback for the three-day trek to Hartford. During the first evening of his journey, Washington stayed at the home of an acquaintance at King's Ferry, not far below Verplanck's Point, and there to his delight he was joined for dinner by Benedict Arnold, recently named the new commander of the American installation at West Point. Arnold was a long way from his post, but he explained that he had come downriver to see that a damaged beacon had been repaired. Washington thought nothing of it. In fact, if he thought about it all, Washington likely admired Arnold's pluck, as he had made a long, arduous journey despite still being hobbled from the wound he had suffered in the fighting at Bemis Heights.[11]

Rochambeau and Ternay traveled by carriage from Newport to Hartford—a tiny town that a French officer characterized as "not worth lingering" in—where for two days they met with Washington. Numerous officers and aides had accompanied the leaders on both sides. Lafayette, Henry Knox, and Alexander Hamilton were among the fifty or so in Washington's entourage. But when the three commanders got down to business, Lafayette, who took notes and served as a translator, was the only other person in the room. The French were impressed by Washington, finding him to be grave and dignified, contemplative, businesslike, and meticulous. Right off the bat, the French told him that a New York campaign was out of the question until the remainder of their forces arrived. Strangely, Washington, who since 1778 had steadfastly opposed Congress's nearly unanimous entreaties to invade Canada—sometimes arguing that it should not be considered as it might result in France reclaiming the region—broached the subject of a joint Franco-American campaign to take Quebec. The French were not interested. In the end, the two sides agreed to do nothing until French naval superiority was attained, but thereafter the "reduction of New York" was to be "the most important and most decisive" priority. It was agreed that the Allies would best be served at the time of the New York campaign by having a joint "land army" totaling thirty thousand men, a sufficient number for a siege operation. That would require the Americans to furnish some twenty-five thousand men for the enterprise. The senior officers also tackled the thorny matter of what to do should the anticipated French reinforcements not arrive. If that was the case when winter set in and the armies were immobilized, at least a portion of Ternay's French navy was to undertake "an expedition . . . against the enemy in the Southern states."[12]

Washington had gotten all that he could reasonably have expected to attain and was in good spirits when he started back to New Jersey, but as he wished to inspect West Point, which he had not seen in ten months, the commander took a different route on returning to his army. Washington was wont to refer to West Point as of "great importance," but Knox better expressed the feelings of the commander: The post must be "regarded, by every person of judgment as the object of greatest importance, on the Continent, and to the maintenance of which every thing else ought to give place."[13]

Seven months earlier, Washington had named General Robert Howe, who had defended Savannah against Colonel Archibald Campbell's attack in December 1778, to command the forces at West Point. Soon thereafter, Arnold approached Washington about having that assignment, pleading—truthfully it appears—that his leg was healing so slowly that he could not handle an arduous field command. Washington brushed aside his entreaties, indicating that for the time being the British posed no threat to that vital post. But following the arrival of Rochambeau's army and the danger it faced in July and August from a possible attack by Clinton and Arbuthnot,

Washington prepared to move his army into position for action in New York. This was the point when Clinton, like a clairvoyant, had predicted that Washington would assemble every available man to protect the French—or West Point, if threatened—and that the rebel commander's strategy might include an attack on New York in the event that the British went after the French in Newport. Washington was indeed contemplating an attack on New York should the British assail the French, and he hoped that Arnold would be part of the campaign should it materialize. Aware that Arnold's leg had by midsummer healed to the point that he could again ride a horse, Washington offered him command of the left wing of the army that was earmarked for advancing on Britain's outposts in northern Manhattan.

Washington had long admired Arnold as a brave, daring, and fearless officer who excelled at leading men. He had divined those qualities in Arnold during his first weeks in command of the Continental army, and Washington selected him to lead one wing of the incursion into Canada in the autumn of 1775. Arnold's heroism in that undertaking, conceivably the most challenging assignment faced by any American commander in the Revolutionary War, confirmed Washington's judgment, and in the years that followed he had stuck with Arnold through thick and thin. He badly wanted him back in the field in the summer of 1780. But to his surprise, Arnold begged off, once again asserting that his leg would not permit him to take on the rigors of a field command. Instead, he again asked to be named commandant at West Point. Washington, in retrospect, said that he was surprised by Arnold's response and thought he behaved strangely. At the time, however, the unsuspecting Washington simply took Arnold at his word. He moved Howe into a field command in the Highlands and, on August 3, put Arnold in charge of West Point.[14]

What Washington could not know was that he was dealing with a would-be traitor. Arnold's turn toward treason sprang from many sources. He justifiably felt that Congress had treated him shabbily, promoting junior officers over him, quite belatedly awarding him the promotion that he felt he had earned, and refusing to grant him the back pay that was his due. Nine months after his wounding, while still hobbling on a cane and unable to mount a horse, Arnold accepted appointment as military governor of Philadelphia following its June 1778 evacuation by Clinton's army. Washington had made the appointment, and it was one of his poorest decisions. Putting a man of Arnold's temperament in Philadelphia made the likelihood of substantial trouble almost inescapable. Immodest and overbearing, assertive and contentious, and driven by a stubborn yearning for wealth and social prestige, Arnold soon clashed with powerful Philadelphians. Some came to distrust or dislike him for hobnobbing with presumed Loyalists and eventually marrying Peggy Shippen, the daughter of a reputed Philadelphia Tory. Some were disgusted by his lavish lifestyle. Some saw, or suspected, unsavoriness in many of his financial dealings, including war profiteering and misusing state property. Before long, Arnold was indicted by Pennsylvania authorities on several counts of financial misdealing. He was found guilty on two of the charges.

His seething anger led him to open clandestine discussions with the British as early as April 1779, but he and Clinton did not come to terms until midsummer 1780, soon after word of the fall of Charleston reached New York. It was a time when the rebels' ongoing troubles in the southern states seemed to many, including perhaps to Arnold, to doom the chances of American independence. After prolonged negotiations, Clinton and Arnold struck a bargain. Arnold, by then the commander of America's Hudson Highland installations—which included West Point—was to surrender that post and the men who garrisoned it. In return for his treachery, Arnold was to become a general officer in the king's army and receive £20,000 if the British actually gained the fortress. He wanted £10,000 if the plan was attempted but failed, though in the end he accepted Clinton's offer of £6,000. Considering that on the eve of the war most skilled craftsmen would have had to work for sixty years or more to earn £6,000, Arnold had negotiated terms that would bring him a considerable fortune. On the other hand, Arnold knew that he would lose his Continental army pension (worth roughly £4,500 when commuted to ten years' full pay). If the United States gained its independence, Arnold was also aware that he would lose the property he owned in Connecticut, which he subsequently estimated to

have been valued at roughly £20,000. Clinton later said that Arnold's remu-
neration was "indemnification for whatever loss of property he might
thereby sustain."[15]

Early in September, having chosen to go for West Point over a strike
against the French in Newport, Clinton hurried his preparations. The details
of Arnold's part of the operation were worked out in encrypted correspondence and discussions through intermediaries. No document outlining the
operation has been found, and it is unlikely the plans were ever committed
to paper. It is known that Arnold had long since provided Clinton with
detailed descriptions of the layout of West Point. Beyond that, postmortem
conjecturing about what Clinton and Arnold had agreed to centered
primarily on three theories. One was that Arnold had agreed not only to
divide the three thousand soldiers inside the facility into small detachments
but to disperse those outside the fortress, steps that would make West Point's
capture a simple task for the British. A second notion, advanced by Lafayette,
was that Arnold would simply surrender the fort and garrison at the appearance of the British force. A third guess was that Clinton would besiege the
installation, whereupon Arnold would request reinforcements from
Washington. As the relief force, perhaps led personally by Washington,
approached West Point, Clinton with superior numbers would overwhelm
it and Arnold would surrender the fort and garrison to the British.

It is known that Clinton envisaged a strike carried out by three thousand
British soldiers who were to be conveyed up the Hudson in a task force of
ships of war and troop transports commanded by Admiral Rodney. As
Clinton had already been readying an expedition to the Chesapeake, he
anticipated that Washington's spies would disclose that the frantic activity
at the docks in New York City was in preparation for yet another British
foray into the southern theater. Indeed, James Madison, a Virginia
congressman in Philadelphia, reported on September 19 that the fleet being
prepared in New York was to sail for either Virginia or South Carolina
within the next seven days.

By that September 19, the redcoats had boarded the transports, and the
force was only hours away from sailing on Clinton's "most important

project" up the Hudson. The orders to weigh anchors awaited only the completion of one last meeting between Arnold and a representative of Clinton for "settling the whole of the plan"—its timing, confirmation of the date of the strike, where General Washington was expected to be when the operation was carried out, and "an absolute certainty" that this was not a ruse and that Arnold indeed intended to turn coat. Clinton chose his young aide and confidant Major John André to confer with Arnold. The meeting was set for the night of September 20. André was in place, but Arnold encountered some hitches. Their meeting was rescheduled for near midnight on the following night. Clinton would not give the order to proceed until André returned to New York and confirmed that everything was set.[16]

Washington departed Hartford for West Point on September 23, about thirty-six hours after Andre and Arnold met. That very morning, a few hours before Washington commenced his long ride, André had been taken into custody by American militiamen near Tarrytown. André was behind American lines and out of uniform, and his captors found papers secreted in his stockings. Two days later, on the morning of September 25, Washington—still in the dark regarding Arnold's treachery—reached West Point. He sent some in his party on to Arnold's headquarters on the east side of the Hudson while he inspected the installation on the west side of the river. Later in the morning, Washington reached Arnold's headquarters and learned that none in his party had seen the commandant. What no one knew was that Arnold, alerted both to André's capture and Washington's pending arrival, had made a run for the *Vulture*, a British sloop of war anchored not far away. For several hours Washington and his men remained in the dark. But in the afternoon, when a messenger brought the papers found on André, Washington understood in a flash that Arnold had defected. He turned to Knox and raged: "Arnold has betrayed me. Whom can we trust now?" Just as quickly, on orders from Washington, Hamilton and others mounted up and chased after Arnold, but to no avail. The renegade had too great a head start. Clinton, "exceedingly shocked" by the "unexpected accident" of André's capture, called off the strike at West Point.[17]

Washington was deeply shaken. He felt personally violated by Arnold's disloyalty. Had Arnold's sedition succeeded, six years of suffering and sacrifice would have been for naught. Arnold had failed, but no one could say what the impact of his sordid act would be on America's already crumbling morale. Nor could anyone predict the response of the recently arrived French. What Washington did know was that he wanted to get his hands on Arnold or, short of that, to have him murdered. He sent John Champe, an intrepid Virginia volunteer with ample combat experience, to Manhattan, where he was to pose as a deserter. He was to kidnap Arnold if possible, kill him if necessary. Champe succeeded in enlisting in the Tory unit that Arnold commanded, but was transferred elsewhere before he could act.[18]

The nation was profoundly shocked by Arnold's treason. His effigy and that of Satan were carried through the streets of Philadelphia and burned before a huge throng. Other towns also staged mock executions. Congressmen denounced his "villainy," "iniquity," and "horrid plot," and blasted his "blackest Treason." Some, such as Samuel Adams, claimed they were not terribly surprised, as there were aspects of Arnold's character that had long caused them to harbor "suspicions" of the general. After all, said one congressman, Arnold was given to "nefarious practices." Another delegate thought Arnold had been "a Scourge to America Since the beginning of the Present War." Some army officers who had served with Arnold denounced him. Within two weeks Thomas Paine issued an essay branding Arnold a "desperado" but claiming to see a rainbow in the incident. With his ever-present keen eye for something reassuring, Paine pointed out that Arnold alone among the army's officers had betrayed the cause in six years of war; that, he claimed, was a sign of the strength of America's "national character." He additionally portrayed Clinton's recourse to the "black business" of "bribery" as confirmation of the enemy's desperation. One publisher proposed that hereafter Arnold's first name should be changed from "Benedict" to "*maledicted*" or possibly "Britain's *Benediction*." More than one screed equated Arnold's act with the greed and bent for luxury that had seized hold of so many on the home front. It was also said that while the country would survive Arnold, one could only wonder if the nation could weather the corruption that was eating at its soul. For his part, Arnold published an address to the Continental soldiery urging them to defect and "join me" in bringing to a "close the scene of our afflictions." It fell on deaf ears.[19]

Others besides Paine lashed out at Clinton for attempting to win the war through such an "unprincipled" tactic.[20] Clinton was not troubled by such barbs, but he was deeply anguished by the "unworthy fate" of Colonel André. Clinton loved and admired his aide, and he beat himself up for having failed to take greater precautions to guard against the young man's capture. Clinton entered into negotiations to free him, but the price the Americans demanded was a swap of André for Arnold, and the British commander could not make that bargain. A week after the plot unraveled, André was executed, leaving Clinton to mourn the tragic loss of this man of "the rarest endowments" of valor, intelligence, and amiability. That was not all that troubled Clinton. André's mission, and death, was in vain. West Point was still in rebel hands, and the French remained unmolested in Newport.[21]

CLINTON'S DOLEFUL FEELINGS that September were brightened by news of successes in South Carolina. In one of his final acts before departing Charleston, Clinton had appointed Major Patrick Ferguson to be the inspector of militia, a vital assignment, for given the British army's chronic manpower shortage after Saratoga, a Loyalist soldiery was crucial for "giv[ing] vigour" to the pacification of South Carolina and Georgia. Clinton's expectation was that in both provinces royal militia composed of young or unmarried men were to be raised; the militiamen might serve for six months annually, and they were to engage in patrol, occupation duties, frontline military service, and the disarming of the "notoriously disaffected." In addition, separate companies of "domestick militia," consisting of men above age forty, were to serve as occupation forces once an area had been cleared of rebel military units. While some quibbled that Ferguson was too much the old-school disciplinarian for militiamen, Clinton disagreed. He considered Ferguson "a very zealous, active, intelligent officer" who, given his charismatic qualities, could recruit Loyalists and mold them to be effective citizen soldiers. Now thirty-six, Ferguson hailed from an affluent Scottish family—his father was a lawyer, his uncle a general officer in the British army—and had studied at a military academy in London before beginning to soldier at age fifteen. He had fought in the Seven Years' War and served in America since the New York campaign. He was severely wounded at Brandywine, losing forever the use of his right arm. In the siege of Charleston, Ferguson had commanded the American Volunteers, an infantry corps of Tory regulars that played a substantive role in closing the last exits from the city.[22]

Clinton's instructions to Ferguson underscored the delicacy with which he believed the Loyalists had to be treated. Ferguson was to negotiate each recruit's length of service and permit each company to elect its officers, though in order to assure the proper degree of "order [and] regularity," he could add a sergeant from the regular army to each company. If he took such a step, Clinton warned, it "must be done with great caution so as not to disgust the men or mortify unnecessarily their love of freedom." Ferguson was also to act "without loss of time," an order with which he instantly complied. He was in the field a day or two after Clinton sailed for New York and was impressed by the Tory turnout. Within three months of the fall of Charleston, seven battalions of militia consisting of more than four thousand men had been formed. Ferguson's success led him to conclude that most South Carolinians were so "disgusted with the rebel government" that only a few "small detachments" of Loyalist militia would be necessary for securing large portions of the province. Ferguson's sparkling reports were echoed by those of Lieutenant Colonel Nisbet Balfour, posted along with six hundred men in Ninety Six, deep in western South Carolina. "I am almost certain of no resistance from the Back Country," Balfour informed Cornwallis early in June. Similarly, Lieutenant Colonel Alexander Innes of the South Carolina Royal Regiment reported to Cornwallis that even "the most violent rebels are candid enough to allow the game [is] up and are coming to make their submission in great numbers." Lieutenant Colonel

Archibald McArthur, a battalion commander in the Highlanders, advised that the "country people in general seem desirous to return to their allegiance" to Great Britain. The bevy of good news, as well as what he was learning on his own, led Cornwallis in June to notify Clinton that there was "an end to all resistance in South Carolina." He would remain in South Carolina for a few weeks, Cornwallis said, but in September, when the Tory militia had been satisfactorily recruited and organized, he intended to make an incursion into North Carolina. He hoped to recruit Loyalists, but also to reduce North Carolina "to its duty." He said there was the "greatest probability" that he could achieve his ends. Once he had succeeded, he went on, North Carolina would become a "barrier" that would prevent the rebels up north from retaking South Carolina and Georgia.[23]

While Ferguson recruited militiamen, efforts to raise Loyalist provincial corps were underway as well. The British had largely ignored the Tories in 1775 and 1776, but by the end of the following year eight Loyalist regiments composed of some 3,700 men, mostly from New York, New Jersey, and Pennsylvania, had come into being. The ranks of the provincial units had swelled to about 6,700 men by the beginning of 1780, and several corps accompanied Clinton to Charleston. Shortages of "articles necessary for troops in . . . the field" inhibited recruiting in South Carolina for several weeks after Charleston's fall, but by mid-August commissions had been issued for raising two provincial corps. Recruiting lagged, though within a year eleven Loyalist regiments within Britain's Provincial Line were posted here and there throughout the southern theater.[24]

The sunny news from the South left Clinton as optimistic as this naturally pessimistic man could be. He notified Germain of Britain's "stage of success" in the South, adding the upbeat prognosis that there was "little resource for domestic insurrection" in South Carolina's backcountry.[25] Nor was it only the turnout by Tories that excited Clinton. He was awed, and heartened, by the number of enslaved people who had fled to the British during and after the siege of Charleston. Clinton exhibited a consistently enlightened view toward America's enslaved inhabitants. In the course of his role in the Carolinas campaign in 1776, Clinton had created a company of Black Pioneers composed of southern slaves. Outfitted with uniforms, the roughly seventy-five initial members worked as laborers alongside regular troops. Clinton mandated that they be "decently clothed" and paid the same wages as privates in the army, directed the company commander to "treat these people with tenderness and humanity," and declared that they "shall be entitled (as far as depends upon me) to their freedom" following the war. By war's end, more than two hundred men were serving in the Black Pioneers. During the year prior to the siege of Charleston, Clinton had issued what came to be known as the Phillipsburg Proclamation, a decree in which he announced that all rebel-owned slaves who fled behind British lines would have "full security" against being sold or surrendered to a claimant, as well as the opportunity to pursue any work they "shall think proper." Clinton said that he had taken the step to stay the hand of the Continental army, which had been accepting African American enlistees for more than a year. However, shortly after Lincoln's capitulation in May 1780, Clinton sent clarifying recommendations to Cornwallis and General James Patterson, whom he named as the military commandant of Charleston.

Clinton suggested that enslaved people owned by Loyalists who had fled to Britain's army were to be returned to their owners, but on the condition that they were not to be punished for having taken flight; if punished, the enslaved people were to be surrendered to royal authorities. Runaway slaves owned by rebels were to serve the British for the duration of the war—Clinton envisaged them assisting the British as pilots, guides, scouts, soldiers, and, above all, laborers—and following Britain's victory they were to be rewarded with emancipation for their faithful service. Although Clinton did not establish it as a mandated policy, he conjectured to his two subordinates that following the war it might be wise to grant the freedmen lands taken from the rebels. Clinton's motivation was a blend of humanitarianism and military strategy, as he hoped that his pronouncements would trigger flights for freedom that would ameliorate his army's manpower needs and undermine morale among rebel slaveowners. He was surprised by the staggering number of enslaved people who risked life and limb to reach his army. So many descended so quickly on the British army that the military and civil authorities were overwhelmed, leading Clinton to take five hundred escapees with him back to New York. One British officer remarked that this was a kind of "property we need not seek, it flies to us and famine follows" among their former rebel owners.[26]

After a month of filing several radiant reports, Cornwallis's letters to Clinton in July took on a disquieting tenor. In part, Cornwallis's changed outlook was the result of communiqués from Colonel Balfour, the commander of the Royal Welch Fusileers and a veteran of nearly twenty years' service who had fought in several important engagements in the war's initial two years and was unequivocally trusted by his commander, who soon would name him commandant of Charleston. In June, Balfour had roamed the backcountry before leading six hundred men to garrison the important post of Ninety Six. At first, Balfour had found "every thing quiet in all this part of the country," though ominously he indicated that this was likely to be true "*only* for a short time." Within two weeks, Balfour thought conditions had worsened. "Things are by no means in any sort of settled state, nor our friends [the Loyalists] so numerous as I expected." A month later, he was decidedly pessimistic, as he was finding "the enemy exerting themselves wonderfully and successfully in stirring up the people."[27] Cornwallis's previous upbeat outlook also deteriorated following word that a detachment from Banastre Tarleton's British Legion led by Captain Christian Huck—a lawyer in prewar Philadelphia who had taken up arms as an officer in the provincial unit—was surprised on July 12 by rebel partisans near the North Carolina border. Huck was killed and about ninety of his men were casualties.[28]

Worse yet, in the days that followed, bands of rebel guerrillas formed and launched raids against British posts, patrols, and supply lines. When the opportunity arose, they even engaged sizable units of Britain's army. The largest irregular force was led by Thomas Sumter, a forty-six-year-old former Indian fighter who had also fought to defend Charleston in 1776. A wealthy planter who sat in South Carolina's assembly, Sumter quit soldiering after the first year of the war and remained inactive even during the siege of Charleston. He might never again have taken up arms had Tarleton's men not burned his plantation in the course of their pursuit of Buford. That "roused the spirit of the lion," some said, and despite his penchant for sarcasm and habit of radiating a superior manner, Sumter drew others to him. Within days of Sumter's initial foray, Colonel Francis Marion, another well-to-do planter who had served as an officer in the Continental army and would be dubbed the "Swamp Fox," formed his own irregular force and launched attacks in the low country between the Santee and Pee Dee Rivers.

Men flocked by the hundreds to these partisan bands. Some soldiered in hopes that American independence would result in meaningful social, economic, and political reforms. Some, mostly Scotch-Irish Presbyterians, were driven by the dream of escaping what they saw as the tyranny of the Anglican Church. Some wanted to settle scores against old personal enemies. Sumter and Marion owned enslaved people and some who joined their guerrilla bands did so in the hope of attaining enslaved people owned by Tories. A great many, perhaps most, fought to revenge heavy-handed actions by British soldiers and their Tory adjuncts, including rapes (at times in the presence of horrified loved ones), assaults, thefts (especially of slaves), the wanton destruction of property, abuse of captives, and seemingly indiscriminate executions. The residents had been left "like sheep among wolves," said one plundered South Carolinian; former governor John Rutledge called the British occupation "Wanton and Savage." "I detest the British Army, and despise from my Soul the mass of unfeeling men who compose its Officers," said one of the province's delegates to Congress. A Georgetown planter declared that he would have welcomed the "returning beams of Royal Government," but he and many of his neighbors had been driven into the arms of the rebels by the "horror of war" visited on them by the "British Commanders, & Officers." Darker urges led some to join the fight as partisans. As in every war, some were drawn to arms because formal hostilities liberated them from civil restraints, freeing them to happily practice malevolence in its basest forms. Men of this sort committed deeds every bit as ghastly as those of their most brutish adversaries, convincing more than one

British officer that backcountry South Carolinians were "more Savage than the Indians." (Cornwallis spoke of the "horrid outrages," including "shocking Tortures and inhuman murders which are everyday" perpetrated by the guerrillas; his counterpart, General Nathanael Greene, later said that the warriors on both sides "pursue each other with as much relentless fury as beasts of prey.") Whatever motivated the partisans, by the end of August somewhere in the vicinity of 1,000 men were serving under Sumter or Marion, and their grizzly strikes were taking a toll. In the thirty days following Huck's demise, approximately 350 regulars and Tories died or were wounded at the hands of the partisans. The royal militia abandoned some sites, and attrition had become a matter of considerable concern for Cornwallis, who was compelled to detach men from other essential duties to search for his guerrilla adversaries.

Just two weeks after notifying Clinton that resistance had ended in South Carolina, Cornwallis advised him, "Affairs . . . do not look so peaceful as they did." He told Clinton about "violent rebels" in the field, adding that their "little blow[s]" had resulted in the death of British officers. He went on to say that he feared their every success would "encourage the enemy," strengthening their hand and giving rise to even more guerrilla sorties. For the first time, too, Cornwallis in July expressed doubts about the value of the Loyalist militia, calling many of these citizen soldiers "useless" and—like General Augustine Prevost a year earlier—insisting that only "a considerable regular force" could pacify South Carolina. (After another six weeks Cornwallis said that these militiamen "fail so totally when put to the trial" that dependence could be placed on "Provincial corps alone.") Despite the dark picture he had painted, Cornwallis assured Clinton, "We have not . . . on the whole lost ground." But after another two weeks Cornwallis noted that the "whole country" north of Charleston between the Pee Dee and Santee Rivers was "in an absolute state of rebellion." In mid-August, a very worried Cornwallis told Clinton that the supply routes that coursed through North Carolina—connecting the northern provinces to South Carolina and Georgia, and over which the arms, ammunition, and stores that sustained rebel military efforts in the low country—must be closed. These supplies, mostly of French origin (though some were derived through successful raids by American privateers), entered the country primarily through New England, after which they flowed south to storage depots in the Hudson Highlands, Morristown, Trenton, and Philadelphia, or sped through Pennsylvania, Delaware, and Maryland to Virginia and ultimately the Carolina and Georgia low country via Charlotte. If the supply chain was not plugged, Cornwallis advised, it would be "impossible to hold" South Carolina, and he revealed to Clinton his intention of launching a foray into North Carolina to seal shut the rebels' lifeline. To protect his right flank, Cornwallis urged Clinton to send a raiding force to the Chesapeake, a measure aimed at tying down North Carolina's militiamen far to the east of Charlotte.[29]

Cornwallis was additionally interested in an incursion into North Carolina as a result of intelligence reports that another American army was forming at Hillsborough, northeast of Charlotte, a successor to the army lost at Charleston. Though loathe to take the field in the region's brutal summer heat, Cornwallis felt that he had no choice, for the partisans in South Carolina would draw sustenance from the new rebel army.

Cornwallis's information concerning the raising of another rebel army was accurate. In the wake of Charleston, the ranking American officer in the Southern Department was Major General Johann Kalb. Although born to Bavarian peasants, he called himself "Baron de Kalb." After serving in the French army in the warfare of the 1740s and 1750s, France's foreign ministry sent him to America in 1768 to assess the likelihood of the colonies going to war with Great Britain. Once war broke out, he volunteered to fight for America, and in 1777 he crossed the Atlantic with Lafayette. Some thought Kalb was similar to Washington in many respects. Like Washington, he was not well educated, but he, too, was courageous and sensible. There were differences, however. While Washington enjoyed wine with his meals, Kalb did not drink and his tastes were simpler; he thrived on the companionability of camp life and existed on a diet of beef and bread. Just before Brandywine, Kalb was commissioned in the Continental army, and during the next three years he served in the North under Washington. But during the Charleston crisis, Kalb was ordered to march with 1,400 Maryland and Delaware Continentals to reinforce General Lincoln. He had gotten as far as Petersburg, Virginia, when he learned of Lincoln's surrender, but he continued on into North Carolina and in July reached Coxe's Mill, not far from Charlotte, where he found some 2,600 Virginia and North Carolina militiamen. Kalb was eager to fight, but he wanted no part of commanding the army, a stance unimaginable on Washington's part. Kalb, who was eleven years older than Washington, may also have believed that he was too old to cope with the rigors of command in light of what one congressman aptly called the "indigested State of our Affairs" in the South. Kalb immediately urged Congress to appoint someone else to head the army in the South.[30]

Congress was divided between those who favored Nathanael Greene—who was known to be Washington's choice to succeed him in case of "an Accident happening"—and the supporters of Horatio Gates, the hero of Saratoga. Throughout the war, congressmen had on occasion sought to bring Washington into the selection of commanders in other departments, but he had steadfastly refused to become involved in what all too often was a process that turned more on political than military considerations. This time, too, Washington stayed out of the congressional battle and, in the end, Gates was awarded the post. Congress, in part, may have spurned Greene because of dustups with authorities that had occurred while he commanded the quartermaster corps during the past two years; in addition, some delegates thought he had been habitually ill-mannered toward Congress, often responding to them "with sneer & sarcasm." Gates, on the other hand, was not only a more experienced leader, but also one whose "perseverance and Indifatigable Industry," as one delegate put it, had made him a proven winner. Many congressmen also recollected that Yankee militiamen had rushed to serve under Gates in the Saratoga campaign. They knew, too, that few southern militiamen had taken up arms to help Lincoln defend Charleston, and most understood that militias would have to be a cornerstone of the rebel military effort in the South. Hoping that Gates could once again work his magic with citizen soldiers, Congress on June 13 appointed him to command the southern army. Its hope, one delegate told Gates, was that his "wisdom, patience, and fortitude" would carry the day.[31]

Even before setting off from his home near present Shepherdstown, West Virginia, Gates was fully aware that he would face staggering odds, though he did not know the half of it. At the time of his appointment, Congress believed that Cornwallis possessed about 5,200 men, an estimate that was nearly 50 percent off the mark. Gates knew for certain that Kalb had come south with far fewer troops than Cornwallis possessed, though he had no idea how many Carolina and Virginia militiamen had been sent to the front since Charleston's fall. As Gates rode south, he knew that he would be taking over an army "without strength" and "a Military Chest, without money." If that weren't bad enough, he believed he would be campaigning in a region that was "apparently Deficit in Public Spirit," an assumption based on the woeful militia turnout during the siege of Charleston. Knowing next to nothing about politics in the South, Gates attributed the citizenry's reluctance to help with the defense of Charleston to the region's harsh summer climate, which, he said, "increases Despondency, instead of animating The Soldiers Arm."[32] At times—late in 1776, for instance—Washington's prospects may have been equally bleak, but seldom in this war had he or any rebel commander faced such daunting challenges as those that confronted Gates in July 1780.

Gates stopped in Richmond to meet with Virginia's governor, Thomas Jefferson. Soon after independence was declared, Jefferson had left Congress, bent on revamping Virginia in ways that were unthinkable so long as it remained a British colony. For Jefferson, the American Revolution was about more than breaking away from Great Britain. It was also about transforming Virginia: broadening property ownership, voting rights, and educational opportunities; breaking the stranglehold on political power exercised by Tidewater planters; modernizing the legal system; instituting religious freedom; and possibly taking steps toward ending slavery. As a member of Virginia's assembly from 1776 into 1779, Jefferson was so focused on reforming his state that the war often appeared to hardly intrude on his thinking. He lived at home ten months out of the year, devoting much of his time to constructing his mansion, Monticello, tending his orchards and gardens, and entertaining British and Hessian prisoners of war captured at Saratoga and sent to out-of-the-way Charlottesville. Jefferson's seeming indifference to the war, not to mention his reform mindedness, created life-long resentments among some Virginians. But he seemed not to care until General Washington, in the winter of 1779, wrote that lacerating letter asking why Jefferson, among others, was not helping the United States in its hour of need. Jefferson admired Washington. He also feared him. No one with political ambitions could afford to make an enemy of Washington. Immediately after learning of the general's displeasure, Jefferson agreed to run for governor of Virginia. He was elected by the assembly in June 1779, taking office six months after Britain's reconquest of Savannah and three weeks after Sir George Collier's devastating raid on Virginia. Both were auguries of what for Jefferson was to be one of the most crisis-ridden gover-norships during the Revolutionary War.

Much of Jefferson's first year in office was consumed with raising the six thousand men that Virginia was to furnish each year to the Continental army and with making preparations for the possibility of another British raid. He devised a network of sentinels and express riders as safeguards against a surprise attack, and additionally erected armories, stockpiled weapons and powder, and constructed batteries on the coast and redoubts at strategic sites along Virginia's rivers, especially the James River. But it was not until the siege of Charleston, eight months after his inauguration, that Jefferson faced his first crisis. Washington exhorted him to send militiamen for Charleston's defense. Jefferson knew that to dispatch too many men was to leave his own state defenseless. Ultimately, he sent four hundred militia-men to Charleston, though they arrived after the entrances and exits to the city had slammed shut. Once word of Lincoln's surrender reached Richmond, Jefferson knew that the war was truly inching toward Virginia's doorstep. North Carolina was all that stood between Virginia and what many, like Cornwallis at the time, thought was the conquered province of South Carolina. When General Gates knocked on his door in July to ask for

Virginia's help in the fight against Cornwallis, Jefferson was left with no doubt that the war was perilously close to his state.[33]

In mid-July, Gates—burly, relentlessly ambitious, seasoned, self-assured, and self-absorbed—rendezvoused with a portion of his southern soldiery at Hillsborough, a hamlet roughly one hundred miles above the South Carolina border. Even before he was settled in, Gates bombarded Congress, Jefferson, and Abner Nash, North Carolina's governor, with demands. In all his years of soldiering, said Gates, "it has hitherto never fallen to my lot to witness a scene of such multiplied and increasing wants." He told Nash that the "Army is like a Dead Whale upon the Sea Shore, a monstrous carcass without Life." He needed arms and ammunition. In addition, his pantry was bare of meat and corn, and with neither Virginia nor North Carolina providing money for the acquisition of provisions, the army was reduced to foraging. Tents were needed as well, and so, too, were axes, hatchets, cartouche boxes (for carrying paper cartridges containing powder and lead balls), and bayonet belts. Two weeks following his arrival, Gates reproached Jefferson and Nash for their "unpardonable Neglect" of the soldiery. A first step in overcoming the army's "deplorable state," he told them, was to have cattle drivers bring "Droves of Bullocks" to the "half Starved" men. Jefferson was able to send axes, tomahawks, and horses, but it would be weeks before many of the other commodities sought by Gates could be sent, and given Virginia's economic distress, some items were unlikely ever to be shipped south.[34]

Thirteen days after entering North Carolina, Gates united with Kalb. Gates learned he possessed a bit more than 4,100 men, of which 1,400 were the Continentals that Kalb had brought south in April. There were also militiamen procured since Lincoln's surrender and a few men who had somehow escaped being taken captive in the debacle at Charleston. Sumter, whose irregular band of cavalry was the closest thing to an intelligence arm available to the army, informed Gates that the rebel soldiery—partisans, militia, and Continentals—outnumbered the king's forces dispersed throughout South Carolina's backcountry. As Cornwallis had posted three regiments in Charleston, Sumter's estimate was reasonably accurate. Within days, Gates also learned that an enemy force was gathering at Camden, not far across the South Carolina border. The British in Camden were commanded by Lord Francis Rawdon, a twenty-six-year-old lieutenant colonel who had brought the reinforcements from New York that Clinton had summoned during the siege of Charleston. Aware that a considerable force under Kalb and Sumter was not far away, and that Gates might be coming after him, Rawdon called in scattered forces from other posts. While Gates knew that the British commander in Camden was strengthening his position, he was apprised by Sumter that for at least the next two weeks the enemy would be substantially inferior in numbers to the force that the rebels could muster.[35]

During the Saratoga campaign, Gates had been a model of caution, adhering to a defensive strategy that he thought was the only viable means of contesting a highly trained, well-equipped regular army. But two weeks after taking command in North Carolina—and just days after reporting to Congress that he faced a "most unpromising prospect" with such a woebegone army—Gates scuttled what had worked for him in New York.[36] He put his army on the road to Camden. He was taking the offensive, planning to attack the inferior British force in Camden and thereafter, piece by piece, capturing all the enemy troops that succeeded in escaping his onslaught.

Gates had settled on taking a gigantic risk. He reckoned that if he could get his army to Camden rapidly, he might score a victory of such magnitude that Cornwallis would be thrown on the defensive, a turn of events that might ensure the safety of North Carolina—and Virginia—for the duration of the war. However, there were good reasons for not undertaking such a hazardous venture at this juncture. Gates faced no imminent threat, though he had to suspect that at some point Cornwallis would come after him. While he told Congress that his army one day would be put on a more sound footing, he knew that would take time and would be realized only after Herculean efforts by Virginia and North Carolina to raise and provision the forces they would contribute.[37] In addition, Gates had been with the army for such a short time that he did not know whose advice was trustworthy. Nor could he adequately assess the quality of the intelligence that he received. Above all, Camden was nearly 175 miles away, his ill-nourished men were not in the best shape, and it was midsummer in a scorchingly hot, humid region. Some of his officers counseled against any action, though the head of North Carolina's militia appears to have encouraged the planned attack. It was Gates's call. The choice he made astounded most of his officers and has perplexed historians. Why would a soldier with twenty years of experience who had never previously been a gambler suddenly decide that this gamble was worth taking?

Gates would have been less than human had he not chafed at his treatment and standing. At Saratoga, he had won America's greatest victory. Yet some among Washington's stalwart backers had scoffed at his achievement, crediting Schuyler with having taken the steps that made the triumph possible, trivializing the victory as an easy accomplishment given Gates's numerical superiority, and even preposterously finding fault with his strategy at Saratoga. Furthermore, since Saratoga, Washington appeared to have done everything he could to keep Gates from gaining more glory. He refused to put him in command in the Rhode Island campaign in 1778, and when nearly every congressman had urged an invasion of Canada—an undertaking for which Gates would have been a logical choice to command—Washington had fought tenaciously against an incursion. All the while, Washington, who had remained inactive for three years, had gained iconic status while Gates languished in the shadows. Now, in July 1780, Gates for the first time since Saratoga had a shot at an important victory, something no other American commander in the South could claim during the past four years and something that Washington had not achieved since Trenton-Princeton. No one can read Gates's mind during that torrid summer of 1780, but his gamble may have sprung from an overweening desire to eclipse Washington. While Gates wisely kept his feelings about Washington a closely guarded secret, there can be no doubt about his commitment to the ideals of the American Revolution. He had moved from England to America in 1772 in part because of the repugnance he felt toward his homeland's political and social systems, and when he signed on in 1775 to soldier against Great Britain, he said he was doing so in the hope of "preserv[ing] the Liberty of the Western World." When he came south to fight in 1780, he confided to Lincoln that when his time was up, he could "die in peace" knowing that he had played a role in making America "Free, and Independent," and assuring "its Future happiness under God." His desire for an iconic status akin to that of Washington was equaled by his dedication to America's cause.[38]

Gates blundered twice before his men took their first step toward Camden. Thinking time was of the essence, he ordered his army to march the shortest route. Had he taken the longer route through an array of settlements that included Charlotte, his army likely would have found adequate provisions. Instead, day after heat-blistered day, the weary men, sweat pouring down their dust-caked faces, slogged through a parched region nearly bereft of food. Gates also opted to leave most of his cavalry behind in North Carolina. Dragoons were the eyes of an army. Ranging far ahead of the advancing soldiery, the horse soldiers could relay information on enemy movements and strength. With no more than sixty cavalry troopers accompanying his army, Gates was proceeding nearly blindly.

Few American soldiers have endured the miseries experienced by Gates's men during the march southward. On August 14, two weeks after setting off, the men were in poor condition when they at last reached Rugeley's Mill, just north of Camden. Ill-nourished for days before the march began, they were weak, hungry, and exhausted as they came to the cusp of battle. Nor were all the men who had begun the march still there. Roughly eight hundred Virginia militiamen had abandoned the army, either from desertion or as their period of enlistment had expired. The horses carrying the few cavalry troopers in Gates's army had suffered too. One dragoon spoke of his "starved, broken-down horse" as the battle approached.[39] Gates now had some 3,400 mostly enervated men. In all likelihood, that led him to abandon his planned strike at the British in Camden. Instead, his thoughts turned in favor of taking up a defensive position. He felt the situation would compel Rawdon to attack, as Britain's supply lines were threatened by Sumter and Marion. Under cover of darkness on the sultry night of August 15, Gates marched his army one final time, hoping to establish a defensive position behind Granny Creek, just north of Camden. Before he reached the creek, Gates's army stumbled into the enemy, which was also on a night march. Gates was surprised. He was even more astonished to learn that the British force he had bumped into was not commanded by Colonel Rawdon but by General Cornwallis, who had set off from Charleston after receiving notification that Gates was approaching Camden. Cornwallis had a reputation for disliking defensive warfare, and in this instance he declared that it was "absolutely necessary to act offensively." He additionally asserted that his army must avoid "any serious insult," as that would curtail the Tories' inclination to turn out.[40] Thus, Gates had been moving south with the expectation of taking the offensive, while Cornwallis had come north to save his post and supply depot at Camden through an offensive operation.

Both commanders had good reasons for retreating without a fight. Given the unexpected size of his adversary, Gates now knew that his debilitated army faced a greater challenge than he had ever imagined. Cornwallis, on the other hand, thought he was outnumbered. His intelligence gatherers had reported that Gates possessed some five thousand men, nearly two thousand more than Cornwallis had mustered.[41] But both commanders felt they had no choice other than to prepare for battle. Gates feared that if he retreated, Cornwallis, with his four hundred dragoons under the feared Banastre Tarleton, would hunt down the rebel army and force a fight at some less desirable site. For his part, Cornwallis's thinking had never changed. He believed that he must act or run the risk of fatally disillusioning the Tories. Besides, even though Gates might have a larger army, it included a great many unseasoned militiamen. Cornwallis was confident that his force, composed mostly of regulars, was superior.

It was hazy and already steamy hot when the sun rose on August 16. In the first pink glow of day, Gates and Cornwallis, and their principal officers, hurried into the field to peer at the other army through their spyglasses. Gates watched as his adversary positioned his units. With little time to spare, he responded with orders for arranging his men. Cornwallis placed his regulars and the Irish Volunteers (a provincial unit that Rawdon had once commanded) on the right side of his line, while Tory militiamen composed most of the contingent on the British left. Adhering to standard military practice, Cornwallis posted two battalions of regulars and Tarleton's dreaded cavalry in the rear. For some unfathomable reason, Gates reacted by positioning his militiamen on his left, compelling his least experienced units to confront the adversary's most experienced troops, and North Carolina militia—widely regarded as undependable—in the vital center. Gates's regulars, under Kalb, were stationed on the rebels' right and would for the most part face Tory militiamen. Like Cornwallis, Gates, too, kept some men in reserve. It may have been that Gates's long-cherished faith in the militia—a conviction nourished by the militiamen's exemplary perfor- mance in the Saratoga campaign—led him to align his force as he did. Perhaps he believed they could hold the line while his regulars manhandled Cornwallis's Loyalist militia. But the militiamen at Saratoga had been fresh and well nourished, and some were battle-hardened veterans. The men at Camden were hardly rested and well fed, and few had ever come under fire.

Gates had intended a defensive stand, but when Cornwallis ordered his right wing to advance, the Americans misjudged the movement, concluding at the last second that their adversary was realigning his troops. Thinking he might take advantage of the confusion arising from the disarray caused by repositioning entire units, Gates in an instant scrapped his defensive scheme and ordered his militiamen to advance toward Cornwallis's regulars. In the open field, the militiamen, to their amazement, discovered that fear- some British veterans in their gaudy red coats were rapidly closing in on them. They saw sunlight glinting off the enemy soldiers' bayonets and heard the British over and over again shouting "Huzza" as they came forward. The menacing cadenced beating of British drums hung in the air. The king's soldiers appeared to embody scorn and malice. They also seemed unruffled and unfazed, and later in fact Cornwallis spoke of his men's "cool intre- pidity." It was enough to unnerve any callow soldier and to sow dread in the hearts of some who had experienced it before. As they came within range, the British opened fire. In the acrid smoke and thunderous din caused by thousands of muskets, it suddenly was difficult to see and nearly impossible to hear one's company commander. Virginia's citizen soldiers knew only that comrades were down, some with macabre wounds, and they knew, too, that they were in grave danger, for the British kept "up a constant fire" and made "use of bayonets as opportunities offered."[42] In the unimaginable tumult, fear turned into panic, and panic led the militiamen to break and run for their lives, speeding through the smoky chaos to escape the killing ground and their enemy's expected savage vengeance. They wanted to escape a ferocious enemy, to avoid being shot or stabbed, and above all else to find a safe spot where Tarleton's allegedly merciless troopers could not reach them.

The flight of these green soldiers brought on the prospect of imminent disaster for all the rebel soldiers still on the battlefield. Despite the target he presented, Gates heroically rode amid the militia seeking to stanch their bolt to the rear, and he called in the reserves, hoping their presence would have a calming effect. All his efforts were in vain. More and more soldiers threw down their arms and fled. The American left had completely collapsed. That was the signal for the British right to wheel and attack the American regulars on Gates's right flank. Assailed now from the front and the left, and seemingly from everywhere by Tarleton's horsemen, whom Cornwallis had unleashed, the American right wing was overwhelmed. There were heavy casualties. Kalb, bayoneted eight times and hit with three musket balls, was among the victims. Kalb and his men had fought valiantly, but now the survivors buckled and they, too, fled, abandoning comrades riven with pain from terrible wounds. Twice more Gates rode among the men in a futile effort to stem the calamity and save the day. Twice again he failed. Men bolted for the nearby woods, hid in a swamp east of the battlefield, and raced up the road they had come down a couple of days earlier. In the end, Gates also ran and didn't stop running until he reached Charlotte sometime in the dark of night. By then he had no idea of the whereabouts of his army.

Over eight hundred rebel soldiers were killed or wounded at Camden, or when hunted down by their pursuers in the long, terror-filled day that followed the engagement. For twenty-two miles, according to one British soldier, the road "was strewn with the wounded and killed, who had been overtaken by [Tarleton's] legion." It was, he added, "a perfect scene of horror."[43] In addition to seizing eight pieces of rebel artillery, "all their ammunition wagons, a great number of arms, and 130 baggage wagons," Cornwallis took some 700 prisoners, a considerable number of whom would perish in captivity. The general added that "there never was a more complete victory." His remark was not braggadocio. It was a statement of fact. Clinton saw it in the same light and heaped effusive praise on Cornwallis for his "signal services." Cornwallis's army had also paid a price for its victory, losing 324 men; but that was less than 10 percent of the British force, whereas more than 40 percent of Gates's army was lost. In a span of just over eighteen months—beginning with the fall of Savannah at Christmas 1778—American forces had lost approximately 7,800 who were killed, wounded, or captured in engagements in the southern theater, a grievous toll and one that nearly equaled Britain's losses in Burgoyne's failed invasion of New York.[44]

For the second time in ninety days an American army had been destroyed in the South. No rebel army stood in Cornwallis's way should he immediately advance into North Carolina. It appeared as if the American rebellion was close to having been quashed from Savannah to the southern border of Virginia, a state that for the first time in the war had experienced a destructive British raid during those demoralizing eighteen months since Savannah fell to the king's army. The catastrophe at Camden ruined Gates's once-exalted reputation. He had committed error upon error, blunders that were crowned by the abandonment of his army, in which some men were continuing to fight. His folly would follow him like his shadow for the remainder of the war. Gates guessed correctly that Congress would replace him. He may also have presumed that he was the object of derision, both for what was called the "absurdity" of his many misconceived decisions and even more for "running away . . . from his whole army," as one critic put it. A Massachusetts congressman who admired Gates predicted immediately that "the Old Gent. Will be sneered at." He was correct. Little time passed before Alexander Hamilton, who had long harbored a bitter loathing of Gates, fearing he would eclipse Washington, whom he regarded as "an Aegis very essential to me," ridiculed the old general. Benjamin Rush, a former congressman and army officer who thoroughly understood the personalities and politics of the Continental army, astutely surmised that the sprays of venom directed at Gates were not solely for what had happened at Camden but also for his victory at Saratoga, a stupendous triumph that had caused some to conclude that Washington was his inferior as a general. A Loyalist newspaper in New York satirically offered a reward of three million dollars to anyone who could provide information leading to the discovery of the late Continental army in the South; the bogus document was "signed" by "HORATIO GATES." But it was no laughing matter for those who sat in Congress. One delegate summed up the setback as "ruinous" for the "Southern States." As New York's Robert R. Livingston put it, every member of Congress knew full well that "our prospects grow more & more faint every day."[45]

The shooting had hardly ended at Camden before Cornwallis apprised Clinton of his forthcoming incursion into North Carolina. The commander in chief did not balk so long as Charleston and South Carolina remained safe, for—as Clinton reminded Cornwallis—they were *the principal and indispensable objects of his attention.* Cornwallis ticked off his objectives: close the supply lines to South Carolina's partisans and the next rebel army that Congress dispatched to the South; spur Loyalists to rally to arms; and destroy the remnants of Gates's army and the rebels' indispensable magazines inside North Carolina. Cornwallis did not move immediately on the heels of Camden. His plan, he told Clinton, was to put his first division in motion during the second week of September, a month after the showdown at Camden. The remainder of his force would march out of South Carolina about ten days later. For a second time, he also beseeched Clinton to send a force to the Chesapeake as a diversion. Barring that, he pleaded for reinforcements.[46]

Clinton subsequently criticized Cornwallis for not having immediately advanced into North Carolina without delay. Had he acted while "terror and dismay" stalked the countryside, said Clinton, Cornwallis could easily have destroyed "the scattered debris" of Gates's army, finishing off the entirety of the rebel military forces in the South.[47] Clinton must have forgotten that moving an army was easier said than done. Cornwallis's men were exhausted and hungry, having made a long, wearying summertime march from Charleston to Camden, after which they immediately went into battle. Moreover, not only did Cornwallis's army have to be resupplied, but steps had to be taken to secure its supply lines, which the likes of Sumter—whom Cornwallis now called "an active and daring man"—would see as a tempting target. Two weeks after Camden, Cornwallis remained "without either flour or meal" and his horses, which had been unable to forage all the while, were "wretched beyond description." Many of his men were sick, felled from their exertions in the merciless heat that Cornwallis characterized as equal to that found in the tropics. Cornwallis's wounded also had to be cared for, the hundreds of prisoners taken at Camden looked after, and the vast horde of military treasures captured at Camden safely dispersed to assorted sites in South Carolina. And before the army could move anywhere, it needed additional horses, wagons, and teamsters.[48]

CLINTON MAY HAVE been disappointed that Cornwallis had not accomplished even more, but there was no denying that a major victory had been won, and it dovetailed nicely with a plan the British commander already had on his drawing board. Before leaving Charleston, Clinton's thoughts had turned to raids along the coasts of Virginia and North Carolina, followed by the establishment of bases on the Chesapeake that would shelter active Loyalists and smooth the way for their further military activities. The arrival of the French army and Ternay's small fleet, and uncertainty about the likelihood of enemy reinforcements, caused Clinton to temporarily shelve his Chesapeake plans. However, by summer's end, he had learned that the French armada was blockaded in Brest and that Cornwallis planned to march his army into North Carolina in September. The time was right for action, and Clinton seized the moment. All along, he had toyed with sending two task forces southward, one to destroy rebel storage depots and installations around Philadelphia, the other to sow terror in Virginia while also pinning down that state's militiamen so that they could not aid their brethren in the Carolinas. But given the lag time in communications between New York and the southern theater, Clinton felt that by the time he learned of Cornwallis's planned incursion into North Carolina, British forces had probably already crossed the border and might even have reached Charlotte. Clinton had to move fast. He jettisoned the mission to Philadelphia and hastily readied a force that was to target the Chesapeake. The expedition was to be commanded by Major General Alexander Leslie, a veteran soldier with twenty-five years' experience who had been part of this war since his arrival in Boston in 1776. Leslie was to sail with 2,500 men. He was to remain in communication with Cornwallis, who, after mopping up around Charlotte, might march eastward and link up with Leslie's men and ships either on the Cape Fear River or the coast, an area known to abound with Loyalists.[49]

The immediate target of Leslie's raiders would be Virginia, where Governor Jefferson had been preparing for just such an attack since his first day in office fifteen months earlier. A few days before Leslie's fleet sailed—it weighed anchor about two weeks after Arnold's treason was uncovered—Washington notified Jefferson that "an embarkation is preparing at New York" and the "prevailing opinion" among his spies was that it was "either bound to Virginia or Carolina." He cautioned Jefferson to remove any magazines situated on inland waterways, straightaway informing the governor that both he and Congress wanted these vital supplies protected so that in time they could be given over to the next southern army that was formed. This was not the first warning of its kind that Jefferson had received, but in every previous instance the enemy squadrons had sailed elsewhere. Not this time. During the third week in October a dispatch rider brought the governor word that "about Sixty Sail" had been spotted in the Chesapeake and that enemy cavalry were already ashore at Portsmouth. Jefferson immediately summoned six thousand militiamen to active duty, but he was not optimistic that the militia could mount a successful defense. Royal naval craft could transport enemy units far more rapidly than militiamen could slog on foot down the Old Dominion's dusty roads. During the raid in May 1779, British forces had time and again come and gone by the time

Virginia's militia officers were alerted to their supposed whereabouts. In addition, as Jefferson told Washington, the British would land mostly hardened veterans, but Virginia's army of citizen soldiers did not include "a single man who [had ever seen] the face of an Enemy" warrior. Many men also lacked adequate arms, most were unaccustomed to military discipline, and nearly all hated "forced Marches and too *Strict* Attention to Order."[50]

Jefferson was pleasantly surprised to discover that Virginia's militia performed reasonably well. Not only had several veteran officers returned home in the wake of Camden, but a recent diminution of the Continental line had left a few experienced officers without a post. Many of the former Continentals rushed to the colors, including twenty-two-year-old James Monroe—who had fought in several engagements, including Trenton, Brandywine, and Monmouth and who was vested with the rank of lieutenant colonel and given command of a regiment. Moreover, Virginia's cavalry, covering the area between rivers, provided the foot soldiers with vital intelligence on enemy movements. But the emergency was not long-lived, despite Leslie's intention of staying awhile to spread destruction, establish permanent bases, and destroy an important supply depot in Petersburg. In fact, he was accompanied by several Tory families who had fled Virginia during the first year of the war and now planned to reclaim the houses and property taken from them by the rebels. But within less than a month Leslie sailed away, a sudden departure that baffled Jefferson. Compared with the destructive raid of 1779, Leslie's had resulted in relatively little damage, save that "Great numbers of negroes . . . had gone over to them." What Jefferson did not know, but suspected, was that Leslie's campaign had been cut short by Cornwallis, who had summoned him to South Carolina. (Leslie had been notified that the early-summer supposition that "the tranquility of South Carolina was assured" had not been borne out, in part because the appearance of Gates's army had "unveiled . . . a fund of disaffection in this province of which we could have formed no idea.")[51]

Although Clinton carped that Cornwallis had not moved with sufficient speed after Camden, a segment of Britain's army was on the road to Charlotte within only three weeks of its stunning victory over Gates. By that time, conditions in the backcountry had deteriorated even further. Partisan hit-and-run raids continued to take a toll on Cornwallis's manpower, and every convoy tasked with running supplies from seaborne Charleston to posts in the interior faced the possibility of assault. Cornwallis's problems mounted when Tarleton fell "dangerously ill" with yellow fever, and during the month in late summer that he lay in sick bay, his troopers were largely immobilized. The guerrillas made the most of it. No less discouraging to the British was that the partisans drew on a seemingly endless stream of recruits. When Sumter, on August 18, suffered his worst drubbing, losing more than five hundred men at Fishing Creek—and barely escaping himself—he replaced all the men who had been lost in a matter of days.[52]

On September 7, Cornwallis marched into the lonesome backcountry that the British had come to distrust. Though he did not have to worry about clashing with a meaningful force of Continental regulars, there were risks aplenty. Aware of the danger that irregulars and a worthy complement of militia might contest him, he had cobbled together a strong force. He set off with a train of thirty-eight wagons and two pieces of field artillery. After three weeks, two additional battalions with two more field pieces joined his army. Cornwallis had advised Clinton that his principal goals were to destroy what was left of Gates's fraught army at Hillsborough and seal shut the rebels' supply line, but he told one of his officers that the "object of marching into North Carolina is only to raise men," to which he added that "there is great reason to believe . . . a very considerable amount" could be garnered. There is no reason to doubt that Cornwallis had in mind achieving all three objectives.

The time for such a move seemed perfect. Like Clinton, Cornwallis believed that North Carolina's Tories would be emboldened by Britain's recent victories at Charleston and Camden, while the rebels, without a potent army to protect them, would lay low. He did not know exactly what to expect, though Cornwallis—true to his aggressive bent—vowed that if "bodies of militia" or guerrilla bands dared to appear, he would "strike some blow" against them. If all went well, he would cap his enterprise by marching eastward to Cross Creek on the Cape Fear River, where the army would take

on provisions shipped up the river from Wilmington. Rested and resupplied, his army—swollen with the bonanza of Tories that he anticipated
reaping—would in November's healthier climate link up with General
Leslie's force and commence operations aimed at taking North Carolina out
of the war, the step that would deal a fatal blow to the rebels' hopes for
holding on to South Carolina.[53]

Cornwallis set off toward Charlotte with a well-conceived plan in mind.
The main army, which he would command, was to consist of around 1,800
men and march directly to Charlotte. Major Ferguson, who appeared to
have no peers when it came to procuring Loyalist volunteers, was to take
about 350 men and comb the region west of Charlotte for recruits while
simultaneously securing Cornwallis's left flank. As Cornwallis and Ferguson
moved northward, Major James Wemyss, a thirty-two-year-old regimental
commander with ten years' service under his belt, was to take a mounted
force of 300 men into the region between Camden and the Pee Dee River
about fifty miles to the east, cleansing it of rebel forces and safeguarding
Cornwallis's rear. As much as he might have liked to have Wemyss's men
with him, Cornwallis acknowledged that the region east of Camden was
especially troublesome. "Every two or three hours I receive an express" with
word of rebel "terrors" that have brought "great distress" to the loyal inhabitants, he said. His instructions to Wemyss broke new ground. To this point,
both Clinton and Cornwallis had presumed that heavy-handedness would
be counterproductive, driving neutrals and even some Tory-leaning deni-
zens into the arms of the rebels. While an adherence to leniency when
dealing with civilians remained the army's official policy, Cornwallis saw
that it was not working. He confided to one of his officers that it was "absolutely necessary to inflict some exemplary punishment on the militia and
inhabitants" of the backcountry. In choosing Wemyss for the inauguration
of his alternative approach, Cornwallis selected a tough and ambitious
Scotsman who would wage a no-holds-barred undertaking. Cornwallis
instructed Wemyss to "disarm in the most rigid manner all persons who
cannot be depended on and punish the concealment of arms and ammunition with a total demolition of the plantation." Loyalist militiamen known

to have defected to the insurgents were to be "instantly hanged." Any rebel militiaman known to have violated the pledge to never again bear arms against Great Britain was also to be dealt with in the harshest manner. Civilians who spread "infamous falsehoods" about Great Britain and its army were to be publicly flogged. Nor was Cornwallis inclined to show mercy toward rebel partisans. "[E]xemplary punishment[s]"—code for capital punishment—were necessary to discourage others from joining the irregulars.[54]

Two weeks before Cornwallis's main army began its tramp northward, Major Ferguson, attired as usual in a plaid hunting shirt over his bright red uniform coat and accompanied by his mistress, Virginia Sal, moved out, crossing to the west of the Catawba River. Cornwallis had been warned by the reliable Balfour that Ferguson was "capricious and violent in his whims" and that it was "impossible to trust him out of sight." Cornwallis himself had complained of Ferguson's "power to do . . . mischief," but the commander also thought him unequaled in his ability to raise recruits. If Cornwallis was apprehensive about Ferguson—and he showed little sign that he was—his greater worry must have been that he was dividing his army in enemy country. That was the height of riskiness, as both Ferguson and Cornwallis were aware that while an abundance of Loyalists inhabited this area, so, too, did a superabundance of rebels. In June, thirty days prior to Cornwallis's incursion, 1,300 Loyalists eager to bear arms had organized into six companies in western North Carolina; their objective had been to march south and join with Cornwallis in the fight in South Carolina. They never made it. A roughly equal number of North Carolina militiamen responded to the threat and in a sharp clash at Ramsour's Mill, about thirty miles west of Charlotte, killed, wounded, or captured about 15 percent of the Tories, sending the lucky survivors scurrying home.[55] Now, in August, Ferguson was starting into that very region with a force barely 20 percent the size of the North Carolina militia that had thrashed the Tories.

But Ferguson's army swelled quickly. Before August ended, he had already disarmed some rebels and recruited roughly 900 Tories, bringing his force up to around 1,200 men. Glib, buoyant, eloquent, and persuasive,

Ferguson had a knack for drawing men to him. He told them of the "false-hoods" disseminated by the rebels, pledged protection for the Loyalists, and in a signed "Declaration" branded the rebels as no better than bandits given to "injustice and cruelty." If you are "real men" who "choose [not] to be pissed upon forever and ever by a set of [rebel] mongrels," you will take up arms and join the fight to reclaim North Carolina, Ferguson told the Tory-leaning settlers. He could only hope that the Loyalist militiamen he raised in North Carolina were better soldiers than those he had recruited over the summer in South Carolina. He had found that those backcountry Tories chafed at "military restraints" and were undependable. On the other hand, Ferguson felt that the southerners needed only to be properly trained and disciplined to render them "very fit for rough and irregular war." After all, they were "excellent woods men, unerring shots, careful to a degree to prevent waste or damage to their ammunition, patient of hunger and hard-ship." That said, Ferguson confided to Cornwallis that a considerable number were "less warlike than the rebels," though he believed they would gain confidence when accompanying "our victorious army" and ultimately prove to be good soldiers when "pitted fairly" against rebel militia.[56]

A portion of the main army under Cornwallis was on the march by the end of the first week in September, advancing to the Waxhaws near the Carolina border, not far from the site of the showdown between Tarleton and Buford three months earlier. Cornwallis paused there for nearly two weeks to await the arrival of the remainder of his force. It was not until September 27, more than a month into Ferguson's campaign, that Cornwallis's army entered Charlotte, a village consisting of twenty houses along two streets, though numerous plantations lay on the town's periphery. By then, both Ferguson and Cornwallis were encountering problems. Ferguson had enjoyed considerable success in raising Tories, but not all residents of the backcountry welcomed his presence or his inflammatory pronouncements. By late in the month, Ferguson had known for days that rebel bands were forming to confront him. Some, in fact, had already struck. Snipers, who he said were firing what he called "skulking shots on the flank," were picking off his men, and now and again small rebel parties ambushed contingents of his strung-out force. Ferguson struck back with attacks of his own, though more often than not the enemy melted away before he could inflict much damage. About a month after he had commenced his march, Ferguson's intelligence gatherers advised that a force of eight hundred men from "over the mountains" in present-day Tennessee—they called themselves "Over Mountain men"—was coming after him. He discounted the report, telling Cornwallis that the rebel band could not exceed 300 men. After eleven days, that rebel force still had not arrived, though by then Ferguson knew not only that he was "in the center of a variety of rebel partys," but that two additional hostile forces totaling some three hundred men were reportedly on the way. He brushed aside those disclosures as well, thinking that the numbers were inflated and that Cornwallis would deal with any enemy units coming from the east. Ferguson did not appear overly concerned. In fact, he hoped to ambush a rebel force from Georgia that he knew was coming his way from Augusta. "We shall be ready to strike at whatever comes within our reach," he said, adding that it would be a grave mistake to "turn our backs on this frontier." Three days later, on October 1, Ferguson displayed real concern for the first time. "There can be no doubt that 800" Over Mountain Men had arrived, he notified Cornwallis, and he added that he soon would be outnumbered. Ferguson advised that he would march his force toward the Catawba River, where he expected to be joined by Cornwallis. Ferguson had not yet reached the river six days later when he took up a defensive position atop King's Mountain, twenty or so miles west of Cornwallis's army.[57]

Cornwallis faced difficulties of his own. He was struck down by a fever, the sort of illness that he had come to think inevitable in what he regarded as the loathsome Carolina climate. Rebels were harassing his force, too, though he was never in as much danger as Ferguson. Still, this veteran of campaigns in New York, New Jersey, Pennsylvania, and lately South Carolina, pronounced the area around Charlotte "the most rebellious and inveterate that I have met with." (Tarleton said the area around Charlotte was "more hostile to England than any others in America.") Furthermore, frequent reports of rebel actions in Georgia and South Carolina led

Cornwallis to worry that in his absence the British might lose control of some sectors that had been gained since the fall of Charleston. In fact, he was having trouble even communicating with the army in South Carolina, as his couriers were so often waylaid in this "so disaffected a country." At the top of his list of worries, however, was Ferguson's safety. "I am anxious about Ferguson. . . . I fear his getting into a scrape," he said early in October.[58]

Ferguson was indeed in trouble. Not long after his men had climbed to the top of King's Mountain, Ferguson had to know that he was in a dreadful situation, for large numbers of rebel fighters were gathering at the base of the outcropping—and they just kept coming. While the precise numbers on both sides are unknown, Ferguson may have had a slight numerical superiority (perhaps 1,100 men to the rebels' 900 or 1,000), but he thought he was heavily outnumbered. Even so, he appears to have felt that his army could hold off the enemy for a couple of days until Cornwallis could rescue him. With the poor performance of Gates's callow soldiers fresh on his mind, Ferguson was convinced that he would have the best fighters, and in his final letter he said, "we do not think ourselves inferior to the enemy" in quality. Ferguson also believed he was in a nearly unreachable position. King's Mountain was not a mountain in the true sense of the word, but rather a very tall hill—roughly the height of a six-story building—and Ferguson presumed that scaling the rugged and steep hillsides would be slow going, so slow that his men could repulse every attempt by the enemy to reach the crest. So confident was Ferguson that during his sixty hours on the summit he did not throw up fortifications of any sort. He appears to have believed that the looming engagement would be a rebel bloodbath. He was a fighter and he was eager for action. Not for nothing had his officers nicknamed him "Bull Dog."[59]

If Ferguson welcomed the fray, so did the men at the bottom of King's Mountain. They were not cut from the same cloth as the militiamen with Gates, many of whom had been reluctant soldiers. These were for the most part gaunt, flinty volunteers, backcountry men who had taken up arms to defend their provinces from the hated would-be royal masters and the even more bitterly despised Tories. Some came from Virginia, some from what now is Tennessee, though most in all likelihood hailed from here and there in North Carolina. These men were accustomed to hard labor and undaunted by the challenge of climbing a hill in the face of the enemy's withering fire. They were handy with rifles and knives, and in a fight they could be as savage as a feral animal. On the road to meet Ferguson's force some of these rebels had captured four Tories. They murdered two captives and left the other two "most barbarously maimed."[60] Whether or not they had read Thomas Paine's *Common Sense*, they believed that the American Revolution, as Paine had written, was an epic struggle to "begin the world over again," and the new world they foresaw was one devoid of monarchs and imperious aristocrats. They knew that Ferguson's men were soldiers for a king and the tiny elite who dominated every facet of life in England. They waited patiently at the foot of King's Mountain, but they were avid for battle with those who bowed to the Crown and a titled nobility that scorned commoners as rabble.

Save for Ferguson, every man who fought on October 8 was an American, and for the most part the men on both sides wore similar attire—long hunting shirts made of coarse fabric and wide-brimmed felt or leather hats. As this might come down to a struggle in close quarters, those under Ferguson attached pine twigs to their hats while the rebels stuffed white paper in theirs. That way they could tell friend from foe. Many of the rebels who had trekked considerable distances for this moment had brought their families and ministers along. They had said their goodbyes to wives and children hours earlier. In the last minutes before the battle their ministers offered a final prayer. Atop the hill, Ferguson's men watched and waited, and many also prayed. Intricate battle plans had been prepared at places like Trenton and Germantown. At Bunker Hill it had been simpler. British soldiers had gone up a hill defended by Yankees. That is the way it was to be at King's Mountain, save that this time it would be the rebels that attempted to reach the peak held by those who fought for the king. There was one other difference. At Bunker Hill, Britain's soldiers had marched in formation up the slope. At King's Mountain the rebels would scurry up the slope, getting off a shot when a target was visible, bolting for shelter (where they could reload), firing again, and dashing to another refuge. One of the rebels later recalled that just before the ascent began he heard his leader cry out, "Shout like hell and fight like devils." Another remembered being instructed that on hearing the first gunshot to "raise a whoop" and rush forward. They followed their instructions to the letter. With a hair-raising war cry learned long ago from Indian adversaries—and what in the Civil War came to be called the southerners' "rebel yell"—the backcountry fighters for American independence set off up the steep slopes. Many began the climb with four or five balls in their mouth so they could reload rapidly.[61]

The footing was often unsure and the climb precipitous, but the rebels moved quickly, lest they become an inviting target. Trees, brush, and boulders were thick on the hillsides, and they provided havens on the way to the next hideaway. One rebel, a sixteen-year-old who had never experienced combat, said later that he "really had a shake on me" when for the first time he took aim and fired at another man. Thereafter, he found it was easier to kill.[62] Some rebels fell, so many that in one sector they retreated before returning to again attempt to scale the slope; they were forced to retreat a second time, but they regrouped and came on once more. The Tories did not have the manpower to adequately defend every sector of the hilltop, nor could they fire their slow-loading muskets quickly enough to completely stop their oncoming enemy. The combination of inexperience, the pulse-pounding frenzy of battle, and having to fire downhill caused many of the Tories' rounds fired to go over the heads of their intended victims. Muskets were potent when fired into a massed enemy, but when the Tories on King's Mountain sought to pick off an adversary who was visible for only an instant while darting from one cover to the next, their firearms were terribly ineffective. Within minutes rebels reached the top the hill on several sides and, given Ferguson's folly of not constructing entrenchments, spotted their exposed adversaries. Thereafter it was akin to target practice. The rebels gunned down their unprotected foe. Knowing they were beaten and hoping for mercy, Tories began throwing down their arms. Ferguson, like Gates only weeks earlier, sought without success to rally his men, and when that failed he attempted to lead a charge. Astride a white horse and easily identifiable in his distinctive attire, he could not have imagined that he could survive. Rebels opened up on him. Shot at least seven times, he tumbled lifelessly from his mount. His death was tantamount to suicide, brought on perhaps by his awareness that Sal had already died in the hail of bullets or that he simply wished to go out in what he imagined would be a blaze of glory.

An indecent spectacle next unfolded. Compassion was in short supply on this bloody hilltop. Crying "Buford! Buford! Tarleton's quarter!" many rebels went on a rampage. What ensued was a carnival of bloodlust. While some of their comrades urinated on Ferguson's body, others calmly butchered captives. One rebel soldier later acknowledged that more than one hundred enemy soldiers were killed following their capitulation, while another subsequently admitted that he had shot the first man he saw waving a white flag of surrender. In time, officers restored order and brought an end to the grisly slaughter. Thereafter, the rebels buried their dead and, following orders, interred Ferguson. But with the prospect of Cornwallis's possible arrival to be reckoned with, the rebels' paramount thought was to get away. By the time they began their descent, they knew they had lost 90 men. They knew, too, that they had killed or wounded 319 Tories and taken 700 captive. The toll would have been higher, but a lucky 200 enemy militiamen had been sent off by Ferguson to forage. The Tory "dead lay in heaps," one rebel later recollected, but if they were to be buried, it would have to be by civilians who lived nearby. With their captives in tow, the rebels descended the hill, ignoring the pleas of the wounded, though they did leave behind one physician to tend to more than 200 gravely injured Tories. Virtually all the wounded who were abandoned faced a certain and, in many instances, an agonizingly slow death. Some lingered until wolves and wild dogs climbed the hill and made meals of them.

If the captives thought they were now safe, they were mistaken. Many were stripped of their shirts and jackets, and nearly all of their shoes, though in early autumn the nights in western North Carolina were chilly. They were taken on a horrid forced march of forty miles without food, during which more ghastly incidents occurred, including the abuse and murder of some prisoners. At Gilbert Town, the rebels instituted a drumhead court that sentenced thirty of the Tories to death. Three at a time were hanged. Nine had been dispatched before rebel leaders called a halt to the massacre, less because their thirst for blood had been satiated than because they feared the truthfulness of a rumor that Tarleton was coming.[63]

Cornwallis, who had abided by Europe's conventions of warfare while seeking to pacify South Carolina, had been appalled by the often ruthless tactics of the partisans. When he learned of the treatment of the prisoners taken on King's Mountain—cruelties that he called "shocking to humanity"—he was all the more convinced that the insurgents in America's backcountry were given to an ineradicable "savage barbarity."[64] Yet, though disgusted and outraged, Cornwallis neither went after the victors at King's Mountain nor marched to Hillsborough or eastward to link up with Leslie. Having failed to recruit a significant number of Loyalists near Charlotte, and knowing that Ferguson's cataclysmic defeat doomed all chances of inducing Tories to rally to the king anytime soon, Cornwallis ordered an immediate retreat back into South Carolina, where he hoped to "secure the frontiers." The only means at hand for achieving that end was to order General Leslie to come from the Chesapeake and augment his army, a move that aborted his costly raid in Virginia.

The British army's march out of North Carolina was a gruesome undertaking. Men and horses were ill and fatigued, and heavy rains that swelled creeks and rivers made the trek an even greater ordeal. Cornwallis suffered a relapse of the illness that had felled him earlier, and another officer had to take command. Cornwallis was too sick to pick up his pen before November 1. Even then, he waited another month before writing to Clinton to inform him both of the disaster at King's Mountain and the abject failure of Major Wemyss's pacification mission, an undertaking that culminated in the wounding and capture of the young regimental commander. In a letter that mingled dismay and sorrow, Cornwallis spoke of what he called the "unfortunate" event at King's Mountain, a calamity that he duplicitously attributed to the rebels having possessed better horses, enabling them to move with surprising speed and pin down Ferguson. As for having risked the division of his army, Cornwallis said only that he had relented to Ferguson's requests that he be allowed to go into the far reaches of the inhospitable backcountry.[65]

Clinton got his first hint of the King's Mountain calamity from rebel newspapers. Remembering Cornwallis's earlier report that the Tory militia was undependable, and aware that several British officers in South Carolina had questioned Ferguson's confidence in the fighting abilities of the Loyalist militia, Clinton feared that the newspaper stories were true. Nevertheless, for days Clinton persisted in the hope that the patriot press was printing fake news or exaggerating the battle's outcome. Perhaps, he thought, Ferguson had suffered only "a little check."

It was November when Clinton learned the grim truth. By then, the trees were bare and his army and those of his adversaries were in winter quarters. Clinton's mood was as gloomy as the season. A general officer who came to headquarters soon after the awful truth of King's Mountain was known found Clinton "the most perplex'd, as well as the most disappointed of all Human beings—all his Dreams of Conquests quite vanish'd, from the desperate situation of our affairs in the Carolinas." Clinton sensed instinctively that the blow suffered at King's Mountain would be akin to the grave damage done to the British at Lexington-Concord or Trenton or Bennington, and always the thrashings had come in the backcountry when the commander—whether Gage or Burgoyne or, now, Cornwallis—had "risk[ed] detachments without proper support." The upshot of those earlier British disasters had been that rebel morale had been bolstered. Clinton knew in a flash that Carolina's rebels would be sustained by King's Mountain and the Tories deflated not just by the conquest of Ferguson but by the "precipitancy" of Cornwallis's retreat from Charlotte. Clinton believed that Cornwallis had erred egregiously in entering North Carolina when he must have known that he lacked the resources to maintain bases within the province that would serve as sanctuaries for the Loyalists. Cornwallis had "encouraged [Loyalists] to show themselves," but his withdrawal from North Carolina had exposed the king's friends to "persecution and ruin," robbing them "forever" of "all their confidence of support from the King's army." Clinton sensed a momentous—and dreadful—turn to the war in the South.[66]

In September, a month before King's Mountain, Clinton's prospects had been promising. The British possessed overwhelming naval superiority, the chances appeared good that Arnold could deliver West Point, Gates and his army had suffered a shattering defeat, reports from South Carolina indicated that the insurgency was in terminal straits, and Cornwallis was expected to rendezvous with Leslie and deal North Carolina—and possibly eastern Virginia—a body blow. But now Clinton knew that he had nothing to show for any of the opportunities that had seemed so glittering only weeks earlier.

Clinton had initially doubted Germain's preaching that southern Tories would rise in great numbers and furnish the fodder for Britain to suppress the rebellion in Georgia and the Carolinas, though in time he had warmed to the notion. After King's Mountain, Clinton turned a more skeptical eye toward rousing southern Loyalists, and his suspicions only grew when Lord Rawdon reported that South Carolina's Loyalists were "wearied" and "dispirited" by Britain's inability to pacify the colony during the two long years since the fall of Savannah. What is more, Rawdon darkly predicted that the "whole country" would "submit as soon as the rebels should enter it."[67] However, Clinton's growing cynicism did not mean that he had altogether written off the potential usefulness of the Tories or of crushing the rebellion in the South.

Increasingly, Clinton believed that the key to success in the South was through a combination of Cornwallis's army and the establishment of British posts on the Chesapeake. The latter, he thought, offered the best hope for establishing sanctuaries for Tory activists and their families, and though his thoughts were yet in gestation, he had begun to reflect on also drawing Britain's friends from Pennsylvania, Delaware, and Maryland into an array of nearby enclaves where they would be safe under the shield of both Britain's army and navy. The Tories could emerge from their havens to cooperate with Britain's armed forces in destructive raids akin to those carried out by Leslie and Commodore Collier, sorties that could disrupt the enemy's trade, eat deeply into its morale, and impede the flow of supplies to rebel armies, militia, and partisans in the low country. A resilient Tory arm could also assist Cornwallis in myriad ways as his army persisted in its efforts to quash the rebellion in South Carolina. Almost immediately after learning of King's Mountain, Clinton took steps toward putting his thinking in motion. He readied another expedition to Virginia, this one under the command of his new general, Benedict Arnold.[68]

CHAPTER 8

NEW DIRECTIONS, NEW HOPE

WHILE CLINTON WAS overwhelmed with bad news in the fall of 1780, Washington glimpsed some rays of hope. He was confident the victory at King's Mountain would have "a very happy influence" on the course of the war in the South. He was also delighted to learn that Congress had addressed the never-ending manpower problem in the Continental army. Under a new law, every man who enlisted after January 1 was obligated to serve for the duration of hostilities, a step the commander had been after Congress to take for six years. If quotas were not filled and conscription was necessary, the draftees would serve a one-year hitch.[1]

Washington was delighted, too, that after much backing and filling, Congress had decided to remove General Gates as commander of the army in the South. North Carolina Governor Abner Nash had complained to Congress about Gates, and the state's assembly left no doubt about its wishes to have a new commander of the southern army. They found a receptive audience in Congress. Several delegates feared that recruiting would lag in the wake of Camden, and others anticipated trouble among militiamen unless Gates was removed. Once again, Congress appealed to Washington to name Gates's successor and, for the first time in the war, the commander agreed to "nominate" someone, though with the understanding that

Congress would actually make the appointment. There was never a moment's doubt about Washington's choice. He recommended General Nathanael Greene, who had already notified both Washington and a South Carolina congressman of his willingness to take on the assignment. Before October ended, Greene was aware he had been selected.[2]

Greene had been among the original thirteen general officers appointed by Congress in 1775. On paper, he had been the least likely to be chosen or to succeed. In his early thirties at the time of his selection, Greene had spent his adult years working in the family's iron business and holding down a seat in the Rhode Island assembly. His only prior military experience—if that is the word for it—had been a year of marching and drilling as a private in a local volunteer company. With hostilities looming in 1775, Rhode Island had created an Army of Observation and named Greene to be its commander (in one fell swoop he jumped from a private to a brigadier general), and two months later Congress named him a general in the new Continental army.

Greene had devoured military manuals and read voluminously on military history, but in the opinion of Henry Knox he was the most callow of all the early general officers. However, General Washington, who had little use for some within the initial batch of generals chosen by Congress, was immediately impressed by Greene's industry and methodical manner, and came to respect his abilities even more during the year-long siege of Boston. By the time Boston was liberated in the spring of 1776, Washington had already decided that if something happened to him, Greene should be named his successor. Two years into the war it was apparent that Washington regarded Greene as his most trusted advisor. Thereafter, Greene held several important posts, though he was routinely passed over for an independent command. Not only had his reputation been sullied by the Fort Washington debacle, but after late 1778 Congress wanted him to manage the quartermaster corps, a key branch of the service that had never been run efficiently. Greene was serving as quartermaster general when Congress first chose Robert Howe, then Benjamin Lincoln, to command its southern army. Greene stepped down from his quartermaster duties early in 1780, but six months later Congress chose Gates for the southern army post. However, in the autumn of 1780 Greene's time had come.

Greene, now thirty-eight, was above average height, stocky, and handsome with engaging blue-gray eyes, and walked with a limp from a youthful injury. (Behind his back, some soldiers referred to him as "the Crab," given his mildly disjointed step.) He was troubled with health issues—he was asthmatic, and his right eye, which had been scarred by smallpox, was occasionally irritated—though the only time he had been truly incapacitated during the war was when he was briefly felled by a virulent fever in 1776. His colleagues thought him friendly and appealing, and liked his sense of humor. Washington was impressed by his leadership skills, attention to detail, and soundness as a tactician and strategist. Not everyone was so dazzled with Greene. Some thought him a sycophant—he had named a son after the commander—and not a few chafed at his proclivity for advising Washington to pursue what they saw as an unnecessarily cautious course.[3]

On learning of his appointment, Greene requested permission to first visit his family in Rhode Island. Washington responded that the southern situation was so perilous that Greene must take command as quickly as possible. Greene, who only days before had been ordered to West Point, rushed to the commander's headquarters in Preakness, New Jersey, for consultation, after fibbing to his wife that the appointment he had been "dreading" had come to pass.[4]

Greene spent five days at headquarters and probably met with Washington daily. As six or eight weeks were often required to exchange letters between the vicinity of Manhattan and the Carolinas, both understood that this was to be the final opportunity for Greene to seek advice or Washington to provide counsel. Sadly, neither minutes nor recollections of their conversations have survived. Given Washington's long reliance on Greene as a strategist and devotee of the Fabian concept, the commander probably amplified on the management of the army, advised how to deal with Congress and the southern governors, and vented on the militia, which the commander hardly esteemed. It is known that Washington gave Greene a free hand, simply telling him "to govern yourself entirely according to your own prudence and judgment." Greene, in turn, likely divulged his plan for a "flying army," a force that could be moved rapidly as exigencies dictated, and he surely sought from Washington as many resources as possible. Washington pitched in by ordering General Steuben to the Southern Department, a step he thought was vital as "an army [is] to be created." Gates had operated with a paltry cavalry arm of only some forty troopers, but Greene wanted more and sought to have as many as six hundred mounted troops accompanying his army. Congress saw the wisdom in this and, against Washington's objections, ordered Colonel Henry Lee and his dragoons to ride to North Carolina, though for the most part Greene would have only about half the number of troopers he hoped for. Washington did agree to furnish Greene with a company of artillery. Greene also knew that he would have the services of General Daniel Morgan, a vaunted soldier who had served for five years in this war before he returned home in 1779 with serious back problems and a roiling anger after having been passed over for promotion following his instrumental role in defeating Burgoyne. But neither his health nor his fury prevented him from answering the call to return to action.[5]

Once Greene bade farewell to Washington, he rode to Philadelphia for a week of talks with Congress, pushed on to Annapolis and Richmond for meetings with the governors of Maryland and Virginia, and with Steuben at his side visited Martha Washington at Mount Vernon. Greene was bowled over by Washington's estate, or so he said. It was "one of the most pleasant places I ever saw," he told the commander, adding in the manner that led others to see him as a toady: "Nothing but the glory of being commander in Chief and the happiness of being universally admird could compensate a person for such a sacrafice as you make" in remaining absent from the plantation. Steuben told the commander in chief that he, too, was "delighted" and "charmed" with the estate, though he told others, "If Washington were not a better general than he was an architect the affairs of America would be in a very bad condition."[6]

The substantive portion of Greene's journey came in his meeting with officials. His conversations with the congressmen were predictably discouraging. The delegates confirmed that in the wake of Charleston and Camden the southern army "exists more in name than substance." It consisted of "but a few ragged soldiers" who faced the "greatest distress imaginable." Furthermore, the congressmen offered next to no hope of furnishing additional men and materials, and Greene's pleas for money— "Money is the Sinews of War, and without a Military Chest, it is next to impossible to employ an army," he advised—had been met with the long-since familiar refrain that the national government was without funds. Before leaving Philadelphia, Greene notified Washington that his men would be properly outfitted only if the northern states furnished every necessity. His message to the southern governors replicated what Gates had said to them six months earlier. Greene wanted food, clothing, wagons, and regular soldiers for his army. An absolute dependence on militiamen, he advised, would be "ruinous to the Country." Greene asked the governors to seek authority from their legislatures to secure whatever the army required, to which he added that the responsibility for actually obtaining what was needed fell on the shoulders of the chief executives. On "your Exertions hang the Freedom and Independence of the Southern States," he said. He further advised Governor Jefferson that Clinton's raids on Virginia would continue until they were unproductive or the British commander was compelled instead to send every available man to Cornwallis in the Carolinas. In a sermonizing manner that many found grating, Greene apprised Jefferson that it was always better to "carry on a War rather abroad than at Home," and he added that the governor could see to keeping the war away from Virginia by furnishing what the southern army required.[7]

Greene began the last leg of his journey to take command during the third week of November 1780, five weeks after learning of his appointment and nearly one hundred days after the cataclysm at Camden. He knew that he faced "a dull prospect." Every one of his predecessors had experienced problems in the South similar to those he would confront, and in the end all had suffered mortifying defeats. Given the glum response of Congress, the woeful record of the southern states in furnishing men and materials, and the deplorable condition of the southern army, Greene confided to a friend, "I think the American cause is at deaths door." He saw only two reasons for hope. Perhaps the outcome at King's Mountain would demoralize the Tories and embolden the supporters of the American Revolution. Furthermore, as the Royal Navy was nowhere to be seen, Greene also believed—and told Washington—that the Allies might inflict "a deadly blow" on the enemy if "Count Rochambeau and Admiral Ternay would suddenly embark their troops and land" in the South.[8] With good reason, Greene was more pessimistic than hopeful, although time would reveal that he possessed some assets that his predecessors had not enjoyed. Greene would have an enhanced cavalry arm, vibrant partisan allies, the assistance of the indomitable Morgan, and a collection of field officers who had survived Camden and gained experience in this gruesome southern war. In addition, in time it would be evident that Greene was superior to those southern commanders who had preceded him.

CLINTON, IN DECEMBER, had received directions from Lord Germain (and the king) based on outdated information. Cornwallis's "glorious success" at Camden was the last news that London had heard of the war in the South, and it led the American secretary to exhort Clinton to act with "Vigour and alertness" in following up that "complete victory." Germain believed that if British forces not only raided Virginia but established bases on its coast, Cornwallis would soon thereafter succeed in adding the Carolinas, and possibly the Old Dominion, to the growing list of southern colonies that had been reduced "to the King's obedience."[9]

Clinton had more up-to-date information. He knew of the disaster at King's Mountain and the failure of Major Wemyss's mission to pacify the region between Camden and the Pee Dee River, and he had received slivers of good news. He was aware that Wilmington, North Carolina, was now in British hands, navigation of the Santee River had been secured, and the area south and southwest of Camden was firmly under Britain's control. Furthermore, Cornwallis had encouraged the Native Americans to strike against several deep backcountry settlements that encroached on their lands, an initiative that was paying dividends in that the Over Mountain Men had returned home to fight the Indians.

Otherwise, most of the news that Clinton received from Cornwallis and Lord Rawdon was unfavorable. Additional partisan bands, called "banditti" by Cornwallis, had formed following King's Mountain, posing threats to several British interior posts. Meanwhile, Loyalists were not stepping forward to bear arms. Cornwallis apprised Clinton of his concerns about the unworthiness of Loyalist militiamen, but he did not divulge his thoroughgoing disenchantment with South Carolina's Tories. Cornwallis told others that the Tories were "timid and stupid," unwilling to take up arms, and undependable when it came to supplying intelligence. (Rawdon had long since advised Clinton that during the previous autumn's incursion into North Carolina, the Tories had not provided "the least information respecting the forces gathering against us.") Clinton knew of Cornwallis's despair, though perhaps not how deep it ran. But worthy leaders find ways to learn of sentiment within their armies, and Clinton appears to have been fully aware that many officers not only shared Cornwallis's disillusionment with the Tories but doubted that the tactics employed since the fall of Charleston could quell the rebellion in South Carolina.

For instance, General Charles O'Hara, who arrived in the province near Christmas, rapidly concluded that London's dependence on the Tories was an "old and fatal delusion." He also surmised that the partisans were inflicting an unsustainable rate of attrition on Britain's forces. But it was not only the guerrillas who committed atrocities. Before Charleston fell, a pro-Revolutionary newspaper in the city carried stories of "execrable outrages" wrought by Loyalists. They "plunder houses, steal horses, abuse women, tie and whip men, and cut their ears off." Militia leaders on both sides summarily executed prisoners. The Tories under "Bloody Bill" Cunningham had followed one engagement by hacking to death twenty-eight captives with their swords. The rebels reciprocated in kind. John McCord, a rebel militia captain, once ordered the execution of fourteen Tory prisoners. When one didn't die by gunshot, his throat was cut, prompting one of the perpetrators to remark that he had "never seen a son of a bitch bleed so much." Miraculously, the victim, who was tethered to a dead prisoner, eventually dragged himself to a shady spot, where women—smelling the pungent odor of the decomposing soldier—found and saved the severely wounded Loyalist soldier. It was grim occurrences of these sorts that prompted O'Hara to recoil in horror at the savagery of southern hostilities, which he labeled "the bloodest War ever produced." He focused largely on the "horrid outrages" committed by the partisans, including "shocking tortures and inhuman murders" that were "beyond every curb of Religion and Humanity," and which had succeeded in cowing the Loyalists. Britain's only hope, in O'Hara's estimation, was to respond in-kind to these depredations. Other officers were not so sure. For instance, Colonel Charles Stuart knew that the British army "planted an incontrovertible hatred wherever we went," but he did not know how to deal with it. Harsh measures might work "if one could be sure of injuring [the rebels] sufficiently," he thought, though he also understood that it would be imprudent to "incur their determined enmity for ever." In the end, he thought the leaders must "weigh their Friendship and their Hatred" and decide accordingly. Clinton never wavered, and neither did Cornwallis. Both were certain that uncompromising severity would be counterproductive, and Cornwallis repeatedly, and sternly, cautioned his officers: "For God's sake no irregularities"; "For God's sake keep your troops under regulation."[10]

In the last weeks of 1780 Clinton waited impatiently for word of Cornwallis's next move. For a considerable time he heard nothing of substance, as Cornwallis revealed that he did not know whether "my campaign [will be] offensive or defensive." During a portion of this period Cornwallis was still slowly recovering from the illness that felled him in Charlotte, but he also was awaiting word of the status of Gates's army in North Carolina. If the Americans chose not to reinforce it, Cornwallis appeared to say, he would focus on the pacification of South Carolina. However, if a new rebel army was fielded, he would go after it in North Carolina. When at last he was aware of Greene's appointment, Cornwallis in January 1781 informed Clinton that he would "use every possible means of putting [South Carolina] into a state of defense" before marching his army back into North Carolina.[11] He recalled that Gates's presence had galvanized the low-country rebels, and he believed that Greene's advance on South Carolina would rally them as well. But it was not just Greene's army that Cornwallis would target. He had come to believe that the solution to suppressing the insurgency in South Carolina lay outside that province. He was convinced that the rebel supply lines that coursed through North Carolina were essential lifelines for any rebel army in the Carolinas, and that army, in turn, was a pivotal ingredient in sustaining the partisans. Once he was joined by Leslie, Cornwallis reported, he would put his army in motion in hopes of shutting down the rebel supply lines and destroying the enemy army.

Clinton had not ordered Cornwallis's second incursion into North Carolina, but he was optimistic about it. Despite the calamity at King's Mountain only a few weeks earlier, Clinton radiated confidence that at last the formula for success in the Carolinas had been found. As Arnold's forthcoming expedition to the Old Dominion would tie down Virginia's militia, robbing Greene of precious manpower, Cornwallis's army would be superior to that of his adversary. Furthermore, the combination of Greene's defeat and Arnold's establishment of a British base on the Chesapeake should induce the Loyalists to take up arms. Clinton, too, had come to believe that the original plan for pacifying South Carolina was unworkable. Chasing after the partisans in the backcountry had been ineffectual. Clinton had conceived the plans for Arnold's mission and the establishment of bases on the Chesapeake, but otherwise he was willing to give Cornwallis a free hand. The greatest difference in the thinking of Cornwallis and Clinton at this juncture was that the commander in chief continued to believe that success required substantial help from the Tories, whereas Cornwallis was inclined to think that such assistance would never be found. For Clinton, North Carolina was to be the proving ground.[12]

AS 1781 APPROACHED, both Clinton and Washington thought it was likely to be the last year of the war, and each looked toward the means of ending the stalemate and securing victory. For Washington, victory could come only through a joint Allied campaign to regain New York. For Clinton, it might come in the South through a series of widely dispersed but interconnected initiatives that would solidify Britain's control of South Carolina and Georgia. Or it might come through repulsing an Allied attack on New York. Both commanders understood that success hinged on naval supremacy. Once, when focusing on the South, Clinton remarked that so "long as we hold the entrance of the Chesapeake, all must go well," and on more than one occasion he said the British hold on New York was secure so long as the Royal Navy remained superior at sea. Whereas Clinton feared losing control of the seas, Washington thought the Allies had to achieve dominance on the seas in order to win the war. So long as the British controlled the seas, he said late in 1780, there was a considerable danger that two or more southern states might be lost, and that would bring a dismaying end to the war.[13]

Washington was hopeful, but of the two he was the least upbeat at the outset of 1781. France held the key to victory, and Washington was in the dark as to whether his ally would have the resources, or the will, to take the necessary steps. Washington found comfort in the belief that "in the hours of our deepest distress and darkness" since 1776, the cause had been saved repeatedly by the "many remarkable interpositions" of "the hand of Providence." Fortune and divine intervention were slender reeds to grasp, but he appeared to have faith that one or the other would safeguard what he often called "our glorious cause" and produce a "happy issue of the present contest." Be that as it may, Washington knew full well that the United States faced what he called "an awful crisis." Clinton agreed that his troubled adversary faced an uncertain future, and it buoyed his expectation of success in the coming year. "I have all to hope, and Washington all to fear," Clinton remarked in January, and he added that without financial help from France—which might or might not be forthcoming—the rebellion could not be "re-spirit[ed]." Later, Clinton reflected that his prospects had been "dark and gloomy" when he assumed command, but that he was "sanguine in my hopes" as he entered this crucial year. It was the first instance during his command that he entered a new year with what he believed was the prospect of great success. His optimism arose from more than his enemy's problems. Not only was Clinton confident that the plans he had made for 1781 promised a "fair and solid effort" at attaining victory, but his spirits were bolstered by Germain's pledge that reinforcements were coming.[14]

Clinton and Washington were different in numerous ways, including their dissimilar backgrounds. Clinton was born into the lap of luxury and privilege, the scion of a well-connected English aristocratic family. Like his father, Clinton chose a military career, and his wealth and the family's influence were useful to his advancement. At age thirty-four, he was appointed groom of the bedchamber to one of the king's brothers, an honor through which he acquired an eminent patron. Eight years later, in 1772, he not only was promoted to the rank of general officer but was elected to a seat in Parliament; two years later he was reelected. Washington's family was more comfortable than most colonial households, though following his father's demise in 1743, the means of providing young George with substantial schooling vanished. Furthermore, he was not the family's oldest son, often a considerable roadblock to success in the eighteenth century. (John Adams, the eldest son in his family, was the beneficiary of a Harvard education, whereas his two brothers' schooling ended after about six years, and they spent the remainder of their lives tending small farms.) Deep into adolescence, Washington found that the best he could hope for was to someday be a locally influential figure. As a result of his work as a surveyor, which he undertook beginning around age sixteen, young Washington began to accumulate property, but it was his soldiering for Virginia in the Seven Years' War that made him both a renowned figure within the colony and a very eligible bachelor. At age twenty-seven, he married Martha Custis, the wealthiest widow in the Old Dominion. During the fifteen years prior to the Revolutionary War, Washington reached the pinnacle within his province. He was revered for his bravery and admired as a wealthy Virginia planter, and year after year he served as a respected member of the colony's assembly. But until the cusp of the Revolutionary War, Washington was neither widely known nor influential outside his colony, and to be sure he was unimportant in the seat of the British Empire.[15]

Clinton, a professional soldier since age fifteen, had served in the British army for thirty-three years when he was named its commander in America in 1778. He was a battle-hardened veteran. Washington had soldiered for only five of his twenty-two adult years before the Revolutionary War. He had never led an army of more than two thousand men, had scant experience commanding men in battle, and was largely unfamiliar with confronting a professional European army. Not surprisingly, Clinton's long military background and his passionate scholarly interest in the art of war made him a more gifted strategic planner than Washington, who had to learn the ropes following his appointment to command the Continental army. Washington's first great test had been the New York campaign in 1776, and for weeks on end he had displayed perplexingly poor judgment and nearly fatal indecision. With time, Washington grew in his post, and by 1781 he was more than a merely capable leader. Clinton respected him, though he could not bring himself to refer to Washington as "General," instead always adding the honorific prefix "Mr." when referring to the American commander. Although frustrated by his inability to lure Washington onto a battlefield, Clinton acknowledged the wisdom of his adversary's generalship. Washington, meanwhile, praised Clinton's leadership. "I see no better purpose to which they can apply their army in america," he remarked of Clinton's strategy in 1779, a view from which Washington never wavered before the summer of 1781.[16]

Washington was an extraordinary judge of others, and the decisions he made regarding those vested with crucial command assignments—and those whom he relegated to the backwater of the war—were almost always the proper choices. A striking exception was his refusal to put Gates in command of the Rhode Island campaign in 1778, a poor decision that could have resulted in untoward consequences for America's cause. Clinton, too, was talented in assessing others. Given Lord Germain's affinity for Cornwallis, Clinton probably had no choice but to leave him in command in the South in the summer of 1780. But despite the lingering tension in their personal relationship, Clinton dealt with his subordinate in a fitting and respectfully professional manner. Clinton additionally made excellent choices when putting the likes of Generals Charles O'Hara, William Phillips, and Alexander Leslie, and Colonels Francis Rawdon and Nisbet Balfour in pivotal positions in the Carolina theater.

Washington had little or no prior administrative experience when he assumed command of the newly created army in 1775. He immediately rebuilt the Continental army, a step that he called "new modeling." His aim was a "respectable army" and his prototype was the British army. Throughout the war, Washington tinkered with the army's organization, at times creating new divisions, mobile reserve forces, a light infantry corps, and a plethora of specialized units, while taking advantage of the presence of experienced officers, as he did in utilizing General Steuben to train the soldiery. During the Valley Forge winter, Congress expressed doubts that Washington possessed the administrative skills to transform the army into a force that could win the war, and four years into the war the army remained troubled by administrative shortcomings. Even so, the army that fought at Monmouth in 1778 was superior to the force that had defended New York two years earlier, and thereafter the army's greatest liabilities were due less to its structure than to its lack of money, manpower, and a naval arm.[17] Clinton, in contrast, took command of a long-established army managed by seasoned officers up and down the line. It functioned relatively smoothly and required little mending by its commander. The British corps of officers was the domain of aristocrats and gentry, and Clinton fit in nicely, not only as he had been to the manor born, but in 1777 the king had invested him with the Order of the Bath. Henceforth, he was Sir Henry Clinton. Clinton attempted only one truly significant reform. A 1779 report by Major John André censured the rampant corruption within the army's commissary system. Clinton responded by creating the Commissary of Captures, a sincere—though not terribly successful—effort to reform the distribution of food and provisions obtained through foraging.[18]

In some respects, Clinton was dogged with greater management responsibilities than Washington. The Continental army generals who exercised responsibility in the Northern and Southern Departments were answerable to Congress, but the British officers in command in West Florida, Georgia and East Florida, South Carolina, Halifax, and Quebec reported to Clinton. They consulted the commander in chief about vacancies and promotions, submitted endless requests for additional arms, manpower, and provisions, and sought direction with regard to Native American diplomacy. Whereas troubled civilian patriots could approach local officials or assemblymen, or even Congress, distressed Loyalists often turned to the commander of Britain's army rather than to New York's royal governor. Clinton was inundated with appeals for aid. For example, the widow of a British soldier who claimed to have lost her hearing while hiding in the woods from rebel pursuers sought help as she now had "nothing to support herself or her infant children"; an ill Loyalist whose house had been burned by rebels requested assistance in finding new living quarters; another Loyalist, who had abandoned a "comfortable living" to aid the British, was now "reduced to absolute want and prays employment"; a New York Loyalist, with the unfortunate name of Nicholas Outhouse, sought rations after being left destitute once his three sons joined provincial regiments to fight for the king. Clinton even had to deal with displaced rebel refugees who wound up in Manhattan. "Humanity and good policy" required it, he said, and indeed he appears to have provided help as much from compassion as from hope that his generosity might lure them into the Loyalist camp. Clinton was additionally besieged with appeals to assist prisoners in the so-called Convention Army taken captive at Saratoga, and hardly a week passed when he did not correspond with Charles Jenkinson, Britain's secretary of war, over an endless array of matters, including promotions, pay, camp necessaries, and conditions in army hospitals.[19]

For all their differences, from 1777 onward the British and Continental armies shared some similarities. The Continental army, as historians have pointed out, "increasingly took on the appearance of a traditional European army." Land-owning farmers and middle-class craftsmen largely disappeared from the ranks after 1776; in their stead, the ranks were composed mostly of propertyless men from the lower social orders, including many recent immigrants and a growing percentage of Blacks, many of whom were enslaved. Clinton, too, commanded a polyglot force of men without property. Some of his soldiers hailed from the home islands, others from German principalities, and after 1778 a considerable percentage were American Loyalists. Furthermore, while a mortified Washington watched as hordes of his officers left his army from 1778 onward, Clinton not only was dogged by the departure of a substantial number of his officers but also by the outright refusal of many experienced officers to accept transfer to the American theater. Both commanders were aware of grumbling in the ranks. Some on both sides thought their commander in chief was surrounded with sycophants, and some in both armies carped that their leader was incompetent to hold such a high position.[20]

Years ago, when the historical profession was swept with fervor by what was known as psychohistory, Clinton was put on the couch by his biographer, William B. Willcox, in collaboration with Frederick Wyatt, a psychologist. Devotees of psychohistory believe that through the "diagnosis" of a historical figure, "a recognizable psychological pattern" could be discovered that would explain unconscious motivations in an individual's behavior. Willcox and Wyatt portrayed Clinton as craving power, though they claimed that subconsciously he felt "he ought not to have it." This resulted in a profound conflict that rendered him "unable to use" the authority he possessed. "[A]t bottom . . . he doubted himself too much to be sure that he was right," a disorder that led to a "paralysis of will" on Clinton's part.[21]

To be sure, Clinton drew up plans of action that were not always acted on, as did Washington and every other commander. But in almost every instance when Clinton backed away from a contemplated operation—as when he failed to carry out his intended attacks on the French in Rhode Island—there were sound military reasons for not pursuing the original plan, and his ultimate decisions were always approved by councils of war. Clinton was cautious, a quality that is often a virtue in military leaders. Had

General Gage been less reckless, he would have been spared the disaster at Bunker Hill; and Rochambeau, an experienced and successful general, had sought to teach Lafayette that a circumspect general neither acted impulsively nor recklessly. Washington understood that in certain circumstances caution was called for, and his conduct after 1778 was anything but impetuous.

To suggest that Clinton was devoid of the will to fight is fallacious. After all, he eagerly went into battle at Monmouth and Charleston, committed troops to Virginia, and was ardent in his support of the invasion of Georgia. The notion that a subliminal paralysis of will destroyed Clinton's effectiveness is similarly ludicrous. When New York was threatened by d'Estaing in 1778, it was Clinton's act of hurriedly readying a force to protect New York Harbor that helped save the city. When a rebel force menaced General Pigot in Newport later that summer, Clinton, in New York, acted so rapidly that his reinforcements reached Rhode Island before d'Estaing could get his fleet from New York to Newport. Weeks later, again responding with alacrity, Clinton sent off a large force that came within a whisker of trapping General Sullivan's army on Aquidneck Island. When a desperate Burgoyne called on him for help in the fall of 1777, Clinton sprang into action and waged a brilliant and daring diversionary campaign in the Hudson Highlands.

Much of Clinton's behavior that Willcox and Wyatt attributed to neuroticism—an obsessive guarding of his privacy, ardency for authority, aloofness, excessive sensitivity, "pedantic zest for detail," and "blaming . . . others" ("transferring his own internal guilt to others," in the authors' psychological jargon)—were behavioral qualities that were also exhibited by Washington. Perhaps he, too, was the victim of "an unconscious psychic conflict over authority," though such a claim could never be proven in his case any more than it could be with regard to Clinton.[22] Both Washington and Clinton appear to have had issues with self-worth, but with regard to their extreme caution and unwillingness to act, it is more likely that both wisely understood that the road to catastrophe was paved with foolhardiness.

Both Clinton and Washington were self-centered individuals who exhibited fragile self-esteem. In 1779, Clinton "with tears in his eyes," opened up to a young confidant, Colonel Charles Stuart, acknowledging his concern that some officers "hated—nay, detested" him and some thought him "incapable of his station." As an inexperienced twenty-three-year-old in 1776, Stuart himself had remarked that Clinton was "incapable of commanding a Troop of Horse," but over the years he came to a more balanced view of his commander in chief. By 1779, Stuart had concluded that much of the grousing directed at Clinton came from those who had been close to General Howe, officers who feared his successor might succeed where their chief had failed; Stuart additionally traced the complaints to rancorous junior officers who had been passed over for promotion and to the breakdown of morale within the army following its manpower reduction in 1778. Patrick Henry recollected that when Washington was appointed to command the Continental army, he wept as he privately confided his fear of being unequal to the task before him.[23] No one thereafter recalled Washington letting down his guard. Unlike Clinton, Washington had a deft touch for hiding what he feared were his inadequacies. He fashioned a reserved and unapproachable countenance, permitting no one to get close enough to him to discover his real or imagined imperfections.

Like Clinton, Washington was aware that some disparaged his abilities. At Valley Forge, he spent countless hours poring over handwriting samples in hopes of learning the identity of the authors of anonymous letters to Congress—passed along by members of the Virginia delegation—that rebuked him. It was probably for the best that Washington was unaware that several officers near to him were among his severest critics. One of his aides, Timothy Pickering, thought him weak, ignorant, and vain, while Alexander Hamilton said that the public's positive perception of Washington's admirable character and extraordinary abilities was "unfounded." The army's first quartermaster general concluded that Washington was "totally unfit for his situation," the commander's first secretary thought him "only fit to command a regiment," and General Kalb said that if Washington ever did "anything sensational" it would be more due to luck or "his adversary's mistakes than to his own ability."[24] The critics of Clinton and Washington were correct at times and incorrect much of the time, but what was beyond dispute was that these two very human individuals were deeply wounded by the merest slight of their character and abilities.

Washington cultivated a reputation of being above politics, though in fact few were his equal as a politician. He dexterously managed his relations with Congress, other general officers, and influential figures that visited camp, and his diplomacy with French officials was masterly. Despite having won a seat in the House of Commons, Clinton was politically inept. Old family ties had given him entrée to the monarch, and George III was perhaps his greatest defender in London. But Clinton lacked the political adroitness necessary to win over powerful legislative figures. Generals Howe, Burgoyne, and Cornwallis worked much harder, and with much greater success than Clinton, in developing a loyal following within pivotal circles at home.

As Clinton destroyed many of his personal papers and Washington's widow burned the letters exchanged between the couple, impenetrable gaps exist in our understanding of the private side of both men. Historians have speculated about whether young, unmarried George Washington was romantically involved with Sally Fairfax, a married woman whose husband was out of the country, or when older if he had a dalliance with Elizabeth Powel, a striking, buxom brunette who was half his age and the wife of an upper-crust Philadelphian. While titillating, the ink spilled over these issue remains nothing but conjecture. On the other hand, it is known that while a young, unmarried soldier in Germany in the early 1760s, Clinton had an affair with a married woman that resulted in the birth of a daughter. Many years later, Clinton, a widower in his late forties, commenced an affair with a married woman—Mary Baddeley, a native of Ireland who had come to America with her husband, a soldier in the British army—that led to the birth of a daughter in 1781 or 1782. Their amorous relationship probably began some seven years following the death of Clinton's wife, commencing in New York while he was commander of Britain's army. Following the death of Mary's husband's in Charleston in 1782, she returned to England with Clinton, who provided for her and his child, as he also cared for the daughter he had fathered in Germany.[25]

By 1781, Washington and Clinton had been repeatedly besieged by challenges and both were frayed by years of toil, disappointment, and despondency. Pulsatingly ambitious, both were haunted by fears that their years of
sacrifice would not be crowned with glory and renown. Clinton confessed
that he hoped to achieve "honor" and "credit." Weighed down with despair
in 1776, Washington mourned that he saw "the impossibility of serving
with reputation," to which he added: "I cannot have the least chance for
reputation." Clinton threatened to quit on numerous occasions. During the
darkest days of the campaign to save New York, Washington acknowledged
that all that stopped him from resigning was that "inevitable ruin will
follow from the distraction that will ensue," an outcome that would eter-
nally blacken his reputation. As the war dragged on year after year, Clinton
conceded, "I am fairly worn out." He added that the life-and-death decisions, military reversals, and frustrations that were his lot had left him
"worn down with grief and mortification." He feared the job had taken
years off his life, sighing that it had left him feeling "greatly impaired." As
early as 1776, Washington acknowledged that he was "wearied to death all
day," every day, with the "perplexing" demands of his position, a station
that robbed him of "all comfort and happiness." He added that he was
"bereft of every peaceful moment." By early 1781 Washington admitted
that throughout his "Morning and Evening hours," indeed during "every
moment," he "pant[ed] for retirement; and for those domestic and rural
enjoyments which in my estimation far surpasses the highest pageantry of
this world."[26] All Washington could do, however, was dream of his beloved
Mount Vernon. He at least was able to spend several months each year with
his wife, Martha, who was at his side while the army was in winter quarters.
At the outset of 1781, four long years had elapsed since Clinton had been
home and seen his children.

No one questioned Clinton's and Washington's courage. Clinton had
come under fire on numerous occasions in the Seven Years' War, once
suffering a dangerous wound. He rushed into harm's way as the debacle at
Bunker Hill unfolded, and he faced danger on the Hudson in 1777, at
Monmouth the following year, and at Charleston in 1780. Washington, too,

had fearlessly faced death on several occasions in this war. At Princeton early in 1777, he led his men in battle against musket-wielding enemy soldiers no farther from him than a pitcher is from a batter on a baseball diamond.

George III expressed his admiration of Clinton's "great military talents" and his "zeal and ability." In 1779, the monarch said that he was "well satisfied with your conduct" and had "great confidence" in Clinton's abilities. Likewise, General Howe said that he had a "high opinion" of Clinton "as an officer and a man." When Howe was instructed by the American secretary to select an "able & intelligent" commander for the operation in North Carolina in 1776, he had not hesitated in tapping Clinton for the assignment. Clinton was also his choice later that year to lead the expedition to take Rhode Island. Even Germain, uneasy as he frequently was with Clinton's cautious nature, spoke of his "strongest disposition" to support the course charted by his commander. Later, once the war was stalemated, Clinton's leadership drew more fire than Washington's. Germain and some in Parliament often pressed for the army to take the field, and not a few high-ranking officers complained about Clinton's unwillingness to take a harsher approach toward the rebels. Meanwhile, Congress clamped a lid on criticism of Washington after the Valley Forge winter, making it more difficult to gauge disaffection. From 1779 onward the only discernible restlessness with Washington was among some public officials in the South who thought the commander obsessed with retaking New York and blind to their tribulations. Otherwise, most in Congress and most officers in the army appear to have concluded that Washington was irreplaceable. Few, if any, thought of Clinton in those terms. As historian Marcus Cunliffe observed, Washington's "appointment was meant to symbolize the spirit of union" among thirteen separate provinces.[27] Aside from the king, no one on the British side was looked on in that manner. Whereas Washington came to be seen by Lafayette as the embodiment of the American Revolution—and by another French officer as the "Atlas of America"—it was unimaginable that even the most successful British general could have attained such an exalted stature among his countrymen.[28]

The public officials with whom Washington dealt, and the officers who surrounded him, were nearly unanimous in testifying to his virtue, honesty, industriousness, and dedication. Neither he nor Clinton was dissolute or unscrupulous. Nor was either man truly beloved. Clinton, shy and introverted, often prickly and at times tactless, was not one to discourage flattery. He struck some as vain and arrogant, traits—according to one scholar—not uncommon among veterans of the German campaigns in the Seven Years' War who "tended to look down upon officers who had had their military education elsewhere." While some military choices he made aroused criticism, Clinton was on the whole respected for his dedication and knowledge of warfare. Washington could be bristly, severe, and scornful; was given to glacial silences; and scrupulously avoided all hints of camaraderie with other officers. Those around him were aware of his volatile temper, terrible "wrath," and "tumultuous passions" that were "almost too mighty for man."

Numerous people commented on Washington's aloofness and Olympian manner, punctuated at times with a seeming inability to even engage in conversation. He kept virtually everyone at a distance, so carefully shielding his private side that even those who spent considerable time in his presence felt they never really knew him. Those who knew or met him were most likely to remember his serious and sober comportment, and to describe his "noble" and "stately" bearing. General Rochambeau spoke of Washington's"noble and patriotic character which ever formed the basis of his conduct." On seeing Washington during the 1776 retreat through New Jersey, James Monroe, a young officer in a Virginia regiment, said he had never seen "a deportment so firm, so dignified, so exalted, but yet so modest and composed." Timothy Pickering offered perhaps the best description of Washington and the feelings that he aroused among his officers: "The dignity of his presence, large and manly, increased by steady, firm, and grave countenance and an unusual share of reserve, forbidding all familiarity, excited no little reverence in his presence." Those traits served Washington well as the commander of an army, but they also prevented him from ever having a friend in the true sense of that word. Washington appeared not to be bothered by his friendlessness. He was content to relate to others in terms of how they could best serve his needs. Clinton was too withdrawn to have many friends, but unlike his counterpart he succeeded in developing several close and lasting relationships with fellow officers.[29]

Washington, who unquestionably radiated qualities of leadership, was the more impressive figure of the two. Clinton struck many as average in every way. He was probably about five feet six inches tall, and in middle age he would best be described as portly. If his portraits bear any resemblance to reality, Clinton was softly handsome and radiated a gentle demeanor. Washington, in contrast, appeared to many to be the epitome of a soldier. He towered above almost every other man, and when weighed at age fifty in 1782 he was a trim 210 pounds. Muscular and solid, he exhibited impressive upper-body strength. Many who met him thought him graceful and the most skilled horseman they had ever seen, a mark of athleticism in the eighteenth century. A Massachusetts soldier saw Washington only once, an occasion on which the hurried commander alighted from his horse; long afterward the young man remembered how Washington "leaped from his saddle" with "the spring of a deer." Washington was neither handsome nor unattractive. The most apt description of Washington's appearance might be "rugged." He struck others as strapping and sturdy with a hard-edged countenance. Together with the demeanor he had long since fashioned—solemn, detached, inaccessible—Washington was what many expected in a commander in chief faced with weighty decisions.

Clinton, who was fifty at the outset of 1781, was two years older than Washington. Both men remained in good health throughout the war, possibly because each craved exercise. Both rode daily. Washington was on his charger early each morning for a lengthy tour of the camp. Clinton cantered about Manhattan. Neither man was given to lethargy and both were committed to their jobs, working long hours day after day. Still, each man lived comfortably. Washington habitually selected large, snug dwellings for headquarters and dined daily at a table laden with food and wine. Clinton spent almost the entirety of his four years as commander in chief in New York City, and given the abundance of abandoned residences, he commandeered four houses for his use. Both commanders frequently derived entertainment in the evenings from plays acted and directed by their officers, and when the wives and daughters of Continental officers spent winters with their loved ones in camp, Washington often enjoyed parties and dances. Clinton found time each day to take up his violin and, intellectually curious, he endeavored to daily set aside a period for wide-ranging reading. Washington's days were largely consumed with continuous meetings, though he was accustomed to a long, relaxing midday meal with a dozen or more officers and guests, repasts at which he said little or nothing, depending on one or more of his aides to keep the conversation flowing. Reports and letters aside, there is no evidence that Washington read anything other than an occasional newspaper. Prior to the war, Washington had played cards regularly and frequently hunted and fished, but on assuming command of the army he abandoned those pursuits, fearing the example that he would set. He sometimes tossed a ball or played cricket with younger staff officers, and when separated from Martha he found it relaxing, and stimulating, to spend his evenings with his aides, loyal, bright, and ambitious young men with whom he may have been more inclined to unbend and speak candidly. Clinton was not one to complain of his inescapable workload, but Washington from time to time grumbled that he had no time for relaxation and amusements. At Morristown, in the harsh winter of 1780, he confided to an acquaintance that he yearned for leisure time, but added: "public duty and social enjoyments are so much at variance that I have little expectation of indulging in the latter while I am under ties of the former."[30]

Both Washington and Clinton were plagued with a persistent shortage of troops, and each frequently insisted that the lack of manpower forced a distressing idleness on him. While true, Washington's and Clinton's inactivity also stemmed from caution and an unwillingness to commit their armies to risky undertakings. Washington had an ally that kept the United States afloat through those desperate years, and he believed that in time the Franco-American forces would act in concert to secure the decisive victory that would win American independence. He shepherded his army for the day when at last the Allies would take the field arm in arm. From late 1779 onward, Clinton was convinced that time was on his side. He was confident that sooner or later his American enemy would self-destruct or that France, in despair, would scuttle its alliance with the Americans. Nevertheless, the expectation of an Allied campaign to take New York was never far from Clinton's mind and he, unlike Washington, thought it imperative to keep his army intact for the inescapable pivotal moment in this war.

The outcome of the war is now known and that has doubtless colored posterity's judgment of Clinton and Washington in incalculable ways. Had the Revolutionary War come to a different end, as it easily could have, aspects of Washington's makeup, thinking, and strategic choices that now are seen as strengths might be viewed as weaknesses; conversely, facets of Clinton's temperament and the choices he made that subsequent generations of historians have seen as weaknesses might today be looked on as assets. After 1778, Washington eschewed risk-taking and scrupulously avoided committing the bulk of his army to hazardous actions, and with the exception of the Charleston campaign, Clinton largely had pursued a similar course. At the dawn of 1781, a strong case might have been made that of the two commanders, Clinton had been the wiser in exercising caution and restraint. However, history sometimes is filled with surprises.

BENEDICT ARNOLD'S CHESAPEAKE enterprise came together in December. His orders were to establish a fortified post at Portsmouth on the Elizabeth River in Virginia, just west of Cape Henry and below the terminus of the James River, a channel known as Hampton Roads, as the James, Nansemond, and Elizabeth Rivers flow into the Atlantic in this area. Arnold could be supplied from the sea year-round at this enticing warm-water port. Moreover, with a frigate or two, he could make sudden forays up those rivers—especially the James—to destroy rebel supply depots, hamper the flow of arms and ammunition to the rebels in the lower South, and disrupt the Virginians' commerce with the outer world. Arnold was also to seek to recruit Loyalists to his force, and as he, too, was now an

American Loyalist, this may have been one of the reasons that Clinton chose him to lead the expedition. Arnold was restricted only in that he was authorized to make "excursions" into the hinterland so long as his absence would not jeopardize his base. But Clinton expected him to take the war to Virginia's interior, and like Leslie before him, Arnold was to target Petersburg and its major supply depot.[31]

Arnold's force put to sea on December 20. It consisted of 1,800 men—mostly Tories, but some British and German regulars were part of his army—and within its ranks were units of foot soldiers, cavalry, riflemen, artillerists, and pioneers, who among other things would work on the fortification at Portsmouth. Roughly one hundred of the soldiers were part of the American Legion, the Loyalist outfit that Arnold had raised after switching sides, a contingent that included many deserters from the Continental army. Over thirty vessels constituted the armada, including troop transports and supply ships, as well as five warships ranging in size from a forty-four-gun juggernaut to a sixteen-gun craft.[32] Six weeks earlier, well before Clinton decided on Arnold's expedition, General Washington had written Jefferson that appearances suggested another task force was being readied and "destined Southward" and that the British might possibly time its arrival for late in the year when the term of enlistments of "the better half of our Army" would expire.[33]

Arnold and his men experienced a rough winter's voyage, reminiscent of the travail visited on Clinton's armada when it sailed for Charleston. But Arnold did not have as far to go, and ten days out of New York rebel lookouts spotted his fleet at the entrance to the Chesapeake, though they were unsure whether it was friend or foe, or whether it was bound for Virginia or the Carolinas, or somewhere else. Jefferson had long before established a sentinel system for the speedy transmission of intelligence, and at 8:00 A.M. on Sunday, December 31, a messenger brought him word of the sighting.

Jefferson could not be certain whether this was the British task force about which Washington had warned or whether the French fleet that for so long had been blockaded in Brest had somehow gotten to sea and sailed for Virginia. Although the former was by far the most likely, Jefferson was reluctant to act until he had better intelligence. Frequent mobilizations had, in the fall, sparked what he called "very dangerous insurrection[s]" among militia units in two counties. Jefferson referred to those disturbances as "dangerous fire" occurrences, meaning that the next mutinies might spread and become generalized, leaving him gun-shy about ordering yet another militia muster unless he knew that it was unquestionably necessary.[34] Jefferson waited to act throughout that Sunday and again all day on Monday. Not until fifty hours had passed was Jefferson assured that this was an enemy armada. He responded at that juncture by summoning the militia and ordering them to assorted sites, including Petersburg on the Appomattox River. But Jefferson's delay in acting was consequential, for by then Arnold's soldiers were coming ashore in Newport News and Hampton. Within two additional days the enemy force was already fifty miles up the James River, about halfway to Richmond. When Jefferson at last reacted, he commanded that the "whole militia from adjacent counties" march to the capital, and he further instructed that government papers be removed from Richmond to safety and that all arms and ammunition that could not be transferred be destroyed. The governor, on horseback, supervised operations, and once assured that as much as possible had been done, he took his wife and three young daughters a few miles farther up the James to the safety of a plantation owned by his relatives.

On Friday, January 5, Arnold, with nine hundred infantry and cavalry, reached Richmond. They entered the city nearly unopposed, as the militia had either not yet reached the James or could not keep pace with the swiftly moving British vessels. While Jefferson stood on a knoll across the river and squinted through a spyglass to better see the destruction unfold, Arnold's men carried as much booty as possible to their ships, a considerable amount of it taken from private residences. But the British also seized seven cannon, numerous river crafts or all sizes, and huge stockpiles of grain. So much was garnered that forty-two vessels were required to transport the spoils. In addition to what was taken, the British spiked fifty-two cannon, destroyed over two thousand small arms, and demolished a rope walk, two warehouses, a foundry, several gun carriages, and huge stores of

powder, flints, rum, cordage, canvas, and hemp. The raiders torched some
public buildings, fires that spread and damaged a few residences and a
church, producing a thick black and gray smoke that hovered over
the capital. Arnold's royal troops wasted little time getting back to the
Chesapeake, though they paused to pillage Berkeley, the handsome estate
of Benjamin Harrison, a leading Virginia revolutionary and signer of the
Declaration of Independence.[35]

A week after splashing ashore in Virginia, Arnold was back in
Portsmouth and supervising the erection of his stronghold. Jefferson,
meanwhile, was widely blamed for the recent catastrophe. So vitriolic were
the attacks that Jefferson and many others presumed his public career
would be finished when his term as governor ended in six months. The
calumny directed at Jefferson was not entirely without reason. A more
timely response would have brought throngs of militiamen to Richmond
and much, perhaps all, of the damage to the capital might have been
prevented. Furthermore, two weeks earlier Steuben had proposed that the
governor garrison a fort that sat atop a high bluff at a crook in the James
River called Hood's Landing; Jefferson had ordered the construction of the
bastion a few weeks earlier, but in mid-December he rebuffed the idea of
posting large numbers of militiamen in the fort, thinking they could
provide more valuable service elsewhere. No one knew whether the fort
could have stopped Arnold before he reached Richmond, but all knew that
the invasion force had easily neutralized the installation on its way to the
capital. Though Jefferson was unaware of it, old friends criticized him in
private, and some officials—Steuben among them—complained to
Washington about the governor's shortcomings.[36]

Washington did not join the throng that was bashing Jefferson. All too
aware of the difficulty in making rapid military decisions, Washington, a
fellow Virginian who knew and respected Jefferson, understood the governor's plight. Washington was aware that Virginia was large and in many
areas only "thinly inhabited," making it nearly impossible to rapidly gather
a sufficient force to defend against an unexpected attack. Washington added
that the many navigable rivers that coursed through the state "greatly

exposed" it to these "kinds of predatory expeditions." More harmful sorties were certain to come, Washington told Jefferson, as they provided helpful diversions for Cornwallis.[37]

THE ENEMY'S INJURIOUS raid in Virginia was not all that Washington had on his mind. In fact, he had much greater worries. Late in the fall he had put his men in winter quarters that stretched from West Point to Morristown, preferring the scattergun approach as it made supplying them much easier. But he had no idea how many men he would have when enlistments expired at the dawn of the new year. He lamented to a neighbor in Virginia that for ages the army had been "without money," the men did not have adequate clothing, provisions were obtained solely by foraging and impressment, and with many enlistments shortly to expire the army soon "shall be (in a manner) without Men."[38]

What Washington did know was that 1781 would be decisive, one way or another. One side might score a major victory leading to peace. Or, if the war was still stalemated at year's end, one or more of the belligerents might decide against continuing the fight. Above all, and with good reason, Washington thought it doubtful that the United States could stay in the fray longer than one more year. Some states had wobbled badly in 1780, and given the nation's collapsed economy and crumbling morale, Washington wondered if his country could even "rub through" the coming year. There were reasons, too, to fear that this might be France's final year as a combatant in a stalemated conflict. Neutral countries throughout Europe, their commerce suffering from the French and British war at sea, were pushing assorted peace proposals. One plan was for France and Great Britain to send delegates to a mediation conference at which, in effect, the crowned heads of Europe would determine the peace terms. Russia and Austria backed the idea of an armistice, followed by peace negotiations between Britain and its former colonies. John Adams, one of America's diplomats in Europe, thought America faced greater dangers on the diplomatic front than Britain posed militarily. He also suspected, but could not prove, "Chicanery" on the part of both France and Britain. He wondered if France was secretly behind the proposals for mediation, a strategy aimed at affording the French the means of an honorable exit from a war in which it had gained nothing. He mused, too, over whether Britain was conniving for a way to secure a separate peace with France, after which it would continue to wage war against its former colonies. But during the spring, all the moves for an immediate peace fizzled, largely because France's foreign minister, Comte de Vergennes, still thought an Allied victory was possible in 1781. Adams was relieved, though he believed—as did Washington in all likelihood—that the Allies must break the war's gridlock in the coming months or unfavorable peace terms would be imposed on the Americans.[39]

As 1780 wound down, Washington reflected on the long-ago hopeful signs that had led him earlier in the year to think the stalemate soon would be broken. In a letter to one of his officers, Washington had ticked off the possibilities that once had seemed so promising: Spain had become a belligerent; France was sending over an army and naval force; England was shaken by domestic disturbances and might find that it was not "in her power to continue the contest." But in the end all the bright hopes had faded, and as 1781 approached, Washington remarked that he saw "nothing before us but accumulating distress."[40]

Washington may have thought that things could not be worse, but on New Year's Day 1781, soldiers in the Pennsylvania Line, in winter quarters at Mount Kemble, near Morristown, mutinied. This was the potentially cataclysmic event that Washington had perhaps most feared, and it was hardly unexpected given that his soldiers suffered privations of every kind and had not been paid during the past twelve months, nor had some received the full cash bounties they had been promised at the time of their enlistment. These outrageous conditions had long amounted to a powder keg that could explode at any moment. At noon on January 3—two days before Arnold reached Richmond—a messenger brought word to Washington's headquarters some seventy-five miles north of New York City that a "most general and unhappy mutiny" had commenced and was still in progress. Two immediate grievances were particularly important catalysts in touching off the explosion. Veteran soldiers had been driven over the brink by the appearance of new recruits whose pockets were stuffed with the cash bounties they had received for enlisting. (Upon enlistment, these men had received about twenty-seven dollars in silver and a promise of two hundred acres following the war.) In addition, many men who had enlisted in the new standing army three years earlier had thought their term of service was for three years and would end on January 1, 1781. Now, however, Congress and the army contended that they had joined the ranks for "three years or the war." They were in the army until the war ended. Underlying these complaints was a burning sense that civilians looked with condescension on the soldiery as undeserving of human rights.[41]

Washington learned that two officers had been wounded, and that the mutineers—some one thousand men, roughly 15 percent of those in the Continental army—not only were in control of their camp but had seized half a dozen field pieces and were marching on Philadelphia. Washington's greatest fear was that the actions of the Pennsylvanians would touch off an epidemic of mutinies, something that might well be helped along if civilian authorities became involved and settled things through a generous offer to the mutineers. He desperately wanted the episode to be handled exclusively by the army. Washington additionally worried that the disgruntled soldiers might, like Arnold, defect to Clinton's ranks in return for money, food, and winter clothing. He knew that beyond a shadow of a doubt Clinton would learn of the uprising and attempt to exploit it. He was correct. Clinton was aware of the mutiny before Washington and quickly sought to find some way of "driving the mutineers to us." He sent two agents into New Jersey to make contact with the rebellious soldiers. They were armed with an unsigned statement declaring that the soldiers had been "defrauded" by the rebel leaders and forced to suffer "every kind of misery and oppression." The crux of Clinton's communication, however, was a promise that the British would award the mutineers their back pay without any obligation to become part of the king's soldiery. He wanted them out of the Continental army as much or more than he wanted them in the British army, though he would take these men if they were willing to soldier for Great Britain. Washington, meanwhile, ordered General Anthony Wayne, in command on the scene, to use force only if the recalcitrant soldiers sought to join with the enemy, and he pleaded with the governors of most of the other northern states to find the money that would mollify their men in the Continental army.[42]

Wayne, with a large force, shadowed the mutineers on the road to Philadelphia and negotiated with the committee of sergeants that the rebellious soldiers had appointed. Representatives from the Pennsylvania government also made contact with the soldiers in Princeton, the step that Washington had dreaded, but it was their participation that led to a settlement in mid-month. They had the resources with which to make a deal. Pennsylvania's proffer—which Wayne had no choice but to quietly accept—was that no one would be punished for the insurrection, Clinton's agents would be turned over to the army, and those in the Pennsylvania Line who had served for three years would be given twenty dollars and a promise of all back pay, as well as the choice of leaving the army or of reenlisting. Roughly half the Pennsylvania Line chose to remain in the army, firm in their support of American independence and, as Washington put it, feeling only "detestation of the insidious . . . Enemy." Clinton's agents were handed over to the army and executed.[43]

Washington was "extremely embarrassed" by the mutiny, fearing its impact on General Rochambeau's thinking. He wrote the French general immediately on learning of the settlement, attempting to put a favorable spin on what had occurred. Most of the rebellious soldiers, he accurately said, were not native-born Americans, though in the end all had acted honorably in choosing loyalty to America over Clinton's "most advantageous propositions." With the exception of the New Jersey Line, the remainder of the Continentals were "chiefly natives" who, he told Rochambeau, would loyally endure the hardships they faced.[44]

Washington acknowledged his "utmost anxiety" throughout the crisis, a riveting fear that was not dashed by the settlement. Despite the auspicious tone of his letter to Rochambeau, Washington worried that other mutinies would erupt, and sure enough within twenty-four hours of dispatching his missive to his ally he was notified of an uprising in the New Jersey Line at

Pompton, about twenty miles north of Mount Kemble. (Clinton's intelligence service was now so streamlined that he was aware of the soldiers' planned insurgence before it occurred.) No one questioned that these mutineers had been inspired by what their counterparts from Pennsylvania had achieved. It soon was evident as well that they had been extended the same back-pay offer by the British that had been promised to the Pennsylvanians. Many in the New Jersey Line were longtime veterans who had fought at Brandywine, Germantown, and Monmouth and had endured Valley Forge and the grim years that followed. They had demonstrable grievances. British spies reported to officers in the king's army that many of these men were "naked and barefooted." They, too, had "reach[ed] the bounds of human patience," as Washington had said of the Pennsylvanians in his communiqué to Rochambeau. Initially, it appeared that the rebellion might quickly collapse. A day or so into the mutiny, the disaffected soldiers learned that New Jersey's assembly, unnerved by the Pennsylvania insurrection, had voted bounties for the soldiery and pardoned all who were involved. That was sufficient for some mutineers, but not all. Many still planned to march on Trenton in the coming days to meet with state officials there on January 30.[45]

Washington had pursued something of a wait-and-see course after learning of the Pennsylvania mutiny. On this occasion, however, he did not hesitate to deal with the insurgents in the most ruthless manner. Only such a response, he believed, could prevent further mutinies. He ordered the commander of New Jersey's militia to ready it for action against the state line, if need be, but his principal reliance was to be on a force of five hundred men drawn from among New Hampshire, Massachusetts, and Connecticut Continentals, virtually all of whom were posted at sites on the Hudson River. The Yankee soldiers were allocated three field pieces and placed under the command of General Robert Howe, whose Continentals would have a three-to-one numerical superiority over the mutineers. Washington's orders to Howe were starkly cold-blooded: Once the rebellious soldiers were disarmed, "you will instantly execute a few of the most active and most incendiary leaders." In the unlikely event that the rough-hewn Howe needed a pep talk, Washington reminded him of "how dangerous to civil liberty the precedent is of armed soldiers dictating terms to their country."[46]

The men assigned to this heart-stopping detail made a long, slow descent into New Jersey, a march hindered from the outset by a twenty-inch snowfall that reduced them to "inexpressible fatigue," in the words of one soldier. They trudged several miles each day and spent nights in houses and barns owned by obliging, or perhaps intimidated, farmers. Four days passed before the last man reached the rendezvous site in Ringwood, roughly eight miles from Pompton. In the interim, Howe learned that New Jersey's officers had negotiated with the mutineers, talks that led the men to end their insurrection and return to their huts in exchange for pardons for their offenses. The last of Howe's men arrived during the day on January 26. He was ready to act that night, committed to carrying out his grisly orders, pardons or no pardons. As winter's dark night descended, Howe gathered his force. The men doubtless knew that their job was to suppress a mutiny, but they likely were unaware of Howe's orders to see to the execution of some of their fellow Continentals. The officers "suffered much anxiety," one later recollected, uncertain whether the men would be "faithful on this trying occasion." Not long after midnight Howe ordered his detachment to step off for Pompton. On reaching the outskirts of the mutineers' camp, Howe paused to make the final arrangements and to address his men. Howe may not have required a special exhortation from Washington, but he believed it necessary to ready his soldiers with an inspirational talk. Unburdened by doubt, he told them that mutiny was a heinous crime that could destroy the cause for which they had sacrificed for so long. There would be no compromising with the insurgents, he added; he and his men had not marched all this way to cosset the mutineers. They must be brought to "unconditional submission," a statement that would seem to indicate that Howe did not share with his men the news that the mutiny had ended days earlier. Nor did he divulge even then that some mutineers would be put to death.

Howe's force then set off the last leg of the nighttime tramp. Once the cantonment in Pompton was sighted, he ordered his men to quietly surround the huts where the rebellious New Jersey soldiers lay sleeping. One last anxious interlude remained. In hushed silence, Howe's force marked time until sunrise. After what must have seemed an eternity, the first sign of light appeared in the eastern sky. The time to act had come. Howe directed his aide de camp to awaken the sleeping soldiers and command them to assemble unarmed on the parade ground. They were given five minutes to fall in line. The New Jersey soldiers quietly complied. In the ruddy light of early day, the men stood motionless, their frozen breath visible in the numbing cold on this winter morning, waiting uneasily for whatever was coming. Howe had previously, and covertly, asked the commander of the New Jersey Line to provide him with the names of those he considered the principal ringleaders of the mutiny. Fifteen names were on the list. Howe next directed several New Jersey officers to concur on one man from each of the three regiments who was most responsible for the mutiny. The three dreadfully unlucky designees were immediately tried. It was drumhead justice. Sentenced to death, the condemned men were marched to an area designated as the killing ground. While they stood trembling in the soiled slush and mud, Howe compelled the other twelve men on the list of those blamed for having incited the mutiny to comprise the firing squad. Some of these men, white-faced and trembling, wept openly when ordered to load the muskets with which they were provided. The proceedings moved so quickly, according to one witness, that the condemned had neither time to plead for mercy nor to pray. The first victim, a sergeant whom the New Jersey officers had fingered as the worst offender of the bunch, was made to kneel on the sodden ground. Three in the firing squad were to aim at his head, three at his heart; the other six were to provide the coup d'grâce. Once he was dispatched, the second doomed man was dealt with. The third man, already on his knees and expecting to take his last breath, was pardoned. He arose on shaky legs, tears streaming down his face. With the bullet-riddled bodies of his two friends lying facedown in the blood-soaked sludge only a couple of feet away, he wept uncontrollably, and so, too, did those in the firing squad who a moment earlier had been about to kill him.

Howe felt that he must do one more thing. He addressed the scores of assembled men in the New Jersey Line. He told them their crime had been enormous, as its "dreadful consequences" could have resulted in the ruination of the entire army and the loss of the Revolutionary War, foiling America's bid for independence. The soldiers were then made to ask their officers to pardon them, after which they were compelled to pledge that they would faithfully do their duty in the future. The January mutinies had been suppressed. There would be no more during 1781.[47]

"WE ARE BANKRUPT with a mutinous army," James Lovell, a Massachusetts congressman, pithily informed John Adams when he learned of the uprising by the Pennsylvania Line. He had long known that the irreparable economic problem could have fatal consequences, and like most, he thought the nation's financial woes were the root cause of the mutiny. Four weeks before the initial uprising Lovell had chronicled the nation's anguish: "Our Distress for money is extreme. We can pay neither our civil officers, nor our Army nor our Loan Interest," and money was lacking to hire "a Brigade of Waggons" to transport supplies—if provisions could be purchased—to the troops. Every other congressman was similarly aware of the need for "replenishing the Public Coffers with the Sinews of War," as a Virginia delegate remarked before he repeated a limerick that was making the rounds: "An army naked, and unpaid / The Public lean on foreign Aid." Further assistance from France was indeed the only recourse. Neither the national government nor the states had the means of raising adequate revenue. Six months earlier, before Rochambeau's army came ashore, Colonel Alexander Hamilton already understood that "If we are saved France and Spain must save us."[48]

With the outcome of the war on the line in 1781, there was only one thing to do. The United States would have to seek another loan from its ally. France, in 1777, had extended a subsidy to the new nation, and during each of the next two years it had made additional loans that sustained the enfeebled United States. Now, if the Continental army was to be a viable force in the coming campaign, it required further help. In November, soon after Greene's selection to command the army in the South, Congress voted to request from France a loan of twenty-five million livres, roughly four million dollars. Time was of the essence. In less than six months the weather would permit the opening of the year's campaign season in the North, and under the most favorable conditions around six months would be needed for French money to reach the Continental army. Nevertheless, two months elapsed after Congress acted before its emissary sailed for France. Weeks passed while Congress debated whether it would be best to have Benjamin Franklin, America's minister to France, make the appeal to Comte de Vergennes or to send an envoy extraordinary across the sea. Many congressmen questioned the energy and capacity of the seventy-five-year-old Franklin; others thought him too passive in his dealings with French officials. In normal times, few would have doubted Franklin's suitability. These were not normal times. After much contention, Congress selected Colonel John Laurens, the aide to Washington who had sought to raise an army of Black soldiers in South Carolina. Laurens had studied in Europe and spoke French, was young and energetic, and was close to the Marquis de Lafayette, who promised to write letters of introduction to French officials.[49] On the other hand, Laurens had no diplomatic experience.

Congress instructed its envoy to first meet with Washington and an array of French officials in America, unless doing so would "retard your voyage." Laurens met with the French minister in Philadelphia before calling on Washington at New Windsor in mid-January. Lafayette was posted nearby, and Laurens spoke with him as well. When the discussions concluded, Washington committed to paper his views "on the present state of American affairs," a compendium of the points that he wished for Laurens to raise in his meetings with Vergennes. It was composed while Washington awaited word on the resolution of the mutiny in the Pennsylvania Line, and it was one of the lengthiest documents that he wrote during the war. With perhaps everything riding on a French loan, nothing could be left to chance.[50]

Washington began with an extended explanation of the causes of America's economic miseries, carefully emphasizing that the problem was in no way due to American fatuousness, though he acknowledged that the

new nation's highly decentralized structure of governance was a major part
of the problem. Otherwise, the excessive costs of the war, economic disruption brought on by hostilities and the domestic revolution, the war's unset-
tling impact on commerce, and inexperience in self-government had all
contributed to the irrevocable financial adversities. However, America's
fundamental problem was its "want of a sufficient stock of wealth," the result
of having been kept for so long in a state of subservience within the British
Empire, a reality that imperial France should understand. Congress and the
states had resorted to several expedients to find sufficient revenue. Nothing
had worked. After years of travail the "patience of the army" was "now
nearly exhausted." Faced with critical shortages of food, clothing, and pay,
the Continental army required "speedy relief, a relief not within the compass
of our means." Furthermore, morale had sunk among civilians who were
"little accustomed to heavy burdens," a remark intended to alert the French
that America could not continue this war much longer.

Apart from money, Washington mentioned two matters that were crucial
to an Allied victory. He hoped his ally would increase Rochambeau's army
to fifteen thousand men and stressed the need for "naval superiority." Allied
naval supremacy would derail Britain's ability to supply its army, inflicting
on Clinton's army the very suffering that had for so long been the companion
of America's soldiery. The minute that Britain no longer possessed naval
dominion, said Washington, Clinton would also be compelled to remain on
the defensive. Furthermore, once the British understood that they had no
"prospect of extending their acquisitions," they would lose interest in "prosecuting the war." One other thing: With naval hegemony, the Allies could
launch "a vigorous offensive."

Washington sought to reassure the French that the loan would be repaid.
America's debts were small, he wrote, and could easily be liquidated with
the postwar revenue derived from the sale of western lands. He additionally
wished France to know that America's longing for independence had not
waned. Though the "people are discontented," their disgruntlement was not
with the war. Morale had suffered given the "the feeble and oppressive
mode" of waging the war that had been necessitated by the lack of revenue.

The citizenry remained ready to make "great and continued exertions" in order to avoid "a reunion with Great Britain" that they abhorred.[51]

Dispatching Laurens in search of a French loan was only one step in a flurry of activity taken to ready the country for the crucial campaign that was coming. Congress authorized John Adams, who had been sent across the Atlantic to serve as a peace commissioner, to travel to Amsterdam in search of a loan. In November, New York and the four New England states sent deputies to what became known as the Hartford Convention, a conclave that eventually appealed to Congress to vote for a national impost, a 5 percent tax on goods imported into the United States. Thomas Paine pitched in with two pamphlets that, among other things, endorsed the proposed impost and urged the states to grant greater powers to Congress, including enhanced-revenue raising capabilities. In February 1781, just days after the New Jersey mutiny was squelched, Congress asked every state to grant it the authority to levy the impost. Three days after it took that action—about the time that Laurens finally sailed—Congress made yet another stab at solving its economic dilemma by creating the Office of Superintendent of Finance. Alexander Hamilton, still in his midtwenties was proposed for the post, but it instead went to Robert Morris, Philadelphia's leading merchant. "Our Finances want a Necker," said a Virginia delegate, a reference to Jacques Necker, a Swiss banker thought to be a financial wizard for having reformed France's troubled royal finances a few years earlier. Not everyone was happy with Morris's appointment, but most thought there was little alternative. A New Jersey congressman summed up the feelings of his colleagues. Naming a businessman who was not a member of Congress had to be an improvement over the Board of Treasury, a panel of congressmen with little knowledge of finance that had consistently "only made bad, worse."[52]

Some who feared the worst from the mutiny crises had, by February, come to think the insurrections may have been blessings in disguise. William Sharpe, a North Carolina congressman, thought the mutinies in the long run would have "salutary effects," for they had spurred Congress to act. Washington thought the same thing. He notified General Greene that the scares had "roused" Congress and the states "from their late supine condition," pushing them into "vigorous & effectual exertions."[53]

GENERAL GREENE HAD arrived in Charlotte on December 2, roughly six weeks after his series of meetings with Washington. In the interim, Gates had remained in command and, in October, had shifted the army westward from Hillsborough to Salisbury, near the forks of the Yadkin River and some forty miles above Charlotte. Having been informed by Congress in the fall that a French squadron might possibly be sailing for Charleston, Gates wished to have his army positioned so that it could rapidly advance into South Carolina. No Allied fleet appeared, and in November, Gates concluded that Cornwallis was going into winter quarters. He followed suit. By then a southern army had gradually come together. On November 25, Gates reported that he had 1,053 Continentals, 1,147 militiamen, and 404 men in Daniel Morgan's rifle corps. Altogether, the southern army consisted of 2,604 men and, as Banastre Tarleton observed, had once again "assumed a tolerable appearance."[54]

Greene would not quite see things in quite the same light when he arrived in North Carolina. He found his army "in a most wretched Condition, destitute of every thing necessary either for the Comfort or Convenience of Soldiers." But it was what he had, and he had to decide how to best use it against the army of Cornwallis.[55]

CHAPTER 9

RISK-TAKING BECOMES THE ORDER OF THE DAY

BEFORE DEPARTING NEW Jersey, General Greene had begun to consider his options in fighting Lord Cornwallis, but he knew it was too early to make final plans. At that juncture, and for the next several weeks, Greene did not know whether Cornwallis had been reinforced after King's Mountain. Nor did Greene know the whereabouts of his adversary. Besides, Greene wanted to assess his own army and its officers before laying his plans. Befitting a former quartermaster general, logistics were uppermost on Greene's mind. To assure that supplies from the northern states that passed through Virginia reached his army, he issued orders for the exploration of the Roanoke, Dan, and Yadkin Rivers to determine whether they were practicable for waterborne transportation. He also directed General Steuben to secure the region around Portsmouth in order to inhibit British incursions into Virginia, a directive that was rendered meaningless when Benedict Arnold soon thereafter occupied that site with a powerful force.[1]

Greene was a whirlwind of activity during his first weeks in North Carolina. Even during his journey to Charlotte, Greene had carefully reconnoitered the landscape, keeping a watchful eye on the rivers he crossed, observing fords, ferries, and other possible crossings. Noting that river upon river coursed through North Carolina, he laid the groundwork for successfully traversing those streams in the event that someday he was faced with having to make a hurried retreat. Unlike Gates, who had imprudently hurried into action, Greene spent weeks making preparations for taking the field. Working with Colonel Thaddeus Kosciuszko, the professional military engineer, Greene set about searching for the bateaux that would be needed for transporting supplies and making river crossings. He appealed to the state assembly to provide him with ample wagons, artisans to keep them running, and teamsters to drive them. He saw to the fabrication of more than twenty strategically located magazines and ordered that a three-day supply of milled grain be stored here and there in patriot-owned gristmills. He undertook "great Alterations" within the quartermaster corps and sought to persuade North Carolina to reform its supply system so that one official "of known Probity" would be vested with "full and ample Powers to call forth the supplies." Operating on the dictum that "Great events often depend on little things," he advised the state's Board of War to establish additional storehouses for arms and other provisions, gather and "stall-feed" large herds of cattle, and "salt down as much pork" as possible. He was horrified to discover that many militiamen raised both by Virginia and North Carolina during September's emergency had never been sent home, with the result that their foraging had "laid waste almost all the Country." He knew that he would have to have militiamen, but he wanted them mustered only when the enemy threatened "immediate ravages" or he was about to take the field. From the outset, he took steps to synchronize his army's actions with those of partisan bands, a step with which Gates had scarcely troubled. Greene had hardly unpacked his bags before he contacted Francis Marion and Thomas Sumter. Among other things, he let them know that they were to be a principal source of his intelligence, the "Eyes" of his army, as he put it. Without their help, he would be "groping in the dark," he said. But he also told them that this war could be won only by the army. Partisan sallies were akin to "the garnish of a table." They would play vital roles in softening up the adversary, though only the army could vanquish the enemy.[2]

Greene received encouraging word from Virginia during December. It had resolved to raise the three thousand Continentals needed to meet its troop quota and by mid-month four hundred of those men were already on the march to join him in North Carolina. In addition, Steuben was sending down 1,500 muskets and bayonets, another 2,000 firearms were coming from farther north, and wagons and artillery horses were on the way as well. Greene needed everything. Long before arriving in the South, he had been advised that the army was in deplorable condition, and he immediately found those reports to be all too accurate. His army was "weak," "half starved," "without tents and camp equipage," and in a "wretched Condition," he said. He told Governor Thomas Sim Lee of Maryland that if the southern army was not strengthened, North Carolina would fall under Britain's thumb, a turn of events that would be "fatal to you" and the potential soldiers languishing at home.[3]

Greene had never previously been in the South, but he was aware of the problems that two of his predecessors, Robert Howe and Benjamin Lincoln, had experienced with southern authorities. Greene resolved not be overbearing in his approaches to the officials. "To effect an entire reformation of the plan and politicks of this Country would be a greater task than that attempted by Martin Luther in the Romish Church," he allowed. Contrary to what some in the North had concluded, Greene soon found that southerners had "Spirit and Enterprize," but they "must go to war in their own way or not at all." In their impatience to drive the British from their states, he learned, southerners at times demanded hasty action, and it led him to think it was perhaps what had caused Gates to act too quickly. "Prudence and Caution," Greene vowed, were to be his watchwords.[4]

Gates had used something of a sledgehammer approach when seeking assistance from the governors of Virginia and North Carolina. Greene sought to reason with them, but behind his velvet-glove manner lurked a menacing threat. If the army was not properly supplied, he told Abner Nash, it would have no choice but to "take what is necessary." For the most part, however, Greene chose his words carefully. The quickest way to ensure the loss of discipline within an army, he advised the governors, was to sow anguish among the soldiery by not adequately feeding and clothing them. He wrote Jefferson that the "Life of a Soldier in its best State is subject to innumerable Hardships," but when ill provisioned the soldier's lot become "intolerable." No man faced with unbearable conditions, he continued, "will think himself bound to fight the Battles" dictated by negligent or indifferent leaders.[5]

Following his arrival in North Carolina, Greene found that Cornwallis was in Winnsboro, South Carolina, to which he had retreated following the debacle at King's Mountain. Situated some twenty-five miles northwest of Camden, and midway between the Wateree and Broad Rivers, it was ideally situated for assisting his two main interior posts, Camden and Ninety Six. The region below it was firmly in British control and abounded with all the foodstuffs his army would need. Cornwallis acknowledged, "We live well here," beyond even his "most sanguine expectations." But he had not gotten soft. All along, Cornwallis had planned to remain in Winnsboro only until General Alexander Leslie arrived to reinforce him, and that force did not disembark in Charleston until mid-December, more than two weeks after Greene reached Charlotte.[6]

While Cornwallis awaited Leslie and Greene readied his army, both generals grappled with their strategic choices. Cornwallis remained convinced that if he focused on South Carolina, conditions in that province were certain to remain irredeemably bleak. He held unwaveringly to the belief that suppressing the rebellion in South Carolina hinged on sealing shut the rebels' supply lines and destroying Greene's army, and both objectives could be achieved only by returning to North Carolina. Success was not assured. Permanent closure of the supply lines would depend almost entirely on what Cornwallis called "the exertions of our friends in that province," a reference to Britain's ongoing reliance on an army of occupation consisting of Loyalist militia. Cornwallis's army would clear out the rebels, after which Tory militiamen would occupy and defend the conquered territory and the areas through which the supply lines ran. The role they were to play was so vital that Cornwallis, contradicting his earlier remarks, stated that Britain's "only chance of putting a favorable end to this war" depended on the activism and exemplary service of the Loyalists. Given his experiences in South Carolina, Cornwallis was skeptical of the Loyalists' grit, privately labeling them "dastardly and pusillanimous," but he saw going into North Carolina and hoping for the most from the Tories as the best of the lamentable choices facing him.[7]

Bringing Greene to battle was Cornwallis's second objective, and marching into North Carolina offered the best hope of getting the latest rebel commander onto a battlefield. Given the outcome at Camden, Cornwallis had to assume that Greene would stand and fight only if the rebel army possessed an overwhelming numerical superiority. Otherwise, Greene would run as Washington had run during the New York campaign in 1776. Nevertheless, Cornwallis could hope. Greene, an inexperienced commander, might blunder. His rebel army might also be caught in an inescapable trap while seeking to cross one of North Carolina's many rivers or between two of those rivers. Or, given that he was an unseasoned commander, Greene, might opt to stand and fight, as had Lincoln at Charleston. Time after time in this war the British had been victorious, or come within a whisker of scoring a colossal triumph, when they got the rebels onto a battlefield. In Canada and on Long Island, in Savannah, Charleston, and Camden, the rebels had gone down, and given another hour of precious daylight at Brandywine, Howe might have destroyed Washington's army; at Monmouth, Clinton had thrown a scare into the rebel army while utilizing only a fraction of his redcoats. If Cornwallis could get Greene on a battlefield, he was confident of victory.

In the first days of 1781, Cornwallis wrote Clinton of his decision to reenter North Carolina. His first foray into the province had ended in disaster, and he knew that this incursion would also include risks. Others were aware of that as well. General O'Hara feared that Cornwallis's undertaking would be eerily similar to that of General Burgoyne in New York's backcountry, with added dangers that the British had not faced in 1777.[8]

Like Burgoyne, Cornwallis would have to cope with a dangerously long supply line, one that might be even more vulnerable to partisan attacks than anything Burgoyne had faced. Moreover, Cornwallis would be taking the field in the winter, long after the summer and fall harvests were in, raising the possibility that the British army would have to face unusually large contingents of rebel militia. The presence of the British army in North Carolina might also draw rebel fighters from every nook and cranny throughout the South, as had occurred in the fall. If O'Hara discerned those dangers, there can be no question that Cornwallis was also aware of them. But Cornwallis was a fighter and risk-taker, and after six months in the South he saw another incursion into North Carolina as the sole hope of bringing Britain's southern strategy to a successful conclusion.

Greene also had choices to make. He could take his army into South Carolina and seek to wear down the enemy through multiple small actions. Or he could remain in North Carolina and wait for Cornwallis's army to come after him, eventually "flee[ing] before them," luring the enemy farther and farther from its supply sources, and deeper and deeper into North Carolina's unfriendly backcountry.[9] To enter into South Carolina would not only put Greene in the lion's den against both Cornwallis and Loyalist militias but also increase his supply problems by a quantum leap. What Greene contemplated prior to reaching Charlotte cannot be known, but by mid-December he had made his choice. The option he chose has been described as "audacious." Clinton thought it an idiotic plan that offered "no hopes of success."[10]

Greene decided to divide his army in the face of a superior adversary. Many commanders who had made such a choice had been burned, including Washington in New York in 1776, Burgoyne in dispatching a division to Bennington, and Cornwallis in sending Ferguson into the wilds of western North Carolina. Now Greene opted to follow suit. His plan was to take the bulk of his army to the Cheraws in South Carolina, an area ripe for foraging. At the same moment, Daniel Morgan was to march six hundred men to the Pacolet River in western North Carolina, the very area beyond King's Mountain where Ferguson had spent his final days recruiting Tories. Greene reasoned that should Cornwallis come after him, Morgan could assail Britain's vulnerable backcountry posts at Camden and Ninety Six, wiping out many of the enemy's gains since the fall of Charleston. If Cornwallis came after Morgan, Greene planned to move against weakly defended posts above Charleston.[11]

Greene's plan was packed with hazards, and it was out of character for him, as he not only had pledged circumspection but in previous years had repeatedly advised Washington against risky choices. In large measure, Greene fixed on this course because of "necessity." He could not find sufficient provisions for his army in and around Charlotte. He also quickly discovered that North Carolina's authorities had "such a high opinion of the Militia" that he did not "expect they will ever raise a single Continental soldier." Those militiamen required training and discipline, as did the discouraged regulars he found on his arrival, and he thought he might make strides in those directions should he be left unmolested in the Cheraws.[12]

Greene had faith in Morgan as well as in his cavalry arm. Washington had reluctantly detached Colonel Henry ("Light Horse Harry") Lee—scion of an old and powerful Virginia family who at age twenty in 1776 had been commissioned a cavalry captain—with 150 horse soldiers to the South. Lee linked up with Colonel William Washington, a distant cousin of the commander in chief, who had led dragoons since 1777 after having been seriously wounded on Long Island and at Trenton. Tall and chubby, with short cropped hair, Colonel Washington had served in the southern theater for the past year and now commanded one hundred troopers. Greene had soldiered with both these cavalry officers and had confidence in them. In addition, within a couple of weeks of taking command, Greene concluded that he was surrounded by a cadre of capable officers. Colonel Lee, in fact, believed that in no time Greene had "infused a spirit of exalted patriotism" within officers and men and won the "durable attachment and esteem of all."[*] Though unpretentious, Greene believed in himself. He had served in this war by leading men on battlefields and by running the army's quartermaster service; in both roles, he had learned how armies functioned and how to keep them supplied so that they could function. On first encountering

Greene, many did not see what Lee called the "fire" that burned inside him, but it was there, and it blazed at a pitch that was foreign to the makeup of both Lincoln and Gates. In ambition, enterprise, daring, and aggressiveness, he exhibited similarities to Benedict Arnold and, possibly, Anthony Wayne. Within the Continental army, only Washington was a better general, and by 1781, as events would demonstrate, Greene was at least his equal.[13]

Greene was aware of the perils he would face and fully mindful that risk-taking sometimes ended in disaster. He knew, too, that at times taking chances led to success. Washington hazarded everything in the two encounters at Trenton and came away with two important victories. The commander in chief had rolled the dice again at Germantown, and while he did not gain a victory, his daring was thought to have been a factor in prompting France to ally with the American rebels. In contrast, Britain's generals had seldom acted audaciously. Had Gage attacked Washington's depleted army in Boston at the outset of 1776, had Howe risked an assault on the entrenched rebels in Brooklyn Heights or against the forlorn Continentals at Valley Forge in 1778, the war might have ended long ago. For that matter, had Clinton dared to go after the French in Rhode Island during the previous July or September there may have been no need for a campaign in 1781.

Greene set off for the Cheraws and Morgan for western North Carolina shortly before Christmas. Morgan had with him 320 Maryland and Delaware Continental infantrymen under Lieutenant Colonel John Eager Howard, 200 riflemen, and Colonel Washington's troopers. Morgan was in some respects the rebel's counterpart to Patrick Ferguson, though he had not been reared in the affluence that the Scotsman had known. Morgan was the son of Welsh immigrants who worked a small farm in New Jersey. While in his teens, Morgan had set out on his own, moving to the frontier in Virginia, where he supported himself for a couple of years by working as a teamster and in whatever manual labor jobs he could find. In the French and Indian War, Morgan was hired as a teamster by the British army, a stint that ended when in a fit of anger he struck a redcoat officer, an indiscretion for which he was punished with a brutal flogging. The beating left him with permanent scars on his back and an indelible hatred of the haughty British.

Later in that same war, while soldiering as a Virginia ranger, Morgan was shot through the mouth. In the years between that conflict and the Revolutionary War, Morgan was often in trouble with the law. But with marriage—a common-law affair—he settled down to a rather prosperous life as a farmer, though in 1774 he once again was drawn to arms, this time against the Indians, an experience from which he learned the ways of irregular war and the utility of the Kentucky rifle in combat.

Morgan secured the command of a Virginia light infantry company at the beginning of the Revolutionary War and was in Washington's camp outside Boston by midsummer 1775. He took part in Arnold's Canadian invasion that fall and was captured in the attack on Quebec. Following his release, Morgan was given command of a ranger corps consisting of one hundred riflemen drawn mostly from the Maryland, Virginia, and Pennsylvania frontiers. Often dressed as Indians and sporting war paint, Morgan's corps inspired fear among British soldiers who thought them barbarians. He gained fame for his exploits in the two big battles of the Saratoga campaign, moving his men about the battlefield by issuing signals via a turkey call. He endured the Valley Forge winter, but a year later, passed over for promotion to the rank of general officer, Morgan quit the army. He remained at home in Virginia for a year, until Gates summoned him in mid-1780. He arrived too late to fight at Camden but remained with the army and was present when Greene arrived.

Morgan was thick and hard, with broad shoulders and heavily muscled arms. Like Ferguson, he went into combat dressed unconventionally, often wearing a long linen hunting shirt with leather leggings and moccasins. He carried a rifle and strapped a tomahawk and scalping knife with a twelve-inch blade around his waist. As was also true of Ferguson, Morgan was a leader, the sort of officer men believed in and wished to serve under, an officer fond of spending time with his men, swapping stories with them, treating them well, and giving the impression that he and his men were fraternal equals. In a sense they were, for Morgan's hardscrabble background resembled that of most of his soldiers. Nearly forty-seven years old in 1781, Morgan was no longer in the best of health, with rheumatism and back problems that left him in constant pain, though he was up for one more campaign against the British.[14]

Greene's orders to Morgan were to act "as your own prudence and discretion may direct," though he cautioned him to be cautious and vigilant. The "object" of Morgan's campaign was to "annoy the enemy," language which suggests that Greene thought it more likely that Cornwallis would come after him rather than Morgan. But a battle in western Carolina could not be ruled out, and if Morgan could "spirit up the people" in that region, he could succeed as the patriots had succeeded against Ferguson. Greene ordered Morgan to establish magazines as he proceeded, filling them with provisions obtained through foraging. He might need these resources if compelled to make a hasty retreat or a hurried dash to assist Greene.[15]

Cornwallis, at Winnsboro, learned almost immediately from his dragoons—his best intelligence gatherers—that Morgan and Greene were on the move in different directions. Yet while Cornwallis was aware that his enemy was moving, he was not sure what they were up to. He guessed that Morgan's intention was to attack the royal outpost at Ninety Six. Greene's descent into South Carolina mystified and worried him. The only logical explanation for Greene's action, Cornwallis thought, was that it had to be part of a plan for him to act in concert with a French fleet. "My anxiety is great," he acknowledged, adding that he thought "with horror of an embarkation" by the French. Lacking both the manpower and the naval superiority to tangle with the Allies along the coast, Cornwallis shifted his immediate focus to Morgan.[16]

By Christmas, Morgan had marched past King's Mountain, crossed the Broad River, and camped on the banks of the Pacolet River, about a dozen miles west of the site of Ferguson's defeat. As he was not pressed by the enemy, Morgan remained in this area for some fifteen days, a stretch during which upwards of four hundred militiamen from the three southern states below Virginia arrived in his camp, increasing his troop strength to nearly nine hundred. His plans were somewhat more ambitious than Cornwallis imagined. After four days on the Pacolet, Morgan advised Greene that if he could create a diversion that would draw away Cornwallis, "I should wish to march into Georgia." That hope was not borne out, but even so Morgan had already won an important little victory. Advised that a force of 250 Georgia Tories—perhaps unaware that a large rebel army was nearby—had advanced into the region and were "insulting and Plundering The good people" who resided in the vicinity, Morgan dispatched Colonel Washington with his dragoons and foot soldiers. Alerted at last, the Tories hastily retreated. They did not escape. Washington caught up with them on December 29 at Hammonds Store House, about forty miles away. In a brief encounter, Washington decimated the Tories, killing, wounding, and taking captive some 200 men. Washington did not lose a single man.[17]

Cornwallis, meanwhile, waited impatiently for Leslie and his 1,900 men to join him. He confided that the "slow progress" of the reinforcements was "vexatious," though in truth Leslie's men were not dallying. They were slogging through a countryside that had been flooded by recurrent winter storms. In early January, Cornwallis felt that he could wait no longer, and he put his men in motion. He had conceived a plan for trapping and destroying Morgan and, with luck, of wiping out Greene as well. The first element in Cornwallis's plan was for Tarleton, with a force of 1,200 men that included cavalry, artillery, and infantry from both regular and provincial units—and accompanied by about thirty local Tories who were to serve as guides—to move north in search of Morgan, last known to be some seventy miles away. Like Morgan, Tarleton was to stay on the west side of the Broad River, and his orders were to "push [Morgan] to the utmost." Tarleton set off at the beginning of the second week in January. Heavy rains pounded the region, swelling rivers that were already swollen. Tarleton's progress, like Leslie's, was impeded. In addition, Tarleton paused to await reinforcements and his baggage, and to forage, hoping to accumulate a four-day supply of food before his hunt for Morgan began in earnest.

Three or four days after Tarleton set off, Cornwallis also marched northward, but he stayed on the east side of the Broad River. When joined by Leslie, Cornwallis would possess some 3,200 men, nearly two-thirds of whom were British or Hessian regulars. Cornwallis anticipated that Morgan would retreat, not fight. The rebels might fall back into the lair of the Over

Mountain Men, which would put them beyond the reach of Tarleton. But if Morgan retreated eastward in hopes of rejoining Greene, the rebel force might wind up in Cornwallis's net. By remaining east of the Broad River, Cornwallis also felt assured that he would be between Morgan and Greene. Should Greene hurry to Morgan's rescue, Cornwallis, with his overwhelming numerical superiority, might—if fortune smiled—fall on Greene's little army while Tarleton decimated Morgan. Cornwallis's progress was slowed by the interminable rainfall, but by January 16 he was between Turkey and Bullocks Creeks, only a dozen or so miles south of King's Mountain. He paused there to await Leslie's arrival.[18]

Morgan's intelligence network was the equal of his adversary's, and he was well informed of Tarleton's advance. Morgan rapidly consolidated his force, which had been detached to assorted locations along the Pacolet and Broad Rivers. He additionally posted South Carolina infantrymen armed with rifles, and led by Andrew Pickens, between himself and Tarleton. On January 14, aware that Tarleton was only thirty miles away, Morgan fell back, but neither to the west nor the east. His retreat was to the north. Morgan knew that he faced great peril, and the following day he wrote Greene asking that his detachment be permitted to march east to connect with the remainder of the army. He explained that he could accomplish nothing that would "balance the risks" he faced, adding that he could not contemplate fighting. It "is essential to our safety to avoid coming to action," he said.[19]

Within hours of writing that letter, Morgan learned that Tarleton had about 1,100 men. Morgan, with 940 men, reckoned that the odds against success were not so bad. He began to search for a suitable place to make a stand. Meanwhile, he continued to retreat, aware that each day he withdrew along the muddy, rutted roads and past desolate wintry forests was another day when Tarleton's provisions would dwindle. Morgan guessed that as the stock in Tarleton's pantry shrank, the royal dragoon might be compelled to send out foraging parties that would be susceptible to surprise attacks. Already, in fact, Tarleton was encountering resistance. As his horsemen and foot soldiers slowed to cross the apparently endless number of cold, rushing streams that coursed through the countryside, they now and then were ambushed by small parties of Pickens's men and North Carolina militiamen who were covering Morgan's retreat. An instant after squeezing off a round—often with deadly accuracy—the pickets vanished into the dark woods. After one or two surprise attacks, Tarleton's foot soldiers advanced with feral vigilance.[20]

But Tarleton kept coming. On January 15 he was near Morgan's old campsite on the Pacolet River. As darkness crept over the area, Tarleton appeared to make a camp. It was a ruse. Once darkness blanketed the countryside, Tarleton put his men in motion once again. By the time the surprised rebel units learned they had been duped, Tarleton was only about six miles away from Morgan's force. Time had run out. A decision had been forced on Morgan. On that same day, January 16, Morgan reconnoitered a site that his scouts had spotted. The locals called it Cowpens. It was a wide, mostly flat meadow that stretched five hundred yards, ending against the Broad River. The terrain sloped gently up toward a slight crest at the north end, behind which the terrain dipped before rising again to a low ridge. It had been a perfect spot for cattle drivers to pause when taking herds of livestock to eastern markets, and Morgan thought it a good choice for his purposes. For one thing, unlike Camden, it was not bounded by swamps and dense forests, the places to which many of Gates's men, in search of refuge, had fled. At Cowpens, there would be no escape. The men would have to stand and fight, or risk the fate of Buford's men.[21]

Morgan convened a council of war. It approved giving battle. A third-hand story goes that once the decision was made, Colonel Washington declared: "No burning, no flying: but face about and give battle to the enemy, and acquit ourselves like men in defense of their baggage, their lives, and the interests of the Country."[22] As Tarleton's force closed to within five miles, Morgan, seething with nerves and determination, awakened his men. "Boys, get up, Benny's coming!" he allegedly bawled.[23] While his men ate a hurried breakfast—Morgan thought it could only help to have soldiers with a full stomach—he hobbled among them, focusing on the militiamen in particular. He talked and told jokes, some ribald. He told them that they needed to get off only three shots, after which they could fall back behind the next line. He reminded the men not to squeeze their trigger until they could see the whites of the enemy soldiers' eyes. Morgan promised that the "day will be ours," after which, when they returned home, "the old folks will bless you, and the girls will kiss you, for your gallant conduct."[24]

Morgan had devised an unorthodox battle plan. His forward units were rifleman from Georgia and South Carolina, skilled marksmen who had honed their skills on star-crossed squirrels, deer, rabbits, and goodness knows what else. Hidden behind the few trees on the site, they were to hold their fire until the enemy was nearly on them, then lay down a volley. If sufficient confusion was sown in Tarleton's ranks, they might get off a second or even a third shot. Thereafter, they were to withdraw to the second rebel line about 150 yards farther back and join the militiamen, where they were expected to cut loose at least two additional shots, always sighting in on enemy officers if possible. Next, they were to fall back behind the third line, the line of Continentals commanded by Colonel John Eager Howard, a twenty-nine-year-old Maryland aristocrat who had seen action at Camden and, before that, had fought in many engagements in the North. Washington's cavalry was behind Howard, but hidden from view by the low knoll. The horse soldiers were to enter the fray whenever Morgan or Washington gave the signal. It was a plan with one particularly dicey element. The militia would come under fire early in the engagement. If they panicked, as had the militiamen who lost their nerve at Camden, the entire scheme might unravel. Another general might have posted the militia elsewhere on the battlefield or incorporated them with the regulars. But almost alone among Continental army generals, Morgan had confidence in militiamen. He had been one himself and he felt they would perform well if well led. He also knew that around three-quarters of the militiamen had already experienced some combat and that most were country boys who were accustomed to firearms and good marksmen. Just to be on the safe side, Morgan allocated twenty-four rounds to each man, eight more than men customarily took into battle. Morgan believed that an ample supply of ammunition would help buck up a man's confidence.

Tarleton had put his men to bed that night but roused them in the wee hours of January 17 for the final advance toward Cowpens. Having been in the field for ten days, his men were tired and hungry, and they were given nothing to eat before setting off through the cold, still darkness. After splashing across Macedonia Creek and arriving at the cusp of what soon would be the field of battle, Tarleton still did not feed his men. It was dark and the temperature hovered in the twenties during the hour or so that Tarleton's cold troopers waited impatiently for sunrise. The moment the first low pink rays shone in the eastern sky, Tarleton dispatched fifty dragoons to clear away any pickets that Morgan might have posted. They ran into the rifle-wielding skirmishers Morgan had posted behind trees near the edge of the battlefield. The rebel pickets squeezed off a salvo. Several horsemen tumbled from their mounts. The remainder retreated precipitously. Tarleton next sent out the light infantry. They did the job, but not before some of them were felled, after which Morgan's advance unit, their initial task having been completed, fell back as planned. To this point, not a single rebel soldier had taken a round.

The time had come for the real battle to begin. It is a virtual maxim of warfare that pre-battle plans fall apart in the shock, fog, and supercharged passion of action. But Morgan's plan played out with nearly uncanny accuracy. Tarleton led off with his infantry. Though on foot, these men moved rapidly, covering two hundred yards in three minutes, huzzaing as they came while drums and fifes filled the air with sounds that foretold impending valor. Morgan said later that they came on as if "they Intended to eat us up." One of his men later recalled that the enemy "advanced as if certain of victory."[25] The rebel soldiers answered with their customary blood-chilling "Indian hallo," and they did not flinch. When the enemy came with thirty-five yards, the militiamen in the second line opened fire with what one soldier remembered as a "sheet of flame" that blew a hole in the British line. "Oh! It was beautiful," he recollected.[26] Tarleton's officers regrouped their men and sent them forward again. This time they got off their first round, though as they were climbing a slight incline, many shots were high of the mark. All the while, Morgan stayed with his militiamen, still telling jokes and urging that they "squinney well" when taking aim.[27] By now, the militia-men were ready with their second shot. That fusillade, too, caused horrific damage within the line of redcoats. Four British Legion companies suffered a 90 percent casualty rate. Two-thirds of the royal infantry officers were killed or wounded.

When the militiamen had fired their three shots, they fell back according to Morgan's plan. To this point, nearly all the damage had been caused by the rebels, but the outcome was far from decided. It would be determined by the performance of Colonel Howard's line of Continentals. The fight in this sector was fierce, as the men on each side fired shot after shot. After ten minutes or so, Tarleton threw in his elite Highlanders regiment, which assailed the American right flank. Simultaneously, Tarleton unleashed his feared cavalry. This would tell the tale. Howard ordered a pullback of about "fifty paces" to better defend his flank.[28] A retreat in battle is perilous, but this one was orderly. The rebels were lucky too. British officers mistakenly presumed that Howard's fallback was a sign that the rebels had once again broken under fire and that another rout, akin to that at Camden, was in the offing. They ordered their men to charge the rebel lines. They charged into a nightmare. Howard's line remained steady and his men poured a merciless fire at the surprised British soldiers. Howard seized the moment. He ordered his men to charge their startled and fazed adversary with bayonets fixed. From each side, the skirmishers and militiamen riddled the enemy with an enfiladed fire. At this very moment, Washington's cavalry appeared as if by magic from behind the knoll that had screened them from sight.

Some British broke and ran. Many threw down their arms, just as Gates's panicked men had done six months earlier at Camden. When the first men fled, it sowed panic. Soon, said a rebel soldier, it was if a "whirlwind" had descended on the frightened British soldiers. To another, the flight of the redcoats was "the prettiest sort of running."[29] With vengeance in their eyes, Morgan's soldiers pursued the fleeing enemy soldiers. The rebels had long memories. They recalled the alleged massacre in the Waxhaws and they looked on Tarleton and his men as inhuman murderers. But now, given the upper hand and driven by the frenzy of killing all about them, it was the rebels who turned ruthlessly on their helpless foes. Many screamed "Buford's play" or "Tarleton's quarter." Some enemy soldiers ran until they were cut down. Many fell to their knees and begged for mercy. Clemency was not always forthcoming, though now and then a horseman swooped up a fallen opponent and hustled him to safety. (A British captain who was saved by Colonel Howard wrote frequently in subsequent years to his savior, thanking him again and again for his mercy at that terrible moment.)[30] Tarleton hurried into battle some two hundred green-clad cavalry who had been kept in reserve, and like Gates at Camden, he bravely rode about the battlefield seeking to rally his men. The rival cavalrymen fought at close quarters, and at one point Tarleton and Washington squared off against each other. Washington was wounded and lost his mount, but he was alive as Tarleton spurred his charger and rode away, perhaps the last British soldier to escape the battlefield. Washington grabbed another horse, rallied his troopers, and chased after Tarleton and his band for twenty-four miles before losing them.

Forty minutes after it began, the Battle of Cowpens was over. For the second time in ninety days the rebels had won a showdown in the Carolinas, and this victory was nearly as complete as that at King's Mountain. More than 100 of the enemy lay dead, and some 800 were wounded and captured. Many in the victorious army were bent on massacring the captives, but Morgan—who had been captured at Quebec in 1775 and eventually gained his freedom in a prisoner swap—held his men in check; later in the year the prisoners were exchanged for about 740 surviving Continentals who had been taken captive at Charleston. With the acrid odor of powder hanging over the battlefield, Morgan took possession of a hoard of 800 arms, several artillery pieces, ammunition, a traveling forge, roughly 100 "valuable" horses, 35 baggage wagons, a cache of specie, and 70 enslaved people. Only 250 British escaped with Tarleton. The rebels lost 73 men, of which a dozen perished. A radiantly jaunty Morgan picked up his nine-year-old drummer boy and kissed him. Then he rode amid the carnage of battle crowing, "Old Morgan never was beaten."[31] As he later accurately put it, he had given his adversary "a devil of a whipping."[32]

The rebels had lost at Camden because of a series of errors committed by Gates. They won at Cowpens as a result of Morgan's brilliant leadership, including the unorthodox manner in which he arranged his forces and the trust placed in him by his men, but also owing to a string of blunders on the part of Tarleton, who was beyond his depth in commanding an operation of such magnitude against an enemy of nearly equal strength. His troops were needlessly famished and spent when they entered the battle, and not all were in place when Tarleton ordered the advance. Convinced that the enemy militiamen would once again panic, Tarleton displayed a misguided recklessness that included sending improperly formed units into action. Another factor was crucial in the rebel victory. For the second time in one hundred days, Cornwallis had divided his army, sending a division into the western Carolina backcountry, and for a second time a rebel force seized the opportunity to fight and destroy an adversary of roughly equal size. Cornwallis had lost a third of his army in the drubbing at King's Mountain. Cowpens cost him roughly a quarter of the army that remained. Altogether, his losses in the two encounters approached two thousand men, more or less the equivalent of the reinforcements that Leslie was bringing.[33]

As long, dark shadows gathered over the landscape in the last minutes of sunlight on January 17, the day of the Battle of Cowpens, a messenger brought the first sketchy account of the engagement to Cornwallis's encampment forty miles or more away. The general was standing outdoors, leaning forward on his sword, when the courier dismounted from his sweat-drenched horse. Cornwallis listened. Then he swore loudly and, according to a witness, pressed his sword into the earth with such fury that it snapped in two. A couple of days later he confided that the news "broke my heart," all the more so as until this moment "Every thing . . . bore the most promising aspect." Given the British Legion's superior numbers, Cornwallis as much as said that he had never doubted that Tarleton's foray would be crowned with "the most brilliant success." Criticism of Tarleton was implicit in Cornwallis's remark, though he never actually said so. The only explanation for the defeat that he provided to Clinton was that when Howard's line wheeled about and unexpectedly fired on the approaching British, it resulted first in "utmost confusion," then in a fatal "panic" that undermined discipline. Writing to Germain on the same day, Cornwallis deceptively minimized the losses and advised the American secretary not to believe the "exaggerated accounts" spread by the rebels. He said nothing untoward about Tarleton. In fact, he lauded his courage and Herculean efforts in attempting to prevent his baggage train from falling into the hands of the rebels.[34]

Cornwallis had hastily retreated from North Carolina in the wake of the disaster at King's Mountain. That was not in the cards this time. His next move was never in doubt. He hoped to track down Morgan and annihilate his force before he escaped or succeeded in reuniting with Greene's portion of the rebel army. On the day after Cowpens, Leslie's force at long last joined Cornwallis. If that was good news for the commander, the bad news was that for a few days Tarleton's tattered cavalry was unable to provide credible intelligence. Within twenty-four hours of learning of Cowpens, Cornwallis was on the move, though for all practical purposes he—like Gates on his march to Camden—proceeded blindly, as nearly everything he was told regarding Morgan's whereabouts was three days out-of-date.[35]

Morgan had lingered at Cowpens only long enough to secure the prisoners and collect as much as possible that the enemy had abandoned. Sometime on the sunny afternoon of the battle, Morgan put his army on the road. On the day after the battle, Cornwallis, at his camp below King's Mountain, received sketchy—and untrustworthy—information that Morgan was retreating in a northwesterly direction, likely hoping to reach Gilbert Town. Cornwallis had two choices. Despite Morgan's head start, Cornwallis could also march for Gilbert Town and hope to catch his adversary there. Or, if he assumed that Morgan would eventually turn eastward to rendezvous with Greene, Cornwallis could advance straight to the north and seek to position himself between Morgan and the Catawba River. Cornwallis chose the former option. For two days, he advanced to the northwest while, unbeknownst to him, Morgan marched eastward. Cornwallis's decision has subjected him to considerable criticism by historians, but he had to guess, and he made a logical conjecture. He reasoned that should Morgan, with his superior intelligence arm, learn that the British awaited him at the Catawba, the rebel army would retreat to the safety of the mountains to the west; Cornwallis would be left emptyhanded. Cornwallis gambled that he could catch his adversary on the road to Gilbert Town. Cornwallis was aware that the option he was taking might lead Morgan to retreat into the mountains, but the British commander thought that would be fine. If Morgan sought a hideaway in the mountains and never rendezvoused with the rebel force in South Carolina, Greene's army would be denied a quarter or more of its already scant manpower. But Cornwallis made the wrong choice, and when he realized his mistake and marched eastward, it was too late. Morgan had already reached the Catawba and begun his crossing.[36]

Morgan was across on January 25. He knew that Cornwallis was coming, though still miles away. He did not know whether his adversary would cross the Catawba and continue his pursuit, "but I am apprehensive he will," Morgan told Greene in a communiqué. Aware that he was outnumbered by about three to one, Morgan knew he would have to run if Cornwallis crossed the Catawba and resumed the chase. However, he thought he could outrun his foe, as he was no longer saddled with the prisoners taken at Cowpens, having sent them off to Moravian settlements in the deep backcountry. Suddenly, Morgan and his men caught a break. They were no more than across the river when the skies opened up and days of rain ensued. The placid river soon turned into a roaring and impassable obstacle. Given what he called the "Badness of the Weather," Morgan knew that Cornwallis—if he was so inclined—could not cross anytime soon.

The little rebel army stayed put for days on the east side of the Catawba, all along hopeful that Greene's army would arrive and join them. When several days passed with no sign of Greene and no word from him, Morgan grew edgy. Greene, in fact, was not dawdling. He had not learned of Cowpens until six days after the battle, about the time that Morgan reached the Catawba. He immediately ordered a celebration, which cherry bounce (a concoction made from rum and cider) turned into a raucous event. Two days later, on the day the last of Morgan's men reached the east side of the river, Greene learned that Morgan was waiting for him at the Catawba. Greene wasted no time. He ordered all units in his force—which were scattered from the upper Pee Dee River in the Cheraws to here and there around Georgetown, almost fifty miles away—to march for Salisbury, a rendezvous point just west of the Yadkin River that Morgan had suggested. Greene also directed that much of the army's stores be brought to Guilford Courthouse, some sixty miles northeast of Salisbury, and he urged North Carolina's governor to summon more militia and direct them to march for the Yadkin. In addition, Greene sent a special appeal to Virginia's Blue Ridge mountaineer riflemen, who had performed in a stellar fashion at King's Mountain, telling them that their appearance would "add new splendor to your own glory . . . and give the world another proof of the bravery of the Mountain Militia." While his army was headed almost due north, Greene, accompanied by a guide, his aide de camp, and a small unit of cavalry, rode northwestwardly for the Catawba, where he expected to find Morgan. Greene sped across the Tory-infested landscape, galloping one hundred miles in a bit more than two days. On January 30, thirteen days after Cowpens and five days after Morgan crossed to the east side of the Catawba, Greene, in the nonstop pelting rain, was reunited with his subordinate. It was the first time in six weeks that Greene and Morgan had seen each other.[37]

Lead elements of Cornwallis's force at last reached the Catawba about forty-eight hours after his prey had completed its crossing and several days before Greene arrived and joined Morgan. "Morgan's movements have been too rapid for me," Cornwallis lamented. But he was not ready to give up the chase. Initially, he clutched to the hope that his Tory guides would be familiar with serviceable fords that would enable him to quickly cross the Catawba. If so, he reckoned that he could "get between General Greene and Virginia," compelling his adversary "to fight without receiving any reinforcement" from the Old Dominion.[38] The torrential rain scotched his dream of a rapid passage across the river. As he waited on the west side of the Catawba, Cornwallis faced a difficult choice. Should he resume the chase once the weather permitted or take his army back to South Carolina?

Cornwallis knew there was no question he would face "infinite danger" if he pursued the rebels through the forbidding interior of North Carolina. But if he abandoned the chase, Cornwallis feared that not only would Britain's southern strategy face "certain ruin" but that his reputation would suffer for having turned his back on a possible fight. In addition, should he retreat into South Carolina, his action might lay waste to Britain's resolve to continue the war. If war-weariness weighed heavily on the Americans, Cornwallis was aware that many in England were also tired of the war, and morale would crumble further when word of King's Mountain and Cowpens reached London. The war was six years old, and England's foreign and colonial trades were suffering, public indebtedness was mounting, a French army was now in America, soon a French navy of consequence might arrive, and Britain's citizenry groaned under high wartime taxation. Besides the customary wartime increase in the land tax that had been imposed at the war's outset, Lord North's government had gradually added carriage, stamp, house, customs, and assorted excise taxes, levies that led to hardships and exacerbated long-standing afflictions within the construction trades and textile industries. Cornwallis must have feared that to quit North Carolina hard on the heels of Cowpens would drive a stake through the British government's willingness to continue hostilities.[39]

Cornwallis made his decision. When possible, he would cross the river and attempt to catch Morgan. His army would have to move fast, faster than it had moved since it set off ten days earlier from his Broad River encampment. All excess baggage must be abandoned. It was a daring and potentially perilous decision. As one of Cornwallis's general officer's remarked, the army was about to move "without . . . necessaries, or provisions . . . in the most barren inhospitable, unhealthy part of North America" while searching for "the most savage, inveterate, perfidious, cruel enemy." Cornwallis knew as much. The coming march, he said, would take his army through "one of the most rebellious tracts in America."[40]

Tents, beds, liquor, superfluous clothing, unneeded wagons, and all the flour on hand were piled high and set to the torch, making a giant bonfire. Cornwallis, stolid as ever, started the process by discarding his own overabundance of possessions. One of his officers, who probably had no idea what the common soldiers really thought when they saw portions of their food and rum consumed in the fire, later wrote that the men's coming deprivation "was acquiesced in without a murmur." Likewise, Cornwallis spoke of the men's "most general and chearfull acquiescence." Cornwallis's stripped-down army would be accompanied by a few wagons that could be used for transporting the sick and wounded, as well as by a few other conveyances loaded with ammunition, scant provender, salt, and medical supplies. The army was ready to move and, according to one officer, "resolved to follow" the enemy "to the end of the world." The step that Cornwallis was taking was as hazardous as that taken by Greene in dividing his army. General Clinton later said that Cornwallis at this juncture should have opted for "returning to restore tranquility [in] South Carolina." Instead, Clinton went on, Cornwallis risked his army by taking it into "an exhausted, hostile country . . . without the means of collecting supplies and even beyond the chance of finding refreshment of any sort." But the long, desperate war had come to this. Throughout the three years beginning in 1778, the leaders on both sides had for the most part shrunk from risk-taking. However, Greene had kicked off 1781 with the riskiest of strategies, and Cornwallis followed suit in setting off on a desperate chase through the enemy's lair.[41]

Cornwallis was resolute and filled with fight, but the stars were against him. There was nothing for the cold and wet soldiery to do but wait out the stormy weather. Finally, at 1:00 A.M. on February 1—about thirty-six hours after the reunion of Greene and Morgan, and their departure for the Yadkin—Cornwallis's army began to wade across the five-hundred-yard-wide Catawba River at Cowan's Ford. Advancing four abreast, the redcoats were about one-quarter of the way across the dark, rushing river when they were spotted by an enemy force of some eight hundred rebel militiamen. These were North Carolinians whom Morgan had posted on the east side of the river. They were led by General William Davidson, a thirty-five-year-old Continental officer who had mostly served in the northern theater and been part of several important engagements since 1776. The militiamen opened up on the slow-moving redcoats, who were wading through the rushing waist-deep water that at most would have been a frigid sixty degrees. The river bottom was thick with smooth rocks as slick as ice. Those who fell were in danger being swept away by the fast current. Some men fell. Others stepped into unseen deep holes that led to their total submersion. Horses slipped, too, dumping their riders into the seething river. The British could not return the militiamen's fire. They were carrying their muskets and cartridge boxes above their heads in a mostly vain attempt to keep them dry. One Carolinian thought the enemy's silence was odd. All he could hear, he said, was "the British splashing and making a noise as if drowning."

Cornwallis, a brave and determined leader, saw what was happening at the very outset of the crossing and splashed into the bitterly cold water to set an example. It was his "usual manner" to act in such a fashion, one of Cornwallis's soldiers later remarked. The general's mount was wounded midway across, but somehow the stricken horse managed to reach the far shore and Cornwallis arrived safely. General Leslie's horse was swept from beneath him, but he was saved by a quick-witted sergeant. Others were not so fortunate. Cornwallis subsequently placed his losses at forty men, though others said that as many as one hundred perished during the crossing. After the British reached the other side and the sun rose, Cornwallis sent his light infantry into action. Davidson was killed in the fighting that ensued, mortally wounded while on his horse directing his pickets. His death and the British infantry's seemingly miraculous recovery and advance sowed panic within the militia ranks, provoking a withdrawal so rapid that one militiaman quaintly characterized it as having made "straight shirt tails."[42]

While Cornwallis's men were struggling to cross the Catawba, Greene and Morgan were headed for Salisbury. Greene did not know what size army he would find when he reached the vicinity of the Yadkin. He did know that the Virginia militiamen who had served with Morgan were departing for home, as the term of their enlistments had expired, and on reaching Salisbury he learned that the turnout by North Carolina's militiamen had been disappointing. (Thoroughly dismayed, Greene exclaimed in a letter, "O that we had in the field as Henry the Fifth said, some few of the many thousands that are Idle at Home.") Greene additionally discovered that his dragoons—which had to be assembled from a wide area around Georgetown before covering the seventy-five miles or more to Salisbury—had not arrived. In an instant, Greene knew there was no possibility of making what he called an "effectual stand" against Cornwallis on the Yadkin.[43] Morgan advised that the army retreat northward to the mountains, postponing a showdown until the rebel force, with its provisions, actually came together. Morgan's concern was not solely about battling Cornwallis. By now the rebels knew that Arnold had landed in Virginia about thirty days earlier, and Morgan—and Greene, too—feared his plan was to put ashore his American Legion somewhere on North Carolina's east coast. That would present twin problems. It might result in the American army being caught between Cornwallis on one side and Arnold on the other. It almost certainly meant that many of North Carolina's militiamen, preoccupied with Arnold, would never link up with the main rebel army.

Greene listened to Morgan, but it was his decision to make. There are indications that the two generals argued heatedly, though in the end Greene overruled Morgan without summoning a council of war. He continued to think that it might be possible to fight Cornwallis at the Yadkin or somewhere between that river and the Virginia border. His immediate goal was to draw Cornwallis after him, luring him to drive his men one taxing mile after another, ever deeper into the tangled rebel backcountry. At this juncture, Greene reckoned that Cornwallis's force outnumbered his by perhaps one thousand men. Greene knew, too, that a quarter of his men were militiamen, whom he generally regarded as unreliable. However, if more militiamen rallied to arms and all went well with regard to the gathering of stores, Greene believed he could succeed in "ruining Lord Cornwallis if he persists in his mad scheme of pushing through the Country." But if his force remained small, "naked and distressed," Greene knew that he would have to outrun Cornwallis to Virginia, where his army could be augmented and reconstituted. Greene called on his "forage masters" to bring to Salisbury the boats he had collected since reconnoitering the province back in November. When he reached that river he would make his next crucial decision. First and foremost, he wanted to fight, and he appealed to North Carolina's militiamen "to fly to arms." If "you will not face the approaching danger your Country is inevitably lost," he warned, adding that if "you neglect to take the field and suffer the enemy to over run the Country you will deserve the miseries ever inseparable from slavery."[44]

In the aftermath of Cowpens, Morgan's force had marched at an astounding clip, averaging some thirty miles a day when not slowed by a river crossing. But the recent heavy rains had turned North Carolina's red clay roads to ooze, and the rebels now moved at a much slower pace. Three full days of marching were required to cover the twenty miles or so from Salisbury to the Yadkin, though Greene's army had a considerable head start on their pursuers and were not endangered during the trek. Nevertheless, even with boats awaiting them, crossing the wind-lashed river would be a challenge. Cornwallis knew the impediments that awaited Greene and he pushed his men hard, hoping to catch the fleeing rebels before they could make the crossing. Cornwallis's pared-down army—which Greene characterized as a "completely equiped . . . Light Infantry" corps—moved faster than Greene's.[45]

Greene found the boats at the Yadkin and hurried his men to make the risky crossing at Trading Ford. There was no time to waste. Certain annihilation would follow if his army was trapped with its back to the river. The rebels made it, barely. The last ones to go across came under fire from the van of Cornwallis's army led by General O'Hara. Without sufficient men to make a stand, Greene knew that he had to continue his flight. Guilford Courthouse was forty-seven miles away and the men were cold, wet, and tired, but fortune smiled on Greene's army. Cornwallis's men had marched day after weary day without the customary rest periods, their diet had fallen short of the army's accustomed level of sustenance, and since the great paring down on the lip of the Catawba, the men had been without the shelter of tents and the comfort of warm, dry clothing through a succession of cold, rainy nights and chilly days. Cornwallis's men were spent. They had to be rested and given a chance to build fires and dry their tattered, soggy uniforms and worn shoes. The horses also needed a break and the opportunity to graze. Cornwallis paused for two days in Salisbury. When ready at last to cross the Yadkin, yet another unruly river, the lack of boats compelled him to march fifty miles to the north to find a passable ford. Five days passed between the breather in Salisbury and the moment the last British soldier crossed the Yadkin. All the while, Greene's army had been on the move. As the rebel soldiers marched, their commander directed the officers to seize wagons and supplies from civilians if what was needed could not be purchased. Greene also appealed yet again to Governor Nash to put more militiamen in the field. "[E]vils are now fast approaching," he warned, and he told the chief executive that if the army was compelled to disperse, nothing could stop Cornwallis's "entire reduction" of the state.[46]

The force under Greene and Morgan reached Guilford Courthouse on February 9, eleven days after their departure from the Catawba. Depleted by the casualties at Cowpens, the onerous march of the past few days, the absence of the men who were escorting the British prisoners to Virginia, the departure of the Virginia militiamen, and the scarcity of North Carolina militiamen, Greene thought his army of some two thousand men far too small to stand and fight. But with Cornwallis thirty miles away, Greene paused and convened his first council of war since taking the field weeks earlier. It was a meeting to decide the army's next step. The decision was hardly in doubt. In fact, Greene had already ordered the army's heavy baggage to be sent to Virginia. The generals wasted little time before unanimously deciding "to avoid a general Action at all Events." A week earlier, Greene had thought it "not improbable from Lord Cornwallises pushing disposition, and the contempt he has for our Army, we may precipitate him into some capital misfortune" that the little rebel army could exploit. No one any longer entertained such a thought. The focus now was on reaching Virginia, where reinforcements would assure Greene's safety. The next morning, after the luxury of twenty-four hours of rest, the army began the last leg of its flight. While the men set off, Greene, in his tent, wrote Jefferson—and, for good measure, Patrick Henry, for in some respects he was more powerful than the governor—to request that fifteen hundred

Virginians be raised to unite with the tattered southern army when it crossed the Dan River into the Old Dominion. That would provide safety for the army for the time being, though Greene had come to the conclusion reached long ago by Benjamin Lincoln: "The Southern States are in such a defenceless condition, that they must fall under the dominion of the enemy, unless reinforcements are immediately sent" by the northern states.[47]

General Morgan attended the conclave, and for all practical purposes it was his final act of the war. Wracked with excruciating joint pain and back troubles—both exacerbated by weeks on his feet and in the saddle—Morgan was convinced that "nothing will help me but rest." The next day, Greene granted him a leave of absence, and Morgan left immediately for home.[48]

The Dan was some forty long miles away. Greene divided his army into two divisions for the final dash. The two were to take separate but parallel roads. Colonel Otho Williams, Morgan's successor, was given command of seven hundred men. They were to take the westernmost road and form "a covering party," a shield, for the main force to the east. Williams's mission was also diversionary. He was to march in the direction of the upper fords of the Dan, hopefully deceiving Cornwallis into thinking that was where the entire rebel army planned to cross into Virginia. As Williams's force would be closest to Cornwallis, he was allotted all the army's 250 dragoons, some under Colonel Washington, the remainder under Henry Lee. These horse soldiers constituted Williams's rear guard and were to engage the royal cavalry should it catch up with them. Otherwise, Williams was to destroy bridges and do what he could to harass the enemy and impede its progress. It was a dangerous undertaking. If caught by Cornwallis, Williams's situation would be hopeless and his losses would offset the damage the British had suffered at Cowpens. Greene, with the remaining 1,300 or so men in his little army, was to march toward the lower fords of the Dan. Greene's men, like Cornwallis's, were weary. Those with Williams were even more sapped. During their days with Morgan these men had marched more than three hundred miles in six weeks. Greene estimated that Cornwallis's men had marched two hundred miles since the day they set off for Gilbert Town twenty-three days earlier. Yet somehow they remained "at our heels," as

Greene put it. The British were thought to be twenty miles away on the day the rebels rested at Guildford Courthouse. The next day, Williams reported that Cornwallis was only six to eight miles behind him, but still at least twenty miles from Greene's force.[49]

Cornwallis exhibited an unyielding resolve to catch the rebels. It was as if every bone-chilling, miserably wet, utterly fatiguing minute that he had endured during the three weeks of chasing his adversaries made him more determined to catch and destroy them. Though men in both armies teetered at the breaking point, neither pursuer nor prey dared rest for long. Men on both sides were roused in the still of night and marched for hours before pausing to eat. If they ate a second meal during the day, it was while marching. There were no rest periods and the treks continued unabated until after nightfall. When at last each long, draining day ended, the men gulped down another cold, cheerless meal before finding a bed on the damp, unwelcoming earth. At most, they slept for six hours. The unlucky ones who were assigned picket or guard duty got even less sleep. Greene surely exaggerated in claiming to have slept for only four hours during the final several days of the chase, though there can be no doubt that he and his men in both divisions, and Cornwallis's as well, were sleep deprived.[50]

A couple of days into the chase, Cornwallis fixed his gaze on Williams. By the fourth day, Greene was twenty-two miles away and within a day of reaching the Dan. Williams, however, was now only four miles up the road from the enemy. Furthermore, British intelligence indicated that the rebels had sufficient vessels at the downstream fords to get Greene's army across but that no boats awaited Williams's. Cornwallis rejoiced that his debilitating pursuit had not been in vain. He would trap Williams against the Dan and annihilate his force.

But Cornwallis had been deceived. On February 13, Williams suddenly changed course. He too now hurried for the downstream crossing. Unless Cornwallis could catch him on the last day of the chase, the entire rebel force would safely cross into Virginia. Cornwallis hoped against hope that Williams "would not escape me without receiving a blow." It was not to be. By 2:00 P.M. on February 14, Greene had gotten his wagons into Virginia, and the men were beginning to cross. Three hours later, in the final faint orange rays of daylight, the last of Greene's men were across. Williams's force arrived a bit later, after the dark stain of night enveloped the area. They found campfires left burning for them by Greene's army; the flames provided illumination for their crossing. Sometime toward midnight the last rebel soldier stepped into Virginia. Several hours passed before the van of Cornwallis's army arrived. They found, in the words of one exhausted rebel, that the rebels were "safe over the river and . . . laughing at [the British] who are on the opposite bank."[51]

A bitterly disappointed Cornwallis praised his men's service "under every species of hardship and fatigue." (Clinton, too, subsequently lauded the "firm alacrity with which the troops . . . bore up against . . . difficulties not frequently the lot" of British soldiers.) Later Cornwallis, with considerable accuracy, reflected that he had been brought up short because the unfortunate weather, bad roads, "exceedingly defective" intelligence, timidity of the Loyalists who had failed to turn out, and "many deep creeks and bridges destroyed by the enemy's light troops." Atop the loss of nine hundred men at Cowpens, Cornwallis's grueling chase had cost him in excess of one hundred men, victims of ambushes, firefights, drownings, and the ghastly privation that was the soldiers' daily handmaiden throughout the excruciating forced marches.[52]

Cornwallis never considered pursuing Greene into Virginia. His force, he said later, was "ill-suited to enter . . . so powerfull a province." The men needed rest and their stock of provisions had to be replenished. Furthermore, Virginia—the most populous of Britain's mainland colonies—was capable of mustering large numbers of militiamen to supplement Greene's army. Cornwallis withdrew to Hillsborough, once Gates's headquarters, to regroup and, as he said in a public statement, to beseech "all loyal subjects . . . to stand forth and take an active part in assisting me to restore order and constitutional government." By now, Cornwallis had a thoroughly jaded view of the Tories, though he hoped that they would interpret Greene's flight as evidence that the king's army was close to regaining predominance in North Carolina. He dispatched recruiters to comb the nearby countryside in search of those willing to accept the rank of captain and raise men for their provincial company, as well as those who would enlist in the Royal North Carolina Regiment. Less than a week after Greene escaped into Virginia, Cornwallis issued a bombastic proclamation pointing to his success in "driving the rebel army out of this province," a step that liberated the inhabitants from the "cruel tyranny under which they have groaned for several years." He additionally invited the Crown's "loyal subjects" to hurry to Hillsborough with their arms and a ten-day supply of food.[53]

CHAPTER 10

FATEFUL CHOICES

GENERAL WASHINGTON HAD last seen Nathanael Greene in October. What he had heard from Greene following his arrival in North Carolina, communiqués penned in December that were weeks old by the time they reached the commander, had not been encouraging. Greene had not been sure his army deserved to be called an army. He advised Washington that the southern states had provided only a few poorly equipped militiamen and that the countryside had been "laid waste" both by winter and militia that had remained on active duty during the last six months. So barren was the region, said Greene, that his army would have to remain on the move foraging for provisions. His only cheery news was that both the partisans and Colonel Washington's cavalry were having some success in harassing the enemy. Greene had also divulged his unorthodox plan to divide his army, a step that Washington, and perhaps Washington alone, regarded as being "supported upon just Military Principles."[1]

Washington, who two years earlier had looked on the war in the South as an inconsequential sideshow, now saw things differently. Given the devastating defeats at Charleston and Camden, and the arrival of a British army under Arnold in Virginia, Washington now understood that Britain might have the means of suppressing the rebellion in three southern provinces, an outcome that would be fatal to the quest for independence. He looked on Henry Clinton's decision to dispatch Arnold as a clever stroke. Given Britain's naval superiority, Washington understood that Clinton was pursuing a game plan that could result in a deadly threat to Greene. Arnold's army could block the flow of supplies to the southern army, pin down Virginia's militia so that it could not assist Greene, and possibly join with Cornwallis in a campaign to snare the rebel army.[2]

Washington wrote Governors Nash and Jefferson, gently chiding the former for North Carolina's failure to meet its manpower quota for the Continental army or to furnish adequately supplied militia forces. He appealed to Jefferson to see the bigger picture. He told Virginia's governor that Britain's "predatory incursions" into the Old Dominion were damaging and dispiriting, but he counseled that the greater danger to realizing independence lay in the lower South. Virginia, Washington added, must provide ample assistance to Greene to assure that Cornwallis was denied victory.[3]

Now fully engaged with regard to the grave dangers posed by Britain's southern strategy, Washington, in December, had approached General Rochambeau about sending men and a fleet to the South, either to destroy Arnold in Virginia or assail the British in Charleston. Washington intimated that the United States would never agree to a peace settlement until the British "relinquish their conquests in South Carolina and Georgia." Washington, like Clinton and the French leaders, understood that the key to breaking the stalemate rested with naval superiority—"how might the enemy be crushed if we had it," he wistfully remarked to one of his young officers—but the question remained: Would it be Britain's navy or France's that was instrumental in the decisive action.[4]

Rochambeau's answer came quickly: His orders not only forbade the division of his army but also stressed that it was to act in concert with the navy. That left Washington with but one choice. If men were to be sent to assist Greene, they must come from the Continental army in the north. Giving up men did not come easily for Washington, who coveted their presence for what he was certain would someday be the war's climatic engagement—a Franco-American attempt to retake New York. However, as no major action was likely in the north before the summer and Greene was in desperate need of immediate help, Washington in February detached three battalions totaling twelve hundred men to the southern theater. He gave the twenty-three-year-old Marquis de Lafayette command of this force.[5]

Given his age and lack of experience, the selection of Lafayette must have struck many as odd. (Lafayette himself confided to an acquaintance that he thought it "ludicrous" that he was vested "at my age" with command of "anything honored by the name of an army.") Furthermore, while Lafayette invariably exhibited great courage, his performance when given small-scale command assignments had at times been tinged with incompetence. There were several senior general officers whom Washington might have considered, and under normal circumstances one of them surely would have gotten the nod. But early in February while Washington was wrestling with the decision of sending a detachment southward, he learned from Rochambeau that a violent nor'easter had severely damaged the British fleet off the eastern end of Long Island. Miraculously, the French navy had been spared. For the time being, naval supremacy had startlingly shifted to France. As Ternay had died of a fever just before Christmas, the French navy was now commanded by Chevalier Charles Sochet Destouches, and he jumped at the opportunity to dispatch a fleet from Newport to the Chesapeake. His goal was to destroy the small fleet that protected Arnold, rendering the turncoat and his little army terribly vulnerable.

Washington was ecstatic. This could be a critical turning point in the southern theater, a feeling made all the more palpable when he learned a week later of Daniel Morgan's astounding victory at Cowpens. But if Arnold's force was to be taken, the presence of ground troops was essential. Washington quickly apprised Jefferson of developments and once again urged him to ready Virginia's militia. However, as Washington was certain the "Militia cannot be depended on for . . . vigorous measures," he decided in favor of deploying "a respectable detachment from this Army" to Virginia. Washington said that he selected Lafayette because he could maintain "an immediate, safe and expeditious communication" with the French naval officers. Perhaps there was more than that to Washington's choice. The marquis had gained considerable experience during the four years since first arriving in America. Moreover, Washington, who was incredibly adroit at judging the capabilities of others, believed in Lafayette.[6]

Washington's orders to Lafayette were conventional, but he took pains to emphasize that should Arnold surrender, the Marquis was not to agree to terms that "may screen him from the punishment due to his treason and desertion." Should Arnold "fall into your hands, you will execute [him] in the most summary way," said Washington straightaway. Jefferson had already offered five thousand guineas for Arnold's capture and two thousand to anyone who killed him. A British officer noted that Arnold had taken to carrying two pistols at all times "to escape being hanged." It was rumored that the "very restless" Arnold slept with a pistol under his pillow.[7]

Washington's expectations for the success of the operation against Arnold dwindled when he learned that Destouches had sent only one heavy warship and three frigates to the Chesapeake. Washington quickly sent off two letters to Rochambeau. He made clear his consternation that Destouches had not sailed "with his whole fleet." Washington observed that Arnold, with the land batteries in his fortress acting in conjunction with the royal vessels in Chesapeake Bay, could either drive away the tiny French squadron or forestall its approach until British naval reinforcements arrived from New York. He also returned to the matter of Rochambeau sending troops to cooperate with the fleet. Washington disclosed that he was sending more than a thousand Continentals, though he despaired that such a small force, even when augmented by militiamen, could penetrate Arnold's defenses. Could not the French send one thousand men and some field artillery with the fleet? He closed his appeal by reminding Rochambeau that the destruction of Arnold's army was of "immense importance to the welfare of the Southern States." Washington's effort was unavailing. By the time his initial letter reached Rochambeau, the French squadron had already sailed. In a few days, Washington was advised that as speed had been essential, Destouches had thought too much time would be squandered in loading troop transports. No French soldiers accompanied the task force. Thereafter, Washington had not expected good news, and late in February he learned that the French squadron had failed to inflict the least damage to Arnold's army.[8]

Captain le Gardeur de Tilly, whom Destouches had appointed to command the abortive French expedition, had found that his deep-draft vessels were unable to navigate the Elizabeth River. His frigate had made an attempt and had immediately run aground. But Tilly had not come away empty handed. He had captured a forty-four-gun British frigate, two privateers, four small transports, and some five hundred marines before returning to Newport on February 25. Four days later Washington received amazing news from a French courier who galloped up to headquarters. Tilly's prizes had led the French, in Newport, to decide almost instantaneously to send another squadron to the Chesapeake, this one commanded by Destouches himself. It would consist of ten warships with 1,120 infantrymen loaded into troop transports and fourteen of the army's field pieces lashed in place. The euphoric Washington dashed to Newport to personally thank Rochambeau and learn what steps needed to be taken to safeguard the French army while the fleet was away. (He soon prevailed on the governors of Massachusetts and Rhode Island to dispatch 1,200 militiamen to ensure Newport's safety.) Washington's sudden trek to Rhode Island may have been counterproductive, as the French arranged an elaborate ceremony for their guest, a step that delayed Destouches's sailing when every minute counted.

Destouches commenced his voyage by sailing one hundred miles into the Atlantic before turning south toward Virginia, a step he thought necessary in order to conceal his fleet from the enemy. He knew that sooner or later the British would learn that he had sailed and send their own fleet to the Chesapeake, but Destouches was gambling that despite his extended odyssey, his head start would enable him to reach the bay before his adversary. He was wrong. Taking an indirect route proved costly. Destouches's squadron required twice the time of Tilly's to reach the Chesapeake, and upon arriving it discovered that a British flotilla of twelve sail under Admiral Arbuthnot was already riding the blue-green waters inside the bay. Despite having sailed from New York thirty-six hours after Destouches weighed anchor in Newport, Arbuthnot had won the race to the Chesapeake.

The British had the most ships. The French vessels, armed with their own guns as well as the heaviest artillery in Rochambeau's army, had the most firepower. But the British had arrived first and taken up a defensive formation that, in the words of historian Nathaniel Philbrick, was tantamount to "an ocean-borne imitation of a land-bound fortress." To reach Arnold and his army, the French would have to fight their way through their adversary's imposing line. What is more, in the unlikely event that he broke through, Destouches and his troops would face great peril while disembarking at Portsmouth. Yet despite the dangers he faced, Destouches ran the risk, and on March 16, in the brief Battle of Cape Henry, suffered losses in the range of two hundred men. But he had inflicted great damage. Had Destouches resumed the fight the next day, he might have destroyed the enemy fleet and in the coming days captured Arnold's army. Or he might have suffered more devastating losses. He did not hazard his fleet and men. By nightfall, Destouches was on his way back to Newport.[9]

Washington's hopes had come to naught. He was unhappy, and so, too, was Clinton, who simmered in silence, convinced that Arbuthnot had missed a golden opportunity to score a decisive victory. Neither said anything publicly, though Washington wrote a family member that had the French acted on his initial recommendation in early February—when the British fleet was immobilized by the great storm—"the destruction of Arnolds Corps would then have been inevitable." Unfortunately for Washington, his letter was intercepted and printed in a Tory newspaper in New York. The embarrassed American commander had to apologize to Rochambeau for what he called his "unjust" accusation, explaining that the letter had been "written in haste, and might have been inaccurately expressed." Rochambeau knew better than to make an issue of it.[10]

NO ONE WAS more disappointed by Destouches's failure than General Greene, but it was not the only letdown he experienced. He had expected to be greeted by reinforcements provided by Virginia when he crossed the Dan, and in fact on the day he paused at Guilford Courthouse he had appealed to Jefferson to provide troops. But no Virginia soldiers had awaited him. He wrote Jefferson a second time to remind him that unless bolstered by the Virginia militia, he could not "risqué a general action." What is more, if trapped and forced to fight, the outcome "could not fail to prove ruinous" to Virginia. He pleaded for men and cavalry and asked Jefferson to place those he sent under Continental officers, saying that they would be more useful than twice the number commanded by militia officers. Greene closed his urgent message with a stern admonition: "The Country is inevitably lost unless decided Measures are taken. You will consider the necessity and act according." Greene additionally pleaded with Washington for more troops.[11]

Jefferson responded by calling out the militia in sectors near the Dan and Roanoke Rivers, and pledged to summon even more men to duty should Cornwallis enter his state. This was life-and-death business, and it led Jefferson to advise Greene to have "no scruples" when it came to seizing private property, including horses. Since the fall of Charleston, Virginia had known that the war would creep toward its doorstep, and it spurred the province to resort to conscription. It drafted one-fifteenth of the men in each militia unit and mandated that they serve in the Continental army for eighteen months. More than a thousand men had been raised, and some had already come under fire.[12]

Cornwallis had not pursued the rebel army once it crossed into Virginia. Afforded breathing room for a change, Greene moved his men to Halifax, a short distance farther down the Roanoke River. As the hamlet sat in the midst of a fertile farming area, Greene put his men to foraging while he awaited reinforcements. He did not have a long wait. Within a couple of days, some eight hundred Virginia militiamen had joined him and more were expected. As the additional troops drifted in, Greene dispatched Colonel Washington to impress "good Dragoon horses," though Greene cautioned him to treat the owners with "tenderness" and have the value of each equine appraised by a civilian official. (His careful approach was unavailing, as Greene in no time was beset by angry farmers.) The rebel army was the only one that grew. Cornwallis's pitch at recruiting in the

George Washington by Jean-Antoine Houdon, plaster, c. 1786. EXHIBITED IN THE NATIONAL PORTRAIT GALLERY, SMITHSONIAN INSTITUTE

Horatio Gates by James Peale, after Charles Willson Peale. NATIONAL PORTRAIT GALLERY, SMITHSONIAN INSTITUTION; PARTIAL GIFT OF MR. LAWRENCE A. FLEISCHMAN

Lord George Germain, by Dorofield Hardy, from the original by G. Romney. WILLIAM L. CLEMENTS LIBRARY, UNIVERSITY OF MICHIGAN

Sir Henry Clinton (1738–1795) by John Smart, c. 1777. NATIONAL ARMY MUSEUM, LONDON

Charles Cornwallis (1738–1805) by Thomas Gainsborough. DE AGOSTINI/GETTY IMAGES

Marquis de Lafayette (1757–1834) by an unidentifed artist, after Joseph Boze, nineteenth century. MARIE JOSEPH PAUL YVES ROCH GILBERT DU MOTIER; COURTESY OF INDEPENDENCE NATIONAL HISTORICAL PARK

Comte d'Estaing by an unidentified artist, c. 1782. LIBRARY OF CONGRESS, PRINTS AND PHOTOGRAPHS DIVISION

John Sullivan (1740–1795) by Richard Morrell Staigg, after John Trumbull, 1876. COURTESY OF INDEPENDENCE NATIONAL HISTORICAL PARK

The Siege of Charleston, hand-colored, after the engraving by Alonzo Chappel (1828–1887).
ANNE S. K. BROWN MILITARY COLLECTION, BROWN UNIVERSITY LIBRARY

Benjamin Lincoln (1733–1810) by Charles Willson Peale, from life, c. 1781–1783. COURTESY OF INDEPENDENCE NATIONAL HISTORICAL PARK

Banastre Tarleton by Sir Joshua Reynolds, c. eighteenth century. PHOTO 12/UNIVERSAL IMAGES GROUP/GETTY IMAGES

Major General Thomas Sumter
(1734–1832), engraved by George
Parker, after a drawing of the
original by William G. Armstrong
(1823–1890). WIKIMEDIA
COMMONS

Benedict Arnold by Benoît-
Louis Prévost, after Pierre
Eugène Du Simitière, c. 1780.
NATIONAL PORTRAIT GALLERY,
SMITHSONIAN INSTITUTION

Le Général ARNOLD

deserte de l'Armée des États-Unis

le 3. Octobre 1780.

Thomas Jefferson (1743–1826) by Charles Willson Peale, from life, c. 1791–1792. COURTESY OF INDEPENDENCE NATIONAL HISTORICAL PARK

Nathanael Greene (1742–1786) by Charles Willson Peale, from life, 1783. COURTESY OF INDEPENDENCE NATIONAL HISTORICAL PARK

Daniel Morgan (1736–1802) by Charles Willson Peale, from life, c. 1794. COURTESY OF INDEPENDENCE NATIONAL HISTORICAL PARK

Henry Lee (1756–1818) by Charles Willson Peale, from life, c. 1782. COURTESY OF INDEPENDENCE NATIONAL HISTORICAL PARK

The Continental Line at Guilford Courthouse. UNITED STATES ARMY CENTER OF MILITARY HISTORY

Comte de Rochambeau by Charles Willson Peale, date unknown. LIBRARY OF CONGRESS, PRINTS AND PHOTOGRAPHS DIVISION

Sketch of American uniforms by Baron Ludwig von Closen, 1781. ANNE S. K. BROWN MILITARY COLLECTION, BROWN UNIVERSITY LIBRARY

Comte de Grasse by Mathilde M. Leisenring, after Jean-Baptiste Mauzaisse.

Battle of the Virginia Capes by V. Zveg, 1962. U.S. NAVY ART COLLECTION, NAVAL HISTORY AND HERITAGE COMMAND

French Artillery Park at Yorktown, illustrated by Sidney E. King. COURTESY NATIONAL PARK SERVICE, COLONIAL NATIONAL HISTORICAL PARK

Washington, Lafayette & Tilghman at Yorktown (1784) by Charles Willson Peale
(1741–1827). COLLECTION OF THE MARYLAND STATE ARCHIVES, MSA SC 1545-1120

region around Hillsborough had not met with success. Many locals made clear to Britain's recruiters that they abhorred the American Revolution, but they would neither take up arms for their king nor make known their hatred of the colonial rebellion, as they feared cruel retribution the moment that Cornwallis's army departed. During his pause, Cornwallis succeeded only in resting his men and replenishing his army.[13]

Cornwallis would have liked to remain in Hillsborough for a spell, but several factors led him to cut short his stay. It was dangerous to remain stationary while in hostile country. Both his army and the detachments he sent off to forage would be the prey of militia and partisans. He was also disappointed by the scarcity of provender around Hillsborough. In fact, the food supply was so meager that he was driven to confiscate livestock from the Loyalists—a step that one redcoat acknowledged "caused much murmuring amongst" the Tories—and slaughter some of his draft horses. After only a week in the tiny village, Cornwallis made ready to move out on learning that Greene had crossed back into North Carolina with some 1,600 men. Greene's small force hardly posed a substantial threat, as the British force numbered some 2,400. But Cornwallis expected the rebel army to grow, and he wished to take advantage of his numerical superiority while it lasted. Cornwallis resolved to take the field in search of an encounter with his adversary, which from his point of view could not come too soon.[14]

An unexpected event also played a role in Cornwallis's departure from Hillsborough. He had dispatched Tarleton, with his reconstituted dragoons, to protect Loyalist militiamen who were assembling and marching to Hillsborough. But Tarleton's horsemen were not the only ones in the field. Greene had sent cavalry under William Washington and Henry Lee to separate areas in search both for horses and Tarleton, and to gather intelligence. After days of fruitless hunting, Lee thought he had discovered Tarleton's whereabouts. On February 25, while en route to his adversary's last known encampment, Lee's troop ran up on a four-hundred-man Loyalist force under Colonel John Pyle, an English-trained physician who had long practiced medicine in Chatham County, North Carolina. Lee never hesitated. He fell on the Tories, who made the egregious blunder of thinking that the approaching green-clad horsemen—their uniforms were nearly identical to those worn by the British Legion—were friends.

Surprised and unprepared for battle, the Tories were slaughtered. Lee later floated the exculpatory story that he never intended to fight but was compelled to do so when the enemy opened fire. One of Lee's men later put the lie to that tale when he acknowledged that a rebel horseman had struck the first blow. The version of the event recounted by Andrew Pickens, who was nearby with his militia, also contradicted Lee's varnished account. Within hours of the incident, Pickens wrote that the moment Lee discovered that Pyle commanded the king's soldiers, he struck. The battle—if that is the right word, for many men under Pyle never fought back—ended quickly. At least one hundred of Pyle's men were killed and, according to Pickens, "the greatest part of the others [were] wounded." Lee did not lose a single man. The British, who felt the Loyalist troopers had been "inhumanely butchered," quickly referred to the event as "Pyle's Massacre," a carefully chosen word that was quite appropriate. As at King's Mountain, rebel soldiers once again were responsible for an atrocity that rivaled the barbarism allegedly committed by Tarleton in the Waxhaws. Hours after the encounter, in fact, after darkness had stolen over the landscape, six prisoners from Pyle's troop were killed in cold blood by North Carolina militiamen shouting "Remember Buford." They were "hewed to pieces with broadswords," said a sickened member of the rebel troop.[15]

Once he learned of the carnage inflicted on Pyle's dragoons, Cornwallis knew in an instant that he had recruited his last Tory soldier in the upcountry between Charlotte to Hillsborough. The Loyalists, previously "cautious and slow," now "became timid to an excess," according to one British officer. It is not difficult to see why. For the fourth time in eight months an armed Loyalist corps had been decimated in North Carolina. The debacle at Ramsour's Mill the previous June, followed in October by the horrendous catastrophe at King's Mountain, the January thrashing suffered by the supposedly indomitable Tarleton at Cowpens, and now, in February, Pyle's Massacre were enough to discourage the heartiest soul who contemplated bearing arms for the royal cause. As soon as he was made aware of the latest disaster, Cornwallis moved on to the west, crossing the Haw River roughly midway between Hillsborough and Guilford Courthouse. He continued his forlorn hunt for Loyalist recruits, but hungering for battle, Cornwallis's main focus was to maneuver in hopes of facing off with Greene. Cornwallis, by temperament, was an aggressive soldier. He did not duck fights. He sought them, though not injudiciously. In this instance, he believed that a victory would justify the gamble he had taken in chasing Morgan and Greene, and it would be balm for the hardships he and his men had borne while tracking the rebel forces through Carolina's backcountry. In addition, like many of his officers, he had come to look on his adversary as brutish, and he was driven by a burning scorn for the rebels. Had Cornwallis been privy to the letters of his enemies, his withering contempt for them would only have increased. Greene shrugged off the horrific blood-bath perpetrated by Lee as useful for hampering Cornwallis's recruiting, while Andrew Pickens rejoiced that it had "knocked up Toryism altogether in this part" of the state.[16]

Although Cornwallis had retaken the field and Colonels Lee and Washington were "hang[ing] on the enemy," Greene kept his distance, biding his time in the belief that even more Virginia militiamen would soon join him. While waiting, he frantically appealed for help from North Carolina, Maryland, and Delaware—"I can effect nothing, unless I am largely reinforced," he pleaded—and yet again he asked General Washington for troops, telling him that it was probably "out of the power" of the southern states to send more men. Greene even wrote the commander of the Bedford County, Virginia, militia begging him to send five hundred "good" riflemen for six weeks' service. At one point, a downcast Greene thought the only way that he would receive ample help from Virginia might be for him to bring his army back into the state and hope Cornwallis followed.[17]

During his first days back in North Carolina, Greene could only guess what Cornwallis intended. At one point he believed the "Old Fox"—as he and others sometimes referred to the British general—might be about to march to Virginia to join with and take command of Arnold's army. As late as the first week in March, Greene suspected that Cornwallis intended to retreat to Cross Creek (present day Fayetteville) on the Cape Fear River, which would link him to Wilmington, from where he could be adequately resupplied. Greene hoped that was not the case. He wanted a crack at his adversary as much as Cornwallis yearned for battle. Greene spoke of "giving Lord Cornwallis a run in turn." At the very least, Greene planned to "gall his rear," that is, to dog his every step until, like Washington at Monmouth, he could attack the tail of Cornwallis's army. But Greene, too, was a fighter, and if his army swelled handsomely, he would seize the chance "of effecting [Cornwallis's] ruin" through a set-piece battle. Greene knew the risks. To be sure that Greene was aware of the peril he faced, Daniel Morgan, now retired on his Virginia farm, wrote to spell out the danger that the American army faced. "Cornwallis will push you till you are obliged to fight him," he warned. He further advised Greene not to give battle until adequate numbers of militia were in camp. To that, Morgan ominously added: if the militiamen will "fight you'l beat Cornwallis, if not, he will beat you and perhaps cut your regulars to pieces." To prevent such a disaster, Morgan added a piece of chilling advice. On the day of battle, Greene should station "picked troops" in the rear of the militiamen "with orders to shoot down the first man that runs."[18]

Greene soon suspected that Cornwallis, too, was looking for a fight, though for several days he guessed that the British general would fight only if he enjoyed a numerical advantage. For eighteen days the two armies played "Hide & Seek," as Otho Williams put it. Cornwallis kept his army moving, looking for an opening. Greene also stayed on the move, forestalling the battle until his army had grown to fighting size. If there was to be a battle, it would occur when Greene was ready. General O'Hara said that all the while the "two armys were never above twenty miles asunder." Throughout the daily movements, he added, the rebels were constantly bent on "avoiding a general action" while Cornwallis was "as industriously seeking it." The main armies may have been far apart, but much of the time skirmishes were occurring between small parties. The rival cavalries also searched continuously for their counterparts. One Virginia officer unfairly concluded that Tarleton's "spirit of enterprize" had "entirely deserted him" in the wake of Cowpens. No one questioned Colonel Lee's venturesome qualities, however. "We . . . exert ourselves to alarm the enemy by night, & to harass them by day," Lee declared. Not every soldier exhibited such spunk. Some rebel militiamen, convinced that regular officers used them only to shield more valuable Continentals, deserted and struck out for home. Others abandoned their forward positions and rejoined their regiments farther to the rear.[19]

Many of the soldiers on both sides were ragged and exhausted. Some had been in the field for seventy or more days. British regulars and some of their Continental counterparts were unwashed, unshaven, unkempt, and unfed, or at least not always provided adequate nourishment. One of Greene's soldiers later recollected that "these were times of great suffering. We had but little to eat, as little to wear, [and were] feeble and worn down." Greene mentioned that he had "not had my cloaths [off] for upwards of six weeks." O'Hara said that most of the British soldiers were "barefoot, naked," and famished, having subsisted for days on turnips and a few ounces of corn. Moreover, since that January day on the Catawba when Cornwallis built his giant bonfire, his men had been without tents. The "Spirit of our little Army has evaporated a good deal," O'Hara acknowledged. This was the South, but it was winter and the temperature hovered around freezing on many nights, the days were often chilly and sometimes downright cold, and it rained on all too many days and nights. Illnesses were commonplace. Colonel Williams complained of excruciating pain in his chest, neck, and shoulders from "Rheumatism," a condition that made it nearly unbearable to stay in the saddle hour after hour. The therapy that he chose to alleviate the pain was to soak his feet in warm water. Early in March, Greene fell victim to "a violent inflammation of my eyes," an affliction that nearly "rendered [him] incapable of business." He sought relief through bleedings and purgatives. Somehow the men on both sides soldiered on. They were incredibly tough men who were accustomed to a harsh existence, though the past two months had taxed them to the limits of their endurance.[20]

Aware that a fight could not be forestalled forever, Greene wrote militia commanders exhorting them to "force" their march and come via the most direct route. A Virginia general officer who had been dispatched with four hundred men by "Barrin" Steuben assured Greene that he was coming by the "neareist and best" way. Meanwhile, Greene moved his army at least every other night, always keeping his intended destination a secret, even among his highest officers. He awakened his army long before dawn each morning, as he believed Cornwallis liked to launch surprise attacks when the first streaks of light appeared in the eastern sky. Each day Greene remained on the lookout for the additional troops that were coming. The mountaineers and militiamen from the Old Dominion were the first to arrive, some 325 altogether, followed soon thereafter by elements consisting of Virginia's conscripted Continentals. By March 11, roughly all the units that had been expected had formed a junction with Greene. Altogether, nearly 3,000 men had trickled in over the span of a dozen or so days, though some soon deserted and Greene sent home many underequipped Georgia and South Carolina militiamen, thinking their only contribution would be to consume the army's provisions. Nevertheless, by the second week in March, the rebel army stood at 4,200, roughly double the number of men Cornwallis possessed. Greene was ready to fight. If he waited, he said, his army was more likely to shrink than to increase. Furthermore, given the paucity of food in this "exhausted Country," he knew that he could not keep his army together too much longer.[21]

However, Greene continued to anguish that Cornwallis "dont wish a general action." Had he wanted a fight, Greene mistakenly reasoned, Cornwallis would have "brought it on" by now. On March 12, Greene did what he could to entice Cornwallis. He marched his army to within eight miles of his foe, closer than ever before. Two days later he posted his men at Guilford Courthouse, a virtual invitation to Cornwallis to attack. Greene had carefully chosen this site, prompting a high-ranking British officer to laud him for having selected "very commanding ground." Greene said he dreaded only two things: "a heavy rain and a Night attack." Rain would damage flints and powder, aborting the use of muskets and encouraging the enemy to attack with bayonets. It required more experience and discipline than American militiamen usually displayed to remain steady when fearsome-looking enemy soldiers advanced brandishing gleaming steel bayonets. Greene distributed tents, not for the men to sleep in but for them to store their muskets and powder at night in the event of rain. Fighting at night was uncommon in this war, but Greene knew that Cornwallis could be unpredictable, and should he attack in the dark, it was likely to unnerve even his veteran soldiers. To guard against Cornwallis coming at night, Greene appealed to Lee: "Dont get surprised, nor let us be so."[22]

Greene continued to doubt that Cornwallis would give battle. The best that would come of this, he said at one point, was that he would "pursue the steps of the Enemy" as he retreated to Cross Creek. Greene misjudged Cornwallis. Nine days earlier, Cornwallis had declared: "I shall do every thing in my power to bring [Greene] to an action," and one of his principal officers, who understood his commander's character, said that his chief "embraced with much satisfaction the proffered opportunity of giving [Greene] battle." Cornwallis never wavered, and though heavily outnumbered, he remained confident of victory. The cherished belief that a ragtag army could not best British regulars, the notion that had helped propel Lord North and his ministers to order the use of force in 1775, had never been entirely abandoned. Cornwallis may also have expected that Greene would err colossally. After all, this was Greene's first independent command and the first time he would be in charge of an army under attack.[23]

Early on the morning of March 15, Greene heard the crackle of distant muskets. He knew that Lee's cavalry had made contact with Cornwallis's dragoons, and for the first time Greene was certain that Cornwallis was on the march to Guilford Courthouse. There would be a battle and it would be at the spot that Greene had chosen. The site was much larger than Cowpens, nearly ten times as long and wide. Some of it was open farmland, but after a few hundred yards that gave way to heavy forest. The woods appealed to Greene, as it would make it more difficult for the enemy to maintain its formations, and that in turn reduced the likelihood of bayonet charges. Greene knew the formula that Morgan had utilized for his success at Cowpens, and in fact Morgan—in the letter in which he had advocated a rear guard to gun down deserters—had taken pains to remind his former commander of how he had positioned his army for the clash with Tarleton. But the terrain at Guilford Courthouse was different, and unlike Morgan, Greene would be up against the main British army and a seasoned commander. Greene followed his own instincts, as he had all along since arriving in North Carolina, though his thinking bore the imprint of Morgan's plan.

Like Morgan, Greene arranged his men in three lines. He placed nearly one thousand North Carolina militiamen in the front line and gave command of some units to regular officers. He positioned his artillery between the militia regiments, while all the rebel cavalry, together with some Continentals and Blue Ridge mountaineers armed with rifles, were deployed on the flanks of the first line. That line was posted at the spot where the farmland met the woods, and the militiamen were asked to fire two shots before they fell back among the winter-bleak trees. Virginia militiamen composed a second line some three hundred yards farther back. Whether or not Greene was aware of it—and it is difficult to image that he did not know—Brigadier General Edward Stevens, commander of one of the two Virginia brigades, had posted forty riflemen some fifty yards behind his line and ordered them to shoot any soldier who ran. Maryland and Virginia Continentals brought up the rear in the third line. The greatest differences in the formation that Morgan had put in place at Cowpens and Greene's in this engagement were that at Guilford Courthouse there were no pickets to surprise the advancing adversary and no cavalry units were hidden in the rear. As the sounds of Cornwallis's approaching army grew louder, Greene emulated Morgan by riding among his men, speaking with them and hoping to instill confidence, though neither he nor any other rebel general could match Morgan as an inspirational leader, at least among militiamen.

Hours passed between the time the American soldiery became aware of the certainty of battle and the appearance of the British army. The men spent that time as men facing battle have always done. Nearly all tinkered with their weapons. Some prayed, some tried to focus on what their officers told them. Neophytes quietly wondered what combat would be like and hoped they would not embarrass themselves in front of their comrades. A great many likely thought of home, pondered how they happened to be at this place at this moment, and longed to be elsewhere. It is likely that every man thought about being wounded or dying before the sun set on this day. Though it was a cool day, many men were sweating. Nearly all were vexed with mouths so dry they could hardly swallow. The most unnerved among them wet their pants.

Near noon the American soldiers at last glimpsed their adversaries. They were marching up New Garden Road, keeping step to the somber beat of drums. Most wore bright red coats, but the Hessians were predominately outfitted in blue coats, and the jaegers—Germans recruited primarily from among foresters and huntsmen—were attired in green coats, as were Tarleton's dragoons. Several minutes passed. It took time for some two thousand men to reach the bucolic area that Greene had selected for the confrontation, and once all the men were present, another thirty minutes passed while Cornwallis formed his lines. He had detached approximately 125 men to the rear to guard the baggage. These men would not come under fire. But the roughly 2,200 that Cornwallis positioned as his last act before going into battle most certainly would experience combat, some for the first time, some for the last time.[24] Cornwallis left no record of his thoughts on the eve of battle, but he had come under fire many times. He would have been terribly cold-blooded not to have been anxious, though his predominant sensation might have been exhilaration. More than nine weeks had passed since he stepped off for North Carolina and at long last he was about to get his shot at the elusive rebel army. What was going through Greene's mind cannot be known, but it must have been a mixture of anticipation, doubts, hope, and disquieting trepidation. If elation was part of his mood, the good weather would have contributed to it. It was a sunny, spring-soft southern day.

Cornwallis placed light infantry, grenadiers, and jaegers on his left under James Webster, who had surprised the Americans at Monck's Corner during the siege of Charleston. On the right, General Leslie commanded the Highlanders, attired in their native kilts, together with most of the Hessians.

Tarleton's Legion, posted in the rear, could be plugged in when and where needed. Cornwallis's army was multinational. In its ranks were men who had grown up in England, Wales, Scotland, Ireland, Germany, and the American colonies.

At last, the moment had come for what Colonel Lee called "this day of blood."[25] The British force moved forward with what one officer said was "order and coolness," manifesting an air of "determined resolution."[26] They advanced across farmland, some of which had been plowed. The land that had been left fallow soon turned from a muted wintry green to a muddy brown. Minutes passed. To some of the waiting rebels it must have seemed an eternity. To others, it was as if the enemy covered the sodden ground in the blink of an eye. Artillery already boomed from both sides, though at this juncture it was largely ineffectual. The American militiamen had been instructed to hold their fire until the enemy was within musket range, roughly fifty or so yards away. The lead elements of the British force pressed forward toward North Carolina's militiamen, who were assembled behind a split-rail fence that offered next to no cover. The British could see their adversaries. They could see, too, that the militiamen were resting their muskets on the fence, steadying them for a more accurate shot. It was an "awful period," thought one of the British soldiers.[27] Suddenly, the British accelerated their pace. Fear overtook many of the citizen soldiers behind the fence. Eager to get off their two rounds and withdraw toward the rear, many militiamen fired their first shot when the adversary was still 150 yards away. It was a wasted shot, far beyond a musket's effective range. Some of the militiamen did not stick around for their second shot and, if Greene was later correct, not a few retreated without having fired a single round.

The dismaying performance of these North Carolinians was not typical of the militiamen in this fight, or even of all the militia from North Carolina. Many appear to have waited with a steely, patient resolve, eyeing the enemy soldiers as they marched resolutely, though unhurriedly, through the open fields, marking time until their intended victims came within range. Suddenly, hundreds of muskets erupted. Many of Cornwallis's men, who had yet to fire a shot, crumpled to the soggy earth. One British officer said that "one half of Highlanders dropt on the spot." Another called it a "most galling and destructive fire." A North Carolinian who watched the British soldiers fall was reminded of the "scattering stalks of a wheat field, when the harvest man passed over it with his cradle."[28] Those who were not hit continued to press forward for a few more feet before pausing momentarily to fire their first round. Now was the moment for the bayonets to come into play. The British charged, their weapons made all the more visible as the spring sunshine glinted off the shiny blades. Because the British had taken a few seconds to aim and fire, and to receive the order for a bayonet charge, most militiamen got off their second shot. Like the first, it blew a gaping hole in the enemy line. But the British who were still standing continued their charge, though when they reached the wooded area where the militiamen had been posted, they discovered that their foe was gone. All the North Carolina militiamen had melted away and were headed for the rear.

Only a few minutes had elapsed since the British began their march. During that time the fighting had resembled other clashes in this war. But as the British made contact with the second line of rebels—and later with the third line—most of the fighting took place in the craggy woods that dotted the site Greene had selected. It became impossible for the British to maintain their prearranged lines. The fighting devolved into contests between small units, more akin to combat in many World War II engagements than to a typical eighteenth-century battle. The British sought to adhere to their age-old established practice. Officers belted out orders. The men followed those orders. But it was next to impossible for soldiers to see their officers in the smoke-filled forest or to hear them in the din of countless muskets and heavy artillery. The Americans followed their instincts. They fired, withdrew a few yards to hide behind a tree or fallen log while reloading, and fired again. The fighting varied from area to area. It was dictated by the terrain and the forest, by low-ranking officers, by the men themselves, and by the trauma and chaos of battle. Here and there the British mounted bayonet charges. In some areas the British gained ground. In other sectors, units "suffered greatly" and were driven back. High-ranking officers were in the midst of the fighting. Both James Webster and O'Hara were wounded. Webster took rounds in both arms and a leg. O'Hara took a ball in the thigh, but returned to fight once his wound was tended, and he continued to lead charges until he was shot again, this time in the torso. Cornwallis was just as valiant. His horse was shot from beneath him, but he grabbed another man's mount and continued to ride about the battlefield "evidently unconscious of his danger," as one of his men later remarked. That second horse was also shot from under him, though the general remained unscathed. Greene, too, was in the middle of the battle and at one point was nearly captured by the British, "having rode in the heat of the action full tilt directly into the Midst of the enemy." At the last minute, Greene was rescued by one of his observant officers.[29]

An hour or more into this ghastly fight the British left wing buckled dangerously, imperiling Cornwallis's entire army. An American attack in that sector at that moment could have resulted in the encirclement of the British force. But Greene did not order the assault, which would have had to be made by the militiamen who had withdrawn to the rear in the early going. After all the risks he had taken since December, at this moment of truth Greene turned his back on an uncertain and chancy move. He almost certainly made the correct decision. Every battle has its surprises, and ordering militiamen, who had already done what was asked of them, to attack veterans would have been acutely hazardous. In the havoc of battle what seems at one second to be a golden opportunity can in an instant turn into disaster. A man with the temperament of Benedict Arnold might have made the gamble. Greene's track record during the past one hundred days made him a likely candidate to chance it, but when the possibly decisive moment presented itself, Greene chose prudence and caution. His behavior was exactly what he had pledged it would be when Congress gave him command of the army.

In the final minutes of the struggle it was Cornwallis who may have taken the greatest risk. According to an apparently true story that later circulated, Cornwallis sought to prevent the collapse of his sagging lines and stop the rebel advance by ordering his artillery to fire into a tangled knot of brawling soldiers. He knew some of his own men would be victims, but it was the only means by which he could stop the fighting long enough to regroup. Not for the first time in combat, and not for the last, a leader saw some of his men as expendable so that a greater good could be served. Cornwallis, a hardened professional soldier, had not shrunk from such a horrendous decision, and his act, however pitiless, may have saved his army. Cornwallis was ready to continue the fight. Greene, however, was finished. In two hours of desperate fighting the rebel army had accomplished much, though to continue the battle was dicey. Greene ordered a withdrawal, a step that enabled Cornwallis to claim he was the victor, as his army controlled the battlefield following the day's final shot. That was exactly the tack that Cornwallis took, telling London that he had won a great victory. He added a second falsehood to his deceptive report. He claimed that the rebels had not stopped running until they were "18 miles from the field of battle."[30]

Given that he had been heavily outnumbered and had to fight an enemy that had carefully selected the battle's site, Cornwallis's army had performed extraordinarily well. His post-battle assessments that his men had fought with "much ardour" and displayed "spirited exertions" were understatements. Nearly 300 of Greene's men were dead or wounded, the British had captured every American field piece, 1,300 stand of arms, and two ammunition wagons, as well as killed every artillery horse that had served the rebel army. But Cornwallis had also paid a heavy price. He acknowledged the loss of 532 of his men, close to 25 percent of those who had gone into battle, an unsustainable rate of attrition. One of his officers said that nearly half of all the British officers had been killed or wounded.[31] Greene had a good chance of replacing the men he lost. Cornwallis faced a more daunting task when it came to overcoming his losses.

The war in the South had become a quagmire for the British. Cornwallis had possessed some 6,500 men when he took command in South Carolina in June 1780.[32] His army was subsequently augmented by reinforcements, the formation of provincial units, and the recruitment of Tory militia, so that in the ten months between assuming command and Guilford Courthouse he had altogether commanded upwards of 11,000 men. Some were short-term militiamen who never saw battle, others were garrisoned in Savannah or Charleston and never took the field, and not a few were scattered throughout backcountry posts and had never come under fire. But in the ten months since taking command, Cornwallis had lost some 3,000 men in four major battles. At a minimum, his army lost another thousand soldiers to disease and desertion, in small skirmishes, encounters with partisans, and the grueling race to the Dan. Despite a catastrophic attrition rate, the British had not gained control of one square inch of territory since the first few days following Lincoln's surrender the previous May.

Following the fighting at Guilford Courthouse, Cornwallis's report to London made it appear as though Greene's army had, like Gates's after Camden, fled in great haste and disarray. Actually, Greene's withdrawal was "conducted with order and regularity," as one of Cornwallis's subordinates noted, and ended after ten miles when the army crossed to safety at Reedy Fork River. Unlike the aftermath of Camden, when the British had vigorously sought to hunt down the scattered remnants of Horatio Gates's army, Cornwallis attempted only a half-hearted pursuit of Greene. On the day after the battle, Greene reported to Congress and Washington, among others, lavishing praise on all his troops save the North Carolina militiamen. He claimed that "Victory . . . was certain" had those men done their duty. That might have been true. It is conceivable that Cornwallis could not have overcome the colossal number of casualties that his army would have suffered had the first line of rebel defenders laid down a steady, concentrated fire. Greene stressed that most of the remainder of his soldiers had displayed a "firmness" that would "forever add a lustre to their military reputation." He took pains to emphasize that the Virginia militiamen in the second line had "behavd nobly" and that his cavalry had "performed wonders." He variously described the engagement as "long, obstinate, and bloody" and "long, bloody and severe," and said it was among the "most bloody actions" of the war. (Likewise, Cornwallis said it had been "one of the bloodiest of this war.") Greene also believed he had achieved something of significance. "The honor of the Day terminated in favour of the Enemy," he acknowledged, for they occupied the battlefield when the last shot was fired. But said Greene, in an assessment with which historians have concurred, Cornwallis's "loss being infinitely greater than ours, I trust the event will ultimately prove advantageous to us." Cornwallis may have drawn the same conclusion, though he did not say so. However, one of his officers pronounced Guilford Courthouse "a victory most honourable and glorious," though "the expense at which it was obtained rendered it of no utility." Foes of the war in London immediately reached the same conclusion. On receiving word of Guilford Courthouse, Charles James Fox told the House of Commons, "Another such victory would ruin the British army."[33]

Greene wrote his wife, "Nothing but blood slaughter prevails here." The killing ground at Guilford Courthouse was a chamber of horrors. It was steeped in blood. The dead were strewn all about—Cornwallis estimated that when the shooting stopped, upwards of three hundred corpses littered the landscape—and the wounded from both sides laid on the inhospitable ground for hours, moaning and pleading for help. Their appalling suffering increased when a cold, steady rain commenced soon after the fighting ended and continued throughout the night. General O'Hara, one of the gravely wounded, later said he "never did, and I hope never shall again, experience two such days and Nights, as these immediately after the Battle." For hours, O'Hara—like untold others—did not receive "the smallest comfort" to alleviate his agony. British officers estimated that at least fifty of their wounded died during that awful night. Dog tired, hungry, and unnerved British soldiers combed the grounds in search of those who might yet be saved. They carried their wounded to a church in nearby New Garden and transported injured rebels to the nearby courthouse. Some wounded were taken to the homes of local Quaker residents. Indeed, when the fighting ended many Quaker families hurried to the battlefield with food, water, and milk for the suffering soldiers on both sides. Even those British soldiers who escaped unscathed faced a miserable night. In addition to searching for fallen comrades, they had not eaten in twenty-four hours and the continuous rain prevented them from making fires to cook a meal.[34]

Within twenty-four hours of the battle Greene knew that Cornwallis was sending off his baggage. There would be no more fighting at Guilford Courthouse. Though the baggage wagons pulled out, Cornwallis kept his army on the battlefield for two days. When he evacuated the site of the fighting, it was first to march to nearby New Garden, a Quaker community. The army's arrival was a gruesome sight, as numerous horses carried injured soldiers and seventeen bloodstained wagons were filled with still more of the wounded. The army lingered there only long enough to find care for the casualties and for Cornwallis to issue another grandiloquent proclamation, this one claiming a "compleat victory." Cornwallis announced that Greene's army had been "obliged . . . to fly with the utmost precipitation towards Virginia," an untrue assertion. He followed his bluster with the customary plea for Loyalists to step forward and fight for their king. In all likelihood, Cornwallis never thought that was likely to occur. Within a day or two he knew for certain that it was a forlorn hope. He later told General Clinton that numerous "inhabitants rode into camp, shook me by the hand, said they were glad to see us and to hear that we had beat Greene, and rode home again." He "could not get 100 men" in this part of North Carolina "to stay with us even as militia," he added.[35] Once he found care for his most grievously wounded men—sixty-four in all—Cornwallis set off for Cross Creek on the Cape Fear River.

It was a grim trek of 180 miles. The army set out with few provisions, and the march lasted thirteen long days. During the bulk of the tramp the army was reduced to foraging for its every scrap of sustenance. Soldiers pilfered from farmers, marauding through their fields and pasturelands, taking what could be found in barns and storage bins, even entering houses to confiscate what they wanted. Patriots and Loyalists alike were victims, and among the latter were some who had fought for the Crown.[36] All the while, the wounded and sick—which Cornwallis estimated to be one-third of his army—were transported by horses if they could sit, by wagons and horse litters if they could not. Either way was ghastly, as the incessant jostling was nearly unbearable. Some died in the course of the journey, including Colonel Webster, for whom Cornwallis especially grieved, as he had regarded him as his most trusted officer. The remainder, having marched hundreds of miles in the past eight weeks, marched yet again, some in threadbare shoes, some in bare feet. Cornwallis pushed his army at the fastest possible pace.

He was aware that Greene was coming after him and he knew that his army was in no shape for another round of combat. Greene was indeed now the pursuer, though in the chaos that followed Guilford Courthouse, the rebels were unaware of the British march until three days after it commenced. That head start prevented Greene from pouncing on his vulnerable enemy.

The bedraggled British soldiery reached Cross Creek in late March, only to be bitterly disappointed at what they found. Not only were large British vessels unable to ascend the too-shallow Cape Fear River, but the river was narrow and the banks on each side were tall, a welcoming invitation to Greene or rebel partisans to wreak devastation on royal shipping. There was nothing to do but resume the march, though Cornwallis knew that his men were "worn down with fatigue" and his army was "in the utmost want of necessaries of every kind." Finally, on April 7, almost three weeks after setting off from New Garden, the British force reached Wilmington, a safe site where the men could recuperate and enjoy ample provisions.[37]

DURING THE PREVIOUS fall, General Clinton told an acquaintance that he believed the "Rebellion would end suddenly in a Crash." Soaring expectations kindled by Benedict Arnold's pending treason may have prompted his prediction. But it may also have stemmed from Rochambeau's temporarily precarious situation in Newport, the rebels' economic troubles, or Washington's difficulty in fleshing out the Continental army. Clinton may even have based his prophecy on the assumption that Cornwallis would succeed in North Carolina, as he made the observation on the eve of the earl's initial entry into that province. Whatever was on Clinton's mind, the crash he foresaw had not occurred in the last months of 1780. Nor had the mutinies in the Continental army in the following January brought down the rebels. Aware of King's Mountain and the clash at Cowpens, but not of Guilford Courthouse, Clinton deep into the spring of 1781 knew that Britain was no closer to winning the war. A New York Loyalist who met frequently with Clinton concluded early that year that the British commander "was confused and anxious on the State of Things in the South

Country." It was a view shared by Admiral Arbuthnot, who advised the same Tory that Cornwallis must be substantially reinforced or the British "would be ruined" in the South. Arbuthnot also joined the ranks of leaders on both sides who understood that 1781 would be a pivotal year. It was "now or never for crushing the Rebellion," he declared.[38]

Judge William Smith, the Tory to whom Clinton and Arbuthnot spoke so freely, discerned something else in these candid conversations. Clinton's ruminations, as well as what the commander shared of Cornwallis's reports, led Smith to fear that deep down both generals believed the war in the South was hopeless. In fact, Smith concluded that the two generals soon would be "opening Batteries against" each other in the blame game that was certain to ensue following Britain's defeat. Smith was dead wrong. Clinton did not think the war in the South was unwinnable. He thought the steps he was taking would turn around the war in the South.

Almost immediately upon learning that Lafayette had been dispatched to Virginia, Clinton countered by sending 2,000 men under his old friend General William Phillips, who was to join with Benedict Arnold's force in Portsmouth and assume command of British military operations in the Old Dominion. After learning a few days later that London was sending him six regiments, Clinton—without waiting for the reinforcements—rushed an additional 1,700 troops to Phillips. Clinton believed the presence of some 5,500 regulars in Virginia—plus whatever number of Loyalists they raised— would not only force Governor Jefferson to recall the militiamen he had sent to the Carolinas but also compel Greene to retreat to Virginia and link up with Lafayette. As Cornwallis would have only Carolina militiamen and partisans to cope with, Clinton believed he "could not fail" to bring about the "restoration of order" in Georgia and the Carolinas.[39]

Clinton saw the British army's presence in Virginia as an all-important step in "interrupt[ing] the course of supplies to the Carolinas." Phillips's army was to destroy "the enemy's public stores and magazines" in Petersburg and along the James River. Moreover, operating hand in glove with Britain's navy, the army was to establish Chesapeake bases. British forces posted in these bases could play an active role in impeding the flow of rebel supplies that cascaded south from Philadelphia into Virginia and on to points south. Clinton had toyed with the idea of a British base, or bases, in the Chesapeake as early as 1776. After the Charleston campaign he was wedded to the notion, and he took his first step in that direction in the autumn of 1780 when he dispatched General Leslie, with a large force, to Virginia. In addition to carrying out destructive raids, Leslie was to establish Britain's inaugural Chesapeake base. Clinton further directed Cornwallis, with the large cache of Loyalists he anticipated gathering that fall on his initial incursion into North Carolina, to rendezvous with Leslie somewhere near the Chesapeake. Clinton's expectation had been that Cornwallis and Leslie would establish additional posts that would be garrisoned with regulars and Loyalist troops drawn from the Carolinas and Virginia. From time to time, the king's soldiers were to sally forth from these bases, interdicting the rebels' chain of communications, closing their supply lines, eradicating enemy storage depots, and generally sowing destruction that aimed to transform stalwart rebels into less devoted supporters of the war. Meanwhile, Royal Navy vessels were to operate on the Chesapeake's tributaries between the Potomac and James Rivers, closing those waterways to rebel traffic.

Clinton's plan had not materialized, for Cornwallis in the wake of King's Mountain had summoned Leslie to South Carolina. Nevertheless, by 1781 Clinton was more than ever convinced that he was on the right track for suppressing the rebellion in the South. He was buoyed by Arnold's blitz along the James River, capped by his damaging assault on Richmond. His sortie had inflicted "a most essential injury to the enemy," said Clinton, and he expected more of the same from Phillips. Like Cornwallis—and because of the pessimistic, but realistic, reports sent him by the earl in July and August—Clinton had concluded that his original plan for suppressing the insurgency in South Carolina was unworkable. After much reflection, he had conceived this bold new plan, and he was confident that it would succeed. The "King's affairs," said Clinton, were "going in the happiest train."[40]

During the winter and early spring of 1781, Clinton made his plans in the dark, as for the longest time he had no knowledge of what was unfolding down south. Cornwallis wrote Clinton, on the day following Cowpens, a letter burnished with false information. He minimized Tarleton's losses, emphasizing instead that the British Legion had "cut to pieces" the rebel cavalry. Thereafter, Cornwallis did not write Clinton again for eighty-two days. (Clinton subsequently remarked that his ignorance of Cornwallis's campaign "probably saved me from many an uneasy hour.") Three days after arriving in Wilmington, Cornwallis at last notified Clinton of his fruitless pursuit of Greene and his failure to destroy the rebel army on finally bringing it to battle. His report to Clinton, like his earlier account of Cowpens, was filled with prevarications. Cornwallis claimed to have had one quarter fewer men than he actually possessed at Guilford Courthouse, and he portrayed Greene's army as nearly twice its actual size. (He told others that Greene's army was "seven times my number.") Cornwallis additionally claimed to have scored a "very complete" and "uniformly successful" triumph over Greene. What followed was more truthful. His men had been too exhausted to pursue Greene's tattered army in the aftermath of the engagement. With Greene at his heels, Cornwallis continued, he had brought his army to Wilmington for rest and refurbishing.[41]

Clinton was an old hand at writing reports and in his day had probably embroidered a few. With a keen eye for fabrication, Clinton was not fooled by what he read. Besides, he had learned from General Phillips, his trusted friend, that Cornwallis's army had "suffered very much" during its pursuit of Greene and that while the performance of his eviscerated force at Guilford Courthouse had been "glorious," the result was "the sort of victory which ruins an army." Clinton responded to Cornwallis's chronicle of the recent battle with cynical clarity. He questioned why Cornwallis had so few men at Guilford Courthouse. Based on his earlier communication regarding the outcome at Cowpens, Clinton did the math and concluded that Cornwallis should have been able to commit considerably more men to the fight against Greene. In his response, Clinton also asked, If Greene was so badly beaten, why had his army been able to shadow Cornwallis's on its march to Wilmington? If Cornwallis's victory had been so decisive, he additionally wondered, why had Greene not been obliged to retreat to Virginia?[42]

Clinton was disappointed, but what most troubled him was something else that Cornwallis said: "I cannot help expressing my wishes that [Virginia] may become the seat of war, even (if necessary) at the expense of abandoning New York. Untill Virginia is in a manner subdued, our hold of the Carolinas must be difficult if not precarious." Clinton was appalled. Cornwallis was suggesting that Clinton turn his back on New York and bring his army to Virginia, fusing it into a giant British force that would attempt to crush the insurgency in the Old Dominion. Clinton was not about to abandon New York. He thought it immoral to abandon New York's Loyalists and militarily unwise to relinquish Britain's "only winter harbor" in the northern theater. Furthermore, the British army's departure from New York would open "a wide door for the enemy to wrest Canada from us."

Cornwallis was advocating a very different strategy from what Clinton had painstakingly put together. While Clinton had earlier approved of Cornwallis bringing his force to the Old Dominion to join with Phillips's army, it was on the condition that the earl would come northward only "after he has made his arrangements in the Carolinas." In short, Clinton expected Cornwallis to remain in the Carolinas so long as those provinces were threatened by Greene and the insurgents had not been brought to heel. Clinton never had the "smallest idea of engaging in solid operations [in Virginia] for the particular purpose of conquering" that province. His "resources were certainly by no means equal to" the conquest of a colony as large and populous as Virginia. Furthermore, putting Britain's army in Virginia would be "attended with great risk" in the event that the Royal Navy lost its "permanent superiority at sea" and the French navy gained control of the Chesapeake.[43] Under similar circumstances, New York would be imperiled too, but for the past five years the British had constructed a defensive labyrinth throughout Manhattan and on Long Island and would be better able to repulse an Allied attack. Clinton lucidly saw a bigger picture than Cornwallis was apparently capable of seeing. Clinton's strategy offered a better chance of surviving an enemy onslaught and successfully implementing the southern strategy.

Having finally heard from his subordinate, Clinton in April wrote Cornwallis and yet again stressed that his "presence in Carolina cannot be so soon dispensed with." To that, Clinton added that attempting to subjugate Virginia would require "considerable time," and time was of the essence. Not long before, Lord Germain had advised him that England "cannot support a protracted war. . . . Every advantage must therefore be seized, every occasion profited of." With a firm grip on reality, Clinton saw that there was no possibility that the British army could reestablish royal control of Virginia during 1781, if ever. Atop that, Clinton was convinced that his strategic plan offered the best chance for suppressing the rebellion in the Carolinas before year's end.[44]

Clinton was sufficiently worried by what he had read in Cornwallis's communiqué that he thought of sailing to Wilmington and resolutely punctuating the necessity for Cornwallis to stay out of Virginia. However, he considered it imprudent to leave New York at this juncture. General Knyphausen, his second in command, was ill and Clinton was reluctant to turn over the reins to a less experienced officer now that the campaign season in the North was at hand. Clinton had frequently sent emissaries to London, and he could have—and should have—sent an aide to meet with Cornwallis, but for some inexplicable reason he did not do so. It was a blunder that changed the course of the war, and quite possibly its outcome.

Rather than boarding a vessel for what likely would have been a round-trip of fewer than twenty-five days, Clinton, on April 30, sent off a second letter to Cornwallis. The commander laid out his belief that "no solid operation can be carried on" to subdue Virginia "before those to the southward of it are totally at an end." But he flinched from stipulating that Cornwallis not come to Virginia. Clinton's hand may have been stayed on that score not only by Germain's recent exhortation to commit "a considerable force" to Virginia, but as the secretary had spoken of having "Cornwallis and Brigadier-General Arnold subdue Virginia." Clinton may also have fooled himself that his numerous previous admonitions for Cornwallis to remain in South Carolina until the insurgency was unmistakably suppressed would be sufficient.[45] Besides, he believed his communiqué would be in Cornwallis's hands within ten days. However, Cornwallis did not receive Clinton's letter for two months.

Though it was not apparent in the emollient tone of Clinton's communiqué, he was exasperated with Cornwallis. During the previous fall Clinton had supported Cornwallis's decision to take the war to North Carolina, confident that "very numerous" North Carolina Loyalists would rally to the king's cause. But when he learned of the disaster at King's Mountain, Clinton privately attributed the calamity to Cornwallis's folly in sending a detachment into the backcountry without adequate support. Once Clinton finally became aware of the truth about the outcome at Cowpens—at the hands of what he called a "trifling corps" of rebels—he concluded that Cornwallis had replicated his previous error by detaching an inadequate force to hunt down Morgan. Clinton additionally believed that in the aftermath of King's Mountain, Cornwallis had done irreparable harm to the task of recruiting Tories by abandoning North Carolina after exhorting the Loyalists to take up arms. Finally, Clinton thought it folly for Cornwallis to have pursued Greene through a barren countryside. When Clinton finally learned the truth—that the chase culminated in the British army having suffered crippling losses at Guilford Courthouse—he was certain that the rigors of having attempted to track down Greene had made the outcome of that battle inevitable. (Clinton would have agreed with Horace Walpole's perceptive quip: "Lord Cornwallis has conquered his troops out of shoes and provisions, and himself out of troops.") Given what he saw as the train of Cornwallis's blunders, Clinton feared that the Loyalists—all along the supposed linchpin in Britain's southern strategy—may now have concluded that the British side in this war was "too contemptible . . . to join."[46]

Clinton did not share his pejorative thoughts with Cornwallis. But the series of misfortunes in North Carolina had solidified his thinking that the southern strategy's success hinged on his multifarious plan that included the presence of Phillips's army in Virginia, establishment and maintenance of Chesapeake bases, and the renewal and continuation of Cornwallis's war against the insurgency in South Carolina. Indeed, Cornwallis's misadventures over the past six months had led Clinton to contemplate the addition of yet another dimension to his overall scheme. His interest had been aroused in what he called "the peninsula" on the east side of the Chesapeake, the region that today is thought of as western Delaware and the Eastern Shore of Virginia and Maryland. Clinton knew that the route from Philadelphia through Delaware to the top of Chesapeake Bay, and from there into Virginia, was the key artery in the flow of rebel supplies to South Carolina and Georgia. He was confident that a significant British force could easily pacify and occupy the peninsula. It was, he said, "a large tract of very fertile land abounding with secure borders on both its shores." The region was "most plentifully provided with every supply an army could want, and had a free access from both the Chesapeake and the sea." A British army ensconced there would be safe, as would be the families of Loyalists who shouldered arms for Britain. From a base, or bases, in this region, the British could not only cripple the rebels' supply lines but launch destructive raids against important enemy targets.[47]

DURING THE MONTH after Guilford Courthouse, both Cornwallis and Greene "reflected very seriously" (as the British general put it) on what to do next, and each vacillated as he pondered his choices.[48] Immediately after the battle, Greene concluded that "Cornwallis will not give up this Country [North Carolina] without being soundly beaten," and he spoke of fighting him repeatedly "in hopes by little and little to reduce him in time." Twelve days after the engagement, Greene still anticipated campaigning in North Carolina, as the "reduction of this State is a capital object with the enemy." He also indicated that he would first retire to Virginia to regroup, and he asked Lafayette to join forces with him for the coming battles in North Carolina. At the same moment, Greene wrote Jefferson asking for more militiamen and warning him, "My misfortune will in some measure become yours"; for if the American army was destroyed in North Carolina, Cornwallis's next stop would be in Virginia. But shortly after Greene became aware that Cornwallis was marching for Wilmington, he reached a crucial decision. Greene concluded that as it would be impossible to strike an entrenched British army that was bolstered by naval prowess, he would "carry the War immediately into South Carolina. The enemy will be obliged to follow us or give up their posts in that state." If Cornwallis pursued him, it would "draw the war out" of North Carolina. If Cornwallis stayed in North Carolina, the British would "lose more" in South Carolina than Cornwallis "can gain" in North Carolina.[49] Greene's choice was potentially one of the riskiest undertaken by any commander in this war. If Cornwallis came after him, Greene would face a numerically superior enemy that might prevent him from getting near his supply lines.

Two days before his army reached Wilmington, Cornwallis said that if the enemy army dropped down into South Carolina—an unlikely step, he thought, though he acknowledged that "this war has taught me to think nothing [was] impossible"—he would "run all hazards" in pursuing Greene's force. Two weeks later Cornwallis still thought it improbable that Greene would "risque his army far down the country," and he continued to insist that should his adversary be so imprudent, he would come after him. But at some point during his stay in Wilmington, Cornwallis began to waffle about the wisdom of keeping his army in the Carolinas. He had no stomach for another round in the field in North Carolina, if Greene in fact remained within that province. Given the size of the province, its countless rivers and creeks, and the enemy's exemplary capability of hampering the supply of British armies on the move in the backcountry, Cornwallis had concluded that it was folly to presume that he could destroy his adversary in North Carolina. What if Greene did go to South Carolina? Cornwallis foresaw two outcomes. One was for him to take up a defensive position somewhere, most likely at Camden, and await Greene's attack. For an offensive-minded general like Cornwallis, such a prospect was unpalatable. The second and most likely scenario was that he would yet again be compelled to chase Greene all about the countryside. Cornwallis wanted no more of that. "I am quite tired of marching about the country in quest of adventures," he declared. He as much as said that he would be no more successful in running down his adversary in South Carolina than he had been in the chase across North Carolina. Besides, there was a danger that his army would be pinioned without subsistence "among the great rivers" in South Carolina, a turn of events that could lead to his defeat or, more likely, his army being rendered "useless."[50] Cornwallis appeared to be searching for a rationale for not doing what he knew Clinton wanted him to do.

Cornwallis's thinking was undergirded by the conclusions he had reached since late in the previous summer about how the war could be won. But more than that shaped the contours of his thoughts. In the aftermath of his Pyrrhic victory at Guilford Courthouse, Cornwallis longed to restore a reputation sullied through the ineffable harm his army had suffered in North Carolina during the past six months, damage for which he bore an inescapable responsibility.[51] It drove him to foolhardy thoughts, including contemplating what military officers are not to do. He began to consider disobeying Clinton's long-standing orders that his sole objective was to crush the insurrection in South Carolina.[52] Cornwallis—who like nearly everyone else thought 1781 was likely to be the final year of the war—had convinced himself that there were only two ways of gaining victory. One was for his army and Clinton's in New York to combine in Virginia. The second was to concentrate virtually all Britain's troops in New York. Either way, he believed, would bring on the war's grand showdown, an epic face-off against the Allies.

Cornwallis, in Wilmington, was still mulling over these thoughts on April 9 when he learned that weeks earlier General Phillips had been sent to Virginia to link up with Arnold's force. That news reshaped his thinking. He appears to have immediately begun to consider marching his army to Virginia, where he would take command of the British forces in the Old Dominion. His thinking along these lines may also have been shaped by the advice of General Leslie, who had concluded in the course of his fall raiding in the Old Dominion that the Virginians "seem tired of the war." But resupplying his army in Wilmington would take another two weeks or more to complete, so Cornwallis did not make an immediate decision. He agonized over his choices. He was certain that a campaign in Virginia offered better hopes for a pivotal British victory than the continuation of desultory actions in South Carolina. But from the beginning his orders had been to remain in the Carolinas until their pacification was complete, and Clinton had steadfastly emphasized that the pivot of his strategy was the conquest of South Carolina and Georgia. While wrestling with his options, Cornwallis learned that Greene was marching toward South Carolina. He was also informed that Greene's pending arrival had aroused a "spirit of revolt" among those who were sympathetic toward the American Revolution. In his candid moments, Cornwallis acknowledged that if he abandoned South Carolina, the British forces that remained in that province would be inadequate for coping with both the rebel army and the partisans. The British troops were "so scattered" in South Carolina, he said, that there was "the greatest danger of [their] being beat in detail." That is, that one British base after another—each garrisoned by a small and vulnerable force—would be lost. He foresaw that if Greene were unopposed by his army, the "worst of consequences" would befall "most of the troops [posted] out of Charleston." But when Cornwallis wrote to Lord Germain, he said nothing along these lines. In fact, he deceitfully told the American secretary that Britain could "maintain what she already possesses" in South Carolina and at the same time "push the war" into Virginia. To others, Cornwallis confessed that the choice he had to make "sits heavy on my mind."[53]

By the beginning of the last week in April, after having "reflected very seriously on the subject" for days, Cornwallis had more or less reached a decision to spurn South Carolina and take command of the British forces in Virginia. He held out hope that his move would induce Greene to withdraw from South Carolina, and he disclosed that the situation "in which I leave South Carolina adds to my anxiety." Cornwallis summoned troop transports from Charleston. Should he change his mind while en route to Virginia, he could take his army back to Wilmington and have it transported to some convenient landing spot on the South Carolina coast.[54]

Cornwallis heard nothing from Clinton while grappling with his decision. As Clinton for the longest time had no idea of Cornwallis's whereabouts, the last missive the earl had received from his commander was written three months prior to the Battle of Guilford Courthouse. While in Wilmington, Cornwallis had written Clinton on April 10, his first words to his commander since January. Given that he could reasonably anticipate receiving a reply within thirty days, and with luck possibly even before the end of April, Cornwallis might have waited in Wilmington until Clinton's response arrived. As it turned out, Clinton penned his riposte on April 30 and it reached Wilmington in the middle of May, two weeks after Cornwallis's departure. One can only wonder if Cornwallis's mind would have been changed by Clinton's insistence that he would not consider a major offensive in Virginia until South Carolina's pacification was complete. Clinton's thinking with regard to Cornwallis's task had remained unchanged since the fall of Charleston nearly a year earlier.[55]

On April 26, Cornwallis's army of 1,435 men stepped off for Virginia.[56] If and when he linked up with Phillips, somewhere in excess of 6,500 British troops would be deployed in Virginia. Cornwallis had not waited to receive the orders from Clinton that he knew would soon arrive. It was as if he departed rapidly so that he would not see those orders.

Days into the march, Cornwallis remained haunted by doubts concerning his choice. On his eighth day out, he wrote a young officer that he was "mov[ing] slowly" in the event that he decided to return to Wilmington. The following day, he was more resolute. "I will return," he declared, when the transports arrived from Charleston.[57]

CORNWALLIS MAY OR may not have been correct in thinking that his presence in the Carolinas in 1781 would contribute nothing toward winning the war during that pivotal year. Clinton, on the other hand, had concluded that "the rebellion in America was at its last gasp," a judgment that drew on many sources, especially intelligence reports stressing that "the French would not ... assist the Americans beyond '81, and ... that America without such assistance could not resist." The conclusion that Clinton reached with regard to America's staying power hardly differed from the message that Washington, in January, had instructed Colonel Laurens to convey to the French. Clinton's convictions had led him to conceive a strategy for this year of crisis that aimed at seeing both Great Britain through the severe challenge it likely faced in New York and the recovery of two or more southern colonies. Whereas Cornwallis appeared willing to gamble everything on one grand clash—which might or might not occur—Clinton's plan was the more realistic and farsighted. If his strategy succeeded and if, as he (and a great many others) imagined, an armistice followed by peace negotiations took place in 1782, Great Britain would be in an excellent position to lay claim to South Carolina and Georgia, and possibly North Carolina as well.[58]

Whether Clinton's fresh approach could have turned around the war in the South can never be known. What is known is that Cornwallis never returned to Wilmington, and his fateful decision to take his army to Virginia drove a stake through the heart of Clinton's painstaking strategic planning.

CHAPTER 11

CHOICES AND FAR-REACHING DECISIONS

CORNWALLIS FOLLOWED A familiar route on his northward trek, staying close to the Cape Fear and Haw Rivers before angling toward Hillsborough and crossing the Neuse and Tar Rivers as he approached Virginia. His destination was Petersburg, where he expected to rendezvous with General Phillips, whom he outranked, and take command of Britain's army in Virginia. Cornwallis had set out anticipating an "exceedingly hazardous" march filled with numerous "unforeseen difficulties," but the slog was easier than he had imagined. Greene did not come north and attempt to block his way and neither partisan bands nor militia assailed him. The soldiers welcomed the unremarkable nature of their journey, much of it made under a kindly spring sun, though there were times when they were pelted by rain or reminded by a razor-sharp wind that southern spring weather could also be cold. The army's food supply ran low after a few days. Food was always available, but provisions grew more meager, and thereafter the men were dependent on Tarleton's cavalry, which ranged ahead and foraged. Cornwallis told Tarleton that he "put the greatest confidence" in him, adding, "I trust to your discretion my honour and future happiness." But to be sure that the trooper did not stir up a hornet's nest of troubles, Cornwallis cautioned Tarleton to be "upon your guard against . . . your own prejudices." Otherwise, the two greatest problems that Cornwallis experienced came when sickness broke out among his men and day after day passed without word from Phillips. The latter was especially worrisome, for Cornwallis would not venture into Virginia until he knew the status of Phillips's army.[1]

Phillips, a veteran soldier who had mostly served in Europe, had come to America as part of Burgoyne's ill-fated expedition. Captured at Saratoga, he had been detained in Charlottesville, where he spent many happy hours at Monticello dining and conversing with his host, Thomas Jefferson. Phillips had been exchanged in 1780 and might have secured appointment as the governor of Canada, but he beseeched Clinton, whom he regarded as a dear friend, for a field command. Immediately upon learning that Washington was sending the Marquis de Lafayette with an army to Virginia, Clinton responded by putting Phillips in command of the expanding British army in the Old Dominion. Phillips arrived about ten days after the Battle of Guilford Courthouse, sailing up the Chesapeake in a formidable armada of thirty-two vessels, including heavy warships. By late March he had linked up with Benedict Arnold's force in Portsmouth and taken command of the British army in Virginia.

Phillips's orders included the now customary "desultory expeditions," and he wasted no time conducting his initial raid. Six days after landing, Phillips dispatched a dozen vessels up and down the Potomac River to sow destruction and fear. For the most part, the raiders were unopposed, though militia units from Fairfax and Prince William Counties took the field and saved Alexandria and several estates from what likely would have been considerable destruction. A captured raider at Alexandria acknowledged that his vessel had been destined for Washington's Mount Vernon and George Mason's Gunston Hall, both of which were to have been torched. Stratford Hall, far down the Potomac and the ancestral home of Colonel Henry Lee, was saved by militiamen led by Lee's father, the county lieutenant. Other sites were not so fortunate. During a span of two weeks the raiders seized small crafts, plundered tobacco warehouses, liberated slaves, and set ablaze houses in both Virginia and Maryland. They eventually reached Mount Vernon. HMS *Savage*, whose crew had recently burned nearby homes in Maryland, docked there under a pleasant morning sun, but spared the mansion when Lund Washington, the general's distant cousin and caretaker of the estate, provided the would-be pillagers with food and drink and an array of sheep and swine. The skipper of the *Savage* offered freedom to interested enslaved people. Seventeen departed with him. It was Lafayette who broke the news of the incident to Washington, advising the commander that Lund's behavior had tarnished the general's reputation. Washington was aghast and immediately upbraided his cousin for bribing the "parcel of plundering scoundrels." He added that he would have preferred to learn that his house and grounds had been destroyed.[2]

Spreading destruction and fear was but one of Phillips's objectives in dispatching the squadron to the Potomac. He had learned that Lafayette's army had approached the Chesapeake in early March, but had come no farther south than Annapolis. Phillips, who was planning raids along the James River, believed his control of the Potomac, albeit temporary, would keep Lafayette at a safe distance. In fact, Lafayette, somewhat like Cornwallis in quitting the Carolinas, had unilaterally decided to abandon Virginia and return his army to the northern theater so that he could participate in the anticipated looming battle for New York. Outnumbered and prey for the Royal Navy, Lafayette concluded that he could do nothing in Virginia. "I Have Entirely Lost Every Hope of An Immediate Operation Against Portsmouth. How much the Disappointment is felt By me," he explained to Governor Jefferson. His army had already begun its trek northward when word arrived from Washington ordering Lafayette not to come north but to "turn the detachment to the southward" and "join [Greene's] southern Army" should it march to Virginia. Washington also promised to reinforce Lafayette's army with eight hundred men under Anthony Wayne. Lafayette had reached Trenton when the commander's orders arrived. He turned around his army. His new destination was Richmond.[3]

Clinton's orders to Phillips had also stressed that he was to establish a suitable base from which his army could operate to destroy enemy magazines and impede the flow of supplies to the Carolinas. Clinton had implied that time was critical, as once Phillips achieved his objectives, his army would be recalled to New York to help with its defense against the Allies' likely summer assault on the city. Phillips moved rapidly. Only three weeks after disembarking, and immediately following the Potomac raids, his army was in motion. On April 18, Phillips—with Arnold at his side—shipped out of Hampton Roads with two thousand men, among them British regulars, Hessians, and provincial units, including the American Legion. By the next morning, the British force spiked cannon in Williamsburg and destroyed a shipyard, naval stores, and vessels along the nearby Chickahominy River. Aside from a small garrison of Virginia artillerists at Yorktown, the rebel militia escaped.[4]

Jefferson had acted promptly on this occasion, ordering militiamen from several counties and hundreds of troops already in the field to march to the defense of Richmond and Petersburg. During the ten days after April 22, the enemy force undertook what Jefferson called a "Circle of Depredation." The royal squadron had sailed up the James, past the verdant countryside with its picturesque trees sporting brightly colored spring petals. The little fleet stopped first at Petersburg, the site of a major depot in the rebels' supply chain. General Steuben commanded the militiamen who defended this town. Although outnumbered two to one and fully aware of the "advantage disciplined troops have over others," Steuben fought. Jefferson's counsel had been that "General actions" involving the militia were to be risked only when the Americans possessed "great advantages"—as Greene had enjoyed at Guilford Courthouse—but Steuben was of a mind to put up a fight, lest the enemy's ravaging be ramped up to even greater levels. The outcome of the Battle of Petersburg was never in doubt, though Steuben's militiamen stayed the course throughout a two-hour-long pitched battle, as had the Virginians under Greene six weeks before. At one point, according to Jefferson, the British "broke twice" and ran "like Sheep till supported by fresh Troops." Jefferson exalted in the militia's performance. Though "Ill armed and untried," the citizen soldiers had "disputed the Ground very handsomely," until Steuben, faced with certain defeat, withdrew to a safe site ten miles away. Although the battle had lasted as long as that at Guilford Courthouse, casualties were small in comparison. Approximately one thousand men had been killed or wounded in the showdown in North Carolina, but about one-tenth that number—roughly equally divided between the two armies—were victims in Petersburg. Once the rebels were gone, Phillips's men destroyed every riverboat they found and some private property, and, according to Jefferson, they "burnt all the Tobacco in the Warehouses." Thereafter, the British ranged into the neighboring countryside, where twenty vessels were seized or demolished and barracks and hundreds of barrels of flour and additional supplies in Chesterfield County were burned. But in the wake of Arnold's raid, the governor had ordered the removal of the supplies stockpiled in Petersburg, so Phillips was disappointed in the amount of destruction wrought by his troops.[5]

Thereafter, Phillips's force set off for Richmond, hoping to lay waste to the capital. However, on reaching Manchester, just across the river, Phillips discovered that the town was well defended. Not only were nearly one thousand militiamen waiting, but Lafayette had "pressed forward by very great and rapid Marches" and arrived the day before with nine hundred Continentals. Seeing that the rebels "were able to meet them on an equal footing," as Jefferson put it, Phillips "thought [it] proper to retire," but not before torching the warehouses and every hogshead of tobacco in luckless Manchester. The capital escaped a second round of devastation, though Jefferson reported that the total cost of Phillips's foray had been "very considerable."[6]

By the time Phillips withdrew down the James, Jefferson knew that Lord Cornwallis was on his way to Virginia. He knew, too, that unless abundant assistance was forthcoming, Virginia likely faced disaster, as it could never gather a sufficient force to contest the "combined Armies" of Phillips and Cornwallis.[7] Cornwallis was a new concern for Jefferson, but Virginia's inability to defend itself against Britain's large, mobile forces had haunted the governor since he took office nearly two years earlier. During 1780, Jefferson had appealed to Washington to furnish more troops to the southern army. In the spring of 1781, at almost the same moment that Cornwallis urged Clinton to bring his army to Virginia, Jefferson exhorted Washington to come and take command of all American forces in the Old Dominion. "[L]end us your personal aid. . . . [Y]our appearance . . . would restore full confidence of salvation," he pleaded. When Washington would not move, Jefferson privately questioned the commander's acumen as a strategist. He carped at Washington's obsession with regaining New York, which he equated with Spain's fixation on retaking Gibraltar, and he concluded that the American commander would be no more successful in his quest than a string of Spanish monarchs had been in their pursuit. Jefferson dared not say anything of the sort to Washington, but he wrote Congress that the northern states—which had received abundant help from Virginia in the first several years of hostilities—had turned a blind eye toward their neighbors in the South. "The Northern States are safe: their independence has been established," said Jefferson as early as September 1780, whereas the South now was the "great scene of action." The South, and the American cause, faced a perilous future unless Congress changed course and acted to provide greater help for the beleaguered region, he added. Jefferson even beseeched the assistance of France's minister to the United States. If the American regulars in Virginia were reinforced and adequately supplied by Congress, and if the French navy blockaded the Chesapeake so that Britain's army in Virginia could not escape, wrote Jefferson in April 1781, the enemy would be "whittled down" by militiamen acting in concert with Lafayette's Continentals. Do these things, said Jefferson, and the course of the war would be "totally changed" within "a single Campaign."[8]

Jefferson was hardly alone in searching for the means of turning around this desperate war. Within ten days of Guilford Courthouse, while both Greene's and Cornwallis's armies were yet in North Carolina, General Steuben concocted a plan that won favor with George Weedon, commander of Virginia's militia, and Richard Henry Lee, the Speaker of the state's assembly. As Virginia had some four thousand militia under arms, Steuben's notion was that one half of those soldiers join with Lafayette's force to bottle up Phillips's army in Portsmouth and prevent it from coming to the rescue of Cornwallis's battered force in the wake of its bloody showdown with Greene's army. The remaining half of Virginia's mobilized militia would "by forced marches" hurry to join with Greene's army, which would assail Cornwallis somewhere in North Carolina. When reinforced, Greene would enjoy an awesome numerical majority and he would be up against Cornwallis's badly pummeled and exhausted army. Lafayette was cool to the scheme, thinking that the British could not be contained in Portsmouth. Instead, he proposed that all four thousand Virginia militiamen be sent with dispatch to link up with Greene for an assault on Cornwallis's army. Before learning of Lafayette's response, Weedon formally presented the original plan to Jefferson and his council, telling them that although Virginia would be "much exposed" for a brief period, the "most decisive Strokes" are often those that are "the least suspected." Lee told Jefferson that the proposition "may save Virginia." But Jefferson and his advisors viewed both Steuben's and Lafayette's plans as gambits with only a slight chance of success and they rejected both schemes. Like Lafayette, they doubted that Phillips's regulars, who were augmented by a powerful naval arm, could be pinioned in Portsmouth. Phillips might join Cornwallis and take up a virtually unassailable defensive position. More likely, Phillips's powerful army might break out of Portsmouth and—with most of Virginia's militiamen in North Carolina—sow widespread destruction within the Old Dominion. Steuben and Weedon were bitter, certain that Jefferson had "not an Idea beyond Local Security" and was unwilling to run risks. Greene was angry as well, though he knew it would be imprudent to assail a governor whose future support he might need. But Jefferson almost certainly had made the proper decision. As it turned out, Virginia's militiamen would have had only ten days, and probably less time than that, to assail Cornwallis's retreating army before it reached the safety of Wilmington. One can never know how the plans conceived by Steuben or Lafayette would have played out, but what looked enticing on paper may have netted nothing but untold destruction within Virginia.[9]

Whatever General Washington thought of Jefferson's decision, he did not revile the governor. Jefferson was not the problem, he said in essence. The culprit was a constitutional system that denied Congress adequate powers for "the purposes of War." Until the national government was vested with the proper authority for waging the national war, "we are doing no more than wasting our time," he insisted. Under the current decentralized arrangement, Washington added, it was well-nigh impossible to project or execute "with certainty . . . any plan whatsoever."

His gloomy outlook notwithstanding, Washington was busy mulling over his choices for the coming campaign season. New York, as Jefferson suspected, was uppermost on his mind, though Washington acknowledged that a grand push to retake Manhattan and the city was out of the question unless France sent a fleet that would give the Allies naval superiority. In fact, when General Rochambeau in March proposed marching his army to the periphery of Manhattan and joining ranks with the Continentals, Washington asked him to defer that option. However, to stay Clinton's hand from sending additional troops to Virginia, he proposed that Rochambeau "circulate a report that you are soon to" rendezvous with the Continental army. Washington might dream of a campaign to retake New York, but he could not ignore the safety of the Hudson Highlands or the southern theater, where danger always lurked. He knew, too, that to focus solely on any one of the three would only put the others at hazard. This was the moment that Washington described as "an awful crisis." But sooner or later, the commander also said, the Allies would have to make one of two choices for the coming summer: Either they would opt for a joint operation against New York, or "large detachments" of Continentals would have to be sent "to the Southward" while the French saw to the defense of the Hudson.[10]

In the meantime, as Rochambeau awaited word of reinforcements and additional supplies, the northern theater remained quiet. Days passed, and then weeks. April came to an end. Washington was cheered by the news of Guilford Courthouse and delighted to learn that Cornwallis had withdrawn to Wilmington, a retreat that "discredit[ed]" him by proving that he "is so far baffled" with regard to his next move. Otherwise, Washington's letters were redolent with despair. He had "not at present an Idea of being able" to undertake a campaign to regain New York. For that matter, with no money and so few men, he wondered if he would be capable of doing anything this year when something absolutely had to be done. Everything depended on France, he said, as "we are at the end of our tether." It is "now or never [that] our deliverance must come." If only France would send "a superior Fleet" and "put us in a conditn to be active by advancing us money, the ruin of the enemys schemes would then be certain," he said. Should France do as he hoped, Washington believed that Clinton would be compelled to give "up all the advantages" he has "gained in the Southern States, or be vulnerable every where." By "every where," Washington appears to have meant that Clinton would not have adequate forces for the defense of New York so long as thousands of redcoats were scattered throughout the South.[11]

May was half gone, and Washington's despondency had deepened. But out of the blue a note from Rochambeau arrived. The French general wanted to confer about a campaign plan for the rapidly approaching summer. Beyond that, Rochambeau said only that his son, Vicomte de Rochambeau, had returned from a mission to Versailles. Three months before Congress dispatched John Laurens to France to plead for money, young Rochambeau had been sent home with a shopping list of items needed by France's armed forces in America. For security reasons, the elder Rochambeau divulged nothing about his son's mission or his own thoughts with regard to military plans. Washington eagerly accepted his ally's invitation and it was agreed that within the week the two would meet in Wethersfield, Connecticut, a small village half a dozen miles below Hartford.[12]

Washington made the one-hundred-mile ride from New Windsor, New York, in sunny and mild spring weather, but it turned dark and cold just as he reached Wethersfield. Bad weather or not, the two commanders saw to the customary ceremonial formalities, which included a parade. A formal dinner followed. Late in the day, once the rituals were out of the way, the generals and their staffs opened what was to be a two-day conference at the handsome three-and-one-half-story home of Joseph Webb, who lived next door to Silas Deane, the envoy Congress had sent to Paris in 1776 in search of whatever he could obtain to help America's war effort. Seated in the home's richly paneled parlor, Rochambeau opened the meeting by discussing his son's journey to Versailles. There was good news and bad news. The welcome tidings included word that France was giving (not loaning) the United States 3.5 million livres, the equivalent of roughly £250,000. Rochambeau's son had brought a bit under half that amount with him, and the remainder was due to arrive in Boston in June. No less gratifying was word that a fleet consisting of twenty ships of the line and 3,200 marines and infantrymen had sailed from France on April 5 for the Caribbean. It was under the command of François Joseph Paul, Comte de Grasse. As both England and France typically withdrew most of their navies from the West Indies in late summer with the approach of the hurricane season, all that Rochambeau chose to share with Washington was that the fleet—which would probably be augmented by an additional ten or so French warships already in the Caribbean—might come to North America in August or September. Rochambeau did not have to mention that if the fleet arrived intact, and if Britain could not come close to meeting it ship for ship, de Grasse's task force—augmented by the eight French vessels in Newport—would have attained the long-cherished naval superiority in American waters. The bad news that Rochambeau shared with Washington was that his request for several thousand additional troops had been denied. France was sending over only six hundred men.

Rochambeau then asked for Washington's thinking with regard to the coming campaign. He was probably not surprised to learn that Washington remained an advocate of a joint operation to retake New York. This was not what Rochambeau wanted to hear, and the discussions that followed were at times tense and heated. According to one observer, the French commander, vexed by his counterpart's intransigence, responded gruffly, even rudely. Rochambeau argued that Britain's hold on New York posed no immediate problem, but its southern operations constituted an urgent and serious crisis. Virginia was imperiled by the presence of a large and growing British army. If the Old Dominion fell, all the Southern states would almost certainly have to drop out of the war. Even if Virginia remained afloat, it was not inconceivable that by year's end the rebellions in the Carolinas and Georgia might wither and die. Washington responded that a campaign for New York would compel Clinton to recall his troops in Virginia, which would solve that state's dilemma.

Rochambeau likely marshaled the same arguments against attempting to overwhelm the British in New York that he had put forth at the meeting in Hartford eight months earlier. The British had occupied New York for five years, during which they would have not only stockpiled provisions in preparation for a lengthy siege but constructed what well could be impregnable defenses. (In fact, even as the Allied generals were meeting, Clinton had "a large number of hands" drawn from both his army and civilian laborers toiling to make what he called "such additions to the works as the engineers judged necessary for the defence of the place.") As the city almost surely could not be taken by storm, said Rochambeau, the Allies would have to conduct a siege operation. But that posed serious problems. An army twice the size that Clinton possessed would be needed for success. Washington's intelligence led him to believe that Clinton possessed no more than eight thousand troops in New York. (He actually commanded more than thirteen thousand.)[13] Guided by the faulty intelligence, and unaware that Cornwallis was en route to Virginia even as they spoke, the Allies reckoned that should Clinton recall all British troops in Virginia—which he was expected to do—the British army in New York would total roughly thirteen thousand. (In actuality, it would have totaled some eighteen thousand men.) Washington acknowledged that he would not possess more than 8,250 Continentals. Hence, the combined force of Allied regulars would just about equal the number of troops that Washington and Rochambeau believed to be under Clinton's command. Washington stressed that there would be "no want of Militia," suggesting his confidence that a sufficient number of militiamen could be mustered to provide the Allied armies with the magical two-to-one majority. Whether or not Rochambeau expressed skepticism on that score is not known, but he surely pointed out that militiamen typically served for about three months and a siege operation was bound to require a great many more months than that.

Although Washington and Rochambeau knew nothing of Cornwallis's decision to march to Virginia, they were aware that Phillips commanded a force of some five thousand troops in the Old Dominion. While Rochambeau thought going after the British in Virginia was the more tempting target, he acknowledged readily apparent problems with that option. Not only might the Allied troops have to cope with the South's harsh summer climate, but conveying the supplies needed by the Franco-American armies would be a colossal undertaking. In addition, Virginia might be so picked over by the armies already in the field that foraging would be next to impossible. Still, given that something had to be done in 1781, Rochambeau was willing to run the risks presented by a southern campaign, though not before late summer. In the end, as both men had probably suspected all along, the issue came down to whether to focus on New York or Virginia. Washington was inflexible. He insisted on a campaign to retake New York, prompting Rochambeau to later remark that Washington "did not conceive the affairs of the south to be such urgency."

On the second day at Wethersfield, the Allies reached an agreement. Rochambeau was under orders from home to comply with Washington's wishes. In reality, as historian Robert Middlekauff has observed, permitting Washington to make the key decisions was a "polite fiction," for the American commander was not about to act unless his ally was at his side. Nevertheless, Rochambeau reluctantly consented to a campaign to retake New York. He also agreed to march his army to New York in the near future and link up with the American army. Washington made one concession. He agreed that should de Grasse's fleet arrive in time to be part of a grand campaign, joint operations were to be conducted "as circumstances should dictate."

The following day, after a third dinner with Rochambeau, Washington rode back to his headquarters in New Windsor. He was no more than gone from Wethersfield before Rochambeau sent de Grasse a record of the conference and informed him that America, and particularly its southern states, faced "a very grave crisis." De Grasse's task force, he went on, could "render the greater service" by sailing for the Chesapeake. However,

Rochambeau added that following the destruction of the enemy's base at Portsmouth, de Grasse should sail for New York. He went on to say that Washington preferred that the squadron not stop in the Chesapeake but sail directly for New York. In all likelihood, Rochambeau guessed that de Grasse's orders were to sail to New York, but he couched his letter in a manner that he hoped would cause the fleet to steer for the Chesapeake, where he believed the admiral might discover the presence of a large British army within the Old Dominion. If Rochambeau's intentions were opaque, those of Minister La Luzerne—who wrote de Grasse three weeks later, by which time he was aware that a British army of some seven thousand men under Cornwallis was in the Old Dominion—were inescapable. La Luzerne emphasized that Virginia faced a "crisis which is so alarming . . . that it appears to me there is no time to lose and for their existence it is necessary to do all you can."[14]

Rochambeau, who had to keep his American ally happy, must have been perplexed by Washington's unbending preference for campaigning to retake New York. Yet there were sound reasons for the American commander's commitment to striking British-held New York. Fearing that time was running out for his war-weary countrymen and their French ally, Washington believed that seeking to regain New York offered the best hope for ending the war hurriedly. Clinton's army had nowhere to go, so a strike against New York ensured the great showdown. There were no assurances that a turn southward would result in a climactic clash against the enemy. The Royal Navy might scoop up and remove the British troops in Virginia prior to the arrival of the Allied armies, or the king's army in the Old Dominion—alerted to the looming crisis during the weeks required for the French and American armies to move from New York to the Chesapeake—might retreat to who knew where in the Carolinas. Furthermore, a campaign to retake New York would be a much less difficult logistical undertaking than that posed by the southern option. To transport the equipment and provisions needed by the Allied armies over a distance of hundreds of miles would be daunting. Washington was additionally aware that his northern soldiers feared the South's miasmic climate, viewing it as a deathtrap. With good reason, Washington was not convinced that his men would march to the Chesapeake. (Rochambeau would later say that "the heat" in Virginia was similar to that of the Barbary Coast—today's Morocco, Algeria, Tunisia, and Libya—and that it took a deadly toll; "at sixty," he said, a Virginia "man is quite decrepid.")[15]

While the war raged that spring and America's beleaguered leaders searched for a means to break the stalemate, Colonel Laurens, the emissary Congress had dispatched to France in search of a loan, was deep into his mission. Laurens, accompanied by his friend Thomas Paine, who paid his own way when Congress refused to pick up his tab, had hurried to Boston and shipped out in mid-February on the *Alliance*, departing at about the same moment that Greene's army won the race to the Dan. The two voyagers were fortunate to reach France. Five days out of Boston the ship was beset by a frightful tempest. Gale-force winds not only repeatedly tossed the *Alliance* toward floating bodies of ice but also ripped asunder the portside quarter gallery only a minute after Laurens exited it. For seven suspenseful hours the passengers and crew expected that at any moment they might meet a horrid end, but as suddenly as the storm had blown up, it subsided. Thereafter, the shaken sailors enjoyed a safe and rapid journey, making landfall in L'Orient after twenty-three days at sea.

While Paine went sightseeing through the French countryside, where he was hailed as a celebrity in village after village, Laurens sped first to Paris, then to Versailles. He quickly discovered that Franklin, stung by Congress's slight, had sprung into action and obtained a gift from the French. Though happy, Laurens had been sent to negotiate, so he set off in search of still more from America's ally. His efforts paid off. Taken together, he and Franklin came up with £500,000, some in the form of a loan and some as a handout, and some of which had to be spent in France.[16] Versailles's benef-icence was due to its eagerness for peace. The threat of a wider war in Europe was growing, and France's economic situation was inauspicious. Wishing to wrap up the war in America quickly, Louis XVI's advisors decided they had two options: Send Rochambeau massive reinforcements, or assume the cost of maintaining the American army. Dispatching additional troops to

Rochambeau would solve nothing, as England would surely respond by committing an equal number of reinforcements to its army in America. On the other hand, providing America with the cash needed to keep the Continental army afloat throughout 1781 might facilitate actions that could result in an Allied victory during this pivotal year.

Laurens spent his final weeks abroad in Paris shopping with the money he had received. He purchased clothing and ammunition for the army, as well as sixteen thousand muskets. Early in June, Laurens and Paine boarded *La Résolute* for the voyage home. With the campaign season in the northern states already at hand, they prayed for a rapid Atlantic crossing. They were disappointed. Their crossing consumed eighty-six distressing days. But Laurens was carrying only a bit more than one-third of the money the French had promised. The remainder of the cash (tons of coins packed into barrels) arrived in Newport and Boston in two separate shipments while Laurens and Paine were still in Paris or making their agonizingly slow crossing. In addition, a bevy of French artillery pieces and six hundred troops came ashore in Rhode Island that summer.[17]

AS THE SUMMER campaign season edged ever closer, Sir Henry Clinton felt overwhelmed with "toil and anxiety." Though confident that he had acted "to the utmost extent" with the resources at his disposal, Clinton sensed that others, and especially the leaders among New York's Loyalists with whom he frequently met, were unhappy with his leadership. Indeed, many were restive with what they saw as his cautious defensive posture. Some believed he should have done more to exploit Washington's recruiting crisis and the January mutinies in the Continental army; some had longed for him to act with greater "Severity" in New Jersey, a tactic that might have compelled Washington to take the field, bringing on a climactic clash of arms. One of the most exasperated of Manhattan's Tories exclaimed in his diary, "Sir Henry does nothing." If Clinton was unaware of what these men were saying behind his back, he was conscious of their warm feelings for Cornwallis, whom they had come to see as an active, forceful, combative general.[18]

Clinton was far more troubled by Lord Germain's unconcealed criticism of his leadership, expressed in a series of communiqués. The American secretary exhorted Clinton to be more active, even seeking to stir him to action by spicing his letters with laudatory remarks about Cornwallis's "rapid and decisive" manner and "vigorous exertions." Germain never missed an opportunity to tell Clinton that he possessed a sufficient number of troops, even quite accurately pointing out that there were now more Americans "in the King's service . . . than the whole of the enlisted troops" in the Continental army. But Germain did even more. Where for years he had spoken of subduing the rebellion in Georgia and the Carolinas, beginning in November 1780 the American secretary spoke of pacifying Virginia as well. "I do not think I am too sanguine in my expectations," he told Clinton. In comments that would weigh heavily on Clinton, Germain also made clear that both he and the king earnestly favored "pushing our conquests" in Virginia. The rebels everywhere faced such monumental problems, Germain preached, that a "speedy suppression of the rebellion" throughout the South was within reach. Retaking all four southern colonies, Germain emphasized to Clinton, "is to be considered as the chief and principal object for the employment of all the forces under your command."[19] These remarks were so similar to Cornwallis's recent communiqué from Wilmington that Clinton assumed the Loyalists, and Cornwallis as well, had influenced Germain's thinking. For Clinton, who was in America and understood the situation, and who was struggling to put together a meaningful strategy for either securing a substantive victory or avoiding a consequential defeat, the intrusion on his independence was insufferable.

When a war is stalemated or going badly, some are certain to become disenchanted with the army's leadership. Washington experienced it in 1776 and 1777 before Congress effectively shut down the complaining. There was no one to shield Clinton. While he was occasionally praised in British publications, Clinton was not infrequently maligned in London newspapers for his army's "*usual* dormant state" in New York. Furthermore, as Clinton knew, the English press pulsated with adulation for Cornwallis. Even after Cowpens and Guilford Courthouse—probably as a result of the Earl's misleading accounts of those engagements—Cornwallis was widely lauded for how he "fights away and beats his Enemies." Extolling his aggressiveness, one journal told readers that Cornwallis marched his army 120 miles in four days whereas General Howe had required sixteen days to advance 18 miles during his pursuit of Washington in the New York campaign. Some screeds openly wondered why such a daring and pugnacious officer was not the commander of Britain's army in America.[20]

Clinton was additionally aware of disaffection within his officer corps, and believed he was "hated" and "detested" by many.[21] Whether or not Clinton was actually loathed, not a few officers were devotees of Cornwallis, who in 1776—and more recently in North Carolina—had been the epitome of combativeness. Moreover, some officers disparaged what they saw as Clinton's overweening tenderness toward the rebels. Clinton was a humane individual. He was a pragmatist as well, and since long before becoming commander of Britain's army he had concluded that the best hope of quashing the colonial rebellion was through acting in a manner that would "gain the hearts & subdue the minds of America." That end, he believed, could best be realized by avoiding ruthlessness. Clinton was also following orders. Since early in the war officials in London bent on winning back the loyalty of the colonists had discouraged barbarism. However, some officers on the front lines in the southern theater, where brutality was a hallmark among partisan bands, saw the necessity to respond in kind. The most hardened British officers had come to think that the only hope of bringing this war to a successful conclusion was through resorting to pitiless terrorism. One spoke of "encouraging all kinds of pillage, plunder, & barbarity." Another contended that "we should . . . give free liberty to the soldiers to ravage at will," for only the harshest actions would make America's "infatuated wretches" understand "what a calamity War is." Similarly, General O'Hara, in 1781, advocated "a War of desolation," of strike after strike in civilian areas that resulted in "Ruin and Devastation" to private property. Terror alone, he thought, could break the Americans' will to continue. Forget what the fallout would be regarding American opinion in the aftermath of the war, he said, for England has already lost the affection of most colonists for years to come.[22]

Clinton never went as far as O'Hara would have liked, though he had long since overcome his reservations about conducting raids against civilian centers so long as the raiders conformed to acceptable eighteenth-century norms of waging war. Thus, his orders always emphasized that his soldiers were to destroy only targets that were essential to the enemy's war-making capability. On the other hand, Clinton did not shrink from inciting the Indians "to take up arms," and in 1781 he sought to have them strike "the back settlements of Pennsylvania and Virginia." As their attacks would fall on civilians, Clinton—in hopes of tying down the state militias that might otherwise aid rebel armies—was fully aware that the Native Americans would practice unbridled terrorism.[23]

Clinton was deeply rankled by his image as a do-nothing commander. His prompt responses had been pivotal in frustrating Count d'Estaing's designs on both New York and Rhode Island in 1778. Despite having been allotted a fraction of the troops that Howe had commanded, Clinton had succeeded in winning back Savannah and Charleston. Furthermore, while threatened in New York by a more experienced rebel army than Howe had ever faced—an army that now was backed by French prowess—Clinton had committed 5,800 troops to the southern theater during the six months after October 1780. Though he could not publicly reveal his military planning, Clinton had conceived a realistic strategy for pacifying the Carolinas and Georgia.

But in May, Clinton was informed by General Phillips that Cornwallis had quit the Lower South and was marching to the Old Dominion, news the earl did not pass along for another thirty days. If Clinton was kept in the dark on that score, neither Cornwallis nor the principal officers he had left behind in South Carolina provided him with an accurate picture of what was unfolding in the wake of the earl's withdrawal. Although Lieutenant Colonel Nisbet Balfour, the new commandant in South Carolina, informed Cornwallis—and Germain—that the colony was now "threatned" with a "general revolt . . . on every quarter" that would "annihilate every remaining vestige of loyalty" unless "speedy assistance is . . . sent," the earl advised Clinton that he had been relieved to learn of the salutary state of affairs in the wake of his departure.[24]

Blind to the reality of affairs in South Carolina, Clinton initially focused on Cornwallis's breach of trust in bringing his army to Virginia. The commander in chief said that he was disappointed, astonished, and "exceedingly hurt." Later, Clinton candidly admitted that his fury knew no bounds, for Cornwallis's action had taken a wrecking ball to his careful strategic planning for 1781, the capstone of which was to have been Greene's defeat by Cornwallis or, if that was not possible, the earl's presence in South Carolina was to have flushed the rebel army out of the lower South. Thereafter, Cornwallis was to have had the means with which to deal effectively with the partisans. Furthermore, sometime during the summer Clinton had expected to summon the bulk of Phillips's army to New York in preparation for the Allied blow, leaving only a skeleton force in Virginia to maintain, with the Navy's assistance, Britain's defensive post in the Old Dominion.

Now an even larger British army was going to be in Virginia, and to what end Clinton did not know. What is more, before May ended, Clinton learned that Greene had not followed Cornwallis to Virginia but had taken his army southward into South Carolina where—given the diminished opposition he would encounter—the commander in chief expected the rebel army to threaten all that the British had achieved in the past year. Washington had responded with unbridled rage at what he thought was General Lee's insubordination at Monmouth. Clinton's first reaction on learning that Cornwallis had not complied with his orders was to threaten to resign, though he had not taken that step. Clinton also considered sailing to the Old Dominion to confront his subordinate, but for reasons that are not clear he abandoned that thought. In fact, he responded to Cornwallis's treachery with amazing mildness, his hand doubtless stayed by the knowledge that Germain would support Cornwallis's move. Clinton told a confidant in London: "My wonder at this move of Lord Cornwallis will never cease. But he has made it, and we shall no more but make the best of it."[25]

Clinton's shock at Cornwallis's disobedience occurred as he was modifying his original plans in light of Phillips's reports from Virginia. Once Phillips was on the ground and inspected the region about Hampton Roads, all along the prospective site for Britain's initial Chesapeake base, he concluded the area would be "*a bad post . . . not calculated for defense.*" Phillips, whose judgment Clinton explicitly trusted, proposed instead that the establishment of a base be put on the back burner until a more suitable location could be found. In the meantime, he wished to take his army into Maryland, hoping to bring Lafayette to battle should he resist the incursion. But should "the Marquis retire upon the approach of a corps of troops against him, Maryland would be defenseless." In that eventuality, Phillips recommended strikes at Annapolis and Baltimore, and even nearby Philadelphia, after which his army would "take posts" in what he saw as the relatively safe "lower counties of Delaware" and Virginia's eastern shore. However, Phillips thought he would need upwards of an additional two thousand men and more heavy artillery to carry out his plan, neither of which Clinton felt that he could spare. Nevertheless, the commander was enticed, and in time Clinton's thinking morphed into the possibility of a surprise raid on Philadelphia.

Clinton knew from experience that many Pennsylvania Loyalists had stepped forward to take up arms during General Howe's brief occupation of Philadelphia. Furthermore, as Maryland had not "been tried as yet," Clinton was avid for testing whether its Tory population would rally to arms for their king. He was also intrigued by the prospect of establishing bases on Virginia's eastern shore from which the British soldiery could time and again interdict the flow of supplies from Philadelphia to the Old Dominion. Aware, too, that Philadelphia was a major storage site "on which the enemy depended for supplies," Clinton saw merit in striking the city's "depots before they could be put into motion against me" during the expected attack on New York. There were still other intriguing reasons for striking

Philadelphia. A successful raid would "disperse the Congress, ruin [American] public credit, and totally overset their schemes and preparations for the [looming] campaign." Clinton additionally presumed that the raid might be harmful to an American bank just now under formation, an institution, he feared, that might "give fresh vigor to their cause" once it became operational.

Clinton was confident that a raid could accomplish these objectives. Indeed, the view at headquarters was that a raid that sowed considerable destruction "may be easily effected." Many of his officers had been posted there during Britain's nearly yearlong occupation of the city and were familiar with Philadelphia and its environs. British intelligence not only considered the city's defensive works insubstantial but reported that Philadelphia was not well defended. Intercepted Continental army correspondence led Clinton to conclude that Washington was so weak he "can only act on the defensive." Even if that turned out to be incorrect, Washington's army was a ten-day march away. Militia would have to defend the city, and they would be overmatched in a lightning raid conducted by a sizable British naval and land force. Clinton thought a brief operation conducted by a force of five thousand to six thousand men could destroy ships, supply depots, arsenals, and even Philadelphia's docks. A shuddering bombardment laid down by the Royal Navy would cause widespread damage to the city, as had occurred when Charleston was shelled. Not only might a successful raid deal a lethal blow to the rebels down south; it would further undermine American morale, which he believed was "at its last gasp." Though notoriously reluctant to relinquish his manpower, Clinton was so excited about this scheme that he was willing to provide three thousand troops to the venture, knowing that doing so would temporarily reduce him to a "Starved defensive" in New York. As the plan took shape, Clinton envisioned the navy conveying the troops from New York to Chester, eighteen miles downriver from Philadelphia. Meanwhile, roughly half the troops in Virginia were to go after Lafayette, destroying him or taking him out of the picture, while three thousand troops under Cornwallis in the Old Dominion would join forces with the British division in Chester. (This may

have been what Clinton had in mind when he remarked that he would
"make the best of" Cornwallis's abandonment of the Carolinas.) The
combined British force would advance on Philadelphia, where it would have
a few days to complete its destructive work before withdrawing. If the results
were as spectacular as hoped, the raid might be followed in time by an
incursion against Annapolis or Baltimore.[26]

Had the plan been acted on, it might have changed the course of the
war. Widespread destruction of rebel supply depots and the fear of similar
assaults elsewhere might have compelled changes in Allied plans for the
coming campaign. At the very least, a successful assault on Philadelphia
would have had a substantive impact on the potency of the campaign the
Allies eventually undertook later in 1781. In addition, the disruption of
the rebels' supply system might have forced Greene to profoundly alter his
strategy, possibly even flushing him out of South Carolina. One can only
guess at the damage to the American cause that would have resulted from
widespread carnage in Philadelphia and the necessity of yet another
congressional flight for safety. But Clinton's planning crashed in June
when he learned that Cornwallis opposed such a venture. Cornwallis,
having read the April and May correspondence between Clinton and
Phillips with regard to striking Philadelphia, weighed in on the issue in a
letter on May 26. Cornwallis declared that the proposed operation "would
do more harm than good to the cause of Britain." In subsequent letters, he
advised that Philadelphia's defenses were stronger than Clinton imagined.
He also warned that so much time would elapse between the sighting of
the royal armada and the arrival of the British troops in Philadelphia that
the rebels could "secure specie and the greatest part of their valuable
public stores" within the city. The only means of inflicting a crushing blow
would be to burn the entire city, and that would require so much "time
and labour" that it could never be carried out, he insisted. Thereafter,
Cornwallis returned to the twin themes he had broached while in
Wilmington: Virginia was the best site for waging offensive war, and only
the conquest of the Old Dominion could lead to the subjugation of the
Carolinas.[27]

There is no way of knowing whether Cornwallis's objections to assailing Philadelphia had merit. With twenty-twenty hindsight, it seems clear that Britain's interest would have been better served had Clinton launched the attack. Clinton thought that was true at the time, and he told Germain of his "mortification" that Cornwallis's objections had scuttled the plan, leaving him with no choice but to "confine [himself] to a very strict defensive" posture throughout the summer.[28] Clinton might have ordered Cornwallis to send the troops. But he knew all too well that Cornwallis was Germain's favorite. He was already bucking the American secretary by resisting Cornwallis's call for a campaign to conquer Virginia. Should he carry out a major operation against Philadelphia without Cornwallis's full support, and should the attack fail as the earl predicted, Clinton knew that he would be recalled in disgrace. Clinton's plan was aborted, dying alongside the promising strategy he had crafted for pacifying the Carolinas.

BEGINNING ON MAY 6, a few days before Washington and Rochambeau met in Wethersfield, and a dozen or more days before Clinton knew that his subordinate had marched northward from North Carolina, Lord Cornwallis, near the Tar River in northern North Carolina, wrote General Phillips three times in five days: "Let me hear from you." "Spare no pains to let me hear from you." "I wish to join you. . . . Let me hear from you by every possible means."[29] Word finally arrived from Benedict Arnold. Phillips was in Petersburg and waiting for Cornwallis. Moreover, Clinton was sending reinforcements from New York that should arrive soon. Cornwallis wasted no time. Within twenty-four hours his army was in motion again. On May 15, he crossed into Virginia without encountering the least resistance. ("No more than 150 men Could Be Raised on this Side of the Roonoke" to resist the invasion, Lafayette anguished.) However, as if an augury of things to come, two days after resuming his trek, Cornwallis heard again from Arnold and the news was not good. Phillips, so robust and durable, was dead. What he had thought was only a "teasing indisposition" had been the first signs of what likely was typhoid fever, and he had succumbed.[30]

Five days after entering Virginia, Cornwallis arrived in Petersburg and took command of the British army. When the three regiments sent by Clinton disembarked at Portsmouth a few days later, the British presence swelled to about 7,200. Cornwallis was aware of the size of his army, but as yet he was unaware that Clinton had rejected his proposal to concentrate the British army either in New York or Virginia. Nor did Cornwallis—who had not yet seen the letters that Clinton had sent to Wilmington—know that he had been ordered to remain in the Carolinas until, as Clinton wrote, he judged that "affairs there are in such a train as no longer to require your presence." Clinton's communiqués arrived in South Carolina around the time that Cornwallis reached Petersburg.[31]

Since February, Cornwallis had written only four letters to Clinton, all in April while his army recuperated in Wilmington. But on his first day in Petersburg, Cornwallis penned a long letter to his commander, and he dashed off three additional communiqués within the week. Cornwallis opened by saying that on reaching Virginia he had learned that a French fleet was crossing the Atlantic, information that had been so widely broadcast within the province that even prisoners taken by the British had heard that de Grasse was en route, though no one knew his destination. Cornwallis said he would undertake no major offensives until he learned more about the potential naval threat, but he would abide by Clinton's orders to Phillips, which he saw following his arrival in Petersburg, Cornwallis defined his immediate mission as one of destroying rebel magazines and supply depots, dislodging Lafayette from Richmond, and, if possible, destroying the marquis's army. Once those missions were completed, Cornwallis added, he would take the army to Yorktown on the York River, which Phillips had thought safer and healthier than Portsmouth. From reading Phillips's correspondence with Clinton, Cornwallis also gleaned that the commander in chief had deferred to the judgment of his late friend and accepted his counsel that Yorktown was the most "proper" site for a "station." (A separate and earlier army report indicated that Yorktown not only "stands high, is healthy, and contains houses sufficient for the accommodation of . . . an Army," but that the topography would facilitate its easy fortification.) Cornwallis advised Clinton that Arnold had requested a return to New York and that he was complying with his wishes. Cornwallis concluded by once again pitching the notion that the best hope of suppressing the rebellion in the South lay in taking the necessary steps to "reduce [Virginia] and keep possession" of it. To accomplish such an undertaking, he said, he would need a much larger army, for to attempt it with "a small force . . . would probably terminate unfavourably." In effect, Cornwallis was once again beseeching Clinton to abandon New York and bring his army to Virginia.[32]

Cornwallis's abandonment of South Carolina and tramp to Virginia had introduced a Mad Hatter aspect to Britain's conduct of the war. South Carolina and Georgia were probably gone, though Cornwallis unscrupulously wrote Clinton that he had every reason to expect "that we shall meet with no serious misfortune" in that sector. Moreover, Cornwallis was in Virginia, but for the time being he intended to do nothing more than Phillips had been capable of achieving with a considerably smaller army.[33] Meanwhile, Clinton, with every plan that he conceived since the previous autumn reduced to rubble, appeared clueless as to his next move. He simply waited to learn whether Cornwallis accomplished anything of significance, including the destruction of Lafayette's army.

On that score, if on nothing else, Cornwallis and Clinton were on the same page. Seeking out Lafayette was the first substantive item on Cornwallis's agenda. He remained in Petersburg only briefly before he crossed the James River at Westover plantation, the sprawling estate of the influential Byrd family. Arnold had used it as a base of operations during his January raid on Richmond, as it was occupied by Mary Willing Byrd, a cousin of his wife, Peggy Shippen Arnold. Like Arnold, Cornwallis planned to set off for the capital from that site, but he had little interest in making yet another raid on the town. His sights were set on Lafayette, and a confident Cornwallis famously boasted: "The boy cannot escape me." For his part, Lafayette crowed that if adequately reinforced, he would make his adversary "pay a toll" for having come to Virginia. At the moment, however, Lafayette was outnumbered by four to one or more, and by as much as "ten to one in mounted troops." He appealed to Jefferson for more militiamen and simultaneously called on Steuben and Peter Muhlenberg, two Continental army generals, and George Weedon, who commanded militia in the field, to link their troops to his. His situation was deplorable, Lafayette told Washington. "We have no Boats, few Militia and less arms." Lafayette had no intention of making a stand until the reinforcements arrived. "[I]f we are caught, we shall all be routed," he said. He wished he could run risks, but perhaps with the lecture that Rochambeau had given him a few months earlier still ringing in his ears, Lafayette acknowledged that he was "Guarding Against My Own Warmth." He was resigned to being "Extremely Cautious in My Movements," he added, for should he attempt "to fight a Battle I'll be Cut to pieces, the Militia dispersed, and the Arms lost."[34]

Once the British marched from Westover, Lafayette pulled out of Richmond and into the backcountry above the capital. Cornwallis, unwilling to engage in yet another futile chase after a fleeing rebel army, did not pursue him. Instead, the British army veered in a more northerly direction. Lafayette correctly presumed that the enemy's target was Hunter's Iron Works in Fredericksburg, an installation that the marquis variously characterized as the "Great Resource of the Southern Department" and "the only support of our operations in the Southward." Cornwallis must have hoped that Lafayette would defend the industrial site, but his adversary marched parallel to the British army, careful to remain about twenty miles to the west. Nevertheless, Lafayette sent out detachments to slow Cornwallis's advance, buying time in the hope that Wayne's Continentals and sufficient numbers of militia would trickle in before the British reached the foundry on the Rappahannock River. If Wayne arrived, Lafayette told Governor Jefferson, his "inferiority will not Be quite So alarming" and he might meet Cornwallis on a battlefield. But neither Wayne nor many militiamen joined him, leaving Lafayette with no choice but to stay on the move. All the while, Cornwallis plodded on toward Fredericksburg, keeping a close eye on the enemy force on his flank and remaining vigilant for any blunder by Lafayette. He planned to pounce should Lafayette err.

Lafayette made no mistakes, and by early June Cornwallis knew not only that he could not bring his adversary to battle but also that "every part of Hunters Works that could be taken out" had been removed by the rebels. The site was no longer "of so much importance," he said. His thoughts turned elsewhere. Cornwallis had learned that the Virginia legislature had opted to hold its annual spring session in remote Charlottesville, a safer site than indefensible Richmond and, fortuitously, the residence of the state's chief executive, whose house, Monticello, sat atop a tall hill overlooking the village. It was too alluring to ignore. Virginia's huge supply depot at Point of Fork, fifty miles west of Richmond where the Rivanna River meets the Fluvanna to form the James, was no less enticing. In fact, that target was all the more tempting once Cornwallis learned that a force under Steuben had been sent to protect it. Cornwallis sent Tarleton with 180 dragoons and 70 mounted infantry to Charlottesville to capture the governor and as many assemblymen as possible. Simultaneously, he dispatched Lieutenant Colonel John Simcoe with three hundred men from the Queen's American Rangers, and a small complement of regulars, to destroy the stores at Point of Fork and Steuben's force. Intelligence reported that Steuben commanded about three hundred militiamen. In reality, he had about three times that number, and most were Continentals.[35]

Two days elapsed before Lafayette, who for all practical purposes was without a cavalry arm to gather intelligence, was aware that Cornwallis had turned his gaze toward different targets. The lapse enabled Tarleton to proceed unopposed toward Charlottesville. Jefferson, whose two-year ordeal as Virginia's governor ended on Saturday, June 2, devoted a portion of the following day to his correspondence and the remainder to enjoying his first day of freedom from public responsibility. He went to bed that night a contented man. Neither he nor any assemblyman in the town below was aware that early that morning the green-clad troops in Tarleton's British Legion had begun their ride for Charlottesville. They covered seventy miles in twenty-four hours, pausing now and then to rest and water the horses. As the force neared the rustic little village, its pace slowed. Tarleton ran upon twelve wagons loaded with arms and clothing for the rebels in the

Carolinas. It was a target he could not let pass, and his men destroyed both the conveyances and their contents. A bit later the Legion stopped at a nearby plantation, where the owner and his guests were captured. The prisoners included two Virginia assemblymen and a South Carolina congressman. As the troopers approached Charlottesville, they encountered roughly one hundred militiamen posted just outside town. The dragoons were not delayed for long. The militiamen were not exactly eager to fight.

Unbeknownst to Tarleton, somewhere around 11:00 P.M., as his force thundered through the hamlet of Louisa, they were spotted by Jack Jouett, a Charlottesville native who was slaking his thirst at the Cuckoo Tavern. As Jouett's father owned the Swan Tavern in Charlottesville, where several legislators had rooms, he knew immediately what the enemy was up to. Jouett climbed his mount and sped away to sound the alert. Like Paul Revere in Boston, Jouett had a speedy charger, and he was aware of shortcuts. Never pausing, Jouett won the race by about ninety minutes. He galloped up the hill to Monticello first and at about 4:30 A.M. pounded on Jefferson's door. Next, he rode to town and spread the alarm. In the gray light of early day, most of the assemblymen packed their belongings, jumped on their horses, and rode for safety. Jefferson, meanwhile, correctly guessed that Tarleton's first stop would be in town, giving him ample time before making a getaway. After posting slaves as lookouts on the steep road leading to the crest of the hill, Jefferson got busy. He hid some precious possessions. He also gathered all the important papers he could lay his hands on, stuffing some in saddlebags and burning the remainder. At some point, he got his wife and two young daughters into a carriage and sent them off to a friend's plantation a few miles away.

As the morning wore on, a detachment of twenty British dragoons under Captain Kenneth McLeod descended on Monticello. Jefferson was gone. Stories subsequently circulated that he rode down the other side of his hill and into the dank, dark forest as the king's soldiers approached his residence, but no one knows precisely how much time elapsed between his escape and the moment when the troopers barged through Monticello's front door. The soldiers remained for eighteen hours, apparently spending

much of their time enjoying good meals and consuming—and pilfering—the owner's wine, but doing no damage to the house. Jefferson later
said, "Tarleton . . . behaved very genteelly with me," which may not have
been the case had the British trooper understood the Virginian's role in
drafting the Declaration of Independence. Meanwhile, Tarleton was not
having much luck in capturing assemblymen. He nabbed only seven
laggards, including Daniel Boone. Tarleton destroyed one thousand arms
and upwards of five hundred barrels of powder in the local armory, but he
left the town intact.[36]

On the same day that Tarleton reached Charlottesville, Lieutenant
Colonel Simcoe, a dashing officer cut from the same cloth as Ferguson and
Tarleton, was en route to Point of Fork, twenty-five miles below
Charlottesville. Simcoe hailed from a privileged background and had
enjoyed a formal education that culminated at Oxford. He had entered the
British army ten years before and soldiered with valor in several engagements in the Revolutionary War before being given command of the Queen's
American Rangers, one of the oldest provincial units, tracing its inception
to 1776. His exemplary service in the Carolinas led Cornwallis to turn to
him for the Point of Fork assignment. While Tarleton's force had ridden
swiftly toward its target, Simcoe's men approached their objective mostly on
foot, covering some fifty miles in two days through what their commander
characterized as "incessant marches" that wore out the shoes of many of the
men, leaving them "absolutely barefooted."

Steuben, who was unaware of the enemy's approach until only hours
before their arrival, possessed some 850 men. Roughly two-thirds of his
men were Continentals, but they were new recruits and just as callow as the
militiamen that composed the remainder of Steuben's army. Their
commander faced a crucial test, for Point of Fork was a vital supply depot.
Virginia's commissioner of the Board of War had exhorted Steuben to do all
within his power to safeguard the facility. "If these stores are lost," the
commissioner had warned, "the whole wealth of the state in its present
situation can never replace them, and the only dependences for General
Greene's army will be almost totally cut off. . . . [T]he loss of these stores will

prove the loss of this country." During the past couple of weeks, since learning of Cornwallis's arrival in the state, Steuben had put his men to work moving the stores to the southern side of the Fluvanna, a wide and deep river that would challenge the enemy's capability to reach and destroy the stockpile of goods. But if it would be difficult for Simcoe to reach the supplies, it was just as difficult for the Virginians to transfer the cache of precious commodities. Not all had been moved to safety by the time Simcoe arrived.

Alerted at last that Simcoe was near, Steuben was also told that the Queen's Rangers numbered one thousand men, more than three times its actual size. Steuben did not know that the numbers were in his favor, and Simcoe did what he could to deceive his adversary into thinking that the British force was numerically superior. He scattered his men along a hillside overlooking Steuben's post and directed them to light campfires to give "the appearance of a numerous corps." Steuben fell for the ruse and withdrew that night. (Cornwallis later said he had "retired with great precipitation.") Stretching credulity, Steuben subsequently claimed that he had not run from a fight but that he was complying with orders issued long ago by Greene to march his force into North Carolina. When no one believed him, he candidly stated that it would have been "absurd to be making a Bravado with a small number of bad Troops against such a force" as Simcoe's. Left to roam at will, the British destroyed 2,500 stand of arms, a "large quantity" of powder, more than sixty barrels of materials used in the making of ammunition, additional barrels of rum and brandy, ten mortars, howitzers, cannon, and a vast array of carpenters' implements and entrenching tools. After departing Point of Fork, Simcoe also burned 150 barrels of gunpowder and a considerable amount of tobacco in warehouses on the James. Steuben, already widely disliked in Virginia, was condemned in many circles for not having resisted Simcoe. Lafayette, in private, was among those who denigrated him. He unfairly charged that Steuben had permitted "our Stores" to be "Destroied By about 30 or 40 men," dubiously adding that had he held off Simcoe for merely twenty-four hours all the stores could have been saved. In confidence, Lafayette remarked, "I am not sorry he [Steuben] is leaving" for North Carolina and urged an investigation into Steuben's conduct. If Steuben had fought, the marquis added, it could be said that "Lord Cornwallis's journey to Virginia Has not produced Him the Smallest Advantage." (Later that month, the Virginia legislature asked Lafayette to conduct an inquiry into Steuben's behavior, but the marquis never ordered a formal investigation.)[37]

Within a couple of days of the raids at Charlottesville and Point of Fork, the assorted divisions of Cornwallis's army rendezvoused at Elk Hill, a plantation owned by Jefferson on the James River. Some five thousand British soldiers remained there for several days while the commander sought to learn if more could be done in the field. His chief discovery was that Virginia had transferred its primary supply route to the Carolinas farther to the west in the Blue Ridge Mountains, which Cornwallis deemed too far away to contemplate going after, at least at this juncture. Instead, he opted to march down the James to Williamsburg, which would bring him to the cusp of Yorktown, the site that Phillips and Clinton had contemplated as a defensive site for the army and useful base for vessels that plied the Chesapeake. When Cornwallis departed Jefferson's property on June 13, he left the plantation—in its owner's words—"an absolute waste." Fields were destroyed and barns and fences burned; the best horses were taken and the remainder killed by having their throats slit. Thirty enslaved people were liberated.[38]

Cornwallis paused for a week in Richmond before resuming the march to Williamsburg, a trek undertaken in June "heat . . . so unbearable that many men" were "lost [to] sunstroke." The British had left the capital intact, but otherwise plundered up and down the James, rounding up herds of cattle, burning thousands of hogsheads of tobacco, and seizing an array of mortars and artillery weapons ("all French," Cornwallis noted wryly). As the British marched downriver, Lafayette shadowed their every step. The American force was growing stronger by the day. Assorted militia units appeared, as did Steuben, who had decided against going to the Carolinas. Furthermore, forty-eight hours following Cornwallis's departure from the capital, General Wayne's long-anticipated Pennsylvania Continentals finally arrived. (One of Wayne's men, a Pennsylvanian on his first trip to the South, was goggle-eyed at the sight of spectators lining the roads, including enslaved people "all naked, nothing to hide their nakedness" and, he noted with horror, standing next to white women.) After a brief respite, Lafayette had Wayne's men back in the field, hopeful that they might intercept Tarleton or Simcoe, both of whom were out and about foraging and gathering intelligence. Lafayette, meanwhile, toyed with an attack on Cornwallis's rear, but he abandoned the notion, and the bulk of the British army reached Williamsburg safely on June 25. However, Simcoe was still in the field and vulnerable. He was attacked at Spencer's Ordinary by a detachment from Wayne's force. A sharp, seesaw firefight ensued, forcing Simcoe to call on Cornwallis for help. In the end, Simcoe's men beat off the attackers before the reinforcements arrived, and by day's end the entire British army was in Williamsburg.[39]

Cornwallis's men relaxed while the army was replenished, but they found the heat so unrelenting that their break from marching was hardly restful. "Everything that one has on his body is soaked as with water from the constant perspiration. The nights are especially terrible, when there is so little air that one can scarcely breathe," one soldier complained.[40] Meanwhile, Cornwallis found two letters from Clinton, the first he had received from the commander in chief since entering Virginia. In one of the missives, Clinton made clear that he wanted some of Cornwallis's men for the defense of New York. Since March, Clinton had planned to recall half or more of the army in Virginia. Now was the time to begin the withdrawal. As Greene was in South Carolina and there was no indication that Washington planned to send reinforcements to Lafayette, whose force consisted mostly of "spiritless . . . militia," Clinton saw no justification for such a large army in Virginia. Wishing to immediately reduce the army in Virginia to some four thousand men, Clinton asked Cornwallis for "a proportion of artillery as can be spared," as well as a couple of regiments, four battalions, and two companies of dragoons, altogether roughly three thousand men.[41]

A Hessian officer declared that this necessitated a "swift change" in Cornwallis's plans, as the "army must go on the defensive." In fact, Clinton's communiqué led to an even more profound change in Cornwallis's thinking.

Irked at the prospect of remaining on the defensive in Virginia, he requested permission to return to South Carolina that portion of his army that had quit the province two months earlier. Suddenly confessing his "most painfull anxiety for the situation of South Carolina," and asserting that he could not "render any service in a defensive situation here," Cornwallis astonishingly proclaimed, "I am willing to repair to Charlestown if you approve of it." With that, Cornwallis rapidly prepared to march to Portsmouth, where there were transports for the conveyance of his men. He also felt that his entire army had to make the tramp. He feared leaving some men in Williamsburg or Yorktown with Lafayette's army poised a short distance away. Also conscious of what he referred to as "the clouds of militia which sometimes pour down on us," he hesitated to risk dispatching only those men bound for New York on what might be a dangerous march to Portsmouth.[42]

All the while, Lafayette's army had been camped at New Kent Courthouse near the Pamunkey River, about twenty miles from Williamsburg, waiting for Cornwallis to "explain himself," as the marquis put it. While dogging the enemy on its descent from Richmond, Lafayette had presumed that Cornwallis's entire army had been summoned to New York. But as the British had received a new supply of clothing while in Williamsburg, and as the distribution of "New Cloathes . . . Seldom precedes an Embarkation," Lafayette began to suspect that Clinton planned to abandon Manhattan and sail for Virginia, a step which would bring Washington and Rochambeau southward as well. However, when Cornwallis's army quit Williamsburg on July 4, Lafayette was thoroughly perplexed. "This devil Cornwallis is much wiser than the other generals with whom I have dealt. He inspires me with a sincere fear, and his name has greatly troubled my sleep," Lafayette acknowledged.[43]

All that Lafayette knew was the enemy was making preparations for crossing the James, about four miles below Williamsburg. That almost certainly meant that they were marching to Portsmouth, but the marquis did not know what would follow. Did Cornwallis plan to remain at that base? Was his army about to embark for New York? Was this the first step on Cornwallis's return to the Carolinas? While Lafayette pondered the possibilities, his immediate problem was how to deal with the enemy as it prepared to cross the James.

He ached for a fight with Cornwallis—and one last chance to gain glory—but he confessed to the new governor of Virginia, Thomas Nelson, that he was "terrified at the Consequences of A general defeat." Should his force be destroyed, it could jeopardize the Allies' chances in what he now suspected was the war's soon-to-be decisive engagement in Virginia. What is more, Lafayette thought the war at present bore "a tolerable face" for the Allies. Not only had the British failed to crush the rebellion in the South, but Cornwallis's march to Virginia would likely be interpreted by the peacemakers—should a peace conference convene in 1782—as retreats that presaged Britain's relinquishment of the three southern colonies below Virginia. In fact, by tracking Cornwallis's weary soldiers on their march to Williamsburg, Lafayette had sought to "let my movements give his the appearance of a [British] retreat" within Virginia. If "the American army is not annihilated" during the summer or fall, said Lafayette, the chances were good that a peace conference would recognize the independence of all thirteen states. That was crucial, he added, for unless all thirteen states were independent, "there is no bond that holds" together the United States. (Washington had reached a different conclusion regarding Cornwallis's baffling abandonment of the Carolinas. Thinking it was part of a grand and puzzling master plan conceived by Clinton, Washington guessed that the enemy hoped to deceive the peacemakers into thinking not only that South Carolina had been pacified but that Cornwallis's marches here and there throughout Virginia had been undertaken to make it appear that Great Britain had reestablished control in the Old Dominion as well.)[44]

Two days after Cornwallis's army marched out of Williamsburg, Lafayette sent out a detachment of five hundred men under Wayne to look for an opening that his army might exploit. While wishing to avoid a general engagement, Lafayette knew that Cornwallis's baggage and an unknown number of his troops had already crossed the river. The marquis thought it might be possible to safely strike the British rear in the course of the enemy's river transit. He brought up most of his army and in mid-afternoon on July 6 ordered Wayne to advance toward Jamestown. Wayne's men had to cross a narrow causeway over marshland before reaching Green Spring Plantation. What Lafayette did not know was that Cornwallis had laid a trap. The British commander had posted pickets in a forest just beyond the bucolic fields at the plantation, but hidden deeper in the woods were thousands of troops, including cavalry. Cornwallis hoped that when the pickets opened fire on the rebels, Wayne would think they were there to protect those last few redcoats who had not yet made the crossing. If the rebels fell for his ruse, they just might rush forward into a snare.

It was a clever plan, all the more so as the long causeway and waterlogged terrain would frustrate a rapid and orderly retreat. If Cornwallis's scheme played out as he hoped, his force could outflank and destroy Wayne, inflicting a horrific defeat on the Americans that would come close to approximating the dreadful hiding that Ferguson's army had suffered at King's Mountain. Cornwallis nearly pulled it off. Wayne set off around 3:00 P.M. and within a few minutes encountered the pickets. A two-hour firefight ensued, during which the pickets ever so slowly retreated. The unsuspecting Wayne was drawn deeper and deeper into the trap. Just as the euphoric Wayne grew certain that a splendid victory was at hand, thousands of red-clad British soldiers burst out of the thick woods. That the Americans did not sustain a catastrophic blow in the Battle of Green Spring was due to two things. Lafayette had at last divined what was happening and rushed in reinforcements to provide cover during what he foresaw as Wayne's inevitable retreat. In addition, the British trap was sprung in the half-light of sunset. Wayne fell back, retreating in the creeping darkness. The retreat went smoothly, in part due to a gutsy stand made by a Pennsylvania unit composed of only sixty men who kept portions of the advancing enemy at bay, but also as Wayne rushed two regiments into the vortex. He later said his men had performed with "such vivacity" that the British were checked and prevented from encircling the retreating rebels, a view subsequently seconded by Tarleton, who lavished praise on the Americans' gallantry. Many British officers thought Cornwallis could have more effectively exploited the opportunity at hand. But the British commander, once the most daring of generals, called it a day even before night fully cloaked the field. Lafayette characterized Green Spring as "a warm and close action," but he had escaped disaster. Even so, his little army had suffered nearly 150 casualties, about 10 percent of his manpower.[45]

In the days following the engagement, Cornwallis crossed the James and made the roughly fifty-mile march to Suffolk, where his army remained for more than a week as preparations were made in Portsmouth—some eighteen miles away—for shipping off several thousand men. Cornwallis's soldiers grumbled at their plight in and around Suffolk, as they were "tormented" by "billions of sand—and biting—flies," not to mention the unforgiving heat and now and then a crashing thunderstorm.[46] But the men did more than swat the insects that pestered them, for Cornwallis sent Tarleton to raid nearby courthouses where supplies earmarked for Greene's army were thought to be stockpiled; dispatched other units to scour the area for additional storage depots; and sent off an infantry regiment to destroy stores and vessels in the shipyard at South Quay, nineteen miles to the southwest. More than a week after Cornwallis reached Suffolk, the process of funneling his troops and weaponry to Portsmouth got underway.

It had not been completed when Cornwallis around July 18 or 19 received two communiqués from Clinton that changed everything. Clinton ordered a stoppage to the "sailing of the expedition" to New York and denied Cornwallis's request to return to South Carolina. Clinton's about-face was prompted by his receipt a few days earlier of a letter from Germain that filled him with disquiet, not to mention anger. Responding to Clinton's revelation that he intended to summon much of Phillips's army to New York during the summer, Germain in early May had written expressing his "great mortification" at Clinton's plans. Germain stated categorically that he, members of Lord North's ministry, and the king were in agreement regarding the "vast importance of the possession of Virginia." Indeed, the "unalterable object" of the monarch's expectation was that "the possession of Virginia" must be realized. He underscored that George III was troubled that Clinton appeared not to understand that the "principal object for the employment of all the forces under [his] command" was to prosecute the war "by pushing our conquests" in the South from Georgia to Virginia. Germain's letter reached New York two weeks after Clinton had written Cornwallis asking that he send some three thousand men from Virginia. Though angry, Clinton was a soldier, and he complied with the orders of his superior. He immediately directed Cornwallis to retain his entire army and "maintain . . . respectable defensive" installations at Yorktown and Gloucester, situated across from each other on the York River.

Clinton was bitter that officials three thousand miles from the colonies, and months behind in their awareness of the current military situation, were impinging on his ability to wage the war as he felt circumstances demanded. Germain's latest letter followed one written sixty days earlier in which the secretary had ludicrously asserted that the rebels were so weak—including in Virginia—that "no resistance on their part is to be apprehended that can materially obstruct the progress of the King's arms in the speedy suppression of the rebellion."[47] Clinton knew that Germain's understanding of the military situation was unrealistic. He additionally feared that by reducing the size of the British army in New York, Germain's intrusiveness would have a catastrophic impact on his ability to defend against the pending Allied attack. What Clinton could not know in July was that the demands of the king and the American secretary would have monumental consequences.

Cornwallis had inspected Yorktown and Gloucester while in Williamsburg and concluded that they were a good choice from the standpoint of providing "effectual protection to . . . battle ships." Furthermore, the army's engineers reported that Yorktown was preferable to Portsmouth, a base which both Arnold and Phillips had thought unsound. The sites might be preferable to Portsmouth, but Cornwallis thought them far from perfect. He advised Clinton that they were "dangerous" places, as an army posted there would be vulnerable if attacked by a formidable rebel force, such as the combined armies of Lafayette and Greene. Nevertheless, Cornwallis complied with his new orders, even remarking that he was "very desirous" to reach Yorktown as soon as possible. He chose to sail back to the Virginia peninsula. His return would be more rapid than by land, feeding the men would be less problematical, and he would not have to traverse the James River in the face of enemy opposition. Several days elapsed while his army dropped down to Portsmouth and the men and their heavy guns were loaded onto transports, a period during which a couple of vessels that had already departed for New York were recalled. Near the end of July, Cornwallis's army at last began its voyage to Yorktown. Some of his men disembarked at Gloucester on August 1. The largest part came ashore at Yorktown the following day.[48] Forty days had elapsed since Cornwallis's army completed the march from Richmond to Williamsburg, and as yet not a spade of earth had been turned in the construction of the defenses of Yorktown. That lost time would soon prove crucial.

Lafayette had long since quit stalking his adversary. In the aftermath of the fight at Green Spring Plantation, he had grown ever more convinced that Cornwallis was returning to the Carolinas. He withdrew to near Richmond to watch and wait. He also had to regroup, as nearly all his officers had lost their horses in the fighting at Green Spring. (He jokingly wrote his sister that his "cursed artillery horses . . . got themselves killed.") His next move, Lafayette guessed, would be to "follow his Lordship" to the Carolinas and "form a junction with Gen. Greene."[49]

DURING A THIRTY-DAY period that began late in June when he reached Williamsburg, Cornwallis received ten communiqués from Clinton. These were the first letters he had seen from his commander since before he took his army to Wilmington nearly three months earlier. The missives were dated between April 30 and July 11, but they did not reach Cornwallis in the order in which they were written. They arrived in clusters, one now, two a few days later, still more on subsequent days. Some missives had been sent to Wilmington, others to Charleston, still others to Virginia.[50] Transporting the correspondence by sea also played havoc with its orderly delivery, as the length of every voyage differed. Moreover, in one instance Clinton waited for ten days between writing and sending a missive, thinking it safer to dispatch it via a convoy that was being assembled.[51] The muddled order in which Cornwallis read Clinton's letters confronted him with something akin to putting together a jigsaw puzzle.

Clinton was consistent on three matters: He was unequivocally opposed to attempting to win control of Virginia; he expected a huge Allied land and naval force to attack New York in the coming weeks, though probably not before late summer; and he was unhappy with Cornwallis's abandonment of South Carolina. Otherwise, Clinton appeared to be disjointed. He spoke of concentrating his manpower in New York and advised Cornwallis that the fifteen hundred men he had brought to Virginia from the Carolinas had not been needed in the Old Dominion. The British soldiery already posted there, said Clinton, had been more than adequate for coping with Lafayette's 2,000 Continentals and the "small body of ill armed peasantry" that composed the state militia. But in another letter he ordered Cornwallis's army to remain in Virginia and "take a defensive station" in either Williamsburg or Yorktown. It was also in this batch of letters that Clinton first ordered that some 3,000 men be sent to New York, only to later rescind the order in a subsequent missive. Strewn amid these irreconcilable dispatches were letters that revealed Clinton's plans to strike Philadelphia, instructed Cornwallis to comply with the orders long ago issued to General Phillips, and urged Cornwallis to go after Lafayette once the deadly southern summer had passed. A confounded Cornwallis appears to have thought Clinton was addled.[52]

Clinton may have appeared to be disoriented, but that was not the case. He wrote some letters before learning that Cornwallis had gone to Virginia, others when he expected Greene to come to Virginia and join with Lafayette, and still others after he had discovered that Greene's army was in South Carolina. Clinton's outlook changed from time to time, though not because he was hopelessly confused. He was coping with the wreckage done to his carefully planned strategy by Cornwallis's march to Virginia, as well as by bewildering intelligence reports that one week pointed to an Allied assault on New York and the next hinted that the Allies intended to focus on the British army in Virginia. Clinton also received conflicting estimates of the likely size of Rochambeau's army by summer's end. Above all, his letters reflected the pressure exerted on him by Germain and the king.

Clinton was continuing to wrestle with his strategic choices. The Allied leaders, on the other hand, had recognized early on in 1781 that they faced one of two choices. A month before the Wethersfield conference, and two months prior to learning that Cornwallis had come to Virginia, Washington knew that the Allied forces would either strike at New York or march for the South. The twenty-three-year-old Lafayette saw the same thing. The "Ennemy [must] either . . . throw a Reinforcement into Newyork or to Come with all their force in this State [Virginia]. In a word, I think the Whole Seat of War, the whole force of the British, that of the French and that of General Washington will be in Virginia or that we will Have But little to do in this Part of the World." Lafayette added that as the "enemy Cannot defend [New York] and Conquer the Southern States," Clinton must choose one or the other. While still in Wilmington, Cornwallis had reached the same conclusion. "If we mean an offensive war," New York will have to be abandoned and the entire British force concentrated in Virginia. "If our plan is defensive," he went on, further campaigning in the southern provinces would have to be suspended and all British forces collected in New York.[53] For the Allies, as for Cornwallis, that was it in a nutshell.

If Washington, Lafayette, and Cornwallis could see that the British must focus all their energies on one theater or the other, why could Clinton not see this? Indeed, that had more or less been Clinton's plan until Cornwallis undercut it. Cornwallis was supposed to be in South Carolina; Phillips was to leave a force of about two thousand in a defensive post in Virginia, probably in Yorktown, and sometime during summer bring most of his men to New York, a step that would increase Clinton's army to more than sixteen thousand men. Such a move would have duplicated the consolidation of the British army in New York that Clinton had ordered two years earlier on learning that d'Estaing was making his second visit to North America. Instead, as the summer unfolded, Clinton had on his hands a large British army in Virginia and a force that he thought was disconcertingly small in New York. As he wrestled with what to do, he faced intrusive pressures and wrenching choices that his adversaries were spared. Unlike Washington and Rochambeau, who could act with a free hand, Clinton's autonomy was impeded by the interference of Germain and the king, who ultimately forced on him decisions for Virginia that he opposed. In addition, the Allied leaders were not worried about relinquishing territory. Their object would be the conquest of the British in either New York or Virginia. But if Clinton brought nearly all his army in Virginia northward in a gamble to save New York, he would surely forfeit the South, the recovery of which had been the cornerstone of British strategy for the past three years.

Clinton's quandary was how to protect British interests in both the northern and southern theaters. Like all military commanders, he faced multiple uncertainties. He did not know when the French fleet would arrive. Nor was he aware of the size or destination of the enemy naval force. He did not know if Washington would order Greene's army to Virginia to join with Lafayette or if the American commander would summon Lafayette to New York. The size of Britain's presence in Virginia hinged in part on whether Washington chose either alternative, or neither. Finally, because of conflicting intelligence reports, Clinton was in the dark concerning French plans to enhance Rochambeau's army. Underpinning all Clinton's thinking—and this was the engine that drove his decision-making—was the belief that the Royal Navy would remain supreme in North American waters.

Clinton made no major moves throughout the summer of 1781. He was convinced that the British would never lose their naval supremacy, and as a result, he would be able to move troops from Virginia to New York, or vice versa, once the Allies tipped their hand. He waited and watched. The one action he might have taken would have been to urge Cornwallis, with his army of 7,200, to immediately go after Lafayette's force of about 2,000 Continentals and whatever number of militia turned out. The destruction of yet another Continental army in the South would not have been inconsequential. Even if that had not occurred, the threat of Lafayette's destruction might have brought Greene back from South Carolina, preserving Britain's long-held gains in that sector. Or, to save an imperiled Lafayette,

Washington might have committed more of his men to Virginia, weakening the Allies on the eve of their expected attack on New York. But Clinton was convinced—obsessively so, as was Cornwallis and to a degree Rochambeau—that the weather in the summertime South was so exceedingly dangerous that Britain's army would suffer a ghastly rate of attrition should it be in the field during those torrid months. What is more, an army cannot live in the field forever. It requires a base through which it can be supplied, and that base has to be secured. Just as Rochambeau had immediately thrown up a defensive perimeter at Newport, Cornwallis was required to put men to work digging breastworks and constructing redoubts at Yorktown and Gloucester. That, in the end, was the charge that Clinton gave to Cornwallis: to fortify his base on the York River and, in the autumn, undertake operations against Lafayette and the rebel supply lines.

Virtually every commander in this war spoke of the strain and lonely responsibilities they endured. Washington and Clinton often mentioned being worn down with anxiety, Cornwallis in April had spoken of decisions that sat "heavy on my mind," and in June Lafayette lamented the "dreadful burden imposed on me."[54] Clinton, too, was emotionally drained. He spoke of the "mortifying circumstances" he faced, the worst of which appeared to be having his "well-weighed" ideas second-guessed by those in London who in turn pushed "crude and oversanguine," and "uninformed," notions.[55]

Washington, on Manhattan in 1776, had been so exhausted and overwhelmed by the cares that accompanied his high-pressure position that he fell victim to such confusion and irresolution that his army was placed in considerable jeopardy. Clinton in 1781 evinced no sign that his cognitive abilities were in disarray. He had designed a capable strategy for a two-front war, only to have it wrecked by Cornwallis's disobedience. Thereafter, he conceived a daring raid on Philadelphia, a strike that might have altered the course of the war had it been attempted. But Clinton abandoned that scheme when Cornwallis objected. Clinton's leadership had always been distinguished by caution and an unwillingness to take chances, and at this moment—which he and virtually every civil and military leader on both sides regarded as the great crisis point of the war—he was not about to act recklessly. Nor did he see any reason to do so.

Clinton had wrestled with his strategic choices throughout the past several weeks since learning of Cornwallis's march to Virginia. As July faded and Cornwallis's army boarded transports in Portsmouth for the voyage back to Yorktown and Gloucester, Clinton continued to believe that the Allies planned operations against New York and that the French fleet would ultimately sail for New York. Just as Rochambeau doubted the wisdom of an attack on British-held New York, Clinton believed that so long as the Royal Navy remained superior to any French fleet, he could withstand all the enemy could throw at him. Clinton trusted that his manpower and defenses would enable him to overcome either an attack or a siege, a judgment based in some degree on his knowledge that whereas his army would consist almost entirely of regulars, 40 percent or more of the soldiery in the Allied army would be callow militiamen. In addition, just as he had expected Washington to muster every available man for the defense of the French in Newport, Clinton anticipated summoning whatever was needed from Virginia to meet the emergency.[56] If his strategy culminated in the enemy's failure to take New York, Clinton believed not only that the Allies would be finished but that the British could thereafter recoup their losses in the South. If he was correct, the war would come to an end with the American rebels having to accept unsatisfactory peace terms. Indeed, perhaps the best the Americans could hope for would be an outcome in which the independence of only some of the thirteen former colonies was recognized.

By late July, Cornwallis had waded through the welter of Clinton's contrary orders. His exasperation was evident in his responses. "In the first you tell me" to do this or that, but in another "dispatch . . . you require" the opposite. What most riled Cornwallis, however, was Clinton's rebuff of his recommendation to attempt the subjugation of Virginia. He now knew that he had come to Virginia for no good reason. He knew, too, that he had baselessly hazarded the loss of everything in South Carolina. Furthermore, as a soldier with an appetite for action, Cornwallis instead faced the prospect of weeks of inactivity. Atop it all, Cornwallis perceived the possible danger in garrisoning his troops in a lonely defensive station near the Chesapeake. In July, he advised Clinton: "I must . . . take the liberty of calling your Excellency's serious attention to the question of the utility of a defensive post in this country which cannot have the smallest influence on the war in Carolina and which only gives us some acres of an unhealthy swamp and is for ever liable to become a prey to a foreign enemy with a temporary superiority at sea."[57]

CHAPTER 12

CORNWALLIS'S GIFT

FOR THREE DAYS after Guilford Courthouse, General Greene had expected Cornwallis's army to strike again. Instead, "of a sudden they took their departure," said Greene, a surprise move that he was slow to discover. When at last he learned that the enemy was moving toward Cross Creek on the Cape Fear River, Greene presumed that Cornwallis planned to return to action in North Carolina after resting and refurbishing his army. On March 23, more than week after what Greene always called "the Battle of Guilford," he put his army in motion to find his adversary. "Our Army is in good spirits," he said, but the militiamen were melting away, having served their time and departed for home "to kiss their wives and sweet hearts." It was also planting time for those who lived on farms. Even as his army dwindled in the aftermath of the great battle, Greene still enjoyed a numerical superiority and he hoped, at a minimum, to assail Cornwallis's rear as his adversary was on the move.[1]

However, Cornwallis's head start was too great to overcome, especially as Greene's progress was painfully slow. His men were compelled to forage in the same countryside that British army had already stripped bare. At times, food was so scarce that his men had no choice but to consume the garbage left behind by the enemy. The search for provisions was not Greene's only worry. He commanded a weary army. His regulars had been in the field almost continuously for nearly four months. Nor was it only the enlisted men who were drained. "The whole family" of officers "is almost worn out," said Greene, who was among the exhausted. For days on end after crossing from Virginia back into North Carolina during the last week in February, Greene and his soldiers had "little to eat, less to drink, and lodge[d] in the woods in the midst of smoke." All the while, he had been confronted with one critical decision after another. Though not a professional soldier, day in and day out Greene had made choices that were part and parcel of what he called "the great and little arts of war." Somehow, he said, he had "blundered through without meeting any capitol Misfortune." But the strain was taxing. On one occasion he fainted, an episode he chalked up to weariness and inescapable anxiety.[2]

Greene could not catch Cornwallis, but he looked forward to a clash once the British army moved out of Cross Creek. He beseeched Jefferson to send provisions and more militiamen, and with candor he told the governor that the military situation remained "precarious." The "least misfortune will bring the war to your doors," he warned. Greene wrote Lafayette about marching his army into North Carolina and forming "a junction of our forces." He also appealed to Congress for troops, though unlike Jefferson he was careful not to accuse the northern states of ignoring the army's Southern Department.[3]

Greene's thinking changed in a flash once he saw that Cornwallis's army was headed for Wilmington. Greene knew that it would be "impossible for us to injure them" deep down on the coast, for Cornwallis not only would rapidly construct a formidable system of defenses, but he would enjoy the protection of the Royal Navy. Furthermore, obtaining supplies in that sector would be problematical. In the final days of March, Greene made another momentous decision, one that he characterized as "critical and dangerous." He decided to take his army into South Carolina. Several factors influenced his thinking. Assuming that Cornwallis would follow him rather than joining the British forces in Virginia, Greene reflected that it was "in our interest to keep the enemy as much divided as possible." Moreover, when Cornwallis came after him, that would "draw the War out of" North Carolina, enabling

Governor Nash to send his militiamen wherever they were needed out of the state. Unaware that Clinton had sent General Phillips to Virginia, Greene also imagined that Lafayette would bring his army to South Carolina and together they would give Cornwallis "a drubbing." First, however, Greene ordered Lafayette to march to Richmond. From there, he said, "you can cooperate either with me or the Militia" in Virginia "as the movements of the Enemy may render necessary." Greene additionally knew that if Cornwallis pursued him, his adversary would not catch up to him for four weeks or more, as the refitting in Wilmington would likely take around twenty days. What is more, the distance that Cornwallis would have to cover from the coast to, say, Camden was considerably farther than the trek Greene would make from his starting point near Cross Creek. Partisan sniping might also slow Cornwallis's progress. Greene was gambling that before Cornwallis arrived, the rebel army could make considerable gains, including capturing British supply depots. Much of Greene's thinking boiled down to a simple conclusion: If he remained in North Carolina, the enemy would continue to hold all their posts in South Carolina; but should Cornwallis do the unthinkable and not pursue him, the British in the end would lose virtually everyplace they had occupied in South Carolina for the past year. Greene admitted that his undertaking would be filled with "risque and difficulty," but so long as he could obtain supplies and keep open a lane of retreat, he "fear[ed] no bad consequences."[4]

Two days before Cornwallis reached Wilmington, Greene set off toward Camden. It was early April and for the most part the days were pleasantly mild, though it was the season when the weather could in no time change from agreeable to miserable. Greene had 1,300 men in his little army. British forces in South Carolina—regulars and Loyalist militia—totaled around 8,000. Greene had some idea of the size of his adversary and was also aware that if Cornwallis returned to the province, British forces would swell by some 1,500 men. Despite the confidence Greene exuded in some of his correspondence, he knew that he badly needed additional manpower, and he called again on Jefferson and Nash, and also on General Steuben, for help. Still unaware of the presence of the large enemy army in Virginia, Greene urged Jefferson to send militia, clothing, and horses, adding that the militia-men would be more useful if they could act in concert with "a superior Cavalry." He also cautioned Jefferson that if Virginia failed to act, his "Army must inevitably fall a Sacrifice." Every step that Virginia took to hold the bulk of the enemy in South Carolina, he added, would help in "keeping War at a distance from" the Old Dominion. Greene straightaway told Governor Nash that he must rise to the occasion. North Carolina, he said, must meet its quota for Continentals and reform its militia (so they won't "disgrace them-selves" again, said Greene with merciless candor), and the assembly has "to lend me all the assistance in their power." That included furnishing horses and wagons, the want of which "distresses us exceedingly." He directed Steuben to inveigh the Virginia assembly to send at least fifteen hundred men and ordered him to find and dispatch suitable cavalry horses, even if they had to be forcibly taken from their owners. He additionally called on Steuben to send him a "very great consumption of cartridges and ammunition."[5]

Greene's entreaties fell on deaf ears in Richmond, where Jefferson was confronted with a formidable enemy force. When Virginia sent no militia-men to South Carolina and the governor additionally spurned Steuben's plan to send much of Lafayette's army to assist in a strike against Cornwallis in North Carolina, Greene simmered with an implacable anger toward Jefferson. Greene thought him incapable of putting the general welfare above that of his state. "If the Governors cannot trust their Generals it is a folly to prosecute the war," he raged. Greene wished that Congress would lean on the chief executives of all the states, none of whom in his estimation could see the bigger picture. Unable to hide his anger, Greene told Jefferson that his myopia might in the end mean that the "Great Expense of blood and treasure" in this war had been for nothing.[6]

Greene was not alone in wringing his hands. With Cornwallis out of the state, the oppressive burden of command on the British side in South Carolina fell on Colonel Nisbet Balfour, the commandant of Charleston and senior British official in the province. His responsibilities included funneling men and supplies to the backcountry, where Lieutenant Colonel Francis Rawdon not only commanded the garrison in Camden but was responsible for the several British posts scattered throughout the hinterland. Balfour, the thirty-eight-year-old scion of a Scottish laird, had fought in several engagements in this war and was among the wounded at Bunker Hill. Tall, with an athletic build and penetrating blue eyes, he looked every bit the soldier. One observer admired Balfour's "well-chiselled" features and described him as "altogether a very fine specimen of physical manhood." Rawdon was eleven years younger and better educated. The product of the Anglo-Irish aristocracy, he had studied at Oxford before entering the army at age seventeen. Three years later, he was a lieutenant leading his men up the bloody slopes at Bunker Hill. He, too, had fought in several key battles in this war, and along the way he had taken command of the Volunteers of Ireland, a Loyalist regiment raised during the occupation of Philadelphia. Like Balfour, Rawdon was tall and strapping, but behind his back some limned him the ugliest man in England. That cruel and tasteless barb was unwarranted. Portraits by Joshua Reynolds and Thomas Gainsborough captured a figure who was plain rather than handsome, but not unsightly.[7]

Balfour first learned that Greene might bring his army into South Carolina a few days after the rebel force set out from Cross Creek. Cornwallis had broken the news, though at that juncture he was still vowing to "run all hazards" in coming after his adversary. Even after Greene had reached the vicinity of Camden, Cornwallis advised Balfour that he could not "conceive it likely [that Greene] would risque his army" by entering South Carolina, though he guessed his adversary might send some light troops to assist the guerrilla bands. After another three days, Cornwallis broke the news to Balfour that he was taking his army to Virginia, a step that should "force Greene to quit South Carolina." Quite at odds with what he was telling Sir Henry Clinton, Cornwallis added that should Greene remain in the state, the British would probably lose their outposts throughout the backcountry, but that "Charleston is not in danger." Curiously, Cornwallis did not write Rawdon until ten days after first sending word to Balfour. When he tardily penned a communiqué to Rawdon, it was to notify him that Camden was in Greene's crosshairs. Even stranger, Cornwallis had to know that Greene would reach his target well before his letter reached Rawdon.[8]

Greene in fact approached Camden on April 19 following a march of two weeks. During his trek, he had appealed to Maryland's chief executive for reinforcements, admonishing him for having failed to provide the manpower that he had promised back in November. Greene had few peers when it came to reminding people of their unfulfilled commitments, and he did so in this instance by telling Governor Thomas Sim Lee, "Had it not been for the very great exertions of Virginia, the Southern States must have fallen" at Guilford Courthouse. To this he added that should the Carolinas fall to the enemy, Lee "may depend upon Virginia and Maryland falling next." He also took steps to secure large numbers of boats, just in case he was compelled once again to make a hurried retreat, and sent out orders to impound wagon horses and move all supply depots from the coast to the interior. Simultaneously, Greene made urgent requests for ammunition. His long-term plans were up in the air. He continued to say that should Cornwallis march for Virginia, he would abandon South Carolina and go north to join with Lafayette. But his immediate focus was on Camden, where he hoped for another battle. "Much blood has been spilt, and more must be spilt, before this Country can regain its liberty," he said near the end of the trek.[9]

Greene's intelligence gatherers overestimated the size of the British garrison at Camden by a third, putting it at nine hundred, and they further advised that a considerable number of British reinforcements were on the way. Some got through, including men from Ninety Six and Tory units that Rawdon said responded to his summons with "great zeal and fidelity." However, the largest force that had been sent to bolster Rawdon never made it, due in part to the resistance of Francis Marion. Greene rapidly concluded that he could not "storm the Town with a prospect of success." Sufficient supplemental troops had arrived to actually bring Rawdon's numbers up to nine hundred. In addition, during the past year the British had constructed a daunting network of defenses at Camden. A palisade surrounded the hamlet, and eight redoubts were strategically placed beyond the town wall. Greene saw that his only choice was to "take a position" and "induce the Enemy to sally" out of its stronghold. He chose a site just north of Camden that locals called a hill—Hobkirk's Hill—but which Rawdon more accurately described as a ridge. It was a heavily wooded area. On its east side—the rebels' left—lay Little Pine Tree Creek and the uninviting Big Pine Tree Creek Swamp, a snake-infested, boggy morass that Greene thought was impassable. Those features led him to believe that his adversary would not come at him from that direction.[10] Rawdon, of course, knew all along where Greene's army was camped, but for several days he resisted the temptation to abandon his secure bastion. Two pieces of intelligence ultimately persuaded him that the time was right to go to battle. He learned that in coming days Greene would be reinforced by Colonel Henry Lee's cavalry and large numbers of partisans. In addition, a rebel deserter had passed along word that Greene had sent his artillery to the rear along with his baggage train.

Rawdon was aggressive and ambitious, and he knew that if he could deal a crumpling blow to his adversary, Britain's occupation of South Carolina would be freed from a truly dangerous threat for the foreseeable future, possibly for the war's duration. He thought the odds favored his success. Though he planned to arm "every [man] that could carry a firelock," including his musicians and drummers, Rawdon would be outnumbered by about four hundred men, but nearly all his men were regulars, and a considerable portion of Greene's army consisted of militia. Rawdon also expected to go into the fight with artillery pieces, whereas Greene would have none.[11]

Greene's battle plan was neither a carbon copy of Daniel Morgan's at Cowpens nor of his own at Guilford Courthouse. He put pickets out front, especially along the southern and western approaches. He planned to put his Virginia and Maryland Continentals in forward positions—the Virginians on his right, the Marylanders on his left—and some militiamen behind them. Colonel Washington's dragoons were stationed on the far left wing, with orders to swing behind Rawdon's force (if the battle unfolded satisfactorily) and prevent its retreat to Camden. The artillery had indeed been sent to the rear, but on the day before the battle—and after the rebel deserter passed along what he believed to be accurate information to Rawdon—Greene ordered that it be brought forward.

On April 25, six weeks after the Battle of Guilford Courthouse and on the very day that Cornwallis began his northward march from Wilmington, Rawdon was ready to fight. His plan was to advance on the rebels from the east, precisely what Greene least expected. Early that morning, Rawdon sent his force on a mile-long circuitous march. The men waded through the menacing swamp that Greene was convinced his foe would avoid. The British soldiers made it through, moving as quietly as possible into and across Little Pine Tree Creek, where they entered thick woods that in places was covered by thick underbrush. "[W]e got into the wood unperceived," Rawdon later wrote, and when he gave the order to attack, his men "came down upon the enemy's left flank." Like Washington on Long Island and at Brandywine, Greene was taken by surprise. It was early in the day, and his quartermaster had just arrived with a two-day supply of provisions. The rebel soldiers were devouring breakfast, or tending to camp chores, when to their astonishment distant gunshots were heard from the direction of the sector where Greene had posted very few pickets. Drums immediately sounded the alarm. The men rushed to their assigned spots in Greene's preconceived plan, though in the disarray and chaos of the moment not all found their units.

Rawdon thought there was "much confusion" among the rebels, a conclusion later confirmed by some of Greene's officers and borne out by failure of the surprised pickets to effectively delay the British advance. Not all the American officers had gotten their forces properly organized when the fighting began in earnest. However, Greene's choice of the battlefield site gave him something of an advantage at the outset. The woods and swamp compelled Rawdon to tightly bunch his front line. It made an inviting target, which Greene exploited by opening fire with his supposedly nonexistent artillery. The cannonade, which the astonished Rawdon characterized as a "shower of grapeshot," blew a large hole in the redcoats' line. A sergeant in Greene's army subsequently said the blow "put the enemy in great confusion," mayhem that Greene exploited by ordering his Continentals to charge forward. All appeared to be going well, so well that Greene anticipated scoring a "compleat victory." But Rawdon did not panic. His men continued to fight, and soon enough, several units joined in a counterattack. Rawdon's assault occurred at the moment that Colonel John Gunby, commander of the First Maryland Continental Regiment, halted an advance to redress his dangerously bowed line of soldiers. The enemy's bayonet charge against the disordered Marylanders sowed such disruption that one company fell apart. That tiny collapse triggered a contagion of disorganization. To restore order, Gunby ordered a pullback. There were times at Monmouth and Guilford Courthouse when stepping back was the prudent choice, as it prevented mayhem and resulted in a salutary—even saving—regrouping. But at Hobkirk's Hill the Marylanders' pullback had a toxic effect. It spawned confusion in other units. Soon, disorder threatened disaster. Greene was in the middle of the fighting seeking to halt the withdrawals, and for a moment it appeared that he and many of the Virginian Continentals might be surrounded. Hard fighting prevented that, but to avert a second Camden catastrophe Greene felt that he had no choice but to order a general withdrawal. It was a more or less orderly retreat that continued for three miles, until Rawdon called a halt to his pursuit. Greene's army survived, but it nearly lost its artillery. Gunners, seeing the battle turn, hid their weapons from the advancing British by rolling the heavy artillery behind a dense thicket. Later, while the fighting continued, the artillerists, grunting under the strain of pushing and pulling guns that weighed hundreds of pounds, retrieved their cannon. Greene himself allegedly pitched in to help drag the cumbersome weaponry into play.[12]

Greene variously characterized the outcome of the fighting as a "little repulse" and "our defeat or rather repulse," and he said he had "come off second best." Rawdon mostly spoke of his "success," though he told Cornwallis that "we routed him totally." The fight had been savage. It was what historian John Buchanan described as "a classic eighteenth-century set-piece battle in which lines of infantry faced each other without attempting to take cover and traded volleys at close range until one line gave way." Under such circumstances, all that saved many from death or a grievous wound was that the principal weapon—the smoothbore musket—was notoriously inaccurate. As it was, the British lost 258 men, one-fourth of those who fought. Greene said that the percentage of his army that was lost was in the same neighborhood, which would suggest that his losses may have approached 350, though he reported a loss of 270 to Congress. Each side also took prisoners. Five men captured by the Americans turned out to be deserters, and following a court-martial all were hanged. "Desertion is a Crime so Dangerous to an army," Greene said later, that he faced an "indispensable necessity of giving some serious example" to his soldiery.[13]

Greene was convinced that he had come close to scoring a great victory, so close that to be denied the triumph left him "almost frantick with vexation at the disappointment." Since his service in the French and Indian War, Washington had found a scapegoat for his principal failings, and Greene himself had been made the fall guy for the debacle at Fort Washington in 1776. Similarly, Greene, prey to mounting anger, attributed his failure at Hobkirk's Hill to Gunby's conduct under fire. Not all of Greene's officers agreed. Although a court of inquiry made up of three officers determined that Gunby's actions had been "extremely improper and unmilitary," there were those in the army who thought Greene's miscues were largely to blame for the battle's outcome. Some held the commander responsible for not having taken adequate steps to prevent being surprised. Others thought Greene had erred in abandoning his defensive position and ordering a charge following the cannonade. Still others thought he had poorly utilized his dragoons. They felt that if Colonel Washington's cavalry had been kept in reserve—as had been the case at Cowpens—and thrown into battle when the British rushed forward to capitalize on the disorder among the Marylanders, the engagement might yet have ended in a spectacular victory akin to that won by Morgan at Cowpens some seventy-five days earlier. Some American officers also blamed the outcome on the cavalry commander more than on Greene or the unfortunate Gunby. Once Washington's dragoons moved out, they had taken such a wide circuit that they barely got into the fight. Indeed, not only did Washington choose an improper route to the rear, but even as the fighting raged, his horse soldiers squandered precious time dealing with the British noncombatants they encountered, men that one officer derisively called the "trumpery of an army."[14]

Greene sank into the valley of despair following the battle. He lamented that his "force and my Talents are unequal to the conflict." Greene's critical remark about his abilities was uncommon, and the more constant theme in his correspondence was that his lack of success was due to the weak hand that he had been dealt. In the immediate aftermath of Hobkirk's Hill, Greene said that he expected Rawdon to come after him yet again, and he pledged to "dispute every inch of ground in the best manner" possible, even if the enemy succeeded in pushing him "back to the mountains." There were times when Greene felt that the war in the South could not be won, and while still aware of the presence of Phillips's large army in the Old Dominion, he remarked that Cornwallis's march to Virginia was a stroke of genius. "Lord Cornwallis," he said, "will establish a chain of posts along James River" that will effectively block the flow of supplies to the Carolinas. If Cornwallis succeeded, "the Southern States, thus cut off, will die like the Tail of a Snake," he added. Greene felt forsaken by Congress and the northern states, and even by General Washington; reading between the lines of his mournful communiqués, Greene seemed to suggest that the commander in chief could have relinquished more men from his habitually inert army. Like Jefferson, Greene felt that no one above the Potomac appeared to understand "the nature of the war and the circumstances" of the southern states. He lashed out, too, at authorities in Virginia, Maryland, and North Carolina. They were not doing enough to assist him. He needed men, horses, wagons, teamsters, artificers, saddles, harnesses, and arms, he said. He urged the authorities in the Carolinas to construct a string of armories and fill them with weapons and ammunition so that his almost constantly moving army could be supplied. Greene was pessimistic that his needs would be met. At this juncture, he believed the Loyalists constituted a majority of the citizenry in large parts of South Carolina and Georgia, and that his army lacked the means to regain control of those two states. After months of fighting, he lamented, "We have many broken bones; spilt much blood and gained but little advantage. Disgrace and not glory has been our portion." With an eye on looming peace negotiations—much as Lafayette and Clinton were focusing on what the diplomats would discern when they sat down at the conference table following this pivotal year—Greene in May declared that "the fate of the Southern States" hung "suspended by a slender thread." At times, Greene felt that he had been sent on a hopeless mission. He confided to a close friend: "I am sick of the service, and wish my self out of the [Southern] Department."[15]

Greene reserved his harshest feelings for Virginia and Thomas Jefferson. He told Congress that Virginia had promised two thousand militiamen, but they never appeared, and he asked the legislators to investigate. He also told Congress that it was absurd to permit the chief executive of a state to command the militia when the nation supposedly was "engaged upon a continental plan." He complained to his friend Lafayette that Jefferson sent neither men nor cavalry horses to the army. When writing Jefferson, Greene tempered his remarks, though he still castigated him for failing to provide the army with horses. Virginia alone among the southern states was "not a frontier State," he told Jefferson, adding that only the Old Dominion possessed the capability to truly assist the army.[16]

No one was more relieved to learn of Rawdon's victory outside Camden than Cornwallis. After learning that Greene had entered South Carolina, Cornwallis—five days into his march to Virginia—remarked that the "thought of Camden distresses me." As the showdown between Greene and Rawdon approached, Cornwallis's anxiety was palpable. "The die is cast," he said nervously, all too aware that much of the blame for a British catastrophe would fall on his shoulders. When word of Rawdon's success reached him, Cornwallis gushed that it was "the most splendid of the war." A victory it was, but Rawdon and Balfour knew better than their commander—and better than Greene for that matter—how grave Britain's situation had become in South Carolina. Cornwallis's four-month absence and his string of failures in North Carolina, together with the arrival of Greene, had strengthened and emboldened the rebels and discouraged the Tories. A few days before Hobkirk's Hill, Balfour acknowledged that parties of up to three hundred partisans "have over run all the country" below Camden, while Ninety Six, to the west, was imperiled by guerrilla bands led by Andrew Pickens and others. Several additional posts were also threatened. Loyalist militiamen were defecting in alarming numbers, a turnabout brought on by a foreboding sense that the future belonged to the rebels, but spurred, too, by the partisans' terrorist tactic of "murdering every [Loyalist] militia officer" as well as "every man . . . who is known to be a loyalist." Writing to Cornwallis, Balfour predicted that if Greene were reinforced so that he could "really come in force," the citizenry would flock to the rebels. The people were "very ripe for" it, he added. It was as close as Balfour ever came to begging Cornwallis to return.[17]

The mere appearance of Greene's army in the province in April had led Balfour to conclude that many British posts in the backcountry were doomed. He was prescient. Within three weeks of Hobkirk's Hill, Forts Watson (some fifty miles below Camden on the Santee), Motte (midway between Watson and Camden), and Granby (thirty-five miles southwest of Camden) had fallen to Lee's dragoons or to the combined forces of Continental cavalry and partisans. So, too, had Orangeburg, a little hamlet only seventy-five miles above Charleston that British regulars had occupied a year earlier just as Clinton sailed from Charleston to New York. Far to the west, Forts Dreadnought and Grierson on the Savannah River fell, and following the surrender of the latter its commander, a British officer, was murdered. Four other posts were besieged, and Georgetown (not quite halfway between Charleston and Wilmington) and Nelson's Ferry (across the Santee from Fort Watson) had been relinquished. Balfour was no longer sure that Charleston could be held. "The enemy having uniformly murdered in cold blood all our militia whom they have been able to get at . . . had not failed also to affect our town folks," he said. So worried was Balfour that he had not sent reinforcements from Charleston to aid Rawdon when Camden was threatened. A few days after the engagement at Hobkirk's Hill, he began calling in many of the garrisons in the hinterland. Balfour needed the manpower, but he also feared the inevitable loss of the posts and the soldiers that garrisoned them. Some of the smaller posts that were overwhelmed by rebel forces had contained upwards of 150 troops, as had some that were abandoned before their foreseeable loss. Camden, on May 10, was the largest to be evacuated and destroyed. Rawdon followed orders in giving it up and marching his men to Charleston. It was a trek that he knew would be dicey. Greene was in his rear, Lee and Marion were between him and Charleston, and, as Rawdon put it, "The whole interior country had revolted." But using rivers and creeks to his advantage, as Greene had done when chased by Cornwallis, Rawdon made it. For good reason, Balfour in mid-May saw only hopelessness. "The general revolt of the province [and] the universal disaffection" convinced him that South Carolina was lost unless the backcountry could be retaken, and it could be regained only if "a very great additional force" sent by Cornwallis, Clinton, or London should "come here immediately." Within a few weeks he reported that the "revolt is universal" and the "minds of the people are bent on their [revolutionary] principles."[18]

The Americans had scored victory after victory that spring, taking one British fort after another together with the provisions they contained. They had captured over eight hundred enemy troops, nearly half of which were regulars. But the British still held Ninety Six, though only because the messages sent from Charleston that ordered its abandonment had been intercepted by rebel forces. Made aware of Balfour's intentions to relinquish the post through the captured messages, Greene (as Colonel Lee later wrote) might have passed on the captured communiqués to the commandant of Ninety Six and offered him safe passage to Charleston in return for giving up the installation without a fight. Curiously, Greene did not choose that course. Most likely, he thought taking Ninety Six would be easy pickings. He knew that his army was twice the size of the post's defenders. Of course, he knew that Balfour could not stand by idly and permit a garrison of some five hundred men to be captured, but Greene guessed that three weeks or more would pass before reinforcements reached Ninety Six and by then the beleaguered British troops would have capitulated. It may be, too, that Greene lusted for the glory of a conquest by arms, a prize that had eluded him. Expecting to possess Ninety Six by early June, Greene felt his spirits soar as his army marched westward over dusty, sun-scorched roads. He was convinced that the fall of Ninety Six, the last backcountry installation still in British hands, would weaken London's claim to South Carolina or Georgia at the peace table. Greene also envisaged this endeavor as his last in South Carolina, after which he would take his army to Virginia and link up with Lafayette for still another confrontation with Cornwallis.[19]

Lieutenant Colonel John Cruger commanded at Ninety Six. A forty-three-year-old New Yorker, Cruger had been raised in an old and prosperous family of Manhattan merchants. Choosing to soldier for the Crown, Cruger had served with the British army since 1776 and in the South since Campbell's expedition to take Savannah in 1778. He was regarded as "a finished gentleman in all his conduct." He was also a tough and tenacious soldier. Hoping that reinforcements were on the way from Charleston, Cruger dug in and prepared to resist, confident that he could hold out until the arrival of the troops that would shore up his little force.

Once Greene's chief engineer, Thaddeus Kosciuszko, saw the installation that housed Cruger's army, he understood the thinking of the redcoat officer. Kosciuszko advised that the rebel army would face formidable obstacles. Ninety Six was an old outpost that antedated the war, and for ages it had sported a sound system of defenses. A star fort with sixteen complex angles guarded the road leading to Ninety Six; the garrison within that fort could pour an enfiladed fire on an approaching enemy. The fort was surrounded by a deep ditch and abatis—sharp wooden stakes that could impale, or at least slow to a snail's pace, any assailant. Ninety Six itself was a town that included numerous log cabins, two blockhouses, and several wells, around which ran a heavy wooden stockade fence. As with the fort, abatis and a wide, deep ditch encircled the palisade. During his first day at Ninety Six, May 22, Greene allowed that "this place [is] much better fortified and [the] garrison much stronger in regular troops than was expected." The next day he solemnly admitted, "Our success is very doubtful." But he persisted.[20]

Rapidly concluding that his cannon could not knock down the stockade, Greene set his men to digging parallels on its east and west sides, deep trenches that would house the artillery as it crept ever closer to the target. Cruger responded by sending out squads at night to surprise the sappers, and they were amazingly successful. Greene not only suffered his initial casualties, but he was compelled to order that new parallels be dug much farther from his objective. As days passed, Greene attempted without success to burn down the stockade. He also conceived a plan to dig a tunnel under the enemy's ditch and blow a hole in the stockade, but by the third week of the siege the tunnel had yet to get under "the ditch of the enemies works" and his men were "wore out with fatigue and hardships." In addition, Greene's supply of ammunition was dwindling, casualties had mounted in the frequent skirmishing, and men who toiled under the blazing summer sun and in the relentless southern humidity were falling ill. Greene fretted that a "proper Army" could have long ago brought the siege to a climax, but he feared that victory would elude "our little force." His parallels had advanced closer to the star fort, yet even when his cannon in the third parallel had closed to within 140 yards of their target, the stronghold withstood the shelling. His army constructed elevated artillery batteries, but they, too, were ineffective. Greene's men built a thirty-foot tower from which riflemen could fire into the fort. Nothing turned the tide. Worse still, on June 9, Greene learned from a Charleston newspaper that six days earlier three British regiments sent from Ireland and a bevy of new recruits had arrived in the city. Now there was no question that reinforcements, which Greene expected to be led by Rawdon, would come to save Cruger. As they would have to cover some 175 miles to reach Ninety Six, Greene called on the partisans to do what they could to delay the advance of the additional troops. But the clock was ticking, and Greene was beset with a brooding expectation of failure. The scapegoat on this occasion was to be Virginia, as it had "not afforded me the support I expected."[21]

Greene's intelligence gatherers kept him abreast of the progress of the enemy's relief force. He had a few days yet, but not enough to reduce Ninety Six through a siege. That left him with three options: intercept and fight the relief force before it reached the fort; call off the siege and depart; or order a mass attack. Greene had too few men to confront the relief force, and given the time and blood invested over the past month, he was unwilling to march away without having attempted a frontal attack. The odds of its success were far from good, but that was his choice. He prepared by issuing calls to South Carolina's militia officers—who had been active in the Savannah River campaign—to hurry with their men to his side. "Let us have a field day; and I doubt not it will be glorious," he wrote, adding, "No time is to be lost." Time ran out before they arrived. On June 18, with the relief force getting closer and closer, Greene gave the order to launch the attack against two sectors of the installation. Grim-faced volunteers in forlorn hope units would lead the way. While under fire, these men, armed with axes, would plunge into the ditch and hack away at the abatis, hoping to clear the way for the assault force.

The bloody fighting lasted for forty-five minutes, and in the end Greene had little to show for it but more casualties. Some men penetrated the stockade. None got into the star fort. Upwards of 150 of Greene's men were killed, wounded, or captured trying, and that number was atop the more than two score casualties that he appears to have suffered during the monthlong siege. Two days later Greene admitted defeat and marched his army away from Ninety Six. It was a cruel blow, and all the more so as he knew that with a few additional days he would have achieved victory, for the last source of water available to Cruger's men had come under the sights of American gunners. Greene said that he was shamed by his defeat. Still furious more than a week later, and on the hunt for a fall guy, Greene wrote Jefferson that his action in preventing Virginia's militia from coming to the Carolinas had been responsible for "the most mortifying and disagreeable consequences." He simply told Congress that he was consoled by the knowledge that "nothing was left unattempted" by his army.[22]

The relief force, which was indeed led by Rawdon, arrived some thirty hours after Greene's departure. Rawdon thought of pursuing his enemy, but his men were exhausted and Greene had a considerable head start. They were already sixteen miles away and behind the Saluda River. After another two days Greene's army was some sixty-five miles away and behind the Enoree River, a tributary of the Broad. Not only was Greene's army far away, but Rawdon was desperately short of supplies, having discovered that Ninety Six was "almost entirely destitute of stores." He had to forage before he could do doing anything else. Though Balfour called Ninety Six Britain's "most commanding and important of all the posts in the Back Country," he nevertheless stuck to his previous decision to abandon the installation. He knew it could be held only by an exceedingly large force and he knew, too, that those men were urgently needed elsewhere. Within a few days, Rawdon abandoned Ninety Six and set off for the coast. He divided his force on the march. He took one route, Cruger another, hopeful that by separating the twin forces the two might harvest a larger recruitment of Loyalists. Though these were not forced marches, fifty or more British soldiers died of heat-stroke or exhaustion during what still was a grueling summer trek.[23]

Greene's destination had been Charlotte, but when learned that Rawdon was not in pursuit, he turned south. Greene became the pursuer, Rawdon the prey. Learning that Rawdon had only four hundred troops, Greene believed that "he may be defeated with ease," and he tracked that wing of the enemy's army, pushing his army down dusty roads and past parched farmland in the sweltering summer heat. After passing through Winnsboro, where Cornwallis had recuperated following his first incursion into North Carolina, Greene pressed on toward Orangeburg, where he rightly presumed Rawdon would pause to rest his men and await supplies. But as Greene approached the town he found Rawdon "so posted that it was impossible to attack him." Greene took up a position eight miles from town, hopeful that Rawdon could be drawn out for a fight, as had been the case at Hobkirk's Hill. "Our men were in high spirits and wished for action," he claimed, but after forty-eight hours Greene discovered that British reinforcements were on the way from Charleston. That news led him to suspend operations. Although his dragoons remained active in hopes of reducing enemy posts in the low country, Greene knew that his army had "sufferd incredible hard-ships" and required "a little relaxation," all the more so as the daily July temperatures and humidity were stuck in the stratosphere and the nights were unpleasantly warm and sultry. In mid-month—just as Cornwallis was on the cusp of settling his army at Yorktown—Greene retreated to the High Hills of Santee, which had a cooler and healthier climate than did the low country and was a site that wealthy planters had long used as a retreat in the sickly summer season.[24]

Greene's depleted army had been in the field for nearly seven months, and the men who had served under him since the campaign was launched the previous December had easily marched more than a thousand miles, fought in at least two major battles, and come under fire in countless small skirmishes. The combined casualty tolls at Cowpens, Guilford Courthouse, Hobkirk's Hill, and Ninety Six exceeded 850. If the losses from disease, the rigors of campaigning, and the toll taken in innumerable minor encounters are factored in, Greene's army had suffered the loss of substantially more than 1,000 men. Greene, who had served five years in the northern theater before coming south, tried to tell a general officer posted in New York just how difficult it was to serve in the Carolinas. The "Northern service is nothing at all," said Greene, adding that American troopers who had not soldiered in the Carolinas had "never seen any thing like war yet." He also remarked that those who had not witnessed war in the Carolinas could "have no Idea of the horrors of the Southern war. Murders are as frequent here as petty disputes are to the Northward."[25]

Greene, like his men, needed a breather. Three days after Hobkirk's Hill, he had offered his best remembered observation: "We fight get beat rise and fight again."[26] That summed up what he had endured, and he anticipated more of the same. By the time he took his army to the High Hills of Santee, Greene had been informed by Washington of the plans made at Wethersfield to assail Clinton in New York. Greene tried to imagine what that would mean. He believed Clinton would abandon Virginia, summoning some or all his troops in the Old Dominion for the defense of New York and sending every last man who could be spared to South Carolina. Like a great many others, Greene suspected there would be a European peace conference in 1782. (His friend Joseph Reed, the chief executive in Pennsylvania, had written him a month earlier, "The finishing the War in America is so obvious that it is impossible to miss it by Accident.") Surely, Greene thought, Clinton would not only do all within his power to hold New York, but he would also make a major effort to reduce Georgia and South Carolina prior to the gathering of the diplomats.[27]

Greene could not see into the future, though since coming south he had never been more upbeat. He was in "good Health," he said in July, and though his "little Army has undergone every Hardship," it had "overcome every difficulty." He believed his "prospects are much mended in this Quarter." Nor was that all. He had learned that Admiral de Grasse was being sent with a large fleet to North America, and he quickly deduced that if it came to the Chesapeake before Clinton removed his troops from Virginia, "Lord Cornwallis's Army, and the fleet and Garrison at Portsmouth would be much in our power."[28]

Greene was additionally buoyed by the praise lavished on him by a war-weary country that appreciated a daring and active general who had racked up military gains. Although he had failed to score a victory in either of his two major battles since April, he deserved acclaim for his daring that led to Morgan's triumph at Cowpens as well as kudos for having debilitated Cornwallis's force in the wild chase across North Carolina and at Guilford Courthouse. Despite his dearth of manpower or resources, the relentless nature of Greene's campaigning—and his welcoming collaboration with the partisans—had succeeded in reducing Britain's claims to all but a tiny toehold in South Carolina.

Greene learned from several sources of Congress's euphoria at his "prudence and Gallantry." "Congress and all America," he was told by a friend, "fully believe that had your force been adequate to the service that you would have expelled your titled enemy and all others from the southern states." Congress lauded his "Wisdom . . . Fortitude and true Courage," and looked toward the day when he would "return crowned with Laurels." Greene was not only nominated for the newly created post of secretary of war, but Congress was considering striking a medal to honor him.[29] Things looked brighter, as Greene had said, but things had looked brighter in the aftermath of Saratoga four long years earlier, and then joy had turned to despair.

CHAPTER 13

MONUMENTAL DECISIONS

IN JUNE, SIR Henry Clinton learned of Nathanael Greene's defeat in April at Hobkirk's Hill, and the overblown accounts that reached him portrayed the British victory as more spectacular than it had been. Led to believe that a great many more than six hundred rebels had been lost—a total equal to half Greene's army—an ecstatic Clinton thought "the rout" was Britain's "most important victory of the whole war." The latest rebel catastrophe, Clinton reasoned, assured that Greene would be too hobbled to achieve much in South Carolina.[1] The misinformation proved to be most unfortunate, for Clinton received the tidings as he continued to mull over his strategic choices for the coming campaign in 1781. Given what he believed to have occurred at Hobkirk's Hill, Clinton was less anxious about Cornwallis's departure from the Carolinas. If he had ever seriously considered ordering Cornwallis to return to South Carolina—and it is unlikely that he was ever close to taking that step—he no longer contemplated that option.

But over the course of the summer, Clinton learned the true magnitude of the disaster unfolding down south. He realized that "the defection of the country was become general" in South Carolina—long-held British posts "were daily dropping into the enemy's hands," was how he put it—and that knowledge stoked his rage toward Cornwallis. Having no doubt that those "heavy misfortunes" were due to Cornwallis's abandonment of South Carolina, Clinton for the first time dared to criticize his subordinate to Lord Germain. To do so was an act of courage, as only three weeks earlier he had received the letter from the American secretary upbraiding him for not pursuing a more aggressive policy in Virginia. That was the communiqué that had led Clinton to change step, terminating the redeployment of a substantial number of troops from the Old Dominion to New York and ordering Cornwallis—and his entire army—to take up defensive positions in Yorktown and Gloucester. As July turned toward August, Clinton had come to clearly understand that Britain's southern strategy was in tatters and that Cornwallis deserved much of the blame for its unraveling, and he additionally apprehended the utter folly of Germain's and the king's insistence on leaving a large army in Virginia. Angry, but also possibly seeking to vindicate himself in the event that he recalled some men in Virginia in preparation for the anticipated Allied attack on New York, Clinton opened up to Germain about all that Cornwallis had done during this crucial year. He had gone into North Carolina "without a force sufficient to protect or provisions to support them." Cowpens had been the result. Thereafter, Cornwallis had persevered in the field even though it was unmistakably clear that few Loyalists in North Carolina would rally to his side. From the start, it had been a misguided campaign, and predictably it had ended with the British army suffering ruinous losses in the pursuit of Greene's fleeing army and at Guilford Courthouse. Even more egregiously, Cornwallis had turned his back on South Carolina, a course of action "full of doubt and ruin" and "in opposition to every principle of policy as well as duty." Cornwallis's foolhardy behavior, Clinton charged, was directly responsible for the ruination of all that the British had realized in a year of dogged and bloody sacrifices in South Carolina.[2]

Deep into August, with Cornwallis's army intact at Yorktown, Clinton sought to make decisions based on what he knew, what he suspected lay ahead, and what he felt could be the consequences of any action that he took or did not take. He feared that should he withdraw too many troops from Virginia, those left behind might be vulnerable to an attack by Lafayette. Or if the British force in Virginia was too small to pose much of a threat, Lafayette might either join Greene in a campaign to take Charleston or come north to link up with Washington, a step that would add to the size of the Allied force that he believed would soon attack New York.

However, as the summer sped past and the likelihood grew of the imminent arrival of Comte de Grasse's French squadron, Clinton appeared to wrestle with the idea of once again summoning some of Cornwallis's army to New York. But Clinton found himself in the uncomfortable position of having to rely on Cornwallis's judgment regarding the proper size of the army in Virginia, and the earl insisted that his army's safety required all of his 7,500 men. Cornwallis said that he based his assessment on the recommendations of his engineers and his own conviction that after two weeks of work on Gloucester's defenses, it remained incapable of withstanding an attack by an enemy force of merely a thousand men. (Cornwallis did not mention it, but only when work was to begin on the fortifications at Gloucester and Yorktown was it discovered that the army lacked the necessary entrenching tools for doing the job. "[N]o one had thought" to bring along the spades and pickaxes from Portsmouth, said a surprised and disgruntled German officer.) Once work did begin, progress was slowed by widespread illness due to "the great heat, which has decomposed our blood too much," according to one soldier. The remedies for the maladies— emetics and bleeding—were counterproductive and likely contributed to what one soldier described as "the land fever turn[ing] into putrid fever." Cornwallis reported, too, that he could not work his men too long each day in Virginia's adverse summertime climate "without ruining their health." Furthermore, he was unable to employ his entire soldiery as manual workers. Some were assigned to foraging parties and others stood guard against a surprise attack. It would be nice to have a supplemental supply of laborers, especially African Americans as "the heat is too great" for whites, Cornwallis said, but "there is a great want of Negroes to work." He had sought African American workers from Portsmouth only to learn that droves of "wretched Negroes" at that base had fallen prey to "some fatal distemper" and "are dying by scores every day." (Expressing shock at the condition of the "poor Negroes," Cornwallis directed O'Hara to find food for them and "some person of the country . . . to take charge of them to prevent their perishing.")[3]

Clinton faced the dilemma that confronted all commanders in this war. He was not on the scene to judge for himself. He had no way of knowing the strength of the enemy forces in Virginia or whether Yorktown and Gloucester could withstand an assault, though from the outset he believed that Cornwallis would lay in a sufficient amount of provisions to enable his army to withstand a siege "to the middle of Nov." Otherwise, Clinton shrank from issuing orders to Cornwallis that might prove to be disastrous. His predicament was not unlike that faced by Washington in 1777 on the eve of the clash at Brandywine. Feeling the need for more troops, Washington had asked Horatio Gates, who was in the fight of his life against General Burgoyne in the Saratoga campaign, to send Daniel Morgan and his corps of riflemen to help in the struggle to save Philadelphia. Gates refused. Washington acquiesced to his refusal. Similarly, Clinton abided by Cornwallis's avowal that he would not be safe with a smaller army.[4]

Clinton's thinking throughout the summer was also shaped by the realization that reestablishing royal control in the South had been the fulcrum of Britain's war effort since the debacle at Saratoga, and he dared not turn his back on the strategy. To do so would be to invalidate three years of sacrifices, including not only the risks that he himself had run in capturing Charleston, but the deaths and injuries suffered by the men he had sent into harm's way. In addition, Clinton remained steadfastly committed to achieving success in the South, and he continued to believe that it was possible. He never embraced the idea that Virginia could be conquered. But Clinton persisted in the belief that in the autumn, following the defeat of the Allies in New York, British forces would suppress the rebellion in the low country.[5]

Throughout the summer, Clinton remained persuaded that the coming Allied attack on New York was the most immediate and dangerous threat that he faced, and he stepped up work to shore up fortifications and build new barriers. Late in the summer, he called to duty many of the 5,500 militiamen in royal units around Manhattan. His fears for New York were not imaginary. Clinton's information on the Wethersfield conference, derived from his superlative spy network and intercepted letters written by Washington and Lafayette, indicated that the Allies intended an operation against New York "with all the force they could collect." Abundant intelligence reports over the years had pointed to Washington's obsession with retaking the city, and in fact from the spring deep into the summer of 1781 the American commander continued to prefer an operation against New York to any alternative. "I am threatened with a siege," Clinton said in June, adding that "the enemy will *certainly* attack" New York.[6] Clinton was aware that if New York was lost, and his army with it, the blow would be greater than that suffered by Britain at Saratoga. The Allies would have unmistakably scored the decisive victory in this war. On the other hand, if the Allied campaign to retake New York failed, Clinton believed—again based on intelligence provided during the past year—that France would essentially drop out of the war by consenting to peace talks that an emasculated America would have to accept. In that event, Britain would be positioned to reestablish its rule over some of its former colonies, leaving London with a shrunken but still substantial North American empire. In choosing a course of action for the crucial weeks ahead, Clinton had to juggle what was necessary for the defense of New York with the safety of his armies in Virginia and the prospects for regaining what was being lost in the low country.

Clinton commanded a bit more than thirteen thousand men in New York, but felt that he needed additional troops to adequately defend the city against what would be a much larger Allied force. It "cannot be doubted," he said, that the Allies could field a force of twenty thousand, for to do so they would need to secure only some eight thousand militiamen from New York and the manpower-rich surrounding provinces. By early in August, thinking the Allied assault could not be far away, his anxiety grew. A month after telling Cornwallis to unload the men on troop transports in Portsmouth and take them instead to Yorktown, Clinton mentioned to Cornwallis his need for more men, artillery, artillerists, and engineers. He even took the extraordinary step of reproducing portions of five letters that he had sent

Cornwallis over the past one hundred days, each of which disclosed his need of men in Virginia to help with the defense of New York.[7] However, by the time Clinton's communiqués reached Yorktown, Cornwallis's situation had changed drastically and he was unable to send any units to Manhattan. By then, too, Clinton had received a remarkable letter from Cornwallis, who was now aware of the disaster unfolding in South Carolina. Confessing "my judgment is liable to error," Cornwallis sheepishly acknowledged, "the measure which I adopted" in coming to Virginia was "Perhaps . . . not the best" decision.[8]

Clinton's planning for the looming crisis was comprehensive and thoughtful. Drawing on the reports of his intelligence service and his many years of experience, Clinton was confident that Britain's armies in Savannah, in Charleston, and on the Virginia peninsula were safe—as was his in New York—so long as the Royal Navy remained supreme in North American waters. He was confident that Britain would not lose its naval supremacy. Britain possessed the world's greatest navy, one that had shattered the French in the Seven Years' War. He had known since May that a formidable French task force under de Grasse was crossing the Atlantic. British intelligence, said Germain, who had informed Clinton of the threat, reported that the enemy squadron consisted of twenty-six ships of the line and 12,000 troops. (Rochambeau, at nearly the same moment, received word from Versailles that it consisted of twenty ships of the line and 3,200 troops. It actually consisted of twenty-eight ships of the line and 3,300 marines.) Germain had further divulged that after dropping off supplies and conducting summertime operations in the Caribbean, de Grasse's fleet would sail for North America. Clinton never doubted that de Grasse would be coming. French fleets had arrived in North America in each of the past three years, two under Comte d'Estaing and the *Expédition Particulière* the previous summer. No one knew de Grasse's destination, and Germain had not speculated on the matter. He had said only the French navy was being sent to "revive the expiring cause of the rebellion."

Throughout the spring and summer, Germain remained jauntily optimistic despite the looming French threat. He declared that he was "not apprehensive" about de Grasse's fleet, for even if the French admiral brought his entire squadron northward, the British navy would be a match for it. Britain's navy in the Caribbean would trail the French task force as it sailed northward, he advised, ultimately joining forces with Britain's fleet in North America to preserve the Royal Navy's superiority. The awesome power of Britain's navy would prevent de Grasse from "giving you any interruption in your operations," Germain counseled. Even in a worst-case scenario, de Grasse would not have time "to do you any material injury." He would come and go rapidly. The French fleet would be on its way back to France or the Caribbean long before a siege operation of many months duration in New York could be completed. Germain's final letter on the subject, penned on August 2, was even more upbeat. Not only did he continue to believe the Royal Navy was up to the challenge, but intelligence—with considerable accuracy—reported that Versailles had decided against providing Rochambeau with additional troops. If Clinton was successful in defending New York against an Allied attack, the American secretary concluded, the outlook would be "most favourable for the King's affairs." Furthermore, during the months needed "to bring on a [peace] negotiation" during 1782, Clinton would have the "advantage in your operations" in Virginia and throughout the South.[9]

Clinton was more concerned than Germain about de Grasse's pending arrival. He told the American secretary that it might be next to impossible "to defend this extensive post" against "so powerful an armament" as that posed by the Allied armies and the French fleet. He also feared that his position in New York would "become very critical" should de Grasse remain "superior at sea" for a several weeks. That said, Clinton, like Germain, doubted that de Grasse could gain "a naval superiority in these seas," and if he did, he could not maintain his advantage for more than roughly thirty days. If that was borne out, Clinton believed the Allied attack could be repulsed.[10] There was another crucial factor that Clinton counted on. So long as the Royal Navy maintained its superiority, in a pinch Clinton could summon troops from Virginia or South Carolina to assist in the defense of New York.

As the summer campaign season advanced and Britain's army in New York remained inactive, and as the news from the southern theater passed from what one Tory called "ticklish" to the "utmost distress," the Loyalists in Manhattan who met from time to time with Clinton grew increasingly depressed and angry. "Nothing is done or seems to be intended to be done," one raged. "What timid policy. . . . What Insignificancy of Conduct!" "Sir Henry is a distressed Man," a "trifler," one who makes plans only to change them and in the end "resolves Nothing." He was "insensible" to the dangers he was bringing on through his inertia, one alleged. It was said that Clinton consulted only the "servile" sycophantic officers who surrounded him, and they purportedly made "Use of their General for their own Interests." Nor was it only Tories who groused. Some British officers complained, among them Benedict Arnold, who confided to his Tory friends that he was "disgusted at the Inactivity" and fed up with the "Indecision" and "Defect of a Spirit of Enterprise" that prevailed at headquarters.[11]

These were bitter men, individuals who had cast their lot with the king and were coming to think that American independence, in at least some form, was unavoidable. Those who were not soldiers were unaware of the myriad complexities involved in launching military operations, much less the quandaries faced by a commander charged with devising a winning strategy in a two-front war. They simply knew that they wanted a more aggressive and intrepid commander, someone like Cornwallis. One New York Tory even equated Cornwallis's recent march to Virginia with Alexander the Great's triumphant campaign of conquests.[12]

Many hoped that Clinton would be recalled and Cornwallis named as his replacement. In blasting Clinton for his exceeding caution, these critics overlooked his initiatives in the southern theater and the major commitments he had made to the war in the South since the previous autumn. They complained that he was not cut from the same cloth as Nathanael Greene or Lord Cornwallis, and that was true. Clinton's aversion to risk-taking was more akin to the command style that General Washington had demonstrated during the past four years. From Brandywine and Saratoga onward, Washington was wary and watchful. Initially, he believed that time was on his side, as Britain's fervor for continuing to fight would diminish following France's entry into the war. However, even after Washington discovered that time might be his enemy, he refused to act without the support of his French ally. On assuming command in 1778, Clinton had thought time was against him, but as the war wore on and the American economy and morale crumbled, he came to see time as an asset. By 1781, Clinton felt that if Britain's forces could avoid defeat that year, it was yet possible that London would achieve a victory of sorts in the war. To achieve this end, Clinton believed he must avoid precarious undertakings. During that summer, he considered but rejected a move against West Point. He yet again pondered a major initiative against the French in Rhode Island, labeling it the "same tempting target" that it had been the previous year.[13] But in the end, he declined to act. His object was to remain on the defensive, preserving his army in preparation for the enemy's blow against New York.

Had Clinton known in the middle of the pivotal summer of 1781 what he would know in September, he might have acted differently. But Clinton was not clairvoyant.

IN THE SPRING, Washington had asked Rochambeau to wait a spell before bringing his army to New York to link up with the Americans. Rochambeau obliged, but on June 10—expecting de Grasse's fleet to arrive somewhere in North America before summer's end, and possibly even within the next six weeks—the French army began its journey from Newport to rendezvous with its ally. Not every French soldier made the trek. Those in sick bay could not march and Rochambeau left behind four hundred men to join forces with some five hundred Rhode Island militiamen for the defense of Newport. About seven hundred men had to be assigned to the French naval squadron, which had been depleted by illness and desertions. The fleet, now under Comte Jacques-Melchoir de Barras, who had recently been sent by Versailles to command the squadron, was also to remain in Newport for the time being, as it was possible that de Grasse would come there first. Nearly two hundred soldiers were given temporary duty as teamsters. They were to drive more than one hundred wagons loaded with supplies of every sort, including the baggage of officers, which was limited to a staggering 150 pounds per man. But about three thousand men set off on foot, stirring up great clouds of dust on the summertime march over primitive roads that were deemed unsuitable for handling the army's heavy siege artillery. The siege guns were to be shipped by sea at a later date to wherever the Allied armies eventually chose to go.[14]

The army's march had been carefully planned. Magazines stocked with food and water had been established along the route, as had campsites. Utilizing the eighteenth century's version of a GPS system, almost every step of the 220-mile trek had been outlined by advance scouting parties. For instance,

> Coming out of Voluntown [today's Sterling Hill, Connecticut], leave a road on the left, continue straight ahead, go through a deep wooded hollow through which flows a small brook. Then go uphill. Soon after you come out of the woods, the road forks. Take the left fork. The right-hand fork, which goes up a rather steep little hill and is difficult for wagons, leads into the center of Plainfield. The left hand road, less steep, comes in the far end of town, with Eaton's Tavern on your right.

The plan was for the soldiers to be awakened at 2:00 A.M. and to begin the day's march two hours later. A halt for the day was to be called at noon in order to save the men—garbed in heavy wool uniforms—from illness brought on by excessive exertion in summer's heat and humidity. On many evenings, according to one soldier, "people in the neighborhood came to visit our camps. We furnished the music and they danced. Each day there was a new party." The army was projected to cover up to fifteen miles each day that it marched, which was roughly every third day. Twenty-six days into the march—and on the eleventh day of actually marching—the first French regiments slogged their final mile and established a camp at Philipsburg, New York, close by the 6,300 American troops under

Washington. So precisely had everything been planned that La Luzerne, the French minister, arrived at the same moment from Philadelphia to greet his countrymen.[15]

Rochambeau and Washington knew that the long-anticipated action was coming, though they did not know when or where it would occur. At Wethersfield, they had agreed—as Washington at the time noted in his diary—to join forces "to commence an operation against New York," unless de Grasse established "a Naval superiority" to the "southward" in the Chesapeake.[16] During their conversations in May, the two commanders had been aware that the forces under Arnold and Phillips were in Virginia. It was only much later—six days before the French army marched out of Rhode Island—that Washington learned that Cornwallis had assumed command of the British army in the Old Dominion. What once had been thought to have been a British army of perhaps 4,500 men was now presumed to be a force in the vicinity of 7,000. It was around this time, too, that Rochambeau first informed Washington that he had encouraged Admiral de Grasse to sail for the Chesapeake rather than to New York. Washington greeted that news with greater flexibility than he had displayed at Wethersfield. Perhaps, he said in a communiqué to Rochambeau, an operation in the South would be "more practicable and equally advisable" than a campaign for New York. Yet he closed his letter by urging Rochambeau to request de Grasse to bring his fleet to New York. Washington remained fixated on New York.[17]

Nevertheless, while the French army was tramping toward New York, Washington broached with Rochambeau the notion that the French squadron in Rhode Island might sail immediately for the Chesapeake. Washington passed along intelligence that four hundred reinforcements were being sent from Ireland to Cornwallis, and he argued that the swift arrival of Barras's fleet would prevent the king's army in Virginia from being supplied by sea. It was of the "utmost importance" to reduce the British forces in Virginia "to very great difficulties and distresses," said Washington, though the tenor of his letters suggest that he was more interested in preventing Cornwallis from going on the offensive that summer than in softening him up for a siege down the road. In fact, two weeks after urging that Barras descend on the Chesapeake, Washington swung back to plans that he had made for launching a strike against Clinton in New York.[18]

Meanwhile, Rochambeau was growing steadily more convinced that the Chesapeake must be the focal point of the coming campaign. In May, not long after the meeting in Wethersfield, he wrote de Grasse of the "grave crisis" in the South, though he stressed that the fleet should go where its commander thought it could "render the greatest service." Two weeks later, after learning from de Grasse that he could stay only briefly no matter where he went, Rochambeau—who all along had stressed that a siege of New York would be a protracted affair—once again pitched the Chesapeake in a communiqué to the admiral. Rochambeau characterized his joining with the Continental army outside New York as a "diversion in favor of Virginia," and he advised that the French minister to the United States shared his concern that an American army under Lafayette in Virginia was faced with almost certain destruction by the much larger enemy army.[19]

Rochambeau was not alone in pushing for a Chesapeake campaign. La Luzerne also advocated going after the British in Virginia. Aware that the situation was precarious in the Old Dominion, La Luzerne feared not only the impact that its loss would have on the other southern states but also its consequences for France's commitment to its American ally. Lafayette had taken pains to keep the minister informed, writing roughly every dozen days and stressing the challenges he faced and the importance of frustrating Cornwallis's plans to close the supply routes to the Carolinas. In his first communiqué, written in March as he was setting off for the South, Lafayette told La Luzerne that "General Washington . . . thinks it important for the safety" of Virginia and "honor of American arms" that his little army be sent to that state. Once in Virginia, Lafayette recounted his tribulations and described how he was coping. "We have no money, clothing, shoes, nor shirts, and in a few days we shall be making our meals on green peaches; our feet are torn for lack of shoes and our hands itchy for lack of linens." Going "without a shirt gives a man gall, and the lack of shoes, especially in a forced march, ends up tearing a man's foot," he added. But to that, Lafayette said: "all that will not prevent us from marching if we must." His army was small and vulnerable to being "completely thrashed" if forced into a showdown with Cornwallis, but to avoid certain defeat he vowed to make "suitable use" of "my legs." He needed cavalry and he beseeched La Luzerne to use his "influence to get them for us." In his last letter before the French minister left Philadelphia to join Rochambeau and Washington in New York, Lafayette had advised that if his little army was "not annihilated," Virginia was "not conquered," and Greene was successful in the Carolinas, "the French and Americans arm in arm" could humble Britain's diplomats at the likely peace conference next year. That, he added, would mean an "America independent" with all thirteen states in the Union.[20]

When La Luzerne was greeted by the Allied generals north of Manhattan, he likely soon discovered that Washington preferred an attempt to take New York to a campaign in Virginia. In fact, just as the French army was setting out on its journey from Newport, Washington had written Rochambeau with a new proposal. Alter the course of your march and bring your army more rapidly, Washington had exhorted. Clinton had sent a large detachment to forage in New Jersey, Washington advised, adding that it had "so weakened their posts" at the northern end of Manhattan—Forts George, Knyphausen, and Tryon—that they were open to attack. Washington added that he was organizing a nighttime foray under General Lincoln that would bear a resemblance to Anthony Wayne's spectacular assault at Stony Point two years earlier. Lincoln would strike within seventy-two hours, on the night of July 2. If successful, Washington added, it "will be of the utmost consequence to our future operations."[21] Rochambeau complied, though he appears to have done so reluctantly. He abhorred night battles, thinking them too risky for all but specially trained units. Furthermore, even if the attacks were successful, Rochambeau knew that it would not guarantee success in reclaiming New York City, as all of Britain's network of interior defenses would yet need to be taken. Rochambeau may well have suspected that Washington was seeking to lock the Allies into the New York operation at the expense of going after Cornwallis in Virginia.[22]

French units earmarked for the operation set off on July 1, and the next day the Americans marched on their target from Peekskill. Washington emphasized that all depended "absolutely on secrecy and surprise." Neither was achieved. Lincoln had been advised that if his operation was detected, or if he failed to take all three forts, he was to withdraw immediately, "as we shall not be in a situation to support you." Lincoln did not take any of the forts and, after losing about one hundred men, retreated to safety. Washington was left to write Rochambeau, "I am sorry to say that I have not had the Happiness to succeed," though he claimed that having reconnoitered the enemy's positions and works, the operation would provide "very essential Benefit . . . to future operations" in the conquest of New York.[23]

Three days later, in the wilting heat of July 6, the last men in Rochambeau's army reached Dobbs Ferry, the principal rendezvous site, which occupied high ground on the east bank of the Hudson. The French soldiers had marveled at the countryside they passed through, mistakenly thinking Connecticut was the most fertile state in America and a bit surprised that its farms yielded nearly everything that was grown in France. One officer, who had traveled widely in his more than thirty years in the French army, gushed that Connecticut sported "some of the handsomest houses and best people" he had ever encountered. But as the army approached the Hudson, the French soldiers saw the unmistakable ravages of war. An artilleryman "felt very sad" for the Americans who had been subjected to "the horrors and cruelty of the English." He saw nothing but "burned woodlands, destroyed houses, and fallow fields deserted by the owners." Another of Rochambeau's soldiers spotted numerous "very handsome" homes that had been abandoned, leaving gardens and lawns overgrown with weeds that stood two feet tall. Once they reached Dobbs Ferry, the French soldiers tried to pitch their tents under leafy shade trees and near gurgling brooks, leading at least one to describe his camp as a "sylvan abode." Later, he recalled his six weeks' stay at this site as a time of "perfect happiness." Some officers frequently dined with their Allied counterparts. They enjoyed an abundance of food and were satisfied with its preparation, but some were put off that the "table was served in the American style." That is to say, salads, meats, vegetables, and desserts were "put upon the table at the same time" rather than in separate courses, and the diners were expected to eat the bounty "on the same plate."[24]

The French had hardly arrived before they passed in review before Washington. The next day the Americans paraded for Rochambeau. The reaction of the French to the Continentals ran the gamut. One thought they looked "rather good," while another was struck by their "destitution: the men were without uniforms and covered with rags; most of them were bare-foot." Several were surprised by the number of African American soldiers, who by now comprised roughly 5 percent of all American regulars and nearly three-quarters of Rhode Island's soldiery. The Black soldiers impressed a French officer as "merry confident, and sturdy." An aide to Rochambeau thought them "the most neatly dressed, the best . . . armed, and the most precise in . . . maneuvers" of all the American soldiers. One French soldier was troubled by the remarkably large aggregate of young boys and old men among the American regulars, and he wondered if they were up to the rigors of military service. However, another French officer admired "the American troops tremendously! It is incredible that soldiers composed of men of every age, even of children of fifteen, of whites and blacks, almost naked, unpaid, and rather poorly fed, can march so well."[25]

Days passed, and then weeks, without word from de Grasse. Was he coming? Was his destination the Chesapeake or New York? For the great bulk of the soldiery each day was business as usual, with most tending to customary camp duties. Many officers were left with time on their hands. Few used it as wisely as Alexander Hamilton, long an aide to Washington but since June 30 the commander of a New York light-infantry battalion. With nothing of "importance to occupy [his] attention," Hamilton drafted four long essays for a New York newspaper under the title "The Continentalist." His tracts assailed the new nation's decentralized govern-mental structure, an arrangement that thwarted the "general interest" of the United States. The "disorder" of "our whole system" threatens success in the war, he stressed. But it could be corrected if the states agreed to "ENLARGE

THE POWERS OF CONGRESS." Hamilton said nothing about Washington's generalship, which he had privately criticized, though he may have intended a swipe at the commander when he asserted that a mistake had been made through underestimating "how difficult it must be to exhaust the resources of a great nation . . . like that of Great Britain." [26]

If some found that time was heavy on their hands, Washington remained busy. He complained that his "load of business, and constant hurry" meant that he had "to husband time." With the exception of brief letters to his stepson and a brother, Washington's correspondence was confined to the business at hand. He penned letter after letter to governors, the Board of War, and Congress, and in most he pleaded for supplies. He met with visitors to camp, none of whom were more important than Robert Morris, the superintendent of finance. Washington and Morris huddled for three days discussing the army's needs in the coming campaign, whether in New York or Virginia. The topics they discussed included better means of conserving provisions, improving the storage and distribution of clothing, the location of supply depots around Manhattan and along the route to Virginia, and the details of moving ordnance by sea from Rhode Island to New York or Virginia. [27]

Throughout the summer, Washington was careful, too, to stay in touch with Lafayette. Fearful that any letter he wrote might fall into the wrong hands, Washington, on July 13, simply told Lafayette that he would soon "communicate matters of very great importance to you." He advised the young commander to ready his army for something big and to establish a "Chain of Expresses" between Virginia and Dobbs Ferry to expedite the flow of orders. Washington met frequently with his allies, and he and Rochambeau reconnoitered the area in the event that New York would in the end be their target. Sometimes patrolling British soldiers fired on the two commanders, on one occasion killing a bodyguard of Washington's. In another instance, recounted by Rochambeau, he and Washington "fell asleep, overcome with fatigue, at the foot of a hedge," and were awakened by "fire from guns on enemy vessels." They not only had overslept but had "forgotten the hour of the tide." They had to hurry, Rochambeau wrote, to the "mill dam on which we had crossed over the inlet that separated us from the mainland; we found it covered with water. Two small boats were brought up," and the commanders were rowed to safety.[28]

CLINTON, IN NEW York City, knew when the French army departed Rhode Island and when it arrived and joined forces with its ally. But during the next six weeks he did not move against the Allied armies. Some of his officers thought a successful attack by the army and a squadron of naval craft "would be productive of the best consequence," possibly even putting it "out of the power" of the Allied armies to launch a campaign that fall. At least one of those officers thought Clinton's hand was stayed because of his inability to obtain a large portion of Cornwallis's troops from Virginia. New York's Tories were beside themselves with fury at the commander's inertia. As rebel militia had not yet been summoned, they could not believe that Clinton did not strike the relatively small enemy force north of the city. Their anger only increased after August 11, the day Clinton's long-awaited reinforcements arrived, and he still did not move. One Loyalist, at his wit's end with such "shameful Inactivity," wrote officials in London championing Cornwallis's virtues and, if only by implication, passing along his stinging judgment of Clinton.[29]

Clinton was not about to emerge from his sturdy defensive emplacements, but he did consider taking action in August. Following the departure of Rochambeau's army for New York, Clinton spotted the opportunity for a joint naval and land assault on Barras's squadron in Newport and the handful of enemy troops with it. Intelligence reported that the small French fleet was "totally unprotected," as the army's heavy siege guns—which were to be shipped later to Rochambeau—had been removed to near Providence; furthermore, there were fewer than 1,500 French regulars and rebel militia in Newport. Clinton consulted officers who had been posted in Rhode Island under General Pigot in 1778 and earlier, seeking information on the best landing spot, knowledgeable pilots, and refugees who might be helpful. This opening was even more attractive than the opportunities that Clinton had considered the previous summer and fall, but it, too, slipped through his fingers. Admiral Thomas Graves, who had served under Arbuthnot and succeeded him at almost the same instant that Rochambeau's army began its march from Rhode Island, had sent most of his fleet to patrol off near Boston for an expected French convoy laden with supplies. Graves's fleet was gone for four weeks, during which time it never spotted the enemy ships. When the empty-handed royal vessels finally returned to Sandy Hook, Clinton pushed hard for a joint expedition against Newport. Graves consented, but would not move until four of his ships, including the massive seventy-four-gun *Royal Oak* (which had been sent to Halifax for repairs) were out of dry dock and serviceable. "[E]verything was got in readiness for the expedition," Clinton subsequently stated, but by the time Graves had "a sufficient force," de Grasse had arrived and the foray was out of the question.[30] Yet again, a golden opportunity in Rhode Island had been lost. In this instance, had Barras's fleet been destroyed, de Grasse would have been stripped of a substantial number of vessels that he was counting on, an outcome that might have profoundly altered the course of events in the coming weeks.

AT A JULY 19 conference with Rochambeau, Washington remained committed to a campaign to take New York, and as late as August 1 his diary entries demonstrate that he still expected to besiege Clinton army's on Manhattan. But his outlook was changing, not so much because he glimpsed the possibilities offered by shifting to Virginia, but because of the disappointing response of several northern states to his calls for troops and supplies. He was coming to conclude that he had "neither men, nor means adequate" for a protracted operation against the British in New York. To his mind, Massachusetts and Connecticut were the worst offenders. He railed that for the past sixty days John Hancock, the governor of Massachusetts, had not even answered his letter calling for a shipment of powder. They were hardly the only states that let him down. Recruiting had gone badly everywhere that year. Only about 50 percent of the quotas assigned the states had been met. Some states had sent scores of men, whereas they had been expected to send hundreds or thousands. As July wound down, a bitterly disappointed Washington admitted in private that he could "scarce see a ground upon wch to continue my preparations against New York." Years later, Washington sought to convince the public that all along he had favored going after Cornwallis in Virginia in preference to an offensive against Clinton in New York. That was not the case. Deep into that summer he clutched to his plan for attacking New York, though ultimately his troop shortages brought him around to the conclusion that Rochambeau had long championed: It was preferable "to strike the enemy in the most vulnerable quarter," and that was in Virginia.[31]

Because of the uncertainty regarding de Grasse's plans, the Allied armies had taken steps since early July to prepare for both a Virginia and a New York campaign, though they sought as much as possible to conceal their interest in Cornwallis. However, it was only when an air of inevitability developed about turning instead to Virginia that the Allied commanders set out in earnest to deceive Clinton into believing that he was about to be besieged. Pilots that were to guide the French fleet were made conspicuous in the hope of convincing the British that de Grasse's arrival at Sandy Hook was imminent. Dispatches revealing that "the militia are to be embodied," one of the last steps usually taken prior to a campaign, had a way of falling into enemy hands. Bread ovens, a routine accompaniment of a siege army, were constructed on the periphery of Manhattan, and boats were hurriedly brought in. Both were meant to be signs that the Allied armies had no intention of departing. Throughout the Allied armies' stay at Dobbs Ferry, Clinton received strikingly good information from his intelligence network. He knew that only minimal numbers of rebel militia had come to camp, that the Allies had neither siege guns nor cavalry, and that the enemy had moved some supplies to the west side of the Hudson. All appeared to be signs that Washington and Rochambeau were not planning an assault or siege of New York. But those tidbits could as easily mean that de Grasse's northward voyage had been delayed and that the Allies did not wish to summon the militia or ship the siege guns until it was absolutely necessary to do so. Furthermore, on August 17 intelligence reported that a few days earlier de

Grasse had written Rochambeau that he was sailing for the Chesapeake with his entire fleet. Clinton ran the report past Admiral Graves, who dismissed it as due to a "heated imagination." Clinton mulled it over before concurring. Clinton's struggle to sort the real from the fanciful in the daily intelligence reports was the age-old quandary that military commanders have always faced. He later said only that the enemy's machinations had not deceived him, although it was during the second week of the Allied campaign of deception that Clinton for the first time in a spell wrote Cornwallis about "embark[ing] the troops you can spare me for operation here." However, Clinton may not have been duped by the enemy so much as he was the victim of self-deception. His undoing may have sprung from his fixation on the notion that the Allied blow must inevitably fall on New York.[32]

In the meantime, the French and American armies planned their march to Virginia, and Washington, who could not ignore the defense of the Highlands above Manhattan during his absence, had to decide which units to take with him and which to leave behind. He named General William Heath, whom he had kept out of a combat role following disappointing performances in 1776, to command one artillery regiment, seventeen infantry regiments, and a handful of dragoons—altogether about 2,000 men—in the Highlands. Washington would take nearly 6,300 troops to Virginia. Rochambeau would have a bit more than half that number. By early August, the two commanders were prepared for a campaign in Virginia, if de Grasse indeed had sailed for the Chesapeake.[33]

Day after wickedly hot day passed in the first half of August without word of any kind from the French task force. Washington remained busy. As had been his practice throughout the war, he spent considerable time poring over the sentences handed down by courts-martial. Most involved desertion, and in every instance Washington approved the court's decisions that the culprits be flogged on the bare back. Two officers were cashiered, one a captain who had struck and kicked his major. Two men were sentenced to death, one for mutinous behavior, the other for desertion and reenlisting under a different name in order to scoop up a cash bounty. Washington pardoned the deserter, but the mutineer went to the gallows, one of some forty Continentals who were executed in this war. Other matters also occupied his time. He took steps to preserve the health of the army's horses, which soon would face the ardors of pulling heavy wagons and cumbersome artillery in a painfully long march. He sought tents for what might be a protracted siege. He alerted George Clinton, the governor of New York, to a suspected Tory kidnapping plot. Above all, Washington continued to call on the states to meet their manpower quotas lest "the Campaign will waste away as the last did in a fruitless attempt to get men."[34]

Toward mid-month Washington received a string of important letters from Lafayette. In July, the young general had written that thirty British transports had arrived at Hampton Roads "full of troops—Most of them Red Coats," but there were some German units. Lafayette initially thought they were reinforcements for Cornwallis. If so, he added, Cornwallis would possess the manpower to control everything south of the James River, and with those troops he could block all supply lines to Greene in South Carolina. But within hours, as the fleet took aboard throngs of liberated slaves who had escaped to freedom behind British lines, Lafayette wrote again to warn that portions of Cornwallis's army and the recently arrived troops must be about to sail to New York to augment Clinton's forces in defending the city. Within days, Lafayette wrote again to say that the vessels had sailed without Cornwallis's army. It had remained in Virginia. Drawing on his intelligence sources, Lafayette disclosed that Cornwallis's force totaled 4,600 men. He missed the mark by nearly 40 percent. In fact, Lafayette's communication was even more badly flawed than that, for when all the sailors attached to the Royal warships in and about Yorktown were counted, there were some 9,000 British servicemen available to Cornwallis. Lafayette's figures may have been off, but on one matter he was on target. On July 31 he wrote Washington: "Should a french fleet Now come in Hampton Road the British army would, I think, Be ours."[35]

Lafayette's missives contained mostly good news, but as they were trickling in to Washington's headquarters, the Allied generals faced an urgent problem. The French squadron under Admiral Barras remained in Newport.

Believing that reinforcements for Clinton were en route from Virginia, the generals wanted Barras in place on the approach to New York to capture the enemy convoy when it appeared. Rochambeau had to handle this matter, and in his communiqué he "strongly pointed out" to Barras the necessity of bringing his fleet immediately. But Barras refused to move until he heard from de Grasse and could sail to join him. Washington, who had been frustrated so often in this war, was not surprised, but he found it to be yet another exasperating disappointment. Rochambeau was no less displeased, and he told La Luzerne of his disgust. But to Washington, Rochambeau simply said: "you can't make these [naval] gentlemen do what they don't want to."[36]

August 13, the thirty-eighth day since the two armies had rendezvoused, passed much like the previous days. Washington issued orders addressing unsavory recruiting practices by some officers, wrote Congress concerning the mistreatment of American prisoners of war in Britain's custody, and dispatched two pilots down the New Jersey coast to provide help to de Grasse just in case he was actually sailing for New York.[37] Washington likely suspected the next day would bring more of the same. It did not.

On August 14, a clear and delightfully cool day, a courier arrived from Newport with the long-awaited news. De Grasse had written Rochambeau in late July that he would soon sail from Cap François (in today's Haiti) for the Chesapeake with twenty-eight ships of the line and 3,200 troops. Unaware that Rochambeau had marched to New York, de Grasse sent the communiqué to Newport. The all-important letter arrived on the eleventh and was opened by Barras, who wasted no time forwarding it to Rochambeau. Three days passed before it reached the Allied commanders. One might have expected Washington's diary to ring with exclamations of joy. But Washington, who was practiced in shielding his emotions from others, was no less restrained in the privacy of his journal. "Received dispatchs from the Count de Barras announcing the intended departure of the Count de Grasse . . . for Chesapeake bay," he wrote dryly. Washington's self-control also sprang from his awareness that de Grasse's fleet was yet at sea, at this juncture perhaps only halfway to its objective. Much could yet go wrong. Cornwallis might escape to the Carolinas. A British fleet might seal the entrance to the Chesapeake. A hurricane might play havoc with de Grasse's task force. Washington did mention in his diary that he had been "obliged . . . to give up all idea of attacking New York."[38] His aching passion to retake that city died hard.

An army could not be moved on the spur of the moment, especially when it involved thousands of men who faced a trek of some 450 miles. Considerable planning had already been undertaken, but now that the march to Virginia was official, a thousand and one last-minute details had to be ironed out. Five long, busy days passed before the men set off. During that time, Washington wrote de Grasse that the "whole of the French Army and as large a detachment of the American as can be spared" will "meet Your Excellency" in Virginia.[39] As a safeguard that his plans would not fall into Clinton's hands, Washington sent word of the coming march to Lafayette and Congress via express riders. The missive to Lafayette contained an order: "you will detain [Cornwallis's] troops untill you hear from me again."[40]

CHAPTER 14

THE TRAP SLAMS SHUT

ON AUGUST 19, FIVE days after Barras's courier brought word that Admiral de Grasse was sailing for the Chesapeake, the Allied armies set off for Virginia. With guidance from the Americans, the French planned the route of their march as carefully as they had charted their trek from Rhode Island a few weeks earlier. Washington needed no guidelines. He had first traveled some of these roads thirty years earlier while a young soldier in the French and Indian War, and as commander of the Continental army he had often led his men through this region. However, none of Washington's previous travels had been as systematically plotted. Army engineers and quartermasters had established magazines and campsites along the route, each designated for specific units.

The two armies did not get off to a good start. Not only did a want of horses slow the French, but on day one a terrific storm swept over the region, making already bad roads nearly impassable. Nevertheless, within twenty-four hours both armies had begun to cross the Hudson River. Six days passed before all the men in the two armies were across and on the move. They formed two columns a few miles apart to speed their march. Washington, concerned that the enemy might attempt to prevent their advance, had placed units composed of his most veteran soldiers nearest the

Hudson. Only the highest-ranking officers knew the destination of the armies, and that information remained a closely guarded secret for several days. As the van of the armies neared Staten Island and Sandy Hook—the latter, as Sir Henry Clinton knew, would be de Grasse's destination if he was sailing for New York—Washington erected a "dummy camp." Campfires were burned each evening, more bead ovens were assembled, and batteries and boats were constructed. So realistic was the deceit, said one Continental, that "our own army no less than the Enemy are completely deceived." To complete the ruse, false information (including bogus contracts for the acquisition of food that supposedly had been foraged) was permitted to fall into the hands of British spies. Everything possible was done with an eye toward forestalling the moment when Clinton, at last aware of the Allies' plans, would send word to Cornwallis of what was coming and ready a relief expedition to the Chesapeake.[1]

During the second day on the road, Washington wrote Lafayette to break the news that the armies were "in Motion" and "destined for the Southern Quarter." He ordered Lafayette to round up as many horses and wagons as possible and, of course, to take every possible step to see that Cornwallis "may not be able to escape you." Given his distance from Virginia, Washington said that he could not advise Lafayette on what steps to take to prevent Cornwallis's flight, but "I am perswaded your Military Genius & Judgment, will lead you to make the best" choices.[2]

On August 30, the armies passed over the Raritan and took much the same route that Clinton's army had traveled following the Battle of Monmouth three years earlier, save that the British had marched to New York City and the Allied soldiers were headed in the opposite direction. Washington was aware that from that moment onward the Allies' "intentions could [no longer] be concealed" from the enemy. Now, too, the men in the two armies deduced that they were headed somewhere on the other side of the Delaware River. If Washington worried about that—and given the fear among northerners about soldiering in the miasmic southern climate, he was indeed most anxious—his day was brightened by the receipt of exceedingly good news. Word arrived that the Royal Navy's squadron that had followed de Grasse from the Caribbean had landed at Sandy Hook and that it consisted of only fourteen ships of the line. When joined with the British warships already in North American waters, the British navy would be inferior to de Grasse's twenty-eight ship task force. A communiqué from Lafayette also arrived that day. The enemy had abandoned Portsmouth and their additional bases in that sector and had "Went Round to York[town]," he reported. Washington at last knew exactly where the hoped-for siege would take place, so long as Lafayette could foil any attempt by Cornwallis to escape.[3]

By September 2 the American army was across the Delaware River, though their ally lagged a bit behind. While the French were still crossing the river, Washington's army paraded to the accompaniment of drums and fife through the streets of Philadelphia in a two-mile-long procession. "The streets being extremely dirty, and the weather warm and dry," one soldier noted, "we raised a dust like a smothering snow-storm, blinding our eyes and covering our bodies with it." Two days later it was the turn of the French army. Their "brilliant appearance and exact discipline," a striking contrast to that of the Continentals, stirred the hearts of the large throng of Philadelphians who gathered for the parade. As a "complete band" played martial tunes, they marched in their white coats faced with green and "with flags flying and cannon at the head of each regiment." The members of Congress stood on the steps of what now is called Independence Hall waving joyously and removing their hats when the French flag passed. Earlier in the day, Thomas McKean of Delaware, the president of Congress, attired in a black velvet coat that struck one French soldier as "singular[ly]" fashionable, had asked Rochambeau if he should salute the French troops. The "King of France usually did," Rochambeau replied, which led McKean, in the words of one congressman, to conclude that he "might do likewise without demeaning himself."[4]

It was a joyous time for McKean, and not solely because of the mounting optimism regarding the coming military campaign in Virginia. On the very day the Continentals paraded through Philadelphia, John Laurens at long last arrived. He had sailed to France early in the year as Congress's representative to seek an urgently needed loan. The French, as desperate as their ally to successfully wind up this war, had been generous. About three-quarters of the booty provided by France had arrived early in the summer. Laurens, who had arrived in Boston while the Allied armies were crossing the Hudson, had made a mad dash to Philadelphia, bringing along transports loaded with 2.5 million livres in specie and the military supplies he had purchased in Paris. Yet while Congress was jubilant and Washington and his generals rejoiced, the arrival of the money stirred a hornet's nest. Word of France's bountiful gift inevitably seeped down to the soldiers, who had not been paid in ages. Before leaving Dobbs Ferry, Washington had appealed to Superintendent of Finance Robert Morris for a month's pay in specie for his soldiers. Over the next three weeks he appealed to Morris on two additional occasions, the last time just after the men had passed through Philadelphia. Washington advised Morris of the "great discontent" among the men but added that a "little hard money would put them in proper temper." In the end, the money brought home by Laurens was spent on other needs of the army, forcing an embarrassed Washington to ask Rochambeau to loan money to Congress. Rochambeau obliged, and Congress agreed that Washington, at the proper moment, could award the soldiers a month's pay in specie.[5]

The armies passed through Chester on September 5 and entered Wilmington, Delaware, the following day. That was where a dispatch rider with important news found Washington. De Grasse was in Chesapeake Bay and had landed his marines, who were to join forces with Lafayette in impounding the enemy in Yorktown. It was now a good bet that Cornwallis could neither escape by land nor be rescued by sea. Washington was exuberant. For the first time since Saratoga and news of the French alliance there was light at the end of what had been a very long tunnel. He wanted to personally break the news to Rochambeau, who had chosen to abandon his horse and sail down the lower Delaware River. When the French commander's vessel was sighted, an exuberant Washington stood on the shore "waving his hat and white handkerchief joyfully." As Rochambeau came ashore, Washington abandoned his legendary formal demeanor and with uncharacteristic warmth and intimacy hugged his fellow commander. With "deep satisfaction," Washington passed along the happy tidings. Rochambeau probably told Washington what he told France's minister of war: "If M. de Grasse is or makes himself master of the Bay, we hope to do some good work."[6]

What was supposed to be the final leg of the march was a twenty-mile tramp to Head of Elk at the top of Chesapeake Bay, the very site where General William Howe's army had disembarked during its 1777 campaign to seize Philadelphia. In 1781, this was to be the embarkation point for the Allied armies, as the men were to sail the remainder of the way. Weeks earlier, Washington had sent out orders and pleas for boats for just this occasion, though he had stressed that the vessels must not appear until just prior to the arrival of the Allied armies, lest Loyalist spies inform Clinton that Cornwallis was the enemy's "next object." General Antoine-Jean-Louis LeBègue de Presele Duportail, one of four French engineers recruited by Benjamin Franklin and Silas Deane in 1777, had become Washington's chief engineer and had overseen the shipment of horses, oxen, flour, cured meat, rum, and boats to the top of the Chesapeake.

Boats were present when the armies arrived, but too few for all the men and equipment. With de Grasse expected to remain for only a brief time, and no guarantee that Lafayette's force could contain Cornwallis forever, the delay caused by the shortage of boats was a potentially fatal problem. Eighty vessels were available, chiefly those used by Chesapeake oystermen. Washington issued orders to "combat load" the boats—that is, to see that the paraphernalia needed for land operations be given first priority. That left boats for only one-third of the soldiery. Improvisation was necessary. Designated units boarded vessels and departed. Additional marching faced those for whom there was no room. These "Very much annoyed" men, in the words of a French officer, set off on foot, some for Baltimore, some for Annapolis, where they would search for any sort of craft that could deliver them to the peninsula between the York and James Rivers in Virginia. It was decided, too, that all of the French army's horses, wagons, and baggage would make the passage from the top of the bay to the James River entirely by land. Those who made the overland journey may have been the lucky ones. Bad weather and contrary winds turned the lengthy voyage down the Chesapeake into a nightmare for those in the smallest crafts. Most of those vessels were stocked with limited quantities of biscuits and cheese, forcing the soldiers to put ashore time and again in search of food, some of which was procured—as a French soldier put it—"not with money, but with musket shots." Because of the frequent stops, the Chesapeake transit turned into an interminable, deprivation-filled trip for many. On average, it took the sailors about eighteen days to reach the peninsula, pretty much the same amount of time required for those on foot, who, according to one French soldier, completed the journey "without having suffered any inconvenience."[7]

While planning was underway concerning how to get the armies from Head of Elk to the vicinity of Yorktown, Washington for the first time notified his men of the arrival of de Grasse's task force, and he accompanied his announcement with a warning and a supplication:

> As no circumstance cou'd possibly have happened more opportunely in point of time, no prospect cou'd ever have promised more important success, and nothing but our want of exertions can probably blast the pleasing prospects before us. The General calls upon all the gallant Officers, the brave and faithful soldiers he has the honor to command to exert their utmost abilities in the cause of their Country and to share with him (and with their usual alacrity) the difficulties, dangers and glory of the present Enterprize.

With his men about to plunge into the South, it was at this moment that Washington chose to promise his soldiers that the award of one month's pay in specie was imminent.[8]

Washington had not been home since the day he departed in May 1775 to take his seat in the Second Continental Congress, a journey that he made just a couple of weeks after the war's first engagements in Lexington and Concord and a month prior to his appointment as commander of the

Continental army. Now that he was not far from Mount Vernon and the armies were two weeks or more from reaching Yorktown, he opted to make a hurried side trip to his estate. He had done all that he could do to shepherd his army to Virginia. All that "now gives me uneasiness," he remarked, was that no word had arrived from Admiral de Barras, but he could do nothing about that. Aching to see his plantation, Washington set off for Mount Vernon accompanied by Rochambeau and the Marquis de Chastellux, one of the three major-generals who came with the *Expédition Particulière*, their staffs and his own. Wishing to squeeze in every possible minute at home, Washington made the 120-mile journey on horseback in two days of hard riding. He and his guests spent four days at the estate. A New Englander on Washington's staff thought Mount Vernon "an elegant seat and situation," was bowled over by the "opulence" surrounding him, and gushed at the "princely entertainment" lavished on the guests. Chastellux was awed by the "magnificent" location of the estate, but said nothing of the mansion, though he noted that Martha Washington was a "chubby woman of about forty or forty-five" who struck him as resembling "a German princess." While not inspecting his farm or tending to his guests, Washington sent off several communiqués to his officers, including one to Lafayette. "We are . . . on our way to you," he wrote, adding in a postscript: "I hope you will keep Lord Cornwallis safe, without Provisions or Forage untill we arrive. Adieu."[9]

ALTHOUGH SIR HENRY Clinton was aware of every step taken by the Allied armies beginning with their departure from Dobbs Ferry on August 19, he did not know exactly what to make of it. The next day one of his staff officers, probably reflecting the commander's puzzlement, despaired that "No certain judgment can yet be formed of their intentions." Later, Clinton said that initially, though only briefly, he thought Washington was merely sending reinforcements to Lafayette in Virginia. He jettisoned that notion when he learned that both Allied armies were on the march. Nine days after the enemy armies departed Dobbs Ferry, and three days before they crossed the Raritan, Clinton wrote Cornwallis that he could not "well ascertain Mr. Washington's real intentions." He rushed detachments to Staten Island, a step that indicated he likely continued to believe that the enemy planned to attack New York.[10]

No hint of desperation shines through in Clinton's correspondence at this juncture. He continued to believe that the Royal Navy would remain sovereign in North American waters. Like the Admiralty in London and the naval officers surrounding him in New York, Clinton did not think de Grasse would be so reckless as to bring his entire fleet to North America, for to do so would leave France's sugar islands unprotected. Furthermore, English officials advised Clinton that they did not believe de Grasse would have the means of bringing all his warships to the American mainland, as some would be needed in the annual convoy that carried home the produce of the French islands and others would inevitably be laid up for repairs. In fact, during August the brigantine *Swallow* arrived in New York from the Caribbean with seemingly convincing information that "the greatest part of [de Grasse's] line of battle ships would go to Europe with" the convoy, tidings that appeared to confirm Clinton's belief that the Allies could not achieve the naval superiority necessary for taking New York or to fatally threaten Cornwallis.[11]

During the spring, London had notified Sir George Rodney, commander of the Leeward Islands Squadron, that a French task force under de Grasse had sailed from Brest for the West Indies on March 22, though at that juncture London estimated that the enemy fleet totaled only about fourteen ships of the line. The Admiralty directed Rodney to attempt to intercept the French task force. Failing that, it was hoped that during the summer Rodney might contest de Grasse's fleet and, at the very least, damage it and reduce its potency prior to its expected voyage to mainland America. When de Grasse did sail north, Rodney was ordered to follow him and join with the navy in North America. The Admiralty looked on Rodney as its most talented admiral. His record throughout his lengthy naval career had been distinguished, and since taking command in the Caribbean in 1779, his performance had been illustrious. In a span of two years, he had seized or demolished sixteen enemy warships, killed or taken captive three enemy admirals, foiled a French attempt to take Barbados, and won control of St. Eustatius. Although during the summer London became aware that the French squadron was considerably larger than it had originally thought, it remained confident that Rodney, together with the navy in North America, could thwart whatever threat de Grasse posed.[12]

Clinton, in New York, had received more or less the same intelligence about de Grasse that London had passed on to Rodney during the spring and summer. Although Clinton had an inkling that the British fleet in the Caribbean was overextended, he and the naval officers in New York never wavered in their belief that the Royal Navy would remain supreme following de Grasse's arrival. Rodney had assured them that he would set off the moment that de Grasse weighed anchor to sail for North America. "[T]hey cannot move but I will be at them," Rodney had declared. De Grasse would, of course, join with de Barras's fleet, but as the French naval force in Rhode Island had only a single-vessel superiority over the Royal Navy in or near New York, Clinton continued to believe that the Royal Navy would remain numerically superior. Late in July, Clinton had been informed that de Grasse had sailed from the West Indies and a British fleet was in pursuit. He did not panic. Indeed, he continued to think that following the coming show-down, the Revolutionary War would end "most gloriously" for Great Britain.[13]

Clinton was a veteran officer who knew that wars were filled with surprises. He knew, too, that the most reasoned assumptions concerning the enemy's plans might be incorrect. What if de Grasse brought a larger-than-anticipated fleet? What if his destination was the Chesapeake? What would that mean for Cornwallis? On three occasions that summer Clinton sent warnings to Cornwallis that de Grasse would be sailing for the American mainland. He additionally advised Cornwallis to prepare his defenses, admonitions to assure that Cornwallis's army remained safe against Lafayette and Virginia's militiamen, as well as de Grasse. However, Clinton did not think Cornwallis would be in mortal danger even if de Grasse came to the Chesapeake. Britain's navy, he remained convinced, would possess the strength to keep the Chesapeake open, facilitating the flow of supplies to Yorktown or even Cornwallis's rescue by sea. In addition, Clinton believed that Cornwallis had stockpiled provisions for ten thousand men, sufficient to see him through into November, and that de Grasse would remain in North America for only a brief time, and certainly not deep into the autumn. If, in a worst-case scenario, de Grasse gained superiority in the Chesapeake and Cornwallis was besieged by Allied armies, Clinton was confident that the British army in Yorktown could hold out until the French fleet departed and relief arrived from New York.[14]

When the Leeward Islands Squadron that was supposedly following de Grasse arrived at Sandy Hook, it was not commanded by Rodney, who was ill with a host of maladies and had sailed for home, but by Admiral Sir Samuel Hood. Rodney had neither intercepted de Grasse back in the spring nor expended much energy thereafter looking for him. For three months during that critical spring and summer, Rodney's fleet never left St. Eustatius, as its commander occupied his time in plundering and overseeing preparations for transporting his booty to England. Early in July, Rodney had informed New York that de Grasse would sail for the mainland with only about half his fleet, underscoring what London had been saying all along. But on the last day of July, Rodney discovered that de Grasse was in fact bringing his entire fleet of twenty-eight ships of the line to the mainland and that he was accompanied by Virginia pilots. Rodney knew that the French task force was almost certainly bound for the Chesapeake. However, for reasons that are unfathomable, Rodney waited eleven days before he passed on this crucial information to New York. Had he acted instantly, Clinton and the naval officers in New York might have discovered the size of de Grasse's fleet and its destination in mid-August, even before Barras's messenger brought Rochambeau and Washington word that the French task force was sailing for the Chesapeake. Armed with that information, Clinton might have taken steps to rescue Cornwallis, to order him to take flight for South Carolina, or to have the British navy in New York seal the Hudson River before the Allied armies could make a crossing and begin their descent to Virginia. But Rodney, whether from illness or enervation, had not quickly sent the precious information that he possessed to New York. In fact, he had not even informed Admiral Hood of the size of the French fleet bound for North America.

Rodney left for England on August 1. Hood, his successor, who had been made aware that de Grasse's fleet had gone to Cap François, from which it would sail for mainland America, did not depart for North America until eleven days later. Clinton had long since made clear that he hoped Britain's Caribbean fleet would arrive prior to the appearance of the enemy task force. As early as June, he had appealed to Rodney to come quickly, as de Grasse's arrival "in great force" was expected sometime in July or August. It would be late August before the Leeward Islands Squadron finally arrived.

When Hood sailed, he was unaware of de Grasse's whereabouts, his destination, or the size of his fleet. Hood sailed with fourteen ships of the line, the most he could scrape together. Rodney had kept two heavy warships for shepherding the loot taken on St. Eustatius back to England. Furthermore, rather than ordering Commodore Sir Peter Parker, the commander of the Jamaica squadron, to provide warships to Hood, Rodney had merely asked him to furnish whatever he could spare. Parker decided that he could not relinquish a single ship of the line.[15]

Hood subsequently told Clinton and the naval officials in New York that he had arrived off Cape Henry, at the entrance to Chesapeake Bay, on August 25 and scouted the area. He said that he had spotted no sign of the enemy fleet. Hood added that he had made contact with some light British vessels in the bay, and they had not seen any French ships. He reached the logical and, as it turned out, the correct conclusion that de Grasse's fleet was not in the Chesapeake. Logbooks from Hood's fleet suggest that he had not gone to the Chesapeake but had sailed directly for New York. Some naval officials later doubted Hood's claim of having searched the Chesapeake, and modern scholarship suggests that Sir Samuel lied to the officials in New York. If so, his prevarication hardly mattered, for even had Hood scoured the Chesapeake, he would not have found the French fleet. It did not arrive in the Chesapeake until after the Leeward Islands Squadron reached New York.[16]

Hood docked at Sandy Hook on August 28, two days before Washington's army crossed the Raritan, the unmistakable sign that it was marching for Virginia. When Hood disclosed that the French fleet was not in the Chesapeake, Clinton and the naval officials in Manhattan—who still had not received Rodney's message of paramount importance concerning the size of the French fleet or its intended target—were more than ever convinced that New York was de Grasse's destination. They guessed that the French task force had sailed for Newport in order to first rendezvous with Barras. Later that same day word arrived that Barras's fleet had sailed three days earlier from Rhode Island for an unknown destination. Britain's high command surmised that Barras's squadron planned to link up somewhere, sometime, with de Grasse's fleet, but they could only guess at the rendezvous site or the combined fleet's eventual destination. As the Allied armies at that moment were still near Staten Island, Clinton for another thirty-six hours or so continued to believe that the long-anticipated attack on New York was imminent.

The moment that Hood arrived at Sandy Hook he relinquished command of the fleet to his superior, Admiral Thomas Graves, since midsummer the successor of Admiral Arbuthnot. Graves was nearly universally respected as efficient and capable, though he had never commanded in battle. He sprang into action with eagerness for the test he faced. Graves readied his fleet, adding his five serviceable vessels to the fourteen that Hood had brought north, and on August 31, when the weather at last permitted, the nineteen British ships of war set off in search Barras's fleet of eight heavy warships and the flotilla of unknown size under de Grasse. Graves was supremely confident. The last word from Rodney that had reached New York was that de Grasse was bringing only twelve to fourteen heavy warships northward. Even if Graves's flotilla encountered a French force of twenty heavy warships, he expected to be "equal fully to defeat any designs of the enemy."[17]

In reality, de Grasse's fleet consisted of twenty-eight ships of the line and five frigates, together with fifteen transports loaded with 3,300 troops. Clinton and Britain's admirals were in the dark on this score. Furthermore, as September dawned they did not know that de Grasse had sailed into

Chesapeake Bay on August 30, five days after Hood had purportedly searched the area around Cape Henry and the day before Graves's squadron had sailed from New York into the Atlantic in quest of the two enemy fleets. At the sight of the French task force, the small British squadron in the bay scurried for safety, some among them hastening toward Yorktown in hopes of finding a safe berth up the York River. De Grasse also hurriedly swung into action. Within twenty-four hours he dispatched one of his ships of the line and two frigates as protection for the transports that conveyed troops to the James River to join with Lafayette's little army. He also sent three ships of the line and another frigate to the York River to block any attempt that Cornwallis might make to escape the Chesapeake. De Grasse's fleet that would soon go to battle for supremacy in the Chesapeake now consisted of twenty-four ships of the line and two frigates.[18]

Sometime after sunrise on the morning of August 31, Cornwallis—whose last communiqué from Clinton with regard to de Grasse had confidently predicted that there was little "probability of the enemy's having a naval superiority in these seas"—received word that French vessels "lie at the mouth" of the York River. Later in the day, Cornwallis got more bad news, which he hurriedly dispatched to Clinton. The Chesapeake teemed with upwards of forty French vessels, "mostly ships of war, and some them very large," though he was unaware of the number of French ships of the line. Cornwallis, who had seldom bothered to write Clinton throughout the first several months of this critical year, flooded the commander with four letters in five days, each redolent with foreboding. The first of these communiqués was penned on the day that Graves and Hood sailed from New York in search of Barras. The last, drafted on September 4, broke the news that enemy troops had disembarked from transports along the James River. (It was a landing that prompted a nearby Pennsylvania soldier to gush, "Never did I behold a more beautiful and agreeable sight." It "spread an universal joy" among the American servicemen, he added.)[19]

Six days passed before the first of Cornwallis's frantic letters reached British headquarters in New York. By then Clinton had long since discovered Allied intentions, although Cornwallis's communiqués brought the first word of the arrival of the French fleet in the Chesapeake. Clinton learned, too, that de Grasse had brought a large fleet to mainland America, but he remained unaware of its exact size.

Although shaken by the realization that the Allies had Cornwallis's army in their sights, Clinton was still confident. Graves and Hood—who had sailed from New York a week earlier and had not been in touch with Clinton since—had on their departure expressed their "fullest confidence" that the Royal Navy would at least equal the united forces of de Grasse and Barras. Furthermore, Clinton persisted in the hope that Britain's admirals could catch and demolish some or all of Barras's fleet before it joined with de Grasse's. Clinton was buoyed, too, by a letter that Cornwallis had dispatched during the third week in August. Cornwallis had reported that Yorktown and Gloucester "would be in a tolerable state of defense" in six weeks, that is by around October 1, which Clinton correctly believed would be the earliest that the Allies could commence siege operations. Furthermore, Clinton was somewhat assured by a note that Germain had sent him two months earlier. Rear-Admiral Richard Digby was sailing with three ships of the line to join the Leeward Islands Squadron, news that appeared to assure that the Royal Navy would be superior to anything the French could put up against it.[20]

Historians have severely criticized Clinton's supposed indecision during the thirteen days between the time the Allied armies began crossing the Hudson and the telltale Allied crossing of the Raritan. According to one, Clinton's "procrastination" in sending relief to Cornwallis was "one of the foremost blunders of the war."[21] The absence of rebel militia and siege guns was perhaps the most compelling evidence during those two weeks that the Allies might not be planning to attack New York, but that neither had been brought to Dobbs Ferry was not proof of the enemy's intentions. Clinton was aware that the siege guns would have to be delivered by Barras from Rhode Island, and it was not until the very eve of Washington's crossing of the Raritan that he learned that Barras had sailed. Even then, Clinton had no idea of that squadron's destination. Furthermore, as the campaign for New York was expected to be a protracted affair and militiamen served for relatively brief periods—as Rochambeau had repeatedly reminded Washington—it was logical that the citizen soldiers would not be summoned to duty until the very last moment, in all likelihood only after de Grasse arrived, and of course by early September he was nowhere to be seen. Given Hood's report that de Grasse had sailed a week or more prior to his departure but was not in the Chesapeake, Clinton until September 2 held to the logical conclusion that the French fleet was bound for New York. Finally, the Allies had taken pains to trick Clinton into believing that the blow was coming in New York, and to some extent their trickery worked. Lacking the information available to historians, Clinton had to contemplate mountains of data, some of which he concluded was reliable and some was unreliable. The task before him was to sort through the myriad shards and attempt to reach the correct conclusion. The decision he reached was incorrect. Clinton failed, but his failing in this pivotal moment was not one of indecision. Had Rodney expeditiously dispatched what he knew to be the true size of de Grasse's fleet and its almost certain destination, or had a bevy of British officials not discounted the likelihood that the entire French task force would sail for North America, Clinton might have responded differently. Not for the first time, or the last time, a military commander reached an errant conclusion as a result of incomplete and incorrect information.

CLINTON RECEIVED THE first of Cornwallis's frenzied communications on September 5. It arrived in New York on the day before Washington learned of de Grasse's arrival. At last, Clinton had been made aware that an enemy fleet was in Chesapeake Bay. He quickly convened a council of war, the first of several that would meet in coming days and weeks. The British generals unanimously approved sending a four-thousand-man relief expedition to Yorktown, and Clinton ordered it to be readied. The feverish, days-long work of loading men and provisions commenced at once. At the same moment, Clinton wrote Cornwallis that the expedition would sail "the instant I receive information from the Admiral that we may venture." Twenty-four hours later, Clinton wrote Germain of the "very alarming" developments that might mean Britain's military situation was "coming fast to a crisis." In a letter with overtones of the construction of his defense should things come to a bad end for Great Britain, Clinton added that "your lordship may be assured that with what I have, inadequate as it is, I will exert myself to the utmost to relieve Lord Cornwallis."[22]

The only other action launched by Clinton during that first week of September was a previously planned raid that targeted a fleet of privateers and merchant vessels in New London, Connecticut. A Loyalist force of 1,700 men under Benedict Arnold descended on the New England town and totally destroyed it, razing some 150 homes.[23] In the days that followed, an anxious Clinton waited impatiently for word from the flag officers near the Chesapeake. He presumed that the Royal fleet and de Grasse's squadron of unknown size would clash off the coast of Virginia, a battle that would determine superiority in Chesapeake Bay and whether or not a relief force could reach Yorktown. Until then, Clinton—and the thousands of men squeezing aboard the steamy transports that would someday presumably be bound for Virginia—marked time.

Meanwhile, Graves's North Atlantic Squadron, which had sailed on August 31 in search of the fleets under Barras and de Grasse had come up empty-handed. It had eventually turned and sailed south, and on September 5—the day that Clinton convened his initial council of war—it approached Lynnhaven Bay at the mouth of the Chesapeake. Through the haze at nine-thirty that morning, the lookout on HMS *Solebay* caught sight of more than twenty sails at the entrance to the bay. Graves had at last found de Grasse. In a matter of hours, he counted twenty-four ships of the line in the enemy squadron. Graves had nineteen ships of the line. The British were outnumbered. The unthinkable had occurred. But Graves was prepared to fight. His copper-bottomed ships were faster than the bulk of the French vessels, and he possessed two ninety-gun ships of the line, whereas de Grasse had but one. Though Graves was unaware of it, his ships were also better manned than those of his adversary, for nearly five hundred of de Grasse's crewmen were elsewhere, engaged in transporting to the James River the troops that were to rendezvous with Lafayette's force.

De Grasse, who was oblivious to the British squadron before it faced him, made the first move. He was intent on getting out to sea, where he could fight a traditional naval battle unhindered by the nearby coastal land of Lynnhaven Bay. Rushing to complete his task, de Grasse's ships were in no discernible order and at their most vulnerable. Some later thought that had Graves struck at that moment he might have gained victory, but Graves had not sailed from New York in battle order and he too faced the necessity of aligning his squadron. It was a time-consuming task. Vessels that were a considerable distance apart could be alerted only through a system of signals, and on occasion alterations in the alignment were necessary because of changes in wind patterns. De Grasse succeeded in rounding Cape Henry and forming his battle line. Finally, well past 4:00 P.M., nearly six hours after the rival fleets had sighted each other, the Battle of the Chesapeake, called by some the Battle of the Virginia Capes, began.

The clash that followed has been described as the most important naval engagement of the eighteenth century, though some historians have argued that it was an unnecessary battle, insisting that de Grasse need not have fought. Given his vast superiority in numbers, they reasoned that de Grasse had only to take a defensive position in the Chesapeake in order to foil Graves's hope of reopening the bay.[24] However, de Grasse was in the dark as to the whereabouts of the Allied armies. He knew they planned to come south, but there was a chance that the British had prevented their descent. Nor could de Grasse predict what the weather would be in coming days. It was good at the moment, but this was hurricane season. In fact, it was around this time in 1778 that Comte d'Estaing's fleet had been badly damaged by the monstrous storm that struck Newport. If something akin to that happened in the late summer of 1781, de Grasse's numerical superiority might disappear in a flash. Furthermore, de Grasse was a fighter. He had come to fight, and out beyond Cape Henry he fought his battle.

The contest lasted roughly two hours, and it began with confusion rife on Britain's side due to a mix-up in the signals displayed by Graves. Graves inexplicably ran up contradictory signal flags. Moreover, the van in de Grasse's battle line was more than a mile ahead of several of his ships, and the distance increased throughout the battle given shifts in the wind direction. The result was that the advance vessels on both sides were very much in the brawl, but the ships in midline fired mostly ineffectually because of their great distance from the target; those in the rear were so far away from their foe that they were never fully engaged. The rival vans suffered extensive, and more or less equal, damage. The British lost some 350 men, de Grasse around 400, and several ships on both sides sustained extensive damage. As nightfall approached, Graves correctly concluded that the battle was shifting in favor of the French, and he hoisted the "discontinue the engagement" signal flag. The crucial battle was over, and de Grasse still controlled access to Chesapeake Bay.

Over the next four days Graves sought to patch up his battered vessels, battled adverse weather (which caused additional harm to a couple of his most heavily damaged ships), and on several occasions held councils of war, each intense and brooding. Five days after the fight, Graves learned that Barras's squadron had at last arrived. It included eight ships of the line, four frigates, and six transports packed with siege guns and supplies. Moreover, Barras was accompanied by eight American vessels loaded mostly with food. De Grasse's squadron now enjoyed an even greater superiority.[25] Graves, bombarded by contradictory advice, was frozen with indecision for three additional days. On September 13, having reached the indisputable conclusion that the French were "absolute masters of . . . navigation" in Chesapeake Bay," he began his voyage back to New York. Barring a providential intervention in the form of a hurricane, Cornwallis's army was not going to escape by sea during the next several weeks, if ever.[26]

Within hours of learning that enemy vessels were at the foot of the York River, Cornwallis had become aware that a formidable—possibly indomitable—French task force was in Chesapeake Bay. If he was going to try to fight his way out, August 31 was the day he should have begun his preparations for taking flight. But Cornwallis did not attempt to escape, and he was subsequently criticized for it by both historians and Clinton, who later said that the army in Yorktown should have darted for safety within twelve hours of discovering that the French had arrived.[27] Historians who agree with Clinton's assessment have pointed to Cornwallis's nearly three-to-one numerical advantage over Lafayette's small army. Their argument is that Cornwallis could have punched through the rebel force, possibly even demolishing it, before marching back to South Carolina "to destroy Greene's Continentals" and deal with partisans. It has even been contended that once Greene was defeated, Cornwallis might have marched back to the Chesapeake to take part in a giant British pincer movement. With Clinton coming south to assail the Allies from one side, and Cornwallis coming north to attack the armies of Washington and Rochambeau from the other side, the British army might have inflicted a mortal blow on its enemy.[28]

It is a rosy picture. But given what Cornwallis knew and did not know during the initial hours after becoming aware of the French presence, and mindful of the obstacles he would face in seeking to escape, his decision to stay put was judicious. Clinton, who was supposedly better informed about such matters, had repeatedly assured Cornwallis throughout the spring and summer that the Royal Navy would maintain its superiority. On August 31, the day that he discovered French vessels near Yorktown, and for at least a week thereafter, Cornwallis was unaware of the actual size of the French task force. Within thirty-six hours of learning that an enemy fleet had arrived in the Chesapeake, Cornwallis was informed that a sizable number of French troops had begun landing on the nearby James River. In a flash he knew the French were there to join with Lafayette's army, a step that would bring the Allied armies closer in size to his own and significantly compound his difficulties should he seek to escape. He also had to assume that in a very short time the enemy force, when augmented by Virginia militiamen, would have superior numbers, though as a knowledgeable professional soldier Cornwallis surely believed that Lafayette's army would be incapable of mounting a successful siege or of breaking through the defensive system he had constructed during the past month. Hence, for several fateful days in early September, Cornwallis not only believed that his army was safe, but he expected Britain's navy to soon regain control of the Chesapeake.[29]

Attempting a breakout was Cornwallis's only other option, and as a professional soldier, and an aggressive one at that, he surely contemplated it. He would have been aware of the mountainous obstacles that stood between him and a successful getaway. An army cannot instantaneously launch a march. The men who were away foraging would have to return, the soldiers across the river in Gloucester would have to link up with those in Yorktown, and wagons would have had to be loaded with provisions, munitions, and the ill and infirm; the artillery that had been erected in defensive lines would also have had to be made mobile once again. By the time the army was ready to move out, it would have had to fight its way through the combined, and potent, Franco-American force under Lafayette. Moreover, while the British had been constructing their fortifications, Lafayette had been doing the same. The young Frenchman hardly exaggerated on September 8 when he wrote Washington that should "Lord Cornwallis come out against such a position as we have, every body thinks that he cannot but repent of it." Cornwallis was aware of the steps that Lafayette had taken and also would have known that even if he somehow succeeded in breaking through the enemy's defenses, his army—which would be bloodied in the fight, leaving him encumbered with wounded—would face a lengthy trek through the unwelcoming Virginia and Carolina backcountry. Food would be in short supply, and he would almost certainly lack sufficient boats for getting across the numerous rivers that would have to be crossed. If Lafayette and his allies pursued the fleeing British—as the earl had chased Morgan and Greene—Cornwallis's army would be especially vulnerable.[30] Cornwallis faced puzzling choices, but given the information at his fingertips in the first days of September, he made a thoughtful and sensible decision. To make a bolt for freedom was to risk the loss of his entire army. By staying put, Cornwallis believed the odds were good that his army could survive the enemy threat.

On September 12, Clinton wrote Lord Germain that the only way to rescue Cornwallis "is by going to him," that is to send a large relief force to Virginia. But if the French controlled the Chesapeake, the relief force would face "certain destruction." He would await word from Graves before doing anything, he advised the American secretary. The very next day Clinton received the bad news regarding the outcome of the Battle of the Virginia

Capes. He immediately convened a council of war. Some officers urged the immediate dispatch of the troop convoy that for the past week had been awaiting orders to sail. However, a majority, including Clinton, thought such a step impractical. Only one ship of the line was available to accompany the convoy. There was a danger that all four thousand men in the relief expedition might be lost. Furthermore, if these men somehow miraculously reached Yorktown and were stuck there for any length of time, Cornwallis would have even more mouths to feed, reducing the number of days that he could hold out. Confident that Cornwallis "had provisions to last him to the end of October," forty-nine days away, the generals agreed to the "less hazardous" option of awaiting the arrival of Admiral Digby. He was known to be coming with at least three ships of the line, but his squadron might be larger if he had succeeded in rounding up additional vessels in the West Indies. In that event, the suddenly enlarged Royal Navy might yet have the means of reestablishing British control of the Chesapeake.[31]

Overnight, James Robertson, the royal governor of New York who was also a lieutenant general in the British army and had attended the gloomy council of war, grew ever more apprehensive. The next morning, he wrote Clinton expressing his misgivings with the decision. All was lost if Cornwallis was compelled to surrender, he warned. "[W]e give up the game if we do not try to risk" sending a relief expedition, dangerous as that course might be. Clinton responded by calling another council of war, this time telling the generals that he was willing to increase the size of the relief expedition to six thousand men should it be decided to hazard such a mission as proposed by Robertson. The governor pressed his case with "Earnestness and all of his Abilities"—which Clinton later characterized as "great"—but once again the council voted to do nothing until Digby arrived.[32]

Only three days elapsed before Clinton summoned another council of war, this one brought on by word from Graves that the French had completely sealed the entrance to the Chesapeake and could not be dislodged. The French stranglehold was so great, Graves had added, that relief ships could not even reach the York River under cover of darkness. The generals learned that Cornwallis's army could not sustain itself through foraging, but yet again they voted that it would be "highly improper" under current conditions to risk sending a relief expedition. The generals convened again two days later and discussed a diversion up the Delaware River to destroy stores around Philadelphia, once Clinton's favorite notion. However, he now thought it "a chimerical project," as no "diversion will induce Mr Washington to stir a man from the object before him." The generals sided with their commander and voted to do nothing. Clinton received more bad news on September 23 when a communiqué sent seven days earlier by Cornwallis somehow got through to New York. Cornwallis broke the news that Barras had joined de Grasse's fleet. "They have 26 sail of the line," Cornwallis reported, considerably underestimating the number of heavy warships in the enemy squadron. To that, Cornwallis added: "This place is in no state of defence. If you cannot relieve me very soon, you must be prepared to hear the worst." Clinton called together his generals that same day and, as always, crisply outlined the issues before them. The generals understood the urgency of the moment. Unless Cornwallis received "the most speedy assistance," his army would be lost and the British war effort would suffer "the most fatal consequences." The time had come to undertake a "great risk" in order to save the force trapped at Yorktown.[33]

The generals were ready to act. The decision now rested with the navy. Additional councils of war convened on September 24 and 26. Now that the fleet had returned to New York from the Chesapeake, the three flag officers—Graves, Hood, and Drake—for the first time that month met with the army's general officers. Digby who all month had been "hourly expected," at last arrived just after the initial meeting. The hope that he would bring several large warships was dashed once lookouts spotted his sails on the horizon. Just as Germain had divulged back in July, Digby's little squadron consisted of only three ships of war. When the officers, including Digby, gathered for the second conclave, they knew that de Grasse possessed overwhelming superiority of numbers and that by taking up a defensive position his fleet would almost surely be indomitable. Clinton would subsequently maintain that he believed de Grasse might have been defeated had the Royal Navy confronted him in a second engagement. At the time, however, he merely told Germain that so long as the French maintained their numerical superiority, "I shall despair of being able by any means to relieve [Cornwallis's] army." The best that Clinton and the other officers appear to have hoped for was that with luck the tides might impede the enemy fleet, enabling Britain's vessels to run past them and reach the York with men and provisions.[34]

All understood, too, that sending men and ships into de Grasse's lair would be the riskiest of risky operations. A staggering percentage of the British army in North America could be lost and with it the entire North American Squadron. Furthermore, if that squadron were destroyed, Britain would without question lose all its possessions in the West Indies. On the other hand, each man had to have been all too aware that a vote to do nothing to rescue Cornwallis's army might well be a career-ending decision. They had to act. It "is not a move of Choice . . . it is of necessity," Clinton told a friend and a young officer.[35]

In what must have been taxing meetings, the two councils of war voted to send a relief expedition consisting of "above 5,000 men" the moment the navy completed the rehabilitation of the vessels damaged in the Battle of the Virginia Capes. The naval officers thought their damaged ships would be sufficiently repaired and outfitted by October 3, and that at the latest the relief fleet could sail for the Chesapeake on October 5.[36] Clinton immediately sent word of the decision in two communiqués to Cornwallis, messages in which he solicited information on the "exact strength of the enemy's fleet and what part of the Chesapeake they appear to be most jealous of." He additionally asked where the expeditionary force "can best . . . form a junction with you," a curious statement that seemed to hint at the prospect that Cornwallis might attempt to fight his way out of the trap and meet the relief force somewhere other than at Yorktown. Clinton was understandably vague as to when the armada might reach the Chesapeake. That was "subject to disappointment," he acknowledged, which could hardly have been news to a veteran soldier like Cornwallis, though when Clinton spoke of "the middle of November" as a possibility, the trapped general at Yorktown had to know that the odds against his rescue were immense.[37]

CORNWALLIS'S TRAVAIL AT Yorktown was not the only sign that the tide of war was running against the British. Spain had declared war on Britain in June 1779 with several strategic objectives in mind, some in the Caribbean and Central America. Spain not only sought to terminate British military and commercial interference in Jamaica and present-day Nicaragua, Honduras, and Belize, but to regain Florida, which it had lost to Britain in 1763 in the Seven Years' War. The reconquest of Florida was crucial in ending the British threat to Spanish commercial trafficking throughout the Gulf of Mexico, and Spain launched its campaign from New Orleans in the summer of 1779, close to the time that Comte d'Estaing set his sights on Savannah. The Spanish were more successful than the French, and by summer's end they had regained control of the lower Mississippi region. Moving rapidly under the leadership of Bernardo de Gálvez, a young military officer and governor of Louisiana, the Spanish next opened a campaign to take Mobile. Putting together an army of 3,400 soldiers and a task force of three ships of the line and four frigates (one of which was a captured British sloop that he took as his personal vessel and imperiously christened *Gálvestown*), Colonel Gálvez overwhelmed the small British garrison of three hundred. The fort at Mobile surrendered in March 1780, just as Clinton's army was preparing to open the siege of Charleston.

Only Pensacola stood in the way of the Spanish campaign to reclaim all of West Florida. Field Marshal Gálvez (he had recently been promoted) went after it in the fall of 1780, but was thwarted when a hurricane—the first of three powerful storms that pummeled the Caribbean and Gulf of Mexico during October—scattered and badly damaged his fleet. Undaunted, he put together a second expedition that sailed from Havana in the winter of 1781 at the same moment that Cornwallis was pursing Greene across North

Carolina. The campaign was long and difficult, as at the outset the British garrison enjoyed an overwhelming numerical superiority. But in time, as reinforcements arrived—including four French ships of the line and an assortment of smaller craft—Gálvez's force grew to be three times the size of the British force. In May, just days before Cornwallis set off from Wilmington, North Carolina, for Virginia, the British surrendered Pensacola. Great Britain had lost control of West Florida. Neither Congress nor Washington appeared to think much of Spain's conquests and Britain's losses, though Gálvez's spirited campaigns had tied down thousands of King George's soldiers, particularly men from Loyalist-rich West Florida who might otherwise have contributed to the pacification of Georgia and South Carolina. (Washington told Spain's agent in Philadelphia that he was delighted at Britain's loss of West Florida, a defeat that was mutually beneficial to Spain and the United States, but he told Congress of his alarm at learning that the 2,500 British prisoners taken at Pensacola were permitted to return to Clinton's army in New York.)

Although Spain never allied with the United States, it had provided aid in addition to tying down British troops in West Florida. In the spring of 1777, prior to declaring war on Great Britain, Spain sent bolts of cloth, thousands of blankets, and twenty-four thousand muskets to the Americans. During the summer and fall of 1778, Spanish ships crossed the Atlantic loaded with thirty thousand additional blankets, shoes, cloth, and uniforms for the beleaguered Americans. Early in 1781 another Spanish fleet arrived in New England laden with six thousand captured British uniforms, including coats, hats, shoes, and shirts. Additional Spanish vessels arrived with clothing for America's soldiery in July 1781. By then, the Continental army had so much clothing that the United States government sold the surplus as a revenue-raising measure. On two occasions during the twelve months before the siege of Yorktown, Spain also provided monetary assistance to the cash-strapped Americans. Altogether, Spain provided 375,000 livres in subsidies and loans, roughly one half of 1 percent of the amount provided by France and Holland. Spanish aid was modest but not an unimportant factor in Britain's ongoing woes of waging what had since 1778 been transformed from a conflict to suppress a colonial rebellion into a gigantic world war.[38]

WASHINGTON AND ROCHAMBEAU arrived in Williamsburg on September 14, twelve days before the councils of war in New York voted to send the relief force to Yorktown. Lafayette was among the first to greet the American commander, whom he had not seen in nine months. He rushed to Washington and embraced him with "an ardor not easily described," one surprised witness remarked, kissing him "from ear to ear."[39] The Allied commanders had reached Williamsburg well ahead of their armies, which were still in transit down the Chesapeake by foot or boat. Lodging in the home of George Wythe, a signer of the Declaration of Independence, Washington on his first night in town enjoyed an "elegant supper" and listened as a band played an overture from a French opera. On following nights he dined first with Lafayette, then with General Steuben. This was also a period of considerable idle time for the men under Lafayette and Wayne, which some filled with fishing and playing billiards. Four days after arriving, Washington and Rochambeau took a small vessel, the *Queen Charlotte*, down the James and out to de Grasse's flagship, the *Ville de Paris*, anchored off Cape Henry. They were accompanied by Generals Duportail and Henry Knox, the head of artillery in the Continental army.[40]

De Grasse, eleven years older than the forty-nine-year-old Washington, was an imposing figure and one of the rare individuals who was actually slightly taller than the American commander. De Grasse, a veteran of three wars, had served in the French armed forces since he was eleven years old. Like Washington, he had little formal education, but again like the American general he was urbane and radiated cordiality. A story that might be apocryphal goes that de Grasse greeted Washington as "*Mon cher petit général!*" If true, it is unlikely the thin-skinned Washington thought it funny, though all who were present supposedly found it most amusing. Washington was in a jubilant mood and, all in all, concluded that the ensuing "Interview," as he called it, was a success. Washington got the answers he hoped for to most of the questions he posed. De Grasse said that his original plan had been to depart by October 15, but he might be able to stay until the end of the month. As the two Allied generals presumed the big guns should be in place and firing no later than the end of the first week in October, they would have roughly twenty-five days to compel Cornwallis to surrender. De Grasse additionally promised to provide two thousand men if the Allies were forced to finish the campaign with an all-out attack on Cornwallis's entrenched army. The admiral agreed to furnish cannon for the coming siege, though not as much gunpowder as the two commanders would have liked. The one disappointment was that de Grasse categorically refused to follow the operation in the Chesapeake by helping the Allied armies liberate Charleston. The meeting concluded with a dinner and a tour of the *Ville de Paris*, after which at sunset Washington's party boarded the *Queen Charlotte* for the trip back to Williamsburg. That journey must have been frustrating for a land-lubber. Contrary winds delayed the excursion for five long days, and it was not until September 22 that the two commanders returned to their soldiers, who at last had begun to reach the peninsula.[41]

Within another four days, the last of the soldiers had arrived, including the troops that had come south with Barras's squadron. Most of the Allied soldiers came up the James or its tributaries, landing here and there on the peninsula, after which virtually all marched to tiny Williamsburg, the rendezvous site that a French soldier described as "not particularly pretty." Nor was it only manpower that was arriving. For a month Thomas Nelson, Jefferson's successor as Virginia's governor, had been wielding the nearly dictatorial powers given him by the assembly to find food for the thousands of troops expected to assemble at Yorktown. The French had the means to purchase comestibles. The Americans lacked what a quartermaster referred to as the "infatuating metal" wielded by the French, with the result that many head of livestock, bushels of wheat, and pounds of flour were simply seized from farmers. Mills were occupied and, now and then, enslaved people were impounded and made to grind wheat. For armies that were about to conduct a siege, entrenching tools were also "indispensably necessary," as Washington put it, and somehow or other they were obtained. Therafter the provisions had to be delivered over long distances, a stupendous operation made all the more difficult by the shortages of wagons, horses, teamsters, and boats. Civilians were impressed into service, and their labor was sometimes overseen by militiamen. Driven by a conviction that a victory that "holds forth the most glorious consequences" for America depended on the success of his operation, Nelson at times was ruthless, likely in a manner that Jefferson could not have matched. Once the stores were on the peninsula, the governor, with considerable efficiency, personally presided over their stockpiling and distribution.[42]

At dawn on September 28 the two armies began the final leg of the march that had commenced at Dobbs Ferry 40 days earlier (though for the French soldiery, the trek had started when Rochambeau's army left Newport 110 days earlier). The armies were organized in two long columns, the Franco-American armies in one, the American militiamen in the other. The men faced a twelve-mile hike in the unforgiving late-summer heat and heavy humidity, conditions that one French soldier described as "incomparably worse than anything we had previously endured." The armies proceeded slowly and took frequent breaks, but even so several men collapsed and some died. In the last pale-pink light of day, more than twelve hours after setting off, the hindmost soldiers reached Yorktown. The Allies had taken "quiet Possession of their Ground in front of the Enemy's Works," as Washington put it.[43]

During the next day or two, Washington and Rochambeau, viewing the landscape through field glasses, got their first good look at the enemy's defenses. They thought them impressive but not insurmountable, which was largely what Cornwallis had told Clinton a month earlier. The fortifications would have been more imposing had building them begun soon after Cornwallis's arrival in Williamsburg on June 25, but more than five crucial weeks passed before work commenced, time wasted by what turned out to be the unnecessary tramp to Portsmouth.

The Allied commanders soon pieced together that Gloucester, across the York River, bristled with fortifications and nearly one thousand men, including Hessians, British regulars, and provincial troops. As it was to be the enemy's escape hatch, if it came to that, Cornwallis had tended to it before he commenced digging at Yorktown near the beginning of September. Work at Yorktown had taken on an increased urgency as the month sped by and Cornwallis grasped the magnitude of his predicament. During the four weeks before the Allied armies assembled, the British constructed outer works that extended several hundred yards from the town; these were tied together by uninviting ravines and swamps that a French engineer characterized as "impracticable for an attack." The inner works stretched up to two thousand yards in a semicircle around the town, each end terminating at the shore of the York River. There were earthworks and parapets, some more than a foot thick and standing a dozen feet aboveground. Seven artillery batteries were positioned along the length of the outer works, and three more stood within the inner works. Eight earthen redoubts, each in essence a small fort, were positioned along the outer works. Three additional redoubts with stout walls and abatis had been constructed beyond the outer works, and a four-pointed redoubt had been built on a high bluff near the beach and a road to Williamsburg. Redoubts, christened Numbers 9 and 10, stood about three hundred yards apart on the southeast side of Yorktown, an open area that Cornwallis correctly judged the weakest section of his line. Cornwallis had ordered the sinking of nearly thirty British ships in the York in hopes of devising an underwater obstruction that would prevent any enemy ship from ascending the river. The British commander had not brought much artillery with him from the Carolinas, though he had gotten hold of several pieces while in Virginia. He had about sixty-five cannon atop the firepower that would be provided by two Royal Navy frigates in the York River.[44]

The disposition of the Allied armies had been agreed to earlier. Some units sealed off roads leading from Yorktown, and more than two thousand men were posted at Gloucester Point to guard against a British getaway in that sector. The Gloucester contingent was a joint operation. Virginia militiamen under General George Weedon composed the majority of that force, while some six hundred men in Lauzun's Legion—a foreign corps made up of men from fifteen or more European countries—were commanded by Armand Louis de Gontaut, Duc de Lauzun, a French cavalry officer. Across the river, on the plain before Yorktown, the French took up positions south and southwest of the tiny village in what soon would be the left wing of the Allied siege lines. The Americans comprised the right wing, all of which was under the command of General Benjamin Lincoln, who had been the besieged at Charleston seventeen months earlier, but now was about to be the besieger. Lincoln's division, closest to the river, was on the far right of the line; a division under Lafayette was to his immediate left; and a third division under Steuben was on the line's far left in an area that abutted the French artillery park. Each Allied army created its own artillery park. They were next to one another, though separated by Beaverdam Creek; the parks were sites where ordnance and ammunition were stored. Washington and Rochambeau set up separate headquarters to the rear and behind the midpoint of what was soon to be the long, snaking Allied siege line. Each commander used a large tent for housing, though on uncomfortably warm nights Washington occasionally slept outside, hoping for a breath of cool air. From their headquarters, the Allied leaders could look over toward tiny Yorktown, where Cornwallis commanded some 9,725 soldiers and sailors. Washington and Rochambeau could also see their own forces: 8,600 French troops, 8,280 Continentals, and 5,535 American militiamen—a grand total of 21,820 men. The Allies had achieved a fraction more than a two-to-one superiority. Washington and Rochambeau were unaware of the exact number of guns that Cornwallis possessed, but the Allied commanders could probably have made an accurate guess that they had around 30 percent more artillery than their adversary.[45]

With one exception, all had gone smoothly during the week leading to the positioning of the Allied armies. On September 23, the Allied commanders received disquieting news from de Grasse. Intelligence had alerted the admiral that the British were sending additional warships under Digby to the Chesapeake. The report was incorrect. Digby had not yet arrived in New York, but de Grasse did not know that, and he immediately informed the generals that he would have to stand out to sea. In a panic,

Washington responded with a lengthy communiqué begging de Grasse not to depart. Even the "momentary absence of the french fleet" could result in Cornwallis's escape, he warned. Washington added that his information indicated that French sources had "exaggerated" the size of Digby's fleet and that the enemy in New York had disseminated word that he was coming to Cornwallis's relief as a ruse to induce de Grasse to depart. Washington burnished his missive by advising that de Grasse held in his hands "the common cause of France and America." Should the French fleet depart, "no future day can restore . . . a similar occasion for striking a decisive blow." If this opportunity slipped through the hands of the Allies, "an honorable peace will be more remote than ever." Rochambeau appealed to de Grasse as well. In the end, the admiral did not depart, prompting Washington to write him once again, this time saying that de Grasse's decision "proves that a great Mind knows how to make personal Sacrifices to secure an important general Good."[46]

With that dustup behind him, Washington radiated confidence that this campaign would be truly epochal. Before the first siege gun was fired he was aglow with the "fairest expectations" and "brilliant prospects" of victory. "I am not apt to be sanguine," he admitted in a grand understatement, but "I think in all probability Lord Cornwallis must fall into our hands." Yet Washington remained a worrier. He feared the arrival of an Atlantic storm or a powerful British relief expedition, and he wrung his hands over the possibility that the siege would not end before de Grasse pulled out. There were so many things that could go wrong. However, Rochambeau, a veteran of these operations—he had experienced fourteen previous sieges—sought to reassure Washington. The outcome, the unruffled French general promised, was "reducible to calculation." Many soldiers shared Rochambeau's confident outlook. Weedon thought the Allies "have got [Cornwallis] handsomely in a pudding bag." Anthony Wayne never doubted that "We have the most glorious Certainty, of very soon Obliging Lord Cornwallis, with all his Army to Surrender." Similarly, Lafayette at the same moment—and before the heavy guns opened up—advised General Greene that while the Carolinas were being "Retrieved By a Yankey," the rest of "Your Country Has

Been Saved By a Virginian." Washington took nothing for granted. He recalled that two years earlier almost to the day d'Estaing and Lincoln at Savannah had possessed a considerable edge in numbers, arms, and naval power, yet their siege had failed. One can only wonder whether Washington was buoyed by the knowledge that Clinton at Charleston had enjoyed all the advantages with which the Allies at Yorktown were blessed and he had triumphed.[47]

As September turned to October, Washington remained uneasy. His sole diary entry for the period between September 30 and October 6 was that "nothing occurred of Importance," though in fact those days were given over to the agonizingly slow job of moving the heavy artillery from the James River to the siege lines. He waited impatiently but knew that things "were fast ripening to a Point."[48]

NOT SINCE JOHN Burgoyne was bearing down on Albany and William Howe on Philadelphia in 1777 had two important campaigns occurred simultaneously. Just four days after the Allies marched from Dobbs Ferry—and one week prior to de Grasse's arrival in Chesapeake Bay—General Greene brought his army down from the High Hills of Santee. Greene's army had rested for a month, during which it had grown slightly, but even as he took the field, his men, as always, suffered shortages of essential provisions. At times, Greene confessed, he was "ready to sink under the load of difficulties that oppress me." His adversities even caused him to change his mind about the failure of his predecessor, Horatio Gates, who Greene now said "did not deserve" the opprobrium heaped on him following his defeat at Camden. Privately, Greene blamed Congress for America's tribulations, blasting its mismanagement of finances and failure to maintain a "due subordination of the States."[49]

Greene emerged with hopes of completely cleansing the low country of British troops outside Charleston and Wilmington. He put his army in motion earlier than he would have preferred, as not all the militiamen he expected had arrived, but he felt that he could wait no longer, for time was running out on the enlistments of many of his Continentals. Furthermore, given that de Grasse's fleet was expected to arrive soon somewhere in North America, Greene guessed that Cornwallis would abandon Virginia and return to the relative safety of the Carolinas. Greene felt that he would face better odds by going up against his adversary before Cornwallis arrived. As always, Greene was also thinking of the diplomatic negotiations that he anticipated in 1782, and he presumed the peace talks were on the minds of the British in Charleston as well. With cooler weather in the autumn, he predicted, the enemy would "make a great effort" to crush the rebels in Georgia and regain as much territory as possible in South Carolina. If the king's army succeeded, those two states might be lost to the United States in the postwar settlement and, together with Florida, would remain colonies within the British Empire. But Greene believed that if he acted quickly, his army might achieve Britain's "final expulsion" from all but Charleston and Savannah. Greene was additionally influenced by intelligence provided by Henry Lee's cavalry, which the general characterized as his "right eye." Lee reported that disaffection was rife within the British army. South Carolina's heat and humidity, as well as a sense of hopelessness, had led to a spike in desertions. Besides, said Lee, Greene's all-important cavalry arm was larger than the number of British dragoon units in the field. Never had there been "so glorious an opportunity of giving a fatal stab to the British tyrant," Lee advised. Greene listened and acted, though he was certain that his force would be numerically inferior.[50]

Greene's immediate target was the force under Lieutenant Colonel Alexander Stewart, now in command of the main British army, as Lord Rawdon had been forced by poor health to return to England. Stewart was a forty-two-year-old with more than a quarter century of military experience, including having fought in Europe in the Seven Years' War. He had arrived in America only three months earlier, part of the reinforcements that London sent over that summer. Some British officers who served with him were put off by his egotistical manner and languid nature, and it was rumored that he drank heavily, but none doubted his bravery. Stewart's army was only fifteen miles southwest of Greene's point of exit from the

High Hills, but recent heavy rains had swollen rivers and creeks between the two armies. Therefore, Greene took a circuitous route to reach his adversary. He crossed the Congaree, swung northward to Camden, forded the Wateree, and descended the Santee, picking up militia units along the way. As he moved farther south, Greene learned that Stewart had shifted forty miles eastward to Eutaw Springs, on the west side of the Santee. Greene now had close to 2,300 men. Stewart's army had once been considerably larger than the rebel force coming after it, but the British force had been depleted by illness. Stewart now had about 2,000 men fit for duty.[51]

Stewart had known for two weeks that Greene's men were in the field and on the march, but his intelligence was shoddy, a deficiency he blamed on the unwillingness of local inhabitants to provide the least information. On September 8—at the moment the Allied armies were beginning their descent down the Chesapeake, a move of which Greene was unaware—the van of the rebel army stumbled on an unarmed British "rooting party" of more than three hundred men sent a few miles from Eutaw Springs to dig for sweet potatoes. Greene knew instantly that his arrival had taken the enemy by surprise. More than one hundred of those spading under a scorching sun were captured, but many escaped and warned Stewart, who used the time that Greene spent aligning his men for battle to ready his own army. The British were prepared by the time the American force marched the final couple of miles to what was to be the battlefield.

The British had attacked at Cowpens, Guilford Courthouse, and Hobkirk's Hill. This time, the American army would attack. Greene organized his army more or less as Morgan had at Cowpens. Carolina militiamen composed the front line. Continental regulars from North Carolina, Virginia, and Maryland made up the second line. Colonel Lee's light dragoons were on the left, South Carolina state troops on the right. Colonel William Washington's cavalry and Delaware Continentals were in reserve. Stewart, like Cornwallis at Guilford Courthouse, was supremely confident, but things did not go as well as he expected. Greene's army performed exceedingly well early on. To the "astonishment" of one of Greene senior officers, the Carolina militiamen advanced "with shouts and exhortations into the enemy's fire, unaffected by the continual fall of their comrades around them." Greene—who once told Congress that militiamen were worthless save for subjugating Tories—was also amazed. Despite "a most tremendous fire" laid down by the enemy, his flinty militiamen kept moving. Later, Greene said, "Nothing could exceed the gallantry of our officers or the bravery of our troops," and he took pains to lavish praise on the militiamen who had "fought with a degree of spirit and firmness." He also commended his Continentals. Although many were new recruits, they performed "with a degree of obstinacy that would have [done] honor to the best of veterans."[52] Where the rawest troops at Cowpens and Guilford Courthouse had been expected to get off only two or three shots before retreating, these men fired upwards of twenty times in the course of their advance. When the American regulars joined the action, the British retreated precipitously.

At times it appeared that the Americans were on the brink of scoring a huge victory, but battles can be capricious. In this instance, three factors deprived Greene of the triumph that appeared to be within his grasp. As the British fell back, sectors of the American force stumbled on the enemy's provisions, a pantry laden with food and liquor. Discipline evaporated in an instant, and for some of Greene's men the pursuit of the enemy had come to an abrupt end. In addition, many of Greene's officers had been wounded or killed. In fact, it is likely that a greater percentage of officers were casualties in this fight than in any another battle waged by an American force in the Revolutionary War. The incapacitation of such a large number of officers foiled all attempts at restoring order. The outcome of battles waged across a wide battlefield sometimes hinges on what occurs in small spheres, and in this instance tenacious resistance by British units scattered here and there stymied the Americans who seemingly had been en route to victory. One such occurrence was eerily similar to what had occurred at Germantown three years earlier. Some British units took refuge in a three-story brick house on the battlefield and from that jury-rigged fort succeeded in stopping the rebels' advance. In fact, the redcoats regrouped and renewed the fight. In another region of the field of battle, the Americans' progress was halted when

Colonel Washington's overzealous cavalry attacked without infantry support, a calamitous blunder that resulted in Washington being bayoneted and captured as well as the wounding or killing of several of his dragoons.

As the morning wore on, Greene concluded, much as he had at Guilford Courthouse, that he had inflicted heavy losses on his adversary, but to continue the fight would result in his army suffering mounting casualties with little attendant gain. Greene pulled out, leaving Stewart in control of the field, just as a battered Cornwallis had been left in possession of the field at Guilford Courthouse. Both commanders subsequently claimed great victories. "We obtained a complete victory," Greene said. Stewart wrote Cornwallis, "I totally defeated him." Greene went on to say it was "the hottest action I ever saw," a "very severe battle, by far the most bloody and obstinate I ever saw," which was pretty much what he had said of Guilford Courthouse. If Greene's claims of victory were inflated, his army nonetheless had dealt the British a severe blow. Stewart's losses totaled some seven hundred men, close to 30 percent of those who saw action. Greene's army paid a heavy price, too, losing more than five hundred men, nearly a quarter of those who had gone into the engagement. While the British tended to the wounded strewn about the killing fields at Eutaw Springs, Greene's men made a tortuous trek to safety. The hot and weary men made the trudge without a drop of water, and many bore the burden of carrying litters laden with their wounded comrades. Greene's retreat ended in the dying light of day. Early the following day, as the sun crept over the eastern horizon, the British abandoned Eutaw Springs and began their own punishing march toward Charleston.[53]

Greene thought he faced at least one additional major battle in the very near future. Convinced that Cornwallis would escape Yorktown before de Grasse's task force arrived, Greene ordered that his sick and wounded be taken to the Waxhaws.[54] Meanwhile, he readied his army to intercept Cornwallis, most likely somewhere in North Carolina.

Greene, of course, was mistaken about Cornwallis and his heavy fighting was over. Throughout what was mostly a tranquil autumn he learned of the praise heaped on him in the weeks that followed Eutaw Springs. Congress lauded his "wise, decisive and magnanimous conduct" and struck a medal in his honor. Greene's image was on one side beneath the words "distinguished leader." The other side was adorned with a depiction of a female "Victory" dancing on the accoutrements of armies and emblazoned with the words "The Safety of the Southern Department." Washington learned of Eutaw Springs before digging commenced on the first Allied parallel at Yorktown, and he sent his congratulations on "the Well fought Battle" and "splendid" victory. A South Carolina delegate to Congress gushed that Greene's leadership had been "truely important, and glorious." Greene was the "firm Patriot, the able General," he added. John Clark, who had served the army in many capacities, told Greene that he deserved "immortal fame." Virginia's Richard Henry Lee said that Greene had just waged "the best fought battle that the American war has produced." Pennsylvania's chief executive Joseph Reed said that Europeans looked on Greene as one of the world's greatest soldiers and southerners thought him their "Deliverer." Greene likely especially treasured a letter from Thomas Paine, whom he admired. Having returned in September from Paris with Colonel Laurens, Paine had just learned the details of Greene's campaigning since January. "How you have contrived without money to do what you have done I have scarcely a conception," Paine wrote, but he thought it had to have been due to Greene's superlative "enterprise, address, management."[55]

Eutaw Springs was Greene's last major battle in the Carolinas. However, small firefights continued for more than a year, hollow engagements that would have no bearing on the war's outcome but which continued to take lives on both sides.

When Greene had come to the southern theater nine months earlier nearly everything below North Carolina was in British hands. His numbers had always been in flux as militiamen came and went and fresh Continentals were plugged in, but Greene had started the previous December with somewhere in the vicinity of 1,500 men, and over the months his losses from all causes had exceeded the size of that original army. He and his men had fought time and again, and his soldiers had slogged across the Carolinas under the cold skies of winter and the blazing summer sun. No other

American army in this war had endured what Greene's army had undergone for such a protracted period, and arguably none had achieved as much. By the time the last shot was fired at Eutaw Springs, Greene and his men had largely driven the enemy back to Charleston, Savannah, and Wilmington. If there was a peace conference in 1782, Greene's army had done what it could to assure that an independent United States would include Georgia, North Carolina, and South Carolina.

Whether there was a peace conference, and whether the United States would exist at the end of this war, depended to a considerable degree on what transpired some four hundred miles to the north of Eutaw Springs at Yorktown, Virginia.

CHAPTER 15

DECISIVE VICTORY

A DOZEN DAYS passed between the arrival of the last French and Continental troops at Yorktown and the moment the siege guns opened fire. The first challenge was organizational. Men had landed over several days at multiple sites along the James River. In addition, during the passage from Head of Elk to the Virginia peninsula, companies had been separated from regiments, and regiments from battalions. Some sixteen thousand regulars had to be sorted out and properly assembled, a number roughly equal in size to the population of Boston, America's third-largest city. In addition, more than five thousand militiamen gradually arrived, and they, too, had to be plugged in. But the most time-consuming aspect of preparing to launch the siege was getting the provisions, equipment, weaponry, and munitions up from the river. The heavy siege guns had arrived at Trebells's Landing, seven miles away. The dearth of wagons and horses slowed the process, as did the need to move artillery that weighed hundreds of pounds or more across the sandy, traction-resistant coastal soil.[1]

Though the days were busy and this was a battlefield site, much of the routine of army life remained as it always had been. Reveille was at sunrise—around 6:00 A.M. on the peninsula in early October—followed by assembling for roll call and inspection. Thereafter, men reported for designated assignments. Some were in fatigue parties that brought in fresh water; others gathered wood and stones that would be used in making abatis, fascines (a bundle of limbs and sticks used to compact soggy ground or for strengthening embankments), and gabions (parcels of rocks for constructing retaining walls). Many performed a variety of unwholesome tasks necessary for keeping the camp hygienic, a few were assigned hospital duty, and nearly every enlisted man at some time or other stood sentry. "Our duty was hazardous but not very hard," a New Englander later recalled, and he added that for once there was an ample supply of food. Just to be sure, however, the men in his unit had brought along a dog from New York, "old Bose," and they set him to tracking hogs that grazed in the nearby woods; in no time, these troopers added fresh pork to their diet.[2] Retreat was sounded by drumbeats at sunset, in the vicinity of 5:30 P.M., and the men came together in their companies for another roll call. As night closed in drummers beat the tattoo, the signal for men to go to their appointed spot (a tent, if fortunate), where they were to remain until reveille the next morning.

Washington and Rochambeau awakened on September 30 to a startlingly welcome site. Cornwallis had abandoned his outer works, a target the Allied commanders had expected to have to take through bloody and time-consuming combat. A happy Washington reported to Congress that the enemy's generosity had given the Allies "possession of very advantageous Grounds," which the two armies immediately occupied. The Allies did not know what to make of Cornwallis's act, nor did some British officers who later complained that their commander had acted "prematurely," taking a step that ultimately reduced the time the army could hold out. There was, however, a rationale behind Cornwallis's step. The previous day a British ship managed to steal through Admiral de Grasse's blockade and deliver to Cornwallis what turned out to be Clinton's impulsive communiqué that "above 5,000 men rank and file, shall be embarked . . . in a few days to relieve you and afterwards cooperate with you." The news changed Cornwallis's thinking. Anticipating that the relief expedition would possibly arrive within about ten days—and that he would not have to hold out as long as he had previously thought—Cornwallis's primary concern now became one of preserving his men for the defense of his inner works. In hopes of avoiding the loss of those who had been slated for defending the outer works, Cornwallis notified Clinton, "I shall retire this night within the [inner] works, and have no doubt, if relief arrives in any reasonable time, York and Gloucester will be both in possession of His Majesty's troops." (To add to his food supply, Cornwallis additionally set some men to the grim task of slaughtering upwards of seven hundred of the army's horses, and once the butchering was completed the bodies were dumped into the York River.) Cornwallis's mood may have improved after hearing from Clinton, but the Allies frame of mind soared at discovering the empty outer works. In an instant, they advanced closer to Yorktown, near enough in fact that for the first time they could "see . . . all the land which surrounds the town."[3]

Washington, in his diary, characterized the initial five days of October 1 as a time when nothing important occurred, but he could not have been more incorrect. Although Washington could not have known it, October 5 was the date that the Royal Navy had given Clinton for the relief expedition to sail from New York. But the fleet was not ready, and the departure date was pushed back to the eighth. That date came and went too as repairs continued on the vessels damaged in the fray in the Chesapeake. Clinton was next advised that the relief expedition would sail on October 12. Washington may not have known of these developments, but he was aware that starting on October 1, French engineers began planning the Allied parallels, though it was not until the rainy night of October 6 that digging began under cover of darkness in both the French and American sectors. Washington committed 1,500 "Fatiegue men" to do the work while another 2,800 covered them in the event that Cornwallis ordered an attack. Customarily, the army's digging was the job of sappers and miners, sturdy men with strong backs and muscular arms who had dug trenches and fortifications from New England to the middle and southern states. But on this occasion, given that time was precious, hundreds of other men were assigned this duty. However, the first to swing a pickax that evening was Washington himself. He rode to the site, dismounted, was handed a pick, and swung it deftly a few times. One of his soldiers, Private Joseph Plumb Martin, who had served in the army for five years, did not recognize this man that he called a "stranger." Only when some French engineers addressed him as "Your Excellency" did Martin deduce the newcomer's identity. Facing backbreaking work for the next several hours, Martin was not unduly impressed with his commander's theatrics. He somewhat sourly noted that Washington "struck a few blows with a pickax that it might be said 'General Washington with his own hands first broke ground at the siege of Yorktown.'" On the whole, however, Private Martin was happy, as he thought the end was in sight. Speaking like a hunter whose quarry had burrowed underground, Martin remarked that Cornwallis was "holed" and "nothing remained but to dig him out."[4]

The men who were digging were spaced three yards apart and forbidden to speak to one another. If the British knew what was occurring and trained their artillery on these laborers, casualties could be excessive. Work went on through the long, dark night. The British did not respond. When the first light of morning washed across the landscape, work was "in such forwardness as to cover the Men from the enemys fire," as Washington put it. Like that of its French counterpart, the American trench stretched for hundreds of yards and was roughly four feet deep and eight to ten feet wide. (One soldier remarked that a carriage could easily have been driven through the trench.) Excavation was only the first step. During the ensuing seventy-two hours, two redoubts and batteries for siege guns were constructed, fascines and gabions properly placed, and artillery and stores brought to the front lines by grimy, sweat-soaked men. Days earlier, Washington had reported to Congress that when the preliminary work was completed "our Fire will begin with great Vigor." That day came on October 9, more than seven weeks after the Allied armies had departed New York. There now was somewhere in the vicinity of twenty-two days remaining until de Grasse would have to be on his way. The French cannonade began two hours before the American shelling commenced, but at 5:00 P.M. all was ready for the Continental army to join in. Once again there was a little ceremony as Washington was given the honor of putting "the match to the first gun." The soldiers listened intently and heard the ball blast through several structures in the little hamlet. What they did not know was that it had allegedly struck a house where several officers were dining, killing Cornwallis's commissary general and a regimental adjutant. A Continental physician, indifferent to the human damage, rejoiced that "Earl Cornwallis . . . received his first salutation." French soldiers shouted, "Huzza for the Americans!"[5]

Yorktown was hammered day after day. Within two days of the opening salvos some fifty guns were blasting away at the enemy. More were in place and active on subsequent days until nearly ninety siege guns rained destruction on the tiny town and those in and around it. At its peak, some 3,600 rounds crashed down daily on the village, the British army's redoubts, and the soldiers hunkered inside the entrenchments. In the daylight hours the balls were visible as tiny black specks streaking through the sky. At night they looked to one soldier "like a fiery meteor with a blazing tail." Americans thought the after-dark show was a "most beautifully brilliant" sight that resulted in "most sublime and magnificent spectacles," exceeded only by the "splendid conflagration" that raged when vessels in the river and structures within the forlorn town caught fire. Soldiers in the American lines put down bets on the exact day that Cornwallis would surrender.[6]

The besieged viewed the havoc from a different perspective. "We could find no refuge in or out of town," said a German under Cornwallis's command. Soldiers and civilians alike, reduced to a molelike existence, sought shelter in basements and under the earthen overhang at the river's edge. Cornwallis, who was using the home of Thomas Nelson, Virginia's governor, as his headquarters, lost his domicile almost immediately. Thereafter, he retreated to an underground bunker that he had his sappers dig beneath what once had been Nelson's lovely gardens, and he conducted his staff meetings in a cave near the river. No one was safe in this maelstrom, though the best protected were the soldiers in the trenches, unless a ball made a rare direct hit. Throughout the ordeal, men in every corner of the British lines were blasted to bits, crushed by falling houses, and horrifically wounded by shrapnel. In all likelihood, many were victims of brain injuries, especially concussions. Cornwallis told Clinton that on average he lost one man an hour during the first seventy-two hours of shelling. A bit later he advised New York, "We continue to lose men very fast," and in fact Cornwallis's casualty list increased by an additional thirty men within six hours of the dispatch of his missive to Clinton. After a day or two, the terrain in and around what once had been a bucolic village was littered with the bloated bodies of horses and men, and sometimes the mangled body of a still-living victim who could not be rescued immediately given the incessant shower of explosives. Prior to the beginning of the Allied onslaught, the British had shelled the Franco-American lines with more than a thousand rounds a day. But a combination of dwindling ammunition and the hazard posed by exposure to the Allies' relentless bombardment soon reduced Cornwallis's return fire to around 120 rounds each day.[7]

Five days after digging had begun on the first French and American parallels, work began on the second, which would bring the powerful Allied guns closer to Yorktown and make them more deadly. The sappers and miners, and their helpmates, began work on the night of October 11. The next morning, as daylight covered the peninsula, Cornwallis discovered the existence of the second parallels within 300 yards of his lines, virtually point-blank range for heavy artillery.[8] From its starting point in the French sector to its terminus in the American, the second parallel extended 750 yards, though it stopped short of the York River. Cornwallis's Redoubts 9 and 10 guarded this region, and the peril was too great to send men armed only with picks and shovels into that zone. If the redoubts were not taken, the Allied commanders believed that it would be another ten days before Cornwallis would have to surrender. But if they could be taken, the American siege line would almost literally be within a stone's throw of the edge of town, and Cornwallis's surrender would come much sooner.[9] Planning for the attack began that same afternoon.

To this point the Allies had been spared heavy fighting and their losses had been slight. In the initial two weeks of the siege, the Americans had lost some 45 men who were killed and wounded, and the French about 185. Chiefly, the soldiers had been laborers and spectators to the dazzling shows put on by the gunners. But Redoubts 9 and 10 would have to be taken by a direct attack, and it was expected to be a bloody undertaking. It was agreed that the French would have responsibility for attacking Redoubt 9, regarded as the stronger of the two posts, as it was occupied by 120 defenders. The Americans were tasked with taking Redoubt 10, the Rock Redoubt, a small fort situated on a bluff overlooking the river and the more distant of the two from the second parallel; it was thought to house about 45 British defenders. While the details of the operations were worked out, the American batteries hammered the redoubts incessantly for forty-eight hours.

The attacks were scheduled for the evening of October 14, and launch time was set for soon after nightfall. Roughly four hundred men comprised the French unit, and a more or less similar number of Americans were to set off against their target. This was in Lafayette's sector, and for the attack on Redoubt 10 he selected light infantry from among three battalions, one commanded by a Frenchman, Lieutenant Colonel Jean Joseph Sourbadere de Gimat, a grizzled veteran of twenty years' military service who, since early in the year, had at Washington's direction commanded a battalion of Yankee soldiers that included numerous African Americans from Rhode Island. Colonel John Laurens, who had returned to the army following his mission to Versailles, was given command of the second battalion, which also was composed solely of New England soldiers. Alexander Hamilton was in charge of the last American battalion, consisting of New Yorkers. Not surprisingly, Lafayette chose Gimat, one of his staff officers, to lead the attack and reap the laurels that success would bring.

Hamilton immediately appealed Lafayette's decision to Washington. No record of their conversation exists, but it is likely that Hamilton argued that to guard against the American public seeing Yorktown as a French operation—already a likely prospect given the paramount roles played by Rochambeau and de Grasse—it was important for the new American nation that an American command this crucial undertaking. Hamilton, of course, wanted the assignment for personal reasons. He, like many other officers, was terribly ambitious. Only twenty-four years of age, he looked forward to a career in politics, beginning with a seat in Congress, which he had recently been advised was his for the taking soon after the successful culmination of the siege. His service in this war was long and unblemished, as he had taken up arms in 1776, serving initially in an artillery company. He had seen combat during his first year with the army, but thereafter as an aide de camp to General Washington he had mostly watched the war from a desk at headquarters, though on occasion he had come under fire. Time and again, he had pleaded for a field command. Washington always refused. He regarded Hamilton as the best and brightest of the more than twenty young men who served as his aides during the course of the conflict, and he refused to part with such a gifted individual.[10]

Late in July, Washington had finally relented. While the army was at Dobbs Ferry and the campaign of 1781 was close to beginning, Washington had vested Hamilton with command of a New York light infantry battalion. Now, on October 12, only days away from becoming a father for the first time, Hamilton beseeched Washington to put him charge of this vital assignment. The commander agreed, overruling Lafayette. Washington, too, saw the need for Americans to be credited with vanquishing Cornwallis, and in all likelihood he also wished to advance the postwar political career of this young man who he saw as amazingly talented. Here was Hamilton's opportunity to win glory. With Hamilton in charge of the operation, Major Nicholas Fish—his close friend since their days as college classmates—took command of the battalion of New Yorkers.[11]

Two days earlier, knowing that in some capacity he soon would be part of a most perilous operation, Hamilton, wrote his wife, Elizabeth, at her family's home in Albany. With guns firing nearby, the bustle of soldiers all about, and the air heavy with the fusty smell of freshly turned earth, Hamilton took up his pen. He told Elizabeth that he expected to be at home with her within four weeks. He hoped, too, that she would "love me better than ever." He cared not whether the child she was carrying was a boy or a girl. "In imagination I embrace the mother and embrace the child a thousand times. I can scarce refrain from shedding tears of joy." He confessed that dwelling on the realization that he was soon to be a father was dangerous for a man under fire. It could "make me but half a soldier," he said. He closed with word that Cornwallis must surrender within five days, and immediately thereafter, he said, "I fly to you. Prepare to receive me in your bosom. Prepare to receive me decked in all your beauty, fondness and goodness." [12]

Two nights later, October 14, as evening tightened its grip on Yorktown, the siege guns stopped. A thick fog scudded across the landscape. The moon was sheathed by clouds, and the darkness was as dark as it could ever be. Hamilton assembled his men, and Washington addressed them, exhorting them to act as courageous and dedicated soldiers. All was ready. Near 7:00 P.M. six shots were fired, the signal to launch the two attacks. The American attack force advanced in two columns. As in earlier assaults on entrenched and fortified positions, sappers and miners—armed with axes—were to clear the redoubt of abatis and other obstructions, after which the battalions under Fish and Gimat would tear into the installation and seek to take it by wielding their bayonets. (Firing muskets at such close quarters and in the darkness was certain to result in the wounding of comrades.) Meanwhile, Laurens's battalion was to circle round and not only guard against any escape attempt but attack from the rear. Hamilton had hoped to surprise the enemy, but they spotted the advancing battalions and opened fire with musket and cannon. The Americans kept coming. In no time, hand-to-hand combat was the order of the day. The men on both sides fought desperately, lashing out with their bayonets, wielding muskets as clubs, and using bare fists in the savage brawl. The strike against Redoubt 10 was over in ten minutes; the French required three times as long to overcome the stouter defense at Redoubt 9. For the Americans, the toll was less than expected, though somewhere around 44 were killed or wounded; the enemy suffered 28 casualties. The French took heavier losses. Washington said that 180 French soldiers were killed and wounded, but around 115 appears to have been a more accurate figure; some 70 British soldiers in Redoubt 9 were victims. [13]

Hamilton, who came through the ordeal unscathed, was elated. Through what he called "a happy coincidence," everything had gone according to plan and Redoubt 10 was "invelopped and carried." As soon as possible, he once again wrote Elizabeth, this time confessing that he had withheld from her his coming involvement in a mission in which their "happiness was too much risked." He told Elizabeth of the attack and quickly assured her that there would be "nothing more of this kind." Washington was effusive in his praise, saying the "bravery exhibited by the attacking Troops was emulous" and the "Intrepidity" of the soldiers had rarely been equaled.[14]

Cornwallis was not as ebullient. He knew that time was fast running out. "My situation now becomes very critical," he said that same evening, for his army was ensconced in "ruined works, in a bad position, and with weakened numbers." His staying power was down to hours, at most another day or two. By the light of a flickering candle in his underground bunker, he drafted a forlorn letter to Clinton: "The safety of the place is therefore so precarious that I cannot recommend that the fleet and army should run great risqué in endeavouring to save us."[15] Overwhelmed by cascading distress, Cornwallis's only hope was for a miracle.

Thirty-six hours after the assaults against the redoubts, Cornwallis struck the French lines, a surprise sortie that claimed about fifty victims before the attackers were beaten back. That night, under a shroud of darkness—it was "dark as a sack," according to one of his officers—Cornwallis tried something greater. He attempted to escape. He readied boats to convey his trapped army in stages across the York to Gloucester, from which the men would seek to break through the Allied forces and make their getaway. The Allies had long expected something of the sort but were taken by surprise when it occurred. Roughly a third of the trapped army in Yorktown was in the first batch to attempt the crossing. Before all had made it, a violent storm struck, with howling winds, lashing rain, and lightning and thunder. Two vessels, helpless in the raging tempest, were swept downstream and ultimately captured by the Allies. Though the storm had played out in the wee hours of the morning, Cornwallis knew that to attempt further crossings was out of the question. The Allies were now aware of his plan, and his little fleet of naval craft had been scattered from pillar to post by the squall. The French dismissed what Cornwallis had attempted as simply the *baroud d'honneur*, a face-saving act by a doomed commander, long a tradition in European warfare. If so, Cornwallis never owned up to it, and in fact he later told Clinton that it was a serious attempt "to get off with the greatest part of the troops." Whatever was in his mind, he came close to acknowledging that he never really expected the escape attempt to succeed and that he had ordered it in the hope that "it might at least delay the enemy in the prosecution of the siege" until relief arrived. (Some British officers, including Banastre Tarleton, thought Cornwallis should have made a run for it earlier. Tarleton later made the somewhat dubious case that had Cornwallis slipped 3,500 infantry and cavalry, together with provisions, across to Gloucester around October 1, those men could have escaped, salvaging at least some of Britain's doomed army. But in so doing, Cornwallis would have turned his back on 6,000 of his men.)[16]

If Cornwallis did not know before daybreak that he could hold out no longer, he soon thereafter was aware that his time was up. That morning the Allies opened a greater bombardment than ever before. Cornwallis knew that his remaining emplacements and many more of his men faced destruction. He could offer no resistance. "We at that time could not fire a single gun," he said later. Disease was eating away at his men and so, too, was despair. His soldiers' "spirits . . . were much exhausted by the fatigue of constant watching and unremitting duty," Cornwallis subsequently wrote. He had done all that he could since the enemy had marched from Williamsburg and taken up positions across from Yorktown eighteen days before. But the point had been reached that it would be "wanton and inhuman to the last degree" to persist and expose his soldiery to further danger.[17]

The cannonade had continued for nearly four hours when suddenly a British officer, attired in the familiar red coat, and a drummer appeared side by side on the parapet guarding what remained of Cornwallis's defenses. The drummer began beating a *chamade*, the time-tested signal among European armies that a besieged force was prepared to negotiate. Within a minute or two, the big guns fell silent. The officer climbed down from the parapet and, accompanied by the drummer who continued to beat the *chamade*, walked slowly toward the American lines. The officer was escorted to Washington's tent. He handed the American commander a message from Cornwallis. The

Britain commander asked for a cessation of the deafening bombardment for twenty-four hours while surrender terms were discussed.[18] It was October 17, the fourth anniversary of General Burgoyne's surrender at Saratoga, and the beginning of the end of what had been a very long, tortuous road for the soldiers, leaders, and civilians on both sides.

Negotiating a surrender was a novel experience for Washington, but he suspected that Cornwallis was primarily interested in buying time. He was correct. Cornwallis had known for two weeks that Clinton and the Royal Navy were readying a relief expedition, and he hoped it might be nearing the Chesapeake. He hoped even more that it might have overwhelmed the French fleet and be closing in on the York River. Every minute could be crucial. Time was precious for Washington too. He never discounted the possibility of an enemy relief expedition getting through. The weather was fine on this day, but in a day or two it could be de Grasse's nemesis, as it had been for Cornwallis only hours before during his presumptive attempt to escape. Washington was not going to be lured into a protracted delay. He gave Cornwallis two hours to put in writing the terms he proposed for discussions. Despite his aversion to "the further effusion of blood," Washington made clear that the shelling would resume in the event that he had not heard from Cornwallis.[19]

All was quiet during those two hours, and it is likely that nearly every soldier on both sides prayed that the guns would never start up again. But they did. When the two hours elapsed without word from Cornwallis, firing began again. Not for long, however. At 4:30 P.M. another flag was seen. The guns again fell silent and the messenger and drummer made another long, slow walk to Washington's headquarters. They brought a communiqué from Cornwallis. He pleaded that he had not had adequate time to flesh out his terms, but the nub of his proposals were clear: His troops at Yorktown and Gloucester were to be permitted to surrender with military honors, after which the English troops would be permitted to sail to England and the Germans to Germany, and that all would pledge to never again serve against the French or the Americans in this war; more vaguely, Cornwallis hinted that the surrender accord should protect the "interests" of both the runaway enslaved people and Loyalists who were with him.[20]

Some time elapsed before Washington replied. He first consulted his generals and then Rochambeau. In the wee hours of a new day, October 18, Washington responded. He was not willing to be as generous as Cornwallis would have liked. He feared that if the British and German troops were permitted to return home, they would be sent elsewhere to fight the French and Spanish while London sent over an equal number of replacements to continue the war in America. What is more, Washington was driven by the fierce conviction that he must be no more generous toward Cornwallis than Sir Henry Clinton had been in the surrender terms he had imposed on Benjamin Lincoln at Charleston. The soldiers would remain in America as prisoners of war. As for the civilians, Washington balked at any commitment until those individuals were "more particularly described." Washington gave Cornwallis two hours to digest his response, but nearly every man—or at least every officer of high rank—knew that the end was near. Hamilton, for instance, joyously wrote Elizabeth that soon "Cornwallis and his army are ours." In a matter of days, he said, he would set off for Albany, to which he added: "Conceive my love . . . how delightful this prospect is to me."[21]

Cornwallis consented but asked that he be permitted to send the HMS *Bonetta*, a large sloop of war, with a fifty-man crew to New York. His aide de camp and "such soldiers as I may think proper" would be aboard the vessel, and it was to carry papers for General Clinton. Cornwallis did not specify the number of persons he wished to crowd onto the *Bonetta*, but he pledged that in response the British army would liberate an equal number of American prisoners. If Washington agreed to negotiate "on these grounds," Cornwallis would appoint two field officers to parley with the Allied representatives. Washington consented and named Colonel Laurens as his deputy; Rochambeau selected Louis Marie, Vicomte de Noailles, the twenty-five-year-old brother-in-law of Lafayette. A truce was declared once the talks began.[22]

Sometime that day the four envoys took seats across a table from one another in the home of Augustine Moore, a local landowner whose substantial dwelling was a bit more than a mile below Yorktown. While the diplomats talked, men on both sides climbed out of their earthworks and stood looking at one another across the scarred, desolate plain. Soon a French band began playing. British bagpipers responded. Whereas men had been trying to kill one another only shortly before, and would do so again if the negotiations failed, an air of civility shrouded the landscape.

From Washington's perspective, the talks went on interminably. He not fancifully thought they dragged because of the deliberate procrastination of the British emissaries Cornwallis had chosen. One issue that spun things out concerned the details of the surrender ceremony, a matter of indifference to all but a handful of officers. The British wished to march to the surrender field with colors flying. Clinton had denied that honor to Lincoln at Charleston and Cornwallis was now to be rebuffed. The only concession made by the Allied envoys was that Banastre Tarleton's dragoons could brandish their swords. A more substantive matter concerned the Loyalists who served in the British army. Cornwallis wanted them to be accorded the same rights as British regulars who were prisoners of war. The Americans insisted that Congress must decide their fate. Night fell. The talks continued. At some point, Laurens and Noailles put their final terms in writing and delivered the document to Washington for his approval. He agreed and directed his negotiators to tell their counterparts that Cornwallis had until 11:00 A.M. to accept or face a resumption of the firing. If he accepted, the British army was to begin marching to the field of surrender at 2:00 P.M. The two British officers got the word around daybreak on October 19. They carried the terms to their commander.[23]

Cornwallis took every minute given him, but as 11:00 A.M. approached, he signed the surrender accord, having spun things out for forty-eight hours since the *chamade* was first beaten. There had been no sighting of the help that Clinton promised to bring. In fact, at almost the same instant that Cornwallis put his signature on the document, the long-delayed relief expedition consisting of twenty-five ships of the line and 7,149 troops—including

Clinton—weighed anchor in New York and began its voyage for the Chesapeake.[24]

Meanwhile, the surrender document bearing Cornwallis's signature was delivered to Washington, who directed an aide to make a brief inscription at the bottom of the document: "Done in the trenches before York Town in Virginia, Oct 19, 1781." His notation came six and a half years to the day since the first shots of this war were fired on Lexington Green. If Washington pulsated with excitement, he would not permit a show of emotion even in the privacy of his diary. Imprisoned as he was by his ineluctable self-control, his entry simply noted that he had demanded Cornwallis's capitulation by 11:00 A.M. and it was "accordingly done."[25]

Among other things, the "Articles of Capitulation" called for the surrender of Cornwallis's soldiers, all seamen, "His Britannic Majesty's" ships, all arms, accoutrements, stores, and the army's military chest. The defeated army was to parade to the field of surrender at 2:00 P.M. with its "colours cased," a trek that was to be accompanied by the army's bands "beating a British or German march." The soldiers were to "ground their arms." The officers were permitted to keep their private property, which all knew would include the enslaved people they owned. The soldiery would become prisoners of war in unspecified locations within Virginia, Maryland, and Pennsylvania, and they were to receive the "same rations of provisions as are allowed to soldiers in the service of America." General Cornwallis and his staff were "permitted to go on parole" to Europe or to any maritime post in North America that was possessed by British forces. As for the Loyalists serving in provincial units, the accord stated that those "Natives or inhabitants of different parts of this country" who were in Yorktown or Gloucester and had joined the British army were "not to be punished on account" of having chosen to serve the king in this war. Finally, the "*Bonetta* sloop war" was free to depart with "dispatches to Sir Henry Clinton" and "such soldiers as he [Cornwallis] may think proper to send to New York . . . without examination" by the French or American authorities.[26]

When Washington signed the surrender document, he knew that the "soldiers" Cornwallis would send to New York aboard the *Bonetta* would in reality be civilian Loyalists who had accompanied his army since its arrival in Virginia the previous May. Washington was not happy with the provision, but Cornwallis had been adamant on this point, and the Allies consented rather than tempt fate by stringing out the negotiations and the siege.

Two surrender ceremonies followed, one involving Cornwallis's soldiers in Yorktown and separate proceedings for those garrisoned in Gloucester. The Yorktown surrender is the best remembered and the only one of the two memorialized in contemporary paintings. It began an hour later than called for in the surrender document, in part because order was breaking down in the British ranks, especially after some of Cornwallis's men succeeded in getting into the army's stores and taking prodigious swigs from the rum pot. The British soldiers marched about half a mile to a meadow that had been designated as the surrender field, tramping under a mild sun on a pleasantly warm and golden afternoon. The road was lined with spectators who, learning that Cornwallis's surrender was imminent, had streamed to Yorktown's environs a day or two earlier in hopes of witnessing a historic event and gloating at the discomfort of the hated enemy. Once the process got underway, it conformed to the script spelled out in the Articles of Capitulation, though one Continental soldier thought the behavior of some of the king's soldiers was "disorderly and unsoldierly," their "step . . . irregular, and their ranks frequently broken," perhaps due to their consumption of intoxicants. A Pennsylvanian noted that the "British prisoners all appeared to be much in liquor." Another soldier said the enemy's "mortification could not be concealed," which he thought delightful as Britain's officers had "always entertained an exalted opinion of their . . . prowess" while steadfastly looking on the Americans as "a contemptible, undisciplined rabble." Not all the American observers mentioned shambling comportment by the enemy soldiers, but many commented on their sullenness. One thought they demonstrated contempt toward the Americans to whom they were surrendering, while another detected "considerable malice" toward the French. (A Hessian who surrendered did not scorn his captors, saying that the American soldiers should not be thought of as "a motley crowd of farmers," as they were "under good discipline and drill in the English style as well as the English themselves.")[27] A French band performed throughout, and for a time an American fife and drum unit struck up "Yankee Doodle." A story that first appeared fifty years after the event claimed that a British band performed the currently popular song "The World Turned Upside Down," but today most scholars think it a myth, as there is no contemporary evidence to substantiate the yarn.

One thing that did most certainly occur is that Cornwallis pleaded illness and failed to appear at the ceremony, an act at which many Americans sneered. They knew that he had "frequently appeared in splendid triumph as the head of his army," perhaps recalling that it was Cornwallis who had led the British army's victory parade in Philadelphia a few days after the Battle of Brandywine.[28] In his stead, Cornwallis dispatched General O'Hara, not yet fully recovered from the serious wounds he had suffered at Guilford Courthouse. The wife of a New York soldier, who had accompanied her husband throughout his service, was present at the ceremony and described O'Hara as "a large, portly man, full face, and the tears rolled down his cheeks" as he approached the Allied victors. He rode to the entourage with Generals Rochambeau and Washington. O'Hara knew full well that Washington was the commander of the Allied troops in this engagement—after all, it was Washington with whom Cornwallis had negotiated—but he asked to approach Rochambeau. He was coldly directed to Washington instead. When O'Hara attempted to surrender his sword to Washington, the American commander bade him to approach General Lincoln, on the grounds that as O'Hara was the second in command to Cornwallis, he must surrender to the second in command in the American army. O'Hara presented his sword to Lincoln. It was a symbolic gesture, and Lincoln returned it after accepting it and holding it briefly.

A similar ceremony was underway simultaneously in Gloucester, where Tarleton was the British commander. Decidedly nervous, Tarleton met with the French commander prior to the ceremony and asked to see the Articles of Capitulation. He must have prayed that they contained an assurance that the Tories of his British Legion would be fairly treated once they laid down their arms. All too aware that he was hated unreservedly, Tarleton also conveyed his apprehension regarding his personal safety. Given his sinister reputation, Tarleton feared that an unforgiving Virginia soldier might shoot him on sight. The French general posted the Virginians in a sector of the field where no one could draw a bead on Tarleton. (A couple of days later a Virginia civilian stopped Tarleton and demanded his horse, claiming it had once belonged to him but had been stolen by the British officer. "You had better give him his horse," General O'Hara advised, and Tarleton parted with his mount.)[29]

The Allies had done a brisk business in prisoners. Slightly more than 7,000 men in Cornwallis's army were made captives, but when the sailors were added, the total number of prisoners of war taken was 8,091. Along with the human captives, the Continental army took control of 168 British cannon, 23 mortars, 15 howitzers, 6 swivel guns, 2,857 muskets, and an incredible abundance of swords, cartridges, and cartridge boxes. Not all the soldiers who had been with Cornwallis at the opening of the siege were able to surrender. Many had not survived. The British and Germans offered differing figures for the total number who had died in the service of the king of England; the British put the figure at 156, the Germans at 309. The two also differed with regard to the number of wounded. The British counted 326, the Germans nearly 600. (Given the number in the king's service known to have been in Yorktown and the number who surrendered, the German figures for those killed and wounded appear to be more accurate.) Seventy men were missing. Some had deserted to the Allies, and some probably simply tried to escape to who knows where. Neither the British nor the Germans made any attempt to count the number of wounded who in time perished because of their wounds. Allied casualties were nowhere near those of their enemy. The combined number of casualties in the two armies was 389, of which about 40 percent were Americans.[30]

No one attempted to count the victims among the runaway slaves who were with Cornwallis's army. Some 250 had been with the army when General Phillips arrived in Virginia in March, but their numbers swelled dramatically over the next few months, and it is believed that a huge train of supposedly liberated enslaved people accompanied Cornwallis to

Yorktown. Some had died in the shelling during the siege and others had perished in a sweeping outbreak of smallpox that commenced before the arrival of the Allied armies. A Virginian who entered Yorktown immediately following the surrender saw hideously mangled corpses "all over the place" including "an immense number of Negroes" who had died "in the most miserable manner." Rochambeau and one of his aides also toured what was left of the village and saw streets littered with "white and Negro arms and legs." In the course of the siege, Cornwallis, hoping to conserve his food supply, had driven "back to the enemy" some of "our black friends," according to a disgusted Hessian officer. It was a "cruel happening," the German added, as these escapees from slavery had aided the British in preparing Yorktown's defenses only in the end to be made "to face the reward of their cruel masters." Cornwallis had urged other Blacks with him to flee, a desperate step taken to rid his army of the carriers of smallpox, conserve food, and save them from the virtual certainty of being returned to slavery. Some runaways tried to get across the York River, and others disappeared into the thick woods throughout the peninsula. Without maps or knowledge of the landscape—which was inhabited by a white population that could be expected to be nearly uniformly unwelcoming toward Black strangers—these individuals had been sent on a drastic, and mostly forlorn, last-ditch dash to conserve the freedom that thought they had secured. In the aftermath of the surrender, a New England soldier ran up on numerous bodies of Blacks in the forests about Yorktown, some with cooked ears of corn in their hands. These were likely but a few of the many who probably died of hunger and exposure, though there is no way of knowing the number who perished or escaped. It is known, however, that many were captured in the days that followed the surrender.

A number of the spectators at the surrender ceremony had attended not only to see history in the making but for an ulterior motive. They had traveled to Yorktown—some from fifty miles or more away—to search for their runaway slaves. In the aftermath of the ceremony, they fanned out through the woods to rummage for their property. Some hired soldiers as bounty hunters. Among those who watched helplessly as this macabre scene played out were the African American soldiers in the Continental army, men who had risked life and limb in quest of American independence and a belief that the cherished promise of natural rights for all proclaimed in the Declaration of Independence would follow the American triumph in the Revolutionary War. These common soldiers were powerless, too, to prevent some Continental army officers who had lost bondsmen from combing the countryside in hopes of finding their chattel. In the hour of his greatest triumph—very nearly his only triumph of any magnitude in this long war—Washington was among those who searched relentlessly for his slaves who had sought a life of freedom. He recovered two of the seventeen who had fled with the British on board the *Savage*, the sloop that had stopped at Mount Vernon in the spring. He sent them back into slavery. Washington also rounded up all the surviving enslaved people of Thomas Jefferson who had departed Elk Hill with Cornwallis early in the summer, sending them to Richmond, where they were eventually claimed by their owner or one of his representatives.[31]

Cornwallis emerged from his lair on the day following the formal surrender. He dined with high-ranking French officers and paid a respectful call on Washington, after which the two rode leisurely through the lines that only recently had been scenes of utter horror. An American who glimpsed the British general described this normally large man as "diminutive," likely the effect of weeks of intense stress and a shrunken diet. A few days later, an unseasonably chilly day, Cornwallis and Washington met again. Observing that the British general was bareheaded, Washington supposedly suggested that he don a hat to avoid falling ill. Cornwallis replied, "[I]t matters not, Sir, what becomes of this *head now*."[32]

On the day following the capitulation ceremony, Cornwallis also wrote Clinton. His letter was the first salvo in what would be a lengthy public quarrel between the two over who was responsible for the disasters at Yorktown and in the southern theater. Without mentioning his disobedient act of bringing his army from the Carolinas to Virginia in the spring, Cornwallis brazenly told Clinton that he had never seen Yorktown in a "favourable light" and, with deep misgivings, had followed the commander's orders in posting his army there. From the outset he knew that he lacked the numbers and the artillery to withstand the Allied siege, he said, but added that early on he had not attempted to escape because of Clinton's pledge to rescue him. Clinton later expressed his astonishment at Cornwallis's first postsurrender remarks, given that he had never "shown any desire of criminating" his subordinate. In fact, in his initial report to Lord Germain following the surrender—penned before he received Cornwallis's barbed note—Clinton attributed the disaster solely to "the inferiority of our naval support.")[33]

Two days after the capitulation at Yorktown, the British and German prisoners of war, guarded by Virginia militia, began their long trek to captivity, some going to Winchester, Virginia, the remainder to Frederick, Maryland. A bit later the convalescents who could travel were sent to Fredericksburg, Virginia. Ultimately, all the prisoners were confined in Frederick—those in Winchester were forced to march to their new detention site in a driving snowstorm—where for eight months many were housed in quarters that one described as "much in ruins" while another lamented their "Masaurable Satuation [miserable situation]." For many, incarceration in Frederick would pose a greater danger than the Allied siege guns. By the time a prisoner exchange finally ended their ordeal, roughly 9 percent of the Germans prisoners had perished and 31 percent of the British detainees had died. The appalling death rate among the British was far greater than that of Union prisoners in the Confederacy's infamous Andersonville prison during the Civil War, and invites speculation of deliberately malign treatment having been visited on the British.[34]

FIVE DAYS AFTER the British and German soldiers had laid down their arms at Yorktown, the rescue expedition that had sailed from New York on October 19 approached Cape Charles, on Virginia's eastern shore near the entrance to Chesapeake Bay. Aware that he was sailing into harm's way, Clinton had prepared his will just prior to departing Manhattan. Aboard the flagship and likely battling seasickness, his habitual companion at sea,

Clinton squinted into the haze, searching for any sign of a friendly or hostile vessel. Tense hours passed before a small craft containing three Englishmen was spotted. Those men were brought aboard. They had bad news. They had escaped Yorktown on the eighteenth, the day of the truce and Cornwallis's initial parleys with Washington. As they never heard the siege guns resume firing, they guessed the negotiations had culminated in Cornwallis's surrender. A bit later, crewmen glimpsed the *Charon*, a forty-four-gun British man-of-war. "[W]e had the mortification" to learn from its captain that "Cornwallis had proposed terms of capitulation to the enemy" seven days earlier, said Clinton. The following day a vessel from New York arrived carrying what Clinton later termed Cornwallis's "desponding" letter in which the general advised against the army and navy attempting to rescue the beleaguered garrison in Yorktown. In the next day or two, additional escapees from Yorktown arrived with word that confirmed the capitulation of the British army.

Now there was no question. Writing to Germain while still aboard ship near the mouth of the Chesapeake, Clinton gingerly broke the unhappy news: "This is a blow, my lord, which gives me the most serious concern as it will in its consequences be exceedingly detrimental to the King's interest in this country." With the perversity of the proverbial individual who whistles past the graveyard, Clinton also told a friend that given "the position we found the french fleet in," the relief expedition would have had "every prospect of brilliant success" if only Cornwallis had not previously surrendered. Whether he really believed that will never be known, but years later, his bitter loathing shining through, Clinton told that same friend that the disaster in Virginia would never have occurred had it not been for Cornwallis's "ill judged, ill timed Plan" of abandoning the Carolinas and bringing his army to Virginia. He most certainly believed that to be the case, and as far as Cornwallis was concerned it was true. What would have been the fate of Phillips's army in Virginia can never be known, though Clinton had said early in the summer that he intended to redeploy most of that force to New York in July. Had he done so, it seems unlikely that Washington and Rochambeau would have marched to Yorktown to square off against an army that might not have exceeded two thousand enemy soldiers. All that can be known for certain is that before departing the Chesapeake, the distraught British commander dispatched many of the troops in the fleet to South Carolina, after which he and the naval officers returned to New York.[35]

Although the French army settled down to winter in Yorktown, most of the Continentals marched back to New York. The men under General Wayne, however, headed south to join up with General Greene's army in South Carolina and Georgia, where some would once again see action. Nor did John Laurens travel north with his comrades. In November, he was given leave to return to his native South Carolina and serve under Greene, and he too fought in small engagements that would have no bearing on the war's outcome. Nine months later, Colonel Laurens, age twenty-seven, was killed in what Greene characterized as "a paltry little skirmish."[36]

The ink was hardly dry on the Articles of Capitulation before Washington sent Tench Tilghman, one of his aides, to transmit the happy tidings to Congress. He arrived in the wee hours of the morning on October 24, the day that Clinton arrived at the entrance to the Chesapeake. Tilghman awakened Thomas McKean, who in turn got word to the night watchman making his rounds through Philadelphia's cold, deserted cobblestone streets. The watchman's job on his lonely trek was to keep an eye out for trouble, especially fire. On this quiet night, the German American on duty acted as a town crier in spreading the news of Yorktown. One resident remembered being awakened by the watchman, who, below his window, barked out an announcement: "Basht dree o'clock, und Gorn-wal-lis ist daken."[37]

CHAPTER 16

RECKONING

MANY ON BOTH sides had mistakenly thought that General Burgoyne's surrender at Saratoga in October 1777 would end the war. When General Cornwallis surrendered at Yorktown four years later, most at once suspected that the Allies had scored the decisive victory that would in time bring the war to an end. That was the response of Britain's prime minister when Lord George Germain, on November 25, brought him news of the military disaster in Virginia. Lord North reacted "as if he had taken a ball in the breast," Germain said later. He paced the room in a highly agitated state repeatedly exclaiming, "Oh God, it is all over."[1]

For the most part North was correct, at least with regard to North America, where there were to be no more major battles. Substantive engagements were waged by the European belligerents on land and sea in the West Indies after 1781, and much political and diplomatic skirmishing remained in England and Europe before there was peace. From the moment that London learned of what some opposition members in Parliament wryly called the "Burgoynishing" of Cornwallis, North's majority steadily shrank.[2] The prime minister fought back, not so much in hopes of continuing the war as from fear that the full-throated cry for an immediate peace would weaken England's negotiating position in the seemingly inevitable peace talks. Even so, North, clutching at straws, opened secret discussions with both American and French diplomats. He hoped that one of the two would accept his peace terms, drop out of the war, and leave the other to contend alone with Great Britain. The Allies refused to take the bait. By early February 1782, North's ministry was nearly finished, and at month's end it was history. The climax came when the House of Commons, by a nineteen-vote margin, adopted a resolution declaring that those who favored "the further prosecution of the offensive war" in America were "enemies to his Majesty and this country." North was gone, and Germain with him. A new ministry was formed that was known to be ready to open negotiations with the Allies, the statecraft that nearly everyone had foreseen a year earlier.[3]

Peace talks began in April in Paris. They moved slowly for several weeks, but by the summer, considerable progress was being made. In November, thirteen months after the surrender in Yorktown, a preliminary treaty that recognized American independence was signed between Great Britain and the United States. Following the conclusion of Britain's negotiations with France and Spain, the formal Treaty of Paris was signed by all parties early in September 1783, very nearly on the second anniversary of the Allied armies' parades through Philadelphia while on their march to Yorktown. While the process played out, the Continental army remained intact, the bulk of it garrisoned at assorted sites in the Hudson Highlands above Manhattan, which was still occupied by the British army. The French army remained in America throughout 1782. During that summer it made a long, leisurely march from the Virginia peninsula to Peekskill, where the Allied armies were briefly united for the final time. In the fall, Rochambeau's army undertook its last American march, a trek to Boston, from which it sailed for home on Christmas Eve. Washington's army was fed, housed, and safe, but unpaid, which made it a powder keg that could explode anytime. It was an anxious period for the commander, who feared mutinies and mass desertions that could potentially be exploited by the enemy.

It is doubtful that Sir Henry Clinton would have seized the moment had such an opportunity presented itself. He had offered his resignation in the aftermath of Yorktown and was waiting impatiently for the arrival of

General Guy Carleton, his successor. When Carleton at last arrived in May 1782, Clinton wasted no time before sailing for England, departing four years almost to the day since his arrival in Philadelphia to take command of the British army.[4] Washington appears to have feared the unfamiliar Carleton, but order prevailed in the American army, in part perhaps because throughout 1782 and into 1783 there were abundant signs that the war was truly winding down. Within a year of Yorktown, Britain's armies of occupation in Savannah and Charleston abandoned those cities, accompanied by thousands of Loyalists, many of whom took their enslaved people with them. In addition, thousands of former slaves emancipated under the terms of Clinton's 1779 Phillipsburg Proclamation departed from Tybee Island and Charleston with the British army; estimates of the number of these freedmen vary from six thousand to eighteen thousand.[5] Four months after the preliminary peace treaty was signed in Paris, Washington and Carleton agreed to a formal armistice that went into effect on April 19, 1783, the eighth anniversary of the beginning of the war. Thereafter, the two sides rapidly negotiated prisoner swaps, and by late July the last prisoner of war in America had been liberated. On the day the shooting officially stopped, Thomas Paine issued the final installment in *The American Crisis* series, a piece that began, "The times that tried men's souls are over."[6]

The armistice, Congress's inability to pay its soldiers, and disorder in the ranks in the West Point encampment—which Washington feared might be a harbinger of troubles elsewhere—spurred demobilization. So many men were furloughed that by June the Continental army had shrunk by 80 percent, to around 1,800 men. The pockets of those who departed were stuffed with what they derisively called "Morris notes," IOUs signed by Superintendent of Finance Robert Morris that supposedly would be redeemable for sound currency within a few months. Few of the men believed such hooey. Many officers, who had the financial wherewithal to get by in the hard times ahead, held on to their notes and redeemed them years later when the American economy had been put on a sound footing, padding their income with the pension that Washington had helped secure for them, and himself, during the Valley Forge winter. Virtually none of the enlisted men enjoyed such luxury. Lacking money to make their long journeys home, most soldiers sold their notes to speculators for pennies on the dollar. These servicemen had been the victims of their government's breach of trust on numerous occasions, and at the very end of their service they were victims one final time.[7]

Jettisoning most of the soldiery quieted the turmoil in the army throughout the summer. Finally, on November 1, newspapers broke the news of the signing of the Treaty of Paris. The next day Washington delivered a farewell address to the army in which he reflected on why the war was won. He thought the victory was "little short of a standing miracle," and he attributed it to both the "interpositions of Providence" and the "unparalleled perseverance" of the officers and men "through every possible suffering." He did not mention French assistance or the roles played by militiamen and southern partisans.[8]

A few days later Carleton informed Washington of the looming date on which the British army planned to evacuate New York. The Continental army, having now dwindled to about 800 men, marched from West Point to the periphery of the city. Throughout the autumn Carleton had sent off 35,010 Loyalists and some 3,000 emancipated slaves to Nova Scotia, Quebec, and the Bahamas. He had also gradually discharged or redeployed some 22,000 men in his army—including 5,818 Americans who were serving in provincial units—to Europe or other parts of the British Empire. Only 1,930 British soldiers remained in New York on November 25, the day the Continentals arrived at the edge of the city, and throughout that morning they boarded troop transports for their departure. As the British soldiers climbed the gangplanks, New Yorkers lined the shore and "threw their hats in the air, screaming and boisterous with joy" at the departure of the despised enemy and the incontrovertible evidence that war was over and the independence of all thirteen states had really been won.[9] When the last ship was loaded and weighed anchor, the Continental army entered the city it had been driven from in the fall of 1776 and paraded down Broadway before a vast and happy throng.

A month later Washington appeared before Congress, now meeting in Annapolis, and resigned his commission. He did not touch on the reasons for America's victory in his second farewell speech, and the only soldiers he thanked were those who had served as his aides. After declaring that the successful conclusion of this war had given the infant United States the "opportunity . . . of becoming a respectable Nation," he formally resigned his commission and took "leave of all the employments of public life."[10]

The Revolutionary War—America's longest conflict until the Vietnam War—was finally over. Those soldiers who made it home, as did Washington on Christmas Eve 1783, were fortunate. It had been a costly war. About 17,500 British and German regulars died, and it is likely that as many as 4,000 Americans who served in Britain's provincial units were among those who perished. The death toll among Loyalist militiamen can never be known, but it must have been considerable. Most scholars agree on the conservative figure of 30,000 for the number of American Continentals and militia who died in this war, though after a careful appraisal of the mortality rate among prisoners of war, one recent study estimated the death toll to have been 35,800. If the more conservative approximation is anywhere close to correct, roughly one free American male of military age in sixteen died, compared with one in ten in the Civil War and one in seventy-five in World War II. Of those who perished, about 7,000 died in combat. Most of the remainder were victims of disease, though as in every war some men met their death in accidents or suicide. Of those known to have been killed in combat, 2,373 died between the action on Lexington Green in April 1775 and Burgoyne's surrender at Saratoga in October 1777. In the period that followed Saratoga, down through Cornwallis's surrender in October 1781, some 4,451 American soldiers died in battle.[11] If the percentage of deaths from disease was the same after 1778 as before—and it was probably much larger given that most of the campaigning in that period occurred in the fever-ridden South—more than 22,000 Continentals and militia died along the way from Saratoga to Yorktown. Approximately 65 percent of America's death toll in this war came after Saratoga. Thousands more on both sides were wounded but survived, and many would suffer painful reminders of their trauma throughout the remainder of their lives.

WHILE COUNTLESS NUMBERS of American soldiers, especially officers, were deferred to by their neighbors and exalted by their local communities, and some like Henry Knox and Benjamin Lincoln were toasted as state or regional heroes, contemporaries throughout the length and breadth of the United States acclaimed two military men as great national heroes—Washington and Nathanael Greene. Charles Lee, revered by many at the outset of hostilities, ran afoul of Washington and his own demons, and was gone from the army years before Yorktown. Horatio Gates, lionized for a time as Burgoyne's conqueror at Saratoga, lost his luster at Camden; exiled thereafter to the backwaters of the war, Gates was left to bemoan the "horrid Solitude" that was his lot.[12] The only Continental officer to rival Washington and Greene in popularity was not an American, but the Marquis de Lafayette.

Fearing a fatal divisiveness, Congress had taken steps during the Valley Forge winter to insulate Washington from his critics. As John Adams noted, Congress not only took pains to hide Washington's "faults and errors" from the public; it sought to transform the general into an iconic figure. In Adams's words, Congress was bent on making Washington the "central stone in the geometrical arch" that was to be the American pantheon, a necessary step in the minds of the congressmen so that an America without a monarch would have a figure around whom the citizenry could rally.[13] Even after the war, no former army officer or public official dared to say anything unbecoming about Washington. For instance, though some knew otherwise, the former commander in chief was widely celebrated for his genius in orchestrating the British disaster at Yorktown. Six years passed after Yorktown before the first book appeared, in Paris, revealing that Rochambeau had been the real architect of the strategic plan that resulted in Cornwallis's surrender, and more than a century elapsed before the full story—including Washington's lengthy opposition to the Virginia campaign—was published in the United States. Washington was rightly acclaimed for his years of sacrificial service and leadership, and for never having abused the powers given him. One example among many was the tribute paid him by the Massachusetts assembly. He was lauded for his "all-wise . . . Conduct in the Discharge" of his duties." The assembly went on to state:

> What trying Scenes have you not passed through! What Hardships have you not endured! What Dangers have you not encountered! May Heaven reward your unremitted Exertions! May you long live, beloved by a grateful Country. . . .
>
> While Patriots shall not cease to applaud that sacred Attachment which you have constantly manifested to the Rights of Citizens—too often violated by Men in Arms—
>
> Your Military Virtues & Achievements will be deeply recorded in the Breasts of your Countrymen & their Posterity, and make the brightest Pages in the History of Mankind.[14]

One congressman described Washington's appearance before Congress to resign his commission as "a solemn and affecting spectacle, such an one as history does not [often] present. The spectators all wept, and there was hardly a member of Congress who did not drop tears." He added that Washington's departure from the public stage was an "inexpressibly . . . affecting" event.[15]

For more than a decade following the war, no one publicly questioned Washington's generalship. But in 1796, Thomas Paine, once one of Washington's greatest supporters, took aim at him in the pamphlet *Letter to George Washington*. Paine's diatribe was brought on by a mistaken belief that Washington was responsible for his incarceration in Paris—and near brush with the guillotine—during the Reign of Terror in the French Revolution. Brimming with fury toward Washington, Paine argued that from 1778 onward the commander "slept away" his "time in the field, till the finances of the country were completely exhausted." He also criticized

Washington for not having attacked the British in Boston in 1775, when he possessed a vastly larger army than his foe, and for his numerous errors the following year during the New York campaign. Thereafter, year after year, Washington's leadership was marked by "little enterprise." It was Gates who scored the victory at Saratoga that brought France into the war, an ally without whom America could not have defeated the British. Nor did Washington have much to do with winning the war in the South, where states that were "over-run by the enemy" were eventually saved by the superior generalship of Nathanael Greene. In truth, Paine concluded, Gates and Greene should be seen as greater national heroes than Washington. Indeed, Washington deserved "but little share in the glory of the final event," the victory at Yorktown, which, Paine said, was due largely to the French.[16]

Paine may have been correct in some of his assertions, but none wished to take up his argument, either because they thought he was wrong or understood that attacking Washington was too risky. Paine learned that truth the hard way. His many hugely popular writings, and his service in the American Revolution, may at one time have made him the most popular figure in America after George Washington. But his philippic against Washington—together with the nearly simultaneous publication of *Age of Reason*, a sweeping attack on the Bible and the theology of Jesus's divinity—drove a stake through his popularity and influence within America. Following Washington's death, in 1799, hundreds of towns throughout the land held memorial services in his honor. When Paine died, in 1809, not a single newspaper published a eulogy, and only fourteen acquaintances attended his burial.[17]

Curiously, none of the major Founders—neither important fellow Virginians such as Thomas Jefferson, James Madison, and James Monroe; nor John Adams, who had played an instrumental role in Washington's appointment as commander; nor Alexander Hamilton, who by far had been the closest to the commander in chief—rebutted Paine. Only Adams even privately commented on Paine's reviling of Washington, and he merely said the pamphleteer had been "insane" to take on such a lionized figure.[18]

Hamilton never penned a public tribute to Washington's generalship, though on Independence Day 1789 he delivered a passionate tribute to the merits and contributions of Nathanael Greene. Hamilton lauded Greene's "calm intrepidity and unshaken presence of mind" in saving South Carolina and Georgia when "the spirit of their people [was] dejected and intimidated" and "the flame of resistance [was] scarcely kept alive." His exploits, Hamilton added, sprang from "a plan conceived with so much wisdom" that it "may without exaggeration be denominated a master piece of military skill and exertion."[19]

Thomas Paine was a polemicist with an ax to grind, not a dispassionate historian. Washington deserved better. He crucially won the affection and admiration of his officers, a corps of ambitious men who under another leader might have posed a grave threat to republicanism and civilian hegemony. Under his leadership, the Continental army grew to be a respectable military force, one that in the war's latter years was praised by some enemy officers as in some respects the equal of the British army. Who could have imagined, asked a Hessian officer, that out of "this multitude of rabble" an army could have been constructed that "could defy kings."[20] Washington grew to be an accomplished manager of the army. No one can read Washington's day-to-day orders and correspondence and come away unaware of the time, energy, and ability that he devoted to the administration of the Continental army. He also exhibited a deft feel for working with Congress and governors, and it is difficult to imagine anyone who could have exceeded his ability in managing relations with French ministers, generals, and admirals. He was unsurpassed in his talent for judging others. Washington quickly found Henry Knox and put him in command of the army's artillery. It took him only a few weeks to see potential in Greene that no one else discerned. Conversely, he rapidly spotted flaws in some of his officers, William Heath and Israel Putnam among them, and shuttled them to rear echelons, just where they belonged in the estimate of most historians. Washington's keen judgment was repeated countless times in the selection of lower-ranking field officers.

Congress may have worked diligently to make Washington a figure to be revered, but the veneration in which he was held before and after Yorktown was due in some measure to his own adeptness in winning the public's adulation. Perhaps because he had commanded an army in Virginia in the 1750s and had sat in his colony's assembly for years, Washington came to his command post with a deft feel for what to do and not to do. More than a year before Yorktown, Lafayette told Comte de Vergennes that Washington was seen by the public as the "guardian spirit of America," a man who had won his countrymen's respect through his sober, selfless, steadfast, scandal-free, and patriotic service.[21]

Washington, in 1775, was an amateur soldier suddenly vested with responsibility for leading an army of callow officers and soldiers against the professional British army. At times, principally during his initial thirty months on the job, his lack of professional training was readily apparent. He erred time and again in the New York campaign in 1776 and blundered badly in the Battles of Brandywine and Germantown the following year. He had problems making rapid decisions, a flaw that could be—and in his case nearly was—disastrous in the heat of battle. America's cause may have been abetted in that Washington never again had to make momentous decisions while under fire in all the years that followed the engagement at Monmouth in June 1778. Moreover, despite his reputation for selflessness, his fear of Horatio Gates, Saratoga's hero, led Washington to refuse to put him in charge of the campaign to retake Newport in 1778. It may also have been a factor in his opposition to a Canadian invasion in 1778 and 1779, an under-taking that Washington finally embraced in 1780 immediately after learning of Gates's humiliating defeat at Camden, a crushing loss that took him out of the picture as one to command the invasion army.

Washington was painfully slow to recognize the dangers posed by Britain's embrace of a southern strategy, strangely unwilling to provide counsel to General Lincoln during the Charleston campaign, and for the longest time reluctant to part with many men from his immobile army to assist in the fighting in the South. Washington additionally looked on the militia with a jaundiced eye. To be sure, militiamen were not the equal of his Continental regulars, but Greene and Daniel Morgan understood how to effectively utilize them in ways that Washington never comprehended. Today, the Washington of lore is often seen as a daring leader. That judgment hinges almost solely on his laudable audacity in the two battles of Trenton and the attack on the British at Germantown. During the four years that Paine characterized as the time when Washington slept in the field, the commander in chief displayed little dash. He might have attempted to break the stalemate through an invasion of weakly held Canada. Even a limited thrust at Canada might have been sufficient to compel the enemy to withdraw some or all of its troops from the South. Given the numerical superiority of a combined force of Continentals and militia that Washington could have enjoyed throughout 1779 and 1780, he might have struck repeatedly at the British defensive installations ringing New York. Over time, these pinpricks might have drained the strength of the enemy, much as the repeated guerrilla strikes and Greene's valorous assaults in the South led to an alarming attrition in Britain's armed forces. But the boldness that Washington had once exhibited was nowhere to be seen after Monmouth, as France's frustrated foreign minister, Comte de Vergennes, complained. Today, some see Washington's inaction in all those years as the height of wisdom, given that the war was eventually won. But had America failed to achieve independence, or had a tiny new nation of fewer than thirteen states emerged from hostilities—and either of those possibilities appeared to be quite likely deep into 1781—Washington's strategic judgment would not have seemed so sound. Some might speculate that after his repeated brushes with disaster early in the war, and the criticism those instances sparked about his generalship, Washington after 1778 feared to act without the sanction of his ally.

Wars can be lost through excessive caution. But caution can also contribute to victory. Once France entered the war, Washington understood that Franco-American power offered the United States its best chance for victory. Thereafter, he wisely refrained from taking risks that could weaken his army and ultimately diminish Allied strength whenever the decisive moment arrived. Paine saw Washington's repeated unwillingness to fight as a liability. Sir Henry Clinton, a savvy professional officer, saw Washington's conduct as sagacious.

A generation ago James Flexner, one of the general's biographers, labeled Washington the "indispensable man" for the American cause.[22] Washington made mistakes and had his shortcomings, but he was the best choice to command the Continental army. None among the initial batch of general officers that Congress chose in June 1775 was his equal. Only Greene in time appeared to have the necessary qualities for performing as well as Washington, but he was not equipped for the job during the early years of hostilities. There were times when the cause was fortunate to have survived Washington's blunders and deficiencies, but taken as whole the new nation was blessed to have had him as its commander.

NOT SO LONG ago a historian summed up the outcome of the Revolutionary War with the observation that "in the last analysis it was Washington and the army that won the war for American independence."[23] Many contemporaries, and over the decades not a few historians, have come to pretty much the same conclusion. However, such a judgment raises questions. Did America win the war, or did Britain lose a war it could have won? Do other American generals deserve credit alongside Washington for America's victory? How important was French assistance in the war's outcome? What of the sacrifices made by thousands of American militiamen? Did the partisan warriors not make significant contributions to America's victory? What exactly was Washington's role in America's triumph?

Britain could have, and should have, won the war in 1775 and 1776, and it still might have subdued its foe in 1777. There were five instances during the first three years of the war when Britain might have dealt crushing blows to the colonial insurgency. Had the ministry gone to war with an adequate army in place in the colonies, it might have inflicted a crumpling wallop on the first day of hostilities. Two months later it was within the grasp of General Thomas Gage to score a nearly bloodless, and dispiriting, victory over the rebels at Bunker Hill. General William Howe might have destroyed half of the Continental army had he assaulted the rebel redoubts in Brooklyn Heights in September 1776. Given the supremacy of both his army and naval wing, Howe had it within his power to annihilate the remainder of Washington's army that languished in Manhattan in subsequent weeks. Had Howe come up the Hudson to link his army with Burgoyne's during 1777, the catastrophe at Saratoga in all likelihood would have been averted, and it is conceivable that a great British victory might have been won.

Each of those opportunities was missed, and the third year of hostilities ended with Burgoyne's surrender, a turn of events that led many in England to conclude that it was hopeless to continue the war. But Britain persevered, though with a new strategy, a southern strategy that aimed at reclaiming Georgia and South Carolina, and possibly more. Lord George Germain, the American secretary who stitched together the southern strategy, believed the South teemed with Loyalists who were eager to bear arms for Great Britain. Germain insisted that their numbers, and the prowess of Britain's army and navy, would tilt the balance and lead to the recovery of some of the former southern colonies.

It was left to Sir Henry Clinton, named commander of Britain's army in America in the spring of 1778, to make the new strategy work and salvage something for his country from this war. Throughout the three and one half years that followed, Clinton faithfully sought to comply with Germain's orders, which hardly varied from one year to another: maintain Britain's hold on New York; seek to bring Washington to battle, but discontinue attempts to subdue the rebellion in the northern provinces through major offensive operations; and vigorously prosecute the war in the South.[24] From the beginning Clinton felt hamstrung, and with good reason. France entered the war just as Clinton assumed command. He also had to contend with a more experienced and better furnished American adversary than had existed in previous years. What is more, Clinton took command of an army that was stripped of about 40 percent of its manpower.

Many on both sides had thought the war was nearly over when France allied with the United States in 1778. Instead, hostilities dragged on for four additional years. Within a year of Saratoga the war was stalemated. The Allied victory that only shortly before had seemed a certainty had become far from certain. Two years later, at the dawn of 1781, American leaders including Washington, members of Congress, and the diplomat John Adams feared for the cause. The infant nation was bankrupt, mutinies had erupted in the Continental army, and war-weariness was pummeling the populace's will to maintain the fight. Above all, there were unmistakable signs that French staying power was waning after three futile years as a belligerent. Washington confessed that he had nearly lost hope of achieving victory, and he had lots of company. Some feared a total collapse in the new nation's ability to continue to fight. Adams worried that the major powers in Europe would convene a peace conference to impose a settlement, a step that would offer France the face-saving means of exiting the conflict. In such an eventuality, there might not be a United States. Or there might be a United States, though it likely would consist of fewer than thirteen states, for at the outset of 1781 Britain had superior claims to South Carolina and Georgia. Furthermore, there was a strong possibility that the United States would be surrounded by British-held territories. If the war ended as an anxious Adams and many other alarmed Americans feared it might, the British Empire in America would remain huge, stretching from Canada through trans-Appalachia and on to include two or three southern colonies as well as several islands in the West Indies. The independent United States, girdled by a mighty and hostile foreign power, would have little chance of expanding. In fact, the prospects for a truly independent and sustainable United States would be gloomy. The bright promise of a new world of greater opportunities for a greater percentage of the population—the dream that had stirred so many to seek freedom from colonial status—would melt away.

Like his adversaries, and for the same reasons, General Clinton thought that 1781 would be this war's decisive year. He was convinced that France would drop out of the war if the Allies failed to score a decisive victory that year, and he knew the Americans would be unable to continue their insurgency without French assistance. Even with French help, the Americans, drained and in precarious straits, might be incapable of continuing the fight beyond 1781.

Throughout the initial months of that crucial year, Clinton, anticipating an Allied campaign to retake New York, sought to have a sufficient number of troops on hand to meet what he believed would be the enemy's inevitable challenge. As always, he also adhered to the southern strategy. Once a skeptic, Clinton had come to think it was possible to quash the insurgency in the lower South. His thinking had evolved slowly, but it was in place by early in 1781, and it involved a multipronged strategy. Earl Cornwallis was to contend with the rebels—regulars, militia, and partisans—in South Carolina, and he was to remain there until that province was pacified. Meanwhile, Clinton committed several thousand troops to Virginia between January and March, steps taken to lighten Cornwallis's burden in the Carolinas. Not only would the presence of the British army compel Virginia to keep its militia at home, but the king's troops were to plug the arteries through which the rebels moved supplies to the lower South. Acting in concert with the Royal Navy, the army in Virginia was also, in time, to establish Chesapeake bases. Clinton believed that these secure havens would entice the Loyalists to take up arms and that the British army—including Loyalist provincial military units—could launch destructive raids from these sites, sorties that over time would have a withering impact on the southern colonists' will to continue the rebellion. In the spring, Clinton added to his strategic formula the notion of a lightning raid on Philadelphia to destroy supply depots and wreak devastation in the city. If successful, it could play havoc with the Allies putative plan to attack New York. From the beginning, Clinton additionally envisioned withdrawing the lion's share of the army in Virginia during the summer to bolster the British presence in New York, a step that might have led the Allies to abandon all thoughts of attacking their adversary in Virginia.

Clinton's strategic moves in the South in 1781 were aggressive. Elsewhere, he adhered to a risk-averse strategy. He believed that time was on his side.

Just as Washington sought to preserve his army until the time came when the French were capable of joining in a major operation, Clinton wanted to safeguard his army for the impending showdown in New York. If he survived the Allied onslaught in New York, and if his strategy succeeded in largely pacifying Georgia and South Carolina, Clinton believed the war would end favorably for Great Britain.

Clinton's well-crafted plan was one of five strategic schemes that materialized in 1781. Nathanael Greene's was the most ingenious and daring. He violated a cardinal maxim of warfare by dividing his army in the face of a superior force, and it paid dividends at Cowpens in January. Once his army was reunited and reinforced with militia, Greene fought Cornwallis at Guilford Courthouse, a bloody confrontation that debilitated the British army in North Carolina. Almost alone among America's leaders after 1777, Greene had taken risk upon risk, and his successes in the first seventy-five days of 1781 changed the direction of the war.

General Rochambeau had a plan, too, and it also was a gamble attendant with abundant hazards. He grasped the glittering possibilities that could result from a combined land and naval strike at the army of General William Phillips, later that of Cornwallis, in Virginia. The sheer audacity of Rochambeau's plan was breathtaking. In an age when communications were plodding and often unreliable—weeks were often required to transmit messages from North America to the West Indies—it was almost preposterous to imagine that armies deployed above New York City could succeed in rendezvousing in Virginia at just the right moment with a naval squadron sailing north from the Caribbean. In addition, the odds against achieving the element of surprise that would prevent the quarry in Virginia from escaping were considerable. Should any element of Rochambeau's plan miscarry, the Allies would squander what might well be their final chance to conduct a campaign for the long-sought pivotal victory. As was the case with Greene's scheme, Rochambeau's plan was filled with risks, and it was spawned by a measure of desperation. He, too, was convinced not only that 1781 was likely to be the last year of this war, but that no other option had a decent chance of success.

Cornwallis also had a plan. His grew from a belief that under present conditions the rebellion in South Carolina and Georgia could never be suppressed. It was not that he lacked an adequate force of regulars, he said, but that "our friends," the Loyalists in the Carolinas, were timid and unwilling to join him in the fight. In essence, Cornwallis had come to think that the underlying assumption behind the southern strategy—that the presence and assistance of huge numbers of southern Tories would make possible the pacification of the South—was fundamentally flawed. He thought a new approach was necessary. The full power of the British army must be brought together in Virginia to take that colony out of the war and that—and that alone, he thought—would enable the British to reclaim its "hold [on] the more southern provinces."[25] Hoping to pressure Clinton into acquiescing to his strategic thinking, Cornwallis in April 1781 marched his army to Virginia.

While he focused on Virginia, Cornwallis's principal conceit was that Britain's army must be consolidated. He preferred that the consolidation occur in Virginia, though New York would do. Although he never fully explained his thinking, Cornwallis appears to have believed that the Allies would have to make their move against the united British force, wherever it was deployed, bringing on a grand showdown. That climactic engagement would decide the war, much as the Seven Years' War in America had for all practical purposes terminated with Britain's victory over France in a decisive face-off in 1759 on the Plains of Abraham outside Quebec. Cornwallis's plan made sense, but it was not flawless. The Allies might have ignored the combined enemy army, especially if it was in New York, and assailed British-held Charleston, which was occupied by a substantial force. Furthermore, combining Clinton's army in New York with the army in Virginia would necessitate the abandonment of one of those two sites. After years of hostilities, either New York would be relinquished or all of the South would be jettisoned. After six years of warfare, Britain's success or failure would depend entirely on one engagement. If Britain won that battle, or at least foiled the Allies, it could claim a victory of undetermined proportions in this war. If Britain lost the battle, it would lose everything in America.

Washington had a plan for 1781 as well. His gaze was fixed on New York. From his September 1780 meeting with Rochambeau in Hartford into the following summer, Washington remained wedded to the idea of a joint Allied campaign to retake New York. As the plan never came to fruition, no one can know how it would have played out. Rochambeau, a professional soldier with considerably more experience in such things, doubted that it could succeed.

Of the plans devised by the leaders of the armies of Great Britain, France, and America, only Rochambeau's was put into effect. It cannot be known how Clinton's and Washington's designs might have fared. But on the face of it, achieving a decisive victory through an attack on New York— Washington's cherished project—was a long shot. In contrast, Clinton's multifarious stratagem was less risky and more sound. It held out the plausible prospects of Great Britain getting through 1781 without suffering a catastrophic defeat while Cornwallis succeeded in suppressing the insurgents in Georgia and South Carolina. Clinton's hoped-for raid on Philadelphia, if successful, would in all likelihood have had profound impact on Allied planning during this crucial year. In short, it could have been a game changer.

Deep into the summer of 1781—more than six years into this grim, bloody conflict—the war's outcome was far from known. American independence might yet be secured; its bid for independence might be foiled; or an independent United States consisting of fewer than thirteen states might come into being. Winning or losing this war hinged on decisions made, actions taken, and initiatives not pursued throughout that pivotal year.

Yorktown did not come about overnight. It was the result of momentous decisions and a chain of events on a long, twisting road from Saratoga to the historic siege in this once bucolic spot in Virginia. Before 1781, French squadrons had twice come to North America and, for the Allies, nothing substantive had come of either visit. Had Comte d'Estaing inflicted ruinous blows to Britain's war effort on either occasion, the war might have been brought to an end years before Yorktown. Had General Augustine Prevost pressed his advantage at the gates of Charleston in the spring of 1779, South

Carolina might have dropped out of the war, changing the complexion of hostilities in the South in unfathomable ways. Had the British successfully attacked West Point or destroyed either General John Sullivan's army or the French in Newport, or had Benedict Arnold's treason not been a narrow miss, only Virginians who lived on the peninsula between the York and James Rivers would have ever heard of Yorktown.

Particularly crucial occurrences took place during the year before Yorktown. In the aftermath of Clinton's capture of Charleston, the pacification of South Carolina began well enough. However, within weeks the British army not only experienced worrisome disruptions at the hands of rebel partisans but also learned that the willingness of Loyalists to fight for their king had dimmed in the face of the guerrillas' savage reprisals. Cornwallis answered by twice bringing his army to North Carolina, initiatives undertaken to recruit Loyalist troops and plug the flow of rebel supplies into South Carolina. Both campaigns ended in failure. "[N]o good whatsoever resulted from all his exertions" outside South Carolina, was how Clinton put it. First there was the debacle at King's Mountain one year before Yorktown. Clinton characterized the calamity as Cornwallis's Trenton. Next, against armies commanded by Daniel Morgan and Greene, forces in which half or more of the soldiers were militiamen, the British suffered a severe setback at Cowpens and debilitating losses at Guilford Courthouse. Thereafter, Cornwallis took his army to Virginia, leaving "two valuable colonies behind him to be overrun and conquered" by the rebels, as a bitter Clinton remarked. The result of Cornwallis's unauthorized act, Clinton added, was that the southern colonies "are gone from us and I fear are not to be recovered."[26] Clinton might have added that the addition of Cornwallis's army to the British forces already in Virginia created such a tempting target that it helped wean Washington from his fixation on New York.

Cornwallis's misguided decision to abandon South Carolina in the spring of 1781 made a shambles of Clinton's carefully constructed strategic plan. Not only was Clinton's vision of twin campaigns in Virginia and South Carolina ruined, but Cornwallis's opposition to the planned strike against

Philadelphia was, as intended, the death knell for a scheme filled with intriguing possibilities. Cornwallis achieved nothing by coming to Virginia that could not have been accomplished by Britain's army already posted there. When faced with the Allied siege, Cornwallis's decision to hastily withdraw from the outer defenses at Yorktown, though plausible given what he knew at the time, shrank the time required for the Allies to bring about their adversary's surrender. Had Cornwallis compelled the Allies to fight to remove him from the outer defenses, it is conceivable that the siege might still have been in progress when Clinton's relief expedition arrived at the Chesapeake or when de Grasse felt that he had to depart.

In the wake of the news of the disaster at Yorktown, recriminations and finger-pointing were the order of the day in England. Cornwallis fared surprisingly well. Arriving back in England more than six months before Clinton, Cornwallis succeeded in putting forward his vindication. He was well connected politically and adroit with those who shaped public opinion, areas in which Clinton readily admitted his deficiencies. He was "no match" for one so "artful and designing" as Cornwallis, Clinton acknowledged. Furthermore, after word of Yorktown reached England, the opposition faction in Parliament, struggling to bring down Lord North's government and end the war, was better served by assailing the government's reasons for continuing the war than by attacking the conduct of the generals who had fought the war.

Defenders of the government—and some officials, including Germain—reviled Clinton, portraying him as irresolute, overly cautious, surrounded by sycophants, too weak to provide the leadership that had been needed, and without a strategic plan.[27] Much of the press blamed Clinton for Yorktown, especially for not having acted to stop the Allied armies once they crossed the Hudson and began their march to Virginia. One newspaper carped that Great Britain had been "ill served" by all three of its commanders in chief during this war and many in one fashion or another portrayed Clinton has having been outgeneraled by Washington.[28]

Historians have hardly differed from contemporaries in their appraisal of Clinton. Over the years, he has been portrayed as capricious, indecisive,

overly cautious, muddled and confused, persistently inactive, lacking a strategic vision or a master plan, and fatally inhibited by his subliminal sense of
inadequacy. He has been limned as "crippled by self-distrust," "timid," and
"easily cast down by minor reverses," and as a leader who spent much of his
time "devising reasons for inaction." Clinton was "his own worst enemy,"
wrote one scholar, a judgment that neatly summed up the assessment of
most historians during the past seventy-five years.[29] If Washington did not
deserve all the acrimony visited on him by Thomas Paine—or his critics
during the Valley Forge winter—Clinton did not merit the many reproaches
directed at him. The time is long overdue for reassessing Clinton.

He was a good general. In the first three years of the war, prior to
assuming command, Clinton's advocacy of wise tactical and strategic
choices was unequaled among the army's senior leaders. He foresaw the
blunder that General Gage was about to make at Bunker Hill in 1775 and
urged another approach. It was Clinton who conceived the move that led to
Britain's victory on Long Island in 1776. Had Howe listened to Clinton's
recommendations as the ragtag American army retreated across New Jersey
that autumn, General Washington might have suffered a war-altering
thrashing. Clinton rapidly perceived the folly of General Howe's decision to
campaign for Philadelphia rather than to unite with Burgoyne in 1777.
During those years, he demonstrated more than strategic acumen. When
given responsibility for taking Newport in 1776, Clinton carried out the
operation flawlessly, and the steps that he took in New York's Highlands in
1777 when attempting the rescue of Burgoyne's imperiled army were daring
and brilliantly conceived and implemented.

Much of the faultfinding directed at Clinton once he commanded
Britain's army was unfounded. For the most part, the notion that he shrank
from bold, even daring, action is ludicrous. He responded with energy and
zeal to multiple crises during his initial four months as commander,
including going into battle with Washington at Monmouth, springing into
action when threated by d'Estaing in New York and Rhode Island, and
rushing a force to Newport in the late summer of 1778 that came close to
annihilating Sullivan's American army. There was no sign of indecisiveness

on Clinton's part in any of these actions. He was the very embodiment of audacity in each response. Nor were his commitments of large forces to invade Georgia and South Carolina—campaigns that led to the capture of Savannah and Charleston—the acts of an indecisive or timorous commander. In 1780 and again the following year, Clinton was committed to risky operations against the French in Rhode Island, only to be frustrated on both occasions by the Royal Navy. He was avid for acting in concert with Benedict Arnold in 1780 in what he knew might be a perilous operation to claim West Point, only to be thwarted when the plan unraveled following John André's capture. Despite having been stripped of much of his army at the very outset of taking command, Clinton between 1778 and 1780 had time and again acted decisively or been willing to undertake intrepid initiatives.

Perhaps Clinton should have hazarded an attack on West Point in 1779, but he was wary of acting when his knowledge of the enemy's strength was unknown, on the whole an admirable stance for a military commander. Risk-taking sometimes leads to great rewards, but it can have tragic results. General John Burgoyne took several risks during his invasion of New York in 1777 and eventually surrendered his army at Saratoga. Cornwallis chanced multiple perilous moves in the inhospitable North Carolina back-country, and the results were grievous losses at King's Mountain and Cowpens as well as an intolerable casualty toll at Guilford Courthouse. Two years after declining to attack West Point, Clinton's army remained intact and strong, and prepared for what he believed would be the war's pivotal campaign in 1781.

The best case for asserting that Clinton blundered egregiously before 1781 would be his failure to move against the newly arrived French army under Rochambeau in Rhode Island in July 1780. Clinton had over-whelming naval superiority on his side and could have mustered an armed force that was superior in numbers to the army that Rochambeau had brought to America. To have acted, and acted successfully, might have led to a victory of such proportions that the American quest for independence would have been foiled. But Clinton was in the dark with regard to the size of the enemy force, and by the time the navy could have acted, the French had been allotted ample time to prepare their defenses. To attack an entrenched professional army assisted by vast numbers of Yankee militiamen would have been a perilous operation, one attended with far greater risks than d'Estaing faced in making a similar attack in Savannah a few months earlier. D'Estaing, and the Americans with him, paid heavily for their undertaking and they failed to destroy their adversary.

At times, Clinton's preference for caution was due less to irresolution than to his well-founded conviction that time was his friend and the Allies' enemy. With the American insurgency hampered by economic woes, recruiting difficulties, and faltering morale, Clinton was often guided by the clear-sighted belief that more was to be gained from avoiding defeat than from rolling the dice in hopes of gaining a victory. His thinking was essentially identical to that of Washington throughout most of the period from 1778 onward. It was a perspective that helped make Washington an American icon. In the eyes of many, it made Clinton a failure.

To condemn Clinton as ruined by subconscious fears of inadequacy—an idea linked to the psychohistory craze of a bygone era—is an allegation that simply cannot be proved. Taking into account the almost total lack of documentation concerning Clinton's private and confidential thoughts, the idea of suggesting that unconscious motivations paralyzed his will to act is absurd on its face. In fact, given the considerable number of actions that he undertook, it is surprising that the notion gained resonance with so many historians.

The charge that Clinton lacked strategic vision, and was without a master plan, is preposterous. His original scheme for the pacification of Georgia and the Carolinas had to be retooled following the advent of partisan warfare and the setbacks that Cornwallis repeatedly experienced in the Carolina backcountry. Thereafter, the strategy that Clinton formulated— Phillips's army in Virginia providing the assistance that Cornwallis required to pacify South Carolina and Georgia—was well conceived and might have succeeded. But it was ruined both by Cornwallis, who abandoned South

Carolina, and by the meddling of Lord Germain, who had only the haziest idea of the reality of the war in the South.

It is true that Clinton had not contested the Allied armies when they crossed the Hudson in August 1781. Convinced that New York was their target, he was not about to abandon the defensive network in Manhattan that the British had spent five years developing to fight his adversaries in a set-piece engagement. No general worth his salt would have done such a thing. By the time Clinton at last discovered that the Allied force was headed for Virginia, it was too late to act. Clinton had been fooled. But it was not due to irresolution or confused thinking on his part. The reports of his intelligence service never dissuaded him from the belief that the Allies planned a campaign to take New York, a conviction seemingly substantiated both by the disclosure brought by the *Swallow* and the news conveyed by Rear Admiral Hood—days after the Allies crossed the Hudson—that de Grasse's task force was not in the Chesapeake. Had Admiral Rodney expeditiously dispatched the information that he possessed in July concerning de Grasse's strength and destination, Clinton almost certainly would have responded differently. But Clinton acted in the dark during that crucial August. His decision came down to an educated guess. This was a war, like many other wars, of errant guesses. British leaders had guessed that the colonists would never stand and fight against regulars, Washington had guessed that Fort Washington could withstand a British attack or siege, and Germain, among others, guessed that de Grasse would never bring his entire fleet to North America. Clinton, in August 1781, guessed that the Allies were targeting New York. Clinton guessed wrong.

Clinton may not have been a great general, but he was an accomplished, diligent, and thoughtful commander who was far more active than his critics have admitted. Despite the limited size of his army, the coalition of enemies that he faced, and the two-front war with which he grappled, he came stunningly close to avoiding the British defeat that many had seen as virtually inevitable after Saratoga. Indeed, he nearly salvaged something— perhaps a considerable amount—for a government which had continued to wage this brutal American war in the years following Saratoga. Clinton was a better general than his contemporary critics and most historians have argued.

HISTORY CAN PLAY many tricks. Both Washington and Clinton had strengths and weaknesses. Washington's leadership qualities were superior. Clinton, an experienced professional soldier, was the better strategist, and as late as summer 1781 he understood better than Washington how to achieve what his country was fighting for. Washington did not see Yorktown coming. Clinton did not see it coming until it was too late. But it came. For Washington, it came through the help of his ally. For Clinton, it came about in large measure because of a succession of ill-conceived actions by Cornwallis and several Royal Navy commanders. Once Yorktown came, Washington's iconic stature was solidified, and Clinton's reputation was largely ruined.

Clinton's failure had many sources, but among the most important was Lord Germain's ruinous intrusiveness. Whereas Germain had given General Howe a free hand, he overcompensated in the aftermath of the catastrophe at Saratoga. Thereafter, he kept tight reins on Clinton and as never before encroached on his commander's strategic planning. But Germain was three thousand miles away; had never been to America; was at times erroneously influenced by the embroidered, not to mention simplistic, assessments of Tories; and issued orders based on belated and inaccurate information. From the summer of 1780 onward, Germain's preference for Cornwallis—whose boldness and action-prone nature he admired—was an unmistakable undercurrent in many communiqués that he sent to Clinton. Clinton was hardly delusional in recognizing Germain's leanings, and it doubtless was a factor in his not ordering Cornwallis to return to South Carolina in the spring of 1781. Germain additionally foiled Clinton's intention of withdrawing all but some two thousand troops from Virginia during the summer of 1781. Germain's unremitting insistence that the presence of a large army in Virginia was crucial to the "progress of the

King's arms in the speedy suppression of the rebellion" drove Clinton to abruptly order a stop to the removal of troops already underway in July.[30] As a consequence, Britain's maintenance of an army of 7,500 in Yorktown was too tempting for the Allies to ignore.

The Continental Congress had encroached on Washington's strategic choices in 1776, and the American insurgency was fortunate to escape the damage that was done. Congress intruded at times thereafter, but beginning in 1778 it vested Washington with a largely free hand in planning the army's moves. Clinton, and his country's war effort, might have profited had he, too, been the beneficiary of a freer hand in waging the war.

Britain's failure was due in part to the Royal Navy's inability to adequately wage a world war. During three of the four years of Clinton's command, the French for a time gained supremacy in North American waters, fatally so for Great Britain in the late summer of 1781. Yet despite the daunting challenges that the navy faced, it still might have checked de Grasse's squadron. Much of the blame for its failure to have a shot at thwarting the French during that pivotal year was due to the insipid behavior of Sir George Rodney, commander of the Leeward Islands Squadron through most of that summer. Not for nothing would Clinton later exclaim that "Rodney . . . deserved to be ruined for his bad Conduct." Rodney, however, was not solely culpable. The generally superb intelligence system built by the Earl of Sandwich, the first lord of the Admiralty, broke down that year, with the result that London failed to send adequate reinforcements and authoritative warnings to its commanders in New York with regard to the size of the task force that de Grasse would bring to North America.[31] Britain's conduct of the war was additionally hindered in that no official had jurisdiction over both land and naval operations. Clinton early on proposed the creation of the position of supreme commander, but it went unheeded.

So why did America win the war? Morale sagged as the war continued unabated, but it never vanished, and the great majority of men and women on the home front continued to make incredible sacrifices year after year. No Americans were more responsible for winning independence than the thousands of grim-faced soldiers, men who slogged down lonely roads under a blazing sun or while lashed by rain or a raw wind. These were soldiers who slept in the open without tents or in barracks so primitive that in winter the cold seemed to gnaw at the marrow of their bones, men who were often deprived of proper sustenance and adequate clothing and shoes, who not infrequently were unpaid, and who risked their all under enemy fire on bleak and forbidding battlefields. Alongside the sacrifices of the Continentals, untried militiamen who all too often were inadequately prepared for combat answered the call of duty and made substantive contributions in an abundance of clashes, as did resolute and severe partisan warriors.

But these men were not solely responsible for winning independence. Although Washington, probably for reasons of state, ignored the role of French assistance in his two farewell addresses, France's contributions to America's ultimate success were crucial. French aid flowed across the Atlantic prior to the Treaty of Alliance and increased thereafter. Over the years, France provided the Americans with over ten million livres in subsidies and thirty-five million livres in loans.[32] France additionally supplied its ally with a small army and a naval arm, engineering know-how, indispensable equipment, weaponry, munitions, and worthy officers, including Lafayette, Rochambeau, and de Grasse. Without that assistance, the merican insurgency could not have endured or gained victory in 1781. In fact, it may not have survived past 1777, for without the abundance of French artillery and muskets that Horatio Gates possessed, the monumental American victory at Saratoga would have been unimaginable. To be sure, an America devoid of French help could never have imagined the siege at Yorktown.

Other factors were important in the war's outcome. The phenomenal generalship of Nathanael Greene in 1781 had a transformative impact on both the war in the South and General Cornwallis's thinking. Washington's astute managerial skills and inspirational leadership were crucial in sustaining the army, transforming it into a more effective fighting force, and nourishing support for the war in good times and bad. The Allies were helped immensely in that Britain was overextended, burdened with more military fronts than it could manage, taxed with the encumbrances inherent in waging a faraway war, and faced with conducting war in the limitless expanses and forbidding backcountry of North America. When Washington in his farewell to his troops said that the American victory was little short of miraculous, he may have been thinking of those grave—one might almost say amazing, even wondrous—errors committed by Generals Gage, Howe, and Cornwallis, and the shortsightedness of the enemy's naval commanders in 1781. Or he may have meant that the Allies profited from generous measures of luck, including opportune storms on Long Island in 1776 and on the night of the surprise attack at Trenton, a timely nightfall at Brandywine in 1777, and the many alluring opportunities his enemy had not acted on.

The journey from Saratoga to Yorktown was long, tortuous, and bloody, and it might have ended quite differently. When independence was declared, William Ellery, a congressman from Rhode Island, said that it was one thing to declare independence, but another to win it.[33] Five years after declaring independence, it was finally won at Yorktown, a triumph that promised—as Washington said in his farewell to the army—"a glorious period" filled with "enlarged prospects of happiness" that "almost exceeds the power of description."[34]

ACKNOWLEDGMENTS

Debts accumulate in the course of writing of a book, and it is with gratitude that I acknowledge the support, help, and guidance provided by many people. I am particularly grateful to Jim Sefcik, for his encouragement and advice, to Tom Lindsey for generously sharing his research on the number of officers who abandoned the Continental army after 1778, and to Terese Austin for the numerous ways in which she helped with my visit to the William L. Clements Library at the University of Michigan in Ann Arbor. I am thankful that Larrie Ferreiro, Robert Selig, Eric Schnitzer, Don Hagist, Robert Kilpatrick, Eugene Procknow, Patrick Hannum, and Stephen Taaffe took the time to answer queries that I posed. I can't begin to count the ways that Catherine Hendricks has helped me, not only with this book but with others over the years. Sarah Gourley, Mirian Nauenburg, and Beth Sheppard helped me with newfangled machines, and sometimes oldfangled machines, in the course of my research in the library. Lindsey Winchester kindly and helpfully responded to my pleas to secure books and other materials from my office in the library that was shuttered for several months during the initial period of the COVID-19 pandemic. Lorene Flanders, Chris Huff, Beth Sheppard, and Andrea Stanfield graciously supported my research and writing by providing an office that I have used on weekday mornings during the three and a half years that I worked on the book. Angela Mehaffey and Margot David in the interlibrary loan office of the Irvine Sullivan Ingram Library at the University of West Georgia unfailingly met my frequent requests for books and articles. Julie Dobbs, Chris Harris, and Caroline McWhorter helped me out of numerous scrapes with my computer.

Geri Thoma, my literary agent, supported my hope of writing this book and provided encouragement—and much more—in seeing to its inception.

Maureen Klier is a wonderful copy editor and it was my good fortune to work with her once again.

This is my first book with Anton Mueller, who was supportive and understanding, and a storehouse of ideas.

Sammy Grace, Simon, Clementine, and Katy will never read this book, but they enrich my life and that makes the often-trying work of writing a bit easier.

Carol, my wife, has always supported my writing, and her understanding and patience has been crucial to my literary and scholarly activities.

SELECTED BIBLIOGRAPHY

PRIMARY SOURCES

Abbot, W. W., et al., eds. *The Papers of George Washington: Confederation Series.* Charlottesville, VA, 1992–1997.

Blanchard, Claude. *The Journal of Claude Blanchard.* Edited by Thomas Balch. Albany, NY, 1876.

Boyd, Julian P., et al., eds. *The Papers of Thomas Jefferson.* Princeton, NJ, 1950–.

Campbell, Colin, ed. [Archibald Campbell]. *Journal of an Expedition Against the Rebels of Georgia in North America.* Darien, GA, 1981.

Carter, Clarence E., ed. *The Correspondence of General Thomas Gage with the Secretaries of State.* Reprint, New York, 1969.

Chase, Philander, et al., eds. *The Papers of George Washington: Revolutionary War Series.* Charlottesville, VA, 1985–.

Chastellux, Marquis de. *Travels in America in the Years 1780, 1781 and 1782.* Edited by Howard C. Rice. Chapel Hill, NC, 1963.

Clinton, Sir Henry, Papers. William L. Clements Library, University of Michigan, Ann Arbor.

Clinton, Sir Henry. *The American Rebellion: Sir Henry Clinton's Narrative of His Campaigns, 1775–1782, with an Appendix of Original Documents.* Edited by William B. Willcox. New Haven, CT, 1954.

Closen, Ludwig von. *The Revolutionary Journal of Baron Ludwig von Closen, 1780–1783.* Edited by Evelyn Acomb. Reprint, Chapel Hill, NC, 1958.

Commager, Henry Steele, and Morris, Richard B., eds. *The Spirit of 'Seventy-Six: The Story of the American Revolution as Told by Participants*. Indianapolis, IN, 1958.

Dann, John C., ed. *The Revolution Remembered: Eyewitness Accounts of the War for Independence*. Chicago, 1980.

Davies, K. G., ed. *Documents of the American Revolution*. 21 vols. Dublin, Ireland, 1972–1981.

Ewald, Johann, *Diary of the American War: A Hessian Journal*. Edited by Joseph P. Tustin. New Haven, CT, 1979.

Fitzpatrick, John C., ed. *The Writings of Washington*. 39 vols. Washington, DC, 1931–1944.

Foner, Philip S., ed. *The Complete Writings of Thomas Paine*. 2 vols. New York, 1945.

Ford, Worthington C., ed. *Journals of the Continental Congress, 1774–1789*. Washington, DC, 1904–1937.

Greene, Samuel Abbot, ed. *My Campaigns in America: A Journal Kept by Count William de Deux-Ponts, 1780–1781*. Boston, 1868.

Hamer, Philip, et al., eds. *The Papers of Henry Laurens*. Columbia, SC, 1968–.

Hamilton, Philip, ed. *The Revolutionary War Lives and Letters of Lucy and Henry Knox*. Baltimore, 2017.

Historical Manuscripts Commission, *Report on American Manuscripts in the Royal Institution of Great Britain*. 4 vols. London, 1904–1909.

Idzerda, Stanley, et al., eds. *Lafayette in the Age of the American Revolution: Selected Letters and Papers, 1776–1790*. 5 vols. Ithaca, NY, 1976–1983.

Jackson, Donald, et al., eds. *The Diaries of George Washington*. 6 vols. Charlottesville, VA, 1978.

Lamb, Roger. *An Original and Authentic Journal of Occurrences During the Late American War from its Commencement to the Year 1783*. Dublin, 1809.

Lee, Henry. *Memoirs of the War in the Southern Department of the United States.* Philadelphia, 1812.

Lesser, Charles, ed. *The Sinews of Independence: Monthly Strength Reports of the Continental Army.* Chicago, 1976.

Mackenzie, Frederick. *Diary of Frederick Mackenzie, Giving a Daily Narrative of His Military Service as an Officer of the Regiment of Royal Welsh Fusiliers During the Years 1775–1781 in Massachusetts, Rhode Island and New York.* Reprint, New York, 1968.

Rice, Howard C., Jr. and Anne S. K. Brown, eds. *The American Campaigns of Rochambeau's Army, 1780, 1781, 1782, 1783.* 2 vols. Princeton, NJ, 1972.

Rochambeau, Jean-Baptiste-Donatien de Vimeur, Comte de. *Memoirs of the Marshall Count de Rochambeau.* Reprint, New York, 1971.

Rogers, George C., ed. "Letters of Charles O'Hara to the Duke of Grafton," *South Carolina Historical Magazine* 65 (1964): 158–80.

Ross, Charles, ed. *Correspondence of Charles, First Marquis Cornwallis.* 3 vols. London, 1859.

Saberton, Ian, ed. *The Cornwallis Papers: The Campaigns of 1780 and 1781 in the Southern Theater of the American Revolutionary War.* 6 vols. Uckfield, UK, 2010.

Scheer, George F., ed. *Private Yankee Doodle: A Narrative of Some of the Adventures, Dangers and Sufferings of a Revolutionary Soldier.* Boston, 1962.

Scheer, George F., and Hugh F. Rankin, eds. *Rebels and Redcoats.* Cleveland, OH, 1957.

Showman, Richard K., et al., eds. *The Papers of Nathanael Greene.* 13 vols. Chapel Hill, NC, 1976–2005.

Simcoe, John. *Simcoe's Military Journal: A History of the Operations of a Partisan Corps Called the Queen's Rangers.* Reprint, New York, 1968.

Smith, Paul H., ed. *Letters of Delegates to Congress, 1774–1789.* 25 vols. Washington, DC, 1976–2000.

Smith, William. *Historical Memoirs, From 26 August 1778 to 12 November 1783.* Edited by William H. W. Sabine. New York, 1971.

Stedman, Charles. *The History of the Origin, Progress, and Termination of the American War.* 1794. Reprint, New York, 1969.

Stevens, Benjamin F., ed. *Facsimiles of Manuscripts in European Archives Relating to America, 1773–1783.* 25 vols. Reprint, New York, 1970.

———. *The Campaign in Virginia, 1781. An Exact Reprint of Six Rare Pamphlets on the Clinton-Cornwallis Controversy.* 2 vols. London, 1888.

Syrett, Harold C., and Jacob E. Cooke, eds. *The Papers of Alexander Hamilton.* 25 vols. New York, 1961–1987.

Tarleton, Benjamin. *A History of the Campaigns of 1780 and 1781 in the Southern Provinces of North America.* Reprint, Cranbury, NJ, 2005.

Thacher, James. *Military Journal of the American Revolution.* Reprint, New York, 1969.

Uhlendorf, Bernhard, ed. *The Siege of Charleston.* Reprint, New York, 1968.

Wortley, Mrs. E. Stuart, ed. *A Prime Minister and His Son: From the Correspondence of the 3d Earl of Bute and of Lt.-General The Hon. Sir Charles Stuart.* London, 1925.

101 KEY SECONDARY BOOKS ON THE WAR, 1778–1781

See chapter 1's endnotes for numerous worthy books on the war between 1775 and 1777. The following is a list of 101 books that I recommend for understanding the war in the period between 1778 and the decisive Allied victory at Yorktown in 1781. Numerous other worthy books can be found throughout the endnotes.

Alden, John. *Charles Lee, Traitor or Patriot?* Baton Rouge, LA, 1951.

Allison, David K., and Larrie D. Ferreiro, eds. *The American Revolution: A World War.* Washington, DC, 2018.

Atwood, Rodney. *The Hessians: Mercenaries from Hessen-Kassel in the American Revolution.* Cambridge, UK, 1980.

Babits, Lawrence E. *A Devil of a Whipping: The Battle of Cowpens*. Chapel Hill, NC, 1998.

Babits, Lawrence E., and Joshua B. Howard. *Long, Obstinate, and Bloody: The Battle of Guilford Courthouse*. Chapel Hill, NC, 2009.

Bass, Robert D. *The Green Dragoon: The Lives of Banastre Tarleton and Mary Robinson*. Orangeburg, SC, 1973.

Bennett, Charles E., and Donald R. Lennon. *A Quest for Glory: Major General Robert Howe and the American Revolution*. Chapel Hill, NC, 1991.

Billias, George A., ed. *George Washington's Generals*. New York, 1964.

———. *George Washington's Opponents*. New York, 1969.

Black, Jeremy. *War for America: The Fight for Independence, 1775–1783*. Stroud, UK, 1991.

Bodle, Wayne K. *Valley Forge Winter: Civilians and Soldiers in War*. University Park, PA, 2002.

Borick, Carl P. *A Gallant Defense: The Siege of Charleston, 1780*. Columbia, SC, 2003.

Bowler, R. Arthur. *Logistics and the Failure of the British Army in America, 1775–1783*. Princeton, NJ, 1975.

Braisted, Todd W. *Grand Forage 1778: The Battleground around New York City*. Yardley, PA, 2016.

Brown, Gerald Saxon. *The American Secretary: The Colonial Policy of Lord George Germain, 1775–1778*. Ann Arbor, MI, 1963.

Brown, Weldon. *Empire or Independence: A Study in the Failure of Reconciliation, 1774–1783*. Baton Rouge, LA, 1941.

Brumwell, Stephen. *George Washington: Gentleman Warrior*. New York, 2012.

———. *Turncoat: Benedict Arnold and the Crisis of American Liberty*. New Haven, CT, 2018.

Buchanan, John. *The Road to Charleston: Nathanael Greene and the American Revolution*. Charlottesville, VA, 2019.

————. *The Road to Guilford Courthouse: The American Revolution in the Carolinas*. New York, 1997.

Calhoun, Robert McCluer. *The Loyalists in Revolutionary America, 1780–1781*. New York, 1965.

Callahan, North. *Henry Knox: George Washington's General*. New York, 1958.

Carp, E. Wayne. *To Starve the Honor at Pleasure: Continental Army Administration and American Political Culture, 1775–1783*. Chapel Hill, NC, 1984.

Carpenter, Stanley D. M. *Southern Gambit: Cornwallis and the British March to Yorktown*. Norman, OK, 2019.

Cecere, Michael. *The Invasion of Virginia, 1781*. Yardley, PA, 2017.

Chernow, Ron. *George Washington: A Life*. New York, 2010.

Conway, Stephen. *The British Isles and the War of American Independence*. New York, 2000.

————. *The War of American Independence, 1776–1783*. London, 1995.

Crow, Jeffrey J., and Larry E. Tise, eds. *The Southern Experience in the American Revolution*. Chapel Hill, NC, 1978.

Desmarais, Norman. *America's First Ally: France in the Revolutionary War*. Philadelphia, 2019.

Dull, Jonathan. *A Diplomatic History of the American Revolution*. New Haven, CT, 1985.

————. *The French Navy and American Independence: A Study of Arms and Diplomacy, 1774–1787*. Princeton, NJ, 1975.

Dunkerly, Robert M., and Irene B. Boland. *Eutaw Springs: The Final Battle of the American Revolution's Southern Campaign*. Columbia, SC, 2017.

Dykeman, Wilma. *With Fire and Sword: The Battle of King's Mountain, 1780*. Washington, DC, 1978.

Edgar, Walter. *Partisans and Redcoats: The Southern Conflict That Turned the Tide of the American Revolution*. New York, 2001.

Ferguson, E. James. *The Power of the Purse: A History of American Public Finance, 1776–1790.* Chapel Hill, NC, 1961.

Ferling, John. *Almost A Miracle: The American Victory in the War of Independence.* New York, 2007.

Ferreiro, Larrie D. *Brothers at Arms: American Independence and the Men of France and Spain Who Saved It.* New York, 2016.

Fischer, Joseph R. *A Well-Executed Failure: The Sullivan Campaign Against the Iroquois, July–September 1779.* Columbia, SC, 1997.

Fleming, Thomas. *Beat the Last Drum: The Siege of Yorktown, 1781.* New York, 1963.

———. *Washington's Secret War: The Hidden History of Valley Forge.* New York, 2005.

Flexner, James Thomas. *George Washington and the American Revolution.* Boston, 1967.

Freeman, Douglas Southall. *George Washington: A Biography.* 7 vols. New York, 1948–1957.

Frey, Sylvia. *The British Soldier in America: A Social History of Military Life in the Revolutionary Period.* Austin, TX, 1981.

Gilbert, Alan. *Black Patriots and Loyalists: Fighting for Emancipation in the War of Independence.* Chicago, 2012.

Golway, Terry. *Washington's General: Nathanael Greene and the Triumph of the American Revolution.* New York, 2005.

Gordon, John. *South Carolina and the American Revolution: A Battlefield History.* Columbia, SC, 2003.

Greene, Jerome A. *The Guns of Independence: The Siege of Yorktown.* New York, 2005.

Gruber, Ira. *The Howe Brothers and the American Revolution.* New York, 1972.

Henderson, H. James. *Party Politics in the Continental Congress.* New York, 1974.

Higginbotham, Don. *Daniel Morgan: Revolutionary Rifleman.* Chapel Hill, NC, 1961.

————. *The War of American Independence: Military Attitude, Policies, and Practice, 1763–1789.* New York, 1971.

Higginbotham, Don, ed. *Reconsiderations on the Revolutionary War: Selected Essays.* Westport, CT, 1978.

Higgins, W. Robert, ed. *The Revolutionary War in the South: Power, Conflict, and Leadership.* Durham, NC, 1979.

Hoffman, Ronald, Thad W. Tate, and Peter J. Albert, eds. *An Uncivil War: The Southern Backcountry During the American Revolution.* Charlottesville, VA, 1985.

Hoock, Holger. *Scars of Independence: America's Violent Birth.* New York, 2017.

Huggins, Benjamin L. *Washington's War 1779.* Yardley, PA, 2018.

Huston, James A. *Logistics of Liberty: American Services of Supply in the Revolutionary War and After.* Newark, DE, 1991.

Jones, T. Cole. *Captives of Liberty: Prisoners of War and the Politics of Vengeance in the American Revolution.* Philadelphia, 2020.

Kelsay, Isabel T. *Joseph Brant, 1743–1807: Man of Two Worlds.* Syracuse, NY, 1984.

Kennett, Lee. *The French Forces in America, 1780–1783.* Westport, CT, 1977.

Ketchum, Richard M. *Victory at Yorktown: The Campaign That Won the Revolution.* New York, 2004.

Kranish, Michael. *Flight from Monticello: Thomas Jefferson at War.* New York, 2010.

Lambert, Robert Stansbury. *South Carolina Loyalists in the American Revolution.* Columbia, SC, 1987.

Lawrence, Alexander A. *Storm Over Savannah: The Story of Count d'Estaing and the Siege of the Town in 1779.* Athens, GA, 1951.

Lengel, Edward. *General George Washington: A Military Life.* New York, 2005.

Lender, Mark Edward. *Cabal: The Plot Against General Washington.* Yardley, PA, 2019.

Lender, Mark Edward, and Gary Wheeler Stone. *Fatal Sunday: George Washington, the Monmouth Campaign, and the Politics of Battle.* Norman, OK, 2017.

Longmore, Paul K. *The Invention of George Washington*. Berkeley, CA, 1988.

Lumpkin, Henry. *From Savannah to Yorktown: The American Revolution in the South*. Columbia, SC, 1981.

Mackesy, Piers. *The War for America, 1775–1783*. Cambridge, MA, 1965.

Main, Jackson Turner. *The Sovereign States, 1775–1783*. New York, 1973.

Martin, James Kirby. *Benedict Arnold, Revolutionary Hero: An American Warrior Reconsidered*. New York, 1997.

Martin, James Kirby, and Mark Edward Lender. *A Respectable Army: The Military Origins of the Republic, 1763–1789*. Arlington Heights, IL, 1982.

Mattern, David. *Benjamin Lincoln and the American Revolution*. Columbia, SC, 1995.

McBurney, Christian. *The Rhode Island Campaign: The First French and American Operation in the Revolutionary War*. Yardley, PA, 2011.

McDonnell, Michael A. *The Politics of War: Race, Class, and Conflict in Revolutionary Virginia*. Chapel Hill, NC, 2007.

Messick, Hank. *King's Mountain: The Epic of the Blue Ridge "Mountain Men" in the American Revolution*. Boston, 1976.

Middlekauff, Robert. *The Glorious Cause: The American Revolution, 1763–1789*. New York, 2007.

———. *Washington's Revolution: The Making of America's First Leader*. New York, 2015.

Murphy, Orville T. *Charles Gravier, Comte de Vergennes: French Diplomacy in the American Revolution*. Albany, NY, 1982.

Nelson, Paul David. *Anthony Wayne: Soldier of the Early Republic*. Bloomington, IN, 1985.

———. *General Horatio Gates: A Biography*. Baton Rouge, LA, 1976.

Niemeyer, Charles. *America Goes to War: A Social History of the Continental Army*. New York, 1996.

O'Shaughnessy, Andrew Jackson. *The Men Who Lost America: British Leadership, the American Revolution and the Fate of the Empire.* New Haven, CT, 2013.

Pancake, John S. *The Destructive War: The British Campaign in the Carolinas, 1780–1782.* Tuscaloosa, AL, 1985.

Parkinson, Robert G. *The Common Cause: Creating Race and Nation in the American Revolution.* New York, 2016.

Peckham, Howard, ed. *The Toll of Independence: Engagements and Battle Casualties of the American Revolution.* Chicago, 1974.

Philbrick, Nathaniel. *In the Hurricane's Eye: The Genius of George Washington and the Victory at Yorktown.* New York, 2018.

———. *Valiant Ambition: George Washington, Benedict Arnold, and the Fate of the American Revolution.* New York, 2016.

Piecuch, Jim. *The Blood Be upon Your Head: Tarleton and the Myth of Buford's Massacre.* Charleston, SC, 2010.

———. *Three Peoples, One King: Loyalists, Indians, and Slaves in the Revolutionary South, 1775–1782.* Columbia, SC, 2008.

Pybus, Cassandra. *Epic Journeys of Freedom: Runaway Slaves of the American Revolution and Their Global Quest for Liberty.* Boston, 2006.

Rakove, Jack. *The Beginnings of National Politics: An Interpretive History of the Continental Congress.* Baltimore, 1982.

Rankin, Hugh F. *The North Carolina Continentals.* Chapel Hill, NC, 1971.

Raphael, Ray. *A People's History of the American Revolution: How Common People Shaped the Fight for Independence.* New York, 2001.

Ritcheson, Charles R. *British Politics and the American Revolution.* Norman, OK, 1964.

Robson, Eric. *The American Revolution: In its Political and Military Aspects, 1763–1783.* Hamden, CT, 1965.

Royster, Charles. *A Revolutionary People at War: The Continental Army and American Character, 1775–1783.* Chapel Hill, NC, 1979.

Sculley, Seanegan P. *Contest for Liberty: Military Leadership in the Continental Army, 1775–1783.* Yardley, PA, 2019.

Selby, John. *The Revolution in Virginia, 1775–1783.* Williamsburg, VA, 1988.

Shy, John. *A People Numerous and Armed: Reflections on the Military the Struggle for American Independence.* New York, 1976.

Smith, Paul H. *Loyalists and Redcoats: A Study in British Revolutionary Policy.* Chapel Hill, NC, 1964.

Stinchcombe, William. *The American Revolution and the French Alliance.* Syracuse, NY, 1969.

Syrett, David. *The Royal Navy in American Waters 1775–1783.* Aldershot, UK, 1989.

Taylor, Alan. *Divided Ground: Indians, Settlers, and the Northern Borderland of the American Revolution.* New York, 2006.

Theodore Thayer. *Nathanael Greene: Strategist of the American Revolution.* New York, 1960

———. *Washington and Lee: The Making of a Scapegoat.* Port Washington, NY, 1976.

Thomas, Peter D. G. *Lord North.* London, 1976.

Tilley, John. *The British Navy and the American Revolution.* Columbia, SC, 1987.

Tonsetic, Robert L. *1781: The Decisive Year of the Revolutionary War.* Philadelphia, 2011.

Unger, Harlow Giles. *Lafayette.* New York, 2002.

Urban, Mark. *Fusiliers: The Saga of a British Redcoat Regiment in the American Revolution.* New York, 2007.

Valentine, Alan. *Lord George Germain.* Oxford, UK, 1962.

———. *Lord North.* 2 vols. Norman, OK, 1967.

Van Doren, Carl. *Mutiny in January.* New York, 1947.

Ward, Christopher. *The War of the Revolution*. 2 vols. New York, 1952.

Ward, Harry. *George Washington's Enforcers: Policing the Continental Army*. Carbondale, IL, 2006.

Weigley, Russell F. *The Partisan War: The South Carolina Campaign of 1780–1782*. Columbia, SC, 1970.

Whitely, Peter. *Lord North: The Prime Minister Who Lost America*. London, 1996.

Whitridge, Arnold. *Rochambeau*. New York, 1965.

Whittemore, Charles P. *General of the Revolution: John Sullivan of New Hampshire*. New York, 1961.

Wickwire, Franklin, and Mary Wickwire, *Cornwallis and the War of Independence*. London, 1971.

Willcox, William B., *Portrait of a General: Sir Henry Clinton in the War of Independence*. New York, 1964.

Williams, Glenn F. *Year of the Hangman: George Washington's Campaign Against the Iroqouis*. Yardley, PA, 2005.

Wilson, David K. *The Southern Strategy: Britain's Conquest of South Carolina and Georgia, 1775–1780*. Columbia, SC, 2005.

Wood, W. J. *Battles of the Revolutionary War, 1775–1781*. Chapel Hill, NC, 1990.

SIXTEEN IMPORTANT SCHOLARLY ARTICLES ON THE WAR BETWEEN 1778–1781

Berg, Richard. "The Southern Campaigns: The British Effort to Retake the South, 1778–1781." *Strategy and Tactics* 104 (1985): 14–23.

Bowler, R. Arthur. "Sir Henry Clinton and Army Profiteering: A Neglected Aspect of the Clinton-Cornwallis Controversy." *William and Mary Quarterly* 31 (1974): 111–23.

Conway, Stephen. "The British Army, 'Military Europe,' and the American War of Independence." *William and Mary Quarterly* 67 (January 2010): 69–100.

————. "British Army Officers and the American War for Independence." *William and Mary Quarterly* 41 (April 1984): 265–76.

————. "The Politics of British Military and Naval Mobilization, 1775–1783." *English Historical Review* 112 (November 1997): 1179–1201.

————. "To Subdue America: British Army Officers and the Conduct of the Revolutionary War." *William and Mary Quarterly* 43 (July 1986): 381–407.

Kaplan, Roger. "The Hidden View: British Intelligence Operations During the American Revolution." *William and Mary Quarterly* 47 (January 1990): 115–38.

Kyte, George W. "A Projected British Attack upon Philadelphia in 1781." *Pennsylvania Magazine of History and Biography* 76 (1952): 379–93.

Lawrence, Alexander A. "General Robert Howe and the British Capture of Savannah in 1778." *Georgia Historical Quarterly* 36 (1952): 303–27.

Lender, Mark Edward and James Kirby Martin, "'A Traitor's Epiphany': Benedict Arnold in Virginia and His Quest for Reconciliation." *Virginia Magazine of History and Biography* 125 (2017): 315–57.

Lutnick, Solomon M. "The Defeat at Yorktown: A View from the British Press." *Virginia Magazine of History and Biography* 72 (1964): 471–78.

Mackesy, Piers. "British Strategy in the War of American Independence." *Yale Review* 52 (1963): 539–57.

Willcox, William B. "The British Road to Yorktown: A Study in Divided Command." *American Historical Review* 52 (October 1946): 1–35.

————. "British Strategy in America, 1778." *Journal of Modern History* 19 (June 1947): 97–121.

————. "Rhode Island in British Strategy, 1780–1781." *Journal of Modern History* 17 (December 1945): 304–331.

Willcox, William B., and Frederick Wyatt. "Sir Henry Clinton: A Psychological Exploration in History." *William and Mary Quarterly* 16 (January 1959): 3–26.

NOTES

ABBREVIATIONS

AR   William B. Willcox, ed. *The American Rebellion: Sir Henry
            Clinton's Narrative of His Campaigns, 1775–1782, with an
            Appendix of Original Documents.* New Haven, CT: Yale
            University Press, 1954.

CP   Ian Saberton, ed. *The Cornwallis Papers: The Campaigns of
            1780 and 1781 in the Southern Theatre of the American
            Revolutionary War.* Uckfield, UK: The Naval and Military
            Press, 2010.

DAR   K. G. Davies, ed. *Documents of the American Revolution.*
            Dublin: Irish University Press, 1972–1981.

DGW   Donald Jackson et al., eds. *The Diaries of George Washington.*
            6 vols. Charlottesville, VA: University of Virginia Press, 1978.

Facsimiles Benjamin F. Stevens, ed. *Facsimiles of Manuscripts in
            European Archives Relating to America, 1773–1783.* 25
            vols. Reprint, New York: AMS Press, 1970.

GW   George Washington

JCC   Worthington C. Ford, ed. *Journals of the Continental
            Congress, 1774–1789.* Washington, DC, 1904–1937.

LDC   Paul H. Smith, ed. *Letters of Delegates to Congress,
            1774–1789.* 34 vols. Washington, DC, 1976–2000.

LSLP   Stanley Idzerda et al., eds. *Lafayette in the Age of the
            American Revolution: Selected Letters and Papers, 1776–1790.*
            5 vols. Ithaca, NY: Cornell University Press, 1976–1983.

NG	Nathanael Greene
PAH	Harold C. Syrett and Jacob E. Cooke, eds. *The Papers of Alexander Hamilton*. 27 vols. New York: Columbia University Press, 1961–1987.
PGWR	Philander Chase et al., eds. *The Papers of George Washington: Revolutionary War Series*. Charlottesville, VA: University of Virginia Press, 1985–.
PH	*The Parliamentary History of England, from the Earliest Period to the Year 1803*. New York: AMS Press, 1966.
PNG	Richard K. Showman et al., eds. *The Papers of Nathanael Greene*. 13 vols. Chapel Hill, NC, 1976–2005.
PTJ	Julian P. Boyd et al., eds. *The Papers of Thomas Jefferson*. Princeton, NJ, 1950–.
SHCP	Sir Henry Clinton Papers
Smith, *Memoirs*	William Smith. *Historical Memoirs, from 26 August 1778 to 12 November 1783*. Edited by William H. W. Sabine. New York: New York Times and Arno Press, 1971.
TJ	Thomas Jefferson
WLCL	William L. Clements Library, University of Michigan
WW	John C. Fitzpatrick, ed. *The Writings of Washington*. 39 vols. Washington, DC, 1931–44.

PREFACE

1. John Adams to William Tudor, October 7, 1774, in Robert J. Taylor et al., eds. *Papers of John Adams* (Cambridge, MA, 1977–), 2:188.

2. David McCullough, *1776* (New York, 2005); David Hackett Fischer, *Paul Revere's Ride* (New York, 1994), and *Washington's Crossing* (New York, 2004); and Rick Atkinson, *The British Are Coming: The War for America, Lexington to Princeton, 1775–1777* (New York, 2019).

3. Thomas Paine, *Common Sense*, in *Complete Writings of Thomas Paine*, ed. Philip S. Foner (New York, 1945), 1:31.

4. Thomas Paine, *The American Crisis I*, in ibid., 1:50.

5. John Adams to Abigail Adams, April 26, 1777, in L. H. Butterfield et al., eds. *Adams Family Correspondence* (Cambridge, MA, 1963–), 2:224.

6. Paine, *The American Crisis XIII*, 1:230, 235; *AR*, 590; Sir Henry Clinton, *Narrative of Lieutenant-General Sir Henry Clinton*, in Benjamin F. Stevens, ed., *The Campaign in Virginia: An Exact Reprint of Six Rare Pamphlets on the Clinton-Cornwallis Controversy* (London, 1888), 1:13, 15, 21, 24, 28, 43n; Clinton, *Observations on Some Parts of the Answer of Earl Cornwallis to Sir Henry Clinton's Narrative*, in ibid., 1:103, 111; GW, Farewell Orders to the Armies of the United States, November 2, 1783, *WW* 27:223.

CHAPTER 1: BRITAIN'S WAR TO WIN, 1775–1777

1. George III to Frederick Lord North, November 17, 1774, in W. Bodham Donne, ed., *The Correspondence of King George III with Lord North 1763 to 1783* (reprint, New York, 1971), 1:215.

2. Quoted in Bernard Bailyn, *The Ordeal of Thomas Hutchinson* (Cambridge, MA, 1974), 169.

3. Stephen Conway, "To Subdue America: British Army Officers and the Conduct of the Revolutionary War," *William and Mary Quarterly* 43 (1986): 383; Stephen Conway, *The British Isles and the War of Independence* (New York, 2000), 13; Fred Junkin Hinkhouse, *The Preliminaries of the American Revolution as Seen in the English Press, 1763–1775* (reprint, New York, 1969), 159, 162, 168; Solomon Lutnick, *The American Revolution and the British Press, 1775–1783* (Columbia, MO, 1967), 36–41; Troy Bickham, *Making Headlines: The American Revolution as Seen Through the British Press* (DeKalb, IL, 2009), 60, 74; John Ferling, *Independence: The Struggle to Set America Free* (New York, 2011), 43–44; John Alden, *General Gage in America: Being Principally a History of His Role in the American Revolution* (Baton Rouge, LA, 1948), 220–21. On Britain's colonial policies, and the debate it engendered in both England and America, see Justin de Rivage, *Revolution Against Empire: Taxes, Politics, and the Origins of American Independence* (New Haven, CT, 2017). For the general who predicted that a thousand troops could quell the colonial rebellion, see Verner W. Crane, *Benjamin Franklin's Letters to the Press, 1758–1775* (Chapel Hill, NC, 1950), 263n. The "burning two or three of their towns" quote can be found in

Rick Atkinson, *The British Are Coming: The War for America, Lexington to Princeton, 1775–1777* (New York, 2019), 47.

4. Andrew Jackson O'Shaughnessy, *The Men Who Lost America: British Leadership, the American Revolution, and the Fate of the Empire* (New Haven, CT, 2013), 22–23, 48–53. George III is quoted in Alan Valentine, *Lord North* (Norman, OK, 1967), 1:319–20, 314.

5. William Fowler, *Samuel Adams: Radical Puritan* (New York, 1997), 86–87; GW to George Mason, April 5, 1769, *PGWC* 8:177–80; Arthur Lee to GW, June 15, 1777, *PGWR* 10:43.

6. Ferling, *Independence*, 52–87; Declaration of Colonial Rights and Grievances, in David C. Douglas et al., eds. *English Historical Documents* (London, 1956–1970), 9:805–8; John Adams to Joseph Palmer, September 26, 1774, in Robert J. Taylor et al., eds. *Papers of John Adams* (Cambridge, MA, 1977–), 2:173; Adams to William Tudor, October 7, 1774, ibid., 2:188. For excellent studies of 1774, the pivotal year, and the First Continental Congress, see Mary Beth Norton, *1774: The Long Year of Revolution* (New York, 2020), and David Ammerman, *In the Common Cause: America's Response to the Coercive Acts of 1774* (Charlottesville, VA, 1974).

7. George III to North, September 11, November 17, 1774, in Donne, *Correspondence of King George III with Lord North*, 1:202, 215.

8. Alan Valentine, *Lord George Germain* (Oxford, 1962), 118; Thomas Gage to Earl of Dartmouth, September 2, 1774, in Clarence E. Carter, ed., *The Correspondence of General Thomas Gage with the Secretaries of State* (reprint, New York, 1969), 1:370–71; Gage to Lord Barrington, September 25, October 3, November 2, 1774, ibid., 2:654, 656, 659; Minute of a Cabinet Meeting, January 21, 1775, in *The Manuscripts of the Earl of Dartmouth, Prepared for the Historical Manuscript Commission of Great Britain* (reprint, Boston, 1972), 1:372; Stephen Conway, "The Politics of British Military and Naval Mobilization, 1775–1783," *English Historical Review* 112 (1997): 1185; Peter D. G. Thomas, *Tea Party to Independence: The Third Phase of the American Revolution, 1773–1776* (Oxford, 1991), 176–81; Jeremy Black, *War for America: The Fight for Independence, 1775–1783* (Stroud, UK, 1998), 23; Ian R. Christie and Benjamin W. Labaree, *Empire or Independence, 1760–1776* (New York, 1976), 231; David Hackett Fischer, *Paul Revere's Ride* (New York, 1994), 51.

9. One version of Chatham's speech is in *PH* 18:149–60. A second, based on notes taken by Hugh Boyd that were published in 1779, can also be found in ibid., 18:149–56n.

10. Ibid., 18:478–538.

11. Lord Dartmouth to Gage, January 27, 1775, Carter, *Correspondence of General Thomas Gage*, 2:179–81; Conway, *The British Isles and the War of American Independence*, 14.

12. Larrie D. Ferreiro, *Brothers at Arms: American Independence and the Men of France and Spain Who Saved It* (New York, 2016), 33–34. The Benjamin Franklin quote can be found on page xvi.

13. Atkinson, *The British Are Coming*, 52.

14. Fischer, *Paul Revere's Ride*, 309; Christopher Ward, *The War of the Revolution* (New York, 1952), 1:26–27.

15. Fischer, *Paul Revere's Ride*, 184–260, 320–24. See also George C. Daughan, *Lexington and Concord: The Battle Heard Round the World* (New York, 2018). For a succinct account of that historic day, see Atkinson, *The British Are Coming*, 60–76. The Atkinson quote can be found on page 63.

16. William B. Willcox, *Portrait of a General: Sir Henry Clinton in the War of Independence* (New York, 1962), 48.

17. David Smith, *Whispers Across the Atlantic: General William Howe and the American Revolution* (New York, 2017), 3–8.

18. For accounts of the Battle of Bunker Hill, see Richard M. Ketchum, *Decisive Day: The Battle for Bunker Hill* (New York, 1974), and Nathaniel Philbrick, *Bunker Hill: A City, a Siege, a Revolution* (New York, 2013). A succinct account of the engagement can be found in Atkinson, *The British Are Coming*, 103–10. For general accounts of the siege of Boston and the battle, see Richard Frothingham, *History of the Siege of Boston* (Boston, 1849), Allen French, *The Siege of Boston* (New York, 1911), and Louis Birnbaum, *Red Dawn at Lexington: "If They Mean to Have a War, Let it Begin Here"* (Boston, 1986). On Howe's reaction to the carnage, see Smith, *Whispers Across the Atlantic*, 35–38. See also Howe to the British Adjutant General [?], June 22 and 24, 1775, in Henry Steele Commager

and Richard B. Morris, eds. *The Spirit of 'Seventy-Six: The Story of the American Revolution as Told by Participants* (Indianapolis, 1958), 1:132; and Maldwyn Jones, "Sir William Howe: Conventional Strategist," in *George Washington's Opponents*, ed. George Athan Billias (New York, 1969), 47. Clinton's comment is in *AR*, 19; Earl Percy is quoted in Smith, *Whispers Across the Atlantic*, 38.

19. Thomas, *Tea Party to Independence*, 254–65; Valentine, *Lord North*, 1:378–79, 389–95, 407–8.

20. Valentine, *Lord George Germain*, 1–94, 140; Gerald Saxon Brown, *The American Secretary: The Colonial Policy of Lord George Germain, 1775–1778* (Ann Arbor, MI, 1963), 1–25; O'Shaughnessy, *The Men Who Lost America*, 167–70.

21. T. H. Breen, *American Insurgents, American Patriots: The Revolution of the People* (New York, 2010), 207–40. Lincoln's quote can be found in James M. McPherson, "A. Lincoln, Commander in Chief," in *Our Lincoln: New Perspectives on Lincoln and His World*, ed. Eric Foner (New York, 2008), 29. To follow the steps taken by the rebel governments, including local committees of safety, for suppressing Loyalists, see Peter Force, ed., *American Archives*, 4th series (Washington, DC, 1847–1853), vols. 3 and 4.

22. L. H. Butterfield et al., eds. *The Diary and Autobiography of John Adams* (Cambridge, MA, 1961), 3:321–23. On GW's background, see John Ferling, *The First of Men: A Life of George Washington* (reprint, New York, 2010), 1–110; Ferling, *Setting the World Ablaze: George Washington, John Adams, Thomas Jefferson and the American Revolution* (New York, 2000), 3–4, 14–20, 23–25, 28–34, 41–48, 64–67, 71–76, 96–99; Ron Chernow, *Washington: A Life* (New York, 2010), 3–177; and Joseph J. Ellis, *His Excellency: George Washington* (New York, 2004), 3–74. For comments by the congressmen who chose GW and Philadelphians who observed him, see Thomas Cushing to James Bowdoin Sr., June 21, 1775, *LDC* 1:530; Deane to Elizabeth Deane, June 16, 1775, ibid., 1:494; Dyer to Jonathan Trumbull Sr., June 16, 1775, ibid., 1:496; Dyer to Joseph Trumbull, June 17, 1775, ibid., 1:499–500; Hancock to Gerry, June 18, 1775, ibid., 1:507; John Adams to Abigail Adams, June 17, 1775, in L. H. Butterfield et al., eds. *Adams Family Correspondence* (Cambridge, MA, 1963–), 1:215–16; Benjamin Rush to Thomas Rushton, October 29, 1775, in L. H. Butterfield, ed., *Letters of Benjamin Rush* (Princeton, NJ, 1951), 1:92.

23. The quotation can be found in Theodore Thayer, "Nathanael Greene: Revolutionary War Strategist," in *George Washington's Generals*, ed. George Athan Billias (New York, 1964), 111.

24. Kevin Phillips, *1775: A Good Year for Revolution* (New York, 2012), 299.

25. The King's Proclamation, August 23, 1775, *English Historical Documents*, 9:850–51; Orville T. Murphy, *Charles Gravier, Comte de Vergennes: French Diplomacy in the Age of Revolution, 1719–1787* (Albany, NY, 232–33; Jonathan Dull, *A Diplomatic History of the American Revolution* (New Haven, CT, 1985), 48, 57–62; Ferreiro, *Brothers at Arms*, 37–61; Patrick Villiers, "Lafayette," in *The American Revolution: A World War*, ed. David K. Allison and Larrie D. Ferreiro (Washington, DC, 2018), 146; Norman Desmarais, *America's First Ally: France in the Revolutionary War* (Philadelphia, 2019), 3–18.

26. Edward G. Lengel, *General George Washington* (New York, 2005), 105–11; John Ferling, *Almost a Miracle: The American Victory in the War of Independence* (New York, 2007), 75–78.

27. James Kirby Martin, *Benedict Arnold, Revolutionary Hero: An American Warrior Reconsidered* (New York, 1997), 11–84, 100–108; Hal T. Shelton, *General Richard Montgomery and the American Revolution* (New York, 1994), 8–115; Ward, *War of the Revolution*, 1:143–49, 161–77; Atkinson, *The British Are Coming*, 141–63, 195–215. For detailed accounts of the travail of Arnold and his men, see Thomas A. Desjardin, *Through a Howling Wilderness: Benedict Arnold's March to Quebec, 1775* (New York, 2006), and Arthur Lefkowitz, *Benedict Arnold's Army: The 1775 Invasion of Canada During the Revolutionary War* (New York, 2008).

28. *Pennsylvania Gazette*, May 1, 1776.

29. Edward Rutledge to Ralph Izard, December 7, 1775, *LDC* 2:462.

30. Thomas Paine, *Common Sense* (1776), in *The Complete Writings of Thomas Paine*, ed. Philip S. Foner (New York, 1945), 1:3–46.

31. Adams to Patrick Henry, June 3, 1776, in Taylor, *Papers of John Adams*, 4:235; William Ellery to Benjamin Ellery, July 10, 1776, *LDC* 4:430. For the reports of BF's team, see Commissioners to Canada to John Hancock, May 10, 17, 27, 1776, *LDC* 3:64–67; 4:22–24, 80–82. On the military debacle that unfolded in the

wake of the arrival of the British flotilla, see Ferling, *Almost a Miracle*, 108–11; Atkinson, *The British Are Coming*, 288–94; Paul H. Smith, "Sir Guy Carleton: Soldier-Statesman," Billias, *George Washington's Opponents*, 120–22; and Ward, *War of the Revolution*, 1:198–201.

32. Adams to GW, January 6, 1776, *PGWR* 3:37; David Hackett Fischer, *Washington's Crossing* (New York, 2004), 381, 383; Conway, *The British Isles and the War of American Independence*, 15; Rodney Atwood, *The Hessians: Mercenaries from Hessen-Kassel in the American Revolution* (Cambridge, UK, 1980), 51–52, 254. The "O Britons" quote can be found in Stephen Conway, *The War of American Independence, 1775–1783* (London, 1995), 51.

33. GW to Hancock, July 17, 1776, *PGWR* 5:356; Jonathan Trumbull Sr., September 9, 1776, ibid., 6:266–67.

34. The "canvass wings" remark was made by General Charles Lee, among others. Lee is quoted in Eric Robson, *The American Revolution in Its Political and Military Aspects, 1763–1783* (Hamden, CT, 1965), 107.

35. Howe to the Earl of Dartmouth, March 21, 1776, *DAR* 12:83. Howe's "most effectual means" quote can be found in Smith, *Whispers Across the Atlantic*, 62.

36. William Howe to Lord George Germain, July 7, 1776, *DAR* 12:157.

37. *AR*, 41–42; Lengel, *General George Washington*, 144.

38. Edward H. Tatum Jr., ed., *The American Journal of Ambrose Serle* (reprint, New York, 1969), 78–79.

39. Howe to Germain, September 3, 1776, *DAR* 12:218.

40. Quoted in Holger Hoock, *Scars of Independence: America's Violent Birth* (New York, 2017), 79.

41. Smith, *Whispers Across the Atlantic*, 51; Atkinson, *The British Are Coming*, 374.

42. Howe to Germain, September 3, 1776, *DAR* 12:217; Ira Gruber, *The Howe Brothers and the American Revolution* (New York, 1972), 71.

43. Howe to Germain, September 3, 1776, *DAR* 12:218; Ward, *War of the Revolution*, 1:211–37; Fischer, *Washington's Crossing*, 92–101; Gruber, *Howe Brothers*, 111–13. GW to Hancock, August 31, 1776, *PGWR* 6:177.

44. *AR*, 46; Barnet Schecter, *The Battle for New York: The City at the Heart of the American Revolution* (New York, 2002), 183–90.

45. GW to Hancock, September 2, 4, 6, 8, 19, *PGWR* 6:200, 216, 231–32, 248–49, 341; GW to Lund Washington, October 6, 1776, ibid., 6:493; GW to Samuel Washington, October 5, 1776, ibid., 6:486.

46. Howe to Germain, September 25, November 30, 1776, *DAR* 12:232, 258; *AR*, 48; Council of War, October 16, 1776, *PGWR* 6:576; Robert Hanson Harrison to Hancock, October 14 [–17], 1776, ibid., 6:566; John Alden, *General Charles Lee: Traitor or Patriot?* (Baton Rouge, LA, 1951), 142–44.

47. Trumbull to GW, October 31, November 30, 1776, *PGWR* 7:73, 242; ibid., 7:8n, 52n, 69–70n; Douglas Southall Freeman, *George Washington: A Biography* (New York, 1948–1957), 4:221–35. For an excellent brief account of the New York campaign through the Forts Washington and Lee debacles, see Atkinson, *The British Are Coming*, 365–402, 431–62. The "cow catching a hare" quote can be found in Atkinson, page 354.

48. Fischer, *Washington's Crossing*, 121–25; Ferling, *Almost a Miracle*, 154; GW to John Hancock, November 16, 1776, *PGWR* 7:162–65; Edwin G. Burrows, *Forgotten Patriots: The Untold Story of American Prisoners During the Revolutionary War* (New York, 2008), 200.

49. Franklin Wickwire and Mary Wickwire, *Cornwallis and the War of Independence* (London, 1971), 7–90; Hugh F. Rankin, Charles Lord Cornwallis: A Study in Frustration," in Billias, *George Washington's Opponents*, 193–94; O'Shaughnessy, *The Men Who Lost America*, 249–51.

50. Wickwire and Wickwire, *Cornwallis and the War of Independence*, 89; Howe to Germain, December 20, *DAR* 12:267.

51. GW to Hancock, December 5, 1776, *PGWR* 7:262, and also see ibid., 7:274–75n and 292n; Smith, *Whispers Across the Atlantic*, 160–61; Wickwire and Wickwire, *Cornwallis and the War of Independence*, 92–95. GW is quoted in Jones, "Sir William Howe," Billias, *George Washington's Opponents*, 56. The "wretched remains" quote can be found in Ward, *War of the Revolution*, 1:281.

52. *AR*, 55–56; Willcox, *Portrait of a General*, 115–16.

53. Ibid., 7:274n. For more detailed accounts of the chase across New Jersey, see Fischer, *Washington's Crossing*, 125–35; William M. Dwyer, *The Day Is Ours! An Inside View of the Battles of Trenton and Princeton* (New York, 1983); and Richard Ketchum, *The Winter Soldiers* (Garden City, NJ, 1973), 279.

54. Howe to Germain, September 25, 1776, *DAR* 12:232.

55. Valentine, *Lord George Germain*, 144. Howe is quoted in Smith, *Whispers Across the Atlantic*, 175.

56. Robson, *The American Revolution in Its Political and Military Aspects*, 94–105; Atkinson, *The British Are Coming*, 355.

57. GW to Joseph Reed, December 23, 1776, *PGWR* 7:423; Fischer, *Washington's Crossing*, 130, 183, 185, 381; Paul David Nelson, *General Horatio Gates: A Biography* (Baton Rouge, LA, 1976), 72–73; Ferreiro, *Brothers at Arms*, 69.

58. Reed to GW, December 22, 1776, *PGWR* 7:415.

59. William M. Welsch, "Christmas Night, 1776: How Did They Cross?," *Journal of the American Revolution* (December 24, 2018).

60. GW to Hancock, December 27, 1776, *PGWR* 7:454, 459–60n. The best account of the march on Trenton and the engagement, and the most trustworthy figures on casualties, can be found in Fischer, *Washington's Crossing*, 206–62.

61. Dwyer, *The Day Is Ours*, 320; Robert Beale, *Memoirs*, in Dennis P. Ryan, ed., *A Salute to Courage: The American Revolution as Seen Through Wartime Writings of Officers of the Continental Army and Navy* (New York, 1979), 57.

62. Wickwire and Wickwire, *Cornwallis and the War of Independence*, 96–97; Fischer, *Washington's Crossing*, 263–345, 412–13, 419; Atkinson, *The British Are Coming*, 511–54; Howard H. Peckham, ed., *The Toll of Independence: Engagements and Battle Casualties of the American Revolution* (Chicago, 1974), 22–29. The figure for prisoners of war can be found in Atkinson, *The British Are Coming*, 508.

63. Tatum, *The American Journal of Ambrose Serle*, 35, 162, 163; Gruber, *Howe Brothers*, 156–57; Valentine, *Lord North*, 1:421–27; Valentine, *Lord George Germain*, 149–61.

64. *JCC* 2:11–22; 3:331–34; 5:729, 747, 749, 751, 756–57, 762–63, 788–807; Taylor, *Papers of John Adams*, 5:38–40n; Seanegan P. Sculley, *Contest for Liberty: Military Leadership in the Continental Army, 1775-1783* (Yardley, PA, 2019), 51, 58–61; Paul David Nelson, "The American Soldier and the American Victory," in John Ferling, ed., *The World Turned Upside Down: The American Victory in the War of Independence* (Westport, CT, 1988), 36–45; James Kirby Martin and Mark Edward Lender, *A Respectable Army: The Military Origins of the Republic, 1763-1789* (Arlington Heights, IL, 1982), 62–97; Charles Patrick Neimeyer, *America Goes to War: A Social History of the Continental Army* (New York, 1996); Charles H. Lesser, ed., *The Sinews of Independence: Monthly Strength Reports of the Continental Army* (Chicago, 1976), 2–43; William C. Stinchcombe, *The American Revolution and the French Alliance* (Syracuse, NY, 1969), 9.

65. These two paragraphs draw on Howe to Germain, November 30, December 20, 1776; January 20, April 2, 1777, *DAR* 12:264–66, 266–69; 14:33, 64–65; Germain to Howe, March 3, May 18, 1777, ibid., 14:48, 84; [John Burgoyne], "Thoughts on Conducting the War . . . ," February 28, 1777, ibid., 14:41–46; Richard J. Hargrove Jr., *General John Burgoyne* (Newark, DE, 1983), 102–4; Smith, *Whispers Across the Atlantic*, 166; Brown, *American Secretary*, 88–90; Valentine, *Lord George Germain*, 151; Gruber, *Howe Brothers and the American Revolution*, 199–200.

66. Howe to Germain, October 22, 1777, *DAR* 14:242.

67. Howe to Sir Guy Carleton, April 5, 1777, ibid., 14:66; Howe to Germain, October 22, 1777, ibid., 14:242.

68. Philip Schuyler to GW, July 7, 1777, *PGWR* 10:219–21. John Adams is quoted in Richard Ketchum, *Saratoga: Turning Point of America's Revolutionary War* (New York, 1997), 219.

69. For a succinct profile of Burgoyne, see O'Shaughnessy, *The Men Who Lost America*, 123–51.

70. Schuyler to GW, July 10, 17, 1777, *PGWR* 10:245, 312. Also see Ketchum, *Saratoga*, 158–74, 245–49, 251–55, 288–91, and John H. G. Pell, "Philip Schuyler: The General as Aristocrat," in Billias, *George Washington's Generals*, 54–78.

71. Burgoyne to Germain, August 20, 1777, *DAR* 14:162–67. Burgoyne sent two letters to Germain on August 20.

72. Quoted in Henry P. Johnston, *The Campaign of 1776 Around New York and Brooklyn* (Brooklyn, 1878), pt. 2, 38.

73. Burgoyne to Clinton, October 4, 1777, in Mrs. E. Stuart Wortley, *A Prime Minister and His Son: From the Correspondence of the 3d Earl of Bute and of Lit.-General the Hon. Sir Charles Stuart* (London, 1925), 118–19; Clinton to Burgoyne, October 5, 1777, ibid., 119; Marquis de Chastellux, *Travels in America in the Years 1780, 1781 and 1782*, ed. Howard C. Rice (Chapel Hill, NC, 1963), 1:96; Willcox, *Portrait of a General*, 180–81; *AR*, 77; Max Mintz, *The Generals of Saratoga* (New Haven, CT, 1990), 203; Black, *War for America*, 131; Edward G. Lengel, "From Defeat to Victory in the North, 1777–1778," in *The West Point History of the American Revolution*, Clifford J. Rogers, Ty Seidule, and Samuel J. Watson (New York, 2017), 109. Burgoyne's quote can be found in Willcox, *Portrait of a General*, 179–80.

74. The "greatest Conquest" quotation is in Lloyd Brown and Howard Peckham, eds. *Revolutionary War Journals of Henry Dearborn, 1775–1783* (New York, 1971), 111. The other quotation—by Lieutenant William Digby—can be found in Commager and Morris, eds. *Spirit of 'Seventy-Six*, 1:605. On the Saratoga campaign, see Ketchum, *Saratoga*; Mintz, *The Generals of Saratoga*; Hargrove, *General John Burgoyne*; and Nelson, *General Horatio Gates*.

75. GW to George Clinton, July 1, 1777, *PGWR* 10:163; GW to Hancock, July 2, 1777, ibid., 169; GW to William Livingston, July 12, 1777, ibid., 10:256; GW to Heath, July 19, 1777, ibid., 10:339.

76. Quoted in Conway, *The War of American Independence, 1775–1783*, 34.

77. Stephen R. Taaffe, *The Philadelphia Campaign, 1777–1778* (Lawrence, KS, 2003), 50–52; Howe to Germain, August 30, 1777, *DAR* 14:181; Smith, *Whispers Across the Atlantic*, 224.

78. Henry Knox to Lucy Flucker Knox, September 13, 1777, in Philip Hamilton, ed., *The Revolutionary War Lives and Letters of Lucy and Henry Knox* (Baltimore, 2017), 123.

79. Bob Drury and Tom Clavin, *Valley Forge* (New York, 2018), 15.

80. Accounts of the engagement at Brandywine can be found in Taaffe, *Philadelphia Campaign*, 30–78; Ward, *War of the Revolution*, 1:342–54; Ferling, *Almost a Miracle*, 245–50; Lengel, *General George Washington*, 22–41; *PGWR* 11:187–93n.

81. GW to Hancock, September 11, 13, 15, 17, 19, 23, 1777, *PGWR* 11:200, 213, 237, 253, 268, 301; Freeman, *George Washington*, 4:490–99; Taaffe, *Philadelphia Campaign*, 84–87, 90. The "still & quiet" quote is in Aaron Sullivan, *The Disaffected: Britain's Occupation of Philadelphia During the American Revolution* (Philadelphia, 2019), 130.

82. Adams to Abigail Adams, September 1, October 28, 1777, Butterfield, *Adams Family Correspondence*, 2:335, 362.

83. Taaffe, *Philadelphia Campaign*, 93–107; Ward, *War of the Revolution*, 1:362–71; Ferling, *Almost a Miracle*, 253–56; John Ferling, *The Ascent of George Washington: The Hidden Political Genius of an American Icon* (New York, 2009), 134–35. The jester's quip can be found in Jones, "Sir William Howe," Billias, *George Washington's Opponents*, 61.

84. Gruber, *Howe Brothers*, 249; Elbridge Gerry to Adams, December 3, 1777, *LDC* 8:374; Committee at Headquarters to Henry Laurens, December 6, 1777, ibid., 8:380, 381; Cadwalader's Plan for Attacking Philadelphia, November 24, 1777, *PGWR* 12:371; NG to GW, November 24, 1777, ibid., 12:378.

85. In 1765, Parliament expected to annually collect 4 million pounds from the Stamp Act. See Merrill Jensen, *The Founding of a Nation: A History of the American Revolution, 1763–1776* (New York, 1968), 60.

86. [Israel Mauduit], *Observations upon the Conduct of Sir William Howe* (1776; reprint, New York, 1971), 24.

87. Some quotations can be found in Ketchum, *Saratoga*, 442 and 436. The Loyalist's "unanimous sentiment" quote and the "monotonous mediocrity" remark can be found in Jones, "Sir William Howe," Billias, *George Washington's Opponents*, 40, 41.

88. John Harvie to TJ, December 29, 1777, *LDC* 8:494; Laurens to GW, December 24, 1777, ibid., 8:471; William Ellery to William Whipple, December 21, 1777, ibid., 8:456.

CHAPTER 2: A NEW WAR COMING

1. *PH* 19:471, 472, 583, 609, 611, 700, 1072, 1084, 1224; Ira Gruber, *The Howe Brothers and the American Revolution* (New York, 1972), 273–77; George III to North, December 4, 9, 18, 1777, in W. Bodham Donne, ed., *The Correspondence of King George III with Lord North 1763 to 1783* (reprint, New York, 1971), 2:92, 95–97, 101; Piers Mackesy, *The War for America, 1775–1783* (Cambridge, MA, 1965), 155. The "no man with common sense" quotation can be found in Alan Valentine, *Lord North* (Norman, OK, 1967), 1:469; the "so soiled a character" quote can be found in Alan Valentine, *Lord George Germain* (Oxford, UK, 1962), 274.

2. GW to John Augustine Washington, June 10, 1778, *PGWR* 15:375. The minister to Prussia's comment is in William B. Willcox, "British Strategy in America, 1778," *Journal of Modern History* 19 (1947): 101.

3. Leonard W. Labaree et al., eds. *The Papers of Benjamin Franklin* (New Haven, CT, 1959–), 25:lx; Sir Philip Gibbes: Minutes of a Conversation with Franklin, January 5, 1778, ibid., 25:421; David Hartley [?] to BF, February 13, 1778, ibid., 25:663.

4. George III to North, January 13, 1778, Donne, *Correspondence of King George III with Lord North* 2:118–19; Valentine, *Lord North*, 1:509.

5. *PH* 19:762–67; Charles R. Ritcheson, *British Politics and the American Revolution* (Norman, OK, 1964), 258–69; Valentine, *Lord North*, 1:473–510; Peter D. G. Thomas, *Lord North* (London, 1976), 116; Peter Whitely, *Lord North: The Prime Minister Who Lost America* (London, 1996), 174; Andrew Jackson O'Shaughnessy, *The Men Who Lost America: British Leadership, the American Revolution and the Fate of the Empire* (New Haven, CT, 2013), 62; Weldon Brown, *Empire or Independence: A Study in the Failure of Reconciliation, 1774–1783* (Baton Rouge, LA, 1941), 205–26, 244–56; Anthony Gregory, "'Formed

for Empire': The Continental Congress Responds to the Carlisle Peace Commission," *Journal of the Early Republic* 38 (2018): 649.

6. Larrie D. Ferreiro, *Brothers at Arms: American Independence and the Men of France and Spain Who Saved It* (New York, 2016), 16–20, 90.

7. Adams to Henry Knox, September 19, 1779, Robert J. Taylor et al., eds. *Papers of John Adams* (Cambridge, MA, 1977–), 8:152.

8. The foregoing draws on Jonathan R. Dull, *A Diplomatic History of the American Revolution* (New Haven, CT, 1985), 89–96; Alexander DeConde, "The French Alliance in Historical Speculation," in *Diplomacy and Revolution: The Franco-American Alliance of 1778*, ed. Ronald Hoffman and Peter J. Albert (Charlottesville, VA, 1981), 1–37. That Germantown was a factor leading to the Franco-American alliance, see Adams to James Lovell, July 26, 1778, in Taylor, *Papers of John Adams*, 6:318.

9. The initial Walpole quote can be found in Mackesy, *War for America*, 158. For the second, see Horace Walpole to Sir Horace Mann, February 18, 1778, in W. S. Lewis, ed., *Selected Letters of Horace Walpole* (New Haven, CT, 1973), 220.

10. *PH* 19:486, 516, 535, 538, 540, 546, 979, 1006; O'Shaughnessy, *The Men Who Lost America*, 165.

11. O'Shaughnessy, *The Men Who Lost America*, 320–45.

12. Mackesy, *War for America*, 147–61, 180–86; Gerald Saxon Brown, *The American Secretary: The Colonial Policy of Lord George Germain, 1775–1778* (Ann Arbor, MI, 1963), 139–73; O'Shaughnessy, *The Men Who Lost America*, 334, 343; Valentine, *Lord George Germain*, 327–42; N. A. M. Rodger, *The Insatiable Earl: A Life of John Montagu, Fourth Earl of Sandwich, 1718–1792* (New York, 1993), 137, 146, 154, 266–74.

13. Germain to Henry Clinton, March 8, 21, 1778, *DAR* 15:58–59, 74–76; O'Shaughnessy, *The Men Who Lost America*, 294. See also O'Shaughnessy, *An Empire Divided: The American Revolution and the British Caribbean* (Philadelphia, 2000).

14. George III to North, January 31, 1778, in Donne, *Correspondence of King George III with Lord North* 2:125–26; Germain to Clinton, March 8, 1778, *DAR* 15:57–62.

15. Rachel N. Klein, "Frontier Planters and the American Revolution: The South Carolina Backcountry, 1775–1782," in *An Uncivil War: The South Carolina Backcountry During the American Revolution*, ed. Ronald Hoffman, Thad W. Tate, and Peter J. Albert (Charlottesville, VA, 1985), 38, 40.

16. Germain to Clinton, March 8, August 5, 1778, *DAR* 15:60–62, 178.

17. Germain to Clinton, March 8, 1778, ibid., 15:62.

18. Mackesy, *War for America*, 155; Germain to Clinton, February 4, March 8, 1778, *DAR* 13:235; 15:57; William B. Willcox, *Portrait of a General: Sir Henry Clinton in the War of Independence* (New York, 1962), 134, 136–37, 206–8. The "gallant behaviour" quote can be found in Valentine, *Lord George Germain*, 330. The "favorite of everybody" quote is in Willcox, page 208.

19. Henry Laurens to John Loveday, August 9, 1777, *LDC* 7:449; Laurens to Lachlan McIntosh, August 11, 1777, ibid., 7:457; Laurens to Christopher Zahn, August 13, 1777, ibid., 7:476; William Paca to TJ, August 19, 1777, ibid., 7:516; John Adams to Abigail Adams, August 26, 1777, ibid., 7:554.

20. Richard Henry Lee to TJ, August 25, 1777, ibid., 7:550; John Adams Diary in ibid., 8:7; James Duane to George Clinton, October 3, 1777, ibid., 8:46; Lee to George Wythe, October 19, 1777, ibid., 8:146; Elbridge Gerry to Thomas Gerry, October 21, 1777, ibid., 8:156.

21. Duane to Horatio Gates, December 16, 1777, ibid., 8:421–22; Eliphalet Dyer to Gates, November 5, 1777, ibid., 8:233–34; Laurens to Gates, November 5, 1777, ibid., 8:235–36; James Lovell to Gates, November 5, 1777, ibid., 8:237–38.

22. Richard Ketchum, *Saratoga: Turning Point of America's Revolutionary War* (New York, 1997), 439; Carl Burger, *Broadsides and Bayonets: The Propaganda War of the American Revolution* (Philadelphia, 1961), 196; Page Smith, *A New Age Now Begins* (New York, 1976), 2:939, 946; Kenneth Silverman, *A Cultural*

History of the American Revolution: Painting, Music, Literature, and the Theatre . . . 1763–1789 (New York, 1976), 331.

23. For the foregoing paragraphs, see GW to Henry Laurens, January 2, 1778, *PGWR* 13:119; GW to Patrick Henry, March 28, 1778, ibid., 14:336; Alexander Hamilton to George Clinton, February 13, 1778, Harold C. Syrett and Jacob E. Cooke, eds. *The Papers of Alexander Hamilton* (New York, 1961–1987), 1:428; Lovell to William Whipple, October 21, 1777, *LDC* 8:158; Lovell to John Langdon, October 14, 1777, ibid., 8:120; Hancock to Dorothy Hancock, October 1, 1777, ibid., 8:39; Edward Langworthy to William O'Bryen, December 1, 1777, ibid., 8:355; Jonathan Dickinson Sergeant to Lovell, November 20, 1777, ibid., 8:296; Robert Morris to Richard Peters, January 25, 1778, ibid., 8:649; Benjamin Rush to John Adams, October 1, 13, 21, 31, 1777, Taylor, *Papers of John Adams*, 5:299–303, 315–16, 316–19, 323–25; Rush to William Duer, December 8, 1777, in Lyman H. Butterfield, ed., *Letters of Benjamin Rush* (Princeton, NJ, 1951), 1:172; Rush to Mrs. Rush, January 15, 1778, ibid., 1:186; Rush to Gates, April 9, 1778, ibid., 1:208–9; Rush to NG [?], February 1, 1778, ibid., 1:195; Laurens to John Laurens, October 16, 1777, January 8, 1778, in Philip M. Hamer et al., eds. *The Papers of Henry Laurens* (Columbia, SC, 1968–), 11:554–55; 12:275. See also John Ferling, *The Ascent of George Washington: The Hidden Political Genius of an American Icon* (New York, 2009), 148–54.

24. Mark Edward Lender, *Cabal: The Plot Against General Washington* (Yardley, PA, 2019), 108–236. NG is quoted in Stephen R. Taaffe, *Washington's Revolutionary War Generals* (Norman, OK, 2019), 144.

25. Lovell to Samuel Adams, December 15, 1777, *LDC* 8:419; William Ellery to Whipple, December 21, 1777, ibid., 8:456; Laurens to GW, December 24, 1777, ibid., 8:471; Laurens to William Livingston, January 27, 1778, ibid., 8:664; Lovell to Lee, December 28, 1777, ibid., 8:491; John Harvie to TJ, December 29, 1777, ibid., 8:494; William Ellery to Nicholas Cooke, March 1, 1778, ibid., 9:185.

26. John Bannister to Theodorick Bland Jr., May 3, 1778, ibid., 9:569; Gerry to James Warren, May 26, 1778, ibid., 9:751; Samuel Chase to Thomas Johnson,

May 3, 1778, ibid., 9:571; Gouverneur Morris to Robert R. Livingston, May 3, 1778, ibid., 9:590; Lee to John Page, May 4, 1778, ibid., 9:599; Thomas McKean to Caesar Rodney, May 31, 1778, ibid., 9:792; Ferreiro, *Brothers at Arms*, 101. On the views on trade and territorial matters, see William C. Stinchcombe, *The American Revolution and the French Alliance* (Syracuse, NY, 1969), 15–16.

27. Chase to Johnson, May 3, 1778, *LDC* 9:572; Alfred Owen Aldridge, *Man of Reason: The Life of Thomas Paine* (Philadelphia, 1959), 59; Stinchcombe, *American Revolution and the French Alliance*, 16–25; GW to Nicholas Cooke, May 26, 1778, *PGWR* 15:223; GW to John Augustine Washington, May [?], 1778, ibid., 15:285–86; GW to Robert Morris, May 25, 1778, ibid., 221. The "arduous contest" quotation can be found in Aaron Sullivan, *The Disaffected: Britain's Occupation of Philadelphia During the American Revolution* (Philadelphia, 2019), 190. Patrick Henry's comment and the allusion to GW's tears are in Smith, *A New Age Now Begins*, 1054–55.

28. Laurens to John Laurens, May 16, 1778, *LDC* 9:684–85; GW to Robert Morris, May 25, 1778, *PGWR* 15:221.

29. GW to Landon Carter, May 30, 1778, *PGWR* 15:268.

30. *JCC* 11:474. On the hopeless mission of the commission, see Brown, *Empire or Independence*, 244–75.

31. Brown, *Empire or Independence*, 265; Gregory, "Formed for Empire," *Journal of the Early Republic* 38:657–72. The "mixture of ridicule" quote is in Mark Edward Lender and Garry Wheeler Stone, *Fatal Sunday: George Washington, the Monmouth Campaign, and the Politics of Battle* (Norman, OK, 2017), 84.

CHAPTER 3: FROM HOPE TO CONSTERNATION

1. GW to Carter, May 30, 1778, *PGWR* 15:268; Rush to William Gordon, December 10, 1778, in Lyman H. Butterfield, ed., *Letters of Benjamin Rush* (Princeton, NJ, 1951), 1:221; John Adams to Rush, March 19, 1812, in John A. Schutz and Douglass Adair, eds. *The Spur of Fame: Dialogues of John Adams and Benjamin Rush, 1805–1813* (San Marino, CA, 1966), 212; Lovell to Samuel

Adams, January 20, 1778, *LDC* 8:618; Paul K. Longmore, *The Invention of George Washington* (Berkeley, CA, 1988), 204–8; Thomas Fleming, *Washington's Secret War: The Hidden History of Valley Forge* (New York, 2005), 191–92. The "Idolatry" quotation can be found in Bob Drury and Tom Clavin, *Valley Forge* (New York, 2018), 189.

2. GW to Laurens, December 23, 1777, *PGWR* 12:685.

3. Ibid., 12:683; GW to John Hancock, October 13 [–14], 1777, ibid., 11:55n; GW to John Cadwalader, March 20, 1778, ibid., 14:234; Wayne K. Bodle, *Valley Forge Winter: Civilians and Soldiers in War* (University Park, PA, 2002), 5–10, 103–42; Stephen R. Taaffe, *The Philadelphia Campaign, 1777–1778* (Lawrence, KS, 2003), 148–53; E. Wayne Carp, *To Starve the Army at Pleasure: Continental Army Administration and American Political Culture, 1775–1783* (Chapel Hill, NC, 1984), 44, 55–73; James A. Huston, *Logistics of Liberty: American Services of Supply in the Revolutionary War and After* (Newark, DE, 1991), 67–68, 75, 82.

4. GW to Laurens, December 23, 1777, *PGWR* 12:683–87; John Ferling, "Joseph Galloway's Military Advice: A Loyalist's View of the Revolution," *Pennsylvania Magazine of History and Biography*, 98 (1974): 171–88.

5. Quoted in Piers Mackesy, *The War for America, 1775–1783* (Cambridge, MA, 1965), 151.

6. Edward G. Lengel, *General George Washington: A Military Life* (New York, 2005), 272–73; From a Continental Congress Camp Committee, December 10, 1777, *PGWR* 12:588–89; GW to Laurens, December 22, 23, 1777, ibid., 12:667–70, 683–87; Elbridge Gerry to GW, January 13, 1778, ibid., 13:218–19; GW to a Continental Camp Committee, January 29, 1778, ibid., 13:376–404; ibid., 13:695n; 14:551n; Laurens to Lafayette, January 12, 1778, *LDC* 8:572.

7. The above draws on Mark Edward Lender and Garry Wheeler Stone, *Fatal Sunday: George Washington, the Monmouth Campaign, and the Politics of Battle* (Norman, OK, 2017), 60–75; Henry Wiencek, *An Imperfect God: George Washington, His Slaves, and the Creation of America* (New York, 2003), 196–205, 227–32; Seanegan P. Sculley, *Contest for Liberty: Military Leadership in the*

Continental Army, 1775–1783 (Yardley, PA, 2019), 120–22; Stephen R. Taaffe, *Washington's Revolutionary War Generals* (Norman, OK, 2019), 155–56; Douglas R. Egerton, *Death or Liberty: African Americans and Revolutionary America* (New York, 2009), 76–77. On the uniforms, see Larrie D. Ferreiro, *Brothers at Arms: American Independence and the Men of France and Spain Who Saved It* (New York, 2016), 155.

8. GW to a Continental Camp Committee, January 29, 1778, *PGWR* 13:376–404; GW to John Stark, August 5, 1778, ibid., 16:256.

9. GW to Laurens, April 23, 1778, ibid., 14:601; GW, Washington's Thoughts upon a Plan of Operation for Campaign 1778, April 26–29, 1778, ibid., 14:641–42.

10. Commission from Congress to GW, June 19, 1775, ibid., 1:7; Instructions from the Continental Congress to GW, June 22, 1775, ibid., 1:22; GW to the General Officers, April 20, 1778, ibid., 14:567; From a Council of War, May 9, 1778, ibid., 15:83–87; *LDC* 15:9n.

11. Stephen Moylan to GW, May 13, 1778, *PGWR* 15:118; ibid., 15:272n; GW, General Orders, May 5, 1778, ibid., 15:39; Charles Royster, *A Revolutionary People at War: The Continental Army and American Character, 1775–1783* (Chapel Hill, NC, 1979), 250–54.

12. GW to John Parke Custis, May 26, 1778, *PGWR* 15:225; Ira Gruber, *The Howe Brothers and the American Revolution* (New York, 1972), 299; O'Shaughnessy, *The Men Who Lost America*, 207–11.

13. Germain to Clinton, February 4, March 8, 21, 1778, *DAR* 13:235; 15:57, 60, 74–76.

14. Sir Henry Clinton to the Duke of Gloucester, October 10, 1778, Series III: Letterbooks, vol. 254, in SHCP (WLCL); *AR*, 85–86; Stuart to Lord Bute, May 27, 1778, Mrs. E. Stuart Wortley, *A Prime Minister and His Son: From the Correspondence of the 3d Earl of Bute and of Lit.-General the Hon. Sir Charles Stuart* (London, 1925), 125. Clinton's "My fate is hard" comment can be found in William B. Willcox, "British Strategy in America, 1778," *Journal of Modern History* 19 (1947): 109. The "rebellious colonies" quote is in Aaron Sullivan,

The Disaffected: Britain's Occupation of Philadelphia During the American Revolution (Philadelphia, 2019), 187.

15. These two paragraphs draw on William B. Willcox, *Portrait of a General: Sir Henry Clinton in the War of Independence* (New York, 1962), 9–18, 200.

16. The above appraisal of Clinton draws on O'Shaughnessy, *The Men Who Lost America*, 207–20; Willcox, *Portrait of a General*, 3–39; William B. Willcox, "Sir Henry Clinton: Paralysis of Command," in *George Washington's Opponents*, ed. George Athan Billias (New York, 1969), 73–102. The "sporting away" quote is in Willcox, *Portrait of a General*, 108n. The "shy bitch" quotation can be found in O'Shaughnessy, 214.

17. *AR*, 23–38; Clinton to Germain, July 8, 1776, *DAR* 12:162–64; David K. Wilson, *The Southern Strategy: Britain's Conquest of South Carolina and Georgia, 1775–1780* (Columbia, SC, 2005), 36–58; Ira D. Gruber, "Britain's Southern Strategy," in *The Revolutionary War in the South: Power, Conflict, and Leadership*, ed. W. Robert Higgins (Durham, NC, 1979), 213–15. Lee's "acted like Romans" remark, together with Clinton's "blindfolded" comment and the sailor's remark about "such a drubbing," can be found in Rick Atkinson, *The British Are Coming: The War for America, Lexington to Princeton, 1775–1777* (New York, 2019), 325, 340, 341. Atkinson's account of the Charleston action and the events leading up to it can be found on pages 243–56, 323–44.

18. *AR*, 57–58. The quote concerning Newport's value can be found in Atkinson, *The British Are Coming*, 505.

19. Willcox, "British Strategy in America, 1778," *Journal of Modern History* 19 (1947): 108; *AR*, 78–84.

20. Clinton to Germain, June 5, 1778, *DAR* 15:132; *AR*, 89–90.

21. Commissioners for Quieting Disorders to Germain, June 15, September 5, 1778, *DAR* 15:141, 196; Aaron Sullivan, *The Disaffected: Britain's Occupation of Philadelphia During the American Revolution* (Philadelphia, 2019), 184–85; Lender and Stone, *Fatal Sunday*, 83–93, 96–98, 126; Stephen Conway, *The War of American Independence, 1775–1783* (London, 1995), 104.

22. Clinton to Germain, June 5, July 6, 1778, *DAR* 15:132, 160.

23. Council of War, June 17, 1778, *PGWR* 15:414–17. The generals' responses can be found in ibid., 15:419–23, 431–64.

24. Johann Ewald, *Diary of the American War: A Hessian Journal*, ed. Joseph P. Tustin (New Haven, CT, 1979), 135.

25. William S. Stryker, *The Battle of Monmouth* (reprint, Port Washington, NY, 1970), 82, 129.

26. Marquis de Lafayette to GW, June 24, 26, 1778, *PGWR* 15:529, 553; Council of War, June 24, 1778, ibid., 15:520–21. The generals' responses can be found on pages 522–29. For that of NG, see NG to GW, June 24, 1778, ibid., 15:525–26. The NG quote is on page 526. Lafayette's "disgraceful and humiliating" quote can be found in Stryker, *Battle of Monmouth*, 77.

27. GW to Gouverneur Morris, May 29, 1778, *PGWR* 15:261.

28. This quote and "select and strong detachment," above, are in GW to Laurens, June 28, 1778, ibid., 15:578.

29. TJ, Notes of Cabinet Meeting on Edmond Charles Genêt, August 2, 1793, *PTJ* 26:602–3.

30. The account of the Battle of Monmouth draws on Lender and Stone, *Fatal Sunday*, far and away the best book on this engagement. Lee's "I think these people are ours" quote is from *Fatal Sunday*, page 261. GW's "forced the Enemy from the Field" can be found in GW to Laurens, June 29, 1778, *PGWR* 15:587. For Clinton's assessment, see Clinton to Germain, July 5, 1778, *DAR* 15:159–63. The bearing down "with great Spirit" and "field of Carnage and Blood" quotes can be found in Henry Knox to Lucy Flucker Knox, June 29, 1778, in Philip Hamilton, ed., *The Revolutionary War Lives and Letters of Lucy and Henry Knox* (Baltimore, 2017), 147–48. A good account of Lee's actions can be found in Taaffe, *Washington's Revolutionary War Generals*, 165–68.

31. GW, General Orders, June 29, 1778, *PGWR* 15:583; GW to John Augustine Washington, July 4, 1778, ibid., 16:25; Hamilton to Elias Boudinot, July 5, 1778,

Harold C. Syrett and Jacob E. Cooke, eds. *The Papers of Alexander Hamilton* (New York, 1961–1987), 1:512. The "turned the fate of the day" quote can be found in Conway, *War of American Independence*, 105.

32. Ewald, *Diary of the American War*, 136; Elias Boudinot, "Exchange of Major-General Charles Lee," *Pennsylvania Magazine of History and Biography* 15 (1891): 31–32; Lee to GW, June 30, 1778, *PGWR* 15:595–97. Lee wrote three letters to GW on June 30. On Lee's court-martial, see Lender and Stone, *Fatal Sunday*, 390–97.

33. GW to John Augustine Washington, July 4, 1778, *PGWR* 16:25. For a superb appraisal of GW's role at Monmouth, see Taaffe, *Washington's Revolutionary War Generals*, 165–71.

34. Norman Desmarais, *America's First Ally: France in the Revolutionary War* (Philadelphia, 2019), 85; *PH* 20:213.

35. GW to Vice Admiral d'Estaing, July 14, 17, 1778, *PGWR* 16:68, 88; d'Estaing to GW, July 17, 1778, ibid., 16:90; AH to GW, July 20, 1778, ibid., 16:109; *PH* 20:213; Willcox, "British Strategy in America, 1778," *Journal of Modern History* 19 (1947): 111; Willcox, *Portrait of a General*, 238; Jonathan R. Dull, *The French Navy and American Independence: A Study of Arms and Diplomacy, 1774–1787* (Princeton, NJ, 1975), 105–20.

36. GW to Thomas Nelson, February 8, 1778, *PGWR* 13:481; GW to Laurens, November 14, 1778, ibid., 18:149–51; Governor Frederick Haldimand, Sketch of the Military State of the Province of Quebec, July 25, 1778, *DAR* 15:169–71; Haldimand to Germain, October 15, 1778, ibid., 15:221; John Ferling, *Almost a Miracle: The American Victory in the War of Independence* (New York, 2007), 290–93, 316–18; Edmund S. Morgan, *The Genius of George Washington* (New York, 1980), 14–16, 60–63.

37. Clinton to Germain, July 27, 1778, *DAR* 15:173; Willcox, *Portrait of a General*, 247; Christian M. McBurney, *The Rhode Island Campaign: The First French and American Operation in the Revolutionary War* (Yardley, PA, 2011), 76–77, 82–83, 97, 101.

38. McBurney, *The Rhode Island Campaign*, 51; GW to John Sullivan, July 22, 1778, *PGWR* 16:133; ibid., 16:70n; NG to Sullivan, July 23, 1778, *PNG* 2:466; Charles P. Whittemore, *General of the Revolution: John Sullivan of New Hampshire* (New York, 1961), 64–68; Aedanus Burke to Sullivan, *LDC* 8:108–10.

39. These three paragraphs draw on GW to Sullivan, July 22, 1778, *PGWR* 16:133; ibid., 16:178n; GW to Lafayette, July 27, 1778, ibid., 16:185; NG to Sullivan, July 23, 1778, *PNG* 2:466; ibid., 2:482–84n; Willcox, *Portrait of a General*, 247; Richard Buel Jr., *Dear Liberty: Connecticut's Mobilization for the Revolutionary War* (Middletown, CT, 1980), 156; Ferreiro, *Brothers at Arms*, 172; McBurney, *The Rhode Island Campaign*, 81–123.

40. *PNG* 2:482–86n, 490–91n, 501–4n; Willcox, *Portrait of a General*, 243–50; GW to d'Estaing, September 11, 1778, *PGWR* 16:570; GW to NG, September 1, 1778, ibid., 16:459; GW to Lafayette, September 1, 1778, ibid., 16:461; Sir Robert Pigot to Clinton, August 31, 1778, *DAR* 15:190; Christopher Ward, *The War of the Revolution* (New York, 1952), 2:587–95; Lee Kennett, *The French Forces in America, 1780–1783* (Westport, CT, 1977), 7; Ferreiro, *Brothers at Arms*, 178; McBurney, *The Rhode Island Campaign*, 124–32, 152–53.

41. Quoted in Willcox, *Portrait of a General*, 250.

42. McBurney, *The Rhode Island Campaign*, 164, 228; *AR*, 102–3.

43. McBurney, *The Rhode Island Campaign*, 148–69.

44. Ibid., 170–95; Ward, *War of the Revolution*, 2:591–92.

45. Frederick Mackenzie, *Diary of Frederick Mackenzie, Giving a Daily Narrative of His Military Service as an Officer of the Regiment of Royal Welsh Fusiliers During the Years 1775–1781 in Massachusetts, Rhode Island, and New York* (reprint, New York, 1968), 2:391; *AR*, 100, 103.

46. GW to John Augustine Washington, September 23, 1778, *PGWR* 17:110–11; NG to Joseph Reed, October 26, 1778, *PNG* 3:19; NG to John Cadwalader, November 10, 1778, ibid., 3:57; Henry Marchant to Robert Treat Paine, September 19, 1778, *LDC* 10:666.

47. Clinton to Gloucester, October 10, 1778, Series III: Letterbooks, SHCP (WLCL); Willcox, *Portrait of a General*, 252–53; David Syrett, *The Royal Navy in American Waters, 1775–1783* (Brookfield, VT, 1989), 114–15.

48. Council of War, September 1, 1778, *PGWR* 16:452–54. The generals' responses can be found in ibid., 16:470–74, 476–79, 480–85, 486–94.

49. Don Higginbotham, *The War of American Independence: Military Attitudes, Policies, and Practice, 1763–1789* (New York, 1971), 249; GW to Andrew Lewis, October 15, 1778, *PGWR* 17:388; GW to Joseph Reed, November 27–28, 1778, ibid., 18:316; GW to Gouverneur Morris, October 4, 1778, ibid., 17:253.

50. *AR*, 119; Clinton to Germain, September 15, October 8, 25, 1778, *DAR* 15:201, 210, 232. Clinton's "tired of the war" and "One more vigourous campaign" remarks can be found in Willcox, "British Strategy in America," *Journal of Modern History* 19: 119. On the size of Howe's army in August 1776, see Ira Gruber, *The Howe Brothers and the American Revolution* (New York, 1972), 101; and Mackesy, *War for America*, 86, 222.

CHAPTER 4: LAUNCHING THE SOUTHERN STRATEGY

1. [Archibald Campbell], *Journal of an Expedition against the Rebels of Georgia in North America*, ed. Colin Campbell (Darien, GA, 1981), 10.

2. Ibid., 5.

3. Germain to Clinton, March 8, 1778, *DAR* 15:60–61; Clinton to Germain, October 25, 1778, May 21, August 21, 1779, ibid., 15:232; 17:126, 188; Clinton to Gloucester, November 19, December 12, 1778, Series III: Letterbooks, vol. 254, SHCP (WLCL); *AR*, 116.

4. Campbell, *Journal of an Expedition*, ix–x, 29; Howe to Germain, January 17, March 5, 1778, *DAR* 15:30, 54; Clinton to Germain, October 25, 1778, ibid., 15:232; Germain to Clinton, December 3, 1778, ibid., 15:279; Carlisle Commission to Germain, November 16, 1778, ibid., 15:259; Piers Mackesy, *The War for America, 1775–1783* (Cambridge, MA, 1965), 100; Jim Piecuch, *Three*

Peoples, One King: Loyalists, Indians, and Slaves in the Revolutionary South, 1775–1782 (Columbia, SC, 2008), 129. For the conflicting characterizations of Campbell, see John Buchanan, *The Road to Charleston: Nathanael Greene and the American Revolution* (Charlottesville, VA, 2019), 4.

5. Campbell, *Journal of an Expedition*, 5, 11, 101–2n, 107n; Campbell to Patrick Tonyn, December 5, 1778, ibid., 11; *AR*, 110; William B. Willcox, *Portrait of a General: Sir Henry Clinton in the War of Independence* (New York, 1962), 261, 286.

6. Clinton to Germain, October 25, 1778, *DAR* 15:232.

7. Ibid.; David K. Wilson, *The Southern Strategy: Britain's Conquest of South Carolina and Georgia, 1775–1780* (Columbia, SC, 2005), 83; Alexander A. Lawrence, *Storm over Savannah: The Story of Count d'Estaing and the Siege of the Town in 1779* (Athens, GA, 1951), 38–45.

8. Germain to Clinton, December 3, 1778, *DAR* 15:278.

9. Clinton to Germain, December 15, 1778, January 11, 1779, ibid., 15:285–86; 17:28; Todd W. Braisted, *Grand Forage 1778: The Battleground Around New York City* (Yardley, PA, 2016), 53–55. Braisted's book is crucial for detailed information on Clinton's foraging activities during the last six months of 1778. On the British army's logistical problems throughout the conflict, see R. Arthur Bowler, *Logistics and the Failure of the British Army in America, 1775–1783* (Princeton, NJ, 1975), 92–166. See also Norman Baker, *Government and Contractors: The British Treasury and War Supplies, 1775–1783* (London, 1971). Baker attributes Britain's supply issues to numerous causes, including a lack of storage facilities, delays in shipping, damage during voyages, poor packing, poorly organized stowage, weather-related matters, and fraud.

10. GW to John Augustine Washington, September 22, 1776, *PGWR* 6:371–74; GW to Reed, December 12, 1778, ibid., 18:398.

11. GW to d'Estaing, October 27, 1778, ibid., 17:598–99.

12. GW to Richard Henry Lee, September 23, 1778, ibid., 17:98; GW to d'Estaing, October 2, 20, 22, 27, 1778, ibid., 17:222, 478, 517, 598–99; GW to Gouverneur

Morris, October 4, 1778, ibid., 17:254; GW to John Parke Custis, October 26, 1778, ibid., 17:579; GW to Patrick Henry, November 3, 1778, ibid., 18:31.

13. GW to John Parke Custis, May 26, 1778, ibid., 15:224; GW to G. Morris, October 4, 1778, ibid., 17:253; GW to John Jay, April 23, 1779, ibid., 20:176; E. James Ferguson, *The Power of the Purse* (Chapel Hill, NC, 1961), 25–44; Richard Buel Jr., *In Irons: Britain's Naval Supremacy and the American Revolutionary Economy* (New Haven, CT, 1998), 127–31; Albert Bolles, *The Financial History of the United States* (New York, 1870), 1:159–60. The "Bum Fodder" quote can be found in Richard Buel, *Dear Liberty: Connecticut's Mobilization for the Revolutionary War* (Middletown, CT, 1980), 199.

14. GW to George Mason, March 27, 1779, *PGWR* 19:627; GW to John Augustine Washington, November 26, 1778, ibid., 18:305; GW to Reed, December 12, 1778, ibid., 18:397. On prices and price controls, see Anne Bezanson, *Prices and Inflation During the American Revolution: Pennsylvania, 1770–1790* (Philadelphia, 1951); and Eric Foner, *Tom Paine and Revolutionary America* (New York, 2005), 145–61.

15. These two paragraphs draw on GW to Benjamin Harrison, December 30, 1778, *PGWR* 18:450; GW, To the Continental Congress Committee of Congress, January 20, 1779, ibid., 19:38; GW to Richard Henry Lee, September 23, 1778, ibid., 17:98; GW to Henry, October 7, 1778, ibid., 17:294; GW to G. Morris, October 4, 1778, ibid., 17:254; GW to Richard Peters, January 9, 1779, ibid., 18:607; GW to Baron de Knobelauch, March 7, 1779, ibid., 19:392; GW to Laurens, October 24, November 11, 1778, ibid., 17:558; 18:96; and John Ferling, *Almost a Miracle: The American Victory in the War of Independence* (New York, 2007), 279–80.

16. GW to the Continental Congress Committee of Conference, January 8, 13, 1779, *PGWR* 18:595n, 630–31n; Clinton to William Eden, April 4, 1779, in *Facsimilies* 12, no. 1280.

17. GW to Harrison, December 18 [–30], 1778, *PGWR* 18:448–49; GW to Jay, December 13, 1778, ibid., 18:405; *LDC* 11:376.

18. GW to George Mason, March 27, 1779, *PGWR* 19:628; GW to Harrison, December 18 [–30], 1778, ibid., 18:448–50; GW to Thomas Nelson, March 15, 1779, ibid., 19:492.

19. Joseph R. Fischer, *A Well Executed Failure: The Sullivan Campaign Against the Iroquois, July-September 1779* (Columbia, SC, 1997), 9–33; Alan Taylor, *Divided Ground: Indians, Settlers, and the Northern Borderland of the American Revolution* (New York, 2006), 91–94. See also Glenn F. Williams, *Year of the Hangman: George Washington's Campaign Against the Iroquois* (Yardley, PA, 2005); Johann Ewald, *Diary of the American War: A Hessian Journal*, ed. Joseph P. Tustin (New Haven, CT, 1979), 167. The Joseph Brant quotation can be found in Colin G. Calloway, *The Indian World of George Washington: The First President, the First Americans, and the Birth of the Nation* (New York, 2018), 242.

20. For GW's three plans, see GW to the Continental Congress Committee on Conference, January 13, 1779, *PGWR* 18:624–29. For GW's secret thoughts concerning another Canadian campaign, see GW to Laurens, November 11, 1779, ibid., 18:99–100.

21. GW to Schuyler, January 25, 1779, ibid., 19:73–74; GW to Lachlan McIntosh, January 31, 1779, ibid., 19:116–17; GW to Edward Hand, February 7, 1779, ibid., 19:138–39; GW to Sullivan, March 6, 1779, ibid., 19:388–89; GW to Reed, March 3, 1779, ibid., 19:345.

22. GW to Schuyler, January 18, 1779, ibid., 19:18.

23. GW to Sullivan, March 6, 1779, ibid., 19:388–89; GW to Reed, March 3, 1779, ibid., 19:345.

24. GW to James Duane, January 11 [–12], 1779, ibid., 19:612. See also Benjamin Lee Huggins, *Washington's War, 1779* (Yardley, PA, 2018), 18–20.

25. GW to the Continental Congress Committee on Conference, January 8, 20, 23, 1779, *PGWR* 18:594–97n; 19:38–42, 52–56.

26. GW to G. Morris, May 8, 1779, ibid., 20:385; GW to William Fitzhugh, April 10, 1779, ibid., 20:31; GW to Lund Washington, May, 29, 1779, ibid., 20:688; James Thomas Flexner, *George Washington in the American*

Revolution, 1775–1783 (Boston, 1968), 235–39; Kate Haulman, "Fashion and Culture Wars of Revolutionary Philadelphia," *William and Mary Quarterly* 62 (2005): 660.

27. GW to Harrison, December 18 [–30], 1778, *PGWR* 18:449.

28. GW to George Mason, March 27, 1779, ibid., 19:628; GW to Harrison, December 18 [–30], 1778, ibid., 18:448–50; GW to James Warren, March 31, 1779, ibid., 19:673–74; GW to Thomas Nelson, March 15, 1779, ibid., 19:492.

29. GW to Warren, March 31, 1779, ibid., 19:674.

30. John Banister to St. George Tucker, August 11, 1778, *LDC* 10:422.

31. Roger Sherman to Jonathan Trumbull Sr., October 27, 1778, ibid., 11:136; Francis Lewis to George Clinton, December 31, 1778, ibid., 11:391; James Duane to Mary Duane, May 26, 1779, ibid., 12:537; John Fell's Diary, December 16, 1778, January 5, 1779, ibid., 11:349, 416; James Duane to Robert R. Livingston, January 3, 1779, ibid., 11:400; William Whipple to Josiah Bartlett, January 3, 1779, ibid., 11:410; Connecticut Delegates to Trumbull, January 4, 1779, ibid., 11:413; Laurens to Sullivan, January 5, 1779, ibid., 11:418.

32. Duane to Livingston, January 3, 1779, ibid., 11:400; Laurens to Sullivan, January 5, 1779, ibid., 11:418.

33. GW to Warren, March 31, 1779, *PGWR* 19:674; GW to John Armstrong, May 18, 1779, ibid., 20:517–18; Ferguson, *Power of the Purse*, 44.

34. *Common Sense* can be found in *The Complete Writings of Thomas Paine*, ed. Philip S. Foner (New York, 1945), 1:3–46. *The American Crisis* is in ibid., 1:49–239. For Paine's essays on corruption in 1778, see his collection of essays under the heading "The Affair of Silas Deane" in ibid., 2:96–188. The quotations in these paragraphs can be found in his essay "To the People of America," ibid., 2:143.

35. Thomas Paine to GW, January 31, 1779, *PGWR* 19:117.

36. Thomas Paine, *The American Crisis VII* (1778), in *Complete Works of Thomas Paine*, 1:140–57. The quotes can be found on pages 141, 149, 150, 152, 153, 155.

37. Campbell, *Journal of an Expedition*, 13–20; Campbell to Germain, January 16, 1779, *DAR* 17:33–34.

38. Charles E. Bennett and Donald R. Lennon, *A Quest for Glory: Major General Robert Howe and the American Revolution* (Chapel Hill, NC, 1991), 1–99; Marquis de Chastellux, *Travels in America in the Years 1780, 1781 and 1782*, ed. Howard C. Rice (Chapel Hill, NC, 1963), 1:111; Evangeline W. and Charles M. Andrews, eds. *Journal of a Lady of Quality: Being the Narrative of a Journey . . . 1774–1776* (New Haven, CT, 1921), 167. Jeff Dacus, "General Robert Howe's Alleged Treason," *Journal of the American Revolution*, October 3, 2017; Hugh F. Rankin, *The North Carolina Continentals* (Chapel Hill, NC, 1971), 18.

39. Bennett and Lennon, *A Quest for Glory*, 85–99; Campbell to Germain, January 16, 1779, *DAR* 17:34, 36; Campbell, *Journal of an Expedition*, 19–24, 27; Dacus, "General Robert Howe's Alleged Treason"; Wilson, *Southern Strategy*, 65–80; Christopher Ward, *The War of the Revolution* (New York, 1952), 2:679–83. Campbell's quote can be found in Robert L. O'Connell, *Revolutionary: George Washington at War* (New York, 2019), 217.

40. Clinton to Eden, February 5, 1779, *Facsimilies* 12, no. 1258; *AR*, 116–19; Clinton to Germain, May 22, 1779, *DAR* 17:129–30.

41. GW to Lafayette, March 8 [–10], 1779, *PGWR*, 19:402.

CHAPTER 5: THE YEAR OF MARKING TIME

1. GW to William Smallwood and the Field Officers of the Maryland Line, March 2, 1779, *PGWR* 19:335; GW to Mason, March 27, 1779, ibid., 19:627; GW to Jay, March 15, 1779, ibid., 19:487.

2. GW to Jay, March 15, 1779, ibid., 19:487; GW to Israel Putnam, March 27, 1779, ibid., 19:629–30; Jay to GW, February 3, 1779, ibid., 19:124, 124–25n.

3. NG to GW, May 31, 1779, ibid., 20:707.

4. GW, Circular to the States, May 22, 1779, ibid., 20:569; GW to Gouverneur Morris, May 8, 1779, ibid., 20:385.

5. James Thacher, *A Military Journal During the American Revolutionary War, from 1775–1783*, ed. Thomas Bulch (reprint, New York, 1969), 162.

6. GW to Conrad-Alexandre Gérard, May 1, 1779, *PGWR* 20:279–80; GW to Morris, May 8, 1779, ibid., 20:384.

7. GW to Alexander McDougall, March 6, 1779, ibid., 19:384.

8. *AR*, 114, 142; Clinton to William Eden, May 20, 1779, *Facsimilies* 9, no. 997; William B. Willcox, *Portrait of a General: Sir Henry Clinton in the War of Independence* (New York, 1962), 261–63, 273–74.

9. Germain to Clinton, December 3, 1778, January 23, 1779, *DAR* 15:278; 17:44–45.

10. Clinton to Germain, May 22, 1779, ibid., 17:129–30; Clinton to Eden, May 20, 1779, *Facsimilies* 9, no. 997.

11. Clinton to Germain, May 22, 1779, *DAR* 17:129; Willcox, *Portrait of a General*, 270.

12. Clinton to Germain, April 4, May 13, 1779, *DAR* 17:96, 123; Clinton to Eden, May 4, October 10, 1779, *Facsimilies* 9, nos. 993, 1013.

13. Willcox, *Portrait of a General*, 271.

14. Ibid., 272–73; *AR*, 142n; Piers Mackesy, *The War for America, 1775–1783* (Cambridge, MA, 1965), 257–58.

15. *AR*, 119–20.

16. GW, Circular to the States, May 22, 1779, *PGWR* 20:569; GW to John Armstrong, May 18, 1779, ibid., 20:518.

17. Abigail Adams to John Adams, September 10, 1777, October 25, 1778, June 8, 1779, in L. H. Butterfield et. al., eds. *Adams Family Correspondence* (Cambridge, MA, 1963–), 2:340; 3:111, 198; Lucy Flucker Knox to Henry Knox, April 31 [?], 1777, in Philip Hamilton, ed., *The Revolutionary War Lives and Letters of Lucy and Henry Knox* (Baltimore, 2017), 90. See also Edith B. Gelles, *Abigail and John: Portrait of a Marriage* (New York, 2009), 118–21, 137–39.

18. Most of the quotations can be found in Sara T. Damiano, "Writing Women's History Through the Revolution: Family, Finances, Letter Writing, and

Conceptions of Marriage," *William and Mary Quarterly* 74 (2017): 708–9, 719, 720. On John Adams as a creditor, and for Abigail Adams's assorted tactics for dealing with scarcity, see Woody Holton, *Abigail Adams* (New York, 2009), 121–92. Abigail Adams's "pockets full of money" quote can be found in Holton, page 126. For Holton on debtors paying off old debts in worthless money, see Woody Holton, *Unruly Americans and the Origins of the Constitution* (New York, 2007), 8.

19. Abigail Adams to John Adams, June 10, 18, September 29, 1778, June 8, 1779, May 1, November 13, 1780, January 15, April 23, 1781, Butterfield, *Adams Family Correspondence*, 3:36, 47, 95–96, 200, 336; 4:15, 64, 106, 107n. See also ibid., 3:194n. For Adams's comment that the tax burden would be more than the people could bear, see 4:15.

20. Abigail Adams to John Adams, July 12, August 10, September 16, 25, October 1, 9, 1775, March 31, 1776, ibid., 1:243, 272, 279, 284, 288, 297–98, 370.

21. Robert Middlekauff, *The Glorious Cause: The American Revolution, 1763–1789* (New York, 1982), 535–58. The "dreadful consequences" quotation is on page 542.

22. The "plough and hoe" and "no time" for nothing but work quotes can be found in Ray Raphael, *A People's History of the American Revolution* (New York, 2001), 113–14. The remaining quotes, together with others on the travail of the war, can be found in Sarah Hodgkins to Joseph Hodgkins, October 9, November 19, December 10, 1775, February 1, 11, May 23, October 19, 1776, April 26, 1778, in Herbert T. Wade and Robert A. Lively, eds. *This Glorious Cause: The Adventures of Company Officers in Washington's Army* (Princeton, NJ, 1958), 178, 184, 191, 192, 203, 224, 239–40.

23. Lucy Flucker Knox to Henry Knox, August 23, 1777, August 12, 1781, in Hamilton, *Revolutionary War Lives and Letters of Lucy and Henry Knox*, 117, 155.

24. Clinton to Edward Mathew, May 20, 1779, *DAR* 17:125; Roger Kaplan, "The Hidden War: British Intelligence During the American Revolution," *William and Mary Quarterly* 47 (1990): 129; John Selby, *The Revolution in Virginia, 1775–1783* (Williamsburg, VA, 1988), 204–8; Mackesy, *The War for America,*

269–70; Clinton to Eden, May 20, 1779, *Facsimilies* 9, no. 997. Both GW and General Charles Lee referred to the "canvass wings" of the enemy navy. For one of GW's use of the term, see GW to John Augustine Washington, June 20, 1779, *PGWR* 21:198; Lee's can be found in Eric Robson, *The American Revolution: In Its Political and Military Aspects, 1763–1783* (Hamden, CT, 1965), 107.

25. These two paragraphs draw on *AR*, 122–26; Clinton to Eden, June 17, 18, 1779, *Facsimilies* 9, no. 999; Washington to Horatio Gates, June 11, 1779, *PGWR* 21:129–31; GW to William Fitzhugh, June 25, 1779, ibid., 21:242.

26. GW to Jay, June 6, 1779, *PGWR* 21:90; GW to John Augustine Washington, June 20, 1779, ibid., 21:198; Smith, *Memoirs*, 116.

27. Kaplan, "The Hidden War," *William and Mary Quarterly* 47: 117, 129; *AR*, 122, 126, 129, 129n; Council of War, June 6, 1779, *PGWR* 26:326.

28. Gates is quoted in Douglas Southall Freeman, *George Washington: A Biography* (New York, 1948–1957), 5:109. See also GW, Enclosure Contingency Orders, June 12, 1779, *PGWR* 21:154–55; GW to Israel Putnam, June 14, 1779, ibid., 21:175–76; From a Board of General Officers, July 22, 1779, ibid., 21:612–14. For the "too strong" quotation, see Knox to Lucy Flucker Knox, June 29, 1779, Hamilton, *Revolutionary War Lives and Letters of Lucy and Henry Knox*, 149; Thacher, *A Military Journal During the American Revolutionary War*, 133; Marquis de Chastellux, *Travels in America in the Years 1780, 1781 and 1782*, ed. Howard C. Rice (Chapel Hill, NC, 1963), 1:89, 94.

29. Smith, *Memoirs*, 110, 178. The "Nothing surely can be more shameful" quote can be found in Stephen Conway, *The War of American Independence, 1775–1783* (London, 1995), 114.

30. *AR*, 121–22, 126; George F. Scheer, ed., *A Narrative of Some of the Adventures, Dangers and Sufferings of a Revolutionary Soldier, by Joseph Plumb Martin* (Boston, 1962), 161.

31. *AR*, 126, 129.

32. Smith, *Memoirs*, 132.

33. Ibid., 134, 137.

34. Ibid., 109, 122, 137; Frank Moore, comp., *The Diary of the American Revolution, 1775–1781* (New York, 1967), 374–84; *PGWR* 21:375–76n, 378n, 759–68n; Norwalk Officials to GW, July 9, 1779, ibid., 21:403–4; Jonathan Trumbull to GW, July 10, 1779, ibid., 21:429–30; GW to Jay, July 9, August 6, 1779, ibid., 21:397, 759n.

35. Clinton to Gloucester, December 10, 1779, Series III: Letterbooks, vol. 254, SHCP (WLCL).

36. GW to Jay, July 9, 1779, *PGWR* 21:397; GW to Anthony Wayne, July 9, 14, 1779, ibid., 21:410–11, 488; Wayne to GW, July 10, 16, 17, 1779, ibid., 21:432–33, 522, 523, 541–43; GW, Plan of Attack, July 15, 17, 1779, ibid., 21:509–10; GW, General Orders, July 16, 1779, ibid., 21:511; Christopher Ward, *The War of the Revolution* (New York, 1952), 2:596–603; Paul David Nelson, *Anthony Wayne: Soldier of the Early Republic* (Bloomington, IN, 1985), 94–100; George Scheer and Hugh F. Rankin, eds. *Rebels and Redcoats* (Cleveland, 1957), 361–63.

37. Ward, *War of the Revolution*, 2:604–10; *AR*, 139, 147.

38. Clinton to Eden, July 3, 4, 1779, *Facsimiles* 9, no. 1003.

39. Jonathan Dull, *A Diplomatic History of the American Revolution* (New Haven, CT, 1983), 107–113; Dull, *The French Navy and American Independence: A Study of Arms and Diplomacy, 1774–1787* (Princeton, NJ, 1975), 125–43, 155; Samuel Flagg Bemis, *The Diplomacy of the American Revolution* (New York, 1935), 70–93. La Luzerne and GW are quoted in Larrie D. Ferreiro, *Brothers at Arms: American Independence and the Men of France and Spain Who Saved It* (New York, 2016), 116. On GW's trip and talks with the French envoy, see also Substance of a Conference with La Luzerne, September 16, 1779, *PGWR* 22:438–42, 442–44n.

40. GW to Lafayette, September 30, 1779, *PGWR* 22:560; GW to John Sullivan, September 3, 1779, ibid., 22:346; Willcox, *Portrait of a General*, 283, 295.

41. Mackesy, *War for America*, 225, 272–73.

42. Frederick Haldimand to Germain, October 3, 1779, *DAR* 17:231.

43. Germain to Clinton, May 5, 1779, ibid., 17:117; Clinton to Haldimand, September 9, 1779, ibid., 17:204; GW to John Sullivan, May 31, 1779, *PGWR* 20:716–19. For the best accounts of the Sullivan Expedition, see Joseph R. Fischer, *A Well-Executed Failure: The Sullivan Campaign Against the Iroquois, July–September 1779* (Columbia, SC, 1997); Glenn F. Williams, *Year of the Hangman: George Washington's Campaign Against the Iroquois* (Yardley, PA, 2005); Holger Hoock, *Scars of Independence: America's Violent Birth* (New York, 2017), 285–93; and Colin G. Calloway, *The Indian World of George Washington: The First President, the First Americans, and the Birth of the Nation* (New York, 2018), 247–59; John Ferling, *The First of Men: A Life of George Washington* (reprint, New York, 2010), 314–15. See also Isabel T. Kelsay, *Joseph Brant, 1743–1807: Man of Two Worlds* (Syracuse, NY, 1984). On the postwar implications of the Sullivan Expedition, see Calloway, *The Indian World of George Washington* and Susan Dunn, "Our Father, the President," *New York Review of Books* (April 5, 2018).

44. Germain to Clinton, June 25, 1779, *DAR* 17:151.

45. Germain to Clinton, September 27, 1779, ibid., 17:225. On the attempted invasion, see Dull, *French Navy and American Independence*, 143–58; Alfred Temple Patterson, *The Other Armada: The Franco-Spanish Attempt to Invade Britain in 1779* (Manchester, UK, 1960).

46. The quotes can be found in Willcox, *Portrait of a General*, 281, and *AR*, 139n. See also Franklin Wickwire and Mary Wickwire, *Cornwallis and the War of Independence* (London, 1971), 39–40, 105–7, 113–16.

47. Most of the quotes can be found in Willcox, *Portrait of a General*, 86, 230, 281, 282. For Clinton's exuberance at Cornwallis's abilities, see Clinton to Germain, August 20, 1779, *DAR* 17:188.

48. Clinton to Germain, August 21, 1779, *DAR* 17:189; Germain to Clinton, March 3, 1779, ibid., 17:72; *AR*, 143–44; *PGWR* 22:506n. On Arbuthnot's background and character, see John A. Tilley, *The British Navy and the American Revolution* (Columbia, SC, 1987), 163–64, and William B. Willcox, "Arbuthnot, Gambier, and Graves: 'Old Women' of the Navy," in Billias, *George Washington's Opponents*, 267–68.

49. *AR* 145–49, 152; Haldimand to Clinton, May 26, June 18, 1779, *DAR* 17:135–36, 147; Benjamin Lee Huggins, *Washington's War, 1779* (Yardley, PA, 2018), 147.

50. GW to d'Estaing, September 13, 1779, *PGWR* 22:409; GW to Arthur St. Clair, October 4, 1779, ibid., 22:619; Huggins, *Washington's War, 1779*, 75, 127.

51. Jay to GW, September 26, 1779, *PGWR* 22:512; GW to d'Estaing, October 4, 1779, ibid., 22:611–15; GW to Samuel Huntington, October 4, 1779, ibid., 22:629.

52. The above draws on Huggins, *Washington's War*, 128–30, and the editor's note, "Planning for an Allied Attack on New York," circa October 3–7, 1779, *PGWR* 22:394–601. See also GW, Loose Thoughts upon an Attack of New York, October 3, 1779, *PGWR* 22:601–3, and the correspondence concerning the prospective campaign between GW and several generals over a four-day span in early October in ibid., 22:604–21.

53. David B. Mattern, *Benjamin Lincoln and the American Revolution* (Columbia, SC, 1995), 6–50; David K. Wilson, *The Southern Strategy: Britain's Conquest of South Carolina and Georgia, 1775–1780* (Columbia, SC, 2005), 81.

54. Prevost to Germain, January 18, June 10, 1779, *DAR* 17:43, 143; Wilson, *The Southern Strategy*, 82–88, 102.

55. Wilson, *The Southern Strategy*, 102–15; Prevost to Clinton, May 21, 1779, *DAR* 17:127–29; Prevost to Germain, June 10, 1779, ibid., 17:141–43.

56. Committee of Congress to GW, April 28, 1779, *LDC* 12:399; South Carolina Delegates to Rutledge, May 7, 1779, ibid., 12:437; Jay to Henry, May 10, 1779, ibid., 12:452; Jay to Rutledge, August 12, 1779, ibid., 13:362; GW to John Augustine Washington, May 12, 1779, *PGWR* 20:461; GW to Rutledge, May 7, 1779, ibid., 20:371.

57. Committee of Congress to GW, April 28, 1779, *LDC* 12:399; Jay to Patrick Henry, May 10, 1779, ibid., 12:453; Jay to Lincoln, August 12, 1779, ibid., 12:362; Wilson, *The Southern Strategy*, 177–78; Norman Desmarais, *America's First Ally: France in the Revolutionary War* (Philadelphia, 2019), 200–201.

58. *AR*, 150; Stanley D. M. Carpenter, *Southern Gambit: Cornwallis and the British March to Yorktown* (Norman, OK, 2019), 65. For the quotes on alligators, see Alexander Lawrence, *Storm over Savannah: The Story of Count d'Estaing and the Siege of the Town in 1779* (Athens, GA, 1951), 50; and Benjamin Kennedy, ed., *Muskets, Cannon Balls and Bombs: Nine Narratives of the Siege of Savannah in 1779* (Savannah, GA, 1974), 110–11.

59. Lawrence, *Storm over Savannah*, 76–131; Wilson, *The Southern Strategy*, 135–92; Mattern, *Benjamin Lincoln*, 85–87; Ferreiro, *Brothers at Arms*, 201; *AR*, 150. Campbell's remark about Prevost can be found in Lawrence, page 41. Lincoln's account of the toll of battle is in Lincoln to Samuel Huntington, October 22, 1779, *PGWR* 23:232n. D'Estaing's description of the frightful "carnage" can be found in Ferreiro, page 202.

60. Lincoln to Huntington, October 22, 1779, *PGWR* 23:232n

61. Quoted in Lawrence, *Storm over Savannah*, 128.

62. Lincoln to Huntington, October 22, 1779, *PGWR* 23:232n.

63. GW to Schuyler, November 24, 1779, ibid., 23:421; GW to Huntington, November 24, December 7, 1779, ibid., 23:416, 544–46; GW to Schuyler, November 24, 1779, ibid., 23:421; GW to Edmund Pendleton, November 1, 1779, ibid., 23:122.

64. GW to Huntington, November 18, 20, December 7, 1779, ibid., 23:320–25, 329n, 377–79, 544–46.

65. Clinton to Germain, August 21, September 26, November 17, December 15, 1779, *DAR* 17:189, 221, 255, 260; Germain to Clinton, March 31, September 27, 1779, ibid., 17:89, 224; Lafayette to GW, March 18, 1780, *PGWR* 25:83, 84n.

66. For these two paragraphs, see Smith, *Memoirs*, 144, 167–68, 174–77, 181, 183, 184, 187, 189, and Stuart to Lord Bute, November 1, 1779, Mrs. E. Stuart Wortley, *A Prime Minister and His Son: From the Correspondence of the 3d Earl of Bute and of Lt.-General the Hon. Sir Charles Stuart* (London, 1925), 162.

67. Clinton to Eden, November 19, December 11, 1779, *Facsimilies* 10, no. 1032, 1034.

68. AR, 153 and 153n; Wilson, *The Southern Strategy*, 198; *AR*, 156, 158; Smith, *Memoirs*, 200–201.

CHAPTER 6: AMERICA'S SARATOGA

1. GW to Jabez Bowen, December 15, 1779, *PGWR* 23:620–21; GW to William Heath, December 21, 1779, ibid., 23:670–71; GW to William Livingston, December 21, 1776, ibid., 23:676–77; GW to Anthony Wayne, December 28, 1779, ibid., 23:767; GW to Samuel Huntington, December 30, 1779, ibid., 23:779. On GW and espionage, see Alexander Rose, *Washington's Spies: The Story of America's First Spy Ring* (New York, 2006).

2. Huntington to GW, November 11, December 10, 1779, *PGWR* 23:243, 570–71; GW to Huntington, November 18, 29, December 2, 8, 1779, March 27, 1780, ibid., 23:320, 482, 506–7, 556; 25:196; ibid., 486n; GW to Lincoln, December 12, 1779, February 27, March 28, 1780, ibid., 23:584; 24;582; 25:209–10; John Mathews to Lincoln, December 9, 1779, *LDC* 14:257–58; Mathews to Thomas Bee, January 5 [?], 1780, ibid., 14:320; Lovell to Gates, November 11, 1779, ibid., 14:179; Carl P. Borick, *A Gallant Defense: The Siege of Charleston, 1780* (Columbia, SC, 2003), 34–36.

3. John Ferling, *Almost a Miracle: The American Victory in the War of Independence* (New York, 2007), 65, 113, 341–44; Ferling, *The Ascent of George Washington: The Hidden Political Genius of an American Icon* (New York, 2009), 201–202. See also Henry Wiencek, *An Imperfect God: George Washington, His Slaves, and the Creation of America* (New York, 2003), 227–32.

4. Mathews to Lincoln, December 9, 1779, *LDC* 14:257–58; David B. Mattern, *Benjamin Lincoln and the American Revolution* (Columbia, SC, 1995), 89.

5. George F. Scheer, ed., *Private Yankee Doodle: Being a Narrative of Some of the Adventures, Dangers and Sufferings of a Revolutionary Soldier* (Boston, 1962), 169–70, 172; James Thomas Flexner, *George Washington and the American*

Revolution (Boston, 1967), 354–56; Douglas Southall Freeman, *George Washington* (New York, 1948–1957), 5:143–52; Donald Jackson et al., eds. *The Diaries of George Washington* (Charlottesville, VA, 1976–1979) 3:342–52; GW to Lafayette, March 18, 1780, *PGWR* 25:83; Seanegan P. Sculley, *Contest for Liberty: Military Leadership in the Continental Army, 1775–1783* (Yardley, PA, 2019), 138.

6. Editor's note, *PNG* 5:260n; NG to Jeremiah Wadsworth, February 8, 1780, ibid., 5:354.

7. Arthur St. Clair to GW, February 11, 1780, *PGWR* 24:444–46; James Abeel to Richard Kidder Meade, February 13, 1780, and editor's note, ibid., 24:446–49n; GW to St. Clair, February 12, 1780, ibid., 24:157–58; Harry M. Ward, *George Washington's Enforcers: Policing the Continental Army* (Carbondale, IL, 2006), 59–72; Benjamin Huggins, "Raid Across the Ice: The British Operation to Capture Washington," *Journal of the American Revolution*, December 17, 2013; the latter article is in an online journal without page numbers.

8. I am grateful to Thomas K. Lindsey for sharing information from his research on the number of officer resignations during the initial six months of 1780.

9. Continental Congress Committee on Reducing the Army to GW, January 11, 1780, *PGWR* 24:84–85; GW to the Continental Congress Committee on Reducing the Army, January 23, 1780, ibid., 24:221–25; GW to Elbridge Gerry, January 29, 1780, ibid., 24:312–13; GW to Huntington, February 10, April 3, 1780, ibid., 24:433; 25:298–300. For the quotas for each state, see the editorial note in ibid., 24:434n.

10. Committee at Headquarters to the States, August 19, 1780, *LDC* 15:600–603.

11. Thomas Paine, *The American Crisis VIII* (1780), in *The Complete Writings of Thomas Paine*, ed. Philip S. Foner (New York, 1945), 1:158–64.

12. AH to [?], December 1779–March 1780, in Harold C. Syrett and Jacob E. Cooke, eds. *The Papers of Alexander Hamilton* (New York, 1961–1987), 2:236–51, 234–36n. See also Ron Chernow, *Alexander Hamilton* (New York, 2004),

137–38; and the more detailed account in John C. Miller, *Alexander Hamilton: Portrait in Paradox* (New York, 1959), 51–56. Hamilton's quotes on the wealthy can be found in Miller, page 56.

13. E. James Ferguson, *The Power of the Purse* (Chapel Hill, NC, 1961), 48–56; Jackson Turner Main, *The Sovereign States, 1775–1783* (New York, 1973), 250–315; Richard Buel Jr., *In Irons: Britain's Naval Supremacy and the American Revolutionary Economy* (New Haven, CT, 1998), 130.

14. *LDC* 15:113n, 362n, 639n; Committee of Congress to the Committee at Headquarters, June 16, 1780, ibid., 15:328.

15. GW to Fielding Lewis, May [5?], 1780, *PGWR* 25:553–56; GW to John Jay, March 15, 1779, ibid., 19:488.

16. Arthur Lee to John Adams, September 18, 1780, in Robert J. Taylor et al., eds. *Papers of John Adams* (Cambridge, MA, 1977–), 10:185.

17. *AR*, 158–59; Germain to Clinton, March 15, 1780, *DAR* 18:60; Letter of Captain Johann Ewald, February 29, 1780, in Bernhard A. Uhlendorf, ed., *The Siege of Charleston* (reprint, New York, 1968), 23; Diary of Captain Johann Hincrichs, ibid., 121, 125; William B. Willcox, *Portrait of a General: Sir Henry Clinton in the War of Independence* (New York, 1962), 301; "The Narrative of John Robert Shaw," in Don N. Hagist, ed., *British Soldiers, American War: Voices of the American Revolution* (Yardley, PA, 2014), 29.

18. Johann Ewald, *Diary of the American War: A Hessian Journal*, ed. Joseph P. Tustin (New Haven, CT, 1979), 194; Prevost to Clinton, March 2, 1780, in Historical Manuscripts Commission, *Report on American Manuscripts in the Royal Institution of Great Britain* (London, 1904–1909), 2:96; Clinton to Prevost, March 8, 1780, ibid., 2:99; *AR*, 159–60, 162; Piers Mackesy, *The War for America, 1775–1783* (Cambridge, MA, 1965), 340. The "state of nature" quote can be found in Willcox, *Portrait of a General*, 302.

19. Borick, *A Gallant Defense*, 36–37; Lincoln to TJ, January 7, 1780, *PTJ* 3:260–61; TJ to GW, February 17, 1780, ibid., 3:297; GW to TJ, October 6, 1780, *PGWR* 25:414–15n.

20. GW to Lincoln, September 28, 1779, *PGWR* 22:523–24.

21. Huntington to Lincoln, November 11, 1779, *LDC* 14:176; Committee of Congress to Lincoln, November 12, 1779, ibid., 14:180; Larrie D. Ferreiro, *Brothers at Arms: American Independence and the Men of France and Spain Who Saved It* (New York, 2016), 213; Mattern, *Benjamin Lincoln and the American Revolution*, 89–95.

22. *AR*, 163; David K. Wilson, *The Southern Strategy: Britain's Conquest of South Carolina and Georgia, 1775–1780* (Columbia, SC, 2005), 203–205; Mattern, *Benjamin Lincoln and the American Revolution*, 88–94.

23. *AR*, 164; Lincoln to GW, January 23[–24], 1780, *PGWR* 24:235; GW to Steuben, April 2, 1780, ibid., 25:288–89; GW to Lincoln, April 15, 1780, ibid., 25:412.

24. *AR*, 161; Ewald, *Diary of the American War*, 225; Peter Russell, "The Siege of Charleston: Journal of Peter Russell, December 25, 1779 to May 2, 1780," *American Historical Review* 4 (1899): 484; Letter of Ewald, February 29, 1780, *Siege of Charleston*, 29; Borick, *A Gallant Defense*, 49–65; Roger Kaplan, "The Hidden View: British Intelligence Operations during the American Revolution," *William and Mary Quarterly* 47 (1990): 128.

25. Clinton to Germain, May 13, 1780, *DAR* 18:87; Ewald, *Diary of the American War*, 235; Diary of Captain Johann Ewald, *Siege of Charleston*, 61; John A. Tilley, *The British Navy and the American Revolution* (Columbia, SC, 1987), 179.

26. Lachlan McIntosh, "Journal of the Siege of Charleston, 1780," in *University of Georgia Libraries Miscellanea Publications*, no. 7, ed. Lilla Hawes (Athens, GA, 1968), 101; Mattern, *Benjamin Lincoln and the American Revolution*, 88–89. David Ramsay is quoted in Robert G. Parkinson, *The Common Cause: Creating Race and Nation in the American Revolution* (New York, 2016), 479.

27. The correspondence between Lincoln and Whipple can be found in *Original Papers Relating to the Siege of Charleston, 1780* (Charleston, SC, 1898), 17–33.

28. *AR*, 165–66; Clinton to Germain, May 13, 1780, *DAR* 18:87; Robert D. Bass, *The Green Dragoon: The Lives of Banastre Tarleton and Mary Robinson* (Orangeburg, SC, 1973), 31; "Narrative of John Robert Shaw," *British Soldiers,*

American War, 31; John Buchanan, *The Road to Guilford Courthouse: The American Revolution in the Carolinas* (New York, 1997), 196–88; Borick, *A Gallant Defense*, 71–73, 96–108, 121–26, 130–34, 145–60; Wilson, *The Southern Strategy*, 238–39, 246–47. For Tarleton's account of the action, see Henry Steele Commager and Richard B. Morris, eds. *The Spirit of 'Seventy-Six: The Story of the American Revolution as Told by Participants* (Indianapolis, IN, 1958), 2:1103–4.

29. *AR*, 169. The letter explaining that the exit was closed is quoted in Franklin Wickwire and Mary Wickwire, *Cornwallis and the War of Independence* (London, 1971), 131.

30. Willcox *Portrait of a General*, 310–13; Tilley, *The British Navy and the American Revolution*, 174–75, 183, 185; David Syrett, *The Royal Navy in American Waters, 1775–1783* (Aldershot, UK, 1989), 86, 129–30.

31. Clinton to Germain, August 20, 1779, *DAR* 17:188–89; Germain to Clinton, November 4, 1779, ibid., 17:250–51; Willcox, *Portrait of a General*, 314–16; Wickwire and Wickwire, *Cornwallis and the War of Independence*, 12–29. Clinton's "do not think his conduct has been military" comment can be found in William B. Willcox, "The British Road to Yorktown: A Study in Divided Command," *American Historical Review* 52 (1946): 5.

32. Borick, *A Gallant Defense*, 152–54; Hugh F. Rankin, *The North Carolina Continentals* (Chapel Hill, NC, 1971), 228–29; Mattern, *Benjamin Lincoln*, 105–6; Ewald to Baron von Jungkenn, May 13, 1780, in Uhlendorf, *Siege of Charleston*, 417. For Clinton's offer of terms to Lincoln, see *PGWR* 25:576n.

33. These three paragraphs draw on *AR*, 171, 177, 189; Ewald, *Diary of the American War*, 238; Clinton to Germain, May 13, 1780, *DAR* 18:88; Germain to Clinton, March 15, 1780, ibid., 18:60; Diary of Ewald, in Uhlendorf, *Siege of Charleston*, 85, 87; Diary of Johann Hinrichs, ibid., 193; Diary of General Johann von Huyn, ibid., 395; Wilson, *The Southern Strategy*, 205, 225, 234; Willcox, *Portrait of a General*, 305–10; Mattern, *Benjamin Lincoln and the American Revolution*, 107–109; T. Cole Jones, *Captives of Liberty: Prisoners of War and the Politics of Vengeance in the American Revolution* (Philadelphia, 2020),

191–93. The "Blockheads" quote is in Borick, *A Gallant Defense*, 204. For the capitulation terms requested by Lincoln and finally agreed to by him, see ibid., 247–50.

34. Clinton to Gloucester, May 12, 1780, Series III: Letterbooks, vol. 254, SHCP (WLCL); Clinton to Eden, May 12, 1780, *Facsimilies* 7, no. 726.

35. Jim Piecuch, *Three Peoples, One King: Loyalists, Indians, and Slaves in Revolutionary South Carolina, 1775–1782* (Columbia, SC, 2008), 181; Pancake, *This Destructive War*, 148.

36. Proclamation, May 22, 1780, *CP* 1:50. The thrust of his June 1 and 3 proclamations can be found in ibid., 1:83n and 88n. See also, Lord Francis Rawdon to Cornwallis, July 7, 1780, ibid., 1:193.

37. *AR*, 27–28, 176–77.

38. Cornwallis to Clinton, May 30, 1780, *CP* 1:52.

39. Clinton to Cornwallis, May 18, 1780, ibid., 1:45.

40. Bass, *The Green Dragoon*, 79–83; Thomas B. Allen and Todd W. Braisted, *The Loyalist Corps: Americans in the Service of the King* (Tacoma Park, MD, 2011), 27–28; Wilson, *The Southern Strategy*, 242–61; Mark Urban, *Fusiliers: The Saga of a British Redcoat Regiment in the American Revolution* (New York, 2007), 196; Jones, *Captives of Liberty*, 194; Holger Hoock, *Scars of Independence: America's Violent Birth* (New York, 2017), 315–16; Benjamin Tarleton, *A History of the Campaigns of 1780 and 1781 in the Southern Provinces of North America* (reprint, Cranbury, NJ, 2005), 30. Readers should also be sure to see Jim Piecuch, *The Blood Be Upon your Head: Tarleton and the Myth of Buford's Massacre* (Charleston, SC, 2010), 23–40; idem., "Massacre or Myth? Banastre Tarleton at the Waxhaws, May 29, 1780," *Southern Campaigns of the American Revolution* 1, no. 2 (October 2004): 4–10; and C. Leon Harris, "Massacre at Waxhaws: The Evidence from Wounds," 11, no. 2.1 (June 2016): 1–4.

41. *AR*, 176; *CP* 1:35n.

42. Mackesy, *The War for America*, 346; *AR*, 191n.

43. For these paragraphs, see Germain to Clinton, August 5, 1780, *DAR* 17:177; Clinton to Germain, March 9, 1780, May 14, June 4, 1780, ibid., 18:54, 90, 102; James Simpson to Clinton, May 15, 1780, ibid., 18:94–95; Cornwallis to Marriot Arbuthnot, June 29, 1780, *CP* 1:159; Cornwallis to George Turnbull, June 16, 1780, ibid., 1:141; Sir Henry Clinton, *Observations on Some Parts of the Answer of Earl Cornwallis to Sir Henry Clinton's Narrative* (1783), in *The Campaign in Virginia, 1781: An Exact Reprint of Six Rare Pamphlets on the Clinton-Cornwallis Controversy*, ed. Benjamin F. Stevens (London, 1887), 105; Stephen Conway, "To Subdue America: British Army Officers and the Conduct of the Revolutionary War," *William and Mary Quarterly* 43 (1986): 401; Pancake, *This Destructive War*, 79–81; Robert Stansbury Lambert, *South Carolina Loyalists in the American Revolution* (Columbia, SC, 1987), 96; Mackesy, *The War for America*, 342, 346; Ian Saberton, "Was the Revolutionary War in the South Winnable by the British?" *Journal of the American Revolution*, October 10, 2016. Clinton's quote about a force sufficient to hold the South "against the world" can be found in Willcox, *Portrait of a General*, 320. The numbers on the Loyalists who came forward following Lincoln's surrender can be found in Piecuch, *Three Peoples, One King*, 179. Clinton's "strongest reason" comment can be found in Stephen Conway, "The War in Georgia and the Carolinas," in *The West Point History of the American Revolution*, ed. Clifford J. Rogers, Ty Seidule, and Samuel J. Watson (New York, 2017), 157.

44. Clinton to Cornwallis, June 1, 1780, *CP* 1:57, 61.

45. Lafayette to GW, April 27, 1780, *PGWR* 25:501; Benjamin Franklin to Vergennes, February 25, 1779, in Leonard W. Labaree et al., eds. *The Papers of Benjamin Franklin* (New Haven, CT, 1959–), 28:604; Franklin to Committee of Foreign Affairs, May 26, 1779, ibid., 29:553; GW to Lafayette, September 30, 1779, *WW* 16:369; Lafayette to Jean Frédéric Maurepas, January 25, 1780, *LSLP* 2:344–45; Hamilton to Lafayette, ibid., 2:349n; Lee Kennett, *The French Forces in America, 1780–1783* (Westport, CT, 1977), 7–10; Harlow Giles Unger, *Lafayette* (New York, 2002), 93–103, 107–108.

46. Vergennes to Lafayette, March 5, 1780, *PGWR* 25:501–2n; *LSLP* 3:3n; Ferreiro, *Brothers at Arms*, 207–11; Ferguson, *Power of the Purse*, 55–56; Unger, *Lafayette*, 109–10. The "as my own son" quote is in Unger, page 107.

47. Vergennes to Lafayette, March 5, 1780, *PGWR* 25:501–2n; *LDC* 15:163n; Lafayette to Vergennes, May 20, 1780, *LSLP* 3:26; GW to the Council of War, June 6, 1780, *WW* 18:483.

48. Vergennes to Lafayette, August 7, 1780, *LSLP* 3:129; Orville T. Murphy, "The View from Versailles: Charles Gravier Comte de Vergennes's Perceptions of the American Revolution," in *Diplomacy and Revolution: The Franco-American Alliance of 1778*, ed. Ronald Hoffman and Peter J. Albert (Charlottesville, VA, 1981), 140–41.

49. *AR*, 177; Cornwallis to Clinton, June 2, 1780, *CP* 1:55; *AR*, 190, 192; Willcox, *Portrait of a General*, 322–24.

50. AR, 191–92; Willcox, *Portrait of a General*, 323.

51. Ferreiro, *Brothers at Arms*, 218–19; *AR*, 199–200; Germain to Clinton, March 15, 1780, *DAR* 18:60; Clinton to Germain, July 4, 1780, ibid., 18:114; Willcox, *Portrait of a General*, 324. George III is quoted in Mackesy, *The War for America*, 326.

52. The foregoing paragraphs draw on *AR*, 198–208; Clinton to Arbuthnot, July 15, 22, 30, 1780, ibid., 443–45, 447; Arbuthnot to Clinton, July 16, 18, 23, 27, 1780, ibid., 444–46; Captain Henry Savage to Clinton, July 30, 1780, ibid., 446–47; Clinton to Eden, August 18, 1780, *Facsimilies* 7, no. 730; Clinton to Eden, August 14, 1780, SHCP, vol. 118 (WLCL); Clinton to Charles Stuart, August 26, 1780, Mrs. E. Stuart Wortley, *A Prime Minister and His Son: From the Correspondence of the 3d Earl of Bute and of Lt.-General the Hon. Sir Charles Stuart* (London, 1925), 169; Jean-Baptiste-Donatien de Vimeur, Comte de Rochambeau, *Memoirs of the Marshal Count de Rochambeau* (reprint, New York, 1971), 9; Kennett, *French Forces in America*, 24, 33; Willcox, *Portrait of a General*, 325–30; William B. Willcox, "Rhode Island in British Strategy, 1780–1781," *Journal of Modern History*, 17 (1945): 304–16; Freeman, *George Washington*, 5:179–86; Syrett, *Royal Navy in American Waters*, 145–50; Tilley, *The British Navy and the American Revolution*, 184, 191; Mackesy, *The War for America*, 325–27, 348, 351; Willcox, *Portrait of a General*, 337; William B. Willcox, "Arbuthnot, Gambier, and Graves: 'Old

Women' of the Navy," in *George Washington's Opponents*, ed. George Athan Billias (New York, 1969), 271.

53. *AR*, 203n; Autograph Memorandum re Attempt to Poison Sir Henry Clinton, August [?], 1780, SHCP, vol. 120 (WLCL); Willcox, *Portrait of a General*, 331–32.

54. Arbuthnot to Clinton, August 3, 8, 18, 1780, *AR*, 447–48, 449, 451; Clinton to Arbuthnot, August 11, 13, 18, 1780, ibid., 448–51. Clinton described his epic land journey under "every Inconvenience in this inclement season" in Clinton to Arbuthnot, ND, 1780, SHCP, vol. 118 (WLCL). He was so annoyed at being "disappointed" by Arbuthnot's absence that he wrote Lord North complaining of the admiral's behavior. See Clinton to North, August 20, 1780, SHCP, vol. 118 (WLCL).

55. Intelligence Reports to Clinton, August 31, August [?], 1780, SHCP, vol. 120 (WLCL); Clinton to Sir George Brydges (Admiral Rodney), September 18, 1780, in Godfrey B. Mundy, ed., *The Life and Correspondence of the Late Admiral Lord Rodney* (London, 1830), 1:397–400. See also Willcox, "Rhode Island in British Strategy, 1780–1781," *Journal of Modern History* 17 (1945): 313–14.

56. The "tremendously disturbing" quotation can be found in Stephen Brumwell, *Turncoat: Benedict Arnold and the Crisis of American Liberty* (New Haven, CT, 2018), 218. The "gave themselves up for lost" quote is in Willcox, *Portrait of a General*, 337.

57. These two paragraphs draw on Clinton to Germain, October 11, 1780, *DAR* 18:183–86; Clinton to Stuart, September 18, 1780, Wortley, *A Prime Minister and His Son*, 170.

58. For these two paragraphs, see *AR*, 214; Intelligence Report to Clinton, August 19, 1780, SHCP, vol. 118 (WLCL); Clinton Memo to Arbuthnot, August [?], 1780, ibid., vol. 120; Syrett, *Royal Navy in American Waters*, 152–55; Mackesy, *The War for America*, 346. GW had some sixteen thousand men under arms in New Jersey and New York, and he could have raised thousands of New England militiamen. See Charles H. Lesser, ed., *The Sinews of Independence: Monthly Strength Reports of the Continental Army* (Chicago, 1976), 176–77. For

Clinton's quote about his expectation that GW would raise the "whole force of America," see Clinton to Rodney, September 18, 1780, in Mundy, *Life and Correspondence of the Late Admiral Lord Rodney*, 1:400.

59. Clinton to Germain, August 25, 1780, *DAR* 18:153.

60. For these two paragraphs, see Thomas Paine to Blair McClenaghan [?], May 1780, in Foner, *Complete Writings of Thomas Paine*, 2:1184–85; Paine to Joseph Reed, June 4, 1780, ibid., 2:1186–88; Thomas Paine, *The American Crisis IX* (1780), ibid., 1:166–70; GW to Reed, May 28, 1780, *WW* 18:434–35; GW to Congress, July 10, 1780, ibid., 19:150; John Keane, *Tom Paine: A Political Life* (London, 1995), 199–200.

61. Elizabeth Cometti, "Women in the American Revolution," *New England Quarterly* 20 (1947): 329–46; Linda Grant DePauw and Conover Hunt, *Remember the Ladies: Women in America, 1750–1815* (New York, 1976), 86; GW to Esther Reed, July 14, 20, August 10, 1780, *WW* 19:167, 216, 350–51.

62. John Ferling, *The Loyalist Mind: Joseph Galloway and the American Revolution* (University Park, PA, 1977), 51–64. A complete list of Galloway's pamphlets can be found in the bibliography of *The Loyalist Mind*.

63. Peter Whiteley, *Lord North: The Prime Minister Who Lost America* (London, 1996), 183–89; Alan Valentine, *Lord North* (Norman, OK, 1967), 2:238–57.

64. Lovell to Abigail Adams, June 13, 1780, *LDC* 15:314; Schuyler to Robert R. Livingston, June 12, 1780, ibid., 15:307; Thomas McKean to William Atlee, June 12, 1780, ibid., 15:304; Oliver Ellsworth to Jonathan Trumbull Sr., June 6, 1780, ibid., 15:264; William Churchill Houston to William Livingston, June 4, 1780, ibid., 15:245.

65. GW, Circular to the States, June 30, 1780, *WW* 19:104; GW to Jonathan Trumbull, June 18, 27, 1780, ibid., 19:30–31, 82; GW to Reed, June 16, 1780, ibid., 19:18–19; GW to Congress, June 20, 1780, ibid., 18:35; GW to George Clinton, June 20, 27, 1780, ibid., 19:47–49, 84; GW to Robert Howe, June 18, 1780, ibid., 19:24; GW to Robert R. Livingston, June 29, 1780, ibid., 19:90; GW to TJ, June 29, 1780, ibid., 19:97–98; GW to John Augustine Washington, July 6,

1780, ibid., 19:136; GW, Circular to the States, August 27, 1780, ibid., 19:451; Freeman, *George Washington*, 5:184–85.

66. GW to Committee of Cooperation, July 13, 1780, *WW* 19:166; GW to Congress, July 14, 1780, ibid., 19:171; GW to Trumbull, July 14, 1780, ibid., 19:168.

67. GW to Committee of Cooperation, July 13, 1780, ibid., 19:166; GW to Meshech Weare, June 30, 1780, ibid., 19:106.

CHAPTER 7: VICTORIES, SETBACKS, AND MISSED OPPORTUNITIES

1. Lee Kennett, *The French Forces in America, 1780–1783* (Westport, CT, 1977), 41, 48; Larrie D. Ferreiro, *Brothers at Arms: American Independence and the Men of France and Spain Who Saved It* (New York, 2016), 220–22; Charles H. Lesser, ed., *The Sinews of Independence: Monthly Strength Reports of the Continental Army* (Chicago, 1976), 176–77. The "reception on landing" remark is quoted in Stephen Conway, *The War of American Independence, 1775–1783* (London, 1995), 63.

2. GW to Comte de Rochambeau, July 16, 1780, *WW* 19:185–87; GW to Chevalier de Ternay, July 16, 1780, ibid., 19:187–88; GW to Council of War, June 6, 1780, ibid., 18:482–83.

3. GW, Memorandum for Concerting a Plan of Operations, July 15, 1780, ibid., 19:174–76.

4. Lafayette to GW, July 26, 29, 1780, *LSLP* 3:109–11, 113–16; Lafayette to Rochambeau and Ternay, August 9, 1780, ibid., 3:131–36.

5. Lafayette to La Luzerne, August 24, September 10, 1780, ibid., 3:153, 168; GW to Reed, August 26, 1780, *WW* 19:441.

6. GW to Lafayette, August 3, 1780, *WW* 19:313–15; Lafayette to Rochambeau and Ternay, August 9, 1780, *LSLP* 3:131–36.

7. Lafayette to Rochambeau and Ternay, August 9, 1780, *LSLP* 3:131–36; Clinton to [?], September 1, 1780, SHCP vol. 120 (WLCL).

8. Rochambeau to La Luzerne, August 14, 1780, *LSLP* 3:141; Rochambeau to Lafayette, August 27, 1780, ibid., 3:155–56.

9. Kennett, *French Forces in America*, 59.

10. Lafayette to Rochambeau and Ternay, August 9, 1780, *LSLP* 3:131, 133–34.

11. Douglas Southall Freeman, *George Washington* (New York, 1948–1957), 5:186, 190–92.

12. Summary of the Hartford Conference, September 22, 1780, *LSLP* 3:175–78; Conference at Hartford: GW's Answers to Queries, September 22, 1780, *WW* 20:76–78; Conference at Hartford, Summary of a Conversation, September 22, 1780, ibid., 20:79–81. The comment on Hartford can be found in Marquis de Chastellux, *Travels in America in the Years 1780, 1781 and 1782*, ed. Howard C. Rice (Chapel Hill, NC, 1963), 1:76.

13. GW to Trumbull, July 12, 1779, *PGWR* 21:459; Knox to GW, March 29, 1780, ibid., 25:223.

14. GW to Robert R. Livingston, June 29, 1780, *WW* 19:91; GW, General Orders, August 1, 1780, ibid., 19:302; GW to Benedict Arnold, August 3, 1780, ibid, 19:309–11; Nathaniel Philbrick, *Valiant Ambition: George Washington, Benedict Arnold, and the Fate of the American Revolution* (New York, 2016), 273.

15. *AR*, 214. See also Stephen Brumwell, *Turncoat: Benedict Arnold and the Crisis of American Liberty* (New Haven, CT, 2018), 155–232, 302, 322–23; Philbrick, *Valiant Ambition*, 243–80.

16. These three paragraphs draw on Brumwell, *Turncoat*, 251–61; Philbrick, *Valiant Ambition*, 290; James Madison to Joseph Jones, September 19, 1780, *LDC* 16:95–96; Clinton to Germain, October 11, 1780, *DAR* 18:184–86. Clinton's "absolute certainty" quote is in *AR*, 215.

17. Willard Sterne Randall, "Why Benedict Arnold Did It," *American Heritage* 41 (September–October, 1990), 60–73.

18. GW to John Laurens, April 9, 1781, *WW* 21:438; George F. Scheer, "The Sergeant Major's Strange Mission," *American Heritage* 8 (October 1957): 26–29, 98; *AR*, 216.

19. William Churchill Houston to William Livingston, September 27, 1780, *LDC* 16:115; John Hanson to Philip Thomas, October 2, 1780, ibid., 16:124; Benjamin Huntington to Oliver Ellsworth, October [2?], 1780, ibid., 16:129; John Sullivan to Meshech Weare, October 2, 1780, ibid., 16;131; Samuel Adams to Elizabeth Adams, October 3, 1780, ibid., 16:132; Madison to Edmund Pendleton, October 3, 1780, ibid., 16:141; Theodorick Bland to St. George Tucker, October 8 or 9, 1780, ibid., 16:163; Brumwell, *Turncoat*, 305; James Kirby Martin, *Benedict Arnold: An American Warrior Reconsidered* (New York, 1997), 1–10, 424–32; Charles Royster, "'The Nature of Treason': Revolutionary Virtue and American Reactions to Benedict Arnold," *William and Mary Quarterly* 36 (1979): 163–93; Thomas Paine, "The Crisis Extraordinary" (1780) in *The Complete Writings of Thomas Paine*, ed. Philip Foner 1:187–88; Robert G. Parkinson, *The Common Cause: Creating Race and Nation in the American Revolution* (Chapel Hill, NC, 2016), 477, 501.

20. Houston to Livingston, September 27, 1780, *LDC* 16:116.

21. *AR*, 217–18.

22. Ibid., 175–76; Clinton Instructions to Patrick Ferguson, May 22, 1780, *CP* 1:105; Cornwallis to Clinton, June 30, 1780, ibid., 1:160. On Ferguson, see Marianne McLeod Gilchrist, *Patrick Ferguson: "A Man of Some Genius"* (Uckfield, UK, 2003).

23. Ferguson to Cornwallis, June 6, 14, 1780, *CP* 1:102–3, 106–7; Clinton Instructions to Ferguson, May 22, 1780, ibid., 1:103–5; Nisbet Balfour to Cornwallis, June 12, 1780, ibid., 1:84; Alexander Innes to Cornwallis, June 8, 1780, ibid., 1:111; Archibald McArthur to Cornwallis, June 13, 1780, ibid., 1:132; Cornwallis to Clinton, June 30, 1780, ibid., 1:161–63; Cornwallis to Germain, August 20, 1780, *DAR* 18:145; Ian Saberton, *The American Revolutionary War in the South: A Re-evaluation from a British Perspective in the Light of the Cornwallis Papers* (Tolworth, UK, 2018), 2n.

24. Cornwallis to Germain, August 20, 1780, *DAR* 18:145; Paul H. Smith, *Loyalists and Redcoats: A Study in British Revolutionary Policy* (Chapel Hill, NC, 1964), 44–74, 139; Piers Mackesy, *The War for America, 1775–1783* (Cambridge, MA, 1965), 526; David K. Wilson, *The Southern Strategy: Britain's Conquest of South*

Carolina and Georgia, 1775–1780 (Columbia, SC, 2005), 23, 65, 71, 90, 122, 181, 219, 243. Twenty-six Loyalist military units were raised in the South during the war and 150 altogether throughout the six years down to Yorktown. For a compendium of these units, readers should see Thomas B. Allen and Todd W. Braisted, *The Loyalist Corps: Americans in the Service of the King* (Tacoma Park, MD, 2011).

25. Clinton to Germain, August 25, 1780, *DAR* 18:153–54.

26. Clinton's quotes, and materials on the Black Pioneers, can be found in Todd Braisted, "The Black Pioneers and Others: The Military Role of Black Loyalists in the American War for Independence," in *Moving On: Black Loyalists in the Afro-Atlantic World*, ed. John W. Pulis (New York, 1999), 12–13. Otherwise, these two paragraphs draw on Sylvia R. Frey, *Water from the Rock: Black Resistance in a Revolutionary Age* (Princeton, NJ, 1991), 113–15; Douglas R. Egerton, *Death or Liberty: African Americans and Revolutionary America* (New York, 2009), 84–87; Jim Piecuch, *Three Peoples, One King: Loyalists, Indians, and Slaves in the Revolutionary South, 1775–1782* (Columbia, SC, 2008), 215–25; Cassandra Pybus, *Epic Journeys of Freedom: Runaway Slaves of the American Revolution and Their Global Quest for Freedom* (Boston, 2006), 40. The "property we need not seek" quotation was made by John André and can be found in Pybus, 40.

27. Nisbet Balfour to Cornwallis, June 7, 12, 24, July 20, 1780, *CP* 1:79, 84, 239, 253.

28. Francis Rawdon to Cornwallis, July 12, 1780, ibid., 1:200; Enclosure, George Turnbull to Rawdon, July 12, 1780, ibid., 1:201–202.

29. These three paragraphs draw on the editor's note, ibid., 1:149–50; Cornwallis to Arbuthnot, July 14, 1780, ibid., 1:166; Cornwallis to Clinton, July 15, August 6, 12, December 4, 1780, ibid., 1:170, 176–77, 180; 3:38; Cornwallis to Clinton and Arbuthnot, August 23, 1780, ibid., 2:16; NG to Samuel Huntington, December 28, 1780, *PNG* 7:9; Ian Saberton, "Midsummer 1780 in the Carolinas and Georgia—Events Predating the Battle of Camden," *Journal of the American Revolution*, July 15, 2019; Rachel N. Klein, "Frontier Planters and the American Revolution: The South Carolina Backcountry, 1775–1782," in *An Uncivil War: The South Carolina Backcountry During the American Revolution*, ed. Ronald Hoffman, Thad W. Tate, and Peter J. Albert (Charlottesville, VA,

1985), 62, 63, 79, 78; Robert M. Weir, " 'The Violent Spirit,' the Reestablishment of Order, and the Continuity of Leadership in Post-Revolutionary South Carolina," ibid., 74. Good starting points on the South's partisan warfare can be found in Walter Edgar, *Partisans and Redcoats: The Southern Conflict That Turned the Tide of the American Revolution* (New York, 2001); Russell F. Weigley, *The Partisan War: The South Carolina Campaign of 1780–1782* (Columbia, SC, 1970); Hoffman, Tate, and Albert, *An Uncivil War: The Southern Backcountry During the American Revolution*; James A. Huston, *Logistics of Liberty: American Services of Supply in the Revolutionary War and After* (Newark, DE, 1991), 104–62, 243; and Stanley D. M. Carpenter, *Southern Gambit: Cornwallis and the British March to Yorktown* (Norman, OK, 2019), 95–104. For Cornwallis's comments on the Loyalist militia, see Piecuch, *Three Peoples, One King*, 191; and Cornwallis to Clinton, September 22 and 23, 1780, *CP* 2:46. I am grateful for the help provided by Eric Schnitzer on the matter of supply routes.

30. GW to Johann Kalb, April 2, 4, 1780, *PGWR* 25:281, 283; John Armstrong Jr. to Horatio Gates, June 6, 1780, *LDC* 15:259; Stephen R. Taaffe, *Washington's Revolutionary War Generals* (Norman, OK, 2019), 100.

31. Schuyler to GW, April 5, 1780, *LDC* 15:13; Henry Laurens to Richard Henry Lee, August 1, 1780, ibid., 15:531; Samuel Huntington to Gates, June 13, 1780, ibid., 15:312; Richard Howly to Gates, July 28, August 10, 1780, ibid., 15:518, 566; Ezekiel Cornell to Gates, August 20, 1780, ibid., 15:605; John Armstrong Jr. to Gates, June 15, 1780, ibid., 15:319.

32. Hanson to Thomas, June 21, 1780, ibid., 15:355; Gates to Lincoln, July 4, 1780, James Gregory and Thomas Dunnings, eds. *Horatio Gates Papers, 1726–1828* (Sanford, NC), Microfilm, Reel 11.

33. On TJ in the war before June 1779, see John Ferling, *Apostles of Revolution: Jefferson, Paine, and Monroe in the Struggle Against the Old Order in America and Europe* (New York, 2018), 89–99.

34. Gates to TJ, July 19, 22, August 3, 1780, *PTJ* 3:495–96, 501, 524–25; TJ to Gates, August 4, 1780, ibid., 3:526–27; Gates to Abner Nash, July 19, 1780, Gregory and Dunnings, *Horatio Gates Papers*, Microfilm, Reel 11.

35. Kalb to Gates, July 16, 1780, Gregory and Dunnings, *Horatio Gates Papers*, Microfilm, Reel 11; Rawdon to Cornwallis, July 4, 7, 11, 1780, *CP* 1:192, 193–95, 199; Cornwallis to Rawdon, July 15, 1780, ibid., 1:205. Thomas Sumter's estimate of the number of British troops can be found in Paul David Nelson, *General Horatio Gates: A Biography* (Baton Rouge, LA, 1976), 220. On the distribution of British forces, see Saberton, *The American Revolutionary War in the South*, 2.

36. Gates to Huntington, July 20, 1780, Gregory and Dunnings, *Horatio Gates Papers*, Microfilm, Reel 11.

37. Ibid.

38. Gates to Lincoln, July 4, 1780, ibid. On Gates's feelings toward England and America's cause, see Nelson, *General Horatio Gates*, 32–33.

39. Deposition of Guilford Dudley, in John C. Dann, ed., *The Revolution Remembered: Eyewitness Accounts of the War of Independence* (Chicago, 1980), 215.

40. Cornwallis to Rawdon, July 15, 1780, *CP* 1:205.

41. Return of Troops at Camden, August 13, 1780, ibid., 1:233–34; Franklin Wickwire and Mary Wickwire, *Cornwallis and the War of Independence* (London, 1971), 152–54.

42. Cornwallis to Germain, August 21, 1780, *CP* 2:13.

43. The quotation can be found in Wickwire and Wickwire, *Cornwallis and the War of Independence*, 163. The account of the campaign and battle draws on that book and Nelson, *General Horatio Gates*, 220–37. An excellent succinct account can be found in Carpenter, *Southern Gambit*, 104–16.

44. Cornwallis to John Harris Cruger, August 18, 1780, *CP* 2:19; Clinton to Cornwallis, September 20, 1780, ibid., 2:49. On British casualties, see editor's note, ibid., 2:5. The American prisoners were sent to Charleston, where most were confined aboard prison ships; large numbers perished of smallpox and maltreatment. See T. Cole Jones, *Captives of Liberty: Prisoners of War and the Politics of Vengeance in the American Revolution* (Philadelphia, 2020), 197–98.

45. Hamilton to Tobias Lear, January 2, 1800, in Harold C. Syrett and Jacob E. Cooke, eds. *The Papers of Alexander Hamilton* (New York, 1961–1987), 24:155; Hamilton to James Duane, September 6, 1780, ibid., 2:420–21; Hamilton to Elizabeth Schuyler, September 6, 1780, ibid., 2:422–23; Benjamin Rush to John Adams, October 23, 1780, in Robert J. Taylor et al., eds. *Papers of John Adams* (Cambridge, MA, 1977–), 10:303; Rivington's *Royal Gazette*, August 30, 1780, in Henry Steele Commager and Richard B. Morris, eds. *The Spirit of 'Seventy-Six: The Story of the American Revolution as Told by Participants* (Indianapolis, 1958), 2:1134; Lovell to Gerry, September 5, 1780, *LDC* 16:20; John Henry to Thomas Sim Lee, September 2, 1780, ibid., 16:9; Robert R. Livingston to John Jay, August 26, 1780, ibid., 15:624.

46. Cornwallis to Clinton, August 23, 29, 1780, *CP* 2:16, 42; *AR*, 186.

47. *AR*, 214, 224.

48. Cornwallis to Germain, August 20, 22, 1780, *CP* 2:9, 14–15; Cornwallis to Balfour, August 31, 1780, ibid., 2:65; Cornwallis to Arbuthnot, August 23, 1780, ibid., 2:18; editor's note, ibid., 2:25.

49. Cornwallis to Clinton, August 29, 1780, ibid., 2:42; Clinton to Cornwallis, September 20, 1780, ibid., 2:49; Clinton to Alexander Leslie, n.d., ibid., 2:50; *AR* 210, 221, 225. Throughout the autumn, Lord Germain continued to hope that each letter from Clinton would reveal that Cornwallis was "well advanced towards James River" and acting in concert with Leslie. See Germain to Clinton, November 28, 1780, *DAR* 18:237.

50. GW to TJ, September 11, October 10, 1780, *PTJ* 3:639–40; 4:27–28; TJ to GW, October 22, 25, 1780, ibid., 4:59–60, 68; TJ, Steps to Be Taken to Repel General Leslie's Army, October [22?], 1780, ibid., 4:61–64; TJ to Samuel Huntington, October 25, 1780, ibid., 4:67–68; John E. Selby, *The Revolution in Virginia, 1775–1783* (Williamsburg, VA, 1988), 217.

51. TJ to GW, October 25, 1780, *PTJ* 4:69; TJ to Huntington, November 3, 19, 1780, ibid., 4:92–93; 128; Selby, *Revolution in Virginia*, 217–21; Clinton to Germain, November 12, 1780, *DAR* 18:229; Clinton to Stuart, November 1, 1780, Mrs. E. Stuart Wortley, *A Prime Minister and His Son: From the Correspondence of the 3d Earl of Bute and of Lt.-General the Hon. Sir Charles Stuart* (London,

1925), 170; Rawdon to Alexander Leslie, October 24, 1780, ibid., 18:189; Ferling, *Apostles of Revolution*, 101.

52. Carpenter, *Southern Gambit*, 116–23.

53. Cornwallis to Clinton, September 22, 1780, *CP* 2:45; Cornwallis to James Wemyss, October 7, 1780, ibid., 2:222; editor's note, ibid., 2:26.

54. Cornwallis to Rawdon, August 4, 1780, ibid., 1:226; Cornwallis to Wemyss, August 28, 31, October 7, 1780, ibid., 2:208–9, 210, 222; editor's note, ibid., 1:155; 2:27. For two useful essays concerning violence against civilians by both sides in this war, see Mark Edward Lender and James Kirby Martin, "Liberty or Death! *Jus in Bello* and Existential Warfare in the American Revolution," in *Justifying Revolution: Law, Virtue, and Violence in the American War of Independence*, ed. Glenn A. Moots and Phillip Hamilton (Norman, OK, 2019), 147–67; Benjamin J. Carp, " 'Disreputable among civilized Nations': Destroying Homes During the Revolutionary War," ibid., 168–89.

55. Balfour to Cornwallis, June 24, 27, July 12, 1780, *CP* 1:237, 242, 249; Carpenter, *Southern Gambit*, 90–93.

56. Ferguson to Rawdon, ND, *CP* 2:142–43; Ferguson to Cornwallis, August 29, ibid., 2:147; Ferguson, "Declaration," September 9, 1780, ibid., 2:150–52; editor's note, ibid., 2:27; Hank Messick, *King's Mountain: The Epic of the Blue Ridge "Mountain Men" in the American Revolution* (Boston, 1976), 88–89.

57. Ferguson to Cornwallis, September 14, 19, 28, October 1, 1780, *CP* 2:149, 154–55, 159, 162; Rawdon to Leslie, October 24, 1780, ibid., 2:55; editor's note, ibid., 2:27–28; Ian Saberton, "George Hanger—His Adventures in the American Revolutionary War," *Journal of the American Revolution*, February 17, 2017.

58. Cornwallis to Balfour, October 3, 7, 1780, *CP* 2:106–7, 116; Banastre Tarleton, *A History of the Campaigns of 1780 and 1781 in the Southern Provinces of North America* (reprint, New York, 1968), 160.

59. Ferguson to Cornwalllis, October 6, 1780, *CP* 2:165; Wilma Dykeman, *With Fire and Sword: The Battle of King's Mountain, 1780* (Washington, DC, 1978), 31; John Buchanan, *The Road to Guilford Courthouse: The American Revolution in the Carolinas* (New York, 1997), 229.

60. Quoted in Piecuch, *Three Peoples, One King*, 199.

61. Thomas Young, "Memoir of Thomas Young," *Orion* 3 (1843): 86; James Collins, *A Revolutionary Soldier* (Clinton, LA, 1859), 52–53.

62. Collins, *A Revolutionary Soldier*, 52–53.

63. Accounts by participants can be found in Commager and Morris, *Spirit of 'Seventy-Sex*, 2:1142–45; Young, "Memoir of Thomas Young," *Orion* 3:87; Anthony Allaire, *Diary of Lieut. Anthony Allaire* (reprint, New York, 1968), 31–32. For detailed accounts of the encounter, see Messick, *King's Mountain*; Christopher Ward, *The War of the Revolution* (New York, 1952), 2:739–45; W. J. Wood, *Battles of the Revolutionary War, 1775–1781* (Chapel Hill, NC, 1990), 196, 200–202; Dykeman, *Fire and Sword*, 58–76. See also the accounts in Holger Hoock, *Scars of Independence: America's Violent Birth* (New York, 2017), 320–21; Jones, *Captives of Liberty*, 200–203; and Carpenter, *Southern Gambit*, 124–28. The casualty figures for the Tories vary widely. The figure that I have used can be found in Mackesy, *The War for America*, 345.

64. Cornwallis to William Smallwood, November 10, 1780, in Charles Ross, ed., *Correspondence of Charles, First Marquis Cornwallis* (London, 1859), 1:67.

65. Cornwallis to Leslie, November 12, 1780, *CP* 3:39–40; Cornwallis to Clinton, December 3, 1780, ibid., 3:24–25; Rawdon to Leslie, October 24, 1780, ibid., 2:55; Rawdon to Clinton, October 28, 1780, *DAR* 18:216; Clinton to Germain, December 16, 1780, ibid., 18:258; Wickwire and Wickwire, *Cornwallis and the War of Independence*, 219–22. On Wemyss's failed mission, see Wemyss to Cornwallis, September 20, 30, 1780, *CP* 2:215, 217; Robert Gray to Cornwallis, September 30, October 7, 1780, ibid., 2:218, 223; editor's note, ibid., 2:26.

66. These two paragraphs draw on Clinton to Germain, October 30, 1780, *DAR* 18:217; Charles O'Hara to the Duke of Grafton, November 15, 1781, in George C. Rogers, ed., "Letters of Charles O'Hara to the Duke of Grafton," *South Carolina Historical Magazine* 65 (1964): 169; *AR*, 226–28; William B. Willcox, *Portrait of a General: Sir Henry Clinton in the War of Independence* (New York, 1962), 350, 353.

67. Rawdon to Clinton, October 28, 1780, *DAR* 18:216.

68. Clinton to Germain, December 16, 1780, ibid., 18:257.

CHAPTER 8: NEW DIRECTIONS, NEW HOPE

1. GW, General Orders, October 27, 1780, *WW* 20:258; GW to the President of Congress, October 15, 1780, ibid., 20:189; Douglas Southall Freeman, *George Washington* (New York, 1948–1957), 5:226–27; 230.

2. NG to John Mathews, October 3, 1780, *PNG* 6:336; NG to GW, April 22, 1779, ibid., 3:423; GW to NG, October 14, 22, November 8, 1780, ibid., 6:385–86, 424–25, 469–71; ibid., xvi, 336–37n; John Mathews to GW, October 6, 1780, *LDC* 16:159; Paul David Nelson, *General Horatio Gates: A Biography* (Baton Rouge, LA, 1976), 241.

3. On NG's background and traits, see Theodore Thayer, *Nathanael Greene: Strategist of the American Revolution* (New York, 1960), 15–278. Also see Thayer, "Nathanael Greene: Revolutionary War Strategist," in George Athan Billias, ed., *George Washington's Generals* (New York, 1964), 109–36; Terry Golway, *Washington's General: Nathanael Greene and the Triumph of the American Revolution* (New York, 2005), 5, 29–30, 37, 90–91, 140, 149, 154–58, 172; Stanley D. M. Carpenter, *Southern Gambit: Cornwallis and the British March to Yorktown* (Norman, OK, 2019), 132.

4. NG to GW, October 16, 19, 1780, *PNG* 6:396, 412; GW to NG, October 18, 1780, ibid., 6:410; NG to Catherine Greene, October 15 or 16, 21, 22, 1780, ibid., 6:397–98, 415, 418, 421.

5. GW to NG, October 16, 18, 22, 1780, ibid., 6:396, 410, 425; Lafayette to NG, November 10, 1780, 6:477; Ezekiel Cornell to NG, September 19, 1780, ibid., 6:299; Henry Lee to NG, October 25, 1780, ibid., 430–31; editor's notes, ibid., 6:xvii, 427n, 431n, 450n, 529n.

6. NG to GW, November 13, 1780, ibid., 6:478, 480n.

7. NG to GW, October 31, 1780, ibid., 6:447–48; NG to Samuel Huntington, October 27, 1780, ibid., 6:436; NG to Thomas Sim Lee, November 10, 1780, ibid., 6:473–74; NG to TJ, November 20, 1780, ibid., 6:491–93.

8. NG to Alexander McDougall, October 30, 1780, ibid., 6:446; NG to GW, November 3, 1780, ibid., 6:462.

9. Germain to Clinton, November 9, 1780, *DAR* 18:223–24.

10. Stuart to Bute, September 16, 1778, Mrs. E. Stuart Wortley, in *A Prime Minister and His Son: From the Correspondence of the 3d Earl of Bute and of Lt.-General the Hon. Sir Charles Stuart* (London, 1925), 168–69; Cornwallis to John Harris Cruger, November 23, 1780, *CP* 3:273; Cornwallis to Tarleton, December 18, 1780, ibid., 3:352; Cornwallis to Clinton, December 4, 29, 1780, ibid., 3:24, 25, 28, 30; Cornwallis to Balfour, November 10, 12, 17, 1780, ibid., 3:68, 71, 75; editor's note, ibid., 3:6; O'Hara to Duke of Grafton, November 1, 1780, January 6, 1781, George C. Rogers, ed., "Letters of Charles O'Hara to the Duke of Grafton," *South Carolina Historical Magazine* 65 (1964): 159, 171; Clinton to Alexander Innes, February 19, 1780, in Historical Manuscripts Commission, *Report of American Manuscripts in the Royal Institution of Great Britain* (London, 1904–1909), 2:93; Andrew Jackson O'Shaughnessy, *The Men Who Lost America: British Leadership, the American Revolution, and the Fate of the Empire* (New Haven, CT, 2013), 268. Rawdon's remark concerning intelligence can be found in Clyde R. Ferguson, "Carolina and Georgia Patriot and Loyalist Militia in Action, 1778–1783," in *The Southern Experience in the American Revolution*, ed. Jeffrey R. Crow and Larry E. Tise (Chapel Hill, NC, 1978), 186. For accounts of atrocities see Robert McCluer Calhoon, *The Loyalists in Revolutionary America, 1760–1781* (New York, 1965), 476, 492–93. Clinton is quoted in Robert M. Weir, " 'The Violent Spirit,' the Reestablishment of Order, and the Continuity of Leadership in Post-Revolutionary South Carolina," in *An Uncivil War: The South Carolina Backcountry During the American Revolution*, ed. Ronald Hoffman, Thad W. Tate, and Peter J. Albert (Charlottesville, VA, 1985), 74.

11. Cornwallis to Clinton, December 3, 1780, January 6, 1781, *CP* 3:24, 33–34; Clinton to Germain, January 25, 29, March 1–16, 1781, *DAR* 20:43–45, 51–52; 68–72; Roger Kaplan, "The Hidden View: British Intelligence Operations During the American Revolution," *William and Mary Quarterly* 47 (1990): 131.

12. Cornwallis to Clinton, December 3, 1780, *CP* 3:27; Clinton to Cornwallis, November 6, December 13, 1780, ibid., 3:22, 32.

13. Clinton to Gloucester, January 12, 1781, November 1, 1780, Series III: Letterbooks, vol. 254, SHCP (WLCL); GW to James Duane, October 4, 1780, *WW* 20:118; GW to John Laurens, January 30, 1781, ibid., 21:162.

14. GW to John Armstrong, March 26, 1781, *WW* 21:378; Clinton to Stuart, January 20, 1781, in Wortley, *A Prime Minister and His Son*, 171; Sir Henry Clinton, Narrative of Lieutenant-General Sir Henry Clinton, in Benjamin F. Stevens, ed., *The Campaign in Virginia: An Exact Reprint of Six Rare Pamphlets on the Clinton-Cornwallis Controversy* (London, 1888), 1:10; *AR*, 274.

15. William B. Willcox, *Portrait of a General: Sir Henry Clinton in the War of Independence* (New York, 1962), 5–35. On GW prior to the Revolutionary War, see John Ferling, *The First of Men: A Life of George Washington* (reprint, New York, 2010), 1–110; Ferling, *Setting the World Ablaze: George Washington, John Adams, Thomas Jefferson, and the American Revolution* (New York, 2000), 2–91; Ron Chernow, *Washington: A Life* (New York, 2010), 3–184; Joseph J. Ellis, *His Excellency: George Washington* (New York, 2004), 3–72.

16. GW to Lincoln, September 28, 1779, *PGWR* 22:324.

17. GW's "respectable army" quote can be found in James Kirby Martin and Mark Edward Lender, *A Respectable Army: The Military Origins of the Republic, 1763–1789* (Arlington Heights, IL, 182), 47. See also Mark Edward Lender, *Cabal: The Plot Against General Washington* (Yardley, PA, 2019), 108–236; Stephen R. Taaffe, *Washington's Revolutionary War Generals* (Norman, OK, 2019), 47, 108, 130–34, 191; Edward G. Lengel, *General George Washington: A Military Life* (New York, 2005), 272–73, 279–80.

18. R. A. Bowler, "Sir Henry Clinton and Army Profiteering: A Neglected Aspect of the Clinton-Cornwallis Controversy," *William and Mary Quarterly* 31 (1974): 111–22.

19. Mary Driscoll to Clinton, November 27, 1779, in Historical Manuscripts Commission, *Report on American Manuscripts in the Royal Institution of Great Britain* (London, 1904–1909), 2:67; John Ackerman to Clinton, December 5, 1779, ibid., 2:70; Richard Minifie to Clinton, December 9, 1779, ibid., 2:70–71; Nicholas Outhouse to Clinton, October 9, 1779, ibid., 2:49; Matthew P. Dziennik,

"New York's Refugees and Political Authority in Revolutionary America," *William and Mary Quarterly* 77 (2020): 75. For the appeals from Clinton's subordinates, including General William Phillips, who wrote often about the plight of the Convention prisoners, and the correspondence between Clinton and the secretary of war, see the indexed volumes 1 and 2 of the *Report on American Manuscripts* cited above.

20. Willcox, *Portrait of a General,* 141; Stephen Conway, "The British Army, 'Military Europe,' and the American War of Independence," *William and Mary Quarterly* 67 (2010): 69–100; Stephen Conway, "British Army Officers and the American War of Independence," *William and Mary Quarterly* 41 (1984): 265– 72. The two quotations can be found on pages 71 and 97 of Conway, "The British Military" essay. The quotation can be found in Martin and Lender, *A Respectable Army,* 94.

21. Frederick Wyatt and William B. Willcox, "Sir Henry Clinton: A Psychological Exploration in History," *William and Mary Quarterly* 16 (1959): 3–26.

22. Ibid., 8, 10, 20.

23. Charles Stuart to Lord Bute, July 9, 1776, August [?], 24, November 1, 1779, in Wortley, *A Prime Minister and His Son,* 83, 149, 150, 152, 155, 162; Douglas Southall Freeman, *George Washington: A Biography* (New York, 1948–1957), 3:439–40.

24. GW to Patrick Henry, March 28, 1778, *PGWR* 14:336; ibid., 1:2n; John Adams to Benjamin Rush, March 19, 1812, in *The Spur of Fame: Dialogues of John Adams and Benjamin Rush, 1805–1813,* ed. John A. Schutz and Douglas Adair (San Marino, CA, 1966), 213; Hamilton to Phillip Schuyler, February 18, 1781, Harold C. Syrett and Jacob E. Cooke, eds. *The Papers of Alexander Hamilton* (New York, 1961–1987), 2:565–66; Jonathan G. Rossie, *The Politics of Command in the American Revolution* (Syracuse, NY, 1975), 192; John Ferling, *The Ascent of George Washington: The Hidden Political Genius of an American Icon* (New York, 2009), 148–49.

25. Chernow, *Washington,* 55, 83, 646; James Thomas Flexner, *George Washington: The Forge of Experience, 1732–1775* (Boston, 1965), 184–86, 195–205; Flexner,

George Washington and the New Nation, 1783–1793 (Boston, 1969), 314–22; Willcox, *Portrait of a General*, 38n, 59, 60, 69, 174, 198–99, 453–54, 470.

26. *AR*, 85; GW to Lund Washington, September 30, 1776, *PGWR* 6:441–42; GW to Armstrong, March 26, 1781, *WW* 21:378. Clinton's "fairly worn out" and "grief and mortification" comments can be found in Willcox, *Portrait of a General*, 270, 451.

27. Marcus Cunliffe, "George Washington's Generalship," in *George Washington's Generals*, ed. Billias (New York, 1964), 13.

28. Germain to Clinton, December 3, 1778, November 4, 1779, September 6, 1780, *DAR* 15:278; 17:250; 18:163; Robson, *The American Revolution*, 169. The "Atlas of America" quote can be found in *George Washington's Generals*, ed. Billias, xii.

29. Willcox, *Portrait of a General*, 59, 65; William B. Willcox, "Sir Henry Clinton: Paralysis of Command," in *George Washington's Opponents: British Generals and Admirals in the American Revolution*, ed. George A. Billias (New York, 1969), 75, 96; Mackesy, *The War for America*, 213; Ferling, *First of Men*, 256–57; Jean-Baptiste-Donatien de Vimeur, Comte de Rochambeau, *Memoirs of the Marshall Count de Rochambeau* (reprint, New York, 1971), 104; Stuart Gerry Brown, ed. *The Autobiography of James Monroe* (Syracuse, NY, 1959), 24. Pickering's comment can be found in Chernow, *Washington*, 199, as can the comments of French officers on page 377. Gouverneur Morris's comments on GW's "tumultuous passions" can be found in Ellis, *His Excellency*, 272.

30. GW to Robert Morris, February 4, 1780, *PGWR* 24:375. On GW's habits and character, see Ferling, *First of Men*, 249–66. Clinton's possession of four houses can be found in Mackesy, *The War for America*, 402. The "spring of a deer" quote is in John C. Dann, ed., *The Revolution Remembered: Eyewitness Accounts of the War for Independence* (Chicago, 1980), 409. On Clinton's height, see William S. Stryker, *The Battle of Monmouth* (reprint, Port Washington, NY, 1970), 33.

31. Clinton to Cornwallis, November 6, December 13, 1780, *CP* 3:21, 32; Clinton to Arnold, December 14, 1780, ibid., 3:55–56; Mark Edward Lender and James Kirby Martin, "A Traitor's Epiphany: Benedict Arnold in Virginia and His Quest

for Reconciliation," *Virginia Magazine of History and Biography* 125 (2017): 322, 325. The *Virginia Magazine* is hereafter cited as *VMHB*.

32. Michael Cecere, *The Invasion of Virginia, 1781* (Yardley, PA, 2017), 13–14; Lender and Martin, "A Traitor's Epiphany," *VMHB* 125:324–25.

33. GW to TJ, November 8, 1780, *WW* 20:336.

34. TJ to Virginia Delegates in Congress, October 27, 1780, *PTJ* 4:77.

35. Cecere, *Invasion of Virginia*, 11–30; Lender and Martin, "A Traitor's Epiphany," *Virginia Magazine of History and Biography* 125:331–34, 338–39; TJ, Diary of Arnold's Invasion and Notes on Subsequent Events in 1781 [The 1796? Version], December 31, 1780, January 1, 1781, *PTJ* 4:258–59; Arnold's Invasion as Reported by TJ in the *Virginia Gazette*, January 13, 1781, ibid., 4:269–70; Depositions of Archibald Blair, Daniel Hylton, and James Currie, October 12, 1796, ibid., 4:271–72; TJ to GW, January 10, 1781, ibid., 4:333–35; TJ to George Weedon, January 10, 1781, ibid., 4:335–36; Arnold to Clinton, January 21, 1781, *CP* 576–80; Major Edward Brabazon, Return of Captured Arms and Ammunition . . . Taken and Destroyed at Richmond and Westham, ND, ibid., 5:81–83; John Selby, *The Revolution in Virginia, 1775–1783* (Williamsburg, VA, 1988), 222–25; Michael Kranish, *Flight from Monticello: Thomas Jefferson at War* (New York, 2010), 167–99.

36. Kranish, *Flight from Monticello*, 203–4; Selby, *Revolution in Virginia*, 223–24; Michael A. McDonnell, *The Politics of War: Race, Class, and Conflict in Revolutionary Virginia* (Chapel Hill, NC, 2007), 402; Steuben to TJ, December 15, 1780, *PTJ* 4:209; Larrie D. Ferreiro, *Brothers at Arms: American Independence and the Men of France and Spain Who Saved It* (New York, 2016), 228.

37. GW to Benjamin Harrison, March 21, 1781, *WW* 21:342; GW to Rochambeau, January 29, 1781, ibid., 21:152; GW to TJ, February 26, 1781, ibid., 21:191.

38. GW to Mason, October 22, 1780, ibid., 20:242.

39. GW to NG, December 13, 1780, ibid., 20:469; GW to Sullivan, November 20, 1780, ibid., 20:373; William Stinchcombe, *The American Revolution and the*

French Alliance (Syracuse, NY, 1969), 153–59; Jonathan Dull, *A Diplomatic History of the American Revolution* (New Haven, CT, 1983), 123; Orville T. Murphy, "The View from Versailles: Charles Gravier Comte de Vergennes's Perceptions of the American Revolution," in *Diplomacy and Revolution: The Franco-American Alliance of 1778*, ed. Ronald Hoffman and Peter J. Albert (Charlottesville, VA, 1981), 140–41; Vergennes to Lafayette, August 7, 1780, April 19, 1781, *LSLP* 3:129; 4:47; John Adams to the President of Congress, June 23, July 11, 1781, Robert J. Taylor et al., eds. *Papers of John Adams* (Cambridge, MA, 1977–), 11:384, 411; Adams to Vergennes, July 13, 16, 18, 21, 1781, ibid., 11:413–17, 420–21, 424–29, 431–33; Adams to Congress, July 11, 14, 15, 1781, ibid., 11:410–12, 418–20; Austro-Russian Proposal for Anglo-American Peace Negotiations, with John Adams's Translation [July 11, 1781], ibid., 11:408–10.

40. GW to John Cadwalader, October 5, 1780, *WW* 20:122.

41. GW to Anthony Wayne, January 3, 1781, ibid., 21:55; Robert Tonsetic, *1781: The Decisive Year of the Revolutionary War* (Philadelphia, 2011), 12; Lender and Martin, *A Respectable Army*, 128. The "most general and unhappy mutiny" quotation can be found in Freeman, *George Washington*, 5:235.

42. *AR*, 240–41. The quotation from the British army's communiqué can be found in Carl Van Doren, *Mutiny in January* (New York, 1947), 85–86.

43. Committee on the Pennsylvania Mutiny to Reed, January 8, 1781, *LDC* 16:559–60; Committee on the Pennsylvania Mutiny Draft Proclamation, January 10, 1781, ibid., 16:585; Committee on the Pennsylvania Mutiny to GW, January 10, 13, 15, 1781, ibid., 16:587, 592, 600; GW to Sullivan, January 16, 1781, *WW* 21:113; Tonsetic, *1781*, 11–26; Freeman, *George Washington*, 5:236–42; Van Doren, *Mutiny in January*, 150–203.

44. GW to George Clinton, January 13, 1781, *WW* 21:95; GW to Rochambeau, January 20, 1781, ibid., 21:120–21.

45. GW to Rochambeau, January 20, 1781, ibid., 21:121; Van Doren, *Mutiny in January*, 204–14; Kaplan, "The Hidden View: British Intelligence Operations During the American Revolution," *William and Mary Quarterly* 47 (1990): 132.

46. GW to Howe, January 22, 1780, *WW* 21: 128–29.

47. The foregoing draws on James Thacher, *A Military Journal During the American Revolutionary War, from 1775–1783*, ed. Thomas Bulch (reprint, New York, 1969), 251–53. See also Charles E. Bennett and Donald R. Lennon, *A Quest for Glory: Major General Robert Howe and the American Revolution* (Chapel Hill, NC, 1991), 133–35.

48. Lovell to John Adams, January 2, 1781, *LDC* 16:537; Lovell to Elbridge Gerry, November 30, 1780, ibid., 16:406; Theodorick Bland to Richard Henry Lee, February 6, 1781, ibid., 16:681; Hamilton to Laurens, June 30, 1780, *PAH* 2:347–48.

49. E. James Ferguson, *The Power of the Purse* (Chapel Hill, NC, 1961), 40, 126; Huntington to Laurens, December 1, 1780, *LDC* 16:407; Thomas McKean to Adams, December 18, 1780, ibid., 16:459; Huntington to La Luzerne, December 20, 1780, ibid., 16:273; Oliver Wolcott to Jonathan Trumbull Sr., December 18, 1780, ibid., 16:461; Lafayette to GW, December 9, 13, 16, 19, 26, 1780, *LSLP* 3:254, 257, 267, 269, 273, 274n.

50. Editor's note, *LSLP* 2:274n.

51. GW to Laurens, January 15, 1781, *WW* 21:105–10.

52. Joseph Jones to GW, February 21, 1781, *LDC* 16:733; William Churchill Houston to McKean, March 31, 1781, ibid., 17:107; John Ferling, *John Adams: A Life* (reprint, New York, 2010), 228–29; Jack Rakove, *The Beginnings of National Politics: An Interpretive History of the Continental Congress* (Baltimore, 1979), 281–83; Thomas Paine, *Public Good* (1780), in *The Complete Writings of Thomas Paine*, ed. Philip S. Foner (New York, 1945), 2:303–33; idem., *The Crisis Extraordinary* (1780), ibid., 1:171–89.

53. William Sharpe to NG, January 30, 1781, *PNG* 7:223; GW to NG, February 2, 1781, ibid., 7:240.

54. Paul David Nelson, *General Horatio Gates: A Biography* (Baton Rouge, LA, 1976), 240–51. Tarleton's quote can be found in Nelson, page 251.

55. NG to TJ, December 6, 1781, *PNG* 6:530.

CHAPTER 9: RISK-TAKING BECOMES THE ORDER OF THE DAY

1. NG to Edward Stevens, *PNG* 6:512–13; NG to Steuben, November 22, 1780, ibid., 6:501.

2. NG to Stevens, December 1, 1789, ibid., 6:513; NG to Edward Carrington, December 4, 1780, ibid., 6:516–17; NG to the North Carolina Board of War, December 7, 18, 1780, ibid., 6:548, 598; NG to Nash, February 3, 1781, ibid., 7:241; NG to Steuben, November 27/28, 1780, ibid., 6:507, 508; NG to GW, December 7, 1780, ibid., 6:543; NG to Francis Marion, December 4, 1780, ibid., 6:519–20; NG to Thomas Sumter, December 12, 1780, January 8, 1781, ibid., 6:563–64; 7:74–75; Stanley D. M. Carpenter, *Southern Gambit: Cornwallis and the British March to Yorktown* (Norman, OK, 2019), 134, 179; Theodore Thayer, *Nathanael Greene: Strategist of the American Revolution* (New York, 1960), 290–91.

3. Steuben to NG, December 15, 24, 1780, *PNG* 6:584, 609; NG to Catherine Greene, December 7, 1780, ibid., 6:542; NG to GW, December 7, 1780, ibid., 6:543; NG to Henry Lee, December 18, 1780, ibid., 6:595.

4. NG to Nathaniel Peabody, December 8, 1780, ibid., 6:554; NG to Henry Knox, December 7, 1780, ibid., 6:547.

5. NG to Nash, December 6, 1780, ibid., 6:534; NG to TJ, December 6, 1780, ibid., 6:530.

6. Cornwallis to Rawdon, November 23, 1780, *CP* 3:167; Cornwallis to Clinton, December 22, 1780, ibid., 3:28; editor's note, ibid., 2:32; Balfour to Cornwallis, December 14, 1780, ibid., 3:112.

7. Cornwallis to Alexander Leslie, November 12, 1780, ibid., 3:40; Cornwallis to Rawdon, January 12, 1781, ibid., 3:250.

8. O'Hara to Duke of Grafton, November 1, 1780, in George C. Rogers, ed., "Letters of Charles O'Hara to the Duke of Grafton," *South Carolina Historical Magazine* 65 (1964): 161.

9. NG to La Luzerne, December 29, 1780, *PNG* 7:19.

10. Christopher Ward, *The War of the Revolution* (New York, 1952), 2:751; Terry Golway, *Washington's General: Nathanael Greene and the Triumph of the American Revolution* (New York, 2005), 241; *PNG* 6:587n; *AR*, 245.

11. NG to [?], January 1–23, 1781, *PNG* 7:175–76; NG to Steuben, December 28, 1780, ibid., 7:11.

12. *AR*, 245; NG to Hamilton, January 10, 1781, ibid., 7:89–90.

13. Golway, *Washington's General*, 237; John Buchanan, *The Road to Guilford Courthouse: The American Revolution in the Carolinas* (New York, 1997), 298, 352. The Lee quotations are in Thayer, *Nathanael Greene*, 291–92.

14. The foregoing draws on Don Higginbotham, *Daniel Morgan: Revolutionary Rifleman* (Chapel Hill, NC, 1961). See also Higginbotham, "Daniel Morgan: Guerrilla Fighter," in *George Washington's Generals*, ed. George Athan Billias (New York, 1964), 291–316.

15. NG to Morgan, December 16, 1780, *PNG* 6:589–90.

16. Cornwallis to Balfour, December 29, 1780, January 3, 1781, *CP* 3:118, 121; Cornwallis to Rawdon, December 31, 1780, January 1, 3, 1781, ibid., 3:235, 237, 239.

17. Morgan to NG, December 31, 1780, *PNG* 7:30–31; editor's note, *CP* 3:11.

18. Cornwallis to Balfour, December 29, 1780, *CP* 3:118; Cornwallis to Tarleton, January 2, 1781, Henry Steele Commager and Richard B. Morris, eds. *The Spirit of 'Seventy-Six: The Story of the American Revolution as Told by Participants* (Indianapolis, IN, 1958), 2:1155; Franklin Wickwire and Mary Wickwire, *Cornwallis and the War of Independence* (London, 1971), 252–56. Leslie's voyage from Virginia to South Carolina had been slowed by bad weather, which also caused the loss of most of his horses; they had to be replaced in Charleston before Leslie could set off to rendezvous with Cornwallis. See Leslie to HC, December 20, 1780, in Historical Manuscripts Commission, *Report on American Manuscripts in the Royal Institution of Great Britain* (London, 1904–1909), 2:223.

19. Morgan to NG, January 15, 1780, *PNG* 7:128.

20. Morgan to NG, January 4, 15, 1781, ibid., 7:50, 127; Lawrence E. Babits, *A Devil of a Whipping: The Battle of Cowpens* (Chapel Hill, NC, 1998), 48–61; Buchanan, *Road to Guilford Courthouse*, 312.

21. Buchanan, *Road to Guilford Courthouse*, 316–17.

22. Quoted in Babits, *A Devil of a Whipping*, 54.

23. Quoted in Buchanan, *Road to Guilford Courthouse*, 318.

24. Thomas Young, "Memoirs of Thomas Young," *Orion* 3 (1843): 88.

25. Morgan's quotation can be found in Higginbotham, *Daniel Morgan*, 137, while the other quote is the account of James Collins in Henry Steele Commager and Richard B. Morris, eds. *The Spirit of 'Seventy-Six: The Story of the American Revolution as Told by Participants* (Indianapolis, 1958), 2:1156.

26. Young, "Memoirs," *Orion* 3:100.

27. Quoted in Babits, *A Devil of a Whipping*, 87.

28. Morgan to NG, January 19, 1781, *PNG* 7:154.

29. The "prettiest sort" quote can be found in Young, "Memoirs," *Orion* 3:101. The remaining quotes are from Babits, *A Devil of a Whipping*, 119–20.

30. John Ferling, *Almost A Miracle: The American Victory in the War of Independence* (New York, 2007), 486.

31. James Collins, *Autobiography of a Revolutionary Soldier* (Clinton, LA, 1859), 57; Higginbotham, *Daniel Morgan*, 142.

32. The standard account of the Battle of Cowpens, on which this summary draws, is Babits, *A Devil of a Whipping*, 81–136. The following are also useful: Morgan to NG, January 19, 1781, *PNG* 7:152–55; editor's notes, ibid., 7:155–61n; Higginbotham, *Daniel Morgan*, 135–55; Robert D. Bass, *The Green Dragoon: The Lives of Banastre Tarleton and Mary Robinson* (New York, 1957), 152–62; Banastre Tarleton, *Campaigns of 1780 and 1781 in the Southern Provinces* (reprint, North Stratford, NH, 1999), 215–18; Buchanan, *Road to Guilford Courthouse*, 319–26; W. J. Wood, *Battles of the Revolutionary War* (Chapel

Hill, NC, 1990), 221–26; T. Cole Jones, *Captives of Liberty: Prisoners of War and the Politics of Vengeance in the American Revolution* (Philadelphia, 2020), 210–11.

33. Carpenter, *Southern Gambit*, 139–41.

34. Cornwallis to Rawdon, January 21, 1781, *CP* 3:251; Cornwallis to Clinton, January 18, 1781, ibid., 3:36; Cornwallis to Germain, January 18, 1781, ibid., 3:47; Wickwire and Wickwire, *Cornwallis and the War of Independence*, 269.

35. Editor's note, *CP* 4:3; *PNG* 7:179.

36. Morgan to NG, January 23, 1781, *PNG* 7:178, 179n.

37. Morgan to NG, January 23, 24, 25, 28, 29, 199–202, 1781, ibid., 7:178–79, 190–93, 211, 215–16; NG to Isaac Huger, January 30, 1781, ibid., 7:219–20; NG to William Campbell, January 30, 1781, ibid., 7:218; Lewis Morris to Nash, January 28, 1781, ibid., 7:208–9; NG to President of Congress, January 31, 1781, ibid., 7:225–26; NG to Marion, January 25, February 11, 1781, ibid., 7:194–95, 281; Huger to Marion, January 28, 1781, ibid., 7:208; NG to Officers Commanding the Militia in the Salisbury District, January 31, 1781, ibid., 7:227–28; Thayer, *Nathanael Greene*, 308–10. Morgan wrote two letters to NG on both January 23 and 24.

38. Cornwallis to Rawdon, January 25, 1781, *CP* 3:252; Cornwallis to Germain, March 17, 1781, ibid., 4:12.

39. Cornwallis to Rawdon, January 25, 1781, ibid., 3:252; editor's note, ibid., 4:3; Stephen Conway, *The British Isles and the War of American Independence* (New York, 2000), 51–54.

40. The "without baggage" quotation can be found in Wickwire and Wickwire, *Cornwallis and the War of Independence*, 277–78. See also Cornwallis to Germain, March 17, 1781, *CP* 4:14.

41. *AR*, 261–62; Cornwallis to Germain, March 17, 1781, *CP* 4:13; Charles Stedman, *The History of the Origin, Progress, and Termination of the American War* (1794; reprint, New York, 1969), 2:326. The "without a murmur" quotation can be found in editor's note, *CP* 4:4, while the "to the

end of the world" can be found in Wickwire and Wickwire, *Cornwallis and the War of Independence*, 278.

42. Cornwallis to Germain, March 17, 1781, *CP* 4:14; Rogers, "Letters of Charles O'Hara to the Duke of Grafton," *South Carolina Historical Magazine* 65 (1964): 175. The account of the British army's harrowing crossing of the Catawba draws on Wickwire and Wickwire, *Cornwallis and the War of Independence*, 281–83; Carpenter, *Southern Gambit*, 183; Hugh F. Rankin, *The North Carolina Continentals* (Chapel Hill, NC, 1971), 63, 120, 143, 165–66, 247–48, 250, 269; George H. Scheer and Hugh F. Rankin, eds. *Rebels and Redcoats* (Cleveland, 1957), 437–38; Roger Lamb, *An Original and Authentic Journal of Occurrences During the Late American War from Its Commencement to the Year 1783* (Dublin, 1809), 343; *PNG* 7:244n. The "usual manner" comment can be found in Lamb's account.

43. NG to Steuben, February 3, 1781, *PNG* 7:243; Thayer, *Nathanael Greene*, 309.

44. NG to Huger, January 30, February 1, 1781, ibid., 7:220, 231; NG to GW, February 9, 1781, ibid., 7:268; NG to the President of Congress, January 31, 1781, ibid., 7:226; NG to the Officers Commanding the Militia in the Salisbury District of North Carolina, January 31, 1781, ibid., 7:227–28; Thayer, *Nathanael Greene*, 311.

45. NG to GW, February 9, 1781, *PNG* 7:268.

46. NG to Joseph Marbury, February 2, 1781, ibid., 7:235; NG to Pickens, February 3, 1781, ibid., 7:241; NG to Nash, February 3, 1781, ibid., 7:241; editor's note, *CP* 3:4.

47. Proceedings of a Council of War, February 9, 1781, *PNG* 7:261–62; NG to Steuben, February 3, 1781, ibid., 7:243; NG to Huger, February 5, 1781, ibid., 7:251; NG to GW, February 9, 1781, ibid., 7:268; NG to TJ, February 10, 1781, ibid., 7:271; NG to Patrick Henry, February 10, 1781, ibid., 7:270; NG to Morgan, February 10, 1781, ibid., 7:271; Thayer, *Nathanael Greene*, 316.

48. Morgan to NG, January 24, 1781, *PNG* 7:191.

49. NG to GW, February 15, 1781, ibid., 7:293; Otho Williams to NG, February 11, 13, 1781, ibid., 7:283, 285.

50. NG to Williams, February 14, 1781, ibid., 7:287.

51. Williams to NG, February 13, 1781, ibid., 7:285–86; NG to Williams, February 13, 14, 1781, ibid., 7:285, 287; editor's notes, ibid., 7:287.

52. Cornwallis to Germain, March 17, 1781, *CP* 4:15; editor's note, ibid., 4:5; Return of Casualties in North Carolina Prior to the Battle of Guilford, ibid., 4:62–63; *AR*, 261.

53. Cornwallis to Germain, March 17, 1781, *CP* 4:15; Cornwallis to Rawdon, February 21, 1781, ibid., 4:45; Cornwallis, Draft Warrant to Raise a Provincial company, n.d., ibid., 4:56; Cornwallis, Warrant to Raise Men for the Royal North Carolina Regiment, February 22, 1781, ibid., 4:55; Cornwallis, A Proclamation, February 20, 1781, ibid., 4:55.

CHAPTER 10: FATEFUL CHOICES

1. NG to GW, December 7, 28, 1780, *PNG* 6:543; 7:7–11; GW to NG, January 9–11, February 2, 1781, *WW* 21:86–87, 171.

2. GW to TJ, February 6, 1781, *WW* 21:191; GW to Laurens, January 30, 1781, ibid., 21:162; Douglas Southall Freeman, *George Washington* (New York, 1948–1957), 5:252.

3. GW to Nash, January 23, 1781, *WW* 21:133–34; GW to TJ, February 6, 1781, ibid., 21:191–92.

4. GW to Rochambeau and Ternay, December 15, 1780, ibid., 20:480–81; GW to Laurens, January 30, 1781, ibid., 162.

5. Freeman, *George Washington*, 5:255.

6. Lafayette to La Luzerne, June 16, 1781, *LSLP* 4:1781; GW to Rochambeau, February 7, 1781, *WW* 21:197–98; GW to NG, February 27, 1781, *PNG* 7:363–64; GW to TJ, February 21, 1781, *PTJ* 4:683–84.

7. GW, Instructions to Lafayette, February 20, 1781, *WW* 21:253–56; Stephen Brumwell, *Turncoat: Benedict Arnold and the Crisis of American Liberty* (New Haven, CT, 2018), 314–15.

8. GW to Rochambeau, February 15, 19, 1781, *WW* 21:229–32, 246–48; GW to the Officer Commanding the French Squadron in Chesapeake Bay, February 20, 1781, ibid., 21:259–61; GW to NG, February 27, 1781, *PNG* 7:363–64; Steuben to NG, February 22, 1781, ibid., 7:333; Freeman, *George Washington*, 5:262.

9. The account of the naval activities draws on Nathaniel Philbrick, *In the Hurricane's Eye: The Genius of George Washington and the Victory at Yorktown* (New York, 2018), 55–72; Larrie D. Ferreiro, *Brothers at Arms: American Independence and the Men of France and Spain Who Saved It* (New York, 2016), 226–31; and Lee Kennett, *The French Forces in America, 1780–1783* (Westport, CT, 1977), 94–101. The Philbrick quote can be found on page 56 of *Hurricane's Eye*.

10. *AR*, 255; GW to Lund Washington, March 28, 1781, *WW* 21:386; GW to Rochambeau, April 30, 1781, ibid., 22:17.

11. NG to TJ, February 10, 1781, *PNG* 7:271; NG to GW, February 15, 1781, ibid., 7:294; NG to TJ, February 15, 1781, *PTJ* 4:615.

12. TJ to NG, February 18, 19, 1781, *PTJ* 4:648, 654; Michael Cecere, "Picking Up the Pieces: Virginia's Eighteen-Months Men of 1780–81," *Journal of the American Revolution*, October 15, 2019.

13. NG to William Washington, February 16, 17, 1781, *PNG* 7:298, 305; NG to GW, February 28, 1781, ibid., 7:370; NG to Joseph Reed, March 18, 1781, ibid., 7:449; Cornwallis to James Henry Craig, February 21, 1781, *CP* 4:25; editor's note, ibid., 4:6; Return of Troops, January 15 to April 1, 1781, ibid., 4:61–62.

14. Charles Stedman, *The History of the Origin, Progress, and Termination of the American War* (1794; reprint, New York, 1969), 2:334–35; Roger Lamb, *An Original and Authentic Journal of Occurrences During the Late American War from Its Commencement to the Year 1783* (Dublin, 1809), 348; Returns of British Troops, March 1, 1781, *CP* 4:61–62; NG to GW, February 28, 1781, *PNG* 7:369; NG to Lee, February 17, 1781, ibid., 7:301–2.

15. Lee to NG, February 25, 1781, *PNG* 7:347–48; Pickens to NG, February 26, 1781, ibid., 7:355; Henry Lee, *Memoirs of the War in the Southern Department of the United States* (Philadelphia, 1812), 1:308–11; Deposition of Moses Hall, in

John C. Dann, ed., *The Revolution Remembered: Eyewitness Accounts of the War of Independence* (Chicago, 1980), 202; Stedman, *History*, 2:333–34; Cornwallis to Germain, March 17, 1781, *CP* 4:15; John Buchanan, *The Road to Guilford Courthouse* (New York, 1997), 364.

16. Stedman, *History*, 2:334; Pickens to NG, *PNG* 7:358; NG to Reed, March 18, 1781, ibid., 7:449.

17. Lee to NG, February 16, 1781, *PNG* 7:298; NG to the NC Legislature, February 15, 17, 1781, ibid., 7:290–91, 303–4; NG to TJ, February 15, 1781, ibid., 7:298; NG to GW, February 15, 1781, ibid., 7:294; NG to James Callaway, February 17, 1781, ibid., 7:299–300.

18. NG to Joseph Clay, February 17, 1781, ibid., 7:300; Williams to NG, February 26, 1781, ibid., 7:361; NG to Richard Caswell, February 18, 1781, ibid., 7:309; NG to John Butler, February 23, 1781, ibid., 7:334; NG to GW, February 28, 1781, ibid., 7:369; NG to Campbell, February 18, 1781, ibid., 7:309; Morgan to NG, February 20, 1781, ibid., 7:324.

19. Cornwallis to Germain, March 17, 1781, *CP* 4:16; O'Hara to Duke of Grafton, April 20, 1781, in George C. Rogers, ed., "Letters of Charles O'Hara to the Duke of Grafton," *South Carolina Historical Magazine* 65 (1964): 177; NG to GW, March 10, 1781, *PNG* 7:423; Williams to NG, February 28, 1781, ibid., 7:373; Lee to NG, February 23, 1781, ibid., 7:336; Charles Magill to TJ, *PTJ* 5:115.

20. Deposition of Garret Watts, in Dann, *The Revolution Remembered*, 195; O'Hara to Duke of Grafton, April 20, 1781, Rogers, "Letters of Charles O'Hara to the Duke of Grafton," *South Carolina Historical Magazine* 65: 177; NG to Catherine Greene, March 18, 1781, *PNG* 7:446–47; Williams to NG, February 18, 1781, ibid., 7:315; NG to Lee, March 5, 1781, ibid., 7:395.

21. NG to Campbell, February 24, 1781, *PNG* 7:341; Thomas Rowland to NG, February 26, 1781, ibid., 7:353; Campbell to NG, March 3, 8, 1781, ibid., 7:383, 411; NG to Lee, March 9, 1781, ibid., 7:415; NG to GW March 10, 1781, ibid., 7:422; NG to Joseph Reed, March 18, 1781, ibid., 7:450; NG to Congress, March 16, 1781, ibid., 7:433; Theodore Thayer, *Nathanael Greene:*

Strategist of the American Revolution (New York, 1960), 326–27; Returns of British Troops, March 1, 1781, *CP* 4:61–62.

22. NG to Lee, March 9, 1781, *PNG* 7:415; Thayer, *Nathanael Greene*, 327. The "very commanding ground" quote can be found in Stedman, *History*, 2:337.

23. NG to Lee, March 14, 1781, *PNG* 7:430; William Pierce to James Read, March 14, 1781, ibid., 7:431; Cornwallis to Craig, March 5, 8, 1781, *CP* 4:26; Stedman, *History*, 2:337; Franklin Wickwire and Mary Wickwire, *Cornwallis and the War of Independence* (London, 1971), 292.

24. Rodney Atwood, *The Hessians: Mercenaries from Hessen-Kassel in the American Revolution* (Cambridge, UK, 1980), 45; editor's note, *CP* 4:8

25. The quote is in Buchanan, *Road to Guilford Courthouse*, 381.

26. Stedman, *History*, 2:338–39.

27. Lamb, *An Original and Authentic Journal of Occurrences*, 361.

28. The "most galling and destructive fire" quote is in Stedman, *History*, 2:339. The two additional quotes can be found in Buchanan, *Road to Guilford Courthouse*, 375.

29. Lamb, *An Original and Authentic Journal of Occurrences*, 349–50; Stedman, *History*, 2:341; NG to Catherine Greene, March 18, 1781, *PNG* 7:446.

30. Cornwallis to Germain, March 17, 1781, *CP* 4:19. The key books on this battle, on which my account draws, are Lawrence E. Babits and Joshua B. Howard, *Long, Obstinate, and Bloody: The Battle of Guildford Courthouse* (Chapel Hill, NC, 2009), and Buchanan, *Road to Guilford Courthouse*, 372–83. Good succinct accounts can be found in Christopher Ward, *The War of the Revolution* (New York, 1952), 2:784–94; editor's note, *PGN* 7:436–41n; and Stanley D. M. Carpenter, *Southern Gambit: Cornwallis and the British March to Yorktown* (Norman, OK, 2019), 198–204.

31. Stedman, *History*, 337; Cornwallis to Germain, March 17, 1781, *CP* 4:18; Return of Casualties in the Battle of Guilford, March 15, 1781, ibid., 4:64–65; O'Hara to Grafton, April 20, 1781, Rogers, "Letters of Charles O'Hara to the Duke of

Grafton," *South Carolina Historical Magazine* 65 177; NG to Samuel Huntington, March 16, 1781, *PNG* 7:435; NG to Morgan, March 20, 1781, ibid., 7:455.

32. Clinton to Cornwallis, May 18, 1780, *CP* 1:45; Wickwire and Wickwire, *Cornwallis and the War of Independence* (London, 1971), 135.

33. Stedman, *History*, 2:341, 343, 344; NG to Huntington, March 16, 1781, *PNG* 7:433–35; NG to TJ, March 16, 1781, ibid., 7:441; NG to GW, March 17, 18, 1781, ibid., 7:445, 451–52; NG to Catherine Greene, March 18, 1781, ibid., 7:446–47; NG to Joseph Reed, March 18, 1781, ibid., 7:448–51; NG to Morgan, March 20, 1781, ibid., 7:455–56; Cornwallis to Clinton, April 10, 1781, *CP* 4:109. Charles James Fox's comment can be found in Wickwire and Wickwire, *Cornwallis and the War of Independence*, 311.

34. NG to Catherine Greene, March 18, 1781, *PNG* 7:446; Cornwallis to Germain, March 17, 1781, *CP* 4:18–19; O'Hara to Duke of Grafton, April 20, 1781, Rogers, "Letters of Charles O'Hara to the Duke of Grafton," 177; Stedman, *History*, 346; Babits and Howard, *Long, Obstinate, and Bloody*, 170–75.

35. NG to Sumter, March 16, 1781, *PNG* 7:442; Babits and Howard, *Long, Obstinate, and Bloody*, 180; Cornwallis, Summons to Arms, March 17, 1781, *CP* 4:57–58; Cornwallis, Proclamation, March 18, 1781, ibid., 4:58–59; Cornwallis to Clinton, April 10, 1781, ibid., 4:110.

36. Cornwallis to Germain, April 18, 1781, *CP* 4:104; Carpenter, *Southern Gambit*, 208.

37. For the two foregoing paragraphs, see Cornwallis to Clinton, April 10, 1781, *CP* 4:110; NG to Lee, March 22, 1781, *PNG* 7:461; Wickwire and Wickwire, *Cornwallis and the War of Independence*, 314–16; Carpenter, *Southern Gambit*, 209. Cornwallis's "utmost want" quote can be found in Wickwire and Wickwire, *Cornwallis and the War of Independence*, 316.

38. Smith, *Memoirs*, 334, 387, 399, 417.

39. For these two paragraphs, see ibid., 405–6; *AR*, 273, 276; Clinton to William Phillips, March 10, 1781, *DAR* 20:84; *PNG* 7:459n.

40. *AR*, 230, 237; Clinton to Cornwallis, November 6, 1780, *CP* 3:22; William B. Willcox, "The British Road to Yorktown: A Study in Divided Command," *American Historical Review* 52 (1946): 4, 7, 9.

41. *AR*, 273; Cornwallis to Clinton, January 18, April 10, 1781, *CP* 3:35–36; 4:109–10.

42. Clinton to Cornwallis, April 30, 1781, *DAR* 20:128–29: Cornwallis to William Phillips, April 10, 1781, *CP* 4:114; Phillips to Clinton, April 3, 16, 19, 1781, ibid., 5:25, 43, 49.

43. These two paragraphs draw on *AR*, 235, 290; Cornwallis to Clinton, April 10, 1781, *CP* 4:111; Germain to Clinton, January 3, 1781, *DAR* 20:30; Clinton to Germain, April 23–May 1, 1781, ibid., 20:114. Clinton's "made his arrangements in the Carolinas" quote can be found in Willcox, "The British Road to Yorktown: A Study in Divided Command," *American Historical Review*, 52 (1946): 11.

44. Clinton to Cornwallis, April 30, 1781, *DAR* 20:129.

45. *AR*, 306; Clinton to Cornwallis, April 30, 1781, *DAR* 20:129–30; Germain to Clinton, February 7, March 7, 1781, *DAR* 20:56, 76.

46. *AR*, 240–48, 259–69; Germain to Clinton, November 9, 1780, February 7, 1781, *DAR* 18:224; 20:56; Smith, *Memoirs*, 405. Walpole's quip can be found in Don Higginbotham, *The War of American Independence: Military Attitudes, Policies, and Practice, 1763–1789* (New York, 1971), 386, n35.

47. The two paragraphs draw on *AR*, 211, 273, 291–92; Clinton to Germain, August 25, 1780, *DAR* 18:153.

48. Cornwallis to Clinton, April 24, 1781, *CP* 4:113.

49. NG to GW, March 18, 29, 1781, *PNG* 7:452, 481; NG to TJ, March 27, 1781, ibid., 7:471–72; NG to Lafayette, March 29, 1781, ibid., 7:478; NG to Steuben, March 27, 1781, ibid., 7:474.

50. Cornwallis to Balfour, April 5, 6, 21, 1781, *CP* 4:42, 44, 121; Cornwallis to Rawdon, April 15, 1781, ibid., 4:121; Cornwallis to Germain, April 18, 1781, ibid., 4:106; Cornwallis to Phillips, April 10, 1781, ibid., 4:114–15; Cornwallis to Clinton, April 24, 1781, ibid., 4:113.

51. Hugh F. Rankin, "Charles Lord Cornwallis: Study in Frustration," in *George Washington's Opponents: British Generals and Admirals in the American Revolution*, ed. George Athan Billias (New York, 1969), 202, 205, 223.

52. Clinton to Cornwallis, June 1, 1780, *CP* 1:57, 61. Many times thereafter Clinton made clear that Cornwallis's paramount objective was to crush the rebellion in South Carolina.

53. Cornwallis to Germain, April 23, 1781, ibid., 4:107; Cornwallis to Phillips, April 24, 1781, ibid., 4:116; Cornwallis to Clinton, April 23, June 30, 1781, ibid., 4:112; 5:105; Leslie to Clinton, November 19, 1780, in Historical Manuscripts Commission, *Report on American Manuscripts in the Royal Institution of Great Britain* (London, 1904–1909), 2:211.

54. Cornwallis to Germain, April 24, 1781, *CP* 4:108–9; Cornwallis to Clinton, April 23, 24, 1781, ibid., 4:113; Cornwallis to Phillips, April 24, 1781, ibid., 4:116.

55. Clinton to Cornwallis, April 30, 1781, ibid., 4:128–30.

56. Wickwire and Wickwire, *Cornwallis and the War of Independence*, 321.

57. Cornwallis to Craig, May 3, 4, 1781, *CP* 4:166.

58. *AR* 293.

CHAPTER 11: CHOICES AND FAR-REACHING DECISIONS

1. Cornwallis to Phillips, April 24, 1781, *CP* 4:116; Cornwallis to Tarleton, May 5, 8, 1781, ibid., 4:157, 162; Cornwallis to Balfour, May 3, 1781, ibid., 4:176; Franklin Wickwire and Mary Wickwire, *Cornwallis and the War of Independence* (London, 1971), 325–26.

2. Clinton to Phillips, March 10, 1781, *DAR* 20:84; Lafayette to GW, April 23, 1781, *LSLP* 4:60–61; GW to Lund Washington, April 30, 1781, *WW* 22:14–15; Michael Cecere, *The Invasion of Virginia, 1781* (Yardley, PA, 2017), 94–101; Ron Chernow, *Washington: A Life* (New York, 2010), 399–400; John Selby, *The Revolution in Virginia, 1775–1783* (Williamsburg, VA, 1988), 270–71.

3. Lafayette to TJ, March 27, 1781, *LSLP* 3:418; GW to Lafayette, April 5, 6, 1781, ibid., 4:7, 8; Harlow Giles Unger, *Lafayette* (New York, 2002), 132–38.

4. Clinton to Phillips, March 10, 1781, *DAR* 20:84; Arnold to Clinton, May 12, 1781, ibid., 20:142–45; Cecere, *Invasion of Virginia*, 101–103.

5. TJ to Speaker of the House of Delegates, May 10, 1781, *PTJ* 5:626; TJ to GW, May 9, 1781, ibid., 5:623–24; Steuben to James Innes, April 23, 1781, ibid., 5:543n; TJ to Steuben, April 26, 1781, ibid., 5:559; Michael A. McDonnell, *The Politics of War: Race, Class, and Conflict in Revolutionary Virginia* (Chapel Hill, NC, 2007), 436; Selby, *The Revolution in Virginia*, 272–73.

6. TJ to GW, May 9, 1781, *PTJ* 5:623–24; TJ to the Speaker of the House of Delegates, May 10, 1781, ibid., 5:626. On the raids at Petersburg and Richmond, see Cecere, *Invasion of Virginia*, 103–14.

7. TJ to GW, May 9, 1781, ibid., 5:624; TJ to the Speaker of the House of Delegates, May 10, 1781, ibid., 5:627.

8. TJ to Philip Mazzei, May 31, 1780, *PTJ* 3:405; TJ to GW, July 2, 1780, May 28, 1781, ibid., 3:478; 6:33; TJ to President of Congress, September 3, 14, 1780, ibid., 3:589, 648; TJ to Chevalier de La Luzerne, April 12, 1781, ibid., 5:421–22.

9. Steuben to NG, March 27, 1781, *PNG* 7:474; NG to Steuben, April 6, 1781, ibid., 8:60; Proposal by Steuben for an Expedition Against Cornwallis, March 27, 1781, *LSLP* 3:419–21, 421n; George Weedon to TJ, March 27, 1781, *PTJ* 5:267; Richard Henry Lee to TJ, March 27, 1781, ibid., 5:262–63; editor's note, ibid., 5:275–77n.

10. For these two paragraphs, see GW to Steuben, April 4, 18, 1781, *WW* 21:414, 469; GW to Rochambeau, April 7, 1781, ibid., 21:427; GW to William Fitzhugh, March 25, 1781, ibid., 21:375–76; GW to John Armstrong, March 26, 1781, ibid., 21:378; GW to Rochambeau, April 7, 1781, ibid., 21:426.

11. GW to NG, April 22, 1781, ibid., 21:492; GW to Lafayette, April 11, 1781, ibid., 21:444; GW to John Laurens, April 9, 1781, ibid., 21:439.

12. GW to Rochambeau, May 14, 1781, ibid., 22:86; Lee Kennett, *The French Forces in America, 1780–1783* (Westport, CT, 1977), 77–78, 104–5.

13. *AR*, 304.

14. Kennett, *French Forces in America*, 108; Jonathan R. Dull, *The French Navy and American Independence: A Study of Arms and Diplomacy, 1774–1787* (Princeton, NJ, 1975), 242–43. Jean-Baptiste-Donatien de Vimeur, Comte de Rochambeau, *Memoirs of the Marshall Count de Rochambeau* (reprint, New York, 1971), 44–46, 50–51.

15. The section on the Wethersfield conference draws on the following: Baron Ludwig von Closen, *The Revolutionary Journal of Baron Ludwig von Closen, 1780–1783*, ed. Evelyn Acomb (Chapel Hill, NC, 1958), 86; Claude Blanchard, *The Journal of Claude Blanchard*, ed. Thomas Balch (Albany, NY, 1876), 104; *DGW* 3:369–70; Conference with Rochambeau, May 23, 1781, *WW* 22:105–7; GW to NG, June 1, 1781, ibid., 22:146; GW to NG, June 1, 1781, *PNG* 8:336; Edward Lengel, *General George Washington* (New York, 2005), 331–32; James Thomas Flexner, *George Washington in the American Revolution* (Boston, 1967), 429–30; Douglas Southall Freeman, *George Washington* (New York, 1948–1957), 5:284–90; Chernow, *Washington*, 401–2; Kennett, *French Forces in America*, 104–106; Larrie D. Ferreiro, *Brothers at Arms: American Independence and the Men of France and Spain Who Saved It* (New York, 2016), 236–39. Rochambeau's comment about GW and the war in the South can be found in Flexner, 429. The "polite fiction" comment can be found in Robert Middlekauff, *Washington's Revolution: The Making of America's First Leader* (New York, 2015), 227. Clinton's comment regarding the work underway to strengthen New York's defenses can be found in *AR*, 320. Rochambeau's request to de Grasse can be found in Ferreiro, 238. On Clinton's troop strength in New York, see Clinton to Germain, April 5–20, 1781, *DAR* 20:104. At roughly the time of the Wethersfield conference, Clinton mentioned having 11,700 troops, though by the summer campaign season reinforcements had brought his army to nearly 14,000. For his comment on Virginia heat, see Rochambeau, *Memoirs of the Marshall Count de Rochambeau*, 110–11.

16. E. James Ferguson, *The Power of the Purse: A History of American Public Finance, 1776–1790* (Chapel Hill, NC, 1961), 126–27.

17. Paine to James Hutchinson, March 11, 1781, in *Complete Writings of Thomas Paine*, ed. Philip Foner (New York, 1945), 2:1192; Ferreiro, *Brothers at Arms*, 234–36. See also John Ferling, *Apostles of Revolution: Jefferson, Paine, Monroe,*

and the Struggle Against the Old Order in America and Europe (New York, 2018), 119–21.

18. *AR*, 293, 300; Smith, *Memoirs*, 386, 388, 396, 399, 407.

19. Germain to Clinton, November 9, 1780, March 7, May 2, 1781, *DAR* 18:224; 20:76, 132.

20. Solomon M. Lutnick, "The Defeat at Yorktown: A View from the British Press," *Virginia Magazine of History and Biography* 72 (1964): 471.

21. Andrew Jackson O'Shaughnessy, *The Men Who Lost America: British Leadership, the American Revolution, and the Fate of the Empire* (New Haven, CT, 2013), 229.

22. O'Hara to Grafton, November 1, 1780, in George C. Rogers, ed., "Letters of Charles O'Hara to the Duke of Grafton," *South Carolina Historical Magazine* 65 (1964): 160; Stephen Conway, "To Subdue America: British Army Officers and the Conduct of the Revolutionary War," *William and Mary Quarterly* 43 (1986): 393, 394. The Clinton quote can be found in Conway's essay, page 381.

23. *AR*, 292.

24. Balfour to Cornwallis, May 21, 1781, *CP* 5:275–76; Cornwallis to Clinton, May 20, 1781, ibid., 5:88.

25. For these two paragraphs, see *AP*, 284, 288, 300–301; Clinton to Germain, May 18, 1781, *DAR* 20:145–46; Clinton to Eden, May 11–June 10, 1781, *Facsimilies*, 7:748; Frederick Mackenzie, *Diary of Frederick Mackenzie, Giving a Daily Narrative of His Military Service as an Officer of the Regiment of Royal Welsh Fusiliers During the Years 1775–1781 in Massachusetts, Rhode Island, and New York* (reprint, New York, 1968), 2:522.

26. These three paragraphs draw on *AR*, 293, 306–7, 320; Clinton to Cornwallis, June 11, 1781, ibid., 531; Phillips to Clinton, April 15, 18, 1781, ibid., 510–11; ibid., 306–7; Clinton to Phillips, April 26–30, 1781, ibid., 515; Phillips to Clinton, April 16, 1781, *CP* 5:43–44; Clinton to Cornwallis, June 11, 1781, ibid., 5:95–97; Clinton to Germain, July 13, 1781, *DAR* 20:186–87; Mackenzie, *Diary of Frederick Mackenzie*, 2:561; Clinton to the Duke of Gloucester, July 24, 1781, Series III: Letterbooks, vol. 254, in SHCP (WLCL); George W. Kyte, "A Projected

British Attack upon Philadelphia in 1781," *Pennsylvania Magazine of History and Biography* 76 (1952), 379–93.

27. Phillips to Clinton, April 15, 1781, *AR*, 511; Clinton to Phillips, April 30–May 3, 1781, ibid., 518–19; Cornwallis to Clinton, May 26, June 30, July 26, 1781, *CP* 5:89, 105; 6:13–14. Before learning of Cornwallis's objections to striking Philadelphia, Clinton wrote him about his views on the matter in a letter of June 11, 1781. For that missive, see *CP* 5:97.

28. Clinton to Cornwallis, June 11, 1781, *CP* 5:95–97.

29. Cornwallis to Phillips, May 6, 8, 10, 1781, ibid., 4:151–52.

30. Arnold to Cornwallis, May 12, 16, 1781, ibid., 4:152, 153; Cornwallis to Tarleton, May 14, 15, 1781, ibid., 4:163–64; Phillips to Cornwallis, May 6, 1781, ibid., 5:69; Lafayette to Morgan, May 21, 1781, *LSLP* 4:118.

31. Clinton to Cornwallis, April 30, 13, 1781, *DAR* 20:129, 94.

32. Cornwallis to Clinton, May 20, 26, 27, 1781, *CP* 5:87–91; Phillips to Clinton, April 3, 4, 16, 1781, ibid., 5:26, 48; Substance of Conversations Between Clinton and Phillips, enclosure in Clinton to Phillips, April 11, 1781, ibid., 5:56; Extracts from Information Given to the Commander in Chief, Respecting the Posts in the Chesapeak, ND, in Mackenzie, *Diary of Frederick Mackenzie*, 2:457; William B. Willcox, *Portrait of a General: Sir Henry Clinton in the War of Independence* (New York, 1962), 397. Clinton had learned of de Grasse's fleet from Germain weeks earlier. See Germain to Clinton, April 4, 1781, *DAR* 20:99; Clinton to Germain, June 9–12, 1781, ibid., 20:156.

33. Cornwallis to Clinton, May 20, 1781, *CP* 5:88. For Clinton's instructions to Phillips, see Clinton to Phillips, March 10, 1781, *DAR* 20:84.

34. Cecere, *Invasion of Virginia*, 22–23; Lafayette to La Luzerne, May 22, 1781, *LSLP* 4:120; Lafayette to the Vicomte de Noailles, May 22, 1781, ibid., 4:122–23; Lafayette to GW, May 8, 24, 1781, ibid., 4:88, 130–31; Lafayette to TJ, April 25, May 28, 31, 1781, ibid., 4:62–63, 136–37, 148–49; Lafayette to Steuben, May 29, 31, 1781, ibid., 4:140–41, 150–51; Lafayette to NG, May 18, 1781, ibid., 4:112–13; Lafayette to Weedon, May 28, 1781, ibid., 4:137–38. Cornwallis's purported boast that Lafayette could not escape him can be found in James Thacher, *A*

Military Journal During the American Revolutionary War, from 1775–1783, ed. Thomas Bulch (reprint, New York, 1969), 300.

35. These two paragraphs draw on Lafayette to Weedon, May 3, 1781, *LSLP* 4:78; Weedon to Lafayette, June 1, 1781, ibid., 4:158; Lafayette to GW, May 4, 1781, ibid., 4:83; Lafayette to TJ, May 28, 31, 1781, ibid., 4:136, 149; Lafayette to Wayne, May 29, 1781, 4:141–42; Lafayette to NG, June 3, 1781, ibid., 4:164; Cornwallis to Clinton, June 30, 1781, *CP* 5:104; editor's note, ibid., 1:10.

36. Banastre Tarleton, *A History of the Campaigns of 1780 and 1781 in the Southern Provinces of North America* (reprint, Cranbury, NJ, 2005), 295–97; TJ to William Gordon, July 16, 1788, *PTJ* 13:363; Michael Kranish, *Flight from Monticello: Thomas Jefferson at War* (New York, 2010), 283–86; Dumas Malone, *Jefferson and His Time* (Boston, 1948–1981), 1:355–57; Cecere, *Invasion of Virginia*, 122; Cornwallis to Clinton, June 30, 1781, *CP* 5:104.

37. These three paragraphs draw on Lieutenant Colonel John Simcoe, *Simcoe's Military Journal: A History of the Operations of a Partisan Corps Called the Queen's Rangers* (reprint, New York, 1968), 212–20; Thomas B. Allen and Todd W. Braisted, *The Loyalist Corps: Americans in the Service of the King* (Tacoma Park, MD, 2011), 88–89; editor's note, "The Legislative Request for an Inquiry into the Conduct of General Steuben," *PTJ* 6:619–39; William Davies to Steuben, May 12, 1781, *PTJ* 6:631; Cornwallis to Clinton, June 30, 1781, *CP* 5:104; Lafayette to La Luzerne, May 22, June 16, 1781, *LSLP* 4:121, 186; Lafayette to GW, June 18, 1781, ibid., 4:194–95; editor's note, ibid., 4:435; Selby, *Revolution in Virginia*, 280; Cecere, *Invasion of Virginia*, 124–26. Steuben's quote can be found in editor's note, "The Legislative Request," *PTJ* 6:629. Six weeks after the sacking of Point of Fork, Lafayette claimed, "What Has Been lost . . . is in Great Measure Recovered." See Lafayette to NG, July 4, 1781, *LSLP* 4:231. For a rebel accounting of the losses, see *PTJ* 6:635n.

38. Cornwallis to Clinton, May 26, 1781, *CP* 5:89; Matthias von Fuchs to Cornwallis, May 23, 1781, ibid., 5:154; TJ to Gordon, July 16, 1788, *PTJ* 13:363.

39. Johann Ewald, *Diary of the American War: A Hessian Journal*, ed. Joseph P. Tustin (New Haven, CT, 1979), 314; Cornwallis to Clinton, June 30, 1781, *CP* 5:104; LSLP, 4:211n; Lafayette to Weedon, June 16, 21, 1781, ibid., 4:189, 190n,

205; Lafayette to Steuben, June 22, 1781, ibid., 4:206; Lafayette to Wayne, June 25, 1781, ibid., 4:212; Lafayette to NG, June 27, 1781, ibid., 4:216; William Feltman, *The Journal of Lieut. William Feltman, of the First Pennsylvania Regiment, 1781–82* (Philadelphia, 1853), 5; Cecere, *Invasion of Virginia*, 129–34. Lafayette put his losses at Spencer's Ordinary at twenty-five. It appears that each side suffered between thirty and sixty casualties. See Lafayette to Nelson, June 28, 1781, *LSLP* 4:217–18.

40. Ewald, *Diary of the American War*, 314.

41. Clinton to Cornwallis, June 11, 1781, *CP* 5:96.

42. Cornwallis to Clinton, June 30, 1781, ibid., 5:105–7; Cornwallis to Leslie, May 24, July 2, 8, 1781, ibid., 5:160, 175, 179; Ewald, *Diary of the American War*, 315.

43. Lafayette to Thomas Sim Lee, June 25, 1781, *LSLP* 4:210; Lafayette to Wayne, June 30, 1781, ibid., 4:222; Lafayette to Vicomte de Noailles, July 9, 1781, ibid., 4:241.

44. Lafayette to Nelson, July 1, 1781, ibid., 4:228; Lafayette to La Luzerne, June 16, 1781, ibid., 4:186; GW to TJ, June 8, 1781, *WW* 22:189.

45. Wickwire and Wickwire, *Cornwallis and the War of Independence*, 341–47; Cecere, *Invasion of Virginia*, 135–43; Cornwallis to Clinton, July 8, 1781, *CP* 5:116–17; Lafayette to NG, July 8, 1781, *LSLP* 4:236–38; Lafayette to GW, July 8, 1781, ibid., 4:239; Lafayette to Allen Jones, July 10, 1781, ibid., 4:241. Wayne's quote can be found in Cecere, page 141.

46. Ewald, *Diary of the American War*, 318.

47. For these two paragraphs, see Clinton to Cornwallis, July 8, 11, 1781, *DAR* 20:181, 185; Germain to Clinton, May 2, March 7, 1781, ibid., 20:132, 76.

48. Cornwallis to Clinton, July 17, 26, 1781, ibid., 5:138; 6:14–15; Engineer's Report to Cornwallis, July 25, 1781, ibid., 6:16–17; Cornwallis to Leslie July 14, 15, 20, 1781, ibid., 4:186, 188, 194, 195; Leslie to Cornwallis, July 15, 1781, ibid., 4:186, 187; Wickwire and Wickwire, *Cornwallis and the War of Independence*, 348–52.

49. Lafayette to de Noailles, July 9, 1781, *LSLP* 4:240; Lafayette to Jones, July 10, 1781, ibid., 4:241; Lafayette to Nelson, July 10, 12, 1781, ibid., 4:242, 243.

50. Arnold to Clinton, May 12, 1781, *DAR* 20:144–45; Clinton to Germain, May 18, 1781, ibid., 20:146.

51. Clinton to Cornwallis, June 8, 1781, *CP* 5:124.

52. Clinton to Cornwallis, June 11, 15, 28, May 29–June 1, June 8, 19, July 8, 11, 1781, ibid., 5:96–97, 98, 102, 114, 118–20, 124, 135–36, 140–42. Clinton's letters are cited in the order in which Cornwallis read them. One of Clinton's orders was in an accompanying note. See also Thomas Tonken to the Navy Board, March 16, 1781, ibid., 4:102.

53. Lafayette to NG, June 20, 21, 1781, *LSLP* 4:198, 203; Cornwallis to Phillips, April 10, 1781, *CP* 4:114–15.

54. Cornwallis to Clinton, April 23, 1781, *CP* 4:112; *AR*, 293; Lafayette to La Luzerne, June 16, 1781, *LSLP* 4:187.

55. *AR*, 319.

56. Clinton to Cornwallis, June 19, July 11, 15, 1781, *CP* 5:135, 143; 6:20; Clinton to Germain, June 9–12, July 3, 1781, *DAR* 20:155–56, 170.

57. Cornwallis to Clinton, July 8, 26, 1781, *CP* 5:116; 6:14–15.

CHAPTER 12: CORNWALLIS'S GIFT

1. NG to Samuel Huntington, March 23, 1781, *PNG* 7:465; NG to Reed, March 18, 1781, ibid., 7:450.

2. NG to Catherine Greene, March 18, 1781, ibid., 7:446–47; NG to Reed, March 18, 1781, ibid., 450; NG to GW, March 18, 1781, ibid., 7:452; Theodore Thayer, *Nathanael Greene: Strategist of the American Revolution* (New York, 1960), 332–33.

3. NG to TJ, March 27, 1781, *PNG* 7:471; NG to Huntington, March 23, 1781, ibid., 7:465; NG to GW, March 29, 1781, ibid., 7:481.

4. NG to Lafayette, April 3, 1781, ibid., 8:34; NG to GW, March 29, 1781, ibid., 7:481; NG to Steuben, April 2, 1781, ibid., 8:24–25.

5. NG to TJ, March 31, April 6, 1781, ibid., 8:17–18, 58; NG to Nash, April 3, 13, May 2, 1781, ibid., 8:36–37, 89, 191; NG to Steuben, March 22, 1781, ibid., 7:463; Thayer, *Nathanael Greene*, 339–40.

6. NG to Lafayette, June 9, 1781, *PNG* 8:367; NG to Steuben, April 6, 1781, ibid., 8:60; NG to TJ, April 28, 1781, ibid., 8:167.

7. Editor's notes, *CP* 1:35–36, 151–52; editor's note, *PNG* 8:152–53.

8. Cornwallis to Balfour, April 5, 6, 21, 24, 1781, *CP* 4:43, 44, 121–22, 123; Cornwallis to Rawdon, April 15, 1781, ibid., 4:121. Rawdon had guessed that "Camden is Greene's object" long before he heard from Cornwallis. See Rawdon to Balfour, April 13, 1781, ibid., 4:174.

9. NG to Thomas Sim Lee, April 7, 1781, *PNG* 8:62; NG to Henry Lee, April 12, 1781, ibid., 8:85–86; NG to Sumter, April 14, 15, 1781, ibid., 8:94, 100; NG to Richard Caswell, April 11, 1781, ibid., 8:79; NG to Davies, April 11, 1781, ibid., 8:80; NG to William Davie, April 14, 1781, ibid., 8:92.

10. Rawdon to Cornwallis, April 26, 1781, *CP* 4:181; NG to Huntington, April 27, 1781, *PNG* 8:155.

11. Rawdon to Cornwallis, April 26, 1781, *CP* 4:180–81; NG to Huntington, April 27, 1781, *PNG* 8:155; John Buchanan, *The Road to Charleston: Nathanael Greene and the American Revolution* (Charlottesville, VA, 2019), 93.

12. Rawdon to Cornwallis, April 25, 26, 1781, *CP* 4:179, 180–82; NG to Huntington, April 27, 1781, *PNG* 8:155–57; editor's note, ibid., 8:157–60. Good accounts of the battle can be found in Christopher Ward, *The War of the Revolution* (New York, 1952) 2:802–8; Thayer, *Nathanael Greene*, 344–45; and especially Buchanan, *Road to Charleston*, 91–101. See also Hugh F. Rankin, *The North Carolina Continentals* (Chapel Hill, NC, 1971), 325–26.

13. Rawdon to Cornwallis, April 25, 1781, *CP* 4:179; Return of [British] Killed, Wounded, and Missing, April 25, 1781, ibid., 4:182–83; NG to Nash, May 2, 1781, *PNG* 8:190; NG to Huntington, April 27, 1781, ibid., 8:157; NG to Reed, August 6, 1781, ibid., 9:135; editor's note, ibid., 8:158–59; General Greene's Orders, April 30, 1781, ibid., 176–76. The Buchanan quote can be found in *The Road to Charleston*, 95.

14. NG to Catherine Greene, May 15, 1781, *PNG* 8:259; General Greene's Orders, May 2, 1781, ibid., 8:187; editor's note, ibid., 8:160n.

15. Recollection of a Conversation Between NG and Colonel William R. Davie, May 9, 1781, ibid., 8:225–26; NG to Reed, May 4, 1781, ibid., 8:199–201; NG to Alexander McDougall, May 17, 1781, ibid., 8:276; NG to the Board of War, May 2, 1781, ibid., 8:188.

16. NG to Huntington, May 5, June 9, 1781, ibid., 8:206, 363; NG to Lafayette, June 9, 1781, ibid., 8:366; NG to TJ, June 27, 1781, ibid., 8:464–65.

17. Cornwallis to Balfour, April 30, May 20, 1781, *CP* 4:175–76; 5:274; Cornwallis to Rawdon, May 20, 1781, ibid., 5:286; Balfour to Cornwallis, April 20, 26, May 21, 1781, ibid., 4:171, 177; 5:277.

18. Balfour to Cornwallis, April 20, May 21, 1781, ibid., 4:171–72; 5:276–77; Balfour to James Wright, July 20, 1781, Historical Manuscripts Commission, *Report on American Manuscripts in the Royal Institution of Great Britain* (London, 1904–1909), 2:303; editor's note, *PNG* 8:xii–xv; NG to Huntington, May 14, 1781, ibid., 8:250–51; Pickens to NG, May 25, 1781, ibid., 8:310–11, 311n; NG, A Proclamation, June 9, 1781, ibid., 8:370, editor's note, ibid., 8:359–60; Thayer, *Nathanael Greene*, 345–54.

19. NG to Lafayette, June 9, 1781, *PNG* 8:367; NG to Nash, June 9, 1781, ibid., 8:369; ibid., xiii; Balfour to Cornwallis, May 21, 1781, *CP* 5:276; Rawdon to Cornwallis, May 24, 1781, ibid., 5:290–91; Buchanan, *Road to Charleston*, 144–45.

20. Editor's note, *CP* 1:258n; NG to Lee, May 22, 1781, *PNG* 8:291–92; NG to Lafayette, May 23, 1781, ibid., 8:300; Thayer, *Nathanael Greene*, 355–56. The "finished gentleman" quotation can be found in Buchanan, *Road to Charleston*, 141–42.

21. Rawdon to Cornwallis, June 5, 1781, *CP* 5:291; NG to William Smallwood, June 9, 1781, *PNG* 8:372; NG to Marion, June 10, 1781, ibid., 8:374; NG to Sumter, June 10, 17, 1781, ibid., 8:375, 376, 404; NG to Nash, June 12, 1781, ibid., 8:381; NG to Huntington, June 20, 1781, ibid., 8:419; ibid., 8:423–24n; Thayer, *Nathanael Greene*, 359.

22. NG to Sumter, June 17, 1781, *PNG* 8:405; NG to Elijah Clarke, June 17, 1781, ibid., 8:404; NG to Huntington, June 20, 1781, ibid., 8:422; ibid., 8:424–25n; NG

to Lafayette, June 23, 1781, ibid., 8:445; NG to TJ, June 27, 1781, ibid., 8:463–64; Ward, *War of the Revolution*, 2:816–22.

23. Rawdon to Cornwallis, August 2, 1781, *CP* 6:63–64; Balfour to Germain, June 27, 1781, ibid., 6:219; Ward, *War of the Revolution*, 2:823–24.

24. Ichabod Burnet to Sumter, June 25, July 3, 1781, *PNG* 8:458, 484; NG to Marion, July 1, 10, 1781, ibid., 8:479, 514; NG to Pickens, July 15, 1781, ibid., 9:10–11; NG to Thomas Burke, July 16, 1781, ibid., 9:19–20.

25. NG to McDougall, May 17, 1781, ibid., 8:276; NG to Catherine Greene, June 23, 1781, ibid., 8:443.

26. NG to La Luzerne, April 28, 1781, ibid., 8:168.

27. NG to Thomas McKean, July 17, 1781, ibid., 9:30; NG to GW, July 17, 1781, ibid., 9:32; Reed to NG, June 16, 1781, ibid., 8:399.

28. NG to Jeremiah Wadsworth, July 18, 1781, ibid., 9:41; NG to La Luzerne, June 22, 1781, ibid., 8:437.

29. Weedon to NG, April 14, 1781, ibid., 8:96; GW to NG, April 18, 1781, ibid., 8:116; Henry Knox to NG, June 7, 1781, ibid., 8:358–59; ibid., 8:365n; McKean to NG, July 26, 1781, *LDC* 17:448; James Varnum to GW, August 20, 1781, ibid., 17:543; Thayer, *Nathanael Greene*, 353.

CHAPTER 13: MONUMENTAL DECISIONS

1. *AR*, 295; Rawdon to Cornwallis, April 26, 1781, *CP* 4:181.

2. *AR*, 296–97, 310–12; Clinton to Germain, July 18, August 9, 1781, *DAR* 20:193, 214. For the hurtful letter that Germain had written in May—mentioned previously in chapter 11—see Germain to Clinton, May 2, 1781, ibid., 20:132.

3. Cornwallis to Clinton, August 16, 22, ibid., 6:24, 27–28; O'Hara to Cornwallis, August 5, 9, 11, 17, 1781, ibid., 6:44–45, 48, 49, 52; Cornwallis to O'Hara, August 4, 7, 10, 1781, ibid., 6:44, 46, 48; Johann Ewald, *Diary of the American War: A Hessian Journal*, ed. Joseph P. Tustin (New Haven, CT, 1979), 325.

4. These two paragraphs draw on Clinton to Cornwallis, June 11, 15, 19, July 11, 15, 1781, *CP* 5:96, 98, 136, 143; 6:20; Cornwallis to Clinton, July 24, 1781, ibid.,

6:15; Clinton to Germain, April 5–20, May 18, June 9–13, July 13, 15, 18, 1781, *DAR* 20:104, 146, 156, 186–88, 190, 193; Disposition of H.M's Ships, July 4, 1781, ibid., 20:173; Clinton to Stuart, October 12, 1781, in Mrs. E. Stuart Wortley, *A Prime Minister and His Son: From the Correspondence of the 3d Earl of Bute and of Lt.-General the Hon. Sir Charles Stuart* (London, 1925), 172; GW to Gates, September 24, 1777, *PGWR* 11:310; Gates to GW, October 5, 1777, ibid., 11:392–93.

5. Clinton to Germain, July 13, 18, 1781, *DAR* 20:187, 192.

6. Clinton to Cornwallis, June 8, 11, 1781, *CP* 5:124, 96; William Smith to Stuart, November 3, 1781, Wortley, *A Prime Minister and His Son*, 173; Thomas B. Allen and Todd W. Braisted, *The Loyalist Corps: Americans in the Service of the King* (Tacoma Park, MD, 2011), 70; Lee Kennett, *The French Forces in America, 1780–1783* (Westport, CT, 1977), 106–7; Roger Kaplan, "The Hidden War: British Intelligence Operations During the American Revolution," *William and Mary Quarterly* 47 (1990): 133.

7. Clinton to Cornwallis, July 15, August 11, 1781, *CP* 6:21–22, 24; Clinton to Cornwallis, August 2, 1781, *DAR* 20:212–13; Clinton to Germain, July 13, 18, 1781, ibid., 20:186, 193; Clinton to Phillips, March 10, 1781, ibid., 20:84.

8. Cornwallis to Clinton, July 24, 1781, *CP* 6:12.

9. These two paragraphs draw on Germain to Clinton, April 4, July 7, August 2, 1781, *DAR* 20:99, 175, 206; Larrie D. Ferreiro, *Brothers at Arms: American Independence and the Men of France and Spain Who Saved It* (New York, 2016), 236.

10. Clinton to Germain, June 9–12, July 3, August 9, 1781, *DAR* 20:156, 170, 216; Clinton to Cornwallis, July 15, 1781, *CP* 6:21.

11. Smith, *Memoirs*, 415, 417, 424–31.

12. Ibid., 419.

13. *AR*, 277–78, 320–21, 325, 327; Clinton to Germain, April 5–20, 1781, *DAR* 20:104–5; William B. Willcox, *Portrait of a General: Sir Henry Clinton in the War of Independence* (New York, 1962), 400–402; John A. Tilley, *The British Navy and*

the American Revolution (Columbia, SC, 1987), 244–46; David Syrett, *The Royal Navy in American Waters, 1775–1783* (Brookfield, VT, 1989), 171, 179–85. Clinton's "same tempting target" quote can be found in Willcox, page 401.

14. Kennett, *French Forces in America*, 106–12, 114.

15. Itinerary of the Marches of the French Army from Providence to the Camp at Philipsburg, 1781, in Howard C. Rice Jr. and Anne S. K. Brown, eds. *The American Campaigns of Rochambeau's Army, 1780, 1781, 1782, 1782* (Princeton, NJ, 1972), 2:21–107; Alexandre Berthier, Journal, in ibid., 1:247; Kennett, *French Forces in America*, 115–17; Ferreiro, *Brothers at Arms*, 239–40; *DGW* 3:390n. The quotation providing directions is in Rice and Brown, 2:22.

16. *DGW* 3:369, 376.

17. GW to Rochambeau, June 13, 1781, *WW* 22:208.

18. NG to GW, May 16, 1781, *PNG* 8:273; GW to Rochambeau, June 17, 19, 30, 1781, *WW* 22:230, 235, 293.

19. Ferreiro, *Brothers at Arms*, 237–39.

20. Lafayette to La Luzerne, March 8, April 10, 22, May 9, 22, June 16, 1781, *LSLP* 3:384; 4:23, 55, 89, 121, 186–87.

21. GW to Rochambeau, June 30, 1781, *WW* 22:293.

22. Kennett, *French Forces in America*, 115–17.

23. GW, Instructions to Lincoln, July 1, 1781, *WW* 22:301–4; GW to Rochambeau, July 3, 1781, ibid., 22:324–25.

24. Jean-Francois-Louis de Clermont-Crèvecoeur, Journal of the War in America . . . , in *The American Campaigns of Rochambeau's Army, 1780, 1781, 1782, 1782*, eds. Howard C. Rice Jr. and Anne S. K. Brown (Princeton, NJ, 1972), 1:28–32; ibid., 1:249n; Berthier, Journal, in ibid., 1:249–50. For the complaints about the food service, see Ron Chernow, *Washington: A Life* (New York, 2010), 405.

25. Clermont-Crèvecoeur, Journal, in *American Campaigns of Rochambeau's Army*, 1:33–34; Claude Blanchard, *The Journal of Claude Blanchard, 1780–1781*, ed.

Thomas Bulch (reprint, New York, 1969), 107; Ludwig von Closen, *The Revolutionary Journal of Baron Ludwig von Closen, 1780–1783*, ed Evelyn Acomb (reprint, Chapel Hill, NC, 1958), 91–92; Kennett, *French Forces in America*, 114. The "neatly dressed" and "I admire" quotations can be found in Chernow, *Washington*, 334 and 404.

26. Alexander Hamilton to Philip Schuyler, February 18, 1781, in Harold C. Syrett and Jacob E. Cooke, eds. *The Papers of Alexander Hamilton* (New York, 1961–1987), 2:565–67; Hamilton to James McHenry, February 18, 1781, ibid., 2:569; [Alexander Hamilton], "The Continentalist," nos. 1, 2, 3, and 4 [July–August 1781], ibid., 2:649–52, 654–57, 660–65, 669–74.

27. James A. Huston, *Logistics of Liberty: American Services of Supply in the Revolutionary War and After* (Newark, DE, 1991), 267–68.

28. GW to John Augustine Washington, July 15, 1781, *WW* 22:385–86; GW, Instructions for Reconnoitering the Enemy's Posts at the North End of York Island, ibid., 22:370–72; Clermont-Crèvecoeur, Journal, in *American Campaigns of Rochambeau's Army*, 1:37–38, 38n; Jean-Baptiste-Donatien de Vimeur, Comte de Rochambeau, *Memoirs of the Marshall Count de Rochambeau* (reprint, New York, 1971), 58–59; GW to Lafayette, *LSLP* 4:247–48; *DGW* 3:398–99, 408.

29. Frederick Mackenzie, *Diary of Frederick Mackenzie, Giving a Daily Narrative of His Military Service as an Officer of the Regiment of Royal Welsh Fusiliers During the Years 1775–1781 in Massachusetts, Rhode Island, and New York* (reprint, New York, 1968), 2:581–82; Intelligence Report to Clinton, June 29, 1781, vol. 161, SHCP (WLCL); Smith, *Memoirs*, 428–30.

30. Clinton to Germain, August 20, September 4, 1781, *DAR* 20:217, 221–22; Clinton to Graves, July 6, 1781, *AR*, 539; Graves to Clinton, July 9, 1781, ibid., 542–43; ibid., 320–28; Mackenzie, *Diary of Frederick Mackenzie*, 2:597–98, 602; Kaplan, "The Hidden War," *William and Mary Quarterly* 47:134; Tilley, *The British Navy and the American Revolution*, 244; Syrett, *The Royal Navy in American Waters*, 184–85; William B. Willcox, "Arbuthnot, Gambier, and Graves: 'Old Women' of the Navy," in *George Washington's Opponents: British Generals and Admirals in the American Revolution*, ed. George Athan Billias (New York, 1969), 276–79.

31. Conference at Dobbs Ferry, July 19, 1781, *WW* 22:396–97; *DGW* 3:397, 404–405, 371n; GW to Noah Webster, July 31, 1788, W. W. Abbot et al., eds.

The Papers of George Washington: Confederation Series (Charlottesville, VA, 1992–1997), 6:413–15, 415–16n.

32. Douglas Southall Freeman, *George Washington: A Biography* (New York, 1948–1957), 5:313; *AR*, 333; Clinton to Germain, August 9, 1781, *DAR* 20:216; Intelligence Reports to Clinton, July 27, 28, 30, 31, 1781, vol. 167, SHCP (WLCL); Clinton to Cornwallis, August 11, 1781, *CP* 6:24; Mackenzie, *Diary of Frederick Mackenzie*, 2:565–66; Kaplan, "The Hidden War," *William and Mary Quarterly* 47: 135.

33. GW to William Heath, August 19, 1781, *WW* 23:20–23; Jerome Greene, *The Guns of Independence: The Siege of Yorktown, 1781* (New York, 2005), 18; *The Sinews of Independence: Monthly Strength Reports of the Continental Army*, ed. Charles H. Lesser (Chicago, 1976), 208.

34. GW, General Orders, August 1, 3, 4, 5, 8, 9, 10, 1781, *WW* 22:442–45, 455, 460, 461–63, 482–84, 485–86, 487–88; GW to William Fitzhugh, August 8, 1781, ibid., 22:481; GW to George Clinton, August 10, 1781, ibid., 22:491.

35. Lafayette to GW, July 30, 31, August 6, 11, 1781, *LSLP* 4:288–90, 290–91, 299–300, 311–12; Greene, *Guns of Independence*, 33. The "Be ours" quotation is in the marquis's letter of July 31 and can be found in *LSLP* 4:291.

36. GW to Lafayette, July 30, 1781, *LSLP* 4:289; Kennett, *French Forces in America*, 121.

37. GW, General Orders, August 13, 1781, *WW* 22:494–95; GW to the President of Congress, August 13, 1781, ibid., 22:495–96; GW to Patrick Dennis, August 13, 1781, ibid., 22:497.

38. *DGW* 3:409–10; Mackenzie, *Diary of Frederick Mackenzie*, 2:587.

39. GW to de Grasse, August 17, 1781, *WW* 23:7–11.

40. GW to Lafayette, August 15, 1781, *LSLP* 4:330.

CHAPTER 14: THE TRAP SLAMS SHUT

1. Jean-Francois-Louis de Clermont-Crèvecoeur, Journal of the War in America. . . . , in *The American Campaigns of Rochambeau's Army, 1780, 1781, 1782, 1782*, ed. Howard C. Rice Jr. and Anne S. K. Brown (Princeton, NJ,

1972), 1:40–43; *DGW* 3:414, 413n; GW, General Orders, August 19, 1781, *WW* 23:19; GW, Answers to Questions Proposed by . . . Rochambeau, August 22, 1781, ibid., 23:36; Douglas Southall Freeman, *George Washington: A Biography* (New York, 1948–1957), 5:314; Lee Kennett, *The French Forces in America, 1780–1783* (Westport, CT, 1977), 132.

2. GW to Lafayette, August 22, 1781, *LSLP* 4:340.

3. Clermont-Crèvecoeur, Journal, in *American Campaigns of Rochambeau's Army*, 1:43; *DGW* 3:414–16; James Thacher, *A Military Journal During the American Revolutionary War, from 1775–1783*, ed. Thomas Bulch (reprint, New York, 1969), 271; Lafayette to GW, August 25, 1781, *LSLP* 4:357. For the routes taken after departing New York, the works of historian Robert A. Selig are indispensable. See Robert A. Selig, *The Washington-Rochambeau Revolutionary Route in the Commonwealth of Pennsylvania, 1781–1783: An Historical and Architectural Survey* (Philadelphia: Pennsylvania Society of Sons of the Revolution; Pennsylvania Society, Sons of the American Revolution, 2007); Selig, *The Washington-Rochambeau Revolutionary Route in the State of New Jersey, 1781–1783: An Historical and Architectural Survey*, 3 vols. (Trenton: New Jersey Historic Trust, Department of Community Affairs, 2006) "Historical Background." In *Washington-Rochambeau Revolutionary Route. Resource Study and Environmental Assessment* (Boston National Park Service Northeast and Capital Regions, 2006), pp. 9–26; Selig, *March to Victory: Washington, Rochambeau, and the Yorktown Campaign of 1781*, U.S. Army Center for Military History no. 70–104–1 (Washington, DC, 2005); Selig, *The Washington-Rochambeau Revolutionary Route in the State of Delaware, 1781–1783: An Historical and Architectural Survey* (Dover: State of Delaware, 2003); Selig, *Revolutionary War Route and Transportation Survey in the Commonwealth of Virginia, 1781–1782: An Historical and Architectural Survey* (Richmond: Virginia Department of Historic Resources, 2009); Selig, *The Washington-Rochambeau Revolutionary Route: Statement of National Significance* (Boston: National Park Service Northeast and Capital Regions, 2003).

4. Clermont-Crèvecoeur, Journal, in *American Campaigns of Rochambeau's Army*, 1:45–46; Jean-Baptiste-Antoine de Verger, Journal, ibid., 1:134; Thacher, *Military Journal*, 271; Thomas McKean to Rochambeau, September 4, 1781, *LDC* 18:11; Samuel Livermore to Meshech Weare, September 4, 1781, ibid., 18:7.

5. *LDC* 18:5n; New York Delegates to George Clinton, September 9, 1781, ibid., 18:27; GW to Robert Morris, August 17, 27, September 6, 1781, *WW* 23:12, 52, 89; Edward G. Lengel, *General George Washington: A Military Life* (New York, 2005), 335; Kennett, *French Forces in America*, 133–34.

6. Freeman, *George Washington*, 5:321–22; James T. Flexner, *George Washington in the American Revolution* (Boston, 1967), 444. Rochambeau's "good work" quotation can be found in Kennett, *French Forces in America*, 134.

7. For these two paragraphs, see GW to Robert Morris, August 2, 1781, *WW* 22:450; GW to Samuel Miles, August 27, 1781, ibid., 23:54–55; Clermont-Crèvecoeur, Journal, in *American Campaigns of Rochambeau's Army*, 1:52–53, 55; Kennett, *French Forces in America*, 135; *PGWR* 10:389n; Robert L. Tonsetic, *1781: The Decisive Year of the Revolutionary War* (Philadelphia, 2011), 129–30, 142; Nathaniel Philbrick, *In the Hurricane's Eye: The Genius of George Washington and the Victory at Yorktown* (New York, 2018), 173; James A. Huston, *Logistics of Liberty: American Services of Supply in the Revolutionary War and After* (Newark, DE, 1991), 270. The "musket shots" quotation is in Kennett, page 137.

8. GW, General Orders, September 6, 1781, *WW* 23:94.

9. GW to Louis Le Bèque duportail, September 7, 1781, ibid., 23:101; *DGW* 3:419–20, 419n; GW to Lafayette, September 10, 1781, *LSLP* 4:397; Marquis de Chastellux, *Travels in America in the Years 1780, 1781 and 1782*, ed. Howard C. Rice (Chapel Hill, NC, 1963), 1:298n; 2:597.

10. Frederick Mackenzie, *Diary of Frederick Mackenzie, Giving a Daily Narrative of His Military Service as an Officer of the Regiment of Royal Welsh Fusiliers During the Years 1775–1781 in Massachusetts, Rhode Island, and New York* (reprint, New York, 1968), 2:593; *AR*, 326–28; Clinton to Cornwallis, August 27, 1781, ibid., 562; Roger Kaplan, "The Hidden War: British Intelligence Operations During the American Revolution," *William and Mary Quarterly* 47 (1990): 136.

11. Mackenzie, *Diary of Frederick Mackenzie*, 2:598–99.

12. Andrew Jackson O'Shaughnessy, *The Men Who Lost America: British Leadership, the American Revolution, and the Fate of the Empire* (New Haven, CT, 2013), 292–93.

13. Piers Mackesy, *The War for America, 1775–1783* (Cambridge, MA, 1965), 418–19; John A. Tilley, *The British Navy and the American Revolution* (Columbia, SC, 1987), 241–42, 248–49; William B. Willcox, *Portrait of a General: Sir Henry Clinton in the War of Independence* (New York, 1962), 409–11; Clinton to Rodney, June 28, 1781, *AR*, 533. Rodney's "cannot move" quotation can be found in Willcox, page 411.

14. Clinton to Gloucester, September 20, 1781, Series III: Letterbooks, vol. 254, SHCP (WLCL); Clinton to Cornwallis, June 8, 19, July 8, 1781, *CP* 5:128, 135, 142.

15. These three paragraphs draw on O'Shaughnessy, *The Men Who Lost America*, 308–11; Philbrick, *In the Hurricane's Eye*, 145; Tilley, *British Navy and the American Revolution*, 241–44.

16. Philbrick, *In the Hurricane's Eye*, 161, 305–306; Samuel Hood to Clinton, August 25, 1781, *AR*, 562.

17. Tilley, *British Navy and the American Revolution*, 248–52.

18. Larrie D. Ferreiro, *Brothers at Arms: American Independence and the Men of France and Spain Who Saved It* (New York, 2016), 181–82.

19. Clinton to Cornwallis, July 15, 1781, *CP* 6:21; Cornwallis to Clinton, August 31, September 1, 2, 4, 1781, ibid., 6:29–30; William Feltman, *The Journal of Lieut. William Feltman, of the First Pennsylvania Regiment, 1781–82* (Philadelphia, 1853), 12.

20. Clinton to Cornwallis, August 27, 1781, *AR*, 562; ibid., 327, 329; Cornwallis to Clinton, August 22, 1781, *CP* 6:27–28; Germain to Clinton, July 7, 1781, *DAR* 20:175; David Syrett, *The Royal Navy in American Waters, 1775–1783* (Altershot, UK, 1989), 186.

21. Franklin Wickwire and Mary Wickwire, *Cornwallis and the War of Independence* (London, 1971), 336, 347; Eric Robson, *The American Revolution i1n Its Political and Military Aspects, 1763–1783* (New York, 1966), 136; Ron Chernow, *Washington: A Life* (New York, 2016), 413. The quotation is from Chernow.

22. Clinton to Cornwallis, September 6, 1781, *CP* 6:33; *AR*, 328–29, 331; Clinton to Germain, September 7, 1781, *DAR* 20:223.

23. Willard M. Wallace, *Traitorous Hero: The Life and Fortunes of Benedict Arnold* (reprint, Freeport, NY, 1970), 278–83.

24. William B. Willcox, "Arbuthnot, Gambier, and Graves: 'Old Women' of the Navy," in *George Washington's Opponents: British Generals and Admirals in the American Revolution*, ed. George Athan Billias (New York, 1969), 280; Syrett, *Royal Navy in American Waters*, 192.

25. Kennett, *French Forces in America*, 136.

26. The account of the Battle of the Virginia Capes draws on Philbrick, *In the Hurricane's Eye*, 179–96; Ferreiro, *Brothers at Arms*, 260–62; Tilley, *British Navy and the American Revolution*, 256–63; and Syrett, *Royal Navy in American Waters*, 192–204; Stanley D. M. Carpenter, *Southern Gambit: Cornwallis and the British March to Yorktown* (Norman, OK, 2018), 239–43. See also Graves to Clinton, September 9, 1781, *AR*, 567.

27. Jerome Greene, *The Guns of Independence: The Siege of Yorktown, 1781* (New York, 2005), 22.

28. Carpenter, *Southern Gambit*, 248.

29. Cornwallis to Clinton, September 16, 1781, *CP* 6:34.

30. Clinton to Cornwallis, June 8, 19, July 11, 1781, *CP* 5:125, 135, 142; Lafayette to GW, September 8, 1781, *LSLP* 4:393; Willcox, *Portrait of a General*, 433. Had Cornwallis attempted to escape, he would have had to leave behind the two thousand or more former slaves who had fled to his army for protection and liberty, though there is no evidence that his final decision was shaped by the ethical dimensions posed by abandoning the runaway slaves with him in Yorktown. See Cassandra Pybus, *Epic Journeys of Freedom: Runaway Slaves of the American Revolution and Their Global Quest for Liberty* (Boston, 2006), 49–50.

31. Clinton to Germain, September 12, 1781, *DAR* 20:230; *AR*, 337–38; Willcox, *Portrait of a General*, 429.

32. Extract of Minutes of Councils of War, September 14, 1781, *AR*, 569–70; Smith, *Memoirs*, 453. Robertson is quoted in Willcox, *Portrait of a General*, 431.

33. Extracts of Minutes of Councils of War, September 17, 19, 23, 1781, *AR*, 571–72, 572, 573; Clinton to Germain, September 26, October 14, 1781, *DAR* 20:232, 241; Cornwallis to Clinton, September 16, 1781, *CP* 6:35.

34. Clinton to Cornwallis, September 24, 1781, *CP* 6:36; *AR*, 339–40; Clinton to Germain, September 12, 1781, *DAR* 20:230; Willcox, *Portrait of a General*, 434.

35. Clinton to Gloucester, October 16, 1781, Series III: Letterbooks, vol. 254, SHCP (WLCL); Clinton to Stuart, October 12, 1781, Mrs. E. Stuart Wortley, *A Prime Minister and His Son: From the Correspondence of the 3d Earl of Bute and of Lt.-General the Hon. Sir Charles Stuart* (London, 1925), 172.

36. Extracts of Minutes of Councils of War, September 24, 26, 1781, *AR*, 573–74, 576–77.

37. Clinton to Cornwallis, September 24, 25, 30, 1781, *CP* 6:35–36, 37, 39; Extracts of Minutes of Councils of War, September 24, 26, 1781, *AR*, 573–74, 576–77.

38. Ferreiro, *Brothers at Arms*, 133–37, 160–64, 242–56; Agustin Guimerá Ravina and José María Blanco Núñez, "Spanish Naval Operations," in *The American Revolution: A World War*, ed. David K. Allison and Larrie D. Ferreiro (Washington, DC, 2018), 68–85; José M. Guerrero Acosta, "Uniforms, Supplies, and Money from Spain," ibid., 86–89; E. James Ferguson, *The Power of the Purse: A History of American Public Finance, 1776–1790* (Chapel Hill, NC, 1961), 40–42, 129–34, 129n; GW to Francisco Rendon, October 12, 1781, *WW* 23:211; GW to President of Congress, July 10, 1781, ibid., 22:356–57.

39. Journal of St. George Tucker, in Henry Steele Commager and Richard B. Morris, eds. *The Spirit of 'Seventy-Six: The Story of the American Revolution as Told by Participants* (Indianapolis, IN, 1958), 2:1224; Richard M. Ketchum, *Victory at Yorktown: The Campaign That Won the Revolution* (New York, 2004), 186.

40. *DGW* 3:420n; Feltman, *The Journal of Lieut. William Feltman*, 14–15.

41. *DGW* 3:420–22; Questions Proposed by General Washington to Comte de Grasse, September 17, 1781, *WW* 23:122–25; Flexner, *George Washington*, 449–50; Freeman, *George Washington*, 333–38; Ferreiro, *Brothers at Arms*, 256, 266.

42. Clermont-Crèvecoeur, Journal, in *American Campaigns of Rochambeau's Army*, 1:56; Emory G. Evans, *Thomas Nelson of Yorktown: Revolutionary Virginian* (Charlottesville, VA, 1975), 112–16; *DWG* 3:422.

43. Clermont-Crèvecoeur, Journal of the War in America. . . . , in *American Campaigns of Rochambeau's Army*, 1:56–57; *DGW* 3:422; GW to NG, October 6, 1781, *WW* 23:191.

44. Greene, *Guns of Independence*, 37–67.

45. Ibid., 75, 78, 91–114; Ferreiro, *Brothers at Arms*, 219; GW to Weedon, September 20, 1781, *WW* 23:126; GW to President of Congress, October 1, 1781, ibid., 23:158.

46. GW to de Grasse, September 25, 27, 1781, *WW* 23:136–39, 143.

47. GW to de Grasse, September 25, 1781, ibid., 23:137; GW to McKean, October 6, 1781, ibid., 23:189; Weedon to NG, *PNG* 9:300; Lafayette to NG, October 6, 1781, *LSLP* 4:413; Tonsetic, *1781*, 172. The Anthony Wayne quote can be found in Greene, *Guns of Independence*, 70.

48. *DGW* 3:423; GW to President of Congress, October 1, 1781, *WW* 23:158.

49. NG to Morris, August 18, 1781, *PNG* 9:200; NG to Rush, August 8, 1781, ibid., 9:149; NG to GW, August 6, 1781, ibid., 9:140.

50. NG to GW, August 7, 1781, ibid., 9:146–47; NG to Lee, August 14, 22, 1781, ibid., 9:181, 223; Lee to NG, August 13, 17, 1781, ibid., 9:177, 196; NG to John Sevier, September 1, 1781, ibid., 9:276; editor's note, ibid., 9:333n. The reference to Lee as NG's "right eye" can be found in Theodore Thayer, *Nathanael Greene: Strategist of the American Revolution* (New York, 1960), 374.

51. *PNG* 9:333n; John Buchanan, *The Road to Charleston: Nathanael Greene and the American Revolution* (Charlottesville, VA, 2019), 218–20. On Colonel Stewart, see editor's note, *CP* 5:295; and Buchanan, page 215.

52. NG to GW, September 17, 1781, *PNG* 9:362; NG to McKean, September 11, 1781, ibid., 9:329. For NG's comment on the worthlessness of militia, see Buchanan, *Road to Charleston*, 67.

53. NG to Thomas Burke, September 17, 1781, *PNG* 9:355; NG to McKean, September 11, 1781, ibid., 9:329; NG to Lafayette, September 17, 1781, ibid., 9:358; Alexander Stewart to Cornwallis, September 9, 1781, *DAR* 20:227. For

excellent succinct accounts of the engagement, see *PNG* 9:333–38n; Thayer, *Nathanael Greene*, 375–80; and Buchanan, *Road to Charleston*, 218–34. For a detailed account, see Robert M. Dunkerly and Irene B. Boland, *Eutaw Springs: The Final Battle of the American Revolution's Southern Campaign* (Columbia, SC, 2017).

54. NG to Lee, September 25, 1781, *PNG* 9:392.

55. McKean to NG, November 2, 1781, ibid., 9:519–21; GW to NG, October 6, 1781, ibid., 428–29; John Mathews to NG, October 22, 1781, ibid., 9:455–56; John Clark to NG, October 25, 1781, ibid., 9:487; Richard Henry Lee to NG, October 28, 1781, ibid., 9:494; Reed to NG, November 1, 1781, ibid., 9:510; Thomas Paine to NG, September 10, 1781, ibid., 9:317–18.

CHAPTER 15: DECISIVE VICTORY

1. *DGW* 3:425; Robert L. Tonsetic, *1781: The Decisive Year of the Revolutionary War* (Philadelphia, 2011), 172.

2. George F. Scheer, ed., *Private Yankee Doodle: A Narrative of Some of the Adventures, Dangers and Sufferings of a Revolutionary Soldier* (New York, 1968), 237–38.

3. *DGW* 3:423; Clinton to Cornwallis, September 24, 1781, *CP* 6:35; Cornwallis to Clinton, September 29, 1781, ibid., 6:36; Samuel Abbot Greene, ed., *My Campaigns in America: A Journal Kept by Count William de Deux-Ponts, 1780–81* (Boston, 1868), 135; Banastre Tarleton, *A History of the Campaigns of 1780 and 1781, in the Southern Provinces of North America* (reprint, Cranbury, NJ, 2005), 387; James Thacher, *A Military Journal During the American Revolutionary War, from 1775–1783*, ed. Thomas Bulch (reprint, New York, 1969), 280.

4. William B. Willcox, *Portrait of a General: Sir Henry Clinton in the War of Independence* (New York, 1962), 436; *DGW* 3:423–24; GW to President of Congress, October 1, 1781, *WW* 23:158; Scheer, *Private Yankee Doodle*, 230, 231–32.

5. *DGW* 3:424–25; GW to President of Congress, October 1, 1781, *WW* 23:158; Thacher, *Military Journal*, 283; Jerome A. Greene, *The Guns of Independence: The Siege of Yorktown, 1781* (New York, 2005), 148–91.

6. Thacher, *Military Journal*, 283–84; William Feltman, *The Journal of Lieut. William Feltman, of the First Pennsylvania Regiment, 1781–82* (Philadelphia, 1853), 18.

7. Cornwallis to Clinton, October 11 and 12, 1781, *CP* 6:40; Wickwire and Wickwire, *Cornwallis and the War of Independence* (London, 1971), 377.

8. Cornwallis to Clinton, October 12, 1781, *CP* 6:40;

9. Alexander Hamilton to Elizabeth Hamilton, October 12, 1781, in Harold C. Syrett and Jacob E. Cooke, eds. *The Papers of Alexander Hamilton* (New York, 1961–1987), 2:678.

10. Ibid., 2:677. For a lengthy account of Hamilton's military service, see Ron Chernow, *Alexander Hamilton* (New York, 2004), 72–166.

11. Greene, *Guns of Independence*, 237–38; Chernow, *Alexander Hamilton*, 53. Of Major Fish, Hamilton said, "I prize him both as a friend and an officer." See Hamilton to Elizabeth Hamilton, August 16, 1781, *Papers of Alexander Hamilton*, 2:666.

12. Hamilton to Elizabeth Hamilton, October 12, 1781, *Papers of Alexander Hamilton*, 2:677–78.

13. An excellent account of the attack can be found in Greene, *Guns of Independence*, 236–53, on which this paragraph draws. See also Hamilton to Lafayette, October 15, 1781, *Papers of Alexander Hamilton*, 2:679–81. The casualty figures provided by GW can be found in *DGW* 3:427. More accurate figures are available in Thomas J. Fleming, *Beat the Last Drum: The Siege of Yorktown, 1781* (New York, 1963), 288.

14. Hamilton to Lafayette, October 15, 1781, *Papers of Alexander Hamilton*, 2:679–81; Hamilton to Elizabeth Hamilton, October 16, 1781, ibid., 2:682; *DGW* 3:427.

15. Cornwallis to Clinton, October 15, 1781, *CP* 6:40–41.

16. Johann Ewald, *Diary of the American War: A Hessian Journal*, ed. Joseph P. Tustin (New Haven, CT, 1979), 337; Cornwallis to Clinton, October 20, 1781, *CP* 6:127; Tonsetic, *1781*, 195; Tarleton, *A History of the Campaigns 1780 and 1781 in the Southern Provinces*, 380–82.

17. Cornwallis to Clinton, October 20, 1781, *CP* 6:127–28.

18. Greene, *Guns of Independence*, 283, 457; Cornwallis to GW, October 17, 1781, *CP* 6:112.

19. GW to Cornwallis, October 17, 1781, *CP* 6:113.

20. Cornwallis to GW, October 17, 1781, ibid., 6:113.

21. GW to Cornwallis, October 18, 1781, ibid., 6:114–15; Hamilton to Elizabeth Hamilton, October 18, 1781, *Papers of Alexander Hamilton*, 2:683.

22. Cornwallis to GW, October 18, 1781, ibid., 6:115.

23. Greene, *Guns of Independence*, 287–89.

24. David Syrett, *The Royal Navy in American Waters, 1775–1783* (Altershot, UK, 1989), 216–17.

25. *DGW* 3:430.

26. Articles of Capitulation, October 19, 1781, *CP* 6:117–21.

27. Thacher, *Military Journal*, 289–90; Feltman, *Journal of Lieut. William Feltman*, 22; Scheer, *Private Yankee Doodle*, 241; Ewald, *Diary of the American War*, 340.

28. Thacher, *Military Journal*, 290.

29. The foregoing account of the two surrenders draws on Greene, *Guns of Independence*, 290–303. For the description of General O'Hara, see John C. Dann, ed., *The Revolution Remembered: Eyewitness Accounts of the War for Independence* (Chicago, 1980), 245. On Tarleton losing his horse, see Feltman, *Journal of Lieut. William Feltman*, 24; and Thacher, *Military Journal*, 292.

30. Greene, *Guns of Independence*, 307–309.

31. For these two paragraphs, see Ewald, *Diary of the American War*, 335; Scheer, *Private Yankee Doodle*, 241; Henry Wiencek, *An Imperfect God: George Washington, His Slaves, and the Creation of America* (New York, 2003), 248; Douglas R. Egerton, *Death or Liberty: African Americans and Revolutionary America* (New York, 2009), 90; Cassandra Pybus, "Thomas Jefferson's Faulty Math: The Question of Slave Defections in the American Revolution," *William and Mary Quarterly* 62 (2005): 256–57; Cassandra Pybus, "Thomas Jefferson and Slavery," in *A Companion to Thomas Jefferson*, ed. Francis D. Cogliano (Chichester, UK, 2012), 274–75; Ludwig von Closen, *Revolutionary Journal, 1780–1783*, trans. Evelyn M. Acomb (Chapel Hill, NC, 1958), 155.

32. Thacher, *Military Journal*, 302. For the description of Cornwallis, see Dann, *The Revolution Remembered*, 245.

33. Wickwire and Wickwire, *Cornwallis and the War of Independence*, 387; Ron Chernow, *Washington: A Life* (New York, 2010), 419; Cornwallis to Clinton, October 20, 1781, *CP* 6:125; *AR*, 346; Clinton to Germain, October 29, 1781, *DAR* 20:253.

34. T. Cole Jones, *Captives of Liberty: Prisoners of War and the Politics of Vengeance in the American Revolution* (Philadelphia, 2020), 226–36; Jones, "'Elated with Victory, and Reeking with Revenge': The Yorktown Prisoners and the Laws of War in Revolutionary Virginia," in *Justifying Revolution: Law, Virtue, and Violence in the American War of Independence*, ed. Glenn A. Moots and Phillip Hamilton (Norman, OK, 2019), 210–39. The two quotations can be found in Jones's essay "Elated with Victory," pages 225 and 229.

35. For these two paragraphs see Clinton to Germain, October 29, 1781, *DAR* 20:252; Disposition of H.M.'s Ships, July 4, 1781, ibid., 20:173; Willcox, *Portrait of a General*, 439; Clinton to Gloucester, December 28, 1781, April 24, 1789, Series III: Letterbooks, vol. 254, SHCP (WLCL).

36. NG to Otho Williams, September 17, 1782, *PNG* 11:670.

37. *DGW* 3:433; GW to Weedon, November 3, 1781, *WW* 23:325–26; John Ferling, *A Leap in the Dark: The Struggle to Create the American Republic* (New York, 2003), 241; Elias Boudinot to Hannah Boudinot, October 21, 1781, *LDC* 18:151.

CHAPTER 16: RECKONING

1. Alan Valentine, *Lord North* (Norman, OK, 1967), 2:274.

2. Francois van der Kemp to John Adams, November 26, 1781, Robert J. Taylor et al., eds. *Papers of John Adams* (Cambridge, MA, 1977–), 12:89.

3. Valentine, *Lord North*, 271–300; Peter Whiteley, *Lord North: The Prime Minister Who Lost America* (London, 1996), 195–208.

4. William B. Willcox, *Portrait of a General: Sir Henry Clinton in the War of Independence* (New York, 1962), 461–63.

5. Robert G. Parkinson, *The Common Cause: Creating Race and Nation in the American Revolution* (Chapel Hill, NC, 2016), 463, 561–62, 565, 567–68.

6. Guy Carleton to GW, April 6, 1783, *DAR* 21:161–62; GW to Carleton, April 9, 21, 1783, *WW* 26:307–8, 345–48; GW to the General Officers of the Army, April 17, 1783, ibid., 26:328–29; GW to Congress, April 18, 1783, ibid., 26:330–34; GW, General Orders, April 18, 1783, ibid., 26:334–37; Thomas Paine, *The American Crisis XIII*, in *Complete Writings of Thomas Paine*, ed. Philip S. Foner (New York, 1945), 1:230.

7. For good accounts of this trying period, see William M. Fowler Jr. *American Crisis: George Washington and the Dangerous Two Years After Yorktown, 1781–1783* (New York, 2011); and Thomas Fleming, *The Perils of Peace: America's Struggle for Survival After Yorktown* (New York, 2007).

8. GW, Farewell Orders to the Armies of the United States, November 2, 1783, *WW* 27:222–27. The quotes can be found on page 223.

9. Parkinson, *The Common Cause*, 575; Paul David Nelson, *General Sir Guy Carleton, Lord Dorchester: Soldier-Statesman of Early British Canada* (Cranbury, NJ, 2000), 171–73; Return of Loyalists Leaving New York, November 24, 1783, *DAR* 21:225–26.

10. GW, Address to Congress on Resigning His Commission, December 23, 1783, *WW* 27:284–85.

11. This paragraph draws on the figures in Howard H. Peckham, ed., *The Toll of Independence: Engagements and Battle Casualties of the American Revolution*

(Chicago, 1974). As stated in the text, the figure of thirty thousand total deaths among American soldiers and sailors is a conservative estimate, for no one knows how many of the wounded subsequently died, no record exists of the toll exacted among the partisan warriors in the southern theater in 1780 and beyond, and many militia records are no longer available, if they ever existed. The estimate that the death toll was nearly thirty-six thousand can be found in Edwin G. Burrows, *Forgotten Patriots: The Untold Story of American Prisoners During the Revolutionary War* (New York, 2008) 200–201.

12. Quoted in Paul David Nelson, *General Horatio Gates: A Biography* (Baton Rouge, LA, 1976), 282.

13. Adams to Benjamin Rush, March 19, 1812, in John A. Schutz and Douglass Adair, eds. *The Spur of Fame: Dialogues of John Adams and Benjamin Rush, 1805–1813* (San Marino, CA, 1966), 212.

14. John P. Kaminski and Jill Adair McCaughan, eds. *A Great and Good Man: George Washington in the Eyes of His Contemporaries* (Madison, WI, 1989), 22–33. I am indebted to Larrie Ferreiro for the historiography on the strategic planning that culminated in Cornwallis's surrender at Yorktown. The book that first revealed Rochambeau's pivotal role was François Soulès, *Histoires des troubles de l'Amérique Anglaise* (Paris, 1787). The first to reveal GW's resistance to a southern campaign may have been Edward Channing, *A History of the United States* (New York, 1912), 3: 326–27.

15. James McHenry to Margaret Caldwell, December 23, 1783, Kaminski and McCaughan, *A Great and Good Man*, 28–29.

16. Thomas Paine, *Letter to George Washington*, Foner, *Complete Writings of Thomas Paine* 2:695, 719, 720.

17. John Ferling, *Apostles of Revolution: Jefferson, Paine, Monroe, and the Struggle Against the Old Order in America and Europe* (New York, 2018), 381. On the circumstances leading Paine to publish his attack on Washington, see pages 276, 287–89, 293–96.

18. Page Smith, *John Adams* (Garden City, NY, 1962), 2:904; Hamilton to Martha Washington, January 12, 1800, in Harold C. Syrett and Jacob E. Cooke, eds. *The Papers of Alexander Hamilton* (New York, 1961–1987), 24:184–85.

19. Alexander Hamilton, Eulogy on Nathanael Greene, July 4, 1789, Cooke, *Papers of Alexander Hamilton*, 5:345–59. The quotations can be found on pages 350, 351, and 355.

20. Quoted in Andrew Jackson O'Shaughnessy, *The Men Who Lost America: British Leadership, the American Revolution, and the Fate of the Empire* (New Haven, CT, 2013), 359.

21. Lafayette to Vergennes, July 19, 1780, *LSLP* 3:100.

22. James T. Flexner, *George Washington in the American Revolution* (Boston, 1967), 531–52.

23. David McCullough, *1776* (New York, 2005), 293.

24. Germain to Clinton, March 8, 21, 1778, *DAR* 15:58–59, 73.

25. [Earl Cornwallis], *An Answer to That Part of the Narrative of Sir Henry Clinton, Which Relates to the Conduct of Lieutenant-General Earl Cornwallis* (1783), in *The Campaign in Virginia 1781: An Exact Reprint of Six Rare Pamphlets on the Clinton-Cornwallis Controversy*, ed. Benjamin Franklin Stevens (London, 1888), 70, 80.

26. *AR*, 226–27, 270–71; Clinton to Cornwallis, *CP* 5:97; Willcox, *Portrait of a General*, 353.

27. These two paragraphs draw on *AR*, 363; Willcox, *Portrait of a General*, 448–55. The quote can be found in Willcox, page 448.

28. Solomon M. Lutnick, "The Defeat at Yorktown: A View from the British Press," *Virginia Magazine of History and Biography* 72 (1964): 475–76.

29. Franklin Wickwire and Mary Wickwire, *Cornwallis and the War of Independence* (London, 1971), 336, 341, 347; Don Higginbotham, *The War of American Independence: Military Attitude, Policies, and Practice, 1763–1789* (New York, 1971), 69; Eric Robson, *The American Revolution in Its Political and Military Aspects, 1763–1783* (New York, 1966), 136; Piers Mackesy, *The War for America, 1775–1783* (Cambridge, MA, 1965), 213, 409, 515; Robert Middlekauff, *The Glorious Cause: The American Revolution, 1763–1789* (New York, 2007), 576; Ian Saberton, *The American Revolutionary War in the South:*

A Re-evaluation from a British Perspective in the Light of the Cornwallis Papers (Tolworth, UK, 2018), 25; Stanley D. M. Carpenter, *Southern Gambit: Cornwallis and the British March to Yorktown* (Norman, OK, 2019), 71.

30. Germain to Clinton, March 7, 1781, *DAR* 20:76; Germain to Cornwallis, June 4, 1781, ibid., 20:151.

31. Quoted in O'Shaughnessy, *The Men Who Lost America*, 346. Clinton's remark about Rodney can be found on page 311.

32. Norman Desmarais, *America's First Ally: France in the Revolutionary War* (Philadelphia, 2019), 233.

33. William Ellery to Benjamin Ellery, July 10, 1776, *LDC* 4:430.

34. GW, Farewell Orders to the Armies, November 2, 1783, *WW* 27:224.

INDEX

A NOTE ON THE AUTHOR

JOHN FERLING is professor emeritus of history at the University of West Georgia. He is the author of many books on the American Revolution, including *The Ascent of George Washington*; *Almost a Miracle*; *A Leap in the Dark*; *Whirlwind*, a finalist for the 2015 Kirkus Book Prize; and, most recently, *Apostles of Revolution: Jefferson, Paine, Monroe, and the Struggle Against the Old Order in America and Europe*. He and his wife, Carol, and their three cats live near Atlanta.